Common Places

INTEGRATED READING AND WRITING

SECOND EDITION

Lisa Hoeffner
McLennan Community College

Kent Hoeffner
McLennan Community College

Mc
Graw
Hill
Education

COMMON PLACES: INTEGRATED READING AND WRITING, SECOND EDITION

Published by McGraw-Hill Education, 2 Penn Plaza, New York, NY 10121. Copyright
© 2019 by McGraw-Hill Education. All rights reserved. Printed in the United States of
America. Previous edition © 2015. No part of this publication may be reproduced or
distributed in any form or by any means, or stored in a database or retrieval system,
without the prior written consent of McGraw-Hill Education, including, but not limited to,
in any network or other electronic storage or transmission, or broadcast for distance
learning.

Some ancillaries, including electronic and print components, may not be available to
customers outside the United States.

This book is printed on acid-free paper.

1 2 3 4 5 6 7 8 9 LMN 21 20 19 18

ISBN: 978-1-259-79564-0 (student edition)
MHID: 1-259-79564-0 (student edition)

ISBN: 978-1-260-10536-0 (instructor's edition)
MHID: 1-260-10536-9 (instructor's edition)

Brand Manager: *Penina Braffman*
Product Developer: *Beth Tripmacher*
Marketing Manager: *Marisa Cavanaugh*
Content Project Manager: *Lisa Bruflodt*
Buyer: *Susan K. Culbertson*
Designer: *Debra Kubiak*
Content Licensing Specialist: *DeAnna Dausener*
Cover Image: *Shutterstock/Thomas Barrat*
Compositor: *Lumina Datamatics, Inc.*
Printer: *LSC Communications*

All credits appearing on page or at the end of the book are considered to be an
extension of the copyright page.

Library of Congress Cataloging-in-Publication Data

Names: Hoeffner, Lisa, author. | Hoeffner, Kent, author.
Title: Common places : integrated reading and writing / Lisa Hoeffner,
    McLennan Community College, Kent Hoeffner, McLennan Community College.
Description: Second Edition. | New York : McGraw-Hill Education, [2019]
Identifiers: LCCN 2017039723 | ISBN 9781259795640 (softcover : student edition :
    acid-free paper) | ISBN 1259795640 (student edition : acid-free paper) |
    ISBN 9781260105360 (instructor's edition) | ISBN 1260105369 (instructor's edition)
Subjects: LCSH: English language—Rhetoric—Problems, exercises, etc. |
    Report writing—Problems, exercises, etc. | Reading
    comprehension—Problems, exercises, etc. | College readers.
Classification: LCC PE1413 .H553 2019 | DDC 808/.042076—dc23

LC record available at https://lccn.loc.gov/2017039723

The Internet addresses listed in the text were accurate at the time of publication. The
inclusion of a website does not indicate an endorsement by the authors or McGraw-Hill
Education, and McGraw-Hill Education does not guarantee the accuracy of the
information presented at these sites.

mheducation.com/highered

About the Authors

LISA HOEFFNER

Lisa Hoeffner earned a PhD in English with a specialization in rhetoric from the University of Houston. She has taught a wide range of courses over the past twenty-five years, including English composition and rhetoric, reading, critical thinking, American and British literature, world literature, humanities, and business writing. Since 1998, Dr. Hoeffner has served in two positions—professor of English and professor of reading—at McLennan Community College in Waco, Texas.

In addition to her teaching role, Dr. Hoeffner is focusing on curricular redesign in developmental education. She serves as grant director for a Texas Higher Education Coordinating Board grant awarded for work on improvement and innovation in developmental education. With the advent of integrated reading and writing in Texas, she has provided leadership for colleges and universities across the state that are creating integrated reading and writing (INRW) programs. She has designed and led training workshops and webinars to prepare faculty to teach INRW and to help institutions create INRW programs. She has also provided leadership to public school districts implementing INRW programs as college and career preparatory classes.

Dr. Hoeffner has a passion for teaching and for innovative technologies. She designed and taught her first online freshman composition class in 1999 and has since developed and taught online courses for developmental students. She is thrilled that she is able to bring both passions to bear in her development of *Common Places* and the Connect IRW: *Common Places* Master Course.

Dr. Hoeffner is a recipient of several awards, including the National Institute for Staff and Organizational Development (NISOD) Excellence Award. She has written and published scholarly articles and poetry, and she has presented her work in developmental education nationally. A native Texan, Dr. Hoeffner enjoys exploring the flora and fauna of regional ecosystems, cooking, and dreaming about living off the grid.

KENT HOEFFNER

Kent Hoeffner earned a BA from Texas A&M University in College Station, an MDiv from Golden Gate Seminary in Mill Valley, California, and a PhD from Southern Seminary in Louisville, Kentucky. Before working in higher education, Dr. Hoeffner was employed in the mental health field, working primarily with adolescents with social and emotional difficulties. During that time, he also taught adult basic education and GED preparation classes.

Dr. Hoeffner has served at McLennan Community College since 2001, first as the division director for liberal arts and currently as a professor of philosophy. In addition to teaching introductory courses in philosophy, he has also taught and developed courses in critical thinking and logic. In 2007, he developed McLennan's first online philosophy course, and since then he has continued to develop and teach various online courses.

Recently, Dr. Hoeffner renewed his long-standing involvement in academic advising by joining a group of faculty in a grant-funded intensive advising program focused on improving the success of developmental students. He regularly mentors students who need help in the areas of successful academic behaviors, self-advocacy, and the development of college-level reading and writing skills.

His background in foreign languages and logic contributed to his talents for creating the sentence-combining and grammar units in *Common Places*, and his expertise in teaching critical thinking and student mentoring helped shape the text. When he is not teaching, advising, or writing, Dr. Hoeffner enjoys following the Dallas Cowboys, reading, and traveling.

Brief Contents

Contents

PART 1   READING AND WRITING AS INTEGRATED PROCESSES 1

©Doug Steakley/Getty Images

©Blend Images–Peathegee Inc/
Getty Images RF

©MBI/Alamy Stock Photo RF

©Ana Abejon/Getty Images RF

©Michael Babwahsingh

©In Green/Shutterstock.com RF

©Joe McDaniel/Getty Images RF

©Lisette Le Bon/Purestock/
Superstock RF

©Felix Behnke/Getty Images RF

©Terry J Alcorn/Getty Images RF

CHAPTER 9   Inferences and Tone 290

©Aaron Lindberg/Getty Images RF

PART 2 INTEGRATED READING AND WRITING PROJECTS 365

©Doug Sherman/Geofile RF

Left: ©Ion Chiosea/123RF RF;
Middle: ©tupungato/123RF RF;
Right: ©JGI/Jamie Grill/Blend
Images RF

CHAPTER 11 Three Integrated Reading and Writing Projects 366

Step-by-Step Guidance and Projects also available individually in McGraw-Hill Create™

PART 3 ADDITIONAL SKILLS 453

©Phanuwat Nandee/123RF RF

©senkaya/123RF RF

Source: nasaimages.org/NASA

Available only in McGraw-Hill Create™

©Dimitri Otis/Getty Images RF

PART 4   WELL-CRAFTED SENTENCES 497

©BananaStock/Jupiterimages RF

©Brand X Pictures/ PunchStock RF   ©Dusty Pixel photography/Getty Images RF

UNIT 2   Spelling and Word Choice 548

©Sergey Novikov/123RF RF

UNIT 3   Punctuation and Mechanics 571

©Jupiterimages/Getty Images

Available only in McGraw-Hill Create™

Editing and Revising Practice

A. EDITING FOR SENTENCE ERRORS

B. EDITING FOR PRONOUN ERRORS

C. EDITING FOR VERB ERRORS

D. EDITING FOR PUNCTUATION ERRORS

E. EDITING FOR ERRORS INVOLVING COMMONLY CONFUSED WORDS

F. REVISING FOR SENTENCE VARIETY

G. REVISING FOR ORGANIZATION

H. REVISING FOR CLARITY

I. REVISING AND EDITING FOR COMBINED ERRORS

Grammar and Mechanics Handbook, from *Common Ground*

PART 5 THEMATIC ANTHOLOGY OF READINGS 581

©Don White/Superstock

©Sam Edwards/Caiaimage/Getty Images RF

THEME Triumphing over Adversity 582

©Pamela Moore/Getty Images RF

©Boris Ryaposov/123RF RF

©DAJ/Getty Images RF

Available only in McGraw-Hill Create™

©AP Images

©svetikd/iStock/Getty Images RF

Preface

Those of us in the classroom realize that teaching reading and writing together requires more than just combining our old, separate reading and writing pedagogies. We have embraced a more rhetorical pedagogy, one that helps students read from a writer's point of view and write with an imagined reader ever present.

We wrote the first edition of *Common Places* to provide that pedagogy. Throughout the book, we accelerate learning by consistently integrating skills. Students are challenged to develop their literacy skills by engaging in real-world, college-level integrated reading and writing projects. By developing their skills in this context, students acquire the literacy skills they need to pass challenging college-level courses.

In addition to integrating and accelerating instruction, the pedagogy of *Common Places* is unique among reading and writing texts because it embeds content designed to foster the emotional intelligence development, metacognition, and problem-solving skills our students often lack.

Features of *Common Places*

The text employs a number of features aimed at helping students master the skills of reading and writing in an integrated fashion.

- We provide scaffolded instruction for students, presenting reading and writing processes from the ground up.

- We prompt students to think their way through the steps we provide. Rather than asking students merely to follow steps, we walk them through how to think about reading and writing tasks.

- We present models of every skill, even prerequisite skills. Models reduce the learning curve by helping students master a skill more quickly and confidently.

- We provide an abundance of opportunities to work on skills. Practices interspersed throughout the text build individual skills, and more comprehensive Chapter Activities at the end of most chapters include additional integrated reading and writing opportunities.

- We present text patterns as tools, not as ends in themselves. Students are guided to select and combine patterns of development that fit writing purposes—informing, analyzing, evaluating, and persuading—and provide the best support for particular audiences.

- We present readings, examples, and exercises to foster emotional intelligence and problem solving—as well as reading and writing skills.

- We prompt students to practice metacognition. Like emotional intelligence, metacognitive skills are correlated with higher GPAs and a greater capacity to learn.

- In Part 4, "Well-Crafted Sentences," we use sentence combining to help students develop true grammatical competency.

- Throughout the text, we embed grammatical tips, as Grammar Focus features, when doing so is appropriate. These tips help instructors teach grammar in context on an as-needed basis.

- For Part 2 ("Integrated Reading and Writing Projects"), Part 5 ("Thematic Anthology of Readings"), and the skills chapters, we select high-interest readings of various lengths from a variety of sources, such as textbooks, Web sites, academic journals, and newspapers, all analyzed for Lexile level.

- In Chapter 11, we provide complete theme-based integrated reading and writing projects. Each project features readings on a specific topic and requires students to read and analyze the selections and then integrate them effectively into their own source-based essays.

- We present the reading and writing process as one integrated progression in the Quick Start Guide to Integrated Reading and Writing Assignments. This brief guide at the start of the text articulates the steps in the reading and writing process and enables students to engage in the process immediately. The visual illustration that accompanies the guide serves as an easy reminder of steps in the IRW process.

Revisions to the Second Edition

In the second edition of *Common Places*, we have streamlined instructional explanations where possible, increased graphic presentations of content, and included even more embedded readings and activities for metacognitive and emotional intelligence development. These are the key changes in the second edition:

- Chapter 1 provides an in-depth introduction to the importance of emotional intelligence, problem solving, metacognition, and self-advocacy.

- In the *Instructor's Manual*, we have added tips for using particular assignments and additional readings to foster emotional intelligence, problem-solving, and metacognition.

- In every chapter, new graphics replace dense sections of text, making the text more readable and more visually friendly.

- We have created additional samples of student writing, which include eight Model Student Papers, in the skills chapters as accessible models for students to use. The model papers are listed in the table of contents for easy reference.

- New and updated readings reflect students' concerns and interests. At least 16 percent of non-student example readings are new, taken from sources like *The New York Times, The Washington Post,* government resources, and textbooks on a range of subjects. In addition, 50 percent of the project reading selections available in the text or in Create™ are new, as well as 40 percent of the text anthology readings. With fifty readings in *Common Places* and nearly one hundred readings in Connect IRW *Power of Process*, instructors will find engaging readings for any student audience or Lexile range.

- A new introduction to Chapter 11, "Three Integrated Reading and Writing Projects," follows one student through the entire process of completing an integrated reading and writing assignment and serves as a ready guide to the three integrated reading and writing projects that follow it.

- We have created a summary-writing project, Project 1 in Chapter 11, that guides students through the process of reading to write a summary.

- We have created a new theme, in Part 5, "Thematic Anthology of Readings," on the topic of fast food, a subject we believe will interest students and prompt critical thinking.

- We have changed the structure of the Connect *Common Places* Master Course. We have made the Master Course even more easy to use and have added *Power of Process* reading assignments followed by brief comprehension quizzes.

- We have uploaded all *Common Places* reading selections into the Connect *Common Places* Master Course so that instructors can assign the readings in *Power of Process* or use the readings for other creative applications.

- In addition to updating content quizzes, we have created application tests for each of the skills chapters. These tests are housed both in the instructors' resources and Connect *Common Places* Master Course.

- We have created four comprehensive exams that test students on the most important integrated reading and writing skills. We have housed these in both the Connect *Common Places* Master Course and instructors' resources.

- The Grammar and Mechanics Handbook from *Common Ground*, the lower-level companion text in this program, is available in Create™ and can be added to *Common Places*.

The Learning Support System of Common Places, Second Edition

The *Common Places* program is a coherent, integrated approach to learning that consists of a number of components that can be tailored to course needs.

Connect Integrated Reading and Writing: The *Common Places* Master Course.   Connect is a highly reliable, easy-to-use homework and learning management solution that embeds learning science and award-winning adaptive tools to improve student results. Connect IRW addresses the specific needs of integrated reading and writing courses and various redesign models of instruction. It teaches reading and writing skills as a complementary process by contextualizing the material within thematic disciplinary readings and authentic writing models. In addition to the innovative content, revolutionary learning technology drives the integration of reading and writing skills through a selection of corresponding toolsets.

In the *Common Places* Master Course, which you can copy to your own Connect account and adapt as you wish, you will find various Connect IRW assignment types aligned to every chapter of the *Common Places*, Second Edition, text to accelerate learning. These features align with the chapters in *Common Places*:

- *LearnSmart Achieve* topics
- Chapter reading quizzes
- Chapter application quizzes
- Vocabulary practices and quizzes
- *Power of Process* assignments built around selected chapter readings
- *Power of Process* assignments built to foster particular reading and writing skills
- *Writing Assignments* that include rubrics for outcomes-based assessment and detailed grade and course reports
- *PowerPoint* presentations that introduce concepts and skills
- Discussion board prompts that follow *PowerPoint* presentations

Contact your local McGraw-Hill representative to copy the course to your Connect account.

LearnSmart Achieve.   *LearnSmart Achieve* offers students an adaptive, individualized learning experience designed to ensure the efficient mastery of reading and writing skills in tandem. By targeting students' particular strengths and weaknesses, *LearnSmart Achieve* customizes its lessons and facilitates high-impact learning at an accelerated pace.

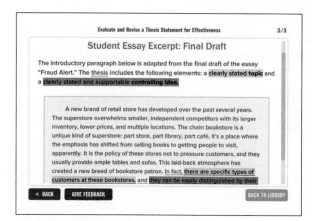
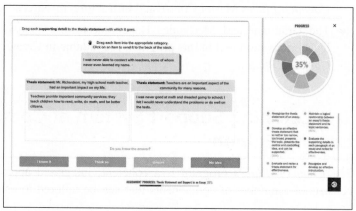

Power of Process.   One overarching goal is at the heart of *Power of Process*: for students to become self-regulating, strategic readers and writers. *Power of Process* facilitates engaged reading and writing processes using research-based best practices suggested by major professional reading and writing organizations.

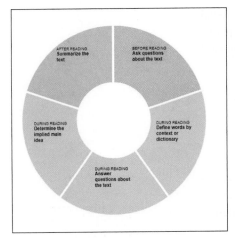

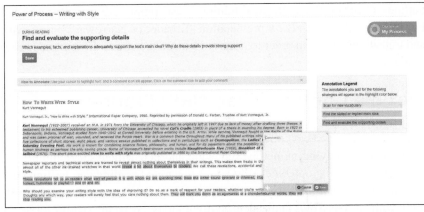

Thematic, Leveled Question Bank.   A thematic, leveled e-book reader and question bank provide dozens of compelling readings and assessment options that instructors can incorporate into their syllabuses. Four pre-built assessments, aligned with the same topics and learning objectives in *LearnSmart Achieve*, may be used as static pre- and posttests for a range of courses.

Book-Specific Resources for Instructors

The following teaching resources are downloadable from the Online Learning Center. Please contact your local McGraw-Hill representative for the username and password to access these resources.

Annotated Instructor's Edition.   Dr. Hoeffner draws on her extensive experience in the classroom—as well as the experiences of many other seasoned IRW faculty—to offer pedagogical ideas that are effective and easy to use. On-page tips suggest innovative ways to present the topics in each chapter. The *Annotated Instructor's Edition* also alerts instructors to teaching resources such as handouts, quizzes, and *PowerPoint* presentations, as well as to assignments and resources in Connect IRW.

Instructor's Manual.   The *Instructor's Manual* is written with the diverse needs of IRW instructors in mind. Faculty new to teaching reading will appreciate the brief presentations of theory that accompany the reading pedagogy in the textbook, as well as the suggestions for how to teach some of the more difficult reading skills. Faculty new to teaching writing will find helpful the suggestions for grading strategies, managing the paper load, addressing grammatical issues, and teaching MLA and APA styles.

Handouts, Exercises, and Graphics.   These copy-and-go pages, useful for in-class, hands-on practice, make preparing for class easier, and they give instructors a way to present material to students whose learning styles benefit from kinesthetic activities.

Topical *PowerPoint* Presentations.   The *PowerPoint* presentations for *Common Places*, Second Edition, are short, fun for students, and powerful. Unlike traditional textbook-supplied *PowerPoint* presentations that simply provide chapter outlines, *Common Places*, Second Edition, presentations are topical and highly visual. For instance, the *PowerPoint* presentation "Broader or Narrower?" starts with photos and transitions to text in order to teach students to recognize differences in the breadth of ideas.

Flexible Content for any IRW Program: Customize *Common Places* with Create™

After closely studying numerous statewide and department curriculum frameworks and student learning outcomes (SLOs) for integrated reading and writing courses, we designed *Common Places*, Second Edition, as a program of content flexible enough to align with various SLOs and course configurations. As an alternative to the content in the national edition, instructors may use McGraw-Hill Create™ to arrange chapters to align with their syllabus, eliminate those they do not wish to assign, and add any of the *Common Places*, Second Edition, content available only in Create™ to build one or multiple print or e-book texts, including Connect IRW access codes—for customized texts for the entire sequence of IRW courses or for a single course. McGraw-Hill Create™ is a self-service Web site that allows instructors and departments to create customized course materials using McGraw-Hill's comprehensive, cross-disciplinary content and digital products. Through Create™, instructors may also add their own material, such as a course syllabus, a course rubric, course standards, and any specific instruction for students.

The following content is available *only* in Create™ for *Common Places*: a chapter on taking reading and writing exams, one additional project, a unit of editing and revising practice, and two additional thematic anthology units ("Television and Stereotypes" and "The Rules of Attraction"). Also, instructors who want a traditional, but level-appropriate, handbook for their students have the option of adding, in Create™, the Grammar and Mechanics Handbook from *Common Ground*, the lower-level text in this program.

A Final Word

Since the publication of the first edition of *Common Places,* we have had the opportunity to meet so many wonderful people who are passionate about teaching and equipping students for success. It has become clear to us that the task of educating students with reading and writing skills is far more than a job. It is a mission, one that stems from a belief in human potential and one that, for many instructors, arises from a desire to see greater equality of opportunity in the world.

We are very excited about the second edition of *Common Places*. We would love to hear from you as you use this new edition. Please feel free to e-mail either of us with questions or suggestions. The feedback we receive from users is invaluable in our continuing effort to improve the book's approach and presentation. We wish you the very best as you equip your students for real, life-changing successes.

Lisa Hoeffner
Lhoeffner@mclennan.edu

Kent Hoeffner
Khoeffner@mclennan.edu

A Word from the Lead Author, Lisa Hoeffner

Many of the ideas in this book come from the rich conversations I have had with colleagues across the country. I have no doubt this would be a different book without the conversations I've had with colleagues and the amazing, teaching-centered folks at McGraw-Hill. I'd like to especially thank Linda Stern, our editor, for her insightful guidance every step of the way. She has managed to herd cats with good humor! I would also like to thank Kelly Villella and Penina Braffman, both of whom have shared the vision for this book and have expertly guided its progression. Kelly is a visionary and a workhorse, a rare combination. And Penina's insights into teaching have made her contributions invaluable. I've also learned a lot from Ashley Sandoval, another fine mind at McGraw-Hill. A big thank you goes to Beth Tripmacher for her constant help, quick wit, and smart ideas. In addition, I would like to thank Lisa Pinto for her insights and enthusiasm along the way.

I am also very grateful to my colleagues at McLennan Community College, especially Linda Crawford, Bill Matta, and Fred Hills. Their support and kindness are representative of the kind of colleagues I am lucky to work with at McLennan.

I would also like to thank the crucial work of all the faculty reviewers of the second edition for their invaluable guidance: Elizabeth Acosta, *El Paso Community College;* Solmaria Benavides, *San Jacinto College – Central*; Joanna Bolick, *Asheville-Buncombe Technical Community College*; Elizabeth Braun, *Catawba Valley Community College*; Krysten Buchanan, *Catawba Valley Community College*; Grisel Cano, *Houston Community College – South, Southeast, Central*; Dennie M. Combs-Norman, *San Jacinto College – Central*; Kathleen Cuyler, *Coastal Bend College – Beeville*; Patricia A. Davis, *Houston Community College – Southwest*; Christina Marie Devlin, *Montgomery College – Germantown*; Tammy Donaldson, *Del Mar College – East*; Ruth Engel, *Tarrant County College – Trinity River*; Mary Sue Fox, *Central New Mexico Community College*; Heidi Giffin, *Central Piedmont Community College*; Stacey Higdon, *Houston Community College – Central*; Cynthia Holland, *Northeast Alabama Community College*; Theodore Johnston, *El Paso Community College – Rio Grande*; Vicky Krug, *Westmoreland County Community College*; Suzanne Labadie, *Oakland Community College, Royal Oak*; Gus P. LaFosse, *Kilgore College*; Desmond Lewis, *Houston Community College – Northwest*; Wei Li, *Lone Star College – North Harris*; Sharon Lockett, *Lee College*; Jacquelyn Minor, *Tarrant County College – Southeast*; Eric Niemi, *Chattanooga State Community College*; Sandra Padilla, *El Paso Community College*; Alexandria Piland, *Central New Mexico Community College – Westside;* Karen Redding, *University of North Georgia, Oconee;* Joan Reeves, *Northeast Alabama Community College*; Michael Rice, *San Jacinto College – Central*; Nancy Risch, *Caldwell Community College and Technical Institute*; Vanessa Sekinger, *Germanna Community College*; Justin Williams, *Navarro College – Corsicana*; and Mary Zamarripa, *San Jacinto College – Central.*

I am most grateful for the patience and support of my family: Hannah, Abby, Seth, Richard, and Gail. And without Kent, my constant companion and co-author, I couldn't have done it. Thank you.

Lisa Hoeffner

Quick Start Guide
To Integrated Reading and Writing Assignments

This brief reference guide will walk you through the integrated reading and writing process, giving you guidance for your assignments from the first day of class.

GETTING STARTED

Analyze your assignment.	Ask yourself: Is the assignment clear and complete? Is research required or allowed? What are the formatting and length guidelines? Highlight or underline key words. For additional clarity, reword the topic as a question to be answered.
Identify your purpose.	Ask yourself: What is my purpose as I read the assigned texts? When I write, will my purpose be to inform, to entertain, to evaluate or analyze, or to persuade?

WORKING WITH READINGS

Preview the reading and think about the topic.	Use four strategies to examine a text before reading it. Preview by looking at title headings, illustrations, and context. Predict the topic. Recall what you already know about the topic. Ask questions you hope the reading will answer.
Read and annotate the text.	Annotate the thesis statement, major supporting points, and supporting details. Annotate any key words associated with the issue. Mark at least three potential quotes.
Outline each reading.	Write a brief outline that includes the thesis statement and major supporting points. Summarize the article in two or three sentences. In your summary, include the source's bibliographic information (author's name, title, and publication information), the topic, the writer's main idea, the major supporting points, and the significant supporting details.
Summarize each reading.	Summarize the article in two or three sentences. In your summary, include the source's bibliographic information (author's name, title, and publication information), the topic, the writer's main idea, the major supporting points, and the significant supporting details.
Prepare an information sheet for each reading.	List the source's bibliographic information and any general notes. Add your outline, your brief summary, issues addressed in the reading, key words, and the quotes you have identified. *For more ideas, go back to "Read and annotate the text," "Outline each reading," and "Summarize each reading."*

DEVELOPING YOUR ESSAY

Synthesize your sources.	If you are using several sources, determine how the sources agree and differ. Use a graphic organizer, such as an issues chart, to categorize and organize the ideas.
Prewrite to develop your ideas.	Use prewriting strategies (discussion, simple listing, clustering, the 5 W's + 1 H questions, freewriting, and freetalking) for topics, major supporting points, and supporting details. *For more ideas, go back to "Analyze your assignment."*
Construct a thesis statement.	Write a thesis statement – a complete sentence in which you articulate your topic and your main point about the topic. Check that your thesis statement is not a statement of fact, a question, or an announcement and that it is not too broad or narrow.
Develop support for your thesis statement.	Determine your major supporting points. Develop supporting details for each major supporting point as content for your essay. Select text patterns (narration, definition, illustration, classification, comparison-contrast, cause and effect, process analysis) and features (such as reasons, examples, and explanations) to express the supporting details. *For more ideas, go back to "Prewrite to develop your ideas."*

Add source materials to your outline.	Start with your topic and thesis statement. Express each major supporting point in a complete sentence. Add supporting details. Jot down ideas for the introduction Indicate in your outline where you might use information from the summaries you wrote, the quotes you identified, and any other source information. *For more ideas, go back to "Read and annotate the text" and "Prepare an information sheet for each reading."*
Write a complete draft of your essay.	Using your outline for guidance, write an introduction, body paragraphs, and a conclusion. Use the major supporting points as topic sentences for body paragraphs. Write as many paragraphs as you need to develop fully the essay's main idea. Decide where to place your thesis statement. Keep your audience's needs in mind as you write. Frequently reread your paper from the beginning to check the flow of ideas, to add needed information, and to reword passages for clarity.
Integrate ideas and quotes from sources correctly.	Follow these rules: (1) Copy direct quotations exactly from the source. (2) Integrate a quoted fragment grammatically into a complete sentence. (3) Use an attributive tag to integrate a quotation into your writing. (4) Start and end a quotation with quotation marks. (5) Place the sentence's period inside the quotation marks; if a parenthetical reference ends the quotation, place the period after the reference. *For more ideas, go back to "Read and annotate the text" and "Prepare an information sheet for each reading."*

FINISHING YOUR ASSIGNMENT

Check that you have met assignment requirements.	Review your annotated assignment to make sure the content of your essay meets the requirements of the assignment. *For more ideas, go back to "Analyze your assignment."*
Revise for organization and unity.	Ask yourself: Is the essay's organization logical? Do all the paragraphs relate to the main idea? Have I used transitions effectively? Make any necessary changes. *For more ideas, go back to "Create an outline to organize your essay."*
Revise for development.	Ask yourself: Have I answered readers' potential questions? Have I included enough support for my thesis statement? Have I explained unfamiliar terms? Make any necessary changes. *For more ideas, go back to "Prewrite to develop your ideas."*
Revise for clarity.	Ask yourself: Are my words concrete and specific? Is my tone appropriate? Are all pronoun references clear?
Create a works cited or references list.	If you used sources, create an MLA works cited list or an APA references list. *For more ideas, go back to "Integrate ideas and quotes from sources correctly."*
Check for plagiarism.	Make sure you have given credit to sources: (1) Check that each summary, quotation, and idea from a source is credited with an attributive tag (*Jones said, . . .*) or a parenthetical reference. (2) Check that each source cited in your essay is listed correctly in the works cited or references list.
Edit your essay using SMART TRACS.	Check for grammatical errors that you have had trouble with in the past. Run a spell-checker. Use other methods, such as SMART TRACS, to find errors. S = Spelling　　　　　　T = Tense consistency M = Missing words　　　　R = Rhythm A = Accurate punctuation　A = Active voice R = Repeated words　　　　C = Confusing words T = Terminal punctuation　S = Sources
Put your essay in the proper format.	Follow your instructor's directions for formatting your paper in MLA style or APA style.

QUICK START GUIDE
to Integrated Reading
and Writing

GETTING STARTED

Put your essay in the proper format.
Edit your writing using SMART TRACS.
Check for plagiarism.
Create a works cited or references list.
Revise for clarity.
Revise for development.
Revise for organization and unity.
Check that you have met assignment requirements.

FINISHING YOUR ASSIGNMENT

Integrate ideas and quotes from sources correctly.
Write a complete draft of your essay.
Add source materials to your outline.
Create an outline to organize your essay.
Develop support for your thesis statement.
Construct a thesis statement.
Prewrite to develop your ideas.
Synthesize your sources.

DEVELOPING YOUR ESSAY

Prepare an information sheet for each reading.
Summarize each reading.
Outline each reading.
Read and annotate the text.
Preview the reading and think about the topic.

WORKING WITH READINGS

Identify your purpose.
Analyze your assignment.

Reading and Writing as Integrated Processes

©Doug Steakley/Getty Images

Emotional Intelligence and Your Pathway to Success

©Blend Images–Peathegee Inc/Getty Images RF

It takes determination and self-knowledge to overcome obstacles to personal success. What challenges do you face? Are you juggling work, study, and parenting responsibilities? Are you struggling with financial resources? How can you keep a positive point of view and work actively toward achieving your goals?

Chapter Objectives

After completing this chapter, students will be able to do the following:

- Define and practice emotional intelligence.

- Define and practice critical thinking.

- Describe the foundations for college success.

What does being smart have to do with being successful? The answer depends on what you mean by "smart." Take the case of Brandon. Brandon was the valedictorian of his high school class. He would sleep through his calculus class because he thought the work was so "tedious and boring," yet his calculus average was 99. Clearly, Brandon's traditional intelligence—which we often call IQ—was very high. After high school, he left home to attend a top-notch university on a full scholarship.

You might think that a student like Brandon would become a highly paid engineer or a renowned chemist, but that's not what happened. After his first semester of college, Brandon's grades were so poor that he dropped out. High school had been so easy that Brandon had not prepared himself for college. Thinking he could study at the last minute, Brandon would often go to parties instead of working on academics. And Brandon also had trouble emotionally. His new environment was nothing like his hometown, so Brandon struggled with fitting in and had bouts of loneliness.

Brandon was extremely smart, but as his story shows, being smart isn't always enough to find happiness and success in life.

People who are successful in life usually possess three essential characteristics: emotional intelligence, critical thinking skills, and grit—the willpower to do what it takes to succeed. In this chapter, we will discuss each of these characteristics and how they affect your success in both college and life.

Developing Emotional Intelligence

Emotional intelligence is different from IQ. **Emotional intelligence,** sometimes called EQ, is your ability to understand and manage your own emotions as well as understand and relate to the emotional needs of others. How many professional athletes can you think of who have destroyed their opportunities for success because of poor decisions they made "off the field"? Almost always, these athletes who cannot manage themselves have poor EQ skills. In the same way that a brilliant guy like Brandon needs EQ to thrive, so also do gifted athletes. And if these exceptional people need EQ, average people need it even more!

The good news is that we *can* increase our emotional intelligence by practicing healthy EQ habits. We will look at three strategies in depth.

EMOTIONAL INTELLIGENCE STRATEGIES

1 Understand your emotions and put them into words.

2 Recognize emotional responses and their consequences.

3 Change emotional responses.

Strategy 1: Understand Your Emotions and Put Them into Words

We experience emotions all the time, and sometimes we let those emotions control us. The problem is, we do not always know when our emotions are controlling us. The first requirement for EQ is to realize when you are experiencing an emotion and to name that emotion. Then, you can make intentional choices about how to react to the emotion. Look at Mia's responses, which follow, to see why this step is so important.

POOR EQ

Mia: I'm so sick of studying. I hate this stuff. I'm going to text Kayla and see what she's doing. I need to get out of here.

GOOD EQ

Mia: Wait a minute. I'm feeling bored. I know that when I feel bored, I want to give up. I need to do something to change this feeling so that I can keep studying. I really want to keep studying because I am determined to become a veterinarian!

The first step in exercising emotional intelligence is understanding and naming your feelings so that you can decide on a suitable response to them.

©kho/123RF RF

At first, Mia has a poor EQ response because she doesn't recognize her emotion and try to change her response. Then, Mia has a realization. She identifies her emotion—boredom—and sees that giving in to her emotion will keep her from reaching her goal of becoming a veterinarian. By naming the emotion and confronting it, Mia can try to find creative solutions that will help her either change her emotion or deal with it in a productive way.

To improve your EQ, start jotting down every emotion you have. It's easy to jot down major emotional responses such as anger or sadness, but we sometimes overlook the less intense—but equally important—emotions. Keep a small pad of paper with you, or use the Notes app on your smartphone. Log your emotions and keep track of them. To get started, use the "Common Emotions" chart to review the various emotions that most of us experience frequently. If you are unsure of the meaning of some of these words, refer to a dictionary or thesaurus for more information.

COMMON EMOTIONS			
Positive Feelings	**Sad Feelings**	**Fearful Feelings**	**Angry Feelings**
amused	alienated	accused	angry
cheerful	apathetic	cautious	annoyed
compassionate	apologetic	confused	bitter
confident	ashamed	fearful	bored
curious	belittled	frantic	burdened
determined	dejected	guilty	deceived
enthusiastic	depressed	helpless	defiant
excited	disappointed	lonely	disgusted
happy	distracted	paranoid	enraged
mischievous	embarrassed	regretful	envious
optimistic	excluded	shocked	frustrated
pleased	gloomy	shy	hateful
protective	grieving	trapped	hostile

(continued)

COMMON EMOTIONS *(continued)*			
Positive Feelings	**Sad Feelings**	**Fearful Feelings**	**Angry Feelings**
proud relieved surprised sympathetic thankful	hopeless humiliated hurt inadequate miserable pessimistic sad self-pitying	undecided unwelcome upset weak	indignant insulted jealous provoked resentful stubborn

PRACTICE 1

Naming Your Emotions

Choose a recent four- to six-hour period of time. For example, you might choose this morning or yesterday evening. Fill in the chart below with all of the emotions you experienced during that time. Try to remember at least three emotions. In addition, write down what triggered, or brought on, the emotion, and write down your reaction to the emotion. Use additional sheets if necessary. A sample has been provided.

Date/Time	Emotion	Trigger	My Reaction
Thursday, 6 p.m.	Angry	I was hungry and tired, and my roommate had eaten the last burrito.	I slammed the fridge door and stormed out. Went to a fast-food place and ate too much.

Strategy 2: Recognize Emotional Responses and Their Consequences

If you have ever seen a toddler have a temper tantrum, you have seen the power of emotions! When we fail to recognize and control our emotions, we often act inappropriately. We might make hasty decisions that affect our lives and the people we love, or we might act out in ways that cause us to lose our jobs, our opportunities, or even our lives. Once you become adept at recognizing and naming your emotions, you will start to notice that emotions are sometimes followed by irrational thoughts.

When you experience an emotion, get in the habit of analyzing the thoughts the emotion brings with it. By doing this, you will be able to think more clearly and act more reasonably. Do not react immediately. Give yourself a few minutes to think. Notice what happens to Keith's response when he takes a moment to reflect.

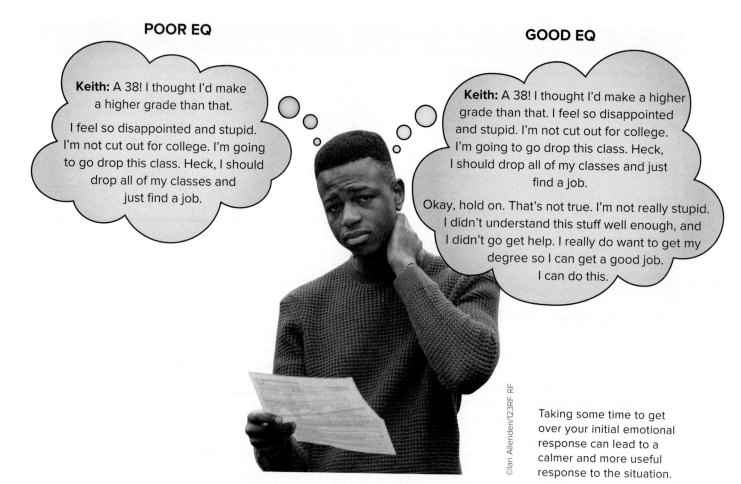

POOR EQ

Keith: A 38! I thought I'd make a higher grade than that.

I feel so disappointed and stupid. I'm not cut out for college. I'm going to go drop this class. Heck, I should drop all of my classes and just find a job.

GOOD EQ

Keith: A 38! I thought I'd make a higher grade than that. I feel so disappointed and stupid. I'm not cut out for college. I'm going to go drop this class. Heck, I should drop all of my classes and just find a job.

Okay, hold on. That's not true. I'm not really stupid. I didn't understand this stuff well enough, and I didn't go get help. I really do want to get my degree so I can get a good job. I can do this.

©Ian Allenden/123RF RF

Taking some time to get over your initial emotional response can lead to a calmer and more useful response to the situation.

It is easy to see how failing to control your emotions might lead to making poor choices in life. Work on taking the time to think about your feelings, correct irrational thoughts, and make decisions that are in keeping with your life goals.

PRACTICE 2

Controlling Emotions

Think of a time when you experienced an emotion and reacted too quickly. Perhaps you were angry and lashed out at someone, or perhaps you were having a lot of fun and made a reckless decision because you didn't think about the consequences of an action. Write two paragraphs. In the first paragraph, explain the emotion, your feelings, and what happened when you acted on the feelings you had. In the second paragraph, write about how you could have controlled the emotion appropriately if you had taken time to think about your feelings and react differently. Explain how you could have reacted and how the outcome of the situation would have been different. Use a separate sheet for your paragraphs.

Strategy 3: Change Emotional Responses

When you have a strong emotion, you need a strategy for gaining control over how you react to it. Use these three methods for controlling your emotional responses.

Reframe.　Strong emotions often lead us to irrational thoughts. Earlier, you saw that when Keith received a low grade on a paper, he started thinking the worst: "I'm stupid. I'm not cut out for college." If Keith does not rethink his response, he might actually begin to believe these irrational thoughts. Then he may do something unwise, such as drop out of college.

Reframing is looking at a problem or situation from a different point of view. You can reframe irrational thoughts by stepping back for a moment and trying to find a new way to think about the situation. Keith received a bad grade, and of course, he felt disappointed. But maybe there are other, more rational ways to think about what just happened. If Keith is honest with himself, he may say, "Okay, I know I didn't study as much as I should have." Or if he *did* study a lot, he can still reframe: "I didn't do well, but that doesn't mean I can't learn this stuff. I will just have to learn to study a new way and will need to get a tutor. I can learn anything if I really want to."

By reframing your thoughts, you can control emotions and make better decisions, decisions that enable you to reach your life's goals.

PRACTICE　3

Reframing Emotional Responses

Read each of the following scenarios. In the box provided, write a few sentences about how each person could reframe the situation and his or her emotional response in a more positive way.

Scenario	Poor EQ Response	How to Reframe the Response
1. Trinity is fuming. She is sitting in her car, waiting for her friend, who is running late—again. Her friend is always late, and Trinity has had it. She feels irate!	*I've had it. I'm sick and tired of Shelly always being late. She can just find her own ride. I'm leaving.*	
2. Marco has been doing homework for his psychology class for an hour and a half. He looks through the packet he has to complete and realizes he will have to do another two hours of work to finish it. He feels discouraged and angry.	*I hate this stuff. I can't believe I've been sitting here for almost two hours on a beautiful Sunday when all my friends are playing football. I'm not doing this stupid stuff. It's just busy work anyway. That teacher just wants to make us miserable. Doesn't she know we have lives outside of class???!*	

(continued)

Scenario	Poor EQ Response	How to Reframe the Response
3. Jill is ecstatic. Her college team just won the championship and everyone around her is celebrating. Her friends are going to a party that will probably last all night, but Jill knows she shouldn't go because she has a big project due in a few days and must work on it.	*No way am I sitting around here working on this project tonight. Heck with studying! Let's party!*	

Become More Flexible.   Sometimes we go through unnecessary anguish because we simply aren't flexible enough. Let's go back to the toddler example. It's common to see a young child have a tantrum for seemingly minor reasons such as not getting to eat dessert before dinner. With a bit of flexibility, the toddler could talk herself into waiting for dessert and spare everyone her tantrums, but toddlers' brains aren't developed well enough to think logically. Adult brains, however, are!

When we intentionally become more flexible, we change an emotional state. For instance, it's easy to get frustrated and angry when you are waiting in a long line. And if someone cuts in line, those feelings intensify. How can we use flexibility to change these feelings?

First, we can develop flexibility on a practical level. If you are waiting in line and have another appointment for which you might be late, think of the options at your disposal. You don't have to continue to wait in the line. You can leave and come back later. Alternatively, you can be late for the next appointment. If you are usually on time, people will probably be forgiving. But you have to remember that fact and talk yourself into feeling more flexible! Another option is to simply use your phone to call and reschedule the next appointment. Or you can question the reason you are in line. Perhaps the thing you are waiting for is not worth the wait. You do not *have* to do anything. No one is forcing you to stand in line. By thinking of alternatives, you can be more flexible and control your situation—and the emotions that go with it.

Flexibility is especially important in college. Imagine that you just had a fight with your girlfriend or boyfriend, and you have to go to class. You may be tempted to sit in the back row, slump down, text friends during class, and tune out. But you know that those behaviors won't help you reach your goals. You've already gone through all the trouble of getting to class. What a waste if you are going to just tune out!

So think of other alternatives. You might tell yourself, "I have all afternoon to think about our fight. I will spend this class time tuning in and spend the rest of the day thinking about what I want." Or you might challenge yourself, like this: "Okay, I am challenging myself to control this emotion. I'm going to act the opposite of how I feel. I'm going to sit up, participate, listen, and tune in. Let's see if I can do it." Thinking about alternatives can enable you to have flexibility when you have to deal with emotions that can sabotage your success.

PRACTICE 4

Practicing Flexibility

Read the following scenarios and notice the problems caused by inflexible thinking. In the space provided, write down flexible alternatives the person can use to help control the situation and the feelings that go with it.

Scenario	Poor EQ Response	Flexible Thinking Alternatives
1. Matt is about to take a math test. He studied all weekend and thinks he is prepared, but right before class, Matt is feeling fearful and almost sick. His hands are getting clammy and he is worried that he won't remember anything.	Matt starts thinking, "I am so bad at math. I'm going to fail this test. I can't remember anything. I'm never going to be able to pass a college math class."	
2. Ashley's eight-year-old daughter came home from school crying and said, "My teacher made fun of me in front of the whole class. She hates me, and now she wants the other kids to hate me too!"	Ashley instantly feels angry and protective. She starts looking for the teacher's phone number and mutters, "Nobody makes fun of my child!" She plans to give the teacher an earful.	
3. L'Vinia's sister just had a baby. Everyone is posting pictures on social media, and L'Vinia is sitting in a government class. She is so excited and is tempted to leave class. She is having a hard time concentrating.	L'Vinia thinks, "I can't concentrate anyway, so this class isn't doing me any good." Then she tunes out and joins the fun by responding to social media. OR L'Vinia slips out quietly and gets to the hospital as quickly as she can.	

Develop an Internal Locus (Center) of Control. Who controls you? As a toddler, you were controlled by your parents. As you grew up, you increasingly began to control your own behaviors. As adults, we exercise a lot of control over our lives, but we also know that some things—such as getting cancer or being laid off—are beyond our control. People who have an **external locus of control** tend to believe that most of their life situations are beyond their control. Conversely, people who have an **internal locus of control** tend to believe that although some things are beyond their control, for the most part, they are in control of their lives.

People who believe they are in control of their lives tend to feel more emotionally stable than people who believe life controls them. A person with an internal locus of control can deal with hard times better than a person with an external locus of control. Read through the next scenario to see how Leah's locus of control affects her thinking.

EXTERNAL LOCUS OF CONTROL ("LIFE IS CONTROLLING ME!")

Leah: My financial aid was denied! Nothing good ever happens to me. They didn't give me financial aid. Now what am I supposed to do? I guess they don't want me to succeed. They said I've been denied. There is nothing I can do. I'm so discouraged.

INTERNAL LOCUS OF CONTROL ("I'M STILL IN CHARGE")

Leah: My financial aid was denied! I'm discouraged. This is strange. I really thought I had everything figured out. I must have made a mistake in my thinking or figuring. I'm going to appeal this decision and see if I can at least get a student loan. If I can't, then I'm going to figure out what I need to do to be eligible for financial aid next semester. I'm going to go online and see who I need to talk to.

©Piotr Marcinski/iStock/Getty Images RF

When you believe that you, and not outside circumstances, are mostly in control of your life, you also believe that you have the ability to resolve issues that arise.

People who do not think they can affect their life circumstances often make assumptions that lead to bad decisions. If Leah believes she has no control over her financial aid, she may give up the dream of going to college. On the other hand, suppose she takes control of the situation and believes that she *can* change the course of her life. Then, she may learn that there are other financial aid options available to her. And she may learn how to get financial aid the next semester.

It is true that we cannot control everything that happens to us, but how we react to life can make a big difference to our success. One way to gain an internal locus of control is to change the scripts that run through our minds. Here are some examples.

Instead of . . .	Say . . .
I never have any luck.	Things didn't go my way this time, but next time I'll do things differently.
They did this to me.	I've found myself in a bad situation, and I'm going to get out of this situation.
It doesn't matter how hard I try, I just can't wake up on time.	I am determined to find a way to wake up on time.
There is nothing I can do about the bus schedule.	I can figure out a way to solve the bus schedule problem.
The test was unfair.	I didn't do a good enough job on the test.

To develop an internal locus of control, try these things:

- **Take responsibility.** You have to take responsibility for the successes—and failures—in your life. That can be difficult. It's hard to admit when we make mistakes, but blaming our circumstances on others will lead to only more failure.
- **Refuse to be a victim.** Think of yourself as a person in control. It is true that sometimes we are victims, but we can reclaim control of our lives by taking positive actions that eliminate fear and hopelessness.
- **Find solutions.** Don't allow life's setbacks to destroy your dreams. Think creatively and find solutions. Ask other people to help you solve problems. Reach out to people who can help. Take an active part in your success and in regaining control of your life. Above all, *do something.* Don't let life happen to you. Take actions that help you regain a sense of control over your life.
- **Think positively.** You have to believe that you can control your life. If you have no hope, you will not be able to find solutions to the problems that threaten success. Believe that where there is a will, there is a way. Start a belief journal. Write down everything you believe you are capable of and go over those beliefs every day.

PRACTICE 5

Developing an Internal Locus of Control

Think about a time when you felt as if you were not in control. Write a paragraph about the situation and how the situation made you feel. Include in your paragraph how you reacted to the situation. Did your reaction help you regain your sense of control? Did your reaction reinforce your feeling that you had no control? How could you have acted differently in order to regain a sense of control? See the example paragraph for a model. Use a separate sheet for your paragraph.

Example:

Before my freshman year of high school, my family moved to a new city. I had always played basketball, so I was pretty confident that I would make the team at the new school. I went to tryouts in the summer, and I did great. But then I learned that I had not been picked for the team. I was crushed and angry. As I got to know the kids at that school, I decided that only the kids who had always gone to school in that district were going to be chosen. They didn't like outsiders. That's what I *thought*. I thought that I couldn't have affected the outcome. So I felt sorry for myself and didn't try out the next year. Then I noticed that a new kid did try out and *he made the team.* So I realized that maybe there was a chance for me. I tried out before my junior year and made the team that time. I played my last two years and realized that the coach was a great guy. He just hadn't seen me play enough to put me on the team my freshman year. What I learned from this is that I thought I had no control, and it cost me two years of playing basketball. If I had realized that I really had the control all along, I would have stopped feeling sorry for myself and would have tried out before my sophomore year. I learned that you have to rise up and take control of what you want.

Thinking Critically

While emotional intelligence helps us to navigate and control our feelings, critical thinking helps us to improve our logic and problem-solving abilities. **Critical thinking** is the practice of forming and asking key questions about the texts you read and the situations you encounter in life. Critical thinkers go on to answer these key questions in order to form rational judgments and find creative solutions to problems.

An Example of Critical Thinking

While critical thinking sometimes relies on having background knowledge, it also involves being able to predict difficulties, question assumptions, and solve problems. In the workplace, being able to think critically often separates managers from lower-level employees.

Consider this scenario: Monica is a clerk at a rental car agency. It is a busy Friday afternoon, and lines of people are waiting to pick up rental vehicles for weekend travel. Monica's supervisor, Fred, who is the store manager, has to leave suddenly to handle a family emergency. Monica and Jill, another entry-level employee, are the only rental clerks available. They are managing to keep the lines moving and keep customers happy, much to Monica's relief.

A customer whom Monica recognizes—an administrative assistant for the local university's sports program—comes in the door. He greets Monica by name; he has done so much business with the rental agency that he has developed a warm relationship with all the employees. In fact, the agency relies on the university's business to meet its sales goals each month.

He bypasses the line of customers and asks to have a private word with Monica. An unexpected situation has come up, he says, and the basketball team needs three vans immediately. Monica doesn't even have to look at her computer to know that the agency's last three vans have already been reserved by customers who are waiting in line. She checks anyway, and sure enough, the vans are reserved. Pulling Jill aside, she asks her advice. Jill has no idea what to do. Monica texts Fred, but she gets no answer. She calls a nearby agency, but they have no vehicles available.

What should Monica do? Should she lease the vans to the loyal university customer and turn away the people who already have reservations? Surely, the company would do better financially to retain the university's business than to satisfy three casual customers. But would such an action be fair? What would her boss do, she wonders? What are the things she should consider to make this decision?

Monica needs to examine her assumptions and ask questions in order to solve this problem. First, she can articulate her goals in the situation: accommodate a long-time customer, accommodate new customers, retain as much business as possible, and retain the company's reputation for good service. She may realize that "solving" the problem does not necessarily mean providing the vans. Perhaps explaining her efforts and demonstrating her concern will preserve the company's reputation for fairness and good service even if the vans aren't available. As Monica thinks through her ideas, she may come to realize that being honest, fair, and as helpful as possible would generate the best outcome for her goals.

©RubberBall Selects/Alamy Stock Photo RF

Health-care professionals use critical thinking to ask questions that lead them to a correct diagnosis. For example, if a patient presents with seizures, a nurse or physician's assistant might ask him whether he has a history of neurological disorders. Knowing the right questions to ask requires critical thinking.

This same kind of thinking is required in college courses. Sometimes courses will require you to simply memorize information, a task that does *not* involve thinking critically. Often, however, your instructors will push you to think critically by requiring you to use that information in unpredictable ways. For example, on a math test, you may see problems that are not like the ones you studied and reviewed but whose solutions are possible if you apply the knowledge you have learned. In applying your knowledge to solve these problems, you are thinking critically, the way Monica has to think.

How Critical Thinking Affects Reading and Writing Skills

Just as there is more to running a rental car agency than following a list of instructions for checking out cars, there is more to comprehending a text than merely understanding its literal meaning. Critical reading requires us to ask questions: What does this writer want me to believe? How might this writer benefit if I believe what he has to say? What assumptions is he making? Do I agree with those assumptions?

Good writing also depends on critical thinking. We can teach a computer to construct grammatically correct sentences, but a computer cannot write convincing essays. It cannot analyze its audience, and it cannot analyze its own assumptions. It cannot think of the critical questions that need to be asked. Such questions include much more complex inquiries than simply "How many pages should this essay be?" Effective writers ask a variety of questions that help them focus their writing. For example, a writer might ask herself whether she should use the term *woman* or *lady* in a composition. She might wonder if an audience is likely to respond more positively to one term than the other. Her analysis can help her choose the more appropriate term for her purpose. This kind of critical questioning will help her anticipate readers' responses and consequently become a better writer. Just as Monica's questions can help her determine the right course of action, critical thinking about your writing will help you determine how to word your ideas and communicate your thoughts effectively. Practice your critical thinking skills by completing the exercise that follows.

Thinking Critically

The following passage describes a scheduling problem for Lin, a freshman in college. Read the passage, and then use critical thinking to answer the questions on a separate sheet of paper.

Lin lives with his parents and is in his second semester in college. He is considering renting an apartment with his best friend. The apartment is within walking distance from campus, so Lin believes he will save on gasoline and make better use of campus resources if he lives in the apartment. Lin would need to work about twenty-five hours a week to afford the apartment and related expenses. His part-time job offers him only fifteen hours a week, but he plans to ask his supervisor for more hours. He has three weeks to decide whether he wants to rent the apartment or remain at his parents' house.

1. List the questions Lin should ask before making this decision.
2. List the potential problems that could arise if Lin were to rent the apartment with his friend.
3. Which of these potential problems could Lin prevent or overcome?
4. If these problems were to occur, how would they affect Lin?
5. Based on your critical thinking, is this a risk worth taking? Why or why not? What advice would you give Lin? Explain in a paragraph.

Succeeding in College

Researchers who study the reasons for college success and the obstacles preventing it have identified several characteristics of successful students:

- Students who succeed are self-directed.
- Students who succeed use resources effectively.
- Students who succeed manage their time well.
- Students who succeed are self-reflective.

Students Who Succeed Are Self-Directed

People who are self-directed are in charge of their own learning experiences. They find a way to learn. They do not depend solely on a textbook or on an instructor or on having the perfect learning situation. They do not wait for an instructor's advice to go to a tutoring center. They take the initiative to find the resources they need for success. In short, they demonstrate grit—the determination to persevere, despite difficulties, in achieving their goals.

Angela Duckworth, a professor of psychology at the University of Pennsylvania, has studied the effects of grit. Duckworth's research has shown that two qualities—grit and self-control—are essential for success. If you have ever started a project that was tedious, time-consuming, and difficult, you know how hard it can be to finish the project. People who have grit finish, regardless of the difficulties and the tedium.

Once you are determined to succeed, you can look for the tools to help you succeed. Notice the different approaches that Ron can take in the scenario shown here.

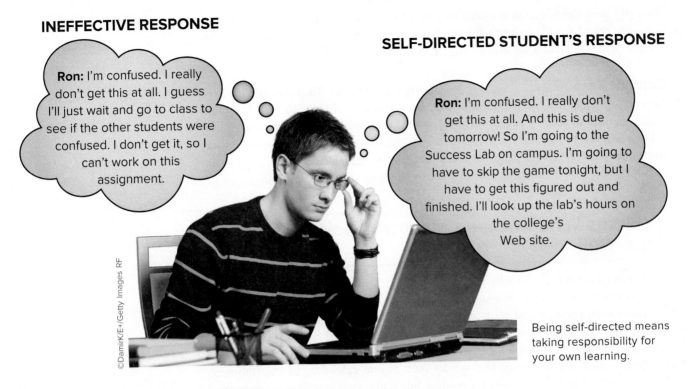

INEFFECTIVE RESPONSE

Ron: I'm confused. I really don't get this at all. I guess I'll just wait and go to class to see if the other students were confused. I don't get it, so I can't work on this assignment.

SELF-DIRECTED STUDENT'S RESPONSE

Ron: I'm confused. I really don't get this at all. And this is due tomorrow! So I'm going to the Success Lab on campus. I'm going to have to skip the game tonight, but I have to get this figured out and finished. I'll look up the lab's hours on the college's Web site.

©DamirK/E+/Getty Images RF

Being self-directed means taking responsibility for your own learning.

Students Who Succeed Use Resources Effectively

Resources are the tools that are available to you as you work on a task. To succeed in college, you need to use a variety of tools: your textbooks, the learning labs on campus, your supportive friends and family, computer software, Web sites, and so on. Identifying the correct tools to use for academic tasks requires careful thinking, and it also requires that you know what tools are at hand. Two categories of tools, in particular, can assist your journey through college: human resources and content resources.

Human Resources.   **Human resources** are the people around you who can provide help:

- Your instructors are your best resources. Do not hesitate either to visit your instructors during their office hours or to e-mail them. Professors welcome their students' questions and office visits.
- Look around your classes to identify peers with whom you might be able to connect. Consider swapping e-mail addresses with one or two classmates so you can discuss assignments or keep up with class notes in case of absences. Of course, always use care about giving your personal information to anyone. A campus e-mail address is a fairly safe way to chat with a classmate, but it might *not* be wise to give out your phone number or address.
- You can also form study groups to discuss course assignments. Such groups can meet on a regular basis or only when necessary.
- Lab instructors or tutors can also be excellent resources for professional feedback on papers or for help with complex assignments.
- If your campus has a writing center, use it. Writing center instructors or tutors are specially trained to help with reading and writing assignments. Do not hesitate to ask a writing center instructor for help with any course that requires writing.
- Additionally, student success counselors and librarians have been trained to help students succeed.

Once you have identified the available human resources on your campus, take the next step—use them! Regularly interacting with instructors and others on campus who are there to help will make a significant difference to your academic success.

Content Resources. Textbooks, library reference books, *YouTube* and *Teacher-Tube* videos, reading comprehension Web sites, online writing labs (OWLs), and search engines are only a few of the content resources that can help you succeed in college. These resources can often help you with questions you have about coursework and careers. Librarians can help you locate a wealth of valuable content resources. In addition, writing textbooks and carefully chosen Internet sites can be useful.

Students Who Succeed Manage Their Time Well

Time management is a necessity in almost every area of life. The color-coded time management plan created by one student, Dana, is shown below.

Good time management starts with assessing your time commitments honestly and carefully. Logging your commitments on a calendar—whether on paper, on a computer, or on your smartphone—is one way to realistically view what you need to get done. There are a variety of ways to sync online calendars to smartphones. Use technology to help you when possible, but make sure that you manage your electronic devices and that they do not manage you:

- Turn off your phone when you study.
- Use your phone's alarm and calendar to keep track of due dates.
- Make your use of social media a reward to be enjoyed *after* you have finished your course work for the day.

Dana's Time Management Plan

Time	Sun.	Mon.	Tues.	Wed.	Thurs.	Fri.	Sat.
6 a.m.							
7							
8		Class	Class	Class	Class		
9		Class	Class	Class	Class		
10		Class	Class	Class	Class		
11							
Noon		Lab/study	Lab/study	Lab/study			
1 p.m.		Lab/study	Lab/study	Lab/study			
2	Work	Lab/study	Lab/study	Lab/study			
3	Work	Lab/study					
4	Work						
5							
6							
7							
8	Study time	Study time	Study time	Study time	Study time		
9							
10							

KEY

Class
Family/children
Lab/study time
Study time
Work

To make a time management system, use a simple chart that lists the days of the week and the hours of each day. Input your commitments, and schedule your study time. Be sure to leave some hours open for flexibility. Post your plan and make others aware of it so they can help you follow it.

Students Who Succeed Are Self-Reflective

Reflecting is simply taking time to think about something in order to understand it or learn from it. *Self-reflection* is looking at your behaviors and feelings from the outside so that you can see yourself more objectively.

We can all think of someone—perhaps an acquaintance, a friend, or even a family member—who makes the same mistakes repeatedly. Perhaps this person is always late or cannot maintain a relationship. It is easy to see the person's faults, and most likely, we can see what causes his failures. But it is much more difficult for us to view ourselves as objectively. Self-reflection is an attempt to do just that.

To practice self-reflection, imagine floating to the top of a room and looking down at yourself, noting the things you are saying and doing. The goal is to be able to see yourself as others see you. Think about yourself as a student. Which of your behaviors sabotage your success? Which behaviors work for you? Self-reflective analysis will help you view your strengths and weaknesses more objectively so you can become the kind of learner and person you want to be.

©Halfdark/Getty Images RF

According to Plato, the ancient Greek philosopher Socrates said that "The unexamined life is not worth living." What do you think Socrates meant?

PRACTICE 7

Using Success Strategies

You have read about four characteristics of students who are successful in college. Think about your own habits and traits as a college student, and answer these questions on your own paper.

1. Provide an example of a time when you were a self-directed student. Alternatively, provide an example of a time when you were not self-directed enough. Explain what happened in the scenarios you present.

2. What keeps you from being more self-directed as a student? Explain.

3. Make a list of resources (human or content) that you plan to use this semester. Include at least one resource that you have never used before.

4. Provide an example of an occasion on which you managed your time well. Provide an example of a time when you did not use good time-management strategies. Explain what happened in both scenarios.

5. What potential time problems might you face this semester? How will you deal with them so that your college work is not affected? Explain.

6. Think about a favorite teacher you had in the past. How would he or she describe you?

7. When you reflect on yourself as a student, what strengths do you see? What weaknesses do you see? What potential do you have to excel? Explain.

CHAPTER ACTIVITIES

⊘ A READING AND WRITING ASSIGNMENT

The critical thinking, reading, and writing skills we discuss in this text not only apply to college success but also affect workplace success. What follows is an article entitled "Are You an Ace or a Joker?" As you read the article, underline at least three important pieces of advice that you will use to prepare for a future career. A writing assignment follows the article.

Are You an Ace or a Joker?

Two guys—let's call them Ace and Joker—have associate's degrees from the same community college. They have obtained basically the same level of academic knowledge and the same technical skills. They both held jobs while in high school and in college. Yet Ace is a much more attractive job candidate to managers who are recruiting workers. Why?

Everyone would agree that having basic knowledge and stock technical abilities is essential for career readiness. However, in addition to academic and technical competencies, a third category of abilities is critical for career readiness: employability skills.

Employability skills, sometimes called *work-readiness* or *job-readiness skills,* are a set of competencies and behaviors that are necessary for *every* type of job. Acquiring them *and* being able to demonstrate to prospective employers that you possess them are crucial to employment success.

Foundational Skills

Being a good employee depends on some very basic, foundational skills. While these qualities may seem too obvious to be highlighted, employers express frustration at how few workers possess them.

Joker pads his time sheet by adding a half-hour here and fifteen minutes there. Ace is totally honest about the hours that he works.

Honesty and trustworthiness are indispensable qualities in the workplace. If an employer cannot trust a worker, every aspect of the work environment becomes overly complicated.

Ace shows up for work on time every single day. Joker comes in on time some days but straggles in a few minutes late about as often. Ace finishes his assignments on time; Joker frequently has excuses about why he was unable to get an assigned project completed by the deadline.

Dependability is vital. Employees need to show up on time every day (unless they have a valid excuse). Completing every task is another dimension of dependability. A staff member who completes tasks as assigned, without prompting and by the deadline, is a very valuable employee.

(continued)

When Ace goofs up, he admits it; when he borrows an idea from coworkers, he gives them credit. Joker, on the other hand, frequently tries to blame others when things go wrong, and he regularly takes credit for the insights and accomplishments of others.

Employers greatly appreciate staff members who take responsibility for their own decisions and actions. If you make a mistake, own it. If someone else came up with a worthwhile idea, give credit where credit is due.

Ace is aware of the benefits of his job, and he remembers all too well the frustration and discouragement he felt when he was unemployed. Joker, on the other hand, seems to consistently see only the negative side of his job.

Having a positive attitude toward work is a wonderful characteristic. You don't have to "whistle while you work," but being upbeat matters. Nobody relishes working with a grumbler; coworkers and supervisors alike appreciate someone with a can-do attitude.

Joker catches on to new tasks quickly, but he often tires of doing the work and fails to complete assignments. If Joker is the hare, Ace is the tortoise. He sees every project through to the end.

Workers need to exert high levels of effort and persistence. Working hard and keeping at it will not only enable you to accomplish more, but your persistence will be noticed by colleagues and superiors. To some employers, a college degree is more important as evidence of perseverance than of knowledge.

Whenever an unexpected crisis occurs, Joker freaks out and has a hard time recovering. Ace, however, rolls with the punches; he is able to adjust on the fly.

Flexibility is highly valued by employers. Many of us like routine; however, in every work environment, unanticipated events occur, often upsetting the regular order of affairs. Workers who can adapt to changing situations are especially valuable.

Ace "looks the part." He comes to work dressed and groomed appropriately. Joker, conversely, will often show up for work looking disheveled, lacking some part of his uniform, and generally resembling a slob.

Understanding and following the dress code or uniform guidelines should be a given in every work context. Employees must always be presentable and pay attention to personal hygiene.

Interpersonal Skills

In most work environments, there are three groups with whom a person interacts: customers or clients, coworkers or colleagues, and managers or supervisors. Relating well to all three groups is vital for success in the workplace.

(continued)

Many of Joker's customers view him as a jerk. Ace's goal, on the other hand, is to help all his customers feel better about their day after their encounter with him.

Anyone who works with customers must be friendly and polite and must respond appropriately to their requests. Although it is not always the case that "the customer is always right," that assumption is an excellent beginning point in dealing with customers.

Everybody likes a team player, and that is how Ace's colleagues characterize him. Joker's associates, in contrast, comment about how they often have to do his part of an assignment.

Good employees respect and work well with coworkers, even those they do not like. It's crucial to be compatible enough with everyone in the workplace to make a successful team. Consider basketball as an analogy. Although it would be great if the players on a team liked one another, it is not really necessary. As long as they communicate with one another and each player performs his or her role, they can be successful as a team.

Joker always seems to be in conflict with his supervisor. Different jobs, different managers—it doesn't seem to matter; there's always tension between Joker and his boss.

The manner in which employees relate to their supervisors is absolutely critical to job success. Employees must treat their supervisors with respect, despite their personal feelings toward them. As an employee, you must respect the *role* even if you do not respect the *individual.*

If Ace's boss tells him that he could do better work, Ace views it as a "gift" from his supervisor. Ace wants to be better at what he does, so he appreciates guidance in that regard—even if he doesn't necessarily enjoy being corrected.

Effective employees take constructive criticism to heart and consider it carefully. No one enjoys being criticized, but effective employees understand that their supervisors offer criticism to guide, not to insult. Good workers don't reflexively reject criticism. Rather, they use it to gain insight and improve their performance on the job.

Whether relating to customers, coworkers, or supervisors, employees inevitably encounter conflict at work. Being able to resolve conflict successfully is a very important interpersonal skill. The successful resolution of conflict lies between two extremes. One extreme is to react to a clash defensively and aggressively. The other extreme is to respond by withdrawing and acting as though no issue exists. Neither of those reactions is productive. If conflict is respectful, honest, sincere, and kind, then it isn't confrontational at all—and it can be very fruitful!

Problem-Solving Skills

Every job involves problem solving: How can we produce our goods or provide our services faster, better, more efficiently? How do we address the

(continued)

roadblocks that inevitably arise? It's not surprising that problem-solving skills routinely rank at the top of the list of desirable traits for prospective staff members. Problem solving involves both critical thinking and creative thinking.

> *When Joker sees a problem at work, he criticizes his supervisors for not having solved it. On the rare occasions when Joker has a suggestion, he throws out an idea without having thought it through. He skips steps—he tends to go from A to C without explaining how to get there, and then he is unhappy when no one thinks his plan is worthwhile. Ace constructs a plan with his audience in mind—whether that is customers or his boss or someone else. He realizes that they cannot fill in unexplained gaps.*

Critical thinking involves recognizing and clarifying a problem. What issue, precisely, is it that needs to be addressed? Identifying possible solutions and then ranking them in terms of preferability is a next step. Constructing a step-by-step explanation as to how the approach selected would be implemented is the final stage. (You can see how courses in math and science provide students with training in critical thinking; although the particular issues in a job setting may not be algebra problems or chemistry experiments, the *method* learned in these academic courses can be applied in a multiplicity of situations.)

> *Joker never seems to come up with any fresh ideas. He offers the same, tired approaches even when they have not worked in the past or when new issues arise on the job. Ace, in contrast, thinks creatively.*

While critical thinking emphasizes the rigorous, analytical type of thinking that we associate with math and science, creative thinking is just as important. Innovative thinking is highly valued in most work environments. Just as the relationship between critical thinking and courses in math and science is clear, so too is the parallel between creative thinking and "artistic" academic courses. Courses in the visual and performing arts—drama, music, art, dance—provide examples of how artists conceive new and imaginative creations. Moreover, academic study in areas less commonly thought of as creative can be very helpful as well. Engineering, marketing, and education courses—to name a few—promote innovative thinking, too.

Conclusion

The skills described here are the attributes that workforce managers repeatedly indicate they desire in their employees. People who are looking for employment opportunities—or better jobs than they currently hold—must possess both employability skills and specific job skills. Additionally, when applying for a job, people need to convey their employability skills in the application process. Employability skills can be added to a résumé, discussed in an interview, or demonstrated while networking. Perhaps most importantly, a person who demonstrates these employability skills in every aspect of his life will impress potential employers as unique.

Who would not want to hire Ace?

Questions for Consideration

1. What are employability skills? Write two to three sentences defining them.

2. How do employability skills differ from academic and technical skills?

3. Read through the section describing the foundational skills employees should have. In what other contexts are these skills important? Explain.

4. On the left side of a sheet of paper, list all the employability skills discussed in the article. Next to each skill, write a sentence explaining whether you possess the skill, are working on acquiring the skill, or have not developed the skill yet. How would an employer view your abilities as a potential employee on the basis of the list you created? Which of these skills do you plan to work on developing? Explain in a paragraph.

Responding to the Reading

1. Which of the employability skills are actually EQ skills? Explain.

2. Choose three employability skills that you need to develop more fully. Write a paragraph about each skill in which you do the following:

   - Explain why you believe you need to develop the skill.
   - Provide an example of a time when you would have been more successful if you had possessed the skill.
   - Finish the paragraph with ideas for how you can develop the missing skill.

3. Using the "Employability Skills" article for ideas, write an essay in which you identify the top five employability skills required for a job in which you are interested. Explain why each skill is important for the job you choose. For example, if you would like to be a nurse, you might discuss the importance of problem solving.

⊖ ADDITIONAL ASSIGNMENTS

1. Think of a job or a class you had in the past in which discipline and behavior were not good. What was the problem? What could your employer or instructor have done differently to make student or worker behaviors more acceptable? Write two or three paragraphs to explain.

2. Think of a time when you made a decision without thinking critically about it. Perhaps you told a lie to a person you loved or bought something expensive on an impulse. What decision did you make? What process did you use to make the decision? Why do you think you made the decision without thinking critically? What steps should you have taken to make a better, more-informed decision? Write two or three paragraphs to explain.

3. Think about a time in your academic life when you failed an assignment. Was the failure brought on because of a problem in emotional intelligence, a problem in critical thinking, or a problem that you could have avoided by using a college success strategy? Explain your answer in a paragraph.

4. Earlier you read about Ace and Joker. With which character do you identify the most? Why? Explain.

EMOTIONAL INTELLIGENCE

We all have good moods and bad moods. People who are "emotionally intelligent" can explain their moods and the likely reasons for them.

They can do something else, as well: they can find ways to regulate their moods when doing so is desirable. Psychologists suggest that people who can control their moods have much better relationships and are happier and more successful than people who cannot. Have you ever intentionally *controlled* a mood? For example, perhaps you went to work one day feeling irritated and snapped at your coworkers. Realizing the effects of your mood on others, you decided to breathe deeply, relax, and say only kind things the rest of the day. If you have managed to control a mood, what methods worked for you? What might have happened if you had not taken control of your mood? Explain in a paragraph.

METACOGNITION

Metacognition is the ability to understand how you learn and how you think. People who are successful in college, usually have developed their metacognitive skills. To develop yours, consider the following activity:

Think about a college or high school class that you found very difficult. Imagine that you can watch a video of how you behaved (studied, attended, listened, questioned, spoke, read, and so on) during that class. What would the video show you doing? Describe the video in a paragraph. What insight can you gain by looking at yourself *from outside*?

One way to learn new skills and techniques is to use the skills and techniques of experts as a model. What skills—physical or mental—have you practiced or even perfected by observing other people at work?

Chapter Objectives

After completing this chapter, students will be able to do the following:

- Use reading to improve their writing.

- Annotate a text for its content and features.

- Determine the meanings of words and build vocabulary.

The writer Stephen King has said, "If you don't have time to read, you don't have the time (or the tools) to write. Simple as that." What King means is that to become a good writer, you have to read. And the more you read, the better you can write.

When was the last time you read something for pleasure? Anything you read—romance novels, entertainment Web sites, and even magazines about interests such as hunting or decorating— will help you to improve your vocabulary and become a better writer.

If you have trouble understanding what you read, two tools—annotation and vocabulary strategies—can help your comprehension. In this chapter, you'll learn how to use these tools to become a better reader as well as a better writer.

Using Reading to Improve Writing

Whether you are reading for school, work, or pleasure, reading has an effect on your writing ability.

Reading to Become a Better Writer

When you read, you begin to understand on an unconscious level how language works. Have you ever started using a word you learned from a friend? If so, you probably did not make an intentional decision to use that word; the word just began to appear in your vocabulary. Although you are not consciously aware of it, your brain records information such as words and phrases. (Think about all the clichés you have learned unintentionally—for example, *seeing eye to eye, easy as pie, love is blind.*)

Our brains also record information about the features of texts we read. For example, if we read several texts that begin with questions, we sometimes find ourselves writing a text that starts with a question. Reading can help you on an unconscious level by teaching you grammar, sentence structure, organization, and other concepts. This unconscious process of acquiring language is one reason that reading is so important.

Writing to Become a Better Reader

One of the ways the brain learns is by *constructing information.* Think about it. What is the difference between these scenarios?

A. An instructor wants you to learn the definitions of four words, so he gives you a handout that provides the words and their definitions. You look over the handout and carefully memorize each word.

B. You go to your doctor, and she tells you that you have a disorder. There are four words she uses that you don't quite understand, so you write them down. When you get home, you look up the words, read about their meanings on the Internet, and then jot down definitions in your own words. After your work, you understand the words clearly.

Which of these scenarios would result in a real, permanent change to your vocabulary? Brain scientists would tell us that scenario B is much more likely to help you learn the words permanently. When you are an active participant in your learning, you are constructing knowledge. Looking up a term and defining it in your own words is a much more active way of learning than memorizing is.

Writing also improves your reading by giving you a way to make sense of texts. When you put a text into your own words, you are actively participating in understanding the text. You can't summarize a text without understanding it. Thus, writing helps you to work out your understanding so that you can find the words to express a text's meaning. Even using a pen to make notes or underline words while you read is a type of writing, a way you can interact with the text to create meaning.

PRACTICE 1

Explaining How Reading and Writing Work Together

Answer each of the following questions. Use your own words.

1. Explain how reading can make you a better writer.

    _____

    _____

2. Why would writing a summary of a text help you understand a text more fully than just reading it?

    _____

    _____

Developing Annotation Skills

Dr. Bowen, a popular college professor, regularly strolled through the aisles of her classroom and looked at her students' books. One day, she said to her students, "If you have not highlighted and annotated the reading you were to have done for homework, you may leave class now." Many students had to leave. As you are reading your homework assignments, imagine that Dr. Bowen is your instructor. You may find that you engage with the material in a way that helps you understand it better.

Dr. Bowen realized that students who did well in her class read critically: that is, they read to figure out not only *what* the writer was saying but also *how* the writer was communicating the message. She expected her students to use annotation as a way to read critically and actively. **Annotation** is reading a text and marking it to make a note of important concepts and features, ask questions, or add your ideas to the text. When you read actively, or critically, you are engaged in a conversation with the writer. Think of annotation as a way to deepen that conversation.

Annotation Tips

Many of the annotation tips shown here require that you write in your books. You may not be comfortable writing in books because you have always been told that marking books ruins them (true for a library book!), but writing in your books is one of the best ways to make sure that you're getting the most out of the time you spend reading. Study the tips in the chart on the next page for what to annotate when you read.

Think about how convenient it would be to have the writers of the texts we read sit next to us during the reading process. We could ask a variety of questions, such as these:

- What did you mean by that phrase?
- How do you know this information?
- Why did you choose to include an example in this spot but not in this spot?
- Is this story true?
- Would you please define that term for me?

These are the kinds of questions it is valuable to think about and note in the margins of the texts you read. By "voicing" your questions in annotations, you become more aware of needing answers to those questions; consequently, you will be more likely to look for possible answers as you continue reading. Marking significant features or content in a text will also help you remember those items.

TIPS FOR ANNOTATING READINGS	
Mark new information	Mark only information that is new to you. If you already know something, there's no need to mark it.
Use highlighters sparingly	If the page is covered with yellow by the time you're finished reading, the important information won't stand out. Only about 20 percent of a page should be annotated, and even less than that should be highlighted.
Focus on vocabulary	Save the yellow highlighter for definitions to make them stand out. Circle words you do not know. Look them up and write the definition in the margins.
Use different colors	Use different colored pens for different types of information. For example, underline the main idea of a paragraph in red and write "main idea" in the margin. Use a blue pen to write your questions in the margins.
Talk to the text	Ask the writer questions: "Why true?" "Always the case?" Note when you agree or disagree with the text. Make connections between different parts of a text: "Said something different on p. 50." Make connections between the text and your experience: "Just like M's habits."
Make comparisons	Start a dialogue between the text you are marking and others you have read. Do the authors agree with one another? Make notes in the margins about others' views: "Smith disagrees; says air pollution is only getting worse."
Develop a system of codes	Use a question mark for something you aren't sure about, an exclamation point for something you find interesting, and a star next to the main idea.
Use sticky notes	Write a word or two on a sticky note so you can quickly find the important information you have flagged: "Stats about pollution." Use these notes sparingly, like a highlighter. Too many make it hard to identify what is important.
Summarize	When you're finished reading, put the main ideas in your own words. Summarizing is an excellent way to make sure you've understood the reading.

PRACTICE ❷

Assessing the Value of Annotations

Look at each example of annotation below, and determine whether the annotation is likely or unlikely to be useful to you as you learn the material. Explain your reasoning.

1. Is this annotation useful? Explain why or why not. _____

   _____

   The amygdala is the part of the brain responsible for processing and regulating emotions and for storing and retrieving memories. Part of the (limbic) system, the amygdala is located deep within the two hemispheres of the brain. It is a small, almond-shaped mass of tissue.

   Isn't the limbic system related to nerves? (go back and check)

   (continued)

2. Is this highlighting useful? Explain why or why not. _____

_____

> The amygdala is the part of the brain responsible for processing and regulating emotions and for storing and retrieving memories. Part of the limbic system, the amygdala is located deep within the two **hemispheres** of the brain. It is a small, almond-shaped mass of tissue.

3. Is this annotation useful? Explain why or why not. _____

_____

> The amygdala is the part of the brain responsible for processing and regulating emotions and for storing and retrieving memories. Part of the limbic system, the amygdala is located deep within the two hemispheres of the brain. It is a small, almond-shaped mass of tissue.

4. Is this annotation useful? Explain why or why not.

_____

> The amygdala is the part of the brain responsible for processing and regulating emotions and for storing and retrieving memories. Part of the limbic system, the amygdala is located deep within the two hemispheres of the brain. It is a small, almond-shaped mass of tissue.

VCW hemisphere

For every Vocabulary Collection Word (VCW), give your in-context idea of the word's meaning and then look up the word's dictionary definition.

Amygdala
1. regulates emotions
2. retrieves memories

DEF:
Amygdala: part of brain, processes emotions/memories/almond shaped/deep inside 2 hemispheres

Annotating a Text's Content

Annotations that concern the **content** of a text are about the ideas the writer presents. Your primary responsibility as a reader is to understand the content of the text. It is usually a good idea to start the reading process with these questions in mind:

1. What is the reading's topic?
2. What is the writer saying about the topic?
3. What kinds of details does the writer give to support the topic?
4. What is important to remember about the topic?
5. Which terms are new or need defining?
6. Which phrases or sentences are confusing?
7. Are there any important lists, processes, or explanations you will need to know?
8. What questions come to mind as you read?

Content annotations concern anything in the text that helps you understand its meaning. For example, if the first paragraph defines a term, make a note of the definition in the margin. You will probably need to know that term as you read through the text. If you find an idea later in the text that you believe is important, make an annotation by jotting down "impt. idea" or putting a star in the margin. If a part of the reading is confusing, jot down a question mark or simply note "confusing." Later you can reread the confusing sections and see if they make more sense or ask for help in understanding them.

The following example shows how Zoe, a student, annotated a textbook passage for content. The passage is from *Foundations of Parasitology*, 9th edition, by Larry Roberts, John Janovy, Jr., and Steve Nadler.

Notice the following features of Zoe's annotations:

- She annotated definitions.
- She marked places where she had questions.
- She wrote out her questions in annotations.
- She used green for confusing information.
- She used yellow for definitions.

Parasitology is largely a study of symbiosis, or, literally, "living together." Although some authors restrict the term symbiosis to relationships wherein both partners benefit, we prefer to use the term in a wider sense, as originally proposed by the German scholar A. de Bary in 1879: Any two organisms living in close association, commonly one living in or on the body of the other, are symbiotic, as contrasted with free living. Usually the symbionts are of different species but not necessarily.

Symbiotic relationships can be characterized further by specifying the nature of the interactions between the participants. It is always a somewhat arbitrary act, of course, for people to assign definitions to relationships between organisms. But animal species participate in a wide variety of symbiotic relationships, so parasitologists have a need to communicate about these interactions and thus have coined a number of terms to describe them.

Handwritten annotations:

DEF: parasitology (like parasites)
DEF: symbiosis (a relationship where both parties get something/depend on the other)
A. de Bary (1879) (gave def.)

DEF: symbionts (the organisms in the symbiotic relationship)
Parasitology: study of symbiotic relationship (betw. 2 symbionts)

Huh? the nature of the interactions? What does this mean?

(random)

Animals (organisms) have parasitic (symbiotic) relationships with other animals (organisms).

Developing a simple system will help ensure that your annotations make sense to you when you go back to review them later.

Annotating a Text's Features

Annotating a text's features makes you more aware of the choices a writer has made to communicate her message. This awareness of writing features, in turn, can open up a world of possibilities for your own writing.

Writers make choices about the ways they communicate their messages to particular audiences. The chart "Common Text Features" presents some of the features often used by writers. Don't worry if you do not know what all of these are. As you learn more about the features of texts, you will feel more comfortable finding these features and using these terms.

COMMON TEXT FEATURES	
Main ideas	**Thesis statement:** The main idea of an essay **Topic sentence:** The main idea of a paragraph
Organizing strategies	**Introduction:** One or more paragraphs at the beginning of an essay that introduce the topic and create interest in the reader. **Conclusion:** One or more paragraphs at the end that bring the essay to a close. **Sequence of information:** Use of time, space, or level of importance to organize information.

(continued)

COMMON TEXT FEATURES *(continued)*	
Main ideas	**Thesis statement:** The main idea of an essay **Topic sentence:** The main idea of a paragraph
Details and text patterns	**Analogy:** An example that explains something unfamiliar by comparing it with something more familiar. **Anecdote:** A brief story that illustrates a specific point. **Cause and effect:** How one circumstance brought about or resulted from another. **Comparison and contrast:** How one item or event is similar to or different from another. **Concrete example:** Specific information that helps the reader understand the writer's point. **Definition:** The meaning of a word or concept. **Explanation:** A description of how something is constructed, how a task is performed, or how something works. **Hypothetical example:** An example that asks the reader to imagine something that is not currently true. **Use of sources:** Citing experts so the reader knows where information is coming from.
Language features	**Questions:** Use of questions to focus readers' attention or engage their emotions. **Repetition:** Use of a word or a phrase several times for emphasis. **Rhetorical question:** A question that the writer asks to make a point but does not expect the reader to answer. The answer may be provided in the text, or it may be self-evident. **Sentence variety:** Use of sentences of different lengths and types to create interest. **Tone:** Use of specific language to convey the emotion the author feels or wants the reader to feel. **Transition:** A word, phrase, or sentence that moves the reader from one idea to another, such as *first, next,* and *after that.* **Wit, sarcasm:** Use of humor to get the point across. Sarcasm is a kind of humor that relies on saying one thing and meaning the opposite.

Annotating features means looking not so much at *what the text says* but at *how the writer writes.* The more you learn about the strategies writers use to convey their ideas in texts, the more you will find to annotate. The passage that follows has been annotated in different colors to point out the text features. (Your annotations as a student should look more like the sample annotations shown earlier in the chapter—and you might not annotate every feature indicated in this example. The color annotations shown here are used throughout the text to demonstrate important points in the examples.)

In an April 30, 2011, TED Talk, Dr. Leeno Karumanchery explains that the amygdala is the part of the brain from which emotions come, and the frontal cortex is the part of the brain that manages cognition—logical thinking. The amygdala is a very old part of our brains. It formed long before the frontal cortex. Karumanchery explains that when something happens to us, the amygdala springs into action first. For example, if you are jogging and a tiger jumps out of the woods in front of you, the amygdala triggers an emotional response: fear. Stress hormones such as adrenaline and cortisol are released, and we have to make a decision: do we fight the tiger or do we run from it? This decision is referred to as "fight or flight." Instinctively, you will do one or the other to try to save your life.	Detail: Comparison of amygdala vs. frontal cortex Example Detail: Process Detail: Definition of "fight or flight"

(continued)

As Karumanchery notes in his talk, "Understanding Emotional Intelligence: The Amygdala Hijack," when you are confronting a tiger, this fight or flight reaction is a good thing. However, we don't confront tigers very often in the modern world. The amygdala doesn't know that. It still produces our first reaction to threatening events. If someone cuts you off in traffic, for example, the amygdala responds. If your response is to "fight," you may be one of the many people who experience—and engage in—road rage. Although you may rationally know that the car that cut you off was probably not intending to insult *you* personally, your rational brain—the frontal cortex—doesn't kick in immediately.

Example
Detail: Cause/effect of "fight" response

People who react immediately to a threat have problems controlling their emotions. Dr. Karumanchery suggests that one solution is to pause for at least five seconds after something makes you angry. If you pause for a short period of time, the frontal cortex has time to start working. More logical thoughts can take the place of the irrational ones triggered by the emotion. For example, the frontal cortex may remind you that life is too important to get into fights about driving habits! Or the frontal cortex may remind you about road rage stories you've heard in the past so that you can remember the danger of following your initial feelings. By taking time to think before reacting, you can take control over your emotions instead of allowing them to control you.

Detail: Cause/effect of pausing

Detail: Process of frontal cortex

Examples

Main idea

The annotations reveal features such as the use of hypothetical examples, explanations of processes, and comparisons. While you may not yet be aware of all the strategies and features writers use, you can still start annotating the features you find in texts.

PRACTICE ③

Annotating and Highlighting Texts

Highlight content and features in this brief passage from the textbook *Principles of Environmental Science* by William Cunningham and Mary Ann Cunningham. Use the tips for annotating readings presented earlier in this chapter. Write your questions in the margins. Circle words you need to look up in the dictionary. Underline the writer's main idea if you can determine it. Make a comment about the textbook's illustration and caption. Don't worry about finding every single feature; just mark those you can identify.

Metals

Many metals, such as mercury, lead, cadmium, and nickel, are highly toxic in **minute** concentrations. Because metals are highly persistent, they accumulate in food chains and have a cumulative effect in humans.

YOUR ANNOTATIONS

VCW minute

(continued)

Currently the most widespread toxic metal contamination in North America is mercury released from incinerators and coal-burning power plants. Transported through the air, mercury precipitates in water supplies, where it bioconcentrates in food webs to reach dangerous levels in top predators. As a general rule, Americans are warned not to eat more than one meal of wild-caught fish per week. Top marine predators, such as shark, swordfish, bluefin tuna, and king mackerel, tend to have especially high mercury content. Pregnant women and small children should avoid these species entirely. Public health officials estimate that 600,000 American children now have mercury levels in their bodies high enough to cause mental and developmental problems, while one woman in six in the United States has blood-mercury concentrations that would endanger a fetus.

Mercury contamination is the most common cause of impairment of U.S. rivers and lakes. Forty-five states have issued warnings about eating locally caught freshwater fish. Long-lived, top predators are especially likely to bioaccumulate toxic concentrations of mercury.

Developing Your Vocabulary

We are constantly exposed to new words, both in what we read and in what we hear. An unfamiliar word is an opportunity to learn and develop your vocabulary. Three ways to learn a new word are to consult a dictionary, to use word parts to determine the word's meaning, and to use context clues to **speculate** as to what the unfamiliar word means.

VCW speculate

Using Dictionaries

The quickest and easiest way to learn the definition of a word is to use a dictionary. These days, online dictionaries are more commonly used than printed versions. When you do an online search for a word's definition, you will get a lot of results. As with many online searches, not all results are equally valuable. Look for dictionary sites that provide multiple definitions of the word, a pronunciation guide, examples of how the word can be used in a sentence, and information about the word's history. These three online dictionaries are all good choices: *Merriam-Webster, Oxford Dictionaries,* and *American Heritage Dictionary.*

Regardless of the type of dictionary, the entries will typically look about the same. A quick review of dictionary features will help you understand some of the helpful dictionary elements you might overlook. See the sample dictionary entry that follows.

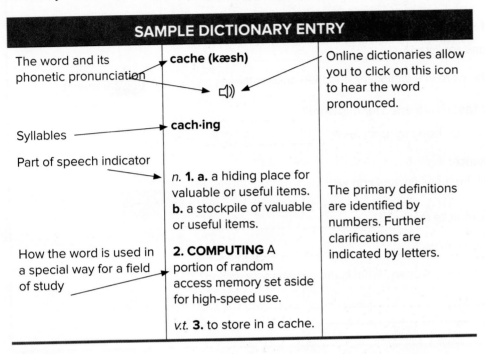

SAMPLE DICTIONARY ENTRY

The word and its phonetic pronunciation — **cache (kæsh)**

Online dictionaries allow you to click on this icon to hear the word pronounced.

Syllables — **cach·ing**

Part of speech indicator —

n. **1. a.** a hiding place for valuable or useful items. **b.** a stockpile of valuable or useful items.

The primary definitions are identified by numbers. Further clarifications are indicated by letters.

How the word is used in a special way for a field of study —

2. COMPUTING A portion of random access memory set aside for high-speed use.

v.t. **3.** to store in a cache.

The numbers *1, 2,* and *3* indicate that there are three different definitions of the word *cache.*

To choose the correct meaning, follow the steps in "How to Find the Correct Definition" on the next page. We will use the three steps to figure out the correct definition of *cache* in this example sentence.

Example: We found a *cache* in the wall where outlaws used to hide money and weapons.

HOW TO FIND THE CORRECT DEFINITION

1 IDENTIFY THE WORD'S PART OF SPEECH.

In the sentence, *cache* is used as a noun.

2 FIND THE DEFINITION MATCHING THE PART OF SPEECH.

Definitions 1 and 2 show what the word means as a noun.

3 READ THE SENTENCE WITH THAT DEFINITION IN MIND.

Definition 1a fits the meaning of the sentence, so it is the correct definition.

To get the most out of dictionaries, read definitions slowly and carefully. Don't skip over the information about the part of speech. It can help you think more clearly about the word itself as well as remember the word's meaning.

PRACTICE (4)

Using a Dictionary Effectively

Complete the definition exercises that follow.

1. Word: *geocaching*. Find the word in a dictionary, and then answer these questions:
    a. How many parts of speech are listed for this word? _____
    b. How many definitions are listed? _____

2. Word: **transient**. Find the word in a dictionary, and then answer these questions:
    a. How many parts of speech are listed for this word? _____
    b. How many definitions are listed for this word? _____

3. Read the following sentence:

    The lobby was filled with beautiful flowers and with the *exquisite* aroma of rich perfume.
    a. What do you think *exquisite* means? _____
    b. Divide the word into syllables. _____
    c. Check your definition in a dictionary. What is the dictionary definition?

    _____

    _____

VCW transient

Using Word Parts

One way to increase your vocabulary is to learn the meanings of individual word parts. If you memorize the word parts in the "Common Prefixes," "Common Suffixes," and "Common Roots" charts, you will be well equipped to figure out the meanings of many of the new words you encounter.

Prefixes and **suffixes** are syllables that can be added to a word to change its meaning; prefixes and suffixes cannot stand alone as complete words. Prefixes appear at the beginning of a word, and suffixes appear at the end of a word. **Roots** are syllables that convey the basic meaning of a word. They can appear in the beginning, middle, or end of a word, and sometimes they can stand alone as complete words.

EXAMPLE OF A WORD WITH A PREFIX, ROOT, AND SUFFIX		
Word: microscopic		
Prefix: micro-	**Root:** scop	**Suffix:** -ic
Meaning: small, tiny	**Meaning:** to see	**Meaning:** relating to, characterized by
Definition: Relating to something too tiny to be seen by the unaided eye.		

Study the charts of common prefixes, suffixes, and roots, and complete the practice exercises that follow.

COMMON PREFIXES		
Prefix	**Meaning**	**Example**
anti-	against, opposite	antisocial
auto-	self	autobiography
bi-	two	bicycle
com-, con-	with, together	communicate, context
dis-	not, opposite of	dislike
em-, en-	to cause to be, to put into or onto, to go into or onto	embattle, enable
ex-, exo-	out of, from	exoskeleton
fore-	earlier	foreshadow
hom-, homo-	same	homogeneous
hype-	over, too much	hyperactive
im-	not	impatient
in-, il-, im-	not	insufficient, illiterate, immature
inter-	between	interstate
micro-	small, tiny	microchip
mid-	middle	midline
mis-	bad, wrong	misbehave
neo-	new, recent, revived	neonatal
poly-	many, much	polygon
pre-	before	premarital
pro-	forward	proceed
quad-	four	quadrilateral
re-	again, back	rejoin
retro-	back, backward	retroactive
se-	apart	separate
semi-	half	semisolid
sub-	under, beneath, secondary	subterranean
super-	above, on top of, beyond	superimpose, superintendent
tele-	far, distant	telephone
trans-	across, change, through	transfer, transmit
tri-	three	tricycle
un-	not, opposite of	unhappy
uni-	one, single	unicycle

COMMON SUFFIXES

Suffix	Meaning	Example
-able, -ible	can be done	laughable, edible,
-age	result of an action/collection	manage
-al, -ial	related to, characterized by	parental, trivial
-an, -ian	one having a certain skill, relating to, belonging to	artisan, Haitian
-ation, -ion, -ition, -tion	act of, state of	graduation, isolation
-en	made of, to make	brighten, wooden
-ence, -ance	act or condition of	governance
-ent, -ant	an action or condition, causing a specific action	obedient, inhabitant
-er, -or	person connected with, comparative degree	competitor, greater
-fy	to make, to form into	liquefy
-hood	state, quality, condition of	adulthood
-ic	relating to, characterized by	historic
-ice	state or quality of	cowardice
-ide	chemical	peroxide
-ish	like, having the characteristics of, inclined or trending to	childish
-ity, -ty	state of, quality of	beauty, prosperity
-ive, -ative, -tive	inclined or tending toward an action	active, inquisitive
-ize	to make, to cause to become	energize
-less	without	homeless
-logy, -ology, -ologist	science of, study of, one who studies	psychology, ecologist
-ment	act, process	torment, replacement
-ness	condition, state of	happiness
-ous, -eous, -ious	full of or characterized by	joyous, rambunctious
-ward	characterized by a thing, quality, state, or action	backward, inward
-ways	in what manner	sideways

COMMON ROOTS		
Root	**Meaning**	**Example**
amo, amatum	love	amorous
aqua	water	aquatics
aud, audi, aus	to hear, listen	audiophile
bene, boun, bon	good, well	benefit
biblio	book	bibliography
bio	life	biological
chrom, chron	time	synchronous
dico, dictum, dict	to say, tell, speak	dictation
fact	make, do	manufacture
geo	earth, ground, soil	geological
graph	writing	biography
inter	between	interrelated
junct	join	junction
log, logos	word or study	dialogue
magnus	large	magnificent
meter, metron	measure	thermometer
path, pathos	feeling, suffering	sympathy
phone	sound	phonetics
populous	people	population
pro	for	proponent
scribe, script	to write	transcribe
sol	sun	solar
sonus	sound	sonogram
spectro, spect, spec	to see, watch, observe	prospect
struct	to build	destruction
syn, sym	the same, alike	sync, synonym
terra	land	subterranean
trans	across	translate
visum, video	to see	videographer
vivo	live	vibrant

PRACTICE 5

Using Word Parts to Speculate about Meanings

Use the "Common Prefixes," "Common Suffixes," and "Common Roots" charts to make an educated guess about the meaning of each of the following words. Write the meaning in the provided space. Then consult a dictionary, and write the dictionary meaning in the appropriate space.

1. Word: *bioconcentrates*

   Your best guess: _____

   Dictionary definition: _____

   _____

2. Word: *excommunicate*

   Your best guess: _____

   Dictionary definition: _____

   _____

3. Word: *contamination*

   Your best guess: _____

   Dictionary definition: _____

   _____

4. Word: *benefactor*

   Your best guess: _____

   Dictionary definition: _____

   _____

5. Word: *transcribe*

   Your best guess: _____

   Dictionary definition: _____

   _____

Using Context Clues

A **context** is an environment. The context of a particular word is the sentence in which it appears and sometimes the sentences nearby.

You may have already noticed Vocabulary Collection Words in the margins of this chapter indicated by this icon: **VCW** . This feature is designed to call attention to words you may not know. When you see a VCW word in the text, jot down the word in your notebook. Next, using context clues, make an educated guess about the word's meaning and jot that down. Then go to a dictionary and see if your definition was correct. Write down the dictionary definition in your notebook.

These three steps can help you use context clues effectively to determine definitions.

USING CONTEXT CLUES TO DETERMINE A WORD'S MEANING

1 DETERMINE THE WORD TYPE
Is it a noun, verb, adjective, or adverb?

2 INVESTIGATE THE CONTEXT
What information is provided by the word's sentence or other sentences nearby?

3 FIND A SYNONYM
What other words could logically substitute in the sentence?

Use a reliable dictionary to check your idea of the word's meaning.

Context Clue Step 1: Determine the Word Type. First, identify the word's part of speech.

> **Example:** Ray's stubbornness often leads him to make mistakes. Last year, he told his friends and family that he had decided to buy a new car. Not a single friend or family member *concurred* with his idea, but Ray bought the car anyway. He soon realized that to pay for the car, he would have to drop out of college and work full-time. Ray insists on learning the hard way.

Concurred functions as a *verb* in the sentence. Now that you know the word's part of speech, you can go to the next step.

Context Clue Step 2: Investigate the Context. Examine the *context*— the sentences around the word—to get clues that can help you figure out the word's meaning. One way to do this is to put each idea into your own words, like this:

Example	Put in Your Own Words
Ray's stubbornness often leads him to make mistakes.	Ray's stubbornness →mistakes
Last year, he told his friends and family that he had decided to buy a new car.	Ray told friends and family he wanted to buy a new car.
Not a single friend or family member concurred with his idea, but Ray bought the car anyway.	No one concurred with the idea. He bought the car anyway.
He soon realized that to pay for the car, he would have to drop out of college and work full-time. Ray insists on learning the hard way.	He had to drop out of college to pay for it.

Context Clue Step 3: Find a Synonym. Once you have used the context to understand the writer's point, you can find a synonym to help you define the new word. A **synonym** is a word that means the same thing as another word. For example, *house, home,* and *residence* are synonyms; all mean roughly the same thing.

Take the unfamiliar word out of the sentence, and plug in other words that might make sense. Think through each potential synonym in this way.

Example: Not a single friend or family member _____ with his idea, but Ray bought the car anyway.

Try this: Not a single friend or family member **agreed** with his idea, but Ray bought the car anyway.

If the synonym makes sense *and* if it fits in the context of the sentence and paragraph, you may have found the word's meaning. The only way to be sure is to use a dictionary to check your hunch.

Here's what part of a dictionary entry for *concur* (the present tense form of the verb) might look like.

con·cur (kən-kûr)

*v.***1.**   To share the same opinion; to agree.

2.   To bring something about by combining factors.

3.   To happen simultaneously.

Definition 1 confirms that the synonym *agree* is correct.

Try your hand at using context clues to figure out the meanings of unfamiliar words by completing the following exercise.

PRACTICE ⑥

Using Context Clues

Use context clues to guess the meaning of each of the *italicized* words in the passages below. Follow the three context clue steps described above. Next, use a dictionary to see if your definition is correct. Record your answers.

1.   Mike, the lodge owner, gave us a *convoluted,* hand-drawn map that was impossible to follow.

    Context-based guess: _____

    Dictionary definition: _____

2.   The map was intended to lead us to a gold mine that had long been abandoned by *prospectors* hoping to find their fortunes.

    Context-based guess: _____

    Dictionary definition: _____

3.   After hiking aimlessly for half an hour, we decided that the *pragmatic* thing to do would be to walk back to the lodge and ask for clearer instructions.

    Context-based guess: _____

    Dictionary definition: _____

4.   Mike laughed and gave us a list of *enumerated* instructions. We could easily follow the ten instructions he gave us.

    Context-based guess: _____

    Dictionary definition: _____

Acquiring New Vocabulary

The key to adding to your vocabulary is *using* the words you learn. "Expanding Your Vocabulary" gives some ways to start using new words and in order to develop your vocabulary.

EXPANDING YOUR VOCABULARY

Keep a Vocabulary Log	• Write new words in a notebook. • Write new words on note cards. • Use an online flashcard tool to keep track of new words.
Intentionally Use the New Words on Your Log	• Think of a context for using the word. • Use the word in that context, and make a note in your log. • Use new words in e-mails, texts, and class work.
Use Technology	• Study words on *Vocabulary.com*. • Download apps for your smartphone that help you increase your vocabulary.
Read	• Always keep reading materials on hand and read them. • Keep track of your reading on a chart or log. • Read for pleasure. Regardless of what you read, your vocabulary will improve!

CHAPTER ACTIVITIES

➔ READING AND ANNOTATING

Frederick Douglass was born into slavery around 1818 in Maryland. Around the age of twelve, his master's wife began teaching him the alphabet. After being reprimanded by her husband, she stopped her lessons, but Douglass was determined to read. In his remarkable story, he explains how learning to read and write was a major factor in his desire to become free. Douglass eventually escaped slavery and became a greatly respected thinker, speaker, and writer. In addition to other writings, lectures, and accomplishments, he told the story of his life in *My Bondage and My Freedom* (1855) and *Life and Times of Frederick Douglass* (1881).

What follows is a paraphrase of a passage from *Narrative of the Life of Frederick Douglass, an American Slave,* published in 1845 by the Anti-Slavery Office in Boston. Read and annotate the paraphrased selection. As you read, think about the character traits Frederick Douglass had. He was a very patient man, but he had many other character traits that helped him succeed in life. Make notes about these traits when you read about Douglass's strategies to learn to read and write.

Learning to Read and Write

By Frederick Douglass

I lived in Master Hugh's family about seven years. During this time, I succeeded in learning to read and write. In order to accomplish this, I was compelled to resort to various strategies because I had no regular teacher.

The plan which I adopted, and the one by which I was most successful, was that of making friends of all the little white boys whom I met in the street. I "converted" as many of these boys as I could find into "teachers." With their kind assistance, obtained at different times and in different places, I finally succeeded in learning to read.

When I was sent to run errands, I always took a book with me and by doing one part of my errand quickly, I found time to get a lesson in before my return. Bread was always available to me at the house but not so for many of the poor white children in our neighborhood. So I would bring extra bread with me on my errands and give some to these hungry little **urchins**. In return, they gave me the much more valuable bread of knowledge.

VCW urchins

I am strongly tempted to give the names of two or three of those little boys as a testimonial of the gratitude and affection I have toward them. However, I believe it is wiser not to do so—not because so doing would injure me but because it might embarrass them in that teaching slaves to read is an almost unpardonable offense in this Christian country. It is enough to say of the dear little fellows that they live on Philpot Street, very near Durgin and Bailey's shipyard.

On occasion, I would sometimes talk the matter of slavery over with them. Sometimes I would tell them that I wished I could be as free as they would be when they became men. "You will be free as soon as you are twenty-one, but I am a slave for life! Do I not have as much right to be free as you have?" These words troubled them; they would express deep sympathy for me and console me with the hope that something would occur by which I might be free.

At this point I was about twelve years old, and the thought of being a slave for life began to weigh heavily on my heart. Just about this time, I obtained a book entitled *The Columbian Orator.* I read it at every opportunity. Among its many interesting ideas, I discovered in it a dialogue between a master and his slave. The slave had run away from his master three times. The book presented the conversation that took place between the two of them after the slave was recaptured the third time. In this exchange, the master presented every pro-slavery argument, and the slave addressed every point. The slave was characterized as saying some very smart, impressive things in reply to his master. The slave was both surprised and delighted regarding the effect of the argument he presented—the master decided voluntarily to emancipate the slave!

The Columbian Orator was a collection of poems, political essays, and other writings. It was widely used in American schoolrooms in the early nineteenth century to teach reading and speaking.

In the same book, I encountered some of the powerful arguments that Richard Sheridan made regarding the oppression of Catholics in Britain. I read his ideas over and over again because they were so interesting. He expressed some of my own thoughts, which had frequently flashed through my mind but

After the Reformation in Great Britain, Roman Catholics were subjected to many restrictions. They could not own land, hold government offices or seats in Parliament, or practice their religion freely without being fined or prosecuted. Richard Sheridan was a writer and member of Parliament who actively supported the expansion of rights for British Catholics.

which died away because I could not put them into words. The key insight that I gained from his works was that truth could have power over even the conscience of a slaveholder. What I learned from Sheridan was a bold **denunciation** of slavery and a powerful vindication of human rights.

Reading these documents enabled me to express my own thoughts and to address the arguments offered for the continuation of slavery. While they relieved me of one difficulty, they brought on another even more painful understanding. The more I read, the more I was led to abhor and detest my enslavers. I could regard them as nothing other than a band of successful robbers, who had left their homes, gone to Africa, and stolen us from our homes, reducing us to slavery in a strange land. I loathed them as being the meanest as well as the most wicked of men.

As I **writhed** under this pain, I would at times feel that learning to read had been a curse rather than a blessing. Learning to read had given me a view of my wretched condition but without any cure. It opened my eyes to the horrible pit of my circumstances but offered no ladder with which I could get out. In moments of agony, I envied the unawareness of my fellow slaves. I have often wished that I myself were an animal and thus ignorant of my **plight**. I thought that I would prefer to be the lowliest reptile rather than myself. Anything—no matter what—to escape from thinking! The contemplation of my situation tormented me. There was no getting rid of it. It was pressed upon me by every object within sight or hearing, animate or inanimate. The silver trumpet of freedom had roused my soul to eternal wakefulness. Freedom now appeared, to disappear no more forever. It was heard in every sound and seen in every thing. It was ever present to torment me with a sense of my wretched condition. I saw nothing without seeing it; I heard nothing without hearing it; and I felt nothing without feeling it. Freedom—it looked from every star, smiled in every calm moment, breathed in every wind, and moved in every storm.

I often found myself regretting my own existence and wishing that I were dead. If it had not been for the hope of being free, I have no doubt but that I would have killed myself—or done something for which I would have been killed. While in this state of mind, I was eager to hear anyone speak about slavery. I was a ready listener. From time to time, I would hear a reference to the "abolitionists." However, it was some time before I learned what the word meant. It was always used in a context that caused it to be an interesting word to me. If a slave ran away and succeeded in getting clear, or if a slave killed his master, or set fire to a barn, or did anything very wrong in the mind of a slaveholder, it was referred to as the **fruit** of abolition. Hearing the word in this connection very often, I set about to learn what it meant. The dictionary offered me little help. I found it was "the act of abolishing," but then I did not know what it meant for something to be abolished. So I was perplexed.

I did not dare to ask anyone about its meaning, for I was confident that it was something they wanted me to know very little about. After waiting patiently, I came across one of our city newspapers that contained an account of the number of petitions from the North pleading for the abolition of slavery in

VCW denunciation

VCW writhed

VCW plight

VCW fruit

the District of Columbia and of the slave trade between the States. From this time forward, I understood the words "abolition" and "abolitionist" and always drew near when that word was spoken, expecting to hear something of importance to myself and fellow-slaves. The light broke in upon me by degrees.

One day I went down on the wharf, and seeing two Irishmen unloading stone from a scow, I went, unasked, and helped them. When we had finished, one of them came to me and asked me if I was a slave. I told him I was. He asked, "Are ye a slave for life?" I told him that I was. The good Irishman seemed to be deeply bothered by the statement. He said to the other that it was a pity that so fine a little fellow as I should be a slave for life. He said it was a shame to hold me. They both advised me to run away to the North; they said that I would find friends there, and that I would be free. I pretended not to be interested in what they said and acted as though I did not understand them because I feared they might be **treacherous**. White men have been known to encourage slaves to escape, and then, to get the reward, catch them and return them to their masters. I was afraid that these seemingly good men might use me so; but I nevertheless remembered their advice, and from that time onward I resolved to run away. I looked forward to a time at which it would be safe for me to escape. I was too young to think of doing so immediately; besides, I wished to learn how to write, as I might have occasion to write my own pass. I consoled myself with the hope that I should one day find a good chance. Meanwhile, I would learn to write.

The idea as to how I might learn to write was suggested to me by being in Durgin and Bailey's shipyard. I would frequently see the ship carpenters, after hewing and getting a piece of timber ready for use, write on the timber the name of that part of the ship for which it was intended. When a piece of timber was intended for the larboard side, it would be marked thus—"L." When a piece was for the starboard side, it would be marked thus—"S." A piece for the larboard side forward would be marked thus—"L. F." When a piece was for starboard side forward, it would be marked thus—"S. F." For larboard aft, it would be marked thus—"L. A." For starboard aft, it would be marked thus—"S. A." I soon learned the names of these letters and understood their meaning when written on a piece of timber in the shipyard. I immediately began copying them and in a short time was able to make these four letters.

After that, whenever I met any boy whom I knew could write, I would tell him I could write as well as he. The next word would be, "I don't believe you. Let me see you try it." I would then make the letters which I had been so fortunate as to learn and ask him to beat that. In this way I got a good many lessons in writing, which I could not possibly have gotten in any other way. During this time, my copy-book was the board fence, brick wall, and pavement; my pen and ink was a lump of chalk. With these, I learned how to write.

I continued by copying the advanced spelling words in *Webster's Spelling Book* until I could make them all without looking at the book. By this time, my little Master Thomas had gone to school and learned how to write and had filled a number of copy-books with his handwriting. He had brought these

scow: a large flat-bottomed boat.

VCW treacherous

hew: to cut wood coarsely.

copy-book: a blank tablet for practicing handwriting.

Master Thomas: the child of Frederick Douglass's master.

home and shown them to some of our near neighbors and then laid them aside. My mistress would leave the house every Monday afternoon and require me to take care of the house. While she was gone, I used the time writing in the blank spaces left in Master Thomas's copy-book, copying what he had written. I continued to do this until I could write in a manner very similar to that of Master Thomas. Thus, after a long, tedious effort for years, I finally succeeded in learning how to write.

Questions for Consideration

1. What effect did reading have on Frederick Douglass initially?

2. Why was Douglass so motivated to learn to read? Why was he motivated to learn to write?

3. What role did motivation play in Douglass's education?

4. In what ways was Douglass's reading of *The Columbian Orator* important in his intellectual and emotional development?

5. How did reading and writing separate Douglass from the other slaves?

6. Write a paragraph in which you speculate about what life would have been like for Douglass had he never learned to read or write. Use your imagination.

7. Why do you think slave owners prohibited slaves from learning to read and write?

➲ USING MODELS TO PRACTICE COMPOSING

Shaun read Frederick Douglass's "Learning to Read and Write" in his English class and was given an essay assignment. Read Shaun's assignment below, and notice his annotations.

Essay Assignment

In "Learning to Read and Write," we learn not only how Frederick Douglass became literate, but also about the character traits that helped him eventually become a free man. Write an essay in which you discuss the character traits that drove Douglass to become literate. Discuss at least three character traits and their effects on Douglass's life in your essay. Use examples from the reading to support your discussion.

SHAUN'S ANNOTATIONS

Assignment turned into a question: What are the character traits that drove Douglass to become literate?

Discuss character traits (3 or more).

Discuss their effects.

Use examples from the reading.

To respond to the assignment, Shaun reread the narrative and marked every possible character trait he could think of. Here are the first four paragraphs Shaun annotated with Douglass's character traits.

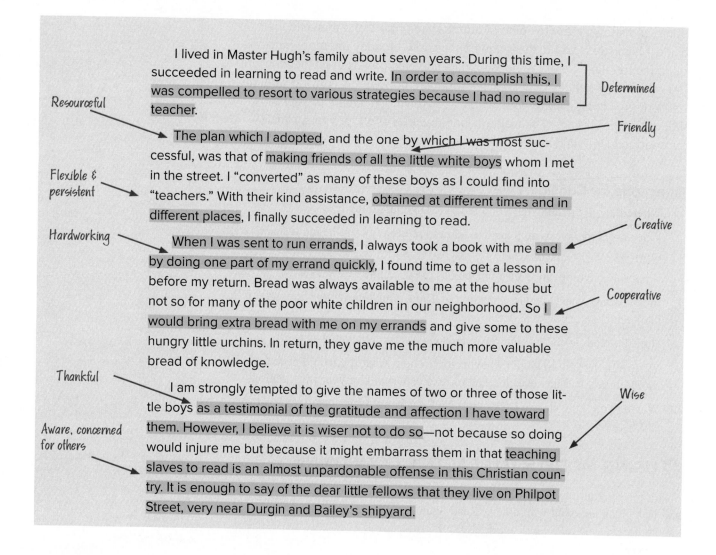

When Shaun finished annotating the entire reading, he made a list of all the character traits he found. Next, he grouped together character traits that were similar, as you can see from the circled numbers in this excerpt from Shaun's prewriting.

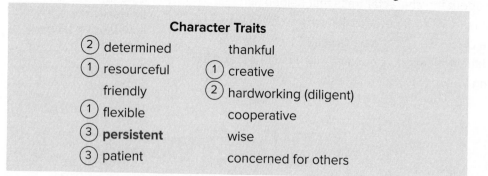

Character Traits

(2) determined   thankful
(1) resourceful   (1) creative
    friendly   (2) hardworking (diligent)
(1) flexible   cooperative
(3) **persistent**   wise
(3) patient   concerned for others

VCW persistent

After identifying the character traits he would discuss in his essay, Shaun wrote a simple outline that included his thesis statement and the major supporting points he planned to use. He decided his essay would be structured like this:

Introduction paragraph

Thesis statement: Frederick Douglass's success in learning to read and write was a result of his resourcefulness, diligence, and persistence.

Major supporting point 1: Without resourcefulness, Douglass would probably not have ever become literate.

Major supporting point 2: While resourcefulness was necessary, diligence and hard work were also important.

Major supporting point 3: Most importantly, Douglass's persistence is the character trait that eventually gave rise to his success.

Conclusion paragraph

After drafting his essay, Shaun revised and edited it, making sure he gave credit to the sources he used. Notice the features of Shaun's writing in the first body paragraph of his essay.

Body Paragraph 1 from Shaun's Essay

Without resourcefulness, Douglass would probably not have ever become literate. Douglass had to come up with his own teachers and his own materials. With the exception of learning the alphabet from his master's wife, every bit of Douglass's reading education was a result of his own resourcefulness. For example, Douglass would get the boys in his neighborhood to teach him by giving them bread and befriending them. He used both bread and the young boys as resources for education. To learn to write, Douglass had to be especially resourceful. Noticing the letters used on wood in the shipyard, Douglass began to copy the letters by writing them with chalk on sidewalks and fences. Another example of Douglass's resourcefulness was in his use of the young Master Thomas's educational materials. Douglass would wait until his mistress left the house and would then use blank spots in Master Thomas's used spelling-books. Because Douglass was resourceful, he was able to use non-traditional methods for learning to read and write.

Main idea of the paragraph (a topic sentence)

Detail: resourcefulness required to learn to read

Example

Detail: resourcefulness required to learn to write

Example

Example

⊖ A READING AND WRITING ASSIGNMENT

Try your hand at writing the remaining paragraphs of Shaun's essay. Using the first body paragraph Shaun wrote as a model, write the remaining two body paragraphs based on Shaun's outline. Alternatively, choose two other items on Shaun's prewriting list to write about. Add an introduction paragraph and a conclusion paragraph to complete the essay. Use the Quick Start Guide to Integrated Reading and Writing Assignments for assistance.

⊖ ADDING TO YOUR VOCABULARY

This chapter's vocabulary words appear below.

denunciation	plight	treacherous
fruit	persistent	urchins
hemisphere	speculate	writhed
minute	transient	

Choose five of the vocabulary words from this chapter that you would like to add to your vocabulary, and think about how you can use them this week. For example, one of this week's words is *speculate.* You can often substitute *speculate* for *guess,* as in the examples that follow.

Example: I don't know if this soup is fattening, but I'd *guess* that it is because it tastes so good.

I don't know if this soup is fattening, but I'd *speculate* that it is because it tastes so good.

List each of the five words you plan to use this week, and make note of a context in which you could use each word.

Example: *Speculate.* I can use this word when I predict what will be on tests or what we'll do in class.

⊖ ADDITIONAL ASSIGNMENTS

1. Reading and writing were arguably the most important skills Frederick Douglass ever acquired. Being literate opened new worlds for Douglass, and eventually he found a way to free himself from slavery. Think about your own life. Have you developed a skill or a relationship that has made a difference in your world? Perhaps you have developed a friendship that has been highly influential, or maybe you have had an experience—such as a job or a vacation—that had a profound effect on you. Write two or three paragraphs about a positive, powerful influence you have had in your life. Explain why this influence affected you, and provide examples of its positive influence.

2. Using Frederick Douglass's essay and your own life experiences, reflect on these questions: What were the effects of hardship on Douglass? What have been the effects of hardship in your life? Explain your thoughts in a few paragraphs.

3. In a variety of career fields, people learn skills by emulating professionals in the field. To emulate is to watch what others do and copy their actions. For example, nursing students spend time as interns emulating the skills of professional nurses in clinics and hospitals. In disciplines such as music, art, and theater, students learn by emulating the masters of their crafts. And in sales and marketing, students learn by emulating the successful techniques of those in the field. Choose a career in which you are interested. How might emulation help you master the content or skills required in this career? Write two or three paragraphs to explain.

EMOTIONAL INTELLIGENCE

One skill that is important for getting along with others is social awareness. The book *Managing Stress* defines social awareness as "the ability to perceive and understand the social relationships and structures in which you and those around you are operating. It involves being able to understand how other people are feeling—and validating those feelings.... And it means understanding that individual happiness is dependent upon assisting others to achieve their own happiness as well."

Write two or three paragraphs explaining what social awareness is. Put the ideas into your own words. Provide an example of a person who is socially aware in a particular situation. Provide another example of a person who is socially *unaware* in a particular situation. For example, a socially aware person may recognize that when the conversation turns to romantic relationships, one of her friends becomes uncomfortable. A person who is socially *unaware* might speak too loudly in class or might dominate a conversation without knowing how he is being perceived by those around him. Finish by offering suggestions for becoming more socially aware.

METACOGNITION

What do you remember after having read this chapter? Without looking back at the chapter, list the major topics this chapter covered. Then review the chapter to see what you missed. Write a short paragraph about how well you remembered the content for each topic.

When you finish, assess your understanding and memory of this chapter. Was it difficult to recall the information you read? Why? What particular material did you remember from the chapter? Why do you think you remembered those items and not others? Did you remember what you annotated better than what you did not annotate? What strategies might you use in the future to better remember the contents of what you read?

Text Credits

Page 24: King, Stephen, *On Writing: 10th Anniversary Edition: A Memoir of the Craft*. New York: Scribner, 2010; Page 29: Roberts, Larry, Janovy, Jr., John, and Nadler, Steve, *Foundations of Parasitology*, 9th ed. New York: McGraw-Hill, 2013. 2; Page 31: Cunningham, William, and Cunningham, Mary Ann, *Principles of Environmental Science*, 7th ed. New York: McGraw-Hill, 2013. 267–68; Fish Consumption Advisory from Cunningham, William and Cunningham, Mary Ann, *Principles of Environmental Science*, 7th ed., Figure 11.20 (p. 268). Copyright © 2009 by McGraw-Hill Education.Used with permission of McGraw-Hill Education; Page 49: *Managing Stress*, MTD Training, 2010. 48.

Previewing Texts and Working with Topics

©Ana Abejon/Getty Images RF

In many careers, previewing materials is essential to getting a job done well. Previewing strategies also help readers and writers keep focused as they work with and create texts.

Sometimes the way you do a job really affects the final result. For example, a high school senior decided to paint his old worn-out car. Not being the mechanical—or artistic—type, he washed his car and dried it, and then he painted it with nine cans of red, high-gloss, bargain-brand spray paint. You can probably imagine the outcome. The painting process he used resulted in the creation of what he and his friends came to call "The Bloodmobile." Indeed, the process he used affected the quality of the outcome.

The same principle is true for reading and writing. The early steps are important. Carefully following these steps will help you confidently begin the integrated reading and writing journey.

Using Pre-Reading Strategies

What you do *before* you read a text can determine whether or not you understand what you read. We call these before-reading steps *pre-reading strategies*. See "Four Pre-Reading Strategies" shown here. Let's look at these.

FOUR PRE-READING STRATEGIES

Previewing

Previewing means looking over a text without reading it word for word. To preview, look over and read each of these parts and ask the questions given in "Preview Questions about Text Elements." The goal of previewing is to get a sense of what a text will present.

PREVIEW QUESTIONS ABOUT TEXT ELEMENTS

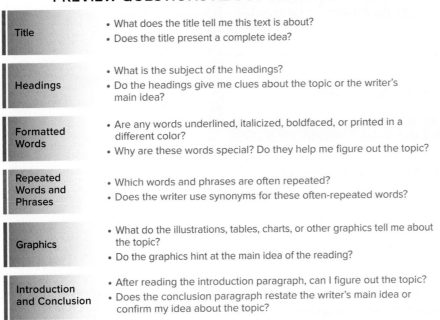

Title	• What does the title tell me this text is about? • Does the title present a complete idea?
Headings	• What is the subject of the headings? • Do the headings give me clues about the topic or the writer's main idea?
Formatted Words	• Are any words underlined, italicized, boldfaced, or printed in a different color? • Why are these words special? Do they help me figure out the topic?
Repeated Words and Phrases	• Which words and phrases are often repeated? • Does the writer use synonyms for these often-repeated words?
Graphics	• What do the illustrations, tables, charts, or other graphics tell me about the topic? • Do the graphics hint at the main idea of the reading?
Introduction and Conclusion	• After reading the introduction paragraph, can I figure out the topic? • Does the conclusion paragraph restate the writer's main idea or confirm my idea about the topic?

A careful preview of the reading can help you figure out what the reading is about—its **topic.** Being able to determine the topic of a reading is one of the most important reading skills. The topic can be expressed in a word or a short phrase. It will not be a complete sentence because a topic does not express a complete thought; it is only the subject or content with which the text is concerned.

Example of a topic: iPads in education

The next example is not a topic because it is a complete thought and is thus presented in a complete sentence.

> **Not a topic:** Although many schools are rushing to purchase iPads for their students, little research shows that learning on iPads is more effective than other methods of learning.

The Title Often Presents the Topic.   A title like "Five Weight-Training Techniques" is very helpful, as it clearly describes the topic of the reading. Not all titles, however, are as revealing. A title like "Alternatives" does not give us much information about the topic.

Headings Give Clues about the Topic.   Flipping through the text to examine its headings and subheadings will give you clues about the topic. Consider the textbook chapter headings in "Previewing Headings."

PREVIEWING HEADINGS

By studying the title, heading, and subheadings of the textbook chapter shown in "Previewing Headings," we can learn several things:

- This chapter is about how humans learn.
- There are theories about how humans learn.
- Two theories are classical conditioning and operant conditioning.

Some readings present a number of different elements, any one of which could be the topic. In such readings, asking what all these elements share may give you the topic of the reading. For example, consider these subheadings from a magazine article:

Biodiesel Engines   Natural Gas Vehicles
Hydrogen-Based Automobiles   Electric Cars

All the subheadings refer to vehicles that use alternative forms of energy. Thus, the topic of the article is likely to be alternative-fuel vehicles.

Formatted Words Are Important for Understanding the Topic.   When you see words that are bold-faced, italicized, underlined, or printed in color, the words are probably important for understanding the text and may help you understand the topic.

Early one morning, Bob is in the shower. While he showers, his wife enters the bathroom and flushes the toilet. Scalding hot water bursts down on Bob, causing him to yell in pain. The next day, Bob is back for his morning shower, and once again his wife enters the bathroom and flushes the toilet. Panicked by the sound of the toilet flushing, Bob yelps in fear and jumps out of the shower stream. Bob's panic at the sound of the toilet illustrates the learning process of **classical conditioning**, in which a *neutral stimulus* (the sound of a toilet flushing) becomes associated with a *meaningful stimulus* (the pain of scalding hot water) and acquires the capacity to elicit a similar response (panic).

This passage illustrates **classical conditioning**. The bold-faced font tells us the term is important.

Two other important terms are in italics: *neutral stimulus* and *meaningful stimulus*.

By noticing the formatted words in this selection, we might conclude that the two italicized words—*neutral stimulus* and *meaningful stimulus*—are important for understanding **classical conditioning**, the term we find in boldfaced letters.

Graphics Will Relate to the Topic and Main Idea.   A preview should also involve looking at any graphics. Graphics include photos, illustrations, charts, tables, and artwork. As you preview readings, you may find infographics, which are illustrations that combine artwork and text to convey information or explain topics. Maps are a common type of infographic, like the illustration shown in "Previewing an Infographic."

PREVIEWING AN INFOGRAPHIC
Before Conditioning

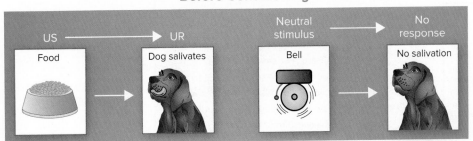

Conditioning   After Conditioning

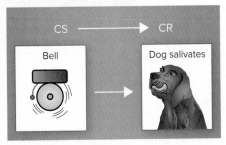

Pavlov's Classical Conditioning In one experiment, Pavlov presented a neutral stimulus (bell) just before an unconditioned stimulus (food). The neutral stimulus became a conditioned stimulus by being paired with the unconditioned stimulus. Subsequently, the conditioned stimulus (bell) by itself was able to elicit the dog's salivation.
Key: US = unconditioned stimulus; UR = unconditioned response; CS = conditioned stimulus; CR = conditioned response.

Repeated Words and Phrases Can Hint at the Topic.   Another method for identifying the topic is to briefly scan the reading. *Scanning,* or *skimming,* simply involves glancing at each paragraph, perhaps reading a sentence or two on each page, and getting a sense of the kind of content and the kind of writing in the text. As you scan the reading, note any words that come up again and again. Look also for synonyms. Imagine skimming over an article and seeing these words constantly repeated:

flying	phobia	fear	nervousness
flights	paranoia	calm	worry
fear of flying	travel	anxiety	uneasiness

These words suggest that the reading's topic is the fear of flying. Notice that some of the words are synonyms. *Anxiety, worry, uneasiness, nervousness, fear*—these words are all somewhat related in meaning. Finding the recurring words and synonyms will help you identify the topic at a glance.

Introduction and Conclusion Paragraphs Can Provide Clues about the Topic   Although previewing usually means looking over a text without reading it closely, go ahead and read the first and last paragraphs during the previewing process. Doing so can help you get an idea about the topic and what the writer is saying about the topic.

PRACTICE 1

Previewing a Textbook Chapter

Study the title, headings, and photo below, taken from a chapter of a textbook entitled *Criminal Investigation.* Then answer the questions that follow.

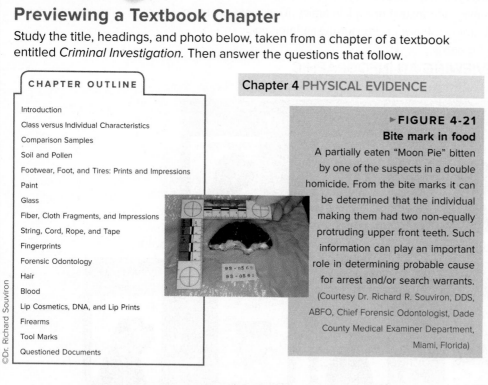

CHAPTER OUTLINE

Introduction
Class versus Individual Characteristics
Comparison Samples
Soil and Pollen
Footwear, Foot, and Tires: Prints and Impressions
Paint
Glass
Fiber, Cloth Fragments, and Impressions
String, Cord, Rope, and Tape
Fingerprints
Forensic Odontology
Hair
Blood
Lip Cosmetics, DNA, and Lip Prints
Firearms
Tool Marks
Questioned Documents

©Dr. Richard Souviron

Chapter 4 PHYSICAL EVIDENCE

▶**FIGURE 4-21**
Bite mark in food
A partially eaten "Moon Pie" bitten by one of the suspects in a double homicide. From the bite marks it can be determined that the individual making them had two non-equally protruding upper front teeth. Such information can play an important role in determining probable cause for arrest and/or search warrants. (Courtesy Dr. Richard R. Souviron, DDS, ABFO, Chief Forensic Odontologist, Dade County Medical Examiner Department, Miami, Florida)

98-0562
98-0561

1. What do you think this chapter is about?

2. For whom do you believe this book is written?

3. What do you think the purpose of this chapter is?

4. The chapter outline lists a number of items, such as hair, blood, and lip cosmetics. What are these? What information do you think the chapter will present about these items?

PRACTICE 2

Identifying Topics

Use previewing to read each passage and identify its topic.

1. Context: A short paragraph found in a community newspaper's opinion section. The writer is a citizen of the community.

    Our town is woefully ill-prepared for flash floods. We do not have a recycling program. Our library has struggled to keep its doors open and has not had funds for new books for two years. In spite of these facts, the City Council is considering installing a new, expensive fence around the city park baseball field. The projects we need the most are not even being discussed. City Council members need to get their priorities in order and consider projects that will benefit all of the citizens in our town, not just sports enthusiasts.

    What is the topic? _____

2. Context: A short reading from a general-interest magazine.

    Although anxiety disorders are common, they often go undiagnosed for years. One reason for this delay in diagnosis is that the symptoms of anxiety can appear to be symptoms of other illnesses.

    In particular, anxiety disorders often produce physical symptoms such as intestinal discomfort, nausea, dizziness, shortness of breath, hyperventilation, and rapid heartbeat. Since these symptoms *can* be caused by physical ailments, people with anxiety often assume their disorder is physical. This assumption can lead them to even greater anxiety and worry because they fear there is something wrong with them and that they may die.

    All of the physical symptoms of anxiety—racing heartbeat, shortness of breath, hyperventilation, dizziness, nausea, and intestinal cramps—can converge on a sufferer at one time. This onslaught of physical symptoms can be terrifying. It can be hard for the victim to believe that the cause is "only anxiety" since the physical symptoms are so real.

    What is the topic? _____

Predicting

After you have previewed the text carefully, a natural step is to make some predictions. Thinking about what you have seen and read, ask yourself the questions in "Making Predictions."

MAKING PREDICTIONS

- What will the text's topic be?

- What do I think the writer will say about the topic?

- Do I think the writer will provide information, or will the writer try to convince me of an opinion?

Jot down your answers before you read. After reading, go back and see if your predictions were correct. The better you get at previewing, the better you will become at making good predictions about what the writer will say.

Recalling

Have you ever read a textbook one day and, the next day, completely forgotten what you read? Most people have had this experience. One trick for understanding and remembering what you read is to tie the new information (what you are reading) to old information (what you already know). For example, if you are reading a chapter about the use of DNA evidence in criminal investigations, think about what you already know about the topic. Your knowledge may come from movies or television shows, but that is okay! By recalling what you already know about the topic, your brain can simply *add* the new information to the existing information. When you try to remember what you have read, your brain has a "file" it can refer to.

One way to recall is to take out a sheet of paper and make two columns. In the left-hand column, make a list of things you already know about the topic. After you read the article, go back and write down information you did not previously know in the right-hand column. Here is an example of a student's recalling activity.

What I Already Know	**What I Learned**
• I watch *Forensic Files*, and I've learned from that show that DNA evidence is really important in some criminal cases.	• There are "DNA Databases" that enable law enforcement to match a DNA sample with a known criminal.
• To get DNA evidence, you need bodily fluids or cells.	• These days, DNA is being used to prove the innocence of some people who have been imprisoned for crimes they didn't commit.
• Sometimes victims of crimes try to leave their DNA at crime scenes.	• The demand for DNA testing is high, so it takes a long time for results to come back.
• One way to get DNA is to swab someone's mouth or to use hair pulled out with roots attached.	

Asking Questions

Finally, before you read, think of some questions you would like the text to answer. By finding the answers to these questions, you will be more likely to understand and remember what you read.

After you preview the text, what questions come to mind? Jot them down. If no questions come to mind, create some questions using the 5 W's and 1 H questions: *Who? What? Where? When? Why?* and *How?* Here are some questions you might ask after previewing a reading on DNA:

- What exactly is DNA?
- Who uses DNA? Do all police departments gather DNA evidence?
- When is DNA useful? When is it not useful?
- How much does a DNA test cost?
- How accurate are DNA tests?
- Where is DNA testing done?
- Why does it take crime labs so long to return DNA results?

After you have created questions, read the selection. Take the time to find and jot down the answers to your questions.

PRACTICE 3

Using the Four Pre-Reading Strategies

What follows is a passage, "Hierarchy of Needs," from *Understanding Your Health*, by Wayne A. Payne, Dale B. Hahn, and Ellen B. Lucas. Use the four pre-reading strategies described in this chapter and summarized in the list below. As you do, write your thoughts on a separate sheet.

- **Preview:** What do you notice when you preview the text?
- **Predict:** What do you predict the topic will be?
- **Recall:** What do you already know about the topic?
- **Ask:** What questions do you have about the text or the topic?

Maslow's Hierarchy of Needs

Abraham Maslow has been one of the most significant contributors to the understanding of personality and emotional growth. Central to Maslow's contribution to twentieth-century American psychological thought was his view of psychological health in terms of the individual's attempt to meet inner needs, what he called the *hierarchy of needs*.

Maslow's theory is a positive, optimistic theory of human behavior. He believed that people are motivated to grow and fulfill their potential, referring to this phenomenon as **self-actualization**. In *Motivation and Personality*, he described self-actualization as "the need to become more and more what one is, to become everything that one is capable of becoming." Maslow differentiated between two categories of needs: **basic needs** and **metaneeds**. Basic needs—physiological needs, safety and security, belonging and love, and esteem needs—are the deficiency needs and are essential and urgent. Metaneeds come into play once the basic needs are met and include spirituality, creativity, curiosity, beauty, philosophy, and justice. Maslow's hierarchy of needs is arranged with the basic needs on the bottom, as they are the most fundamental and powerful needs. Lower-level needs must be met before the next level of

YOUR ANNOTATIONS

ABRAHAM MASLOW'S HIERARCHY

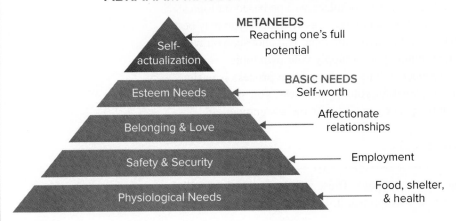

(continued)

needs can be satisfied. Maslow believed that people must fulfill their me-taneeds in order to become completely developed human beings. Left unfulfilled, people can become cynical, apathetic, and lonely.

Maslow arrived at this model by examining people whom he considered to be exceptionally healthy, people he defined as having developed to their fullest potentials. People whom Maslow identified as self-actualized included Albert Einstein, Albert Schweitzer, Eleanor Roosevelt, and Abraham Lincoln. He perceived these people to share similar personality characteristics, such as being self-assured, principled, innovative, compassionate, altruistic, goal-oriented, and internally motivated.

PRACTICE 4

Monitoring Your Understanding

Now that you have completed pre-reading in Practice 3, go on to read and annotate "Maslow's Hierarchy of Needs." When you finish, answer the questions that follow. Use a separate sheet for your answers.

1. What is the topic of this selection?
2. List one prediction you made about this reading. Was your prediction correct or not? Explain your answer.
3. Explain how you used the "recall" pre-writing strategy.
4. On a separate sheet, answer the questions you created during the pre-writing process.
5. How did the pre-reading strategies help you to understand the selection? Do you think your understanding improved by using pre-reading strategies? Explain.

Working with Assigned Writing Topics

Much of the writing you will do in college and the workplace will be based on topics assigned by your instructors or supervisors. For other writing assignments, you may be given a range of topic choices and will need to narrow the topic you choose. You will also encounter writing assignments that require you to supply your own topic.

In some ways, when an instructor selects the topic, the writing process is easier since the first step has already been completed for you. Nonetheless, you should plan to use four strategies to make sure that the paper you write fits the assignment.

Create an Assignment Page

Ideally, you will be provided with an assignment page. These written instructions will tell you exactly what the topic is and how to approach it. If you do not have written directions, then you need to create your own page of instructions. Create an assignment page by listing answers to these questions:

- What is the topic?
- Is research required? If so, what kind of research is expected?
- Is research (or the use of sources such as the Internet) prohibited?
- What is the writing purpose—to inform, to analyze and evaluate, or to persuade?
- What is the due date?
- What is the length requirement?
- What formatting is expected? Has the instructor specified font type and size, spacing, and heading format? Do you need to include a word count? Do you need to use a particular documentation style, such as MLA (Modern Language Association) style or APA (American Psychological Association) style?

Finally, take note of who will be reading your paper. You will need to consider your audience as you make decisions about what to include and how to word your ideas. Often with academic writing tasks, the instructor is the only person who will read what you write. Even though the instructor is an audience of only one, keeping in mind that you are writing for your professor is very important, as it will help you choose content, terminology, and a style appropriate for academic writing. Academic writing assignments always require formal writing, so avoid contractions and slang, use correct grammar and mechanics, and use third person.

Read and Reread the Assignment

A common writing mistake is to write about something that does not address the topic well enough. Understanding the assignment is imperative. Read the assignment instructions twice, making annotations to highlight each particular requirement. Merely reading through assignment instructions in a **cursory** fashion can lead to disastrous results. For example, students in a writing class were asked to write an essay about the morality of physician-assisted suicide, in which a doctor knowingly helps a patient commit suicide. One student wrote a paper on why physicians' assistants should not commit suicide. A second reading of the assignment instructions would have helped this student write on the correct topic.

 VCW cursory

For every Vocabulary Collection Word (VCW), give your in-context idea of the word's meaning and then look up the word's dictionary definition.

State the Paper's Topic in the Form of a Question

If the topic is not offered to you in the form of a question, transform the instructions into a question, as in the following example.

Original instructions: Write an essay in which you examine how credit card companies exploit college students by giving students credit cards, even when the students are unemployed. In your paper, include a discussion of why credit cards can be a problem—especially for college students.

Instructions reworded as questions: How do credit card companies exploit college students, and what are the problems that result from this exploitation?

Seek Help If You Need It

The best way to find help is to talk to your instructor. If your instructor is not available, work with a staff member at a writing lab or tutoring center. If you are confused about the topic or unsure how to begin, seek help before you go any further with your writing.

Developing and Narrowing a Topic for an Essay

Some assignments require you to generate your own topic. The best place to start this process is on a blank sheet of paper. Brainstorm about the subject by writing down everything that comes to mind. Do not evaluate your ideas at this time. Just allow yourself the freedom to write them down.

Brainstorming for Topics

Read "Brainstorming Strategies" on the next page for how to generate ideas for possible topics.

As you search for ideas, be aware that information found on the Internet is not always reliable. Avoid sites that offer papers for sale. Those kinds of Web sites often pop up when you are browsing for topics. Your instructors are familiar with the kinds of papers these Web sites sell or give away, and using a paper written by someone else for your writing assignment is plagiarism.

BRAINSTORMING STRATEGIES

Start with your own interests.	• What are you interested in? What are you passionate about? What aspect of these interests can you write about?
Free your imagination.	• If you had the time, money, energy, and ability, what would you want to learn about? How could you write about these topics?
Reflect on the world around you.	• Which world events affect or interest you? Are there issues about which you are passionate? What might you write about these events or issues?
Think about your life and your history.	• Which of your own experiences or memories might be of interest to others? Do you have experiences that might help others learn lessons?
Visit your college's writing lab, tutoring center, or library.	• Ask someone to help you find a list of hot topics, current issues, or a subject guide.
Check out Internet sites.	• See what other people are talking about by going to sites such as *CNN.com*, *Yahoo News*, or *ProCon.org*. Remember, you are looking for topic ideas, not for actual articles.

PRACTICE 5

Finding Topics of Interest

Imagine that your writing instructor asks you to choose a current event or an issue that is important for your classmates to consider. The assignment is to select the issue and write an informative essay about it. What event or issue would you choose? Use one or more of the topic-selection techniques to choose a topic.

1. Your topic: _____

2. What process did you use for choosing this topic? Explain in one or two sentences:

   _____

   _____

Narrowing Topics

The topic you choose for an essay or other writing assignment (and sometimes even a topic that is assigned to you) needs to be narrow enough for an essay. For example, Raphael was considering majoring in music. His instructor asked students to write an essay that discusses the daily activities involved in a job of interest to them. Raphael decided to write about a job in the music industry. Though Raphael plays several instruments, he did not want to pursue a career as a performer. So he narrowed his topic to jobs that do not include performing music.

To narrow the topic, Raphael started by breaking the subject into parts or types.

Next, he chose one type of music career—being a teacher—to discuss in his essay. After choosing "teacher," Raphael identified the following three kinds of teachers.

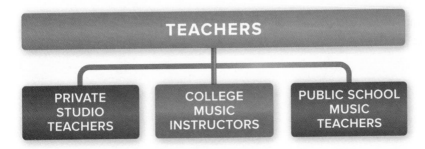

At this point, Raphael determined that these topics could be narrowed even further. Thus he identified three types of "college music instructors."

Raphael was then able to choose a narrower topic—the daily job activities of a band director—that was suitable for his assignment. To check whether he had sufficiently narrowed his topic to fit the scope of an essay, Raphael asked himself the questions shown in "Raphael Narrows His Topic."

RAPHAEL NARROWS HIS TOPIC

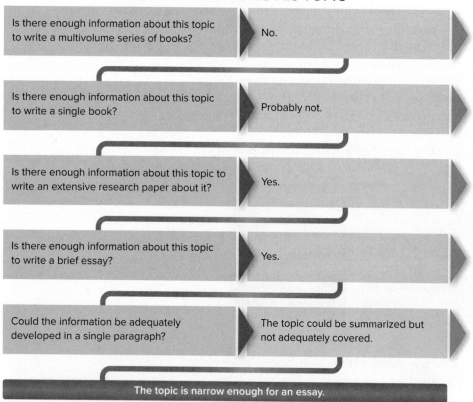

As Raphael did, you can use these questions to determine whether the topics you select are suitable for essays.

> ## PRACTICE (6)
>
> ## Narrowing Topics for Essays
>
> Use the questions in "Raphael Narrows His Topic" to consider each topic that follows. If the topic is suitable for an essay, write "Suitable for an essay." If the topic is too broad, narrow it so that it would be suitable for an essay.
>
> 1. The programming on cable television
>
>   _____
>
> 2. The importance of healthy lunches for schoolchildren
>
>   _____
>
> 3. Dentistry
>
>   _____
>
>   _____
>
> 4. Why teens drop out of high school
>
>   _____
>
> 5. Sleep
>
>   _____
>
>   _____
>
> 6. Stress
>
>   _____
>
> 7. Homelessness
>
>   _____
>
>   _____
>
> 8. Why tattoos are so popular
>
>   _____
>
> 9. Religious tolerance in the United States
>
>   _____
>
>   _____
>
> 10. Cell phones
>
>   _____
>
>   _____

Using Prewriting Strategies to Generate Ideas

Writers do not start at the beginning, go through the middle, and then finish at the end all in a straight line. They might get partway through the writing process only to realize they need to return to an earlier step to clarify their ideas. As you compose, be willing to go back and revise, rethink, and rewrite when your paper would benefit from your doing so.

Prewriting strategies—methods for coming up with ideas—are particularly useful techniques to employ again and again. Once you determine a topic, you can use prewriting to generate ideas. "Guidelines for Effective Prewriting," which follows, will help you get the most benefit from prewriting techniques.

GUIDELINES FOR EFFECTIVE PREWRITING

Use prewriting whenever you need to come up with ideas.	• You can use prewriting at the beginning of the writing process, in the middle, or even at the end when you are revising.
Don't judge what you write down during prewriting.	• The goal is to come up with ideas, not to judge them. Get as many ideas on paper as you can.
If one prewriting technique doesn't work well, try another.	• Sometimes writing a list works; sometimes discussing an idea with friends is a better idea. Use a variety of methods.

Prewriting Strategy: Discussion

Discussing ideas with others can be a useful prewriting strategy. Meet with family, friends, or classmates—in person, online, or by phoning or texting—and talk about your ideas for the assignment. Take notes so that you can revisit the ideas later when you are developing an outline.

PRACTICE **7**

Using Discussion for Prewriting

Imagine your task is to write an essay about a current trend, such as getting a tattoo or wearing a certain style of clothing. You must determine why the trend is popular and how it developed. Use discussion to (1) identify a trend, (2) make a list of the possible reasons for its popularity, and (3) determine, if possible, how the trend developed. Jot down your answers on a separate sheet.

Prewriting Strategy: Simple Listing

Some people love to make lists. Even if you are not one of those people, you might still find that **listing** is a helpful prewriting strategy. First, turn the topic into a question.

For example, Luisa's topic for a writing assignment was the following: *strategies for increasing exercise.*

Topic: Adding exercise to your life
  Question: What are some ways people can get more exercise?
  - go for a walk every day
  - park farther away from entrances
  - take stairs when possible
  - join a gym
  - join a community team (such as volleyball, baseball, and so on)
  - find an exercise partner
  - let their children be their "trainers"
  - buy an exercise machine, such as an elliptical or treadmill
  - buy a video and exercise with it
  - use an online program for motivation
  - hire a personal trainer
  - do chores that require physical exertion, such as washing a car by hand
  - find activities that combine exercise with fun, such as visiting and hiking in parks
  - do the things they liked in childhood, such as bike riding, playing kickball, and so on

Notice that Luisa wrote down everything she could think of. She didn't censor any ideas.

PRACTICE 8

Using Listing for Prewriting

Drawing on your own experience as a student or a parent, think about your K–12 education. Imagine that you plan to write an essay on the changes that could have improved your education. First, turn the topic into a question. On a separate sheet, list at least ten ideas in response to the question.

Prewriting Strategy: Clustering

Clustering, or *mapping,* is a visual method of prewriting. To use clustering, draw a circle in the middle of a sheet of paper, and in that circle write your paper's topic. As you think of an idea related to the topic, put the new idea in a new circle. Use lines to show relationships among ideas. Do not censor any ideas during this process, and do not worry if your result is messy. "Samuel's Clustering Diagram" shows how one student, Samuel, used clustering for an essay about common rites of passage for American youth. (A *rite of passage* is an event or ritual that marks the change from one life stage to another.)

SAMUEL'S CLUSTERING DIAGRAM

PRACTICE 9

Using Clustering for Prewriting

Use clustering to come up with examples or illustrations for an essay. The topic for this essay is *family traditions.* On a separate sheet, first, turn the topic into a question, and then draw a clustering chart to prewrite about this topic. Some items you might consider are types of traditions, problems with traditions, and feelings about traditions.

Prewriting Strategy: 5 W's + 1 H Questions

The 5 W's plus 1 H questions can help you generate ideas about your topic. Think about your topic, and then consider these questions:

Who?   What?   Where?   When?   Why?   How?

Keep in mind that you may not need to use all the information these questions will produce. At this stage, do not censor any information. If you wish, use a computer to type in your ideas. The example below shows Carolina's questions and answers about a particular topic.

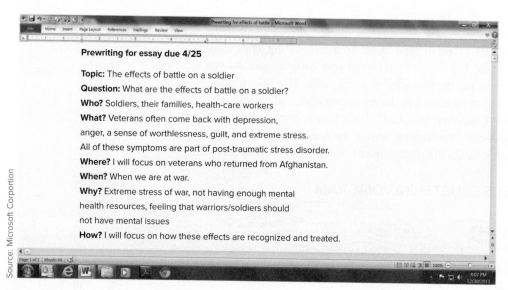

Source: Microsoft Corportion

PRACTICE 10

Using 5 W's + 1 H Questions for Prewriting

Consider the issue of cheating on tests. Use the questions to explore this issue. Write your answers for the following questions on a separate sheet.

Topic: Cheating on tests

1. Who is involved?
2. What happens?
3. Where does it happen?
4. When does it happen?

5. Why does it happen?
6. How does it happen?
7. What can we do to prevent it?

Prewriting Strategy: Freewriting

Freewriting is one of the simplest prewriting methods. To freewrite, simply think about your topic and write everything that comes to mind for a limited period of time, such as three minutes. You do not need to write in complete sentences; it is fine to jot down phrases and words that come to mind. If you cannot think of anything to write, then type or write the topic's key words over and over. The point is not to censor ideas during this stage of writing. The example below shows Anita's freewriting. Notice how she simply recorded everything that came to mind.

VCW deprivation

Topic: sleep **deprivation**

Questions: What are the effects of sleep deprivation? How can one avoid sleep deprivation?

makes it hard to concentrate, makes it hard to stay awake at work and school, can't live life well if you don't get enough sleep, must take time for yourself, set a good example for your kids by going to bed on time, sleep, sleep deprivation, not enough of it, why, because too much is going on, eat dinner too late, too many activities, maybe should cut down on activities, eat a simple dinner like sandwiches, make a time you must go to bed every night, stick to it, teach kids the same, sleep, make room comfortable, nice atmosphere, comfy bed, fluffy pillows

PRACTICE 11

Using Freewriting for Prewriting

Imagine that you are required to write an essay about the decline of manners in public. Give yourself two to three minutes to freewrite. On a separate sheet, write down everything that comes to mind during this time period. If you get stuck, write a key word like *rude* or *polite* or *manners* over and over until you think of new ideas.

Prewriting Strategy: Freetalking

Freetalking is just like freewriting, except you use speech instead of a pen and paper. For two to three minutes, simply talk out loud to yourself about the topic. Consider using a cell phone that records your voice or a small digital recorder. Take your time and think out loud. It might be helpful to imagine you are talking to a friend about the topic. If you get stuck, repeat the topic over and over again. Jot down new ideas as they come to mind.

PRACTICE 12

Using Freetalking for Prewriting

Find a quiet place where you can talk to yourself or to your cell phone or digital recorder without distraction (or embarrassment!). Imagine that you have been assigned a paragraph or an essay on a social issue about which you are very concerned. More specifically, your assignment is to explain why this issue is worth our time and our attention. Examples of such issues are global warming, the **eradication** of poverty in a certain place, and the improvement of every elementary school. Use freetalking to explore why your chosen social issue is important. Write down at least three ideas you discover.

VCW eradication

CHAPTER ACTIVITIES

➡ READING AND ANNOTATING

What follows is an article published on *Greater Good: The Science of a Meaningful Life*, a Web site sponsored by the University of California, Berkeley. Use the four pre-reading strategies covered in this chapter and summarized in the list below. As you use each one, write down your thoughts on the a separate sheet.

- **Preview:** What do you notice when you preview the text?
- **Predict:** What do you predict the topic will be?
- **Recall:** What do you already know about the topic?
- **Ask:** What questions do you have about the text or the topic?

After you complete the pre-reading activities, read and annotate the article. Use annotations to mark key ideas. Additionally, mark any ideas you find interesting. You will use your annotations for a later assignment.

Stumbling Toward Gratitude

By Catherine Price

YOUR ANNOTATIONS

I have a confession: when I go to a bookstore, I like hanging out in the self-help section. I don't know if it's because I think I'll find a book that will solve all my problems, or if seeing all the books on problems I don't have makes me feel better about myself. But whatever it is, I keep going back.

On recent visits, I've noticed a trend: The market has been glutted by books promising the secrets to happiness. That might not seem new (isn't happiness the point of the entire section?), but these aren't touchy-feely self-help titles—they're books by scientific researchers, who claim to offer prescriptions based on rigorous **empirical** research. It's all part of the "positive psychology" movement that has spilled out of academic journals and into best-selling books, popular magazine articles, and even school curricula.

VCW empirical

As I glanced through a few of these titles, two things quickly became clear. First, positive psychologists claim you can create your own happiness. **Conventional** wisdom has long held that each of us is simply born with a happiness "set point" (meaning that some people are constitutionally more likely to be happy than others). That's partially true—but according to positive psychologists Sonja Lyubomirsky and Ken Sheldon, research now suggests that up to 40 percent of our happiness might stem from intentional activities in which we choose to engage.

VCW conventional

Second, in trying to explain which activities might actually help us cultivate happiness, positive psychology keeps returning to the same concept: gratitude. In study after study, researchers have found that if people actively try to become more grateful in their everyday lives, they're likely to become happier—and healthier—as well.

So how do positive psychologists recommend that you increase your level of gratitude—and, therefore, happiness? They endorse several research-tested exercises.

(continued)

These include keeping a "gratitude journal," where you record a running list of things for which you're grateful; making a conscious effort to "savor" all the beauty and pleasures in your daily life; and writing a "gratitude letter" to some important person in your life who you've never properly thanked.

These gratitude exercises all sounded pleasant enough, but would they work for me? While I'm not currently depressed, I'm very aware that depression runs in my family: I'm the only person—including the dog—who has not yet been on Prozac. So I decided to indulge in all three of these exercises over a six-week period, risking the possibility that I might become an insufferably happy and cheerful person.

I emailed University of Miami psychologist Michael McCullough, a leading gratitude researcher, to ask what he thought I could expect as a result of my gratitude overdose.

"If you're not experiencing more happiness and satisfaction in your life after this six-week gratitude **infusion**," he wrote back, "I'll eat my hat!"

Getting Grateful

My first step was to get a gratitude journal. Luckily, a year earlier my recently retired father had stumbled across a bookstore that sold "quotable journals"—blank books with inspiring quotes on their covers. My father, always a sucker for inspiration, sent me seven of them. I settled on one with a cover that said, in all caps, "Life isn't about finding yourself. Life is about creating yourself." Given my experiment in manufactured happiness, this seemed appropriate.

Journal at my side, I decided to start by taking a happiness inventory (available, along with a bunch of other quizzes, at authentichappiness.org, the website run by positive psychology guru Martin Seligman). I scored a 3.58 out of 5, putting myself ahead of 77 percent of participants, but still leaving plenty of room for improvement—as evidenced by my first journal entry.

"It's been a somewhat depressing day," starts my gratitude journal. "Or, rather, week."

At first, it felt a little awkward to keep a journal specifically for gratitude—I felt as if I should plaster my car in cheesy bumper stickers ("Happiness is") and call it a day. But even on that first downbeat afternoon, my journal did make me feel a little better about things. Listing things I was grateful for made me feel, well, grateful for them—and since I'd also decided to jot down moments each day that had made me happy (another positive psychology-endorsed exercise), I had a concrete list of cheerful experiences to look back on when I was feeling down. Thanks to my journal, I know that on January 18th I was happy because I'd exercised, had a good Chinese lesson, and spent 15 minutes dancing around my room to Shakira's "Hips Don't Lie." On January 30th, I was grateful for my **perseverance**, the Pacific Ocean, and the fact that I have really, really good cholesterol.

I've always kept a journal, but once my initial excitement about my new project had passed, my writing schedule felt a bit **contrived**—I often had to force myself to stay awake for a few minutes before bedtime so that I wouldn't miss an entry. But I quickly found that encouraging myself to focus on the good in my life instead of dwelling on the bad was helping me gain a

Prozac: A prescription medication to treat depression.

VCW infusion

VCW perseverance

VCW contrived

(continued)

bit of perspective on things. "The actions in my day-to-day life are actually quite pleasant," I wrote on January 21st, in a moment of insight. "It's anxieties that get me derailed."

It was also good to get in the habit of countering bad things in my day with reflections on the good. For example, on February 1st—which I described as "having a lot going against it"—I wrote that I "spent a bunch of the day cleaning my room and trying to get my new phone to work, went on fruitless errands, ripped out part of a sweater I was knitting, and when I emailed the pattern designer—who goes by 'Yarn Boy'—to ask if he could help me figure out where I'd gone wrong, he sent me an email back telling me to 'take it to a yarn shop.' Thanks a lot, Yarn Ass." And yet the entry ends as follows: "But I did get my phone set up and cleaned my room a bit. Chinese went well. I got cute new barrettes. I worked out even though I didn't feel like it, then I savored the feel of my calf muscles."

That might not sound like much, but trust me: It's an improvement.

Happy Meal

To celebrate finishing my experiment—not to mention filling up my journal—I took my boyfriend out for dinner at a restaurant here in Berkeley called Café Gratitude. It's a place that is **anathema** to my cynical New York roots: cheery waitresses who call everyone "darling," posters on the walls that ask questions like, "Can you surrender to how beautiful you are?" and, worst of all, a menu of organic, vegan dishes, all named with life-affirming sentences. For example, saying to your server, "I am fabulous" means that you would like some lasagna. "I am fun" indicates that you want some toast. Unfortunately, there is no organic, vegan interpretation of "I am about to vomit."

VCW anathema

My boyfriend and I settled on being generous, fulfilled, and accepting (guacamole, a large café salad, and a bowl of rice), and in honor of my experiment, I insisted on ordering the "I am thankful" (Thai coconut soup, served cold). To offset the restaurant's unrelenting cheer, we both ordered alcohol (luckily, even in Café Gratitude, a beer is just a beer).

While nibbling on carrot flaxseed crackers ("I am relishing"), we talked about the past six weeks. McCullough doesn't need to eat his hat—I definitely had experienced moments of feeling happier and more consciously grateful as a result of the exercises, and by the end of my experiment, my happiness index had gone up to 3.92. But I also found that there are times when I need to allow myself to feel bad without fighting against my negative emotions. And my cynical side continues to dream of opening a rival restaurant next door called the **Cantankerous** Café, with menu items like "I am depressed" and "I am resentful."

VCW cantankerous

My biggest question was how long these exercises' effects would last.

"Sometimes positive psychologists sound like we're trying to sell miracles to people. There are no miracles . . . . There are no long-term quick fixes for happiness," said Peterson, when I asked him how I could maintain my happiness boost. "So if you become a more grateful person and you add those exercises to your repertoire, you'll be different six months or a year from now. But if you say okay, I'm done with the story and I'm going back to the way I was, it'll just

(continued)

have been a six-week high. There's nothing wrong with that, but it's not going to permanently change you."

Perhaps that's why, when I got home from dinner, I went straight to my bookcase where I keep stuff my dad has sent me—and picked out another journal.

Questions for Consideration

1. What is the topic of this textbook passage?

2. What is the writer's main point about the topic?

3. What is "positive psychology" according to the author?

4. What is a gratitude journal? Explain and provide an example of what a person might write in a gratitude journal.

5. How can you relate the ideas in this reading to your own life? Explain your answer in two or three paragraphs.

➔ USING MODELS TO PRACTICE COMPOSING

The model essay that follows was written by Kendra, a student in an English class. First, Kendra read and annotated her assignment.

Kendra's Annotated Assignment

Read and annotate "Stumbling toward Gratitude." Catherine Price, the author, suggests that we can have some control over our happiness. Your assignment is to write an essay on the topic of happiness. You will need to narrow this topic.

Read and annotate

Write an essay on happiness

Narrow the topic

To narrow the topic and generate ideas, spend some time thinking about and prewriting on happiness What is it that makes people happy? What do people *believe* will make them happy? Are their beliefs correct?

Prewrite

You might focus on discussing common paths to happiness, or you might focus on false assumptions about what makes us happy. Another idea is to present practices, beliefs, or habits that you believe promote happiness. In your essay, you may refer to Price's article as needed.

Consider these ideas

Refer to Price's essay if desired

Once you have narrowed the topic and come up with ideas, write a draft of your essay. Make sure that you revise and edit your draft. Create a final draft and format it properly before submitting it.

Write a draft
Revise and edit
Put final draft in proper format

Kendra's Prewriting

Kendra used clustering to come up with ideas:

KENDRA'S CLUSTERING DIAGRAM

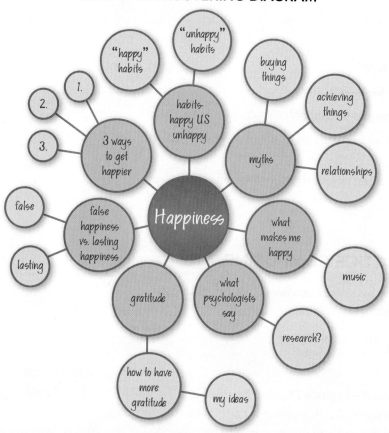

After prewriting, Kendra looked at her ideas. She decided to narrow her paper to focus on myths about happiness.

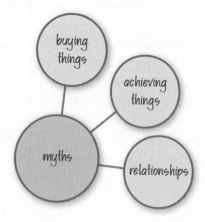

Kendra's Outline

After narrowing her topic, Kendra continued prewriting. She used her ideas to create a rough outline for her essay.

My Outline

Introduction paragraph: I'll talk a little about Catherine Price's ideas, and then I'll end with my thesis statement.

Thesis Statement: Three myths about happiness are that happiness comes from things, that happiness comes from achievements, and that happiness comes from relationships.

Body Paragraph 1: A common myth is that happiness can be bought.

Body Paragraph 2: Another myth is that personal achievements lead to happiness.

Body Paragraph 3: Finally, a common myth about happiness is that to be happy, a person must be in a romantic relationship.

Conclusion paragraph: I'll go back to Catherine Price's ideas to show that happiness comes from inside people.

After creating her rough outline, Kendra continued prewriting. She came up with ideas to put in her body paragraphs and added them to her outline. Next, she wrote a rough draft. She revised and edited her rough draft, and she created a correctly formatted final draft. Here is Kendra's final draft.

Model Student Essay: "Myths about Happiness" by Kendra Hayworth

Hayworth 1	Header
Kendra Hayworth	Heading
Ms. Miller	
DRE 098	
3 November 2017	
Myths about Happiness	Title
Everyone wants to be happy, but it is obvious that not everyone succeeds in finding contentment. Being happy is apparently not that easy. As Catherine Price explains, the study of happiness has become a part of a new field called "positive psychology." One of the insights of positive psychology is that having gratitude is one way to become a more content person, Price notes. Unfortunately, there are many ideas	Introduction paragraph
	Information from article

Hayworth 2

about what makes people happy that are simply wrong. Three myths about happiness are that life satisfaction comes from owning things, that contentedness comes from achievements, and that happiness comes from romantic relationships.

A common myth is that happiness can be bought. Most people, at one time or another, believe this myth. They think that if they can just buy that new car, afford that better apartment, or get that new smartphone they will definitely be happy. But most people know what happens after making purchases like these. There is usually a short period of temporary happiness, but that period is followed by the same cycle. When the "new wears off," the smartphone becomes just another gadget. It does not make its owner happy anymore. It is just a smartphone. People who believe that things can make them happy often move on to the next desired object. Maybe a bigger television will do the trick. Maybe having a great sound system will result in true satisfaction. The problem is, things cannot provide happiness for more than a short period of time. Focusing on things to try to find true contentment is unwise.

Another myth people often believe is that personal achievements lead to happiness. "I'll know I have made it when I graduate." "I'll be so happy if my daughter makes the swim team." "When I lose twenty pounds, I'll be so happy." It is true that achievements bring some happiness to people. But achievements fade. The day after graduation, the graduate wakes up and is the same person. Even though losing twenty pounds can make a person joyous at first, keeping the weight off is always a struggle. Achievements are enjoyed in the moment when they are made. Day-to-day happiness seems to require more than achievements.

Finally, a common myth about happiness is that to be happy, a person must be in a romantic relationship. Many people spend their

Thesis statement

Major Supporting Point 1

Supporting details

Major Supporting Point 2

Supporting details

Major Supporting Point 3

Hayworth 3

waking hours looking for a romantic partner. Some believe that the partner will "complete" them. It is easy to see the falsity of the idea that a romantic relationship is the key to happiness. So many marriages end in divorce, and the number of break-ups for people who are not married is probably even higher. How could a romantic partner be the key to lasting happiness? Even people who do stay together have to work at their relationships. There are plenty of times when it is more difficult to stay in a relationship than to end it. Of course, romance is wonderful when it happens, but like new things and achievements, romance is a temporary thing. So a romantic relationship cannot be the key to a happy life.

Neither material goods, nor personal achievements, nor romantic relationships lead to lasting happiness. So what, exactly, does make people happy? Catherine Price writes about gratitude and how researchers have shown that practicing gratitude results in true, daily happiness. Gratitude is a feeling, and as Price points out, having the feeling more often seems to make people happier. Maybe the key to happiness is changing our minds, changing what goes on inside our heads, and not worrying so much about external things. A first step is recognizing the myths about happiness that so easily lead us in the wrong direction.

Supporting details

Conclusion paragraph

Information from article

Hayworth 4

Works Cited

Price, Catherine. "Stumbling toward Gratitude." *Greater Good*, Greater Good Science Center at UC Berkeley, 1 June 2007, greatergood. berkeley.edu/article/item/stumbling_toward_gratitude.

➡ A READING AND WRITING ASSIGNMENT

Using Kendra's essay as a model, write your own essay about the topic of happiness. Follow the same process Kendra used to plan, draft, revise, and edit her essay.

➡ ADDING TO YOUR VOCABULARY

This chapter's vocabulary words appear below.

anathema	contrived	cursory	empirical	infusion
cantankerous	conventional	deprivation	eradication	perseverance

Choose five of the vocabulary words from this chapter that you would like to add to your vocabulary, and think about how you can use them this week. For example, one of this chapter's words is *cursory*. You can often substitute *cursory* for *hasty*, as in the examples that follow.

Example: I didn't have time to study, so I looked over my notes in a *hasty* fashion.

I didn't have time to study, so I looked over my notes in a *cursory* fashion.

List each of the five words you plan to use this week, and make note of a context in which you could use the new word.

Example: *Cursory.* I can use this word to teach my kids the difference between cleaning their room thoroughly and cleaning their room in a *cursory* way.

➡ ADDITIONAL ASSIGNMENTS

1. In Practice 8, you wrote down ideas about changes that would improve education. Using your prewriting, select two to four changes you believe would transform public education. Write an essay in which you present your ideas.

2. Reread "Maslow's Hierarchy of Needs," a textbook selection from earlier in this chapter. Maslow theorizes that people can work on meeting higher-level needs only after their lower-level needs have been met. Do you agree or not? Write a paragraph explaining your point of view. Provide examples (either real or hypothetical) to support your point of view.

EMOTIONAL INTELLIGENCE
A recent experiment shows the importance of *optimism,* a tendency to feel hopeful and positive about the future. A psychologist tested students at the University of Pennsylvania to determine whether optimism had an effect on grades. The experiment showed that by analyzing the level of optimism students had, researchers could more accurately predict the students' college success than by analyzing their SAT scores! Students who were on the optimistic end of the scale earned better grades than did students who were pessimistic.

Think about optimism, pessimism, and how they affect a person's success. Think of someone you know who is always optimistic. Has optimism made this person a better student or worker? Think of a pessimistic person you know. Has pessimism decreased this person's effectiveness? Write a paragraph in which you speculate on this topic.

METACOGNITION

Did you know that students can change their learning ability over time? If you were never successful in math in the past, that does not mean you cannot learn to do math well now. Your ability to learn can develop and increase over time. What seemed unattainable last year might prove quite achievable this year.

Make a list of your assumptions about your strengths and weaknesses as a learner. Note any subjects about which you have thought, "I'm just not good at that." Next, think of a skill you found difficult at one time but later came to master. Write a paragraph explaining how you learned the skill. Finally, write a paragraph about whether you believe you can learn one of the weak subjects or skills you listed earlier. In your paragraph, explain the reasons for your beliefs.

Text Credits

Page 54: Source: Swanson, Charles R., Chamelin, Neil, and Territo, Leonard, *Criminal Investigation*, 11th ed. New York: McGraw-Hill, 2012; Page 68: Price, Catherine, "Stumbling toward Gratitude," *The Greater Good*, June 1, 2007. Copyright © 2007. The Greater Good Science Center. This article originally appeared on *Greater Good*, the online magazine of the Greater Good Science Center at UC Berkeley. Read more at *greatergood.berkeley.edu*; Page 57: Source: Payne, Wayne, Hahn, Dale, and Lucas, Ellen, *Understanding Your Health*, 12th ed. New York: McGraw-Hill Education, 2012. 37–38; Page 57: Source: Maslow, Abraham H., *Motivation and Personality*, 3rd ed. Longman, 1987; Page 53: King, Laura, *Experience Psychology*, 2nd Edition. Copyright © 2015 McGraw-Hill Education. 171. Used with permission of McGraw-Hill Education.

Main Ideas

If you were blindfolded and could touch only one part of an elephant—trunk, tusk, or leg, for example—what would you guess you were touching?

©Michael Babwahsingh

Chapter Objectives

After completing this chapter, students will be able to do the following:

- Identify topic sentences and implied main ideas in paragraphs.

- Compose topic sentences for paragraphs.

- Identify main ideas in essays.

- Find implied main ideas in essays.

- Compose effective thesis statements.

- Use parallel structure in thesis statements.

In an old parable from India, several blind people each examine a single part of an elephant. Unable to see the whole, the person examining the tail assumes that the item in question is a rope. The person examining a tusk, meanwhile, determines that he is feeling a spear. The body is thought to be a wall, the trunk is mistaken for a snake, and the legs are assumed to be tree trunks. Without any knowledge of the whole—the elephant!—the investigators are led astray.

A written text can also be seen as a whole made up of various parts. While appreciating the individual parts is important, grasping how the parts make up the whole message—the writer's main idea—is crucial to comprehension.

Both reading and writing require us to work with main ideas. In reading, we must be able to identify main ideas, and in writing, we must be able to communicate them. Our focus in this chapter is to see how the identification of particular parts of a reading can lead us to an understanding of the whole—the reading's main idea.

Identifying Topic Sentences and Implied Main Ideas in Paragraphs

The purpose of a paragraph is to communicate a main idea to the reader. The main idea of a paragraph is expressed in a **topic sentence,** and additional sentences in the paragraph are called **supporting sentences.** These additional sentences provide explanations, examples, and other kinds of support to help readers understand the topic sentence. "Characteristics of a Topic Sentence" shows you the four features to look for in a topic sentence.

CHARACTERISTICS OF A TOPIC SENTENCE

A Topic Sentence ...

Expresses the main point in a paragraph	• It gives the exact point the writer hopes the reader will remember or believe.
Expresses the broadest idea in the paragraph	• It includes the ideas given in the paragraph's other sentences.
Presents an idea that requires support	• It makes a point that needs to be explained further or backed up with evidence.
Is a statement, not a question	• It makes a point, so it cannot be a question.

Let's look at a paragraph and try to figure out the topic sentence.

> [1]What is the most important consideration when choosing a career? [2]It is not salary, and it is not status. [3]For many people, the most important factor in finding a career is what the job will require on a daily basis. [4]For example, Leah Reem worked hard in college to become an attorney. [5]After six months on the job, she realized that she hated sitting in an office every day. [6]She often felt too tired to exercise when she got home, and she found herself gaining weight and simply feeling depressed. [7]She began to realize that the daily requirements of legal work were not making her happy, so she quit her job and found a job working with horses. [8]While the new job paid much less, Leah found it very satisfying. [9]If she had known how the daily tasks involved in being a lawyer would affect her, Leah would have chosen a different career field.

First, we will eliminate some of the sentences.

Sentence 1: This sentence is not the topic sentence because it's a question. Topic sentences are always statements.

Sentence 2: This sentence does not tell us what the rest of the paragraph discusses, so it is not the topic sentence.

Sentences 4–9: This long example is being used to support an idea (the topic sentence), so none of these sentences is the topic sentence.

Go back to the paragraph, and cross out these sentences. Now, we are left with one sentence—sentence 3. Does it meet the requirements for topic sentences?

> For many people, the most important factor in finding a career is what the job will require on a daily basis.

We can check that sentence 3 is the topic sentence by asking ourselves whether the sentence has the four characteristics of a topic sentence. "Have I Found the Topic Sentence?" shows our reasoning.

HAVE I FOUND THE TOPIC SENTENCE?

| Does it express the main point in the paragraph? | **Yes.** The paragraph starts with a question, and a question will not be a main point. Also, the paragraph includes a long example. Examples will never be main ideas. They are always used to support another idea. |

| Does it express the broadest idea in the paragraph? | **Yes.** In the paragraph, we have a question, a sentence, and an example. An example is always narrower than the idea it supports.
EXAMPLE: Many fruits contain acids. For example, lemons contain acid.
• Many fruits = broader
• Lemons = narrower |

| Does it express a point that needs support? | **Yes.** The idea that "the most important factor in finding a career is what the job will require on a daily basis" is debatable. Some people will disagree. Thus, the writer will need to provide support to help readers understand and agree. In this case, the support is an example. |

| Is it expressed as a statement, not a question? | **Yes.** The sentence we have chosen has all of the characteristics of a topic sentence. |

The sentence we have chosen has all four characteristics of topic sentences.

Identifying Topic Sentences

In addition to recognizing topic sentences based on their characteristics, you can also use the four-step process in "Identifying a Topic Sentence."

IDENTIFYING A TOPIC SENTENCE

1 Read the paragraph and identify its topic.

2 Figure out the writer's point about the topic.

3 Write a sentence that includes the topic and the writer's point.

4 In the paragraph, find a sentence similar to the one you wrote.

Study the following paragraph to see how the four-step process works. The **bold** print shows repeated words that suggest the topic.

> **Stress management** is an emotional intelligence skill that increases the value of employees in a workplace. Personnel who have methods for relieving **stress** are much less likely to lash out at either coworkers or customers. Additionally, the ability to **control stress** helps workers be more efficient because they are not distracted by tension and worry. Staff who are successful at **keeping their stress levels down** will often rise to a higher level and become especially valued employees.

Here's how we can use the four-step process:

1. Read the paragraph and identify its topic.

Topic: stress management

2. Figure out the writer's point about the topic.

Writer's point: importance of stress management skills for workers

3. Write a sentence that includes the topic and the writer's point.

Our sentence: Stress management is important for workers.

4. Find a sentence similar to the one you wrote.

Topic sentence: Stress management is an emotional intelligence skill that makes employees valuable.

By using these four steps, we created a sentence with a meaning similar to the sentence we found in the original paragraph. We can now check to see if the sentence has the characteristics of topic sentences.

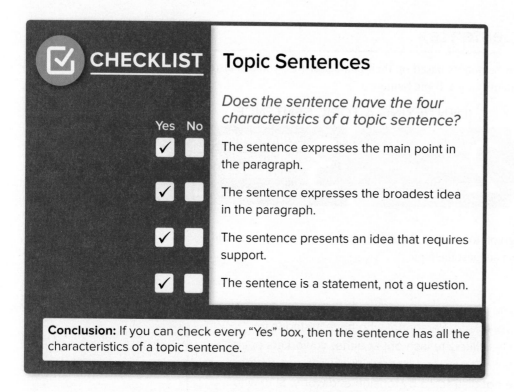

CHECKLIST

Topic Sentences

Does the sentence have the four characteristics of a topic sentence?

Yes   No

[✓] [ ]   The sentence expresses the main point in the paragraph.

[✓] [ ]   The sentence expresses the broadest idea in the paragraph.

[✓] [ ]   The sentence presents an idea that requires support.

[✓] [ ]   The sentence is a statement, not a question.

Conclusion: If you can check every "Yes" box, then the sentence has all the characteristics of a topic sentence.

Considering a Topic Sentence's Placement

In the preceding example, the topic sentence is the first sentence in the paragraph. While a topic sentence is often placed first, it does not have to be. It may be placed in the body of a paragraph or even at the end. The key to finding a topic sentence is not to focus on where it is placed; instead, focus on accurately putting the main idea into your own words. Then you can find the sentence in the paragraph without worrying about where it is placed.

PRACTICE 1

Finding Topic Sentences

Annotate the following paragraph to determine its main idea and topic sentence. Fill in the answers below.

YOUR ANNOTATIONS

What is the difference between a credit card and a debit card? Both can be used instead of cash or checks to make purchases online as well as at places of business. Debit cards are often associated with major credit card companies such as MasterCard and Visa. Yet debit cards function quite differently from credit cards. The fundamental difference is that when you use a credit card, you are actually borrowing money from a bank (the credit card company). That money must be paid back at the end of the grace period (usually about a month), or interest will be charged to you on the amount of the loan. With a debit card, you are spending your own money. Most often the money comes directly out of your checking account. While there are other dissimilarities, the principal difference between a credit card and a debit card is the difference between taking out a loan and spending money that you already have on hand.

(continued)

1. Read the paragraph and identify its topic.

   Topic: _____

2. Figure out the writer's point about the topic.

   Writer's point: _____

   _____

3. Write a sentence that includes the topic and the writer's point.

   Your sentence: _____

   _____

   _____

4. Find a sentence similar to the one you wrote.

   _____

   _____

   _____

Conclusion: If your analysis is correct, you have very likely identified the topic sentence. _____

Finding Implied Main Ideas in Paragraphs

Some paragraphs present an **implied main idea**, an idea that is suggested by the ideas in the paragraph but not stated directly. Readers must figure out the implied main idea and put it into their own words. Use the modified four-step process in "Identifying an Implied Main Idea" to identify the implied main idea, put it into your own words, and create an implied topic sentence.

IDENTIFYING AN IMPLIED MAIN IDEA

1 Read the paragraph and identify its topic.

2 Figure out the writer's point about the topic.

3 Write a sentence that includes the topic and the writer's point.

4 In the paragraph, find a sentence similar to the one you wrote.

If you cannot find such a sentence, the main idea is implied. Use the sentence you wrote as the implied topic sentence.

What follows is a paragraph with an implied main idea, so the paragraph does not have a directly stated topic sentence. As you read the paragraph, pay attention to the terms in bold type. These terms give clues to the topic.

For many years, smoking on airplanes was a **social norm**, an **accepted behavior** in our society. Although travelers could choose to sit in a non-smoking area of the plane, they could not expect to breathe clean air since smoke permeated the plane. By the year 2000, however, smoking had been banned on all commercial flights. Many younger travelers have never flown on a plane where smoking was allowed. Another **changing social norm** we can examine is that of body art. Getting a tattoo used to be a **behavior** associated with rebelliousness—and often lawlessness. Tattoos were for people in gangs, for bikers, for inmates, and for some people in the armed services. Today, tattoos are as common as pierced ears. People from all walks of life choose to get tattoos, and slowly, people are becoming less judgmental about those who have tattoos.

Notice how we can use the process for identifying an implied main idea.

1. Read the paragraph and identify its topic.

> **Topic:** The paragraph gives us two examples of social norms (accepted behaviors), so we will say the topic is "social norms."

2. Figure out the writer's point about the topic.

> **Writer's point:** The writer uses examples of social norms that have changed over time—smoking on airplanes and getting tattoos. So maybe the point is that social norms can change.

3. Write a sentence that includes the topic and the writer's point.

> **Our sentence:** Social norms can change over time.

4. In the paragraph, find a sentence similar to the one you wrote. *If you cannot find such a sentence, the main idea is implied. Use the sentence you wrote as the implied topic sentence.*

> **Implied topic sentence:** There is no similar sentence, so the paragraph has an implied main idea. The sentence we wrote—"Social norms can change over time"—can serve as the implied topic sentence of the paragraph.

When you encounter a paragraph with an implied main idea, write your own implied topic sentence in the margin. You will then be able to go back to the paragraph and read your implied topic sentence to get a quick summary of the paragraph's point.

PRACTICE 2

Finding Implied Main Ideas in Paragraphs

The following paragraph has an implied main idea, not an explicit topic sentence. Use annotations to determine the topic and the writer's point, and then compose your own topic sentence for the paragraph.

Banks frequently make credit cards available to college students. Some people are critical of this practice, but others point out that having a credit card can provide a student with an emergency fund. Not many college students have the luxury of a **robust** savings account. In the event of an emergency, such as a serious health issue, a wrecked vehicle, or stolen textbooks, having a credit card might be a real advantage. Having a credit card also enables a student to begin the process of building credit, which can have long-term benefits. The careful use of credit cards throughout college may mean the student will have built enough credit history to qualify for a home mortgage after graduation.

1. Read the paragraph and identify its topic.

   Topic: _____

2. Figure out the writer's point about the topic.

   Writer's point: _____

3. Write a sentence that includes the topic and the writer's point.

   Your sentence (implied topic sentence): _____

   _____

   _____

YOUR ANNOTATIONS

VCW robust

For every Vocabulary Collection Word (VCW), give your in-context idea of the word's meaning and then look up the word's dictionary definition.

Composing Topic Sentences for Paragraphs

As you use the four-step process to identify topic sentences in readings, you are—at the same time—learning how to write topic sentences. You can follow a three-step process, shown in "Composing a Topic Sentence," for writing a topic sentence.

COMPOSING A TOPIC SENTENCE

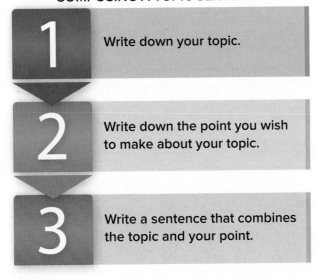

1 Write down your topic.

2 Write down the point you wish to make about your topic.

3 Write a sentence that combines the topic and your point.

For example, suppose you are asked to write a paragraph discussing one type of app that everyone should know how to use. You decide to write about driving navigation apps. "Composing a Topic Sentence: An Example" shows how you might create a topic sentence.

COMPOSING A TOPIC SENTENCE: AN EXAMPLE

1	Write down your topic.	navigation apps
2	Write down the point you wish to make about your topic.	everyone should know how to use them
3	Write a sentence that combines the topic and your point.	One type of app that everyone should learn how to use is a navigation app.

Look over your topic sentence. Make sure that it is a sentence that would require support such as explanations or examples, and make sure it is not a question.

PRACTICE 3

Writing Topic Sentences

Below you will find sets of topics and points about those topics. For each set, write a topic sentence by combining the topic and the point to be made about it. Use the characteristics of topic sentences to check your work.

1. Topic: choosing a career

    Point: how aptitude tests can help

    Your topic sentence: _____

    _____

2. Topic: home water filters

    Point: reasons people use them

    Your topic sentence: _____

    _____

3. Topic: easing mental depression

    Point: how a new hobby can help

    Your topic sentence: _____

    _____

4. Topic: volunteering

    Point: four steps for choosing appropriate volunteering opportunities

    Your topic sentence: _____

    _____

Make it a habit to write out the topic sentences of the paragraphs you read. By doing this, you will improve your ability to write your own topic sentences. Second, you can use the topic sentences you write to grasp the broader idea that unites all of the paragraphs, as you will see later in this chapter.

PRACTICE 4

Identifying and Writing Topic Sentences

The following textbook passage contains three body paragraphs. For each body paragraph, identify the topic and the writer's point about the topic. Write a sentence that combines the topic with the writer's point. If the main idea is expressed in a topic sentence in the paragraph, copy the topic sentence.

Paragraph A

Guilt both alerts us to and motivates us to correct a wrong we have committed. Guilt is a lot like pain. When you cut yourself, you feel pain at the site where the injury occurred. The pain motivates you to repair the injury before it becomes infected and festers. Guilt also motivates us to avoid harming ourselves and others. We refrain from cheating on an exam or from stealing someone's laptop—even when no one is around to see us take it—because the very thought of doing so makes us feel guilty.

1. Topic: _____

2. Writer's point: _____

3. Topic sentence in your words: _____

4. Topic sentence from paragraph or implied topic sentence: _____

_____

Paragraph B

Guilt is frequently regarded as a barrier to personal freedom and happiness. Some of us respond to guilt with resistance, either trying to ignore it entirely or getting angry at the person who "made" us feel guilty. But at the same time, we generally regard a person who feels no guilt—such as a **sociopath**—as inhuman and a monster.

1. Topic: _____

2. Writer's point: _____

3. Topic sentence in your words: _____

4. Topic sentence from paragraph or implied topic sentence: _____

_____

Paragraph C

Guilt is often broadly defined to include shame. However, the two are different. Guilt results when we commit a moral wrong or violate a moral principle. Shame, on the other hand, occurs as a result of the violation of a social norm, or not living up to someone else's expectations for us. Teenagers who

VCW sociopath

(continued)

are lesbian, gay, or bisexual may feel shame for not living up to the expectations of their family, church, or society—but they may not feel moral guilt. Rather than motivating us to do better, shame leaves us feeling inadequate, embarrassed, and humiliated. As good critical thinkers, it is important that we distinguish between guilt and shame.

1. Topic: _____

2. Writer's point: _____

3. Topic sentence in your words: _____

4. Topic sentence from paragraph or implied topic sentence: _____

_____

Identifying Main Ideas in Essays

Just as a paragraph is a group of sentences that expresses and supports one main idea, an *essay* is a set of paragraphs that work together to support a main idea. Essays can appear in **diverse** forms, including magazine articles, scholarly journal articles, brief academic papers, and personal reflections.

VCW diverse

A common thread uniting all essays is that each one uses multiple paragraphs to communicate a main idea to an audience. Usually, a writer introduces the topic, states the main idea, supports or explains the main idea in a series of paragraphs, and offers a conclusion. Not all essays follow this pattern, but most essays include all these elements, which are shown in "An Essay's Structure."

AN ESSAY'S STRUCTURE

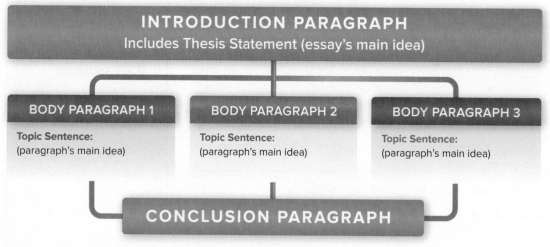

Recognizing the Characteristics of Thesis Statements

The main idea of an essay is its **thesis statement.** The thesis statement provides the writer's topic and the point the writer wishes to make about the topic. Often, a thesis statement is expressed in a single sentence, but sometimes it will span two or three sentences.

Like a topic sentence, a thesis statement has particular characteristics, which you can see listed in "Characteristics of a Thesis Statement."

CHARACTERISTICS OF A THESIS STATEMENT
A Thesis Statement ...

Expresses the most important point in an essay.	• The thesis statement tells readers the exact point the writer hopes readers will remember or believe.
Presents an idea that requires support.	• The thesis statement makes a point that needs to be explained further or backed up with evidence.
Expresses the broadest idea in the essay.	• The thesis sentence includes the ideas presented in the essay's paragraphs.
Is a statement, not a question.	• The idea or opinion in the thesis statement demands explanation, evidence, or discussion in the essay.

Comparing Thesis Statements and Topic Sentences

You may have noticed that the characteristics of thesis statements are similar to those of topic sentences. In fact, thesis statements and topic sentences are similar in that they both communicate main ideas. The difference between them lies in their functions within an essay. If you have only a single paragraph, you will have only one single main idea, expressed either in an explicit topic sentence or in an implied topic sentence. You already know the purpose of the topic sentence: it tells you the most important point of the paragraph.

What happens when paragraphs are put together in an essay? These paragraphs still have topic sentences, and each topic sentence still tells the reader the most important point of its paragraph. However, the paragraphs in an essay serve to support the thesis statement. You can see an example of this in "How Thesis Statements Relate to Topic Sentences."

HOW THESIS STATEMENTS RELATE TO TOPIC SENTENCES

THESIS STATEMENT
Most cultures use storytelling as a way to
reinforce the culture's identity, preserve the culture's history, and
strengthen the culture's values.

BODY PARAGRAPH 1

Topic Sentence:
One reason storytelling is important is that it helps a culture preserve its identity.

BODY PARAGRAPH 2

Topic Sentence:
Another function of storytelling is to preserve a culture's history.

BODY PARAGRAPH 3

Topic Sentence:
Finally, storytelling is used as a way to strengthen a culture's values.

The thesis statement ("Most cultures use storytelling as a way to reinforce the culture's identity, preserve the culture's history, and strengthen the culture's values") contains all three reasons for storytelling, so the thesis statement is broader than each topic sentence. In other words, because the topic sentences each present just a single reason, they are narrower than the thesis statement.

Try your hand at distinguishing thesis statements from topic sentences by completing the exercise that follows.

PRACTICE 5

Distinguishing Thesis Statements from Topic Sentences

In each group below, you will find a thesis statement and several topic sentences. Put an X in the blank for the sentence that is the thesis statement.

1. _____ Cooking at home saves money.

   _____ Knowing how to cook is advantageous in terms of savings, food safety, nutrition, and relaxation.

   _____ Cooking can be a relaxing activity.

   _____ The nutritional value of homemade meals is superior to that of fast food.

   _____ Home cooks can be assured their food is safely prepared.

2. _____ Some people take risks because of a need for sensory stimulation.

   _____ Risk taking is associated with aggression and hostility.

   _____ People who are impulsive are more likely to be risk takers.

   _____ Risk taking is a result of a complex set of human needs, behaviors, and emotions.

3. _____ Attending college with people of all backgrounds helps ease social tensions between groups.

   _____ Diversity on campus leads to diversity in the workforce, which has been shown to benefit businesses.

   _____ As individuals become more educated, their income generally rises.

   _____ Supporting affirmative action in college admissions is in the national interest.

Identifying the Thesis Statement in an Essay

Like topic sentences, thesis statements express a main idea by providing the *topic* and the *writer's point about the topic.* Thus, you can use a process for finding thesis statements that is similar to the one you used for finding topic sentences. The steps in "Identifying a Thesis Statement" will help you.

IDENTIFYING A THESIS STATEMENT

1 Read the essay and identify its topic.

2 Find the topic sentence—whether explicit or implicit—for each body paragraph.

3 Figure out the idea that all the topic sentences have in common.

4 Write a sentence that includes the topic and the idea that all the topic sentences have in common.

5 Find a sentence in the essay that matches the one you wrote. If your analysis is correct, you have very likely identified the thesis statement.

Here is an example of using these five steps.

1. Identify the topic.

> **Topic:** Imagine you have identified the topic of an essay. The topic is weight lifting.

2. Find the topic sentence—whether explicit or implicit—for each body paragraph.

> **Topic sentences:** You have figured out that these are the topic sentences for the body paragraphs:
>
> ■ Weight lifting helps prevent muscle loss resulting from the aging process.
>
> ■ Not everyone knows it, but weight lifting can help with weight loss.
>
> ■ Like many types of exercise, weight lifting can reduce depression.
>
> ■ Even sleep is improved for people who lift weights.

3. Figure out the idea that all the topic sentences have in common.

Shared idea: These sentences all present benefits of weight training.

4. Write a sentence that includes the topic and the idea that all the topic sentences have in common.

Our sentence combining the topic and the shared idea: "As a form of exercise, weight lifting offers many benefits" *or* "Weight lifting can help with weight loss, depression, sleep, and muscle quality."

5. Find a sentence in the essay that matches the one you wrote. If your analysis is correct, you have very likely identified the thesis statement.

Essay's thesis statement: We can now look at the essay and find a sentence that is similar.

PRACTICE 6

Using Topic Sentences to Find the Main Idea of an Essay

Below you will find an essay's topic sentences. Use the topic sentences to make an educated guess about what the essay's thesis statement might be. Put the thesis statement into your own words.

Topic sentence of body paragraph 1: Movement—physical activity of any kind—changes the brain's structure and reduces depression.

Topic sentence of body paragraph 2: Certain types of therapy, especially **cognitive** behavioral therapy, can help with depression.

Topic sentence of body paragraph 3: Learning a new skill, even something as simple as using a new recipe, can lessen depression.

Topic sentence of body paragraph 4: Biofeedback, meditation, and deep breathing contribute to a calmer, less depressed mood.

Write the main idea in a complete sentence: _____

_____

VCW cognitive

Example of Identifying an Essay's Thesis Statement

The following essay contains a paragraph you analyzed earlier in this chapter. Read the essay to see how one student, Sarit, uses the steps you just learned to identify the main idea and thesis statement of the essay.

First, Sarit determines what the essay's topic is by highlighting key words in the title and words that are repeated throughout the essay. Then she identifies and underlines the topic sentence of each paragraph.

Why Emotional Intelligence Matters—At Work

Do you know anyone who is not necessarily the smartest member of a work group but who is a great team player and always seems to contribute significantly? On the other hand, do you know someone who is "book smart" but seems to have a difficult time getting along with coworkers? The first person has high "emotional intelligence." The second person does not. Emotional intelligence (EI) refers to how well people understand their own feelings as well as the emotions of others. Surprisingly, perhaps, being "book smart" is not sufficient for career success. We have learned in recent years that successful employees—those who move the most quickly up the ladder—possess greater emotional intelligence skills than their coworkers.

Awareness of your emotions is one way EI makes you a better employee. Intentionally thinking about how you are feeling is a crucial skill. For example, if you are irritable, you may have a harder time with a planning session at the office than you otherwise would. Realizing that you are grumpy does not instantly make you happy, but it does give you a heads-up that you need to be especially careful as you relate to your coworkers or customers or supervisors. Sometimes people with low emotional intelligence will think their moods justify bad behavior. You may even have heard comments like "Don't mind Jessica; she's always moody." The truth is, Jessica won't be the one getting the promotion.

Empathy means putting yourself in another person's shoes emotionally. Beyond being self-aware, employees who interpret the emotions of others by being empathetic are assets in the workplace. Can you imagine how the other person feels in a given situation? If one of your colleagues has just come from an evaluation with his supervisor and snaps at you when you say "Hello," he might be feeling upset because of what his boss had to say. Recognizing your coworker's emotional situation would help smooth over hurt feelings. Similarly, a salesperson who can empathize with customers will have more pleasant interactions with them; as a consequence, she might even make more sales!

Stress management is another EI skill that makes employees more valuable. A person who has methods for relieving her stress is much less likely to blow up at a coworker or a customer. One who can control her stress is also a more efficient employee because she is not distracted by the tension that has built up inside her psyche. Controlling stress is not always an easy thing to do; people who are successful at keeping their stress level down can rise above their colleagues and become more valued employees.

Unpleasant or difficult situations inevitably occur in the workplace. Workers who are able to adapt fairly quickly when frustrations or disappointments occur will be able to proceed with occupational tasks. Employers can trust employees who are adaptable; such employees will make the adjustments needed to get the work done. Workers who are prone to

(continued)

SARIT'S ANNOTATIONS

Step 1–Identify topic. Emotional intelligence?

Can't be thesis statement–these are questions.

Definition. Maybe the entire essay's main idea is to define emotional intelligence.

Topic–EI and career success?

Step 2–Find the topic sentences.

Topic sentence

Topic–being a better employee??

Emotional intelligence again–topic?

Topic sentence

A benefit of emotional intelligence

Topic sentence

Topic–how emotional intelligence benefits you?

Topic–emotional intelligence at work?

"drama" over frustrations or disappointments will be labeled "difficult" and will not be the ones on the promotion list. Employees who have emotional flexibility are considered more dependable than those who do not.

    Teamwork is crucial in almost every vocation, and EI makes employees better team players. Working well with clients or customers is also critically important in many occupational settings. Being able to recognize and relate to the feelings of others and being aware of your own feelings will increase your ability to work well with others. That is why people with high EI are more successful in their careers than people with low EI.

Topic sentence at end of paragraph

Topic sentence

EI is tied to career success.

Here is how Sarit used the five-step process to figure out the thesis statement of this essay.

1.   Identify the topic.

Topic: emotional intelligence at work

2.   Find the topic sentence—whether explicit or implicit—for each body paragraph.

Topic sentences: Sarit listed the topic sentences:
- Awareness of your emotions is one way EI makes you a better employee.
- Beyond being self-aware, employees who interpret the emotions of others by being empathetic are assets in the workplace.
- Stress management is another EI skill that makes employees more valuable.
- Teamwork is crucial in almost every vocation, and EI makes employees better team players.

3.   Figure out the idea that all the topic sentences have in common.

Shared idea: Sarit realized that these sentences all tell us that emotional intelligence skills can make people better employees.

4.   Write a sentence that includes the topic and the idea that all the topic sentences have in common.

Sarit's sentence combining the topic and the shared idea: "People who have emotional intelligence skills make better employees" *or* "Emotionally intelligent workers make good employees because they are aware of their own emotions, empathetic of others' feelings, capable of managing stress, and good at working in teams."

5. Find a sentence in the essay that matches the one you wrote. If your analysis is correct, you have very likely identified the thesis statement.

> **Essay's thesis statement:** Sarit looked through the essay and underlined this sentence as the thesis statement: "We have learned in recent years that successful employees—those who move the most quickly up the ladder—possess greater emotional intelligence skills than their coworkers."

Sarit notices that two sentences could be the thesis statement. She decides that the first statement, which more fully expresses the main idea, is the thesis statement and that the sentence in the conclusion simply **reiterates** the main idea.

Not all essays will include repeated thesis statements as this example does. As a flexible reader, you need to be aware that essays do not follow a strict formula. Some writers will place the thesis statement in the middle of an essay, and sometimes the thesis statement occurs only at the very end.

VCW reiterate

PRACTICE 7

Finding the Thesis Statement of a Textbook Passage

Read and annotate the following passage from *Lesikar's Business Communication,* a textbook by Kathryn Rentz, Marie Flatley, and Paula Lentz. Use your annotations and the five-step process for identifying a thesis statement. Fill in the answers below.

The Importance of Communication Skills to You

Because communication is so important in business, businesses want and need people with good communication skills. Evidence of the importance of communication in business is found in numerous surveys of executives, recruiters, and academicians. Without exception, these surveys have found that communication (especially written communication) ranks at or near the top of the business skills needed for success.

For example, NFI Research, a private organization that regularly surveys over 2,000 executives and senior managers, recently found that 94 percent of the members "rank 'communicating well' as the most important skill for them to succeed today and tomorrow." A study of skills and competencies needed by accountants strongly supports the value of writing, speaking, and listening, and Deloitte & Touche, ranked by *BusinessWeek* in 2007 as the best place to launch a career, cited communication skills as the "most desirable trait" in a job candidate. Employers surveyed for the National Association of Colleges and Employers' *Job Outlook 2009* also cited "communication skills" and the related traits of "a strong work **ethic**, ability to work in a team, and initiative" as highly prized qualities in job applicants. Recruiters who participated in *The Wall Street Journal*'s latest ranking of MBA programs agreed. They rated "interpersonal and communication skills, a teamwork orientation, personal ethics and integrity, analytical and problem-solving abilities, and a strong work ethic" as most important.

Unfortunately, business's need for employees with good communication skills is all too often not fulfilled. Most employees, even the college trained, do not communicate well. In fact, surveys show that, in the opinion of their employees, even managers and executives who think they communicate well

YOUR ANNOTATIONS

VCW ethic

(continued)

actually fall short. Effective communicators are, therefore, in high demand. Not surprisingly, there is a high correlation between communication skills and income. Even among college graduates, those with higher scores in literacy (use of printed and written information) earn significantly more than lower scoring graduates earn. A study by Office Team revealed that technology magnifies the exposure of one's communications skills, forcing workers to communicate more effectively and **articulately** because these skills will be showcased more. E-mail often results in a sender's language skills being placed in front of different people simultaneously, while audio and video will reveal the caliber of one's verbal and **diplomacy** strengths as well.

VCW articulately

VCW diplomacy

The communications shortcomings of employees and the importance of communication in business explain why you should work to improve your communication skills. Whatever position you have in business, your performance will be judged largely by your ability to communicate. If you perform and communicate well, you are likely to be rewarded with advancement. And the higher you advance, the more you will need your communication ability. The evidence is clear: Improving your communication skills improves your chances for success in business.

1. Write the essay topic: _____

_____

2. Underline the topic sentence for each paragraph, or write the implied topic sentences here: _____

_____

3. Write the idea that all the topic sentences have in common: _____

_____

4. Write your own sentence that includes the essay topic and the idea that the topic sentences have in common: _____

_____

5. Underline the thesis statement and write it here: _____

_____

Finding Implied Main Ideas in Essays

Just as some paragraphs do not have explicit topic sentences, some essays do not contain explicit thesis statements. The main idea—and thesis statement—in such essays is implied. Readers must figure out the main idea through the essay's content. We can use steps from the same process to find implied thesis statements as we use to find explicit ones.

Lucas needs to analyze an essay to determine its main idea for an assignment in his sociology class. He determines that the essay is on the topic of learning disorders in children. To identify the writer's point about the topic, he first annotates the function of each topic sentence.

Topic sentence for paragraph 1: Parents often notice physical difficulties with fine motor skills first.

One symptom of a learning disorder

Topic sentence for paragraph 2: Trouble in particular classes—such as math or reading—is a symptom that may indicate particular learning disabilities.

Another symptom of a learning disorder

Topic sentence for paragraph 3: Some learning disabilities are identified by a child's social behaviors.

Social behaviors–also symptoms

Topic sentence for paragraph 4: Language difficulties can also signal learning disorders.

Language difficulties– another symptom

By looking for a common point that unites all four paragraphs, Lucas can see that they all concern symptoms of learning disorders. Now he is ready to write a sentence combining the writer's topic and main point. Here is Lucas's statement of the essay's implied main idea:

Four types of symptoms are associated with learning disorders in children.
Writer's point about the topic   Topic

Lucas's sentence expresses the implied main idea of the essay. When the thesis statement is implied, write out the thesis statement yourself, as Lucas did. You will have an easier time remembering the essay's main idea if you write it down in your own words.

PRACTICE 8

Finding an Implied Thesis Statement in an Essay

The following essay has an implied main idea. Annotate the essay to determine its topic and topic sentences. On the basis of your analysis, complete the questions that follow.

Summer. The Kenai Peninsula. Wow.

When we leave Dallas, it is 98°F. It is an amazing 68°F when we land in Alaska. It's almost midnight when we pick up the rental car. We proceed to drive the length of the Kenai Peninsula, from Anchorage to Seward, amazed by the amount of daylight. On summer evenings in this part of the world, the sky never grows entirely dark. The sun dips just below the horizon, creating a lingering dusk, and then an hour or two later, the sun gradually peeks above the horizon again. Dusk and dawn are buddies, pals, hanging out together.

Green—everything is green. The mountains are green; the valleys are green; even the water in the dozens of lakes and rivers and creeks that we drive past is emerald green. The mountaintops are the only exception: they are white. Even in July, the mountain crests are still covered with glistening snow.

Salmon are running in the creeks. We stop along the highway and take a few steps to a stream to watch them. In water that is only a couple of feet deep, we see dozens, scores, hundreds of salmon struggling upstream to

YOUR ANNOTATIONS

(continued)

spawn. During their trek from the ocean, the color of their bodies has been transformed from silver to deep scarlet.

   More than once, we come around a curve and happen upon moose beside the road. The size of these animals is startling. They just chew their cud and watch us go by.

   At one point, we exit the highway. We drive a few miles and come face-to-face with an ancient—millions of years old—glacier and the icebergs that it calves. We see icebergs as big as houses in a just-above-freezing lake within walking distance of the highway.

   Alaska. The Kenai Peninsula. Summer. Wow.

1.   Write the essay topic: _____

     _____

2.   Underline the topic sentence for each paragraph or write the implied topic
     sentences here: _____

     _____

     _____

     _____

3.   Write the idea that all the topic sentences have in common: _____

     _____

     _____

4.   Write your own sentence that includes the essay topic and the idea that
     the topic sentences have in common: _____

     _____

Composing Effective Thesis Statements

When you put the main idea of a reading into your own words, you are not only learning how to find thesis statements; you are also learning how to write them. Remember that to find the thesis statement of an essay, you must focus on determining the topic and identifying the point the writer is making about the topic. Similarly, when you compose a thesis statement, you write a sentence that includes your topic and your point about the topic.

Thesis Statements That Are Too Narrow or Too Broad

Because a thesis statement provides the main point of an essay, it must be broad enough to cover everything the writer will include in the essay. Here is an example of how one student, John, composed a thesis statement for an essay.

   John identified his essay topic.

John's essay topic: tips to conquer stage fright

Then John decided that his body paragraphs will present three tips, one in each paragraph.

Body paragraphs:

A paragraph about practice

A paragraph about relaxation techniques

A paragraph about planning

If the thesis statement focuses on only one of the suggestions John plans to discuss in his essay, the thesis statement will be too narrow.

Overly narrow thesis statement: Stage fright can be conquered by setting aside time each day to practice.

Thesis statements can also be too broad.

Overly broad thesis statement: Stage fright is a very common experience.

This statement is too broad to really focus in on John's main idea—that there are several specific ways to conquer stage fright. The key is to write a thesis statement that is just broad enough to cover every point you will be making in your essay. John settled on the following thesis statement.

Effective thesis statement: Stage fright can be conquered by practicing, using relaxation techniques, and planning for mistakes.

PRACTICE 9

Creating Effective Thesis Statements

Below are sets of topic sentences that go with the body paragraphs of different essays. Construct a thesis statement for each set of topic sentences, making sure your thesis statement is neither too broad nor too narrow.

Example

Topic sentences:

- A common effect of recession is unemployment.
- Additionally, businesses lose money in recessions.
- In a recession, most people have less money to spend.

Your thesis statement: *Recessions have negative effects on businesses and individuals.*

(continued)

Set 1

Topic sentences:

- Online courses require students to be self-motivated.

- Additionally, online classes are best for students who have a functional knowledge of computer operations.

- Students who take online courses should have a learning style that is consistent with independent learning.

    Your thesis statement: _____

    _____

    _____

Set 2

Topic sentences:

- Studying economics results in greater knowledge about how consumer goods are priced.

- A course in economics also benefits students by showing how financial decisions have long-term consequences.

- An economics course provides an understanding of how investments work.

- Studying economics helps students understand the **implications** of political decisions on the economy.

    Your thesis statement: _____

    _____

    _____

VCW implications

Set 3

Topic sentences:

- Students need basic Internet skills to be able to succeed in college.

- Students need to know how to do word processing for a variety of tasks.

- The ability to use e-mail and to handle e-mail attachments is another requirement for students.

    Your thesis statement: _____

    _____

    _____

Prewriting and Thesis Statements

You have already learned some methods for prewriting. Prewriting will help you generate ideas about topics, and from your prewriting, you can decide on the main idea you want to communicate. Prewriting will also help you determine the ideas you will use to support your thesis statement.

In the example of prewriting that follows, we see a list of ideas generated by Ben, a student in a writing class, in response to an essay assignment. He has crossed out the ideas he does not want to address and has made notes next to the ones he will include in his essay.

Assignment: Write an essay in which you discuss how failure can be a positive experience. Ideas from prewriting:

- helps people learn about their strengths and weaknesses *(helps people with self-discovery)*
- ~~teaches people to not give up can be motivational~~
- ~~makes people stronger~~
- is actually a way we learn new skills   *(bike riding, for example)*
- teaches people life lessons *(when people fail because of not listening to wise advice or by breaking the law)*

Because of his prewriting, Ben knows what he wants to discuss in his essay. He is ready to write a thesis statement. To write a thesis statement, Ben follows the steps in "Composing a Thesis Statement: An Example."

COMPOSING A THESIS STATEMENT: AN EXAMPLE

1	**Write down your topic.**	*the value of failure*
2	**Write down the point you wish to make about the topic.**	*encourages self-discovery, is a way of learning new skills, teaches life lessons*
3	**Write a statement that combines the topic and your point.**	*Failure is valuable because it encourages self-discovery, provides a way to learn new skills, and teaches life lessons.*
4	**Check that your statement has all the characteristics of an effective thesis statement.**	• *Expresses the most important point in an essay.* • *Presents an idea that requires support.* • *Expresses the broadest idea in the essay.* • *Is a statement, not a question.*

Ben believes that in the long run, it is more important for people to learn life lessons, so he decides to emphasize that idea by putting it last. In his thesis statement, he puts the ideas in the order in which he will present them in the essay.

Ben's thesis statement ("Failure is valuable because it encourages self-discovery, provides a way to learn new skills, and teaches life lessons") provides the main idea of the essay. It also gives readers a clue to the kinds of information the essay will contain and the order in which they will be presented.

PRACTICE 10

Critiquing Thesis Statements

Imagine you are guiding Sharon, who is writing an essay about why people choose to be vegetarians. She plans to discuss these three reasons:

- Some people believe vegetarian diets are healthier than meat-based diets.

- Others choose vegetarianism because of their ethical beliefs regarding the treatment of animals.

- A third reason for choosing a vegetarian diet is concern about the effects of meat production on the environment.

Sharon has written several sentences and wants to know which one would make the best thesis statement, based on the characteristics of thesis statements. Read each numbered sentence, and explain why it would or would not be the best thesis statement. Finally, write your own thesis statement for Sharon's essay.

1. Why is it a good idea to be a vegetarian?

   Your comments: _____

   _____

   _____

   _____

2. Because a vegetarian diet is healthier than a meat-based diet, becoming a vegetarian is a good idea.

   Your comments: _____

   _____

3. People must decide for themselves whether a vegetarian diet is the right choice.

   Your comments: _____

   _____

4. Your thesis statement: _____

   _____

Open and Closed Thesis Statements

Not all thesis statements are explicit about the support the writer will present. **Open thesis statements** do not present the ideas that will be in the body paragraphs but do give a general idea of what the essay will cover.

Open thesis statement:	Making firearms illegal on college campuses is the right policy.

On the other hand, **closed thesis statements** tell the reader exactly what support will be used in the essay.

Closed thesis statement:	Making firearms illegal on college campuses will reduce the potential for violence, keep campuses focused on education, and foster a community of trust.

Closed thesis statements reveal the reasons or supporting points that will be in the essay; thus, the essay is *closed* to other reasons or support.

Open thesis statements are appropriate for essays with body paragraphs that are similar to one another in function. For example, an essay setting out causes of **insomnia** lends itself to a thesis statement such as this one.

 insomnia

Open thesis statement:	Insomnia can be caused by a variety of conditions.
	Topic Writer's point about the topic

The following chart gives examples of open thesis statements.

Type of essay	Open thesis statement
An essay showing how the differences between the public school systems of the United States and Canada affect learning	A comparison of the public school system in the United States with the public school system in Canada reveals significant differences that affect student learning.
An essay offering solutions to the problem of homelessness	Communities can reduce the negative consequences of homelessness by using six strategies that have been proved effective.
An essay in support of making college education free	Making a college education free and available to all citizens makes sense for several reasons.

Closed thesis statements are appropriate when it is important or helpful to readers to reveal the content of the essay in advance. The disadvantage is that such thesis statements can be difficult to compose since they list the specific support that will appear in the body paragraphs. For instance, to convert the open thesis statement about reasons for insomnia to a closed thesis statement, we would need to include particular causes of insomnia.

Closed thesis statement:	Insomnia can have many causes, but the most common ones are stress, medications, and environmental distractions.

The topic is insomnia, and the three causes presented in this closed thesis statement are stress, medications, and environmental distractions.

One key to writing a good closed thesis statement is using parallelism. The Grammar Focus that follows will help you write closed thesis statements that demonstrate parallelism.

Source: Photographs in the Carol M. Highsmith Archive, Library of Congress, Prints and Photographs Division.

The design of this room demonstrates parallelism in that both of the columns are parallel to each other. Can you find other elements that are parallel?

Grammar Focus

Parallelism

Parallelism is the use of consistent structure for all elements in a series of two or more elements. (Hint: Look for a conjunction such as *and* that links the items.)

Bullying in schools is a serious problem because it can <u>cause extreme anguish to victims</u> *and* <u>result in serious physical harm</u>.

The two reasons for the seriousness of bullying are presented in parallel form.

Knowledge of geography is <u>necessary for jobs in commerce</u>, <u>important for careers in sales</u>, and <u>essential for careers in international business</u>.

The three items in the series are presented in parallel form; each contains an adjective followed by a prepositional phrase.

(continued)

Because thesis statements often present series of elements, always check to ensure that your thesis statement is in parallel form. While parallelism is especially important in thesis statements, *every* sentence that presents a series of elements should reflect parallel form.

To use parallelism in sentences, follow these guidelines:

- Identify items in the sentence that could be put in parallel form, usually a series of two or more similar elements joined by a coordinating conjunction (*for, and, nor, but, or, yet, so*).

- Make sure the items in the series are alike in their parts of speech.

Example: During college, Micah liked skiing, jogging, and ~~to skateboard~~ skateboarding.

- Make changes in wording, if necessary, to achieve parallelism.

Example: Trinity teaches special-needs adults to manage their money, practice good hygiene, and ~~the ability to make breakfast, lunch, and dinner~~ prepare their own meals.

COMBINING SENTENCES

The example that follows show how to combine ideas to create thesis statements with parallelism.

Ideas to combine:

- A college education should be free in the United States.

- An alternative to making college free is making a student loan available to anyone who wants one.

Parallel thesis statement: Either a college education in the United States should be free or a student loan should be available to anyone who wants one.

EXPANDING THE CONCEPT

Parallelism is used in sentences, but it is also used in headings and lists, in sets of instructions, and within paragraphs and compositions.

EXERCISES

Combine each set of sentences below into a thesis statement that demonstrates parallelism.

1. Ideas to combine:

- Global warming affects sea levels.

- Global warming creates changes in precipitation patterns.

- Ecosystems are also affected by global warming.

    Answer: _____

    _____

(continued)

2. Ideas to combine:

- One reason to require college algebra for college degrees is to teach students to think **sequentially**.

- The improved use of logic in thinking is another reason college algebra should be required.

- Algebra also creates more flexibility in the way people think.

    Answer: _____

    _____

    VCW sequentially

3. Ideas to combine:

- The use of drones reduces casualities in military troops.

- The cost of military engagement is decreased when drones are used.

- Drones do less damage to cities than traditional warfare does.

    Answer: _____

    _____

4. Ideas to combine:

- Because tablet computers are more expensive than desktop computers, schools should purchase desktop computers rather than tablets.

- Regular desktop computers offer greater functionality than tablets.

- Tablets are much more likely to be stolen than desktop computers.

    Answer: _____

    _____

PRACTICE 11

Writing Parallel Closed Thesis Statements

Combine each of the essay topics below with the point being made about the topic to write a parallel closed thesis statement.

1. Topic: learning a new skill

    Writer's point: helps you grow intellectually, can discover new talents, can be fun and relaxing

    Closed thesis statement: _____

    _____

    _____

2. Topic: wind technology

    Writer's point: advantages—it is renewable; cost of energy production is relatively low; environment is not harmed

    Closed thesis statement: _____

    _____

    _____

(continued)

3. Topic: reasons to shop in thrift stores

    Writer's point: fun, save money, might be rewarded by finding valuable items

    Closed thesis statement: _____

    _____

4. Topic: advantages of using e-mail instead of other forms of communication

    Writer's point: can control your emotional responses to ideas, time is available to think about the ideas involved, discussion of the issue is recorded in the e-mail

    Closed thesis statement: _____

    _____

    _____

    _____

CHAPTER ACTIVITIES

➔ READING AND ANNOTATING

The following is an article that appeared on the Web site *Selfication*. Use these instructions to read the essay.

1. Use prereading strategies before you read the essay word for word. See if you can figure out the topic.
2. As you read, identify the topic sentences—whether explicit or implicit—for each paragraph in this article.
3. Use the process described in "Identifying a Thesis Statement" to determine the essay's main idea. Find the thesis statement in the text, or if the thesis statement is implied, write it in a sentence.

Be sure to annotate the essay as you read.

Fake It Till You Make It: Accomplish Anything You Want by Acting "As If"

By Patrik Edblad

> You must be the person you have never had the courage to be.
> Gradually, you will discover that you are that person,
> but until you can see this clearly, you must pretend and invent.
>
> – Paulo Coelho

YOUR ANNOTATIONS

(continued)

Imagine yourself taking a seat in a waiting room. In just a few minutes you're supposed to get up and walk through the door in front of you to participate in a job interview for your dream job. You've prepared yourself relentlessly, rehearsed all the potential questions that could come up many times over. You set three alarm clocks just in case and showed up 30 minutes early. So far everything's going according to plan and still a quiet panic is spreading inside. When you try to remember what you've been planning to say, your mind goes blank. You feel slightly nauseous; your hands are getting sweaty and your knees seems to be shaking even though you're sitting down.

The Power of Body Language

In hard-pressed, high-stakes situations like these, it's very tempting to close up and make yourself small. You don't want the person next to you noticing your inner turmoil, so you hunch and pretend you have tons of important stuff going on in your phone. This behavior is not unique to humans. You can see it everywhere in the animal kingdom. Just as a dominant animal takes up lots of space, a low power animal tends to crawl up and take up less space. What's really interesting about this is that research has shown that just as low power feelings influence us to exhibit a submissive body language, our body language also affects the way we feel. If you were to force yourself to smile, for example by biting a pencil, it would make you feel happier. This is known as the Facial Feedback Hypothesis (Davis).

Power Posing

Research by Amy Cuddy and her colleagues has shown that by consciously altering your body language, you can change the way you feel in a certain situation. If you go against your natural inclination to hunch and take up as little space as possible when you experience low power feelings, you can actually turn those feelings around. This is done by exhibiting what the researchers call "power posing," which in essence is a fairly straightforward technique. What you do is essentially take up space. Instead of making yourself small, you deliberately spread out and exude confidence. Doing this for just a couple of minutes will significantly increase your testosterone ("the dominance hormone") while decreasing your levels of cortisol ("the stress hormone"), effectively turning these hormone levels to those of powerful and effective leaders. So if you ever find yourself in a situation where you're stressing out, for example before giving a presentation, writing an exam, or freaking out before a job interview as in the example above, remember to "strike a pose." Just a couple of minutes of faking dominant behavior will calm you down and make you feel more confident.

Acting Like an Extrovert

Posing like a powerful person isn't the only way to change your mental state. One study showed that acting like an extrovert, even if you are an introvert,

extrovert: A person who feels energized by being around others. The opposite is an introvert, a person for whom interaction with others is exhausting and draining.

(continued)

makes people all around the world feel happier (Ching). These findings are based on surveys taken by hundreds of people in the US, Venezuela, the Philippines, China, and Japan. Across the board, people reported feeling more positive emotions in daily situations where they either acted or felt more extroverted. These findings support those of an earlier study by Fleeson which focused on the effects of extroverted behaviors such as being talkative, adventurous and having high energy levels. In this study the participants were asked to act in an outgoing way for 10 minutes and then report back how it made them feel. The results showed that even among introverts, acting in an extroverted way boosted their happiness. If you're normally a quiet and withdrawn person, faking outgoing behavior can have a big effect both socially and on your well-being.

Enclothed Cognition

Another way to fake it till you make it is to change your wardrobe. Research has shown that wearing the clothes of people you admire will actually transfer some of their qualities directly onto you (Hajo). In one study the researchers wanted to know if the clothes you wear change your perception of yourself and change your own behavior. To test this, they performed an experiment where college students were given a white lab coat to wear before performing a cognitive test (known as a Stroop test). One group was told they were wearing a doctor's lab coat and the other group was told they were wearing a painter's coat. The group in the "doctor's coat" then preceded to completely blow away the test results of the other group. All the participants knew, of course, that they were not doctors or painters. But it didn't matter. It also didn't matter that they were wearing the exact same kind of jacket. Just believing that they were wearing a doctor's coat was enough to transfer some of the perceived qualities of doctors onto the group. This research shows that if there's a skill or quality you want to develop in yourself, dressing like someone who already possesses it helps you develop it yourself. This isn't magic; it's simply a way to prime your brain to be more disciplined in developing the skills and qualities you want.

Fake It Till You Make It

. . . Or rather "Fake it till you become it," as Amy Cuddy puts it, stems from plenty of research that proves its effectiveness. Whatever you're trying to accomplish, whoever you want to become, there's no need to put it off for the future. Research shows that a much more effective way is to start acting like you're already there:

- If you want to be a writer, start calling yourself a writer.
- If you want to be more confident, act like a confident person.
- If you want to be more social, pretend you're naturally open and talkative.
- If you want to be a runner, start wearing running gear.
- If you want to _____, start faking it! Start faking right now, and your desired behavior, skills and qualities will follow.

(continued)

Works Cited

Carney, Dana R., et al. "Power Posing: Brief Nonverbal Displays Affect Neuroendocrine Levels and Risk Tolerance." *Psychological Science*, vol. 21, no. 10, Oct. 2010, pp. 1363–68.

Ching, Charles M., et al. "The Manifestation of Traits in Everyday Behavior and Affect: A Five-Culture Study." *Journal of Research in Personality*, vol. 48, Feb. 2014, pp. 1–16.

Cuddy, Amy. "Your Body Language Shapes Who You Are." Oct. 2012, www.ted.com.

Davis, Joshua Ian, et al. "How Does Facial Feedback Modulate Emotional Experience?" *Journal of Research in Personality*, vol. 43, no. 5, 1 Oct. 2009, pp. 822–29.

Fleeson, William, et al. "An Intraindividual Process Approach to the Relationship between Extraversion and Positive Affect: Is Acting Extraverted as 'Good' as Being Extraverted?" *Journal of Personality and Social Psychology*, vol. 83, Dec. 2002, pp. 1409–22.

Hajo, Adam, and Adam D. Galinsky. "Enclothed Cognition." *Journal of Experimental Social Psychology*, Jan. 2012, pp. 1–6.

Questions for Consideration

1. The writer thinks pretending can be a useful method for adapting to different situations. Think of someone you know who is successful—perhaps a relative, a friend, a teacher, or a doctor. In what ways do you think this person has used *pretending* as an effective strategy? Explain in a paragraph.

2. We all know people who try to excuse bad behaviors or bad habits by saying, "That's just how I am." Consider a situation in which saying, "That's just how I am," would have negative effects. Reflect on job situations, college responsibilities, and relationships. Write a paragraph in which you examine how such a response would affect a particular situation.

3. Think about the career you aspire to have. In what ways might pretending help you when you start this career? For example, when teachers begin their careers, they have to project confidence in the classroom. Most inexperienced teachers are worried and insecure about their ability to teach well, especially in the first year. When teachers project confidence, parents and students can relax, believing that the teacher has everything under control. In what way will pretending help you adapt to the career you plan to pursue? Write a paragraph to explain.

4. Although we may be unaware of it, we use "faking it" to adapt to situations all the time. If we feel ill, for example, and a coworker asks, "How are you?" many of us will say, "Just fine." These minor acts of pretending make interactions with colleagues more positive. In what ways have you pretended today or in the last few days? Why did you pretend? Did it help your relationships with others go more smoothly? Describe one of your experiences in a paragraph.

➔ USING MODELS TO PRACTICE COMPOSING

What follows is a model essay written by Xavier, a student in an English class. Read through the assignment instructions that Xavier's professor provided.

> **Essay assignment:** Patrik Edblad suggests that pretending ("faking it") can be a very helpful life skill. He presents these techniques: using body language, using power posing, acting like an extrovert, and using clothing. Write an essay in which you discuss how pretending, or "faking it," helps people adapt to a specific new situation. For example, a new employee will not know everything, but by using some of the techniques, the employee might feel more confident and project a more confident image. Make sure your essay includes an introduction, a thesis statement, body paragraphs, and a conclusion. Revise, edit, and format your essay before submitting it.

To start this assignment, Xavier used the prewriting technique of clustering as a method for considering new situations that many people experience.

Next, Xavier chose a topic derived from his prewriting and examined how pretending might be advantageous and disadvantageous in his particular context. He used prewriting to make lists.

> Situation: Death of a loved one
>
> Benefits of pretending:
>
> • Pretending life is normal helps you do the necessary things (wake up, get ready for work, deal with children, go to the job site).
>
> • Pretending can help your kids feel like their lives are in control, even if you don't feel in control.
>
> • Pretending will give you more privacy; other people won't always be asking if they can help or what is wrong.

(continued)

Disadvantages of pretending:

- Pretending takes a lot of energy and effort.
- Pretending might keep you from grieving and experiencing the sorrow so that you can work through it.
- Pretending might set a poor example for children by teaching them to cover up their feelings of sorrow.

Once Xavier finished his prewriting, he created a brief outline that included his thesis statement and the topic sentences for each of his body paragraphs. Notice that he chose not to include all the advantages and disadvantages that he came up with.

Thesis statement: Pretending is a way to adapt to the loss of a loved one, and as a coping strategy, it offers advantages as well as disadvantages.

Body paragraphs:

1. Topic sentence: Pretending life is normal helps parents do the things necessary for everyday life (wake up, get ready for work, deal with children, go to the job site).

2. Topic sentence: By pretending everything is okay, parents can provide a more stable living environment for their children.

3. Topic sentence: Pretending might set a poor example for children by teaching them to cover up their feelings of sorrow.

4. Topic sentence: Pretending takes a great deal of energy and effort.

After creating an outline that includes his thesis statement and topic sentences, Xavier drafted his essay, revised it, and checked it for errors. His final essay appears below. Read it, and annotate at least three features in the essay. For example, if you see sentences that demonstrate parallelism, annotate them. If you find a passage that you believe is worded particularly well, annotate it. Also, annotate the thesis statement and notice where it is placed, and mark the topic sentences.

Model Student Essay: "The Role of Pretending in Times of Grief" by Xavier Lewis

Lewis 1

Xavier Lewis

INRW 0402

Dr. Wright

20 February 2018

The Role of Pretending in Times of Grief

New situations can easily throw us off balance. A new job, a new baby, or a new living situation can be hard to handle. However, most people find methods for adjusting to these new circumstances. One method that can be helpful is pretending. Sometimes by pretending, people can reduce the stress involved in making the transition to a new situation. This is especially true in the case of grief. Pretending is a way to adapt to the loss of a loved one, and as a coping strategy it offers advantages, although there are disadvantages as well.

Pretending that everything is normal helps a grieving person do the things necessary for dealing with everyday life. By pretending that nothing is out of the ordinary, a person is more likely to wake up on time, bathe, tend to chores, go to work, and so on. Pretending, in this case, is a good way to deal with grief. It keeps the grieving person busy, and it allows him or her to do the things that have to get done. Without pretending that life is normal, grieving people might merely stay in bed and cry or quit their jobs out of despair. These actions would add even more complications to adjusting to life without the loved one. Therefore, pretending that nothing has changed is a good way to keep going.

Pretending can help children feel that their lives are in control, even if their parents don't feel in control. Children need stability in their lives. This need for stability doesn't change, even though a parent's life may

Lewis 2

have drastically changed with the loss of a loved one. Parents who recognize their children's need for stability can use pretending as a way to keep their children on an even keel. When parents act as if life goes on as usual, continuing with typical daily activities, children can be comforted and can continue their own lives with fewer disruptions.

While pretending is helpful in many ways, people who are adjusting to grief must realize that pretending, if not used carefully, can have some disadvantages. For one thing, pretending might set a poor example for children by teaching them to cover up their feelings of sorrow. While children need the stability that comes from pretending life is normal, children also need to know it is OK to feel sorrow and to grieve. Therefore, pretending should be used to help life go on, but it should not be used so extensively that there is no room for sorrow.

In addition, pretending takes a lot of energy and effort. It is hard to act as if everything is OK when everything in life has changed so drastically. There must be times of release when those who are grieving can take off the mask of pretending and admit they are exhausted and sad. Having periods of sorrow and periods of productive pretending helps those who are grieving. By reserving energy and effort for only those times when pretending to be normal is necessary, people can reap the advantages of pretending without the disadvantages of it.

No one asks for the sorrow that death brings, but most people go through it sometime in their lives. By pretending that life is normal, people who are grieving can find a way to go on with life—until life really does become normal again, or at least as normal as it can be after a deep loss.

→ A READING AND WRITING ASSIGNMENT

Now that you have read and annotated Xavier's essay, use the same assignment instructions Xavier received to write your own essay on the topic. Follow these steps.

1. Reread Xavier's assignment from "Using Models to Practice Composing."

2. Use prewriting to think about situations in which a person could benefit from using pretending as a coping strategy.

3. Choose one of those situations, and use a prewriting method to determine ways in which pretending might be advantageous and disadvantageous.

4. Use prewriting to write a thesis statement and compose topic sentences for body paragraphs. Plan as many paragraphs as you need to support your thesis statement.

5. Using Xavier's essay as a model, write a complete essay, including an introduction paragraph, body paragraphs, and a conclusion paragraph. Use the thesis statement and topic sentences you have already composed.

6. Follow the Quick Start Guide to Integrated Reading and Writing Assignments to help you with this process.

→ ADDING TO YOUR VOCABULARY

This chapter's vocabulary words appear below.

articulately	diverse	insomnia	sequentially
cognitive	ethic	reiterate	sociopath
diplomacy	implication	robust	

Choose five of the vocabulary words from this chapter that you would like to add to your vocabulary, and think about how you can use them this week. For example, one of this chapter's words is *diverse*. You can often substitute *diverse* for *varied* or *assorted.*

Example: This college offers a *varied* course selection.
This college offers a *diverse* course selection.

List each of the five words you plan to use this week, and make note of a context in which you could use each word.

Example: *Diverse.* I can use this in talking about the career opportunities in my field.

→ ADDITIONAL ASSIGNMENTS

1. Imagine you are starting a new college class, and it is a class you are worried about passing. Which suggestions from Patrik Edblad's essay might help you manage your fears and do better in the course?

2. Reread the textbook passage entitled "The Importance of Communication Skills to You" in Practice 7 in this chapter.

List the qualities employers value. Which of these qualities do you have? Which ones do you lack? Explain actions you can take so that you will have all the qualities employers desire. Write a paragraph or two presenting and explaining your answers.

3. Consider the qualities you explored in assignment 2 above. Now imagine you are writing an essay in which you present four qualities you would like to develop while you are in college. Write a thesis statement for an essay in which you combine the following ideas.

Topic: qualities employers desire in workers

Your point about the topic: qualities you would like to develop for your own advancement

You may write an open or closed thesis statement.

EMOTIONAL INTELLIGENCE

Earlier in this chapter, you read "Why Emotional Intelligence Matters—At Work." In that essay, you read about emotional flexibility. How is emotional flexibility like adaptation? How is it different? Write a paragraph explaining your answers.

METACOGNITION

One way to learn about your strengths and weaknesses as a student is to analyze your graded exams. Find a graded exam on which you received a lower grade than you had expected. On a separate sheet of paper, answer these questions about that exam.

1. What study methods did you use to prepare for the exam?

2. Based on your exam grade, did your study methods work?

3. Look at the questions you missed on the exam. Do the question types have anything in common? For example, on a math test, perhaps you missed the word problems or the problems that require multiplying fractions. On a history test, you may have missed questions based on instructor lectures.

4. Based on the type of questions you missed, what study strategies might have helped you prepare better for these questions?

5. In general, what can you do differently next time to earn an even higher grade?

Text Credits

Page 87: Source: Boss, Judith A., *THINK: Critical Thinking and Logic Skills for Everyday Life*, 2nd ed. New York: McGraw-Hill, 2012. 277; Page 95: Rentz, Kathryn, Flatley, Marie E., and Lentz, Paula, *Lesikar's Business Communication: Connecting in a Digital World*, 12th ed. 3. Copyright © 2011 by McGraw-Hill Education. Used with permission of McGraw-Hill Education; Page 107: Edblad, Patrik, "Fake It Till You Make It: Accomplish Anything You Want By Acting 'As If'" www.selfication.com/mindset/fake-it-till-you-make-it/. Used by permission of the author; Source: Coelho, Paulo, *Eleven Minutes*, translated by Margaret Jull Costa. New York: HarperCollins Publishers, Inc.

Support for Main Ideas

The Capital Gate Building in Abu Dhabi leans an incredible 18°, which makes it the world's farthest leaning building, according to Guinness World Records. How do you think Capital Gate manages to remain upright? In what ways are texts—such as essays and books—like Capital Gate?

Chapter Objectives

After completing this chapter, students will be able to do the following:

- Recognize major supporting points and supporting details in texts.

- Use outlining or graphic organizers to identify major supporting points and supporting details.

- Identify and use transitions.

- Use specific types of supporting details in writing.

At about the age of four, children begin to ask a particular question: "Why?" If you have spent much time with four-year-olds, you probably know the frustration of having to explain *everything:* why broccoli is green, why cars need gasoline, why dinosaurs no longer exist, why it is not OK to talk with your mouth full of food. A part of the maturation process is to wonder about the reasons for things. Curious children need more than a main idea; they need support for that idea, and they will ask "Why?" until they get that support!

As adults, we are not all that different from these curious four-year-olds. We may recognize a writer's main idea, but we may not fully understand why the writer believes as he or she does. We may not understand why the main point is important. We may not even entirely understand the main point unless the writer gives us explanations and examples. A major responsibility for writers is to provide the support needed to communicate their ideas effectively. Readers must also be able to identify supporting details in order to understand a writer's main point correctly.

Recognizing Major Supporting Points and Supporting Details in Texts

The thesis statement of an essay is a strong sentence because it provides the writer's main idea. However, it cannot stand on its own. It requires support, and this support comes in the form of body paragraphs.

Support consists of all the information readers need to fully understand a writer's main idea. Supporting details come in a variety of types: examples, analogies, explanations, short anecdotes (stories), reasons, statistics, quotations, and so on. The support you choose depends on your thesis statement and writing purpose. If you are informing readers, you might use *data* and *explanations* to support your thesis statement. If your purpose is to define a term, you will probably use *definitions* and *examples*.

To be a critical reader, you must be able to identify the supporting materials in texts. This identification begins with a clear understanding of how support provides the structure for an essay.

Major Supporting Points in Essays

In an essay, the **major supporting points** are the ideas that explain, develop, or prove the thesis statement. A common way writers structure essays is to create a paragraph of support for each major supporting point.

In an essay titled "The Importance of Storytelling," the writer's thesis statement presents three functions of storytelling. The major supporting details for the thesis statement consist of three body paragraphs, each presenting a function of storytelling. The illustration "How Thesis Statements Relate to Topic Sentences" shows how the essay's body paragraphs support its thesis statement.

HOW THESIS STATEMENTS RELATE TO TOPIC SENTENCES

THESIS STATEMENT
Most cultures use storytelling as a way to reinforce the culture's identity, preserve the culture's history, and strengthen the culture's values.

BODY PARAGRAPH 1

Topic Sentence:
One reason storytelling is important is that it helps a culture preserve its identity.

BODY PARAGRAPH 2

Topic Sentence:
Another function of storytelling is to preserve a culture's history.

BODY PARAGRAPH 3

Topic Sentence:
Finally, storytelling is used as a way to strengthen a culture's values.

Supporting Details in Essays

Each major supporting point is presented in one or more paragraphs. Within each paragraph, additional details help readers understand the major supporting point. These additional sentences provide supporting details that relate directly to the topic sentence. The supporting details offer further information (examples, explanations, statistics, quotations, anecdotes, and facts) for the topic sentence.

Let's look at an example of how major supporting details work. Read the essay that follows, and notice the relationship between the thesis statement, major supporting points, and details.

The Importance of Storytelling

Think about all the stories you were told when you were a child. Maybe you can remember sitting at the dinner table and sharing funny stories about Aunt Martha or Grandpa Wu. Or maybe your family has stories that get told over and over—because they are hilarious or because they teach an important lesson. Storytelling has always been a part of human cultures. In ancient cultures that did not use writing to preserve history, storytelling was especially important. In fact, long poems such as *Beowulf* and *The Iliad* are primarily stories that were told orally, and these stories helped the people remember their histories. Today, storytelling is still important for a variety of reasons. Most cultures use storytelling as a way to reinforce the culture's identity, preserve the culture's history, and strengthen the culture's values.

One reason storytelling is important is that it helps a culture preserve its identity. *Swapping Stories* is a collection of stories told by the residents of Cajun and Creole communities in Louisiana. As the editor notes, each tale teller "presents a community narrative that **encapsulates**, to a great extent, the shared experiences, values, and sense of humor of his or her neighborhood or cultural background" (Lindahl). Stories that transmit a culture's identity might focus on food, traditions, habits, humor, and community values. For example, many of the Cajun stories focus on hunting and fishing, and this focus reinforces the identity of Cajuns as outdoorsmen. Other stories focus on the importance of food and family. The tradition of making and eating gumbo is part of Cajun culture, so stories about gumbo and other traditional foods are part of the Cajun repertoire.

Another function of storytelling is to preserve a culture's history. Before the invention of writing, history could only be preserved orally. Retelling stories helped ancient cultures remember the past. Today, we still use storytelling to remember our history. Historical novels and films that tell the story of historical events are an important part of our cultural experience. On a more personal level, we tell stories that help younger generations understand and remember their family histories. Amy Tan's *Joy Luck Club* is a novel that presents stories from her mother's experience emigrating to the

YOUR ANNOTATIONS

Thesis statement

Major Supporting
Point 1

VCW **encapsulates**
For every Vocabulary Collection Word (VCW), give your in-context idea of the word's meaning and then look up the word's dictionary definition.

Supporting Details
for Major Supporting
Point 1

Major Supporting
Point 2

Supporting Details
for Major Supporting
Point 2

(continued)

United States from Shanghai, China, in 1949. These stories came from Tan's mother who, as Tan explains, "told stories as though they were happening right in front of her. She would remember what happened to her in life and act them out in front of me. That's oral storytelling at its best" (Gioia 50).

Finally, storytelling is used as a way to communicate a culture's values. Often, stories are used to explain to young people the meanings and reasons for certain values. For example, the story known as "The Boy Who Cried Wolf," one of Aesop's fables, shows why lying is not a good behavior. In addition to reinforcing cultural values, stories provide behavior codes. For instance, a parent may pass on a story to a teen to warn against texting while driving. As Felecia Hodge has noted, for Native Americans, stories present "appropriate and inappropriate behaviors; they provide examples to **emulate** or to shun." Hodge goes on to say, "They teach children and remind adults where they fit in, what their society expects of them, and how to live harmoniously with others and be responsible, worthy members of their tribes." Storytelling transmits values by warning against behaviors that are inconsistent with the cultural group's ethics.

Most people enjoy stories. Perhaps that is why stories are so often the **conduit** used to promote cultural identity, preserve history, and transmit values. Although we might sometimes call a tale "just a story," the stories we listen to and tell are important in profound ways.

Margin notes:
Major Supporting Point 3

Supporting Details for Major Supporting Point 3

VCW emulate

VCW conduit

Works Cited

Gioia, Dana. "Life Is Larger Than We Think." *American Interest,* vol. 2, no. 5, May/June 2007, pp. 47–51.

Hodge, Felicia Schanche, et al. "Utilizing Traditional Storytelling to Promote Wellness in American Indian Communities." *Journal of Transcultural Nursing,* vol. 13, no. 1, 2002, pp. 6–11.

Lindahl, Carl, et al., editors. *Swapping Stories: Folktales from Louisiana.* UP of Mississippi, 1997.

From this example, we can see that the body paragraphs each present a major supporting point. Each of the body paragraphs contains supporting details that back up the major supporting point.

Now let's look closely at the supporting details in one body paragraph. We find two types: supporting details and additional details. The additional details provide more information about the particular supporting details, like this:

One reason storytelling is important is that it helps a culture preserve its identity. *Swapping Stories* is a collection of stories told by the residents of Cajun and Creole communities in Louisiana. As the editor notes, each tale teller "presents a community narrative that encapsulates, to a great extent, the shared experiences, values, and sense of humor of his or her neighborhood or cultural background" (Lindahl). Stories that transmit a culture's identity might focus on food, traditions, habits, humor, and community values. For example, many of the Cajun stories focus on hunting and fishing, and this focus reinforces the identity of Cajuns as outdoorsmen. Other stories focus on the importance of food and family. The tradition of making and eating gumbo is part of Cajun culture, so stories about gumbo and other traditional foods are part of the Cajun repertoire.

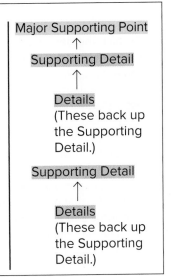

Major Supporting Point
↑
Supporting Detail
↑
Details
(These back up the Supporting Detail.)

Supporting Detail
↑
Details
(These back up the Supporting Detail.)

From the illustration "Layers of Support in an Essay," we can see how levels of detail provide support for a thesis statement.

LAYERS OF SUPPORT IN AN ESSAY

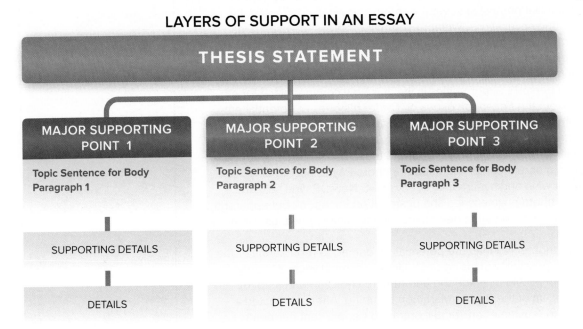

THESIS STATEMENT

MAJOR SUPPORTING POINT 1	MAJOR SUPPORTING POINT 2	MAJOR SUPPORTING POINT 3
Topic Sentence for Body Paragraph 1	Topic Sentence for Body Paragraph 2	Topic Sentence for Body Paragraph 3
SUPPORTING DETAILS	SUPPORTING DETAILS	SUPPORTING DETAILS
DETAILS	DETAILS	DETAILS

PRACTICE 1

Recognizing Major Supporting Points and Supporting Details in Essays

In the following essay, the thesis statement has been annotated for you. Read the essay, and underline the major supporting points. Highlight the supporting details, and draw circles around the additional details.

The Footprint That Does Not Fade

Anyone who uses a cell phone, posts to social media sites such as *Facebook* or *Twitter*, posts comments on Web sites, uploads photos, or even uses a credit or

YOUR ANNOTATIONS

(continued)

debit card has a **digital footprint**—a trail left behind by all of the digital activity in which the person has been involved. A digital footprint provides small bits of information about a person, and all of that information—together—is used to generate a picture of the person's character. Should people be concerned that this information is so readily available to almost anyone who wants it? Probably. Digital footprints can affect a person's reputation, opportunities in life, and personal safety.

VCW digital footprint

Thesis statement

The nature of social networking encourages people to freely post their on-the-spot and **off-the-cuff** comments or photos without thinking carefully about what the information they post says about them. Postings can have serious consequences for one's reputation. For instance, Fox News reported that Janet Dudley-Eshbach, president of Salisbury University, was recently embarrassed by photos she had posted from a personal vacation. One of the photos showed her daughter close to a man, both smiling, and Dudley-Eshbach coming toward the man with a stick. She had included a caption saying she had to "beat off Mexicans because they were constantly flirting with my daughter." The photo and caption—as well as numerous stories about the issue—can still be found on the Internet, although Dudley-Eshbach has pulled her Facebook profile. Another high-profile person affected by his digital footprint is Anthony Weiner, former US representative from New York. Weiner sent "sexts" (sexually explicit texts, including explicit photos) to several women, and when confronted, he originally denied the accusations. Weiner eventually confessed—ashamedly—for both lying and having sent the photos and texts, according to CNN. The scandal ultimately resulted in his resignation as a congressman.

VCW off-the-cuff

In addition to affecting one's reputation, a digital footprint can have serious implications for a person's opportunities in life. It is now commonplace for employers to check out the *Facebook* pages or *Twitter* histories of potential employees. A photo that was meant for only friends to see or an **offhand** comment about hating one's job can give potential employers an impression that can be damaging. Ashley Payne, a twenty-four-year-old teacher in Georgia, recently lost her job when a parent complained about a photo Payne posted of herself holding a glass of wine and a mug of beer, says CBS News. Payne said she tried to make the photo private when she posted it on Facebook but apparently did not succeed. Payne's situation demonstrates how simple postings can have disastrous results.

VCW offhand

Perhaps more frightening than the potential for damaged reputations or the loss of a job is the possibility of losing one's life. Alicia Ann Lynch, a twenty-three-year-old from Michigan, made the unfortunate choice to dress up for Halloween as a victim of the Boston Marathon bombing. After she posted a picture of herself in "costume" on *Tumblr,* outraged people sent her death threats, dug up and circulated nude photos she had posted on the Web, and even harassed her parents. "I've had voice mails where they want to slit my throat and they want to hang me and tear off my face," Lynch said in the *New York Daily News.* Lynch also lost her job, and she probably will not have an easy time finding another one because of the **infamous** digital footprint she now has.

VCW infamous

Educators are now beginning to teach children from a young age to guard their digital footprint. Before the Internet, people could erase their history and start anew. Photos could be ripped up and destroyed; people had the chance to change their reputation if they had made mistakes in the past. These days, a thoughtless posting or photo may be on the Web forever. It is far easier to protect one's reputation than to re-establish it. *Caveat usor* [Latin for "user beware"].

Multiparagraph Support

So far, we have seen how an essay might be structured by presenting each major supporting point in its own body paragraph. What happens, however, if one of the major supporting points requires more than one paragraph of explanation?

In professional essays, writers sometimes use several paragraphs to explain one of the major supporting points. For example, in "The Importance of Storytelling," each body paragraph presents a major supporting point. Let's imagine that the writer has decided to include, in addition, an actual story for each major supporting point. The writer would probably put each story in its own new paragraph. The result would be an essay that has two paragraphs for every major supporting point. A diagram of the essay is shown in "An Essay with Multiparagraph Support."

Writers provide an additional paragraph of supporting details when the point they are making needs significant explanation or discussion. Try your hand at identifying different types of support by completing Practice 2, below.

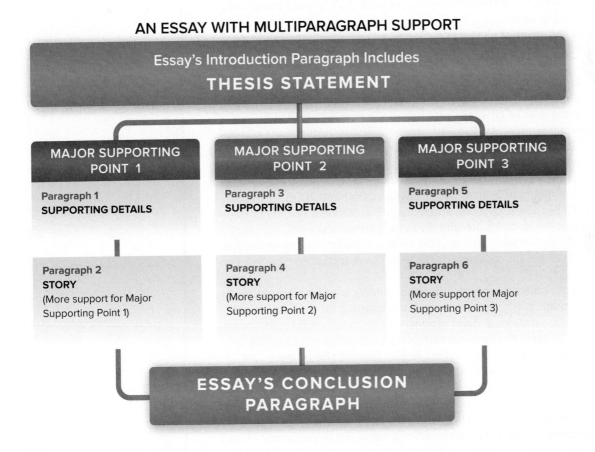

AN ESSAY WITH MULTIPARAGRAPH SUPPORT

Essay's Introduction Paragraph Includes
THESIS STATEMENT

MAJOR SUPPORTING POINT 1	MAJOR SUPPORTING POINT 2	MAJOR SUPPORTING POINT 3
Paragraph 1 **SUPPORTING DETAILS**	Paragraph 3 **SUPPORTING DETAILS**	Paragraph 5 **SUPPORTING DETAILS**
Paragraph 2 **STORY** (More support for Major Supporting Point 1)	Paragraph 4 **STORY** (More support for Major Supporting Point 2)	Paragraph 6 **STORY** (More support for Major Supporting Point 3)

ESSAY'S CONCLUSION PARAGRAPH

PRACTICE 2

Identifying Support in Essays

Read the following essay, which provides an opinion on tar sands oil. You will notice that the thesis statement has been identified. The essay presents three major supporting points, but you will find more than three body paragraphs. Figure out where each major supporting point is, and put brackets around the paragraphs that provide support for the major supporting point.

(continued)

The Most Deadly Oil Yet

The Keystone Pipeline is supposed to provide the United States with endless gallons of cheap crude oil, and we won't have to depend on oil from Saudi Arabia, Venezuela, or other oil-rich countries with whom we have **tenuous** relationships. Those who support the Keystone Pipeline project believe that importing tar sands oil from our neighbor and friend, Canada, will have a significant impact on US oil supplies. Indeed, tar sands oil has been touted as the answer to our oil problems. A close look at what tar sands oil is and the devastation it wreaks, however, will reveal the truth: the use of tar sands oil is an impending disaster, not a miracle.

Canada's countryside, particularly in Alberta, is full of oil. The trouble is that the oil is trapped in sand. Extracting oil from sand is an extremely dirty and environmentally harmful process. To free the sticky oil from the sand, vast amounts of steam (and sometimes toxic solvents) are used. It is a process that increases greenhouse gases by 5%–15%, according to IHS CERA, a research firm. Burning tar sands oil has been shown to produce 20% greater emissions, according to David Strahan.

In addition to the environmental price of tar sands oil, people and animals also pay a high price—with their health, and sometimes with their lives. A number of substances that are linked to cancers and serious diseases, volatile organic compounds, have been found in the area of tar sands oil production at levels of six thousand times normal, according to Think Progress. Cancer levels in the area of tar sands production are now higher than normal, and the Athabascan people who live north of the vast area of tar sands oil production are fearful for their health.

While people worry about cancer, the animals in the area are sick and dying. Kevin Timoney writes in a peer-reviewed article that in the tar sands oil-production areas, large numbers of animals died between 2000 and 2008, including black bears, deer, red foxes, coyotes, and moose. The National Wildlife Federation points out that the tar fields are directly in the path of scores of migratory birds, including American songbirds and the endangered whooping crane. The Athabascans will not eat the local fish because of the potential that the fish contain toxins.

If devastating the environment, endangering animals, and causing cancers in humans is not enough, the dangers posed by transporting tar sands oil might be. TransCanada Corporation, a major producer of tar sands oil, has petitioned the United States to allow the development of a pipeline that would sends tar sands oil components from Canada to Port Arthur, Texas, to be refined. This pipeline would literally run through the backyards of thousands of Americans. It would intersect major rivers and the Ogallala **Aquifer**, a water supply that is used by one-fourth of the irrigated land in America and provides drinking water for two million people, according to Friends of the Earth.

What would happen if the pipeline leaked or a major break occurred? The oil sands product flowing in the pipeline is a heavy, sludgy material, Friends of the Earth points out. If a leak occurs in water, the oil sands material will sink, unlike traditional crude oil. Cleanup efforts would be extremely costly and complicated. Our supply of water may become more valuable than oil itself.

It would be wonderful to do business with our Canadian neighbors and solve our oil problems at the same time—but not at the risk of ruining the environment and endangering our lives and livelihood. The **ecological** and human costs far outweigh any of the touted benefits of this deadly oil.

YOUR ANNOTATIONS

VCW tenuous

Thesis statement

VCW aquifer

VCW ecological

Using Outlining or Graphic Organizers to Identify Major Supporting Points and Supporting Details

One of the best ways to visualize a reading's support is to create a simple outline. The outline should include the reading's title and author, thesis statement, major supporting points, and supporting details. Here is the beginning of an informal outline for "The Importance of Storytelling."

Start with the title.

Write the thesis statement.

List each major supporting point.

List the supporting details for each major supporting point. Do not list the additional details.

Title: The Importance of Storytelling

Thesis statement: "Most cultures use storytelling as a way to reinforce the culture's identity, preserve the culture's history, and strengthen the culture's values."

Major Supporting Point 1: "One reason storytelling is important is that it helps a culture preserve its identity."

    Supporting Detail: "*Swapping Stories* is a collection of stories told by the residents of Cajun and Creole communities in Louisiana."

    Supporting Detail: "Stories that transmit a culture's identity might focus on food, traditions, habits, humor, and community values."

Use complete sentences. If the sentences come directly from the reading, put quotation marks around them.

Major Supporting Point 2: _____

_____

Supporting Detail: _____

_____

Supporting Detail: _____

_____

Major Supporting Point 3: _____

_____

Supporting Detail: _____

_____

Supporting Detail: _____

_____

An outline allows you to reduce the content of a reading into a short, easy-to-read map. In fact, some people create actual visual maps or graphic organizers to take the place of an outline. If you prefer a more visual representation of the information in a reading, you can create a simple graphic organizer.

The purpose of a graphic organizer is to show the relationships among supporting details. Because each essay presents ideas in its own unique way, graphic organizers will not look the same. For example, the graphic organizer for an essay with six major supporting points will look different from one for an essay with four major supporting points.

Hand-drawn graphic organizers are effective for showing relationships among ideas, and they are easy to draw. The hand-drawn organizer below demonstrates the relationships among ideas in an essay on the benefits of encouraging farmers' markets. Notice that the student found it easier to draw the diagram from left to right rather than from top to bottom.

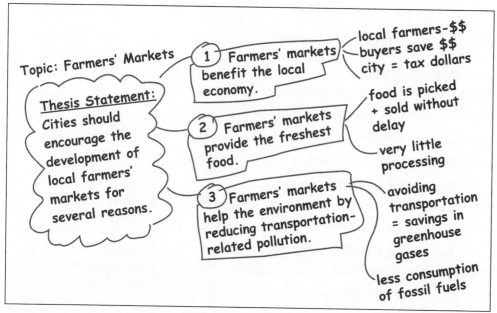

An especially good occasion for using outlining is when you are reading complex material and studying. By putting a reading's major supporting points and supporting details in order, you will be better able to understand the relationships among ideas and remember them later for tests.

PRACTICE 3

Outlining a Reading

Earlier in this chapter, you read "The Footprint That Does Not Fade." Create an outline or graphic organizer for this essay. Use the outline or a graphic organizer presented in this chapter as a model.

Using Transitions

In good writing, the sentences used for support are clearly related to one another. One way to make sure that the relationships between sentences are evident is to use words or phrases that help readers follow the ideas in a text and help writers move smoothly from one idea to another. Notice how the use of the phrase *for example* helps readers see the relationship between these two sentences.

Even cell phone use leaves a digital footprint. For example, a person's cell phone records can reveal that he was traveling between Austin and San Antonio on May 15, 2014, when he made a phone call.

The phrase for example *reveals that the second sentence is meant to elaborate on the first sentence.*

Words and phrases that help the reader move from one sentence to another or from one paragraph to another are called **transitions.** Transitions also help readers recognize a sequence of ideas. If each major supporting point in a text starts with a transition, it is easy to recognize the points. Note the transitions (underlined) in the following example.

Three factors are important to consider in choosing a career. The <u>first</u> factor to consider in choosing a career is personal interest. . . .

The <u>second</u> factor is aptitude. . . .

The <u>third</u> factor that comes into play is the training and education requirements of the career. . . .

When sentences related by transitions indicate a series, the sentences often function in the same way. In this case, the sentences are all major supporting points.

Often, the logic of the supporting details is easier to follow when transitions are used, as in this example.

Good reasons exist on both sides of the debate about whether it is wise to take out student loans. <u>On the one hand,</u> taking out student loans seems logical. College graduates, <u>after all,</u> statistically earn much more than those who do not have degrees. <u>Thus,</u> it seems likely that college graduates will be able to pay off their loans. <u>On the other hand,</u> taking out student loans is fraught with risk. <u>Clearly,</u> college students cannot be certain they will find good jobs after graduation. <u>Additionally,</u> even if they do find good jobs, their entry-level salaries may not be high enough for both a comfortable life and the repayment of student debt.

Transitions show the logical relationships among ideas in this supporting paragraph.

One way to think about transitions is to identify them by their functions, as the table "Common Transition Words and Phrases" demonstrates.

COMMON TRANSITION WORDS AND PHRASES			
Clarification			
for example	in other words	specifically	to demonstrate
for instance	in reality	that is	to explain further
indeed	put another way	to clarify	to illustrate
in fact	simply stated		
Sequences or Time Order			
about	final	next	soon
after	first, second, ... last	now	to begin
as	immediately	often	until
as soon as	in the future	one, another	when
at the same time	later	previously	while
during	meanwhile	simultaneously	

(continued)

COMMON TRANSITION WORDS AND PHRASES *(continued)*

Similarity or Addition

additionally	as well	for instance	moreover
again	besides	furthermore	next
along with	equally important	in addition	plus
also	for another thing	in the same way	similarly
another	for example	likewise	

Contrast

although	even though	on the contrary	otherwise
conversely	however	on the one hand, on	still
counter to	in spite of this	the other hand	yet
despite	nevertheless		

Conclusion or Summary

accordingly	in summary	lastly	the final point
in closing	in the end	the bottom line	to conclude
in short			

Cause and Effect

as a consequence	because	resulting in	therefore
as a result	consequently	so then	thus
at last			

Direction

above	below	next to	there
across	beyond	opposite	to the left
against	here	over	to the right
behind	nearby	overhead	

The example that follows shows the major supporting points that appear as topic sentences in an essay. Notice how the added transitions clarify that these sentences are giving the three major supporting points in the essay. In some cases, the writer has to rewrite the sentences slightly to make the transitions work.

Major supporting points needing transitions:

- Using tar sands oil will reduce the US presence in the Middle East. Canada will provide the majority of the oil the country imports.
- Developing tar sands oil production will greatly benefit the economies of both Canada and the United States.
- Innovations in its production are reducing the potential environmental effects of manufacturing it.

Major supporting points using transitions:

- <u>One reason</u> to support using tar sands oil is that it will reduce the US presence in the Middle East; <u>indeed,</u> Canada will provide the majority of the oil the country imports.
- <u>Another reason</u> for developing tar sands oil production is that it will greatly benefit the economies of both Canada and the United States.
- <u>A final reason</u> for using tar sands oil is that innovations in its production are reducing the potential environmental effects of manufacturing it.

In the following example, the sentences give the supporting details for the final major supporting point of the essay. Notice how the added transitions connect the sentences to one another and provide clues about meaning. Note also that while transitions most commonly appear at the beginning of a sentence, they can also be effective in the middle or even at the end of a sentence.

Supporting details needing transitions:

- Innovations in its production are reducing the potential environmental effects of manufacturing it.
- Producers use less water now. A process that used to take ten barrels of water to produce a barrel of bitumen (the valuable product that is turned into oil) now takes about half of that.
- Some companies plan to recycle water. They plan to share water among themselves to protect the area's aquifer.
- Extraction companies are now beginning to use another method of reaching the bitumen. This method, called THAI (toe-to-heel air injection), does not affect the water supply.

Supporting details using transitions:

- <u>A final reason</u> for using tar sands oil is that innovations in its production are reducing the potential environmental effects of manufacturing it.
- <u>To begin</u>, producers use less water now. A process that used to take ten barrels of water to produce a barrel of **bitumen** (the valuable product that is turned into oil) now takes about half of that, <u>for example.</u>
- <u>Additionally</u>, some companies plan to recycle water. They plan, <u>in fact,</u> to share water among themselves to protect the area's aquifer.
- <u>Moreover</u>, extraction companies are now beginning to use another method of reaching the bitumen. This method, called THAI (toe-to-heel air injection), does not affect the water supply.

VCW bitumen

Try your hand at using transitions to add clarity to supporting ideas.

PRACTICE (4)

Using Transitions

Insert appropriate transitions into the sentences that follow. Reword the sentences if necessary.

1. Major supporting points needing transitions:

    a. Federal student loans are a good financing option because graduates can repay them by participating in loan forgiveness programs.

    b. Students do not have to pay back federal student loans immediately.

    c. Federal student loans do not start **accruing** interest immediately.

    d. The interest rate on federal student loans is generally 3 to 7 percent. This is much lower than that of private student loans.

VCW accruing

(continued)

Answers:

a. _____

_____

b. _____

c. _____

_____

d. _____

_____

2. Supporting details needing transitions:

a. There is a Teacher Loan Forgiveness Program. It is a way to help teachers pay back student loans. Not every teacher is eligible for the program.

b. The program is available only to teachers. Only teachers with Stafford Loans can participate.

c. There are eligibility requirements. A teacher must have worked for five years at a school. The school must be eligible to participate in the program.

d. The teacher must have taken the student loan prior to or during the five years of teaching.

Answers:

a. _____

_____

b. _____

c. _____

_____

d. _____

_____

3. Sentences needing transitions:

a. Over-the-counter medication can be abused. Many people fail to understand this fact.

b. Sleep aids are a commonly purchased over-the-counter item. They are abused.

c. Sleep aids are addictive. People who abuse sleep aids can become dependent on them and unable to sleep without them.

d. Over-the-counter substances that promise to deliver energy are popular. People can abuse these products. They use caffeine-laden products to help them stay awake.

e. Many over-the-counter products can cause dependencies. People should be careful with over-the-counter medication.

Answers:

a. _____

_____

b. _____

_____

(continued)

c. _____

_____

d. _____

_____

_____

e. _____

_____

Using Specific Types of Supporting Details in Your Writing

Although you may not be aware of it, you use supporting details in your conversations all the time. For instance, in a casual conversation with a friend, you may comment about a movie you saw: "That movie was fantastic!" Your friend is likely to ask why you liked it so much. Your response will include supporting details. Notice how your conversation can be outlined in a way similar to an essay.

Thesis statement: That movie was fantastic!

Why?

Support:

- It was a classic epic. (*classification of the movie type*)
- It was so much better than the first movie in the series because the main character, Kudu, didn't win every battle. He seemed much more realistic. (*comparison*)
- The whole movie was in sepia-colored tones, which really added to the oddness of the scenery. (*description*)

We use support without even thinking about it. Moreover, these supporting details come in a wide variety of types.

Recognizing Types of Supporting Details

As you read, become aware of the various types of support writers use and that you have available to you as a writer. The chart that follows lists some of the most common types of supporting details.

COMMON TYPES OF SUPPORTING DETAILS	
Analogy	An example that explains something unfamiliar by comparing it with something more familiar
Cause and effect	How one circumstance brought about or resulted from another
Comparison and contrast	How one item or event is similar to or different from another
Concrete example	Specific information that helps the reader understand the writer's point
Definition	An explanation of the meaning of a word or concept
Description	Sensory information that helps the reader understand a thing or concept
Explanation	A description of how something is constructed, how a task is performed, or how something works
Fact	A statement that is verifiably true

(continued)

COMMON TYPES OF SUPPORTING DETAILS *(continued)*	
Figurative language	Language that expresses ideas in an indirect way, such as metaphors, similes, personification, and hyperbole
Hypothetical example	An example that asks the reader to imagine something that is not currently true
Observation	An account of phenomena or field research
Reason	The rationale or justification for an assertion or claim
Rhetorical question	A question that the writer asks to make a point but does not expect the reader to answer; the answer may be provided in the text, or it may be self-evident
Summaries	A brief recounting of the content of a source
Steps, stages, or phases	A discussion of sequential actions or time periods to depict a process
Testimony	A person's firsthand account of something
Use of sources	Citing external sources, often to prove something: • Citing experts or authorities so the reader knows where the information is coming from and can evaluate its validity • Citing reference books so the information can be considered factual • Citing statistics to provide mathematical information or proof • Citing witnesses to provide evidence or acknowledgments
Visual aid	A photo, diagram, chart, cartoon, or any other graphic representation of content

Thinking Like a Reader to Create Support

Writers select the type of supporting details to use based on the point they are making. To develop supporting details, think about each major supporting point as if you were the reader, not the writer. What questions would you have? What information would you want the writer to add to the paragraph?

One way to anticipate the kind of support an audience might need is to use the "5 W's + 1 H Questions."

5 W'S + 1 H QUESTIONS

WHO? Information about a person or group

WHAT? Explanation of an idea, project, event, or other thing

WHERE? Description of a specific place

WHEN? Information about the timing of an action or historical event

WHY? Explanation of reasons, causes, or effects

HOW? Explanation of the way something happened or could be accomplished

To use the questions, write down the statement that needs to be supported. In the example "Jill Thinks about Her Audience," we can observe one student as she develops support for her essay. Jill has already written a thesis statement, but she needs to figure out the support she will use in her body paragraphs. To do this, she first thinks about what her readers might ask or think.

JILL THINKS ABOUT HER AUDIENCE

My thesis statement: High school students should be required to take a class on personal financial management.

People might ask, "Why?"

People might ask, "Isn't it more important to study reading, writing, and math?"

People might ask, "Can't students learn these things on their own?"

People might say, "Let their parents teach them."

People might say, "I learned the hard way. They can learn the hard way too."

©Thinkstock/Getty Images RF

So how can I respond to these questions and statements? I'll use these reasons in my body paragraphs:

1. Most high school students have very little knowledge about financial matters.
2. Becoming independent requires the ability to manage one's finances.
3. Financial issues are complex and many students do not have the background to learn on their own.
4. The financial choices young adults make can have lasting effects.

By thinking about her audience, Jill develops major supporting points that will help her write her thesis statement and answer her audience's questions. Now that Jill has major supporting points, she can use a similar process to figure out how to support each point. In "Jill Develops Ideas for a Supporting Point," we can see how Jill uses audience analysis to come up with support for her first point.

JILL DEVELOPS IDEAS FOR A SUPPORTING POINT

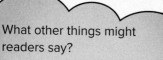

Major Supporting Point 1: One reason to require a personal financial literacy class is that most high school students have very little knowledge about financial matters.

How will readers react?

They might not believe me. I'll need to prove that high school students don't know much about finances. How can I prove that?

- I could do a survey.
- I could find some research to use in my essay.
- I could talk about my own experience.
- I could talk about my friends' experiences.
- I could make up a story (hypothetical example).
- I could tell a story.

I will have to make sure my proof is believable and applies to most high school students, not just me and my friends.

What other things might readers say?

What if they don't know what I mean by "personal financial literacy"?

I need to define that term.

©Thinkstock/Getty Images RF

    As you can see from Jill's experiences, figuring out the kind of support to use in an essay requires thinking like a reader. The more you think like a reader, the better you will be at creating essays that readers find pleasing and satisfactory.

PRACTICE 5

Thinking Like a Reader to Create Support

The following statements are potential major supporting points for different essays. To be developed into a paragraph, each statement would need support. Think like a reader to figure out the kind of support you could use for each statement. The first one is completed as an example.

Major supporting point: Before going to a job interview, applicants should spend time reading about the prospective company.

(continued)

Questions or thoughts readers might have:

a. Why? Will the interviewer expect applicants to already know about the company?

b. What advantage would it be for an applicant to know about the company?

c. What kind of information should the applicant know about the   company?

Types of supporting details you would use in your paragraph:

a. Explanation of why background company knowledge matters

b. Examples of the kind of information applicants should know

c. Examples of interview questions that might be difficult to answer without knowing about the company

1. **Major supporting point:** One strategy for making better grades is to sit at the front of the class.

Questions or thoughts readers might have:

a. _____

b. _____

c. _____

Types of supporting details you would use in your paragraph:

a. _____

b. _____

c. _____

2. **Major supporting point:** Before selecting a career field, it is wise to shadow—or follow around for a day—a person who works in the career you are considering.

Questions or thoughts readers might have:

a. _____

b. _____

c. _____

Types of supporting details you would use in your paragraph:

a. _____

b. _____

c. _____

Developing an Essay from Prewriting to Outlining

Creating the kind of support that will help readers fully understand your thesis statement is an essential part of writing an essay. Usually, when you generate ideas in prewriting, you are already beginning to think about the kinds of information you will use in your body paragraphs. What follows is an example of how Sienna, a freshman writing student, generated supporting details for her assignment.

Analyze the Assignment.   Sienna is taking a class in anthropology, and her instructor has given the class an essay assignment. Sienna's first task is to fully understand the assignment. She reads the assignment and makes annotations.

Assignment Write an essay in which you discuss a rite of passage you have experienced; show readers why this rite of passage was significant.	SIENNA'S ANNOTATIONS *What is a rite of passage?*

By reviewing her class notes, she learns that a rite of passage is an important transitional experience in a person's life, such as marriage, graduation, childbirth, divorce, or even a particular birthday celebration. That information helps her rephrase the assignment as a question.

Sienna's question: What significant rite of passage have I experienced, and why was it important?

Identify the Purpose.   Three other words in the assignment that Sienna annotated are *discuss, show,* and *why.* From these terms she concludes that the purpose of her essay is to tell about her rite of passage and discuss the reasons it was important. Moreover, she is not to discuss just any rite of passage. She must choose one from her own experience. So her purpose is to *inform* her readers about a rite of passage she experienced and *evaluate* its importance.

Prewrite to Develop Ideas.   From class discussions, Sienna discovers that a rite of passage consists of three phases:

Separation

Transition

Reincorporation

Because she recently gave birth to a daughter, Sienna decides to write about how having a baby is an important rite of passage. With that in mind, Sienna rewrites the question her essay will answer.

Sienna's revised question: Why was giving birth to my daughter a significant rite of passage?

Then, using the three phases of a rite of passage, Sienna does some *freewriting*—writing quickly on a subject without pausing to make corrections. During her freewriting, she comes up with ideas about how having a child was a significant experience for her. Afterward, rereading her freewriting, she underlines the important details for each phase. She realizes that the last line of her freewriting answers the question "Why?" so she highlights that line.

Why was giving birth to my daughter an important rite of passage?

Separation: When I was pregnant, I didn't "party" anymore; didn't hang out with the same people; spent more time with my family, especially my mom and husband; entered a new world of doctors, hospitals, and *pain*! I was so sick when I was pregnant.

Transition: When I gave birth, I came home and took care of the baby on my own. Was tired all the time. No peace and quiet! Less money-everything cost so much. No time to shop, go out to eat, exercise. It seemed like work, work, work. Husband was always tired because he helped w/the baby every night and worked all day the next day. We fought. No time for myself. Emotional issues. Sad about losing my free-dom and old body! I wasn't sure I was capable of raising a baby. Every-thing was scary. Read a million Web sites to try to figure it all out.

Reincorporation: One year later, I'm very happy in general. Different expectations. Not a lot of sleep is OK. Learned how to find some time for myself. Have a great daily routine. Feel like I am a competent mom now. Body and weight are adjusting. Feel changed forever-more mature and more like a woman and not a girl.

Construct a Thesis Statement.   Using the material she developed in her pre-writing, Sienna constructs a thesis statement.

> **Thesis statement:** The birth of my first child was a rite of passage that changed me forever.

Notice that Sienna has written an *open thesis statement:* it does not reveal an ex-plicit plan for her essay. Sienna also considered this *closed thesis statement,* which lists the stages she will discuss in each major supporting point:

> The birth of my first child was a rite of passage that involved the stages of sepa-ration, transition, and reincorporation.

Develop Support for the Thesis Statement.   Sienna plans to use each stage in her rite of passage as a major supporting point. Her next task is to create topic sentences for each major supporting point.

Writing Topic Sentences for Major Supporting Points.   Using the three rite of pas-sage phases from her prewriting, as well as the details she developed in the prewriting, Sienna writes topic sentences for her major supporting ideas.

Thesis statement: The birth of my first child was a rite of passage that changed me forever.

Major supporting point 1 (topic sentence): When I became pregnant, I found myself separated from my old life.

Major supporting point 2 (topic sentence): After I gave birth to my daughter, I entered into a tough transition period.

Major supporting point 3 (topic sentence): Fortunately, today I am slowly beginning to see myself in a new way.

Sienna uses transitions while she writes her topic sentences. Notice her use of *When, After, Fortunately,* and *today.* These transitions help signal to readers the major phases through which Sienna passed. We also see some similarity in wording:

When ... I found myself ...

After ... I entered into ...

Fortunately, today I am slowly ...

Both the transitions and the similarities in wording tell readers that these details are the major phases in Sienna's rite of passage.

Anticipating an Audience's Questions. Sienna needs to make sure the supporting details she has developed in prewriting will provide enough information to meet the needs of her readers. One way to do this is to spend time thinking about what readers might want or need to know. By putting herself in the place of the reader, she can predict some of the needs of her audience. The chart below shows some of the audience questions Sienna asks herself about her second major supporting point.

Topic sentence for major supporting point 2: After I gave birth to my daughter, I entered into a tough transition period.

Supporting details:	Audience questions:
▪ Emotional issues—sad about loss of freedom, body image adjustments, marriage was more difficult	▪ What do you mean by "loss of freedom"? Can you provide an example? What kind of freedom will I lose if/when I have children? ▪ How did your body change? How much weight did you gain? ▪ Why was your marriage more difficult? Can you provide an example?
▪ Physical difficulties, never getting enough sleep	▪ What do you mean by "physical difficulties"? ▪ Couldn't you find a way to get more sleep?
▪ Had financial difficulties (baby-related costs)	▪ How much does it cost to have a baby? Do you mean an extra $50/month, or do you mean more like $300–$500/month?
▪ Believed I was not a competent mother	▪ Why were you so down on your mothering abilities? ▪ What tasks were you particularly concerned about?

Listing and Choosing Supporting Details for Each Major Supporting Point.   Sienna returns to her prewriting to find effective supporting details. Although Sienna has already identified some of the supporting details she will use—personal anecdotes and facts about money—she finds even *more specific* examples as she continues thinking about her audience's needs. She plans to add a very short anecdote and some concrete examples to make her essay more informative and enjoyable.

Create an Outline to Organize the Essay.
Sienna now writes a simple outline for her essay. She jots down her three major supporting points—written out as full topic sentences. Under each point, she adds the supporting details she will use. When the supporting details themselves need more explanation or support, she adds them as "details."

Sienna's Simple Outline

Title: Giving Birth: My Rite of Passage

Introduction paragraph

Thesis statement: The birth of my first child was a rite of passage that changed me forever.

Major supporting point 1: When I became pregnant, I found myself separated from my old life.

  Supporting detail: Did not go partying with old friends

   Detail: Was not interested in the same things anymore

  Supporting detail: Spent more time with family and less time doing the things I used to do

Major supporting point 2: After I gave birth to my daughter, I entered into a tough transition period.

  Supporting detail: Emotional trials

   Detail: Sad about loss of freedom, body image adjustments, marriage was more difficult

  Supporting detail: Had financial difficulties

   Detail: Living on one income

   Detail: Paying baby-related costs

  Supporting detail: Afraid I wasn't a competent mother

   Detail: Needed constant reassurance

   Detail: Worried about accidentally hurting the baby

Major supporting point 3: Fortunately, today I am slowly beginning to see myself in a new way.

  Supporting detail: Am a good mother

   Detail: Developed routines that work for the baby

  Supporting detail: More emotionally stable

   Detail: Wake up happy most days

   Detail: Have more confidence and less anxiety

Supporting detail: See myself as grown up

    Detail: Can handle what other women handle

    Detail: Hang out with new group of people, women with children

Conclusion paragraph

Notice that not all of the body paragraphs have the same number of details. Some writers aim to have supporting paragraphs that are roughly the same length, and that is a good goal. However, body paragraphs can have minor variations in the number of details they include and still be effective.

Notice also how coming up with supporting details leads naturally into creating a simple, informal outline for your writing. It is always wise to create an outline before drafting.

PRACTICE 6

Planning Support Paragraphs for an Essay

Using Sienna's work as a model, generate ideas and an outline for an essay on a rite of passage you have experienced. You will use your outline in a later assignment to draft the essay. Follow these instructions.

1. **Start by reading the assignment.** For this assignment, you will write an essay in which you discuss a rite of passage you have experienced. Your essay must show readers why this rite of passage was significant. For details, see "A Reading and Writing Assignment" at the end of this chapter.

2. **Prewrite to develop your ideas.** Choose a prewriting method, such as listing or freewriting, and use it to generate ideas for the topic. First, prewrite about some of the experiences in your life that were rites of passage. Write down each experience, and note why it was significant to you. Do this for at least three experiences.

    Once you have written about three or more rites of passage, choose one to discuss in an essay. If you need to, spend more time prewriting to think of the ways this experience changed you.

3. **Construct a thesis statement.** Write a sentence in which you express the main point you wish to make about the rite of passage you selected for your essay.

4. **Develop support for your thesis statement.** Write a topic sentence for each major supporting point. Consider creating a major supporting point for each significant effect this rite of passage had. Once you have written topic sentences for your major supporting points, list the questions a general audience might have about them. Next, jot down the minor supporting details that would help readers understand each of your major supporting points.

5. **Create a simple outline to organize your essay.** Use Sienna's outline as a model. Include your thesis statement, major supporting points, and supporting details.

CHAPTER ACTIVITIES

➔ READING AND ANNOTATING

What follows is a brief essay about male rites of passage. It begins with an extensive example; the second half of the reading is an explanation of the phases of a rite of passage.

Before reading, use these pre-reading steps summarized here and record your thoughts on a separate sheet.

- **Preview:** What do you notice when you preview the text?
- **Predict:** What do you predict the topic will be?
- **Recall:** What do you already know about the topic?
- **Ask:** What questions do you have about the text or the topic?

Next, read and annotate the essay, and then answer the questions that follow.

Coming of Age: The Importance of Male Rites of Passage

By Brett and Kate McKay

YOUR ANNOTATIONS

The elders of the tribe stood in front of the hut and beckoned for the young man to come out and begin the festivities of the special day. The young man had barely slept the night before, anxiously anticipating the tests he would soon be called to endure. As he rose to meet the elder, he was aware of a great gnawing in his stomach; he had had nothing to eat for the last three days as he purged his body of impurities.

The ceremony soon began. The elders of the tribe pierced his chest, shoulder, and back muscles with large wooden splints. Ropes, which extended from the roof of the hut, were then attached to the splints, and the young man was winched up into the air, his whole body weight suspended from the ropes. Agonizing pain coursed through the young man's body, but he gritted his teeth and tried not to cry out.

While hanging in the air, more splints were hammered through his arms and legs. Skulls of his dead grandfather and other ancestors were placed on the ends of the splints. All the while, the young man cried aloud to the Great Spirit for courage to endure. Eventually, the young man fainted from the loss of blood and the sheer pain of the torture. When the elders were sure he was unconscious, he was lowered down and the ropes were removed. Yet the splints were left in place.

When the young man recovered consciousness, he offered his left pinky to the tribal elders to be sacrificed. He placed his finger on a block and had it swiftly chopped off. This was a gift to the gods and would enable the young man to become a powerful hunter.

Finally, the young man ran inside a ring where his fellow villagers had gathered. As he ran, the villagers reached out and grabbed the still embedded splints, ripping them free. The splints weren't allowed to be pulled out the way they had been hammered in, but had to be torn out in the opposite direction, causing the young man even greater pain and worse wounds. This concluded the day's ceremony.

(continued)

The young man was exhausted and bloodied, but **euphoric**. He had been beyond glad to participate in the ritual. This was the greatest day of his life; today he was a man.

While the coming of age ceremony of the Mandan tribe is a particularly gruesome example, peoples and cultures from prehistoric times onward created rites of passage to initiate boys into manhood. Today, such rites of passage are almost extinct. Boys lack clear markers on their journey to becoming a man. If you ask them when the transition occurs, you will get a variety of answers: "When you get a car," "When you graduate from college," "When you get a real job," "When you lose your virginity," "When you get married," "When you have a kid," and so on. The problem with many of these traditional rites of passage is that they have been put off further and further in a young man's life. Fifty years ago the average age an American man started a family was 22. Today, men (for ill or good) are getting married and having kids later in life. With these traditional rites of passage increasingly being delayed, many men are left feeling stuck between boyhood and manhood. College? Fewer men are graduating. And many that do "boomerang" back home again, spending another few years figuring out what the next step in their life should be. As traditional rites of passage have become fuzzier, young men are plagued with a sense of being adrift.

Of course the process of becoming a man, ceremony or not, does not happen in a single moment. But rites of passage are important in **delineating** when a boy should start thinking of himself as a man, when he should start carrying himself as a man, when the community should start respecting him as a man, and when he should start shouldering the responsibilities of a man. Lacking these important markers, many young men today belabor their childhood, never sure of when they've really "manned up."

What Is a Rite of Passage?

Sociologists have identified three phases that constitute a proper rite of passage: separation, transition, and re-incorporation.

Separation: During this phase an **initiate** is separated in some way from his former life. In the case of the Mandan tribe, the young man was isolated from the village in a hut for three days. In other tribes, boys' heads were shaved and they were ritually bathed and/or tattooed. In a more modern example, when a man has just enlisted in the military, he is sent away to boot camp. His former possessions are put aside, his head is shaved, and he is given a uniform to wear. During the separation phase, part of the old self is extinguished as the initiate prepares to create a new identity.

Transition: During this phase, the initiate is between worlds—no longer part of his old life but not yet fully inducted into his new one. He is taught the knowledge needed to become a full-fledged member of that group. And he is called upon to pass tests that show he is ready for the leap. In tribal societies, the elders would impart to the initiate what it meant to be a man and how the boy was to conduct himself once he had become one. The initiate would then participate in ritual ceremonies which often involved pain and endurance. In the case of the new soldier, he is yelled at, prodded, exercised, and disciplined to prepare him to receive a rank and title.

Re-incorporation: In this phase, the initiate, having passed the tests necessary and proving himself worthy, is re-introduced into his community, which

VCW euphoric

VCW delineating

VCW initiate

(continued)

recognizes and honors his new status within the group. For tribal societies, this meant a village-wide feast and celebration. The boy would now be recognized by all tribe members as a man and allowed to participate in the activities and responsibilities that status conferred. For the soldier, his boot camp experience would come to an end and both his superiors and his family would join in a ceremony to recognize his new status as a full-fledged member of the military.

During all the phases of the process, the men who have gone through the ritual themselves guide the young initiate on his journey. By controlling the rite of passage, the men decide when a boy becomes a man.

Questions for Consideration

1. What is the topic of this reading? What is the main idea, in your own words?

2. Some people have called modern body piercing or tattooing a rite of passage. They believe body piercing and tattooing are very significant experiences that often mark the beginning of adulthood. Do you agree? Why or why not? If you have a piercing or tattoo, did your experience make you feel different about yourself? Was it a true rite of passage? If you do not have a piercing or tattoo, would you predict getting one would be a meaningful rite of passage? Explain in one or two paragraphs.

3. The passage you read concerns male rites of passage. What female rites of passage exist in our society? Make a list. Do each of these rites of passage have a separation phase, a transition phase, and a reincorporation phase? Explain in one or two paragraphs.

4. Some rites of passage seem violent or destructive. Think about the ways young men and women in your culture prove they are moving from adolescence to adulthood. Are any of these ways violent or destructive? Write a paragraph explaining one such rite of passage.

⊙ USING MODELS TO PRACTICE COMPOSING

Earlier in this chapter, you read about the steps Sienna took as she worked on a writing assignment. Below you will find the essay Sienna wrote. Read the essay, and annotate any of the writing features you think are effective. Circle the transitions you find. Be mindful of the support Sienna used. Note any areas where you think she should have included more support.

Model Student Paper: "Childbirth as a Rite of Passage" by Sienna Mendez

YOUR ANNOTATIONS

Mendez 1

Sienna Mendez

INRW 0402

Ms. Cassidy

15 November 2017

Childbirth as a Rite of Passage

There are two worlds—the one before having children, and the one afterward. Most young people, however, do not know about these

Mendez 2

two worlds. Regardless of how much I read about what it is like to have a child, I was not truly prepared for the world I entered after childbirth. Having a baby is a true rite of passage. It is a challenging moment in life, but it also comes with blessings. The birth of my first child was a rite of passage that changed me forever.

When I became pregnant, I found myself separated from my old life. After my long shifts as an emergency room clerk, I used to go out for bar food and drinks with a group of nurses and clerks. When I could not drink anymore, and when I could not stay awake long enough to have fun with the girls, I eventually stopped going. Plus, none of them had children—or wanted children. I still loved my friends, but being pregnant just made things different. I spent far more time with my family than I used to, and gradually my circle of friends became smaller.

After I gave birth to my daughter, I entered into a tough transition period. I was beginning to see what a life change I was in for. I had always been a calm, easygoing person, but I surprised myself with fits of crying or anger. At times I felt really happy, but there were other times when I was sad about losing my freedom, my thin, sexy body, and the fun times my husband and I used to have without the responsibility of a baby.

In addition to those challenges, money problems began to appear. Life just became hard. I had made the choice to quit my job for two years to stay home with our child, but I hadn't realized how different it would be to live on one income instead of two. Baby supplies were so expensive!

Also, I was constantly worried and anxious. I needed reassurance every day, and I spent most of my free time searching for information on the Web or calling my mother in tears. I worried the most about accidentally hurting my child. Were the bottles washed well enough? Was she breathing? I could hardly sleep at night sometimes because of my worrying.

Mendez 3

Fortunately, today I am slowly beginning to see myself in a new way. I truly am a different person than I was a year ago. I have slowly come to believe that I am a good mother. I am not perfect, but no mother is. By developing routines with my baby, I have learned how to manage my day more effectively, even fitting in more time to focus on my coursework.

Better yet, I have become much more emotionally stable. I no longer have fits of tears or anger, and most days I wake up happy and ready to face life. I have far less anxiety about being a mom, and I have developed the belief that now I am really a different person. I am no longer a child. I am proving myself capable of handling what other grown women handle. And even more impressively, I have a group of new friends, mothers with children. I am one of them now.

The transition was not easy, and it is not over. I have a feeling that being a parent will involve many rites of passage. After all, some day my child will leave, and I imagine that that day will be just as hard as the last year has been. With luck, it will result in the same joy.

⊙ A READING AND WRITING ASSIGNMENT

Using Sienna's essay as a model and the material you developed in Practice 6, complete the following assignment:

Write an essay in which you discuss a rite of passage you have experienced; show readers why this rite of passage was significant.

A rite of passage is usually an event or a short period of time in a person's life that is particularly important and results in personal growth. For example, taking care of a loved one who is dying might trigger a reappraisal of life. For the caregiver, this task may be a rite of passage into new insights and a new way of living. Other rites of passage are more formal, such as getting married, having a child, and getting divorced. Think of an event or time in your life from which you emerged changed in some way: perhaps you became "older and wiser," or maybe you had insights that changed the way you live or that helped you mature. You may structure your paper around the ways this rite of passage has affected you, or you may write about each of the three phases Sienna included in her essay planning.

Use the Quick Start Guide to Integrated Reading and Writing Assignments to help you with this process. Be sure to reread your essay carefully for errors.

➔ ADDING TO YOUR VOCABULARY

This chapter's vocabulary words appear below.

accruing	delineating	encapsulates	initiate
bitumen	ecological	euphoric	off-the-cuff
conduit	emulate	infamous	tenuous

Choose five of the vocabulary words from this chapter that you would like to add to your vocabulary, and think about how you can use them this week. For example, one of this chapter's terms is *off-the-cuff*. This term describes something that is said without forethought or preparation. You can often substitute *off-the-cuff* for *unplanned*.

> **Example:** I didn't know my instructor would call on me to explain last night's reading, so I just gave my best *unplanned* answer.
>
> I didn't know my instructor would call on me to explain last night's reading, so I just gave my best *off-the-cuff* answer.

List each of the five words you plan to use this week, and make note of a context in which you could use each word.

> **Example:** *Off-the-cuff.* When I am explaining something to family members but do not have time to get into great depth, I'll let them know my explanation is off-the-cuff.

➔ ADDITIONAL ASSIGNMENTS

1. Practice audience analysis skills by reading the following paragraph. As a reader, what information would you expect the writer to provide? Has the writer of this paragraph met those needs? Analyze the paragraph, and then write a list of recommendations for how the writer could change or add supporting details to meet readers' needs.

    > No one would believe the kinds of things that go on in women's prisons. As a prison guard, I have had the opportunity to get an inside glimpse into the lives of this very isolated world. One prisoner, whom I will call Diva, changed a perfectly ordinary Monday into a day I will never get out of my mind. I am still haunted by that day. Another prisoner had the most unusual visitors, and from the way she looked, you would never have guessed she was the criminal type. My experience as a prison guard has been exceptional.

2. Choose one of the following thesis statements. If you were writing an essay, what major supporting points would you use to effectively demonstrate the thesis statement you selected? What kinds of supporting details would provide evidence for

your major supporting points? Write an informal outline or graphic organizer for the thesis statement you chose.

  a.   All US citizens should have to serve two years in the military.

  b.   Making US citizens serve a mandatory period of two years in the military is a bad idea.

3.   Select a chapter from one of your textbooks for another class or an article from a newspaper or magazine. Create an informal outline or graphic map for the reading you select.

EMOTIONAL INTELLIGENCE

In some ways, starting college is a rite of passage. Think about the three phases of rites of passage: separation, transition, and reincorporation. Think about your experience as a college student. In what ways does becoming a college student require you to experience separation? What kinds of transitions are required of college students? When you finish college, what kind of reincorporation do you expect? Explain in a paragraph or two.

METACOGNITION

Think of a skill you possess that you had to learn. For example, perhaps you know how to work on automotive engines, or maybe you are a great cook, a fabulous guitarist, or a pretty good point guard. Now, think back to a time when you were *not* good at that skill. How did you learn the skill? What did you do in the beginning of the learning process? Did you learn by imitating someone else? Did someone specifically show you what to do? Did you read? Did you talk about the skill? Write a paragraph explaining the way you learned to be good at your skill. Reflect on why that learning method worked for you.

Text Credits

Page 122: Source: Dudley-Eshbach, Janet, "University President Pulls Web Profile" *Associated Press*, October 17, 2007; Page 122: Source: Murphey, Doyle, "Woman Behind Boston Marathon Bombing Costume Blasts Critics" *New York Daily News,* November 6, 2013; Page 141–43: McKay, Brett, and McKay, Kate, "Coming of Age: The Importance of Male Rites of Passage." Copyright © 2008 The Art of Manliness. Reprinted with permission. http://www.artofmanliness.com.

Text Purposes and Text Patterns

From tracks left behind millennia ago, scientists can identify the dinosaurs that once roamed an area. Patterns help us know what to expect, not only in nature, but also in texts.

©Joe McDaniel/Getty Images RF

After completing this chapter, students will be able to do the following:

- Identify the purposes of texts—to inform, to analyze, to evaluate, and to persuade.

- Connect purposes and text patterns.

- Recognize eight text patterns—narration, definition, illustration, classification, comparison-contrast, cause and effect, process analysis, and argument.

- Analyze these eight text patterns as they appear in readings.

- Use these eight text patterns to compose paragraphs and essays.

- Recognize mixed text patterns in a reading, and use mixed text patterns in writing.

Every text has a purpose. In fact, you could probably think of a long list of writing purposes: to reflect, to memorialize, to define, to entertain, to list, to vent frustration, and to make a plea, just to name a few. Most of the texts you encounter in your college and work life will have one or more of these writing purposes: to inform, to analyze, to evaluate, and to persuade.

To compose texts that effectively fulfill their purposes, writers often use text patterns. **Text patterns**—narration, definition, illustration, classification, comparison-contrast, cause and effect, process analysis, and argument—are modes of thought that communicate ideas.

Text patterns help us both as readers and as writers. As readers, we recognize text patterns and expect them to present information in specific ways. As writers, we use text patterns to communicate our thoughts.

In this chapter, we focus on the four writing purposes and learn how text patterns can be used to fulfill these purposes.

Identifying the Purpose of a Text

An important part of exploring a text is to ask yourself, "What is the writer's purpose?" Four common purposes are to inform, to analyze, to evaluate, and to persuade. Knowing the writer's purpose helps you determine the text's meaning and decide on the text's effectiveness.

Writing to Inform

Informative texts are straightforward: they tell readers about a subject. Newspaper articles are usually informative, as are textbooks, reference books, travelogues (travel writing), factual magazine articles, reports, and many scholarly journal articles.

You can identify informative writing by its characteristics:

- It exists to deliver information.
- It uses facts and may include data and statistics.
- It often includes citations from sources.
- It does *not* present the author's opinion; thus, it is unbiased.

Writing to Analyze

To **analyze** is to examine a subject, an event, an object, or a possibility very carefully. Analysis requires that we break a subject into its component parts. To analyze the engine of a car, you would look carefully at the individual parts under the hood. The same principle is true of analytical writing: it requires us to look at the individual components of a subject.

We might also use analysis to understand how past events, such as the Civil War, came to be. We might use analysis to examine current events, such as the privacy threats we face when we use the Internet. We might analyze an object, such as a smartphone or a tablet computer. And we might analyze future actions, such as proposals to change voter registration laws or the potential effects of buying oil from a particular country.

You can identify analytical writing by its characteristics:

- It explains or describes the parts of something.
- It explains or describes how something works or could work.
- It explains or describes how something happened or what might happen.
- It uses facts and credible information.
- It presents the topic in a fair and unbiased way.

Writing to Evaluate

Evaluative texts come to a conclusion about the value or effectiveness of a particular thing, idea, or course of action. Evaluation includes analysis. To evaluate the usefulness of a particular smartphone, for instance, you must first analyze it. You can then evaluate its worth. You might even compare it with another smartphone to make your evaluation.

Because evaluation means making a judgment, it usually involves setting up criteria. Suppose you live in a part of the country where tornadoes are common and you have decided to buy a storm shelter. To evaluate the available shelters, you would first analyze them. You might ask questions such as "What is it made of?" "How large is it?" "Is it inside the home or outside?" "Does it have features such as carpeting?" and "What does it cost?" After completing your analysis, you would decide which criteria are important to you. You may realize that you want a shelter that is inside your home, costs under $3,000, and is made of steel. In this case, your criteria are location, cost, and material. By using these criteria, you will be able to evaluate your options and choose the shelter that best meets your requirements.

You can identify evaluative writing by its characteristics:

- It is based on analysis.
- It generally presents subjects in a fair and unbiased way.
- It uses a fair and clearly stated appraisal process.
- It uses criteria for weighing choices.
- It makes a judgment.

Writing to Persuade

The goal of a great deal of writing is **persuasion.** Some texts that aim to persuade provide explicit arguments; that is, these texts make it clear that they want readers to buy into the point of view they offer. For example, editorials are brief articles written by newspaper editors. Their purpose—by definition—is to persuade readers of a particular point of view. For example, an editorial may describe an editor's opinion about immigration reform with the goal of persuading readers.

Some texts that aim to persuade are more subtle. For example, a Web site may appear to provide information about a product, but when you analyze the site in depth, you may find that the information is just a means to an end: the site's real purpose is to convince readers to buy the product. Persuasive writing is found in almost every genre of writing: fiction and nonfiction books, magazine articles, some newspaper articles, editorials, Web pages, and so on.

You can identify persuasive writing by its characteristics:

- It attempts to sway readers' opinions on a topic.
- It provides evidence for the writer's opinion.
- It is generally written from a biased (opinionated) point of view.
- It appeals to logic, emotions, and credibility to influence readers.

These four writing purposes—to inform, to analyze, to evaluate, and to persuade—will help you understand the choices writers make in their texts.

PRACTICE

Determining a Text's Purpose

Read each text description and make an educated guess about the writer's purpose. Each description presents a different purpose: to inform, to analyze, to evaluate, or to persuade.

1.   An article in a newsmagazine titled "Fences Won't Stop Illegal Immigration"

   Purpose: _____

(continued)

2. "The iPhone versus the Android: Which One Is Best?"—an article in a computer magazine

   Purpose: _____

3. An article in a newspaper titled "Entire City Installs Solar Panels on Its Homes"

   Purpose: _____

4. "Current Trends: The Decline of Marriage"—an article in a popular science magazine

   Purpose: _____

Connecting Purposes and Text Patterns

In both oral and written communication, we depend on recognized patterns of thought to communicate ideas. When you read the phrase "for instance," you realize that you are about to be presented with an example that will help you understand another point the writer is making. When you read "Once upon a time," you mentally prepare to hear a story. These patterns that we use to communicate ideas are text patterns.

The most common text patterns are narration, definition, illustration, classification, comparison-contrast, cause and effect, process analysis, and argument. Often when we communicate, we use more than one text pattern. Consider the paragraph that follows, noticing the variety of text patterns that come into play.

An eclipse is an astrological event that occurs when one object gets in between you and another object and blocks your view. From Earth, we routinely experience two kinds of eclipses: an eclipse of the Moon and an eclipse of the Sun. Sometimes, as the Earth orbits the Sun, it comes between the Sun and the Moon. When this happens, the Earth throws a dark shadow across the Moon. This is known as an eclipse of the Moon, or a lunar eclipse. Sometimes, the Moon passes between the Earth and the Sun. The Moon blocks the light of the Sun and a shadow of the Moon is cast on the Earth's surface. This is an eclipse of the Sun, or a solar eclipse.	Definition Classification Cause and effect Definition Definition

Source: Adapted from http://starchild.gsfc.nasa.gov/docs/StarChild/questions/question6.html.

Text patterns can be used for single pieces of support, as the paragraph above demonstrates, or they can be used to structure an entire essay. A writer who wants to discuss the causes and effects of eclipses in more depth could devote an entire essay to the subject. In such an essay, the writer could use cause and effect as the basic text pattern for the entire text, elaborating on particular causes and effects in each paragraph, for instance.

In the pages that follow, you will learn how to use text patterns in two ways: as supporting details and as the organizational framework for your writing.

Narration

Narration is simply storytelling. Everyone likes a good story. That's why people who are good at writing speeches or sermons frequently add interesting stories to their texts. Have you ever wondered why we enjoy listening to stories? Sometimes the answer is that the stories themselves are simply fun to hear. Perhaps they are funny, or maybe they retell an event that people enjoy recounting.

Another reason we use narration is to make a point or teach a lesson. Aesop's fables are narratives that communicate moral principles. If you have read "The Tortoise and the Hare," you know that the point of the story is to not give up. Because of his persistence, the slow tortoise wins the race.

When writers use narratives, they often do so to make a point. Even if the writer does not explicitly tell readers the point, the narrative should. The narrative should be such a good story and so well told that readers intuitively understand the writer's point in using it. Writing a good story can be challenging. Not only must the story be compelling, but the writer must choose words carefully so that readers can infer meanings.

A political cartoon published on the cover of a July 1908 magazine shows William H. Taft, a Republican hare, racing William Jennings Bryan, a Democratic tortoise, for the presidency. The caption reads, "The Tortoise: If that chap only goes to sleep, I'll win out by a mile." What message was the artist sending with this depiction of a well-known fable? At the time, the artist could not have known that Taft would go on to win the presidential election.

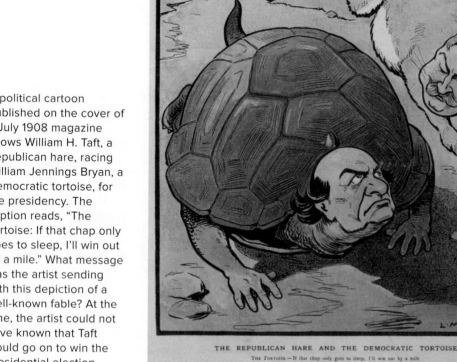

THE REPUBLICAN HARE AND THE DEMOCRATIC TORTOISE.
The Tortoise.—If that chap only goes to sleep, I'll win out by a mile.

Source: Library of Congress, Prints & Photographs Division, Reproduction number LC-DIG-ppmsca-26286 (digital file from original print)

Recognizing the Narration Pattern in Readings

Narrative essays usually present one story that is significant enough to be worthy of its own essay. In a narrative essay, the story *is* the sole content: it speaks for itself.

To identify the narration pattern in a text, look for these characteristics and key words.

CHARACTERISTICS OF THE NARRATION PATTERN

- A meaningful story is told.
- The story has a plot with a beginning, middle, and end.
- The story is told in first-person or third-person point of view.
- Chronological transitions are used to indicate the passing of time.
- Description is used to convey mood, develop characters, create settings, and convey information.

KEY WORDS FOR THE NARRATION PATTERN				
after	finally	initially	not long after	then
as soon as	first, second, third . . .	later	now	today
before	following	meanwhile	once	until
during	immediately	next	soon	when

Narration in Supporting Details

In academic writing, a narrative used as a supporting detail usually takes the form of an *anecdote*—a short, interesting story. Anecdotes are often used as a type of evidence. For example, a veterinarian may write an informative essay about what daily life is like for her. She would very likely use short narratives about different medical cases to help readers get a clear picture of what her days are like.

Narration can also provide a lesson, identify a truth about life, or help readers understand the seriousness of an issue. For example, a writer may tell the story of a soldier who overcomes war injuries to show how success over trauma is possible. Another writer might underscore the dangers of texting and driving with the stories of real people who have lost their lives because of this lethal combination of activities.

Personal stories might also be used as subjects for analysis. For example, researchers often want to analyze personal stories for their research. Hospital researchers may listen to patients' stories to analyze how they can improve their services. These stories can also be used to evaluate hospital programs and make changes. Personal stories and experiences can be valuable bits of research.

In addition to providing material for analysis and evaluation, stories can be persuasive. Suppose the US Congress is considering the passage of a stronger gun control law. Advocates for such a law would be likely to tell their personal stories of tragedy and loss to make their arguments more compelling. These stories can be effective in persuading members of Congress to vote for or against the proposed law.

Finally, short stories are sometimes used to introduce essays. For instance, a writer may use the story of a person who triumphed over obesity to start an essay about effective methods of weight loss. The partial outline that follows demonstrates how narrative can be used as a supporting detail in an essay.

Using Narration as a Supporting Detail

Topic: Why people should work on anger management

Thesis statement: Anger issues should be addressed because they can result in lost jobs, broken relationships, and even death.

INTRODUCTION

  Paragraph 1: Introduction

  Paragraph 2: How anger issues can result in lost jobs (tell Micah's story) . . .

Narration as a Text Pattern

When a writer has a long story that makes a point, the story becomes the focus of the entire essay. In such an essay, narrative is used as a text pattern.

To write a compelling narrative essay, you will need to find a story worth telling, a story that not only is meaningful to you but that you predict others will find meaningful. Remember that you are writing for a general audience. You may love NASCAR, but your readers may not. Similarly, the story of your wedding is probably not going to capture readers' interest unless something unusual happened. Think about the stories you enjoy hearing. What makes them enjoyable? Often these stories appeal to our curiosity about how other people live, help us imagine what being in a particular situation would be like, or describe events that we can relate to.

To use narrative as a text pattern, writers employ features that are common to all narratives. The **plot,** or structure, of the story usually has these elements:

- A beginning
- Rising action that leads to a **climax,** or high point in the action
- The climax itself (usually a conflict)
- Falling action that leads to a resolution of the conflict
- The resolution itself and the ending

Additionally, the narrative should include the details readers expect. Readers want to know information about the characters involved: How old are they? Where do they live? What are they like? Not knowing when an event happened, or not having a clear idea of the order of events in a story, can leave readers confused and dissatisfied. In narrative writing, it is important to include the details that contribute to a story's meaning but to exclude mundane or boring details.

Analyzing a Narrative Text

As you read the narrative essay that follows, "The Chosen One" by Laura Cunningham, see whether you can recognize some of the features of narrative writing. Cunningham's careful choices about plot, time order, details, and wording make her narrative essay particularly effective. As you read, notice the significant features of narrative writing that the annotations point out.

The Chosen One

By Laura Cunningham

A year ago, I boarded a flight to Shanghai during a gale force wind. The plane shivered and taxied back to the hangar twice before takeoff. It is testimony to my anxiety about the purpose of my journey that I felt no fear of flying. I carried with me an empty infant car bed (aptly named the Dream Ride), a three-week supply of diapers, wipes, pediatric antibiotics, bottles and disposable nipples. I was on my way to adopt one of the tens of thousands of baby girls abandoned in China each year.

Chronological transition: helps readers follow the story

Plot element: rising action

Today as I write, my 1-year-old daughter sleeps in a crib in the next room. She lies in the position of trust—on her back, her arms widespread, her face tip-tilted as if for the next kiss.

Chronological transition

A happy ending, so far, for my darling Chinese daughter, and for me. But the journey to Shanghai has somehow not ended. Many nights, I wake at 3 A.M.—yanked from my dream, my heart hammering alarms. At that silent, moonlit time, I remember my choice.

Foreshadowing: The writer jumps to the end of the story and then returns to tell the story from the beginning.

I am embarrassed now to recall the doubt that accompanied me to China. The orphanage had sent a fax (yes, in the new China, orphanages send faxes): "We have a baby for you. We would have taken her picture but it was too cold."

Chronological transition

My concern, if I can articulate the chill gut slide of panic as a "concern," was that somehow I would walk into the orphanage and fail to respond to the baby; that somehow she would not feel like "the right one." I would have to go ahead with the adoption out of momentum, some grim sense of decency, but without the hoped-for love at first sight.

Plot element: The conflict starts to build.

The baby, it seemed from the fax, was already chosen. And while I claimed to love all babies, in my secret, cowering heart I had to admit that I was more drawn to some babies than to others. It wasn't beauty or even intelligence that I required of a baby, but some sign of being, well, simpatico.

More conflict: expression of anxiety about adopting the right baby

I could not see her until the orphanage opened Monday morning. I had arrived in Shanghai on Saturday night. The interval was the high tide of my fear—suspense seemed hydraulic; blood rushed through me at unprecedented speed.

Until Monday I had only the ambiguous answers of Ms. Zhang, the orphanage's emissary who had greeted me at the airport. When I asked: "How old is the baby? How big?" Ms. Zhang answered only with another question:

"What size baby clothes have you brought with you?"

Her response raised some possibility of control, or at least influence. Maybe the baby was not yet chosen. In my sneaking secret chicken heart, I could still pick the best and the brightest star of abandoned baby girlhood in Shanghai.

Plot element: Story approaches its climax—seeing the baby and learning whether she has a choice.

Passing the time until I could meet "my baby," I met another baby at the hotel, already adopted by a single man. (China permits adoptions by foreigners, whether married or unmarried. Its adoption policy is unusual

Chronological transition

(continued)

in that citizens, as well as foreigners, must be at least 35 years old to adopt.) She struck me, however, as not meant to be my baby. She did seem just right for her new father, an American psychologist, who carried with him a sitcom's supply of baby paraphernalia.

Next, I went to the nearest tourist attraction, the Temple of the Jade Buddha, where there was said to be a Buddha to whom mothers pray for a good baby.

Chronological transition

The Buddha glowed in the dim temple. It wasn't jet lag that sent me reeling to my knees before the Buddha. Half-Jewish, half-Southern Baptist, all doubt, I knelt in truest prayer. Let the baby be one I can truly love.

At 9 sharp the next morning I waited in the orphanage, wearing my winter coat indoors (now I understood the fax). Even in midwinter there was no heat. Vapor rose from the thermoses of hot tea carried by the female employees. The translator announced that the baby was being carried in from the nursery building.

"You will have a choice," she said.

Plot element: start of the story's climax section. Notice that this very important sentence stands as its own paragraph.

I looked out the window as she pointed across a courtyard filled with dead bamboo and gray laundry. The window itself was grimy, but through it I saw two women in blue smocks, running toward me. Each held a bundle. There were two babies.

They were swaddled in comforters, their heads completely draped in towels. The first baby was unveiled. There was a staccato of Chinese, translated as: "Pick this one. She is more beautiful. She is more intelligent." Baby No. 1 was the nurses' favorite, a 2-month-old of unsurpassed good looks and robust health. She smiled.

But I could not take my eyes from the second baby, who was revealed almost as an afterthought. She was thin, piteous, a green-complexioned elf, with low-set ears that stuck out. She wheezed. In the pocket of my coat, I held a vial of antibiotics, carried on good advice from a friend.

Plot element: another crucial moment in the story's climax

I had no choice. The second baby was sick. I had medicine impossible to obtain here. I accepted the tiny green baby, gasping and oozing, into my arms. I noticed she also had a bald spot, from lying unmoved in her crib.

Climax: The writer makes a choice.

Shame over my earlier indecision blew from the room like the fetid draft of disease and poverty.

Was it love at first sight? I knew in that instant that we were at the start of our life together.

Love overtakes you at odd moments. I was trying to collect a urine sample, required for a medical test. I held her, her little purple fanny over a rice bowl, in my arms all night. I drew the blankets around us both as a tent to keep away the cold. We waited, silently, all night, until she took a literal "tinkle." Her eyes met mine, on the other side of the world, and I knew Little-Miss-Ears-Stick-Out, With-Tears-in-Her-Eyes was mine, all right.

Plot element: Falling action begins. **Chronological transition**

Within 24 hours, the medicine had taken effect: she turned ivory pink; her eyes cleared. She was beyond my dreams, exquisite, a luminous old soul with contemporary wit. I gazed at her and saw the fatefulness of every mother's choice. It is not the beautiful baby who is chosen, but the chosen baby who becomes beautiful.

Thesis statement: the moral of the story

(continued)

To enter a house filled with unwanted babies is to pass through a door that you can never shut. At 3 A.M., I see the others—the aisles of green cribs holding bundled babies. I try to close my eyes to them, but they refuse to disappear. They are lying there. They are cold; they are damp. I see one baby girl especially. She had an odd genetic defect: the skin of her body was coal black, but her face had no color. She looked as if she were wearing the white theatrical mask of tragedy.

Last Christmas, I was able to choose the green, sick baby over the laughing, healthy one. Would I have had the courage to take one of the others? Would someone? I wake up and see the small faces. They are lying there waiting, waiting to be chosen.

Plot element: resolution. Notice that the resolution leaves readers not totally satisfied. This is intentional.

Source: Cunningham, Laura, "The Chosen One." © 1994 by Laura Cunningham. Reprinted by permission of the author. New York Times Magazine, April 17, 1994.

PRACTICE

Analyzing a Narrative Text

On a separate sheet, answer the following questions about "The Chosen One" by Laura Cunningham.

1. Do you believe this story would be enjoyed by a wide variety of people? If so, why? What are the features that make it appealing? If not, why not? Explain.

2. The writer does not present the story in straight chronological order. Review the story and describe the order in which Cunningham relates the events.

3. What do you think Cunningham means when she writes that her baby appeared "a luminous old soul with contemporary wit"?

4. Cunningham uses figurative language to make her writing vivid and interesting. For instance, she says she is looking for "the brightest star of abandoned baby girlhood." Find two additional passages that use language in a nonliteral way. For each passage, write a few sentences explaining the effect Cunningham's words may have on readers.

5. In what way does the end of the story *not* present a perfect resolution? Why is the tone at the end of the essay not joyous? Explain in a paragraph.

Using Narration in Your Writing

The following steps can guide you through writing your own narrative essay.

1. **Select a story suitable for your narrative essay.** The story you choose for your essay is the most important element of this assignment. You may use a story in which you were involved, or you may tell a story about someone else. Above all, find a story that a general audience will enjoy. Many stories that we personally find entertaining might make a general audience ready for a good long nap. Here are some examples of the types of stories that may be interesting to a general audience.

   - **Stories about ordinary events (like a graduation ceremony or the birth of a child) if the event is unusual in some way.** *Interesting example:* Your high school graduation night when you had a near-fatal car accident. *Not so interesting:* Your high school graduation night when you went to a party with your friends.

- **Stories that tap into something most people are curious about.** *Interesting example:* What it is like to live in a house you believe is haunted. *Not so interesting:* How you rented your first apartment.
- **Stories about something that could happen to the reader but is rare enough to be compelling.** *Interesting example:* What it is like to work in a funeral home. *Not so interesting:* What it is like to work in a clothing store.
- **Stories that give the reader insight into your unique world.** *Interesting example:* How you learned to live with a disability or chronic disease. *Not so interesting:* How you and your sister fight all the time.
- **Stories you find compelling enough to remember.** *Interesting example:* Dad's encounter with a crocodile in Australia. *Not so interesting:* How you found a baby bird on a sidewalk.
- **Stories you yourself would like to read.** *Interesting example:* A story about the variety of cases you have seen in your job as an emergency room technician. *Not so interesting:* A story about how you met and fell in love with your significant other.

2. **Determine the order in which to tell your story.** *How* you tell the story can help readers experience the story in a particular way. Use the order of events to set up tension, anxiety, or any other emotion you would like readers to experience. Sometimes, writers use **foreshadowing**—a hint about events to come in a narrative—to keep readers' interest. Early on in "The Chosen One," the author gives us a clue to how her story resulted in a "happy ending," but we must read to the end of the story to find out what happened.

3. **Create a simple narrative plan, or outline.** Include your thesis statement in your plan. Decide on the major events of the story and the order in which you will tell them, and create a simple outline like the one that follows. Use plot elements—beginning, rising action, climax, falling action, resolution—to structure your narrative.

A Simple Outline for a Narrative Pattern Essay

Thesis statement: Meeting my birth parents was the fulfillment of a dream I have had for a long time. At the same time, it was entirely depressing.

INTRODUCTION: Provide background
Rising action:

- Details about my adoption
- Description of my good life with my adopted family and my persistent longing to meet my birth parents
- Arrangement to meet my birth parents when I turned nineteen
- Anxiety and expectations

Climax: The disappointing encounter with my birth parents

Falling action: The flight back home and the thoughts I had

Conclusion (resolution): Final thoughts

4. **Use creative wording. Figures of speech**—imaginative comparisons between different things—can help readers understand the ideas you wish to convey. For example, instead of just telling readers a room is cold, comparing the room to a meat locker would more effectively convey the same idea. Several figures of speech in particular are useful for writers: personification, metaphor, and simile.

Figure of Speech	Definition	Example
Personification	Attributing human qualities to nonhuman things	*The butterflies danced among the flowers.*
Metaphor	Comparing two unlike things	*Her life is a constant soap opera.*
Simile	Using *like* or *as* to compare two unlike things	*My favorite chair is like a big marshmallow.*

5. **Use descriptive details to create the story's setting.** Descriptive language provides sensory information for readers. By using description, readers can imagine what something looks, sounds, smells, tastes, or feels like. In narrative writing, description helps readers understand characters better. It also helps writers convey a particular mood. For instance, description may convey a sense of eeriness or a sense of peacefulness. Writers also depend on description to create the setting of a story and to render the plot events in a story effectively. In "The Chosen One," Cunningham uses this description, "the tiny green baby, gasping and oozing," to convey the baby's fragility, sickliness, and even lack of appeal.

6. **Make intentional decisions about details and pace.** Cunningham left out details that were mundane so that her story would move at the perfect pace to keep her readers interested. Ask yourself whether the details in your story are necessary. Include details that add value but do not bog down its pace. Use chronological transitions so that readers can keep track of time.

7. **Be very careful about how you word your thesis statement and where you place it.** The thesis statement should not interrupt the narrative. Sometimes placing the thesis statement in the conclusion is an effective strategy for narrative writing since the thesis statement might give away the story's ending if it is placed earlier.

PRACTICE ●

Using Narration in Your Writing

Use the preceding steps to write a narrative essay. Choose one of the following topics, or select your own.

A. Write about a time you witnessed someone acting especially kindly—or especially cruelly—toward another person.

B. Think of an event from your childhood that had an impact on you. Write a brief narrative detailing the event and your feelings about it.

C. Relate a story that your family particularly enjoys retelling. The story might concern something funny that happened, or it might recount a traumatic event that ended well, for example.

If none of these topics appeals to you, come up with your own topic for a narrative essay. Ask classmates or your instructor to give you an honest prediction of how interested (or uninterested) a general audience might be in the story you propose.

Grammar Focus

Verb Tense Choices

As a writer, you must choose the verb tense you will use to convey information. Verbs express more than the action that happens in a sentence. Verb tenses tell when the action takes place—past, present, or future. For example, in each of the following sentences the tense of the underlined verb expresses the timing of the nurse's action.

(continued)

Past: Earlier this morning, the nurse <u>examined</u> the patients' charts.

Present: The nurse always <u>examines</u> the patients' charts at 10 a.m.

Future: Tomorrow morning the nurse <u>will examine</u> the patients' charts.

Even without the phrases *Earlier this morning* and *Tomorrow morning,* readers would know which action already happened (past) and which action will happen (future) because of the verb tense.

For the most part, verbs in a text should remain consistent in tense, although there are places where tenses can change. Follow these guidelines to select the best tense for the information you are conveying.

1. USE PAST TENSE FOR NARRATIVE

Most narratives recount events that have happened. So when writers tell a story, they most commonly use past tense. Note this example from Laura Cunningham's "The Chosen One."

> **Example:** "A year ago, I <u>boarded</u> a flight to Shanghai during a gale force wind. The plane <u>shivered</u> and <u>taxied</u> back to the hangar twice before takeoff."

Present tense is less useful for narratives and is best avoided. If we substitute present tense in the Cunningham quote, the passage is confusing. An essential element of the story is expressed in the phrase *A year ago,* but the present tense verbs conflict with that phrase.

> **Faulty:** A year ago, I <u>board</u> a flight to Shanghai during a gale force wind. The plane <u>shivers</u> and <u>taxies</u> back to the hangar twice before takeoff.

For most verbs, we add *-ed* to the present tense to form the past tense. Some verbs, however, have special forms for the past tense: for example, *bring/brought, drink/drank, eat/ate, feel/felt, is/was, think/thought.* Still others keep the same form in the present and past tenses: for example, *cost/cost, cut/cut, hit/hit.* Consult a dictionary if you are unsure of the past tense form for a verb.

2. USE PRESENT TENSE FOR MOST ACADEMIC WRITING

For almost all academic writing, present tense is the correct tense, even when you are writing about the views of a person who died hundreds of years ago. Note the present tense used in this quotation from *Physical Science,* by Bill W. Tillery.

> **Example:** "Newton's first law of motion <u>is</u> also <u>known</u> as the law of inertia and <u>is</u> very similar to one of Galileo's findings about motion."

Source: Tillery, Bill W. *Physical Science,* 9th Edition. New York: McGraw-Hill Education.

However, when the goal is to compare historical events or beliefs, use past tense, as in this excerpt from *American Authors in the Nineteenth Century.*   *(continued)*

Example: "In the nineteenth century, social changes and the rise of new media <u>revolutionized</u> the way people <u>discovered</u> and <u>read</u> literature. As a result, the audience for American literature <u>grew</u> tremendously, and many authors <u>became</u> celebrities."

Another exception is the use of past tense to describe research processes or studies. Notice the verb tenses in this quotation from "Detroit Exposure and Aerosol Research Study" on the US Environmental Protection Agency's Web site.

Example: "The Detroit Exposure and Aerosol Research Study <u>was</u> a three-year study conducted by the U.S. Environmental Protection Agency (EPA). Its primary objective <u>was</u> to investigate the relationship of select air pollutant concentrations and their sources measured at community air monitoring stations in comparison to those measured in various neighborhoods in Wayne County, Michigan."

3. AVOID UNNECESSARY SHIFTS IN TENSE

Generally, verbs should remain in the same tense throughout a passage. Notice how the shifts in tense in this example are unnecessary and even confusing. In the first sentence, the verbs are in the present tense (*claims, change, processes*), while the verbs in the second sentence are in both the past tense (*wrote*) and the present tense (*act*).

Faulty shift in tense: Margaret Trent <u>claims</u> that social media <u>change</u> the way the brain <u>processes</u> information. She <u>wrote</u> that social media <u>act</u> as "catalysts of neural development."

Corrected: Margaret Trent <u>claims</u> that social media <u>change</u> the way the brain <u>processes</u> information. She <u>writes</u> that social media <u>act</u> as "catalysts of neural development."

Sometimes shifts in tense are acceptable or even necessary, such as when a writer changes from a narrative to another type of writing. Consider this passage from *Physical Science* by Bill W. Tillery. It incorporates the initial sentence we quoted earlier as an example of present tense in academic writing.

Example: "Newton's first law of motion <u>is</u> also <u>known</u> as the law of inertia and <u>is</u> very similar to one of Galileo's findings about motion. Recall that Galileo <u>used</u> the term inertia to describe the tendency of an object to resist changes in motion. Newton's first law <u>describes</u> this tendency more directly."

Source: Tillery, Bill W. *Physical Science*, 9th Edition. New York: McGraw-Hill Education.

Notice that the writer uses mostly present tense (*is known, is, describes*) but switches, appropriately, to past tense (*used*) to explain a historical event.

SENTENCE COMBINING

The example that follows shows how to take sentences that use a variety of tenses, combine them to make smoother and longer sentences, and correct the verb tenses for consistency and appropriateness.

(continued)

Ideas to combine and correct:

- Benjamin Franklin is a scientist and a writer.
- He wrote *Poor Richard's Almanac.*
- He was known for his autobiography.
- Franklin signed the three most important documents of the revolutionary era: the Declaration of Independence, the peace treaty with Britain that ended the Revolutionary War, and the Constitution.
- He is the only person to sign all three.

Consistent and appropriate verb tenses: Benjamin Franklin, a scientist and a writer, wrote *Poor Richard's Almanac* and is known for his autobiography. Franklin also was the only person to sign the three most important documents of the revolutionary era: the Declaration of Independence, the peace treaty with Britain that ended the Revolutionary War, and the Constitution.

EXERCISES

Combine each set of sentences to make smoother, longer ones. Change verb tenses as necessary for consistency and appropriateness. You may change the wording as much as you like as long as you communicate the same ideas.

1. Ideas to combine and correct:
   - I stepped onto the train.
   - From the moment I did, I felt something was not right.
   - An older woman was bundled from head to toe in black.
   - She stares at my old suitcase.
   - "That's my suitcase!" she exclaimed loudly.

   Answer: _____

   _____

   _____

2. Ideas to combine and correct:
   - Werner Heisenberg was a German theoretical physicist.
   - He discovered the Uncertainty Principle.
   - The Uncertainty Principle concerns subatomic particles.
   - It claimed that we can know the position of a particle or its momentum, but not both.

   Answer: _____

   _____

   _____

3. Ideas to combine and correct:
   - The federal law will affect each state.
   - It will require each state to offer free preschool education.
   - According to the law, any child in a school district will be eligible to attend preschool in the district.

   Answer: _____

   _____

   _____

Definition

To *define* is to express the meaning of a term or concept. In textbooks, you will often come across definitions that briefly explain the meaning of a word. These short definitions are a type of support that enable the writer to continue making a larger point.

Other texts, however, focus primarily on defining a term or concept. As a text pattern, **definition** implies going beyond dictionary explanations and providing a more meaningful or important interpretation. For example, a writer may create an entire essay to explain his personal definition of what it is to be a good parent. Such essays use definition, sometimes called *extended definition,* as a text pattern, not merely as a supporting detail.

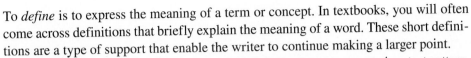

Recognizing the Definition Pattern in Readings

Both uses of definition share some characteristics and key words.

CHARACTERISTICS OF THE DEFINITION PATTERN

- A term or phrase is defined.
- When used as support, a sentence provides a definition. Explanatory sentences may follow.
- When used as a text pattern, the thesis statement concerns the definition in question. Body paragraphs help support the writer's point about the definition.

KEY WORDS FOR THE DEFINITION PATTERN			
consists of	idea	is known as	redefine
define	involves	meaning of	refers to
entails	is characterized by	means	term

Definition in Supporting Details

As a type of support, definitions may appear in any paragraph in an essay. Whenever readers may need help understanding a term or concept, a writer may insert a simple definition. For example, a writer may wish to convince readers that the United States needs to invest more time and effort into safeguarding the Internet. One of the writer's reasons may be that cyberterrorism is a real and dangerous threat. Knowing that not all readers will understand what cyberterrorism is, the writer may define the term and provide an example of how cyberterrorism works. The partial outline that follows shows where a writer may use a definition as a type of support.

Using Definition as a Supporting Detail

Topic: Safeguarding the Internet

Thesis statement: The United States needs to invest more time and effort in safeguarding the Internet.

(continued)

INTRODUCTION

    Paragraph 1

BODY

    Paragraph 2: One of the most serious problems the Internet poses is cyberterrorism.

- Definition: Cyberterrorism is . . .
- An example of cyberterrorism is . . .
- Explanation of example

    Paragraph 3: The reason cyberterrorism is such a threat is . . .

Definition as a Text Pattern

When definition is used as the focus of an essay, it becomes a text pattern. Writers use the definition text pattern for a variety of reasons. First, definition is helpful in explaining new concepts or terms. For example, not all readers know what urban legends are; thus, a writer may help readers get a clear understanding of urban legends by writing an essay that offers an extended definition.

Second, definition allows writers to create their own, unique meanings for terms or concepts. Phrases such as *common sense* or *the American dream* mean different things to different people. A writer may create his own definition of one of these expressions and present it using the definition text pattern.

Third, definition enables writers to analyze the various ways a particular term or concept has been defined. For example, in the history of law, the term *temporary insanity* has been defined differently over time.

And finally, definition is useful for arguing that an ambiguous or controversial term should be defined in a particular way. Some definition essays focus on defining debatable terms or concepts such as *torture*.

An essay that uses a definition text pattern will have a thesis statement that presents the writer's point about the definition. The body paragraphs will include supporting details that work together to convey the writer's point about the definition. The outline that follows shows definition being used as a text pattern. In the example, the writer is presenting her own definition of *family,* and she wants to persuade readers that her definition is sound.

A Simple Outline for a Definition Pattern Essay

Topic: Defining *family*

Thesis statement: A family is a group of people who are committed to and love one another.

INTRODUCTION

    Paragraph 1: How some people and institutions have defined family narrowly

    Paragraph 2: Thesis statement—writer's definition of *family*

(continued)

BODY

Paragraph 3: First characteristic—family members are committed to one another

Paragraph 4: Additional definition—what *committed* means

Paragraph 5: Examples of committed families—nuclear family, single-parent family, nontraditional family

Paragraph 6: Second characteristic—family members *love* one another

Paragraph 7: Additional definition—what *love* means in a family context

Paragraph 8: Examples of families that demonstrate love—nuclear family, single-parent family, nontraditional family

CONCLUSION

Paragraph 9: Why defining the family in a broad way is good for society

Analyzing a Definition Text

In "What I Really Meme Is . . . Anatomy of a Happenin' Thing," author Mary Ann Bell defines a term that is unfamiliar to many people: *meme.* Because the concept of memes is complex, Bell has written an entire essay on the topic. We will examine the components of her essay.

A Definition Text: Introduction and Thesis Statement

Definition texts often begin with an introduction to the term or concept being defined. Bell starts her essay with a definition from *Wikipedia* and then elaborates on that definition.

Introduction Paragraph of "What I Really Meme Is . . . Anatomy of a Happenin' Thing" by Mary Ann Bell

Not long ago, I was relaxing in the den with my daughter and a friend of hers. Out of the blue, my daughter asked, "What is a meme anyway? I keep hearing about them and don't know what they are!" Her friend, a creative writing major, exchanged looks with me. We both knew what the word meant but found it hard to explain. "Well, a meme is, uh," I started. "Never mind!" she replied, "I'll Google it!" Of course, the first hit was from Wikipedia. Also not a surprise, the description there was spot on. Here is what she read to us: A meme is "an idea, behavior or style that spreads from person to person within a culture." It occurred to me that if the three of us with six university degrees between us could not come up with a good definition, then there might be others out there hazy on the concept too—hence, this column.

Thesis statement: The essay starts with a definition from *Wikipedia* and goes on to explain the definition.

Source: Bell, Mary Ann, "What I Really Meme Is . . . Anatomy of a Happenin' Thing," *Internet@* Schools, Vol. 20, Issue 2 (March/April 2013). 24–25. © Copyright 2013 Information Today, Inc. Reprinted with permission.

A Definition Text: Body Paragraphs and Their Organization

Body paragraphs provide information about the definition the writer is proposing. Writers can include many different types of information in the body paragraphs of definition essays. Here are just a few ways writers can elaborate on and provide support for definition texts:

- Dictionary definition of term or concept
- Competing definitions
- History of term or concept
- Example
- Explanation
- Comparison
- Description
- Characteristics

In her article on memes, Mary Ann Bell writes body paragraphs that provide examples, explanations, additional definitions, and historical information about the term.

Body Paragraphs of "What I Really Meme Is . . . Anatomy of a Happenin' Thing" by Mary Ann Bell

One of the easiest and most tempting ways to define "meme" is to offer examples. The ones most readily recognized are those from popular culture. Here are some recent examples that keep cropping up on social networking sites such as Facebook:

- LOLCats/I can has cheezburger?
- Binders of women
- Gangnam-style dancing
- Call me maybe?
- Hey girl (featuring Ryan Gosling)
- Sad Big Bird

In today's social networking environment, the potential is tremendous for an idea, trend, rumor, meme, or anything catchy to spread very quickly. This is the phenomenon we call "going viral," and it is happening every day. Memes can rise up spontaneously or can be intentionally launched. The day after the second presidential debate in 2012, the phrase "binders of women" and iterations thereof spread overnight across the Internet.

Another meme from the campaign is what I call "Sad Big Bird." During the first presidential debate, Mitt Romney said that PBS's funding should be cut to reduce the deficit, even though he "loved Big Bird" as much as anybody. And so, with lightning speed we were treated to pictures of Big Bird standing in welfare lines, looking dejected with friends, and, in general, tugging at the heartstrings of PBS/Sesame Street fans. People wearing Big Bird suits started showing up at campaign rallies. There were people who admitted they remembered very little from the debate other than the threat to off Big Bird.

Similarly this past year, Gangnam-style dancing went viral. And it goes without saying that gorgeous pictures of actor Ryan Gosling, a library fan,

Examples: elaboration of the definition

Another example

More examples
(continued)

offering various completions to the line "Hey girl . . ." are loved by librarians. You can see the collection of these pictures on the site called Hey Girl. I Like the Library Too (librarianheygirl.tumblr.com).

Memes such as these are visual and have a picture or video as the focal point. From these, captions and knockoffs abound. Some hang around for years, such as LOLCats, while others are relatively short-lived. My guess is that "binders of women" will not last far beyond the next months, as the campaign and Mitt Romney's candidacy fade from popular memory. But I am hoping Ryan Gosling does not go away for a very long time.

Who Said That?

How long has this been going on? The term "meme" is actually a coined one, which makes me think it might make it an example of its own definition. As a matter of fact, this term can be tracked back to its originator, Richard Dawkins, and he is alive and well and following memes to this day.

	History of the term and concept

Here is a quotation from an article where he explains: "Our cultural life is full of things that seem to propagate virus-like from one mind to another: tunes, ideas, catch-phrases, fashions, ways of making pots or building arches. In 1976 I coined the word meme (rhymes with cream) for these self-replicating units of culture that have a life of their own." . . .

Remembering back to 1976 and forward, I can think of a number of memes that are still lodged in my brain and, perhaps, in yours as well, if your age allows you to remember that far into the past. One example that I remember in particular is the use and overuse of the phrase "Where's the beef?" The meme stems from TV commercials starring a loveable old lady trying to find a decent meat patty in a fast-food hamburger and promoting Wendy's restaurants. Like all good memes, this one has its own Wikipedia article.

Quotation: traces term to its origin and offers another definition
Examples that go further back in history

A Definition Text: Conclusion

Once the definition of the term or concept has been thoroughly explained and supported, writers conclude their essays. Mary Ann Bell concludes by calling attention to the fact that memes are constantly changing and evolving.

Conclusion Paragraph of "What I Really Meme Is . . . Anatomy of a Happenin' Thing" by Mary Ann Bell

Since the advent of the Internet, the sources, subjects, and recipients have increased exponentially. By making it so easy to combine, change, personalize, and otherwise adapt Internet postings, memes now grow and evolve in countless iterations that can go their merry ways, further mutating along the way.

More explanation: how memes reproduce and mutate

PRACTICE

Analyzing a Definition Text

On a separate sheet, answer the following questions about "What I Really Meme Is . . . Anatomy of a Happenin' Thing" by Mary Ann Bell.

1. What is the purpose of the article?

2. After reading her definition of *meme,* do you have a good understanding of what memes are? If so, what type of body content helped you understand the best? Examples? Explanations? History? Explain. If not, what else could Bell have included to help you understand more clearly?

3. What does Bell mean when she says that memes evolve and change over time?

4. Without looking back at Bell's article, define *meme* in your own words. Provide an example that Bell did not include in her article, if you can think of one.

Using Definition in Your Writing

When your task is to present the meaning of a term or concept, you can use the definition text pattern to structure your writing. The following guidelines can help you through the process of using definition in your writing.

1. Select a topic, and determine your purpose for writing. If you are choosing your own topic for an essay, consider defining a term that may be new to readers, as Mary Ann Bell did when she defined *meme.* Choose a term that will interest readers.

Another approach to finding a topic is to think about terms whose meanings are debated. For example, what does it mean to be *moral*? How do you define *adultery*? You can also choose to define terms that are not necessarily debatable but tend to be defined in personal ways. For example, what does *physical beauty* mean to you? What does *success* mean to you?

If your instructor gives you a term to define, you can move to the next step, determining your writing purpose. Does your assignment tell you whether you are writing to inform, analyze, evaluate, or persuade? Do you want to persuade readers that your definition is the best? Do you want to analyze the way the word has been defined throughout history? Once you are certain about the purpose of the assignment, you can make specific decisions about how you will define the term or concept.

2. Start your prewriting by creating a formal definition that includes term, class, and characteristic. The **term** is the word you are defining, the **class** is the category into which the word fits, and the **characteristic** is simply the quality of the term on which you are focusing, as in the "Definition Model" diagram.

DEFINITION MODEL

1 [DEFINED TERM] Freedom   *is*   **2** [CLASS] a right   *that*   **3** [CHARACTERISTIC] comes with responsibilities

Here are two more examples:

Friendship is a kind of relationship that endures through the ups and downs of life.
term   class   characteristic

A solar panel is a technological device used to generate electricity from the sun's heat.
term   class   characteristic

We can expect that an essay using the definition of *friendship* shown above will give the reader evidence about how friends stand by one another through difficult times.

3. Consider describing the history or background of the term. Unless you are writing a historical analysis, this part of your essay need not be long or extensive. Including a bit of history can make your essay more interesting and can sometimes provide helpful background information. Give credit to any sources you use.

4. Consider using negation in your definition. Negation is a way of defining a term by including an explanation of what the term is *not*. Here is an example from Berkeley's Greater Good Web site:

> Psychologists generally define forgiveness as a conscious, deliberate decision to release feelings of resentment or vengeance toward a person or group who has harmed you, regardless of whether they actually deserve your forgiveness.
>
> Just as important as defining what forgiveness *is*, though, is understanding what forgiveness is *not*. Experts who study or teach forgiveness make clear that when you forgive, you do not gloss over or deny the seriousness of an offense against you. Forgiveness does not mean forgetting, nor does it mean condoning or excusing offenses.

Notice how the definition by negation in the second paragraph of the example helps us understand some of what the author means by *forgiveness*.

5. Determine how you will support your extended definition. Some ideas are providing examples of the way the term has been (or is being) used, citing experts about their definitions of the term, and offering reasons why your definition is appropriate or superior to others. Many types of support can be used to help you make your point. Remember, a definition essay will include a definition, but it will also rely on other support to convey your message.

6. Check your definition for circularity. A **circular definition** includes the term being defined and does not elucidate or clarify meaning.

Ineffective: A Senate committee is a committee composed of members of the Senate.

Effective: A Senate committee is a group of current senators that has specific responsibilities—for example, drafting legislation—regarding a particular area, such as the Armed Services.

7. Write a thesis statement, and construct a simple outline. Remember that although your focus is to define a term, you will need to include support in body paragraphs. The support you choose will help you establish your definition or make your point about the word you are defining.

Using Definition in Your Writing

Use definition as a supporting point in a paragraph and as a text pattern for an essay by completing these two assignments.

1. Write a paragraph in which you define what *social media* means. Provide examples to help readers understand your definition.

2. Use the definition text pattern to write an essay on one of the topics below. Use the Quick Start Guide to Integrated Reading and Writing Assignments for assistance.

   - Define what it means to be educated.

   - Define *egocentrism*. (Note: This definition will require the use of sources. Consult the Quick Start Guide for information about giving credit to every source you use.)

   - Define *freedom of speech*. Provide examples of what the concept means and what it does not mean.

Illustration

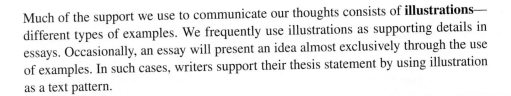

Much of the support we use to communicate our thoughts consists of **illustrations**—different types of examples. We frequently use illustrations as supporting details in essays. Occasionally, an essay will present an idea almost exclusively through the use of examples. In such cases, writers support their thesis statement by using illustration as a text pattern.

Recognizing the Illustration Pattern in Readings

Whether used as a supporting detail or as a text pattern, illustration can be identified by its characteristics and key words.

CHARACTERISTICS OF THE ILLUSTRATION PATTERN

- Illustrations are often used with vague, complex, or broad ideas that are hard to understand.
- Illustrations are more concrete and specific than the ideas they explain.
- Illustrations may appear as examples, visual aids, sample quotes, sample statistics, or other concrete samples.
- Illustrations that are examples can be true or hypothetical.
- Illustrations are often followed by explanations.

KEY WORDS FOR THE ILLUSTRATION PATTERN			
consider	imagine	such as	to clarify
for example	like	support	to explain
for instance			

Illustration in Supporting Details

Illustrations are commonly used as support in essays of all sorts and for all purposes. Any time a concept could be made easier to understand with an example, a graphic, or a sample of some sort, it is appropriate to use illustration. Here is an example of an illustration (underlined) used in an informative text:

> Having the right tools on hand makes the process of completing a difficult task easier. For example, if you are moving everything you own across town, renting an appliance dolly will make moving day less burdensome.

Illustrations can also be actual visuals—graphs, charts, tables, photos, and drawings. Here is an example of an illustration accompanied by a graph in a persuasive text. Note that an explanation of the graph helps readers understand the illustration's significance.

One reason for the decline in sales is that a new superstore opened down the street, as the accompanying graph shows. After the competition's superstore was built in 2008, sales profitability dropped from a high of $3.9 million in 2008 to below $2 million in 2013.

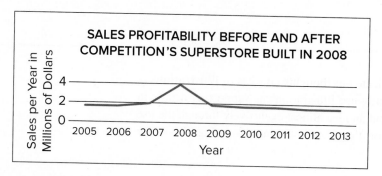

The partial outline that follows includes an example (underlined) as an illustration of the writer's point.

Using Illustration as a Supporting Detail

BODY

Paragraph 1: One of the most serious problems the Internet poses is cyberterrorism.

- Definition: Cyberterrorism is . . .
- <u>An example of cyberterrorism is</u> . . .
- Explanation of example

Paragraph 2: The reason cyberterrorism is such a threat is . . .

Illustration as a Text Pattern

Usually, illustration is used as a type of support in an essay rather than as the text pattern for an entire essay. However, writers sometimes depend on illustrations as primary support for their ideas. While writers may use graphic illustrations, written illustrations are often simply examples. Examples can be taken from the real world or they can be hypothetical.

A **hypothetical example** is one that a writer makes up; it is fictional. As an educated guess, a hypothetical example is based on things that could very likely happen. Even though it is fictional, the example must be realistic: it must portray something that would be typical or likely, not something unlikely to happen.

The type of illustration used depends on the writer's purpose. In an essay whose purpose is to analyze or evaluate, illustrations would likely come from the idea or object being analyzed. For instance, an essay that analyzes a new type of smartphone and evaluates its worth would include examples of the smartphone's features. A writer might analyze the apps built into the phone and provide an example of one of them, or the writer might include a photo as an illustration of the phone's sleek profile.

In persuasive writing, illustrations can be used as proof. Suppose a writer wants to prove that studying math in college results in real-life benefits. One way to prove this point would be to provide specific examples of how mathematical knowledge benefits us in life.

The outline that follows demonstrates how a writer can use illustration as a text pattern for an essay by making illustrations (underlined) the primary method for supporting the thesis statement.

A Simple Outline for an Illustration Pattern Essay

Topic: Choosing a career

Thesis statement: One way to choose a career is to find one that is personally interesting, that harmonizes with one's personality, and that fits one's lifestyle.

INTRODUCTION

    Paragraph 1: Introduction and thesis statement

BODY

    Paragraph 2: In general, the best way to start analyzing careers is to consider personal interests and to find careers that match them.

- Job satisfaction tied to interest
- Chart: shows job satisfaction is tied to interest level
- Anecdote: Leah's choice to quit teaching and open a restaurant
- Need to think creatively about potential jobs
- Example: interest in art, could consider merchandising, industrial painting, even cake decorating or making prosthetics

    Paragraph 3: While a satisfying career will be personally interesting, it should also be a good fit for one's personality.

- Consider whether you like working with people.
- Explanation: introvert/extrovert
- Anecdote: Maddie's first job didn't match her personality.
- Examples: good fit for introverts—programmer, writer, chemist
- Examples: good fit for extroverts—activity director, salesperson, trainer

    Paragraph 4: Finally, finding a fulfilling career requires choosing a job that matches one's lifestyle preferences.

- Examples of lifestyle issues: traveling, hours of work per week, flexibility
- Anecdote: Andre's story about traveling
- Quote: Andre
- Example of lifestyle fit: Cara's flexible job/parenting

CONCLUSION

    Paragraph 5: Concluding thoughts

Notice that the essay will include lots of examples, as well as a chart that illustrates a point, anecdotes used as illustrations, and a quote from Andre, a person whose career choices are used as an illustration.

Analyzing an Illustration Text

What follows is a reading selection, "Subliminal Persuasion," that appears in *Contemporary Advertising,* a textbook by William Arens, Michael Weigold, and Christian Arens. In this selection, the writers use illustration as a text pattern.

An Illustration Text: Introduction and Thesis Statement

The writers start with an example related to the topic, subliminal persuasion. In professional essays, writers may use multiple paragraphs to introduce the topic. In this essay, the introduction—consisting of the long example—spans several paragraphs.

Introduction Paragraphs of "Subliminal Persuasion" by William Arens, Michael Weigold, and Christian Arens

Imagine you could inject an ad message directly into people's minds, bypassing ordinary perception. Consumers would be unable to challenge or ignore your communication—because they would never notice it in the first place. Incredibly, in 1957 James Vicary claimed he had such a technique. The market researcher said that during a movie he had flashed the phrases "Drink Coca-Cola" and "Hungry? Eat popcorn" subliminally (shown the words so quickly people could not detect them). In response, he claimed, sales of popcorn and Coke shot up by 18 percent and 58 percent, respectively.

Illustration—an example of subliminal messaging

As psychologist Anthony Pratkanis notes, "People were outraged and frightened by a technique so devilish that it could bypass their conscious intellect and beam subliminal commands directly to their subconscious." Great Britain and Australia subsequently banned subliminal advertising, and the FCC threatened to revoke the license of any TV station that showed subliminal ads.

Public concern abated when Vicary could not reproduce his effects under supervised tests. He later admitted making them up. But fascination with subliminal advertising reappeared in the early 70s when Wilson Bryan Key published books that claimed to find the word *sex* in hundreds of ads, seeing them in ice cubes from a gin ad and on the surface of a Ritz cracker! And while almost nobody else could see these "embeds," Key sold plenty of books.

Discussion of the illustration

Truth is, not one proven instance where an advertiser has used a subliminal message exists. In fact, doesn't the whole idea seem pretty ridiculous? How can you be influenced by a message that you can't detect? To act on a communication you must understand it, and to understand it you must see it. But the idea of a subliminal message is that you can't see it (otherwise it isn't subliminal). Case closed.

Well, not quite. It helps to separate subliminal advertising (demonstrating that a real advertiser has affected product sales with a hidden message embedded in a commercial) from subliminal influence (demonstrating that people can be affected by a hidden message). Current evidence is conclusive: People can be influenced subliminally.

Thesis statement

Source: Arens, William F., et al., *Contemporary Advertising*, 4th ed. McGraw-Hill Education. 248–49. Used with permission of McGraw-Hill Education; Pratkanis, Anthony R., "The Cargo-Cult Science of Subliminal Persuasion," *Skeptical Inquirer* 16(3), Spring 1992.

As you can see, illustrations are often followed by explanations. Readers need to know *why* they are reading about a particular example, and explanations tie the example to the broader point—the thesis statement or topic sentence—the writer is making.

An Illustration Text: Body Paragraphs and Their Organization

Examples and explanations are the staples of illustration texts. Notice how the body paragraphs consist primarily of these features.

Body Paragraphs of "Subliminal Persuasion" by William Arens, Michael Weigold, and Christian Arens

Demonstrating subliminal influence requires a couple of things. First, you have to present the message (a picture, word, or phrase) so quickly that people can't tell it was there. Psychologists say that something shown for 120 milliseconds (0.12 of a second) or less is undetectable. Second, it has to be proven that the message influences people in some way. For example, a group shown a subliminal message must do something different from a control group that doesn't get the subliminal message.

Dozens of credible research studies have now reported such demonstrations. Consider just one example: A group of researchers wondered what would happen if people who are snake phobic are subliminally presented with a picture of a snake. Phobics typically begin sweating and become anxious when they see a snake photograph, whereas most people are fine. So what happens if snake photos are presented subliminally? The researchers found that even though subjects could not "see" the snake pictures, they responded as if they could: Phobics were anxious, nonphobics were not. So much for the idea that we are immune to messages we can't detect.

> Illustration: example of "snake" study
>
> Discussion

But snakes and phobias are far removed from the concerns of most advertisers. Advertisers want to influence buying behaviors, not fears. Which brings us to research done by three business professors, Yael Zemack-Rugar, James Bettman, and Gavan Fitzimons. In an ingenious experiment, they subliminally presented words related to either sadness or guilt to study participants. Both sadness words (i.e., *sad, miserable*) and guilt words (*guilty, blameworthy*) describe bad feelings. But people act differently when they feel sad as opposed to when they feel guilty. Sad people look for rewards to cheer themselves up, but guilty people deny themselves rewards. So the researchers predicted that in response to subliminal presentation of guilt words, guilt-prone people (as opposed to non-guilt-prone people) would be less likely to buy themselves an indulgence. Conversely, in response to sad words, guilt-prone people as compared with others would be just as likely to buy an indulgence. In fact, their experiments demonstrated these patterns of results. By subliminally influencing specific emotions, the researchers influenced purchase behaviors.

> Illustration—an example of subliminal messaging
>
> Discussion
>
> *(continued)*

An even more direct demonstration that subliminal advertising can work comes from a study done by psychologists Johan Karremans, Wolfgang Stroebe, and Jaspar Claus. They argued that subliminal advertising influences brand preference only when someone is motivated to buy in the first place. In their experiment, people tracked strings of letters on a computer screen. Unbeknownst to the participants, subliminal messages were being flashed every so often. Half of the participants were exposed to the subliminal message "Lipton Ice," and half were exposed to a control word. Later, in a supposedly unrelated second study, participants were asked both how thirsty they were and whether they preferred Lipton or a competing brand. The results: When subjects were not thirsty the two groups showed the same preference for Lipton. But thirsty participants showed a different pattern: Those exposed to the Lipton subliminal message showed a strong preference for Lipton; those in the control group did not. The authors' explanation: Motivation plus subliminal prime equals increased preference for the primed brand.

Taken together, these studies and many others show conclusively that we can be affected by messages presented outside of awareness. Score one for Vicary. But it is a long way from saying this can be done to showing that it is done. In fact, as stated earlier, no one has ever shown that an ad campaign has used subliminal stimuli. And no research backs up Key's claims about "embeds" in print ads.

> Illustration—another example of subliminal messaging
>
> Discussion

Source: Arens, William F., et al., *Contemporary Advertising*, 4th ed. McGraw-Hill Education. 248–49. Used with permission of McGraw-Hill Education.

Since the writers are trying to explain how subliminal persuasion works, they have chosen to use research studies to illustrate their point.

An Illustration Text: Conclusion

The function of any conclusion paragraph is to bring closure to the topic. In this essay, the writers bring closure by making general statements about how people react to the idea of subliminal advertising.

Conclusion Paragraph of "Subliminal Persuasion" by William Arens, Michael Weigold, and Christian Arens

People seem both repelled and attracted by the thought that they can be influenced below the threshold of awareness. It seems to imply a hidden power and dovetails nicely with a universal interest in the idea that not everything is what it seems. Interest in the phenomenon of subliminal advertising won't be going away soon. Especially now that we know it *can* work.

> The simple conclusion paragraph speculates about how people might react to subliminal persuasion and brings closure to the reading.

Source: Arens, William F., et al., *Contemporary Advertising*, 4th ed. McGraw-Hill Education. 248–49. Used with permission of McGraw-Hill Education.

ANALYZING AN ILLUSTRATION TEXT

On a separate sheet, answer the following questions about "Subliminal Persuasion."

1. Why do you think the writers chose to use research studies for their examples?

2. Why would a hypothetical example *not* work in an essay such as this one?

3. Is there a pattern to the writer's organization? For example, does the writer start body paragraphs with examples? When does the writer use explanations?

4. Read each paragraph in the essay but skip over the examples. As a reader, how would you experience the essay if the writer had *not* included examples? Explain your answer.

Using Illustration in Your Writing

The key to using illustration effectively is to consider readers' needs. Has an instructor ever returned to you a writing assignment with the word "Explain" in the margin? The best way to guard against this mistake is to put yourself in the place of your readers and ask yourself, "What information might my readers need explained in more depth?" or "What background information do *I* know that my readers may not know?"

With your audience in mind, you can work through the process of composing an illustration text or selecting illustrations as supporting details. The guidelines that follow can guide you in your illustration writing.

1. Ask yourself how illustration suits your topic and purpose. Some topics lend themselves to illustration more than others do. For example, an essay about how people are judged by their appearances could be developed with illustrations.

On the other hand, an essay explaining how crude oil is refined might not lend itself to the use of examples. Rather, such an essay would more readily be organized by steps or stages.

2. Consider using real examples. If you have access to real-life examples, use them.

3. Consider using hypothetical examples. Hypothetical examples can be just as effective as real-life examples, but hypothetical examples must be believable and likely to happen.

4. Consider using concrete details. Concrete details help us communicate concepts more clearly. For example, a writer might say that her dorm room is uninviting. Yet the term *uninviting* does not create a clear picture for readers. Concrete details about the room—descriptions of fluorescent lights, gray carpet, gray walls, and a mattress on a simple metal frame—can communicate what *uninviting* means and help readers picture the room more clearly.

5. Consider using an extended example. An extended example is carried through an entire essay. For example, if you were writing an essay about immigration reform, the example of one immigrant's experiences might be complex enough to fill an entire essay.

6. Consider using visual aids, facts, data, and statistics. You can illustrate a point in a variety of ways. One way is to provide actual visual aids. In many textbooks, visuals such as charts, photos, and graphics are used frequently. Remember also that any data you use must come from a reliable source, and you must give credit to the source.

7. Write a thesis statement, and construct a simple outline. In general, your thesis statement for an illustration essay will not reference the illustrations you use. Rather, the thesis statement will present your main point, and the illustrations will appear in body paragraphs.

PRACTICE

Using Illustration in Your Writing

Write an essay in which you use illustration as the dominant text pattern. Choose one of the following topics, or select your own.

A. Write an essay in which you respond to the ideas in "Subliminal Persuasion." In what ways other than advertising are people subtly influenced to purchase products? Develop your essay by providing illustrations.

B. Select an economic principle you believe is important to follow in your financial life. For example, one principle is to not keep a balance on credit cards. Another is to buy only items you can afford to pay cash for. Write an essay in which you use illustrations to show the importance of the economic principle you have chosen.

C. Choose a person you admire, explain why, and give examples to show the person's good qualities or actions. The person can be someone you know, a historical figure, or a well-known contemporary.

D. What are the characteristics of a good employee? Explain your view, and give examples to support your ideas.

Classification

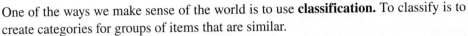

One of the ways we make sense of the world is to use **classification.** To classify is to create categories for groups of items that are similar.

As a text pattern, classification often informs readers about the characteristics of each category of information. An essay about social media, for example, might classify social media into four categories: social networks, blogging Web sites, media-sharing sites, and news-sharing sites. To further explain these categories, a writer might provide the characteristics of each type of social media. While the purpose of such an essay would be to inform, classification is also used to analyze, to evaluate, and to persuade.

Recognizing the Classification Pattern in Readings

Whether classification is used to present details in a reading or as the basic text pattern for a reading, it can be recognized by its characteristics and key words.

CHARACTERISTICS OF THE CLASSIFICATION PATTERN

- Classification presents information in types, groups, or categories.
- It includes discussion of the features associated with each type, group, or category.
- Classification writing often includes examples of the items of each type or in each group or category.
- Classification writing often includes discussion of the similarities and differences of each type, group, or category.

KEY WORDS FOR THE CLASSIFICATION PATTERN			
characteristic	feature	quality	subtype
classify	group	section	trait
cohort	identify	sort	type
distinguish	kind	species	variety

Classification in Supporting Details

Sometimes classification is used to provide helpful information or background knowledge about a subject. Suppose a writer is arguing that adult-onset diabetes can be reversed (an idea that is debatable). One way to begin the discussion would be to provide some background information on diabetes. To do this, the writer might start by classifying diabetes as a metabolic disease. In a body paragraph, she may divide the disease into its two main types: juvenile diabetes and adult-onset diabetes. In this way, classification becomes one of several patterns the writer will use to develop her essay, as this partial outline shows.

Using Classification as a Supporting Detail

Topic: Reversibility of diabetes

Thesis statement: With certain behavioral adjustments, Type II diabetes is reversible for some people.

INTRODUCTION
  Paragraph 1

BODY

  Paragraph 2: Classifying diabetes
  - Classification of diabetes as a metabolic disorder
  - Explanation of metabolic disorders
  - Division of diabetes into types:
    □ Type I diabetes
    □ Type II diabetes

  Paragraph 3: Weight loss and its effect on Type II diabetes
  - Studies from Centers for Disease Control and Prevention
  - Cause-effect discussion

When classification is used as a supporting detail, the discussion of an item's classification is limited, as this outline demonstrates.

Classification as a Text Pattern

While classification can be used as a supporting detail, it can also be the primary function of a text. Classification is often used to inform or to analyze. Informative texts can employ classification to present information so that readers more easily understand it. For example, an introductory biology textbook might include an informative presentation of biological taxonomy—a ranking system for organisms that includes kingdom, phylum/division, class, order, family, genus, and species. A music education textbook might categorize the different types of instruments in symphony orchestras as woodwinds, brass, percussion, and strings, as in the Classification Model diagram.

CLASSIFICATION MODEL

Four Instrument Categories in Orchestras
MAIN CATEGORY

Woodwinds SUBCATEGORY	Brass SUBCATEGORY	Percussion SUBCATEGORY	Strings SUBCATEGORY
Examples: clarinet oboe	Examples: trumpet trombone	Examples: timpani snare drum	Examples: viola cello

While sorting information is a main focus of classification texts, the classification text pattern can also be used to analyze, to evaluate, and to persuade, as these examples demonstrate.

To inform: A magazine article classifying types of financial aid

To analyze: A marketing report presents a breakdown of the types of customers who buy a particular product.

To evaluate: A scholarly journal article on the types of treatment for a psychological disorder evaluates which type helps more people.

To persuade: An essay argues that certain groups of people—such as those with a criminal past or with certain diagnosed mental conditions—should not be allowed to own firearms.

As a text pattern, classification is used to present types, classes, varieties, or groups. Often classification texts are structured so that each type is presented separately, one after another. The discussion of each type or variety includes characteristics that describe the type. The outline below shows how an essay on the types of financial aid available for students might be organized. Notice how each type of financial aid includes a definition, examples, and a discussion of characteristics.

A Simple Outline for a Classification Pattern Essay

Topic: Financial aid available for students

Thesis statement: Three types of financial aid available to college students are scholarships and grants, loans, and work-based aid.

INTRODUCTION

    Paragraph 1: General information about college costs; thesis statement

BODY

    Paragraph 2: First type—scholarships and grants

- Definition of *scholarship* and *grant*
- Examples of scholarships and grants
- Characteristic 1: does not require repayment
- Characteristic 2: is usually competitive and more difficult to get
- Characteristic 3: may be awarded to members of a particular group
- Characteristic 4: might have restrictions on how or where one can use it

    Paragraph 3: Second type—loans

- Definition of *loan*
- Examples of loans
- Characteristic 1: must be repaid
- Characteristic 2: can defer repayment until after college

(continued)

- Characteristic 3: easy to qualify
- Characteristic 4: can use at any college or university

Paragraph 4: Third type—work-based aid

- Definition of *work-based aid*
- Examples of work-based aid
- Characteristic 1: usually does not have to be repaid
- Characteristic 2: sometimes covers more than just tuition and fees
- Characteristic 3: must meet particular requirements to qualify
- Characteristic 4: may be tied to a particular college or university

CONCLUSION
Paragraph 5: Conclusion

Analyzing a Classification Text

The ideas in a classification text must be presented in an order that makes sense for readers. In the preceding example of the types of financial aid, the essay might present types of aid in the order of how easy (or difficult) each type is to obtain or how relevant each is for most students. The writer of the outline above chose to discuss the most desirable type of financial aid first. In a discussion of communicable diseases, a writer may start with the least serious type and progress to the most serious type. The key to determining the order in which to present types is to consider whether audiences might benefit more from one order than another.

A Classification Text: Introduction and Thesis Statement

In an essay that relies primarily on classification for support, the subject being classified i usually presented in the introduction paragraph, and sometimes the thesis statement contains the categories into which items are placed. In the example that follows, the writers tell readers what they will be classifying (types of workers to fire), but they do not reveal the specific categories until the body of the essay.

Introduction Paragraphs of "Three Types of People to Fire Immediately" by G. Michael Maddock and Raphael Louis Vitón

We (your authors) teach our children to work hard and never, ever give up. We teach them to be grateful, to be full of wonder, to expect good things to happen, and to search for literal and figurative treasure on every beach, in every room, and in every person.

But some day, when the treasure hunt is over, we'll also teach them to fire people. Why? After working with the most inventive people in the world for two decades, we've discovered the value of a certain item in the leadership toolbox: the pink slip.

Show of hands: How many of you out there in Innovationland have gotten the "What took you so long?" question from your staff when you finally said goodbye to a teammate who was seemingly always part of problems instead of solutions? We imagine a whole bunch of hands. (Yep, ours went up, too.)

These people . . . passive-aggressively block innovation from happening and will suck the energy out of any organization. When confronted with any of the following three [types of] people—and you have found it impossible to change their ways—say goodbye.

Introduction: leads up to the thesis statement

Rhetorical question: shows that authors are not merely coldhearted executives who like to fire employees

Clue that essay will classify types of employees

Thesis statement

Source: Maddock, G. Michael and Viton, Raphael Louis, "Three Types of People to Fire Immediately," *Businessweek.com*, November 8, 2011. Used with permission of Bloomberg L.P. Copyright © 2011. All rights reserved.

A Classification Text: Body Paragraphs and Their Organization

Body paragraphs in a classification text present the categories, types, or groups into which the writer divides the subject. In the example that follows, the writers create three types of employees to fire immediately: the victims, the nonbelievers, and the know-it-alls. Notice how the body paragraphs include the characteristics or traits of each type of employee.

Body Paragraphs of "Three Types of People to Fire Immediately" by G. Michael Maddock and Raphael Louis Vitón

1. THE VICTIMS

"Can you believe what they want us to do now? And of course we have no time to do it. I don't get paid enough for this. The boss is clueless."

Victims are people who see problems as occasions for persecution rather than challenges to overcome. We all play the role of victim occasionally, but for some, it has turned into a way of life. These people feel persecuted by humans, processes, and inanimate objects with equal ease—they almost seem to enjoy it. They are often angry, usually annoyed, and almost always complaining. Just when you think everything is hum-

Type 1: Headings list types of employees. Alternatively, a topic sentence could introduce each type. The presentation of Type 1 is the writer's first major supporting point.

(continued)

ming along perfectly, they find something, anything, to complain about. At Halloween parties, they're Eeyore, the gloomy, pessimistic donkey from the *Winnie the Pooh* stories—regardless of the costume they choose. Victims aren't looking for opportunities; they are looking for problems.

2. THE NONBELIEVERS

"Why should we work so hard on this? Even if we come up with a good idea, the boss will probably kill it. If she doesn't, the market will. I've seen this a hundred times before."

We love the Henry Ford quote: "If you think you can or think you cannot, you are correct." The difference between the winning team that makes industry-changing innovation happen and the losing one that comes up short is a lack of willpower. Said differently, the winners really believed they could do it, while the losers doubted it was possible.

In our experience, we've found the link between believing and succeeding incredibly powerful and real. Great leaders understand this. They find and promote believers within their organizations. They also understand the cancerous effect that nonbelievers have on a team and will cut them out of the organization quickly and without regret.

If you are a leader who says your mission is to innovate, but you have a staff that houses nonbelievers, you are either a lousy leader or in denial. Which is it? You deserve the staff you get. Terminate the nonbelievers.

3. THE KNOW-IT-ALLS

"You people obviously don't understand the business we are in. The regulations will not allow an idea like this, and our stakeholders won't embrace it. Don't even get me started on our IT infrastructure's inability to support it. And then there is the problem of . . ."

The best innovators are learners, not knowers. The same can be said about innovative cultures; they are learning cultures. The leaders who have built these cultures, either through intuition or experience, know that in order to discover, they must eagerly seek out things they don't understand and jump right into the deep end of the pool. They must fail fearlessly and quickly and then learn and share their lessons with the team. When they behave this way, they empower others around them to follow suit—and presto, a culture of discovery is born and nurtured.

In school, the one who knows the most gets the best grades, goes to the best college, and gets the best salary. On the job, the person who can figure things out the quickest is often celebrated. And unfortunately, it is often this smartest, most-seasoned employee who eventually becomes expert in using his or her knowledge to explain why things are impossible rather than possible.

This employee should be challenged, retrained, and compensated for failing forward. But if this person's habits are too deeply ingrained to change, you must let him or her go. Otherwise, this individual will unwittingly keep your team from seeing opportunity right under your noses. . . .

Hypothetical quotation: follows each heading

Characteristic: Victims feel persecuted.

Characteristic: Victims are often angry, annoyed, and complaining.

Characteristic: Victims look for problems.

Type 2: The presentation of Type 2 is the writer's second major supporting point.

Hypothetical quote

Characteristic: Nonbelievers lack willpower.

Characteristic: Nonbelievers are doubters.

Characteristic: Nonbelievers have a negative effect on teams.

Type 3: The presentation of Type 3 is the writer's third major supporting point.

Hypothetical quote

Characteristic: Know-it-alls are not learners.

Characteristic: Know-it-alls do not seek out new information.

Characteristic: Know-it-alls do not want to fail and relearn.

Characteristic: Know-it-alls can be very smart and seasoned yet have a negative effect.

Characteristic: Know-it-alls may or may not be able to change.

A Classification Text: Conclusion

In this essay, the writers use a very short conclusion paragraph. The first sentence is a restatement of the main idea.

Conclusion Paragraph of "Three Types of People to Fire Immediately" by G. Michael Maddock and Raphael Louis Vitón

You don't want the victims, nonbelievers, or know-it-alls. It is up to you to make sure they take their anti-innovative outlooks elsewhere.

Conclusion: restatement of main idea

Source: Maddock, G. Michael and Viton, Raphael Louis, "Three Types of People to Fire Immediately," *Businessweek.com*, November 8, 2011. Used with permission of Bloomberg L.P. Copyright © 2011. All rights reserved.

PRACTICE

Analyzing a Classification Text

On a separate sheet, answer the following questions about "Three Types of People to Fire Immediately" by G. Michael Maddock and Raphael Louis Vitón.

1. Read through the paragraphs describing "the victims." Besides providing characteristics of this type of employee, what other information do the writers supply? Examples? Explanations? Comparisons? Statistics?

2. Explain this statement: The description of know-it-alls differs from the other two descriptions in that we have to infer their characteristics.

3. The writers use headings to list the three types of workers. Write a topic sentence for each of these types to replace each heading.

4. What is the purpose of this essay? To inform? To analyze? To evaluate? To persuade? (There can be more than one purpose.) Explain your answer.

Using Classification in Your Writing

You can use classification as a text pattern for your writing whenever putting information into categories helps you achieve your writing purpose. The guidelines that follow will help you use the classification text pattern in your writing.

1. Ask yourself whether classification suits your purpose. Not all subjects can be classified. If you have been given an assignment, analyzing the assignment will help you determine whether classification will help you organize your text.

A simple way to think of a classification essay topic is to fill in this sentence:

My topic involves types of _____.

Start with your major. If you are a nursing major, you might choose types of nurses. If you are an education major, you might consider types of teaching jobs. Alternatively, think of a subject or hobby that interests you, and consider how you might divide it into groups such as types of movies, types of wind instruments, or types of alternative fuel vehicles.

For an even more relevant topic, choose to write about something that will help you solve a problem. For an example, one student, Hector, used the topic of financial aid; you saw the outline he created earlier in this chapter. He chose to write about types of financial aid because he needed to know more about how he could afford his college tuition. If you can find a topic that piques your interest and fits the assignment requirements, use it!

2. Use prewriting to determine the items you will classify and to group them into categories. For his essay classifying financial aid, Hector started by listing the aid that he knew was available. He realized that his list included three types of financial aid—scholarships, loans, and work-based aid—and that these types provided convenient categories for classification. His annotated list is shown here.

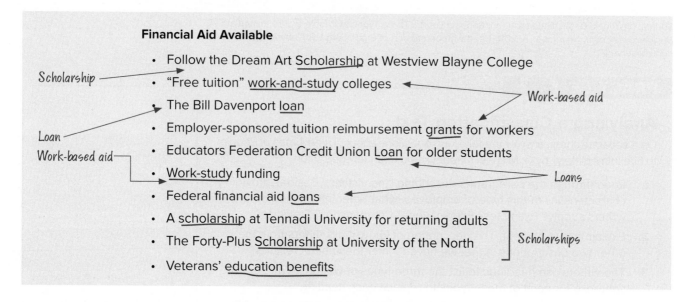

Financial Aid Available

- Follow the Dream Art Scholarship at Westview Blayne College
- "Free tuition" work-and-study colleges
- The Bill Davenport loan
- Employer-sponsored tuition reimbursement grants for workers
- Educators Federation Credit Union Loan for older students
- Work-study funding
- Federal financial aid loans
- A scholarship at Tennadi University for returning adults
- The Forty-Plus Scholarship at University of the North
- Veterans' education benefits

3. Write a thesis statement that uses the classification pattern. Include the groups or categories in your thesis statement. Be sure to arrange the groups in the same order you plan to use in your essay.

4. Write topic sentences for each group or type you are presenting. Use the body paragraphs to present and discuss the characteristics of each category or type. Plan to devote at least one body paragraph to each type or category. You may even need to use two or more paragraphs for the discussion of characteristics.

As shown in Hector's simple outline for an essay on financial aid, the first body paragraph will be rather long. If he ends up using two paragraphs for the first category, he can consider using two paragraphs for each of the remaining categories. Doing so would make his essay more balanced, but it is not necessary. As a general principle, use the number of body paragraphs required to successfully communicate your point.

As you draft, read back over your essay continually so that you can see your writing from a reader's point of view. Make any changes necessary to clarify your ideas and to make your sentences say exactly what you want them to say. Be certain that, after finishing your essay, readers will be able to correctly list the types or groups you discuss. Make sure your writing is clear enough so that they can easily remember the main characteristics of each type.

PRACTICE

Using Classification in Your Writing

Use the preceding steps to write a classification essay. Choose one of the following topics, or select your own.

A. Respond to the article "Three Types of People to Fire Immediately" by writing your own essay about the subject. Can you think of three additional types of people who should be fired? Or perhaps you can think of three types of employees who should be promoted! Write an essay in which you continue the conversation about types of employees and how these types should be treated (hired, fired, demoted, or promoted).

B. Along with all of the benefits we get from the Internet, we also see that some people use the Internet to harm others. What types of Internet abuse can you think of? Write an essay in which you present them.

C. Write an essay classifying one of the following:

- Types of bosses or managers
- Types of vacations
- Types of child care available in your city
- Types of opportunities for volunteering
- Types of poverty
- Types of diets

Comparison-Contrast

Comparing and contrasting are mental activities we do every day. We compare new information we learn in class with information we already know; we contrast a new law with an old law; we take stock of ourselves by comparing and contrasting our qualities with the qualities of others. We also use comparison and contrast to structure our thoughts as we communicate with others in writing.

Technically, to **compare** means to look at the *similarities* between two or more things; to **contrast** means to look at the *differences*. Sometimes, however, people use the term *compare* to mean both: to identify both the similarities and differences. Additionally, comparison-contrast writing always looks at things that are in the same general category. For example, comparing the tourist attractions of one city with those of another is a fair comparison, but comparing the tourist attractions of a city with those of an entire state is not.

Recognizing the Comparison-Contrast Pattern in Readings

To identify the comparison-contrast pattern in a text, look for these characteristics and key words.

CHARACTERISTICS OF THE COMPARISON-CONTRAST PATTERN

- Two or more elements are involved in the comparison and contrast.
- The text presents the differences and/or similarities of these items.
- The text presents an analysis of the items being compared and/or contrasted.

KEY WORDS FOR THE COMPARISON-CONTRAST PATTERN			
although	different	in comparison	on the other hand
but	dissimilar	likewise	otherwise
by the same token	equal	nonetheless	point
criteria	however	on the contrary	similar

Comparison-Contrast in Supporting Details

We make comparisons so often that we are almost unaware we are making them. Think of the times you have been asked a question and used a comparison to answer.

- Oh, my new job? It's different from my old one because I have to answer phones all day.
- This sandwich tastes as if it's been sitting in a car for hours.

A similarity or a difference can be used as a supporting detail in an essay. Suppose, for example, that you are writing an essay to persuade people that it is morally reprehensible to park illegally in handicapped spots. To bring home your point, you may wish to ask readers to compare their health with the health of someone who needs a handicapped parking spot. You might ask readers to put themselves in the place of a person who uses a wheelchair, a person who just had knee surgery, or an elderly person who cannot walk very far. In an outline like the one that follows, you might plan to use these kinds of comparisons.

Using Comparison-Contrast as a Supporting Detail

Topic: Respecting handicapped status

Thesis statement: Illegally parking in spaces designated for handicapped people is a reprehensible act; it shows no empathy for those who need handicapped spaces, does not provide much benefit for the person who does the illegal parking, and shows disrespect for the law.

INTRODUCTION
    Paragraph 1

Body

    Paragraph 2: A person who takes a handicapped parking space without good cause has no empathy for the people who really need such spaces.

- Types of conditions that merit handicapped parking spaces
- <u>Comparison</u>: a person in good health vs. a person who just had knee surgery
- Why people should try to empathize

    Paragraph 3: Another reason no one should illegally park in handicapped spaces is that doing so provides very little benefit to the healthy person and significant hardship to the truly disabled person.

    Paragraph 4: . . .

A comparison or contrast used as support can take up an entire paragraph or as little as one or two sentences.

Comparison-Contrast as a Text Pattern

Sometimes we write essays that provide extended comparisons or contrasts. For example, a writer may compare and contrast buying a car with leasing a car. In such an essay, the writer is likely to present the factors that are important to consumers, such as monthly payments, mileage limits, warranty considerations, and ownership.

For each writing purpose—that is, to inform, to analyze, to evaluate, and to persuade—comparison-contrast can be an effective choice. Comparison-contrast may be used in a history textbook to inform readers about the different capabilities of the Confederate Army and the Union Army during the Civil War, for example.

The writer of an analysis essay can also use comparison-contrast. For instance, the writer may analyze the differences and similarities between two potential careers. If the writer chooses, she can use her analysis to evaluate the two careers and determine which one is best for her. Thus, comparison-contrast can also lead to making evaluative judgments.

Persuasive writing also makes use of comparison-contrast. Arguments about whether to legalize recreational marijuana, for instance, often compare marijuana and alcohol. They may also compare the United States' laws on marijuana use with the laws of other countries. However, writers use comparisons only if doing so will help their side of the argument.

An essay that uses comparison-contrast as a primary text pattern can be organized in one of two ways: block (subject-by-subject) arrangement or point-by-point arrangement. Both arrangements depend on having two or more subjects to compare and particular points of comparison for each subject.

In the **block arrangement,** the writer organizes the discussion by subject, covering all the relevant points first for subject A and then for subject B. In the **point-by-point arrangement,** the writer organizes the discussion by the points of comparison, writing about the first point for both subjects A and B, then about the second point for both subjects A and B, and so on.

For example, we have noted that to compare two subjects—buying a car versus leasing a car—a writer could talk about these points: monthly payments, mileage limits, warranty considerations, and ownership. The graphics here show how a block arrangement of ideas would work. In each graphic, the subject—"Buying" or "Leasing"—is in the center and the points are on the outside.

The sample outlines that follow highlight the differences between the block and point-by-point arrangements.

Block Arrangement	Point-by-Point Arrangement
INTRODUCTION	**INTRODUCTION**
Body	**Body**
Subject 1: Buying	**Point 1:** Monthly payments
• Monthly payments	• Buying
• Mileage limits	• Leasing
• Warranty	**Point 2:** Mileage limits
• Ownership	• Buying
Subject 2: Leasing	• Leasing
• Monthly payments	**Point 3:** Warranty
• Mileage limits	• Buying
• Warranty	• Leasing
• Ownership	**Point 4:** Ownership
	• Buying
	• Leasing
Conclusion	**Conclusion**

The block arrangement can result in some very long body paragraphs if a writer tries to cover all of the points for one subject in a single paragraph. Thus, writers sometimes devote individual paragraphs to each of the points for each subject. Nonetheless, the block arrangement is not always the best choice to discuss subjects that include several points of comparison.

Analyzing a Comparison-Contrast Text

When you read a comparison-contrast text, clearly identify the subjects being compared and the points of comparison. Sometimes the introduction paragraph will help you identify these elements.

A Comparison-Contrast Text: Introduction and Thesis Statement

Comparison-contrast texts often begin with a discussion of the subjects being analyzed. Each subject is introduced, and enough information is provided so that readers understand why the writer is comparing and contrasting the two subjects. The reading that follows, "Economic Systems," comes from *Sociology Matters*, a textbook by Richard Schaefer.

Introduction Paragraphs of "Economic Systems" by Richard Schaefer

> The economy fulfills the basic social function of producing and distributing goods and services. But how is this seemingly amorphous social institution organized? A society's economic system for producing, distributing, and consuming goods and services will depend on both its level of development and its political ideology.
> We will consider the two basic economic systems associated with contemporary industrial societies: capitalism and socialism. In theory, these two economic systems conform perfectly to certain ideals, such as private or collective ownership. However, real economic systems rarely measure up to the ideal types on which they are based. To a greater or lesser extent, most economic systems today incorporate some elements of both capitalism and socialism.

Thesis statement

Source: Schaefer, Richard T., *Sociology Matters*, 6th ed. McGraw-Hill Education, 2013, 252–56. Used with permission of McGraw-Hill Education.

The writer uses a question to introduce the topic: "But how is this seemingly amorphous social institution organized?" His thesis statement answers this question by presenting two organizational systems: capitalism and socialism. We can expect body paragraphs to compare and contrast these two systems.

A Comparison-Contrast Text: Body Paragraphs and Their Organization

The writer has decided to organize his essay using the block arrangement. What follows are the body paragraphs, each of which addresses one subject.

Body Paragraphs of "Economic Systems" by Richard Schaefer (Block Arrangement)

Capitalism	Subject 1
In preindustrial societies, land was the source of virtually all wealth. The Industrial Revolution changed all that. It required that certain individuals and institutions be willing to take substantial risks in order to finance new inventions, machinery, and business enterprises. Eventually, bankers, industrialists, and other holders of large sums of money replaced landowners as the most powerful economic force. These people invested their funds in the hope of realizing even greater profits in factories and business firms.	History of capitalism
The transition to private ownership of business was accompanied by the emergence of the capitalist economic system. Capitalism is an economic system in which the means of production are held largely in private hands, and the main incentive for economic activity is the accumulation of profits. In practice, capitalist systems vary in the degree to which the government regulates private ownership and economic activity.	Definition of capitalism
Immediately following the Industrial Revolution, the prevailing form of capitalism was what is termed *laissez-faire* ("let them do"). Under the principle of *laissez-faire*, as expounded and endorsed by British economist Adam Smith (1723–1790), businesses could compete freely, with minimal government intervention. They retained the right to regulate themselves, operating essentially without fear of government interference.	
Two centuries later, capitalism has taken on a somewhat different form. Private ownership and maximization of profits still remain the most significant characteristics of capitalist economic systems. However, in contrast to the era of *laissez-faire*, today's form of capitalism features extensive government regulation of economic relations. Without restrictions, business firms can mislead consumers, endanger their workers, and even defraud investors—all in the pursuit of greater profits. That is why the government of a capitalist nation often monitors prices, sets safety standards for industries, protects the rights of consumers, and regulates collective bargaining between labor unions and management. Yet in a capitalist system, government rarely takes over ownership of an entire industry.	Changes in capitalism
During the severe economic downturn that began in 2008, the United States moved even further away from the *laissez-faire* ideal. To keep major financial institutions from going under, the federal government invested hundreds of billions of dollars in distressed banking, investment, and insurance companies. Then in 2009, the government bailed out the failing automobile industry, taking a 60 percent interest in General Motors. The Canadian government took another 12 percent.	Capitalism today *(continued)*

Socialism

Socialist theory was refined in the writings of Karl Marx and Friedrich Engels. These European radicals were disturbed by the exploitation of the working class that emerged during the Industrial Revolution. In their view, capitalism forced large numbers of people to exchange their labor for low wages. The owners of industry profited from workers' labor primarily because they paid workers less than the value of the goods produced.

A socialist economic system attempts to eliminate such economic exploitation. Under socialism, the means of production and distribution in a society are collectively rather than privately owned. The basic objective of the economic system is to meet people's needs rather than to maximize profits. Socialists reject the *laissez-faire* philosophy that free competition benefits the general public. Instead, they believe that the central government, acting on behalf of the people, should make basic economic decisions. Therefore, government ownership of all major industries—including steel production, automobile manufacturing, and agriculture—is a major feature of socialism.

In practice, socialist economic systems vary in the extent to which they tolerate private ownership. For example, in Great Britain, a nation with some aspects of both a socialist and a capitalist economy, passenger airline service was once concentrated in the government-owned corporation British Airways. Even before the airline was privatized in 1987, however, private airlines were allowed to compete with it.

Socialist societies differ from capitalist nations in their commitment to social service programs. For example, the U.S. government provides health care and health insurance to those who are elderly and poor through the Medicare and Medicaid programs. In contrast, socialist countries typically offer government-financed medical care to all citizens. In theory, the wealth of the people as a collectivity is used to provide health care, housing, education, and other key services to each individual and family.

Marx believed that the socialist state would eventually "wither away" and evolve into a communist society. Communism refers to an economic system in which all property is communally owned and no social distinctions are made on the basis of people's ability to produce. In recent decades, the Soviet Union, the People's Republic of China, Vietnam, Cuba, and the nations of Eastern Europe were popularly thought of as communist economic systems. However, this viewpoint represents an incorrect usage of a term with sensitive political connotations. All nations known as communist actually fall far short of the ideal type.

By the early 1990s, Communist parties were no longer ruling the nations of Eastern Europe. Just two decades later, in 2012, Moscow had no fewer than 78 billionaires—more than New York (58) and London (39). That year, only China, Cuba, Laos, North Korea, and Vietnam remained socialist societies ruled by Communist parties. Yet even in those countries, capitalism had begun to make inroads.

Subject 2
History of socialism

Definition of socialism

Socialism today

Differences: Socialism and capitalism

Changes in socialism; relationship to communism

Source: Schaefer, Richard T., *Sociology Matters*, 6th ed. McGraw-Hill Education, 2013, 252–56. Used with permission of McGraw-Hill Education.

The author presents roughly the same points when he discusses both subjects: their history, their definitions, their practice today, and their changes over time.

A Comparison-Contrast Text: Conclusion

As is true for any text, the writer must bring the essay to a satisfactory conclusion. Notice how the conclusion for this reading makes an interesting point: the idea that the United States and most other industrialized societies are a combination of capitalism and socialism.

Conclusion Paragraph of "Economic Systems" by Richard Schaefer

In reality, the economy of each industrial society—including the United States, the European Union, and Japan—contains certain elements of both capitalism and socialism. Whatever the differences—whether a country more closely fits the ideal type of capitalism or socialism—all industrial societies rely chiefly on mechanization in the production of goods and services. And all economies, whether capitalist or socialist, change as a result of social and technological advances.

Source: Schaefer, Richard T., *Sociology Matters*, 6th ed. McGraw-Hill Education, 2013, 252–56. Used with permission of McGraw- Hill Education.

This simple conclusion helps readers see that in many ways, communism and socialism are not opposites: rather, both economic systems can exist in a country at the same time. This insight brings closure to the reading.

PRACTICE

Analyzing a Comparison-Contrast Text

On a separate sheet, answer the following questions.

1. If the writer had presented a point-by-point comparison-contrast, how would he have organized his essay? Jot down a brief outline to explain your answer.

2. What is another point the writer could have used for comparing capitalism and socialism?

3. If you were asked to compare and contrast two different homes and then choose the home you liked best, what three points of comparison would be most important to you? Explain why.

4. Remember that one guideline is to compare and contrast things in the same category. Imagine an essay in which a writer claims that Beau's Restaurant—a very expensive steakhouse—is the best place to eat in town. To prove his point, the writer compares Beau's Restaurant with the local McDonald's and Wendy's. Why would such a comparison be unfair?

Using Comparison-Contrast in Your Writing

To use the comparison-contrast text pattern in your writing, follow these guidelines.

1. Ask yourself how classification suits your purpose and topic. If showing the similarities and/or differences between two or more subjects is the primary way you will support your thesis statement, comparison-contrast should be the right text pattern to use for your essay.

2. Determine the specific subjects you will compare or contrast. Be precise about the subjects you are analyzing. If you are comparing high school with college, for example, narrow the subjects to make your topic more manageable. Comparing high school students' attitudes with college students' attitudes is a more precise topic and is more easily planned than a broad comparison of high school and college.

3. Make sure your comparison is fair. It is unfair to compare items in two different categories. Suppose a writer attempts to convince readers that crack cocaine should be a legal recreational drug because some states are making marijuana a legal recreational drug. Many people would say that the drugs are in different categories because crack cocaine is highly addictive and has other attributes that put it in a category of more dangerous drugs. To use comparison persuasively, make sure to choose subjects that are in the same category.

4. Determine whether you will compare your subjects (analyze similarities), contrast them (analyze differences), or do both. Very often, comparison-contrast texts include both similarities and differences. Some writing tasks, however, may require you to choose either to compare or to contrast. For example, a geology assignment may require students to write about the differences in the types of rocks found in their hometowns.

5. Decide whether to use a block arrangement or a point-by-point arrangement. If you are comparing two subjects and have multiple points of comparison, a point-by-point arrangement will usually be more effective. If you are comparing multiple subjects and have only a few points of comparison, a block arrangement will work well.

6. Determine the points of comparison you will analyze. To determine the points of comparison and contrast, think about your writing purpose. To compare two potential careers, a writer might use the comparative points of educational requirements, vacation time and work hours, and potential salary. The points you choose should be the most pertinent points in the discussion. For example, one could compare the type of clothing teachers can wear to work with the type of clothing accountants can wear to work, but this point would not be as important as other points of comparison.

ARRANGEMENTS FOR A COMPARISON-CONTRAST ESSAY	
Block (Subject-by-Subject) Arrangement: Best for just two subjects with multiple points of comparison	**Point-by-Point Arrangement: Best for multiple subjects with only a few points of comparison**
Subject A ■ Point 1 ■ Point 2 ■ Point 3 ■ Point 4 Subject B ■ Point 1 ■ Point 2 ■ Point 3 ■ Point 4	Point 1 ■ Subject A ■ Subject B ■ Subject C Point 2 ■ Subject A ■ Subject B ■ Subject C Point 3 ■ Subject A ■ Subject B ■ Subject C

NOTE: The actual number of subjects and points will vary, as the arrangements above demonstrate.

7. Write a thesis statement, and construct a simple outline. The thesis statement you write should indicate the two subjects being compared. If you choose to write a closed thesis statement, include the points of comparison, like this:

> Determining whether to buy or lease a vehicle requires considering monthly payment, mileage limit, warranty, and ownership status.

PRACTICE

Using Comparison-Contrast in Your Writing

Use the preceding steps to write a comparison-contrast essay. Choose one of the following topics, or select your own.

A. Respond to the reading "Economic Systems." Based on the information in the reading, what do you think life would be like in a socialist country? Compare your idea of life in a socialist country to what life is like in a capitalist country.

B. Select two potential career fields. Choose points of comparison that are important to you, such as salary, type of work, job satisfaction, and typical work hours. Write an essay in which you compare both career fields.

C. What are the differences between courses that require you to master a skill—such as a writing or welding course—and courses that require you to think about information, such as history or sociology? Write an essay in which you discuss at least three points of comparison.

D. Write an essay in which you compare and contrast two movies in the same genre. For example, you could compare two horror movies you have seen. Choose appropriate points of comparison, such as the actors' performances, the plot, and special effects.

Cause and Effect

What caused a bridge to collapse? What are the effects of illiteracy? What will happen if the Arctic ice cap melts? These kinds of questions require that we assess causes and effects. Many subjects lend themselves to thinking about cause and effect; thus, it is common to read analyses of *why* something happened or *what will happen if* certain actions are taken. A discussion of causes and/or effects is called a *causal analysis.*

©Gary Whitton/Shutterstock.com RF

Figuring out causes and effects is not always easy. Scientists may agree that climate change is happening, but world governments cannot agree on the actions that will effectively avert its consequences.

Recognizing the Cause and Effect Pattern in Readings

To identify the cause and effect pattern in a text, look for these characteristics and key words.

CHARACTERISTICS OF THE CAUSE AND EFFECT PATTERN

- The text primarily concerns causes, effects, or both.
- The text concerns phenomena or events.
- The text makes predictions or attempts to explain causes of past events.
- The text examines one cause and/or effect, multiple causes and/or effects, or chains of causes and/or effects.

KEY WORDS FOR THE CAUSE AND EFFECT PATTERN			
as a result	cause	for that reason	so
at last	consequently	if . . . then	therefore
because of	effect	since	thus

Cause and Effect in Supporting Details

An analysis of cause and effect often answers the questions "Why?" and "What if?" In some texts, the writer may use the discussion of a cause or effect (or both) as one type of support among others.

Suppose the United States is considering sending troops to the aid of a foreign country in turmoil (let's call this country Otherland). A reporter is writing an article to evaluate all of the options the United States has. The reporter can provide some background about what *caused* the unrest in Otherland so that readers learn why the United States is considering intervening in the first place. After discussing the causes of the unrest, the reporter can describe the effects of the current situation and then discuss the possible types of action the United States could take. Used in this way, the cause and effect discussion becomes a supporting detail in the reporter's article; other details are likely to be other options that the United States should consider. A partial outline for such an article might look like this.

Using Cause and Effect as a Supporting Detail

Topic: Intervening in Otherland

Thesis statement: The United States needs to consider every possible option before intervening in Otherland.

INTRODUCTION

    Paragraph 1

BODY

    Paragraph 2: History of the problem
- What *caused* the unrest
- Current situation (effects of the fighting, turmoil, etc.)

    Paragraph 3: Option 1—The United States could wait and do nothing for the time being.

    Paragraph 4: Option 2—The United States could send troops.

The article is structured around a list of possible actions; thus, the reporter will likely discuss the potential effects of each action, along with other information, such as the cost of the action, public opinion about the action, and so on.

Cause and Effect as a Text Pattern

Discussions of causes and effects can be complicated. For instance, what causes a recession? Economists can find so many possible causes that figuring out the most likely ones is truly difficult.

Because cause and effect relationships are so complicated, it is not unusual to see entire essays (and books) devoted to explaining these relationships. Such texts are often organized using cause and effect as a text pattern. The cause and effect text pattern may also be used to explain the *domino effect,* a chain reaction that occurs when one effect causes another effect, which causes another effect, and so on. For example, drought causes the price of hay and corn to increase. The increase in hay and corn prices drives up the cost of beef. The increase in the cost of beef is passed along to consumers, and the net result is that consumers have less money after paying for groceries. An essay that discusses a domino effect might be organized chronologically so that the writer begins with the first cause, moves to its effect, discusses the effect as a new cause, and continues this pattern. The illustration "Cause and Effect Models" on the next page shows some kinds of cause and effect relationships that can be used to organize an essay.

CAUSE AND EFFECT MODELS

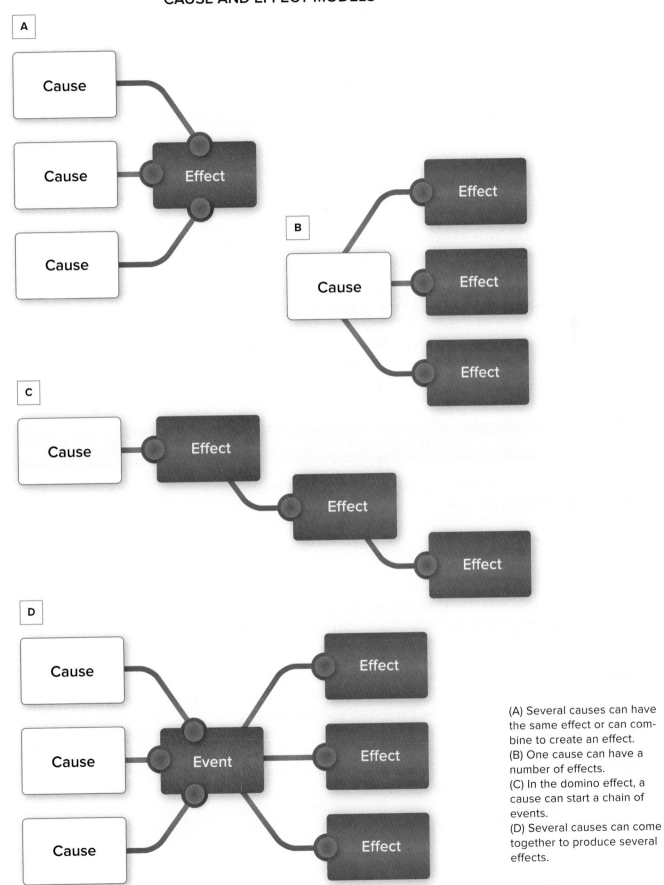

(A) Several causes can have the same effect or can combine to create an effect.
(B) One cause can have a number of effects.
(C) In the domino effect, a cause can start a chain of events.
(D) Several causes can come together to produce several effects.

Essays that present causes and effects can achieve a variety of writing purposes. Informative writing often presents causes, effects, or both. For example, a business textbook chapter might explain the positive effects of Internet marketing. An essay on a successful business might present the good decisions that caused the business to succeed.

Analysis is always required for writing about cause and effect relationships, and sometimes analysis is the primary purpose for writing. An essay that presents an environmental problem, such as the rise of sea levels, might present an analysis of its causes and effects.

Sometimes the goal of a causal analysis is to evaluate. For example, a writer may evaluate different options for helping needy children receive free lunches during the summer. In such an essay, the writer will probably evaluate the potential effects of a number of solutions and will determine the solution that would work the best.

Finally, cause and effect is used extensively in persuasive writing. Any time a writer advocates a certain action, a discussion of that action's effects can be used for support. For example, a writer may argue that buying American-made products benefits American workers. To support that argument, the writer would probably present the effects on workers when Americans buy (or fail to buy) American-made products.

Persuasive writing can also focus on causes. What is causing decreases in the honeybee population? The causes are widely debated; thus, a persuasively focused paper could use a cause and effect text pattern to present a writer's belief—based on evidence—about causes for this phenomenon.

Analyzing a Cause and Effect Text

The writers of effective cause and effect essays organize text elements in the way that best suits the subject, purpose, and reader.

A Cause and Effect Text: Introduction and Thesis Statement

The following article, "Sit with Us," by Colby Itkowitz, appeared in *The Washington Post*. Her introduction consists of background information that will be helpful to readers. Like many journalists, Itkowitz uses very brief paragraphs.

Introduction Paragraphs of "Sit with Us" by Colby Itkowitz

Natalie Hampton spent most of her 7th and 8th grade school years eating lunch alone.	Background information
The new girl at an all-girls private school in Los Angeles, she became the target of a clique of "mean girls" who excluded her from parties, called her names, and even physically assaulted her, she said. They told her she was ugly and would never have any friends. They shoved her in a locker, scratched her, and even threatened to kill her.	*(continued)*

She feared telling on them, afraid of their retaliation. Once a kid who loved going to school, Natalie now dreaded it. She stopped eating; she couldn't sleep. The anxiety became so bad that she had to be hospitalized. Her mom calls it "the darkest period of our lives."

Effects of Natalie's experiences

Natalie switched schools for high school. She chose a school that, when she toured it, seemed to prioritize community. Now a 16-year-old junior, she's happy there, with a group of close friends and extracurricular activities. But she's never forgotten those two dark years when she was bullied and isolated by her peers.

And she hates the idea of other kids going through what she did.

So Natalie came up with an idea that would allow students a judgment-free way to find lunch mates without the fear of being rejected. She developed an app called "Sit With Us," where students can sign up as "ambassadors" and post that there are open seats at their lunch table. A student who doesn't have a place to sit can look at the app and find an ambassador's table and know he or she is invited to join it.

Thesis statement

The introduction gives important background information, and it also presents the effects of Natalie's experiences. This information helps readers understand why Natalie developed a phone app to help her classmates.

A Cause and Effect Text: Body Paragraphs and Their Organization

In the body paragraphs that follow, the writer presents the effects of Natalie's app as well as the positive effects Natalie has experienced from her invention.

Body Paragraphs of "Sit with Us" by Colby Itkowitz

When signing up as an ambassador, students take a pledge that they'll be kind and welcoming to whoever comes to sit with them.

"Lunch might seem really small, but I think these are the small steps that make a school more inclusive," she said. "It doesn't seem like you're asking that much, but once you get people in the mindset, it starts to change the way students think about each other. It makes a huge difference in how they treat each other."

Effects of Natalie's app: School is more inclusive and students treat each other differently

There is research that backs that up. In January, professors from Rutgers, Princeton, and Yale universities found that when students actively take a stand against bullying, and not teachers or administrators, it's more effective. They did so by testing what would happen if a random group of students started actively promoting anti-bullying campaigns at their schools. In the participating schools, they saw a "30 percent reduction in disciplinary reports."

Effects proven by research

(continued)

Bullying is such a serious problem among children and teens that even the White House created an initiative to address it. One statistic shows that 1 in 4 students say they've been bullied in a given school year, and 64 percent of them don't report it.

"If there's one goal of this conference, it's to dispel the myth that bullying is just a harmless rite of passage or an inevitable part of growing up," President Obama said in 2010. "It's not."

The once-bullied Natalie, who is active in the school yearbook, theater and dance, community service, and aspires to study psychology and neuroscience in college, introduced her app on Monday at an assembly in front of her entire school. She's been interviewed on NPR and local television. She's been invited to attend a "Girls Can Do" conference in Washington in November to give a presentation about her experience.

She and her mom, Carolyn Hampton, have scheduled multiple phone conversations with academic administrators all over the country about the "Sit With Us" app and how they can implement it in their schools.

"It's nice to see how resilient she is," Carolyn Hampton said. "It was such a tough period in our lives and she's turned it around and is doing something really positive."

> How inventing the app affected Natalie

Notice that the writer primarily discusses effects. She also provides information on how Natalie's app works. Additionally, she includes information about how serious the issue of bullying is. While discussing effects is important, the writer is free to add other types of information that her readers may need to know.

A Cause and Effect Text: Conclusion

You may remember that the beginning of the article started with Natalie's past. The conclusion takes readers to the present and reports on how Natalie is doing.

Conclusion Paragraph of "Sit with Us" by Colby Itkowitz

When Natalie first started in her new high school, she made friends easily—the way she was before middle school, her mom said. Yet even as a new student, when she saw peers sitting alone, she asked them to join her, Natalie said. Now, many of those kids, are "an essential part of our friend group," she said.

"I'm extremely lucky I got the chance to get out and share my story with other people," she said.

PRACTICE

Analyzing a Comparison-Contrast Text

On a separate sheet of paper, answer the following questions about "Sit with Us."

1. What caused Natalie to create the app?
2. According to the research cited in the article, what is one of the most effective ways to counteract bullying?
3. How could bullying lead to a domino effect? Explain.
4. Think of a time when you observed bullying. What caused the bullying? What was the effect of the bullying?

Using Cause and Effect in Your Writing

Many subjects require that writers address causes and effects. If you are writing a paper and think cause and effect may be a helpful text pattern to use, follow these steps.

1. Ask yourself how cause and effect suits your topic and purpose. Will a discussion of causes and/or effects be the primary focus of your topic? If so, a cause and effect text pattern is appropriate. Events from the past may leave us wondering about their causes, so they are good subjects to consider for such an essay. A topic that prompts us to analyze future effects is also appropriate for the cause and effect text pattern.

2. Analyze the causes and/or effects of your topic. Use questions to help you determine causes and effects.

- What possible causes (or effects) can you think of for the questions you asked in step 1 above? List them. List as many as you can without censoring your ideas.
- Looking back at the causes (or effects) you have listed, ask, "Which of these are the *least* likely or *least* important causes or effects?" Go back to the list and cross out those that are least likely or least important. If a domino effect is involved, write out each cause and effect in the process.
- Select the most likely causes (or effects) to present in your essay.

3. Analyze the logic of the causes and/or effects you will present. It is, unfortunately, common to make logical errors when you are determining causes and effects. Three common errors are confusing correlations with causes, making faulty predictions, and oversimplifying possible causes.

- **Pitfall 1: Confusing correlations with causes.** A correlation is simply a relationship between two things. For example, we have evidence that eating fast food is correlated with having poor health. Imagine, for example, that your friend who eats only fast food (burgers, fries, and shakes, for example) develops a brain tumor? Can we say there is a causal relationship between eating fast food and developing a brain tumor? Although some research shows that fast food and poor health are related, we do not have enough research to know whether eating fast food specifically *causes* brain tumors. In your friend's case, we see a correlation between eating lots of fast food and developing a brain tumor. However, we cannot prove one caused the other.

The correlation pitfall occurs when we assume that because two things appear to be related, one must have caused the other. If you do not have clear evidence linking a cause to an effect, you cannot assume a causal relationship.

- **Pitfall 2: Making faulty predictions.** When we consider taking an action, being able to make accurate predictions is important. Consider drinking and driving. We cannot say that a person who drinks and drives will definitely be involved in an accident. However, we know from evidence that a high percentage of auto accidents involve a driver who has been drinking alcohol. Thus we *can* say that a person who is driving under the influence of alcohol is *more likely* to be in a car accident than a driver who has not been drinking.

  Sometimes it is tempting to make predictions without much evidence because those predictions might help us win an argument or make a point. For example, someone might claim that if Americans agree to gun control laws, then eventually the government will take away people's guns. This is an *unreasonable prediction* because it is not based on evidence. Often, unreasonable predictions are attempts to make the listener fearful and to thus believe the speaker.

  To avoid making faulty predictions, keep the following questions in mind: "How do you know?" and "Would a reasonable person agree with this prediction?" You can avoid this pitfall by making sure you have sound reasons for your predictions, being certain your predictions would be acceptable to a general audience, and having proof to support them.

- **Pitfall 3: Oversimplifying possible causes.** Failing to consider all the possible causes for an event often results in oversimplification. For example, if you come down with a head cold after flying on a plane, you may blame the head cold on your air travel. This thinking, however, has oversimplified the situation. Touching such objects as doorknobs, grocery carts, and escalator rails can introduce germs that cause illnesses like colds. However, colds take several days to incubate. So if you get a head cold two days after flying, it is likely to have been caused by contact with germs before your flight.

  The best way to determine the cause of an event or phenomenon is to make a list of all the possible causes, cross out the causes that are not applicable to the situation, and try to find a cause that is reasonable.

4. Use very careful language to express causes and effects. After finding a reasonable cause, you will then need to use precise language to express the causal connection you have found. Consider this statement of cause:

> Jana's decision to quit her job is probably what made her depressed.

By using *probably,* the writer acknowledges that there may be other causes. Thus, the writer is more accurate, precise, and careful in her language, and this care shows she has thought critically about possible causes.

One way to use more precise language is to use qualifiers, words like *may have, might,* and *likely.* Using qualifiers like these when appropriate will help you make more precise statements about causes and effects.

COMMON QUALIFIERS				
a few	could	may	seems	suggests
all	entirely	might	seldom	the majority
always	few	never	some	unlikely
commonly	many	possibly	sometimes	usually

5. Write a thesis statement, and construct a simple outline. Determine the best way to present the causes and/or effects you will be discussing. Create an outline in which you detail the specific causes and effects you will address and the order in which you will address them.

PRACTICE ⬤

Using Cause and Effect in Your Writing

Use the preceding steps to write a cause and effect essay. Choose one of the following topics, or select your own.

A. Reflect on "Sit with Me," and write an essay in which you discuss how negative experiences can sometimes result in positive outcomes.

B. Write an essay in which you discuss a trend—for example, an increase or decrease in crime on your campus or in your neighborhood—and the causes (or effects) of that trend.

C. Write a cause and effect essay about a good decision you made in life. Explain what caused you to make the decision and the effects of having made the decision.

D. Write an essay in which you discuss the causes or effects of one of the following: alcoholism, faith, a particular disease or condition, worry, a social problem, volunteering, living in a clean (or messy) place.

Process Analysis

Perhaps at some point in your life, you struggled to make sense of the driving directions someone gave you. Or maybe you tried following a bread recipe, only to find that the result was an inedible lump of dough. These kinds of experiences emphasize how important it is to explain processes clearly and accurately.

The **process analysis** pattern usually presents the stages, steps, or phases of a process in a particular order. It can also be used to show how a particular historical event or discovery came about. Certain key words and transitions are often used in process analysis texts.

Recognizing the Process Analysis Pattern in Readings

To identify the process analysis pattern, look for these characteristics and key words.

CHARACTERISTICS OF THE PROCESS ANALYSIS PATTERN

- Process analysis texts provide discussion of a process, procedure, method, course of action, or protocol.
- These texts present a sequence of steps (*first, second, third,* or some other sequencing indicators).
- Process analysis texts provide explanations about how the steps work or how to follow them.

KEY WORDS FOR THE PROCESS ANALYSIS PATTERN				
after	first, second, third . . .	next	stage	to begin
before	later	now	step	to continue
finally	meanwhile	phase	then	to end

Process Analysis in Supporting Details

A writer might briefly explain a process in a body paragraph of an essay to give the audience background information. Suppose a writer is composing a narrative essay to tell the story of someone who immigrated to the United States. The writer may devote a paragraph to explaining the process of becoming an American citizen if this information is necessary for readers to understand the immigrant's story. The partial outline that follows shows where a writer may use a brief explanation of a process as a type of support.

Using Process Analysis as a Supporting Detail

Topic: An immigrant's story

Thesis statement: Despite seemingly insurmountable odds, Robbie Kam-Lin realized his dream of American citizenship.

INTRODUCTION
   Paragraph 1

(continued)

BODY

Paragraph 2: Problems in his native land

Paragraph 3: Getting to the United States

Paragraph 4: The long path to citizenship

- The process of becoming an American citizen

Process Analysis as a Text Pattern

Process analysis can be used for a variety of purposes. For instance, when the sole purpose of an essay is to describe how an event came about or to explain how to perform a task, a writer can use process analysis as a text pattern. In *A Guide to Naturalization,* a brochure published by the US Citizenship and Immigration Services, shown on the next page, process analysis is used to outline the steps a person must take to apply for and acquire US citizenship. Process analysis can also be used to explain a process a writer is proposing, such as a new way to handle incoming orders to improve speed and efficiency. Often the purpose of process analysis texts is to inform. An explanation of how global warming works, for example, could be presented using process analysis.

Explaining a process can also be part of an analysis. A scholarly article in an engineering journal might use process analysis to examine the method used to build a bridge that failed. The purpose of such a discussion may also be to evaluate: by examining processes, one can evaluate the best process to use for a given procedure.

Sometimes writers argue about processes to determine which processes are appropriate, which work the best, or which are the most ethical. For example, what is the best process to use to reunite an adopted child with a birth parent? What process should doctors and hospital staff use to determine whether a person is legally dead? What process should hospitals use for organ donation? These are debatable issues that are appropriate for process analysis papers.

Most process analysis papers can be organized by the stages or phases of the process being described. The outline that follows presents an example of how process analysis can be used to structure an informative essay.

A Simple Outline for a Process Analysis Pattern Essay

Topic: Creating a plan to improve customer service

Thesis statement: Any business can improve customer service by using a five-step process.

INTRODUCTION

Paragraph 1: Introduction and thesis statement

BODY

Paragraph 2: Stage 1—Examining the situation

Paragraph 3: Stage 2—Exploring solutions

Paragraph 4: Stage 3—Implementing a solution

Paragraph 5: Stage 4—Assessing the solution

Paragraph 6: Stage 5—Adjusting or creating a new solution

CONCLUSION

Paragraph 7: Conclusion

What Should I Expect From the Naturalization Process?

Preparing to Apply

- Read *A Guide to Naturalization.*
- Complete the Naturalization Eligibility Worksheet.
- Get an "Application for Naturalization" (Form N-400).
- Visit our website at **www.uscis.gov**.

Completing Your Application and Getting Photographed

- Complete your application.
- Collect the necessary documents.
- Send your application, documents, and fee (DO NOT SEND CASH) to the appropriate Lockbox Facility or Service Center.
- Keep a copy of everything you send to USCIS.

Get Biometics Taken

- Receive an appointment letter from USCIS.
- Go to the biometrics location.
- Get your biometrics taken.
- Mail additional documents if USCIS requests them.
- Wait for USCIS to schedule your appointment.

Being Interviewed

- Receive an appointment for your interview.
- Go to your local USCIS office at the specified time.
- Bring state-issued identification, Permanent Resident Card, and any additional documents specific to your case.
- Answer questions about your application and background.
- Take the English and civics tests.
- Receive case status.

Taking the Oath

- Receive a ceremony date.
- Check in at the ceremony.
- Return your Permanent Resident Card.
- Answer questions about what you have done since your interview.
- Take the Oath of Allegiance.
- Receive your Certificate of Naturalization.

Source: *A Guide to Naturalization*. Washington, DC: US Citizenship and Immigration Services, M-476 (rev. 11/16). 31.

Analyzing a Process Analysis Text

Some specific features are typically found in the introduction, thesis statement, body paragraphs, and conclusion of process analysis texts.

A Process Analysis Text: Introduction and Thesis Statement

The introduction paragraph of a process analysis text usually presents the topic and often includes the thesis statement. The example that follows, "The Three Parts of an Effective Apology," is an article by Christine Carter published on *GreaterGood.com*.

Introduction Paragraphs from "The Three Parts of an Effective Apology" by Christine Carter

People make mistakes all the time. Not just bad people, or weak people. All people. Our mistakes are what make us human. And even when we don't think that we've made a mistake, other people will often find errors in our ways. We human beings are walking offenders. Here's the real question: If we've done something that offends someone else—whether or not we feel we are to blame—should we apologize?

I believe that it almost always serves our highest good to apologize if we've hurt or offended someone else—even if we think the offended person's anger is unjustified, or if we have a perfectly good excuse for what happened. Or if our intentions were all good. We don't repair a fissure in one of our relationships by ignoring it. We initiate a repair by apologizing. But all apologies aren't created equal, of course. (All parents have watched children spit out a forced *"Sorry!"* and known it was worthless.) A good apology is something of an art.

So what makes a good apology? After studying that question extensively, Aaron Lazare developed perhaps the most robust criteria to date for effective apologies. Drawing on Dr. Lazare's work, I've whittled down his ideas to the following three-step method for making a good apology.

Thesis

Source: Carter, Christine, "The Three Parts of an Effective Apology," *The Greater Good*, November 12, 2015. This article originally appeared on *Greater Good*, the online magazine of the Greater Good Science Center at UC Berkeley. Read more at *greatgood.berkeley.edu*.

A Process Analysis Text: Body Paragraphs and Their Organization

The body paragraphs of a process analysis essay describe the steps, phases, or stages of the process in question. Notice that the writer offers explanations and examples to help readers understand each step.

Body Paragraphs from "The Three Parts of an Effective Apology" by Christine Carter

Step 1: Tell Them What You Feel.

Usually, we start by saying "I'm sorry" to express remorse. "I'm sorry" is more effective when we elaborate on our remorseful feelings. For example, "I'm so sorry and sad to hear that my lack of communication has made you so angry and resentful." Or, "I'm so sorry and embarrassed that my comment caused such an uproar."

Step 1 of the process

Explanations and examples

(continued)

Just share the remorseful feelings, please. It is not constructive is suc-
cumb to—and share—feelings of resentment or defensiveness, such as
"I'm sorry . . . you're being so petty and critical."

Step 2: Admit Your Mistake *and* the Negative Impact It Had.

This is the hardest part because it requires admitting responsibility for
our actions or behavior. And this step can feel impossible if we don't really
think we did much wrong, or if our intentions were good.

Ask yourself: How is the other person feeling? What did I do that
caused that feeling? Could I have done something differently?

Empathize with the offended person; the most important thing is that
you demonstrate that you are trying to understand how they feel. (Don't
apologize until you actually do understand how they are feeling; if you
can't put yourself in their shoes, your apology will ring false.)

For example, you might say, "I can see that my comment hurt your
feelings, and that you are feeling misunderstood and uncared for." Or to
your partner you might say, "I know that it was wrong of me to call you out
in front of the whole family, and that you are angry because I've hurt your
credibility with the kids. I'm sure that was embarrassing, and it was a mistake for me to do that."

Step 3: Make the Situation Right.

Good apologies include a reparation of some kind, either real or sym-
bolic. Maybe you create an opportunity for the person you embarrassed to
regain credibility. Or perhaps you admit your mistake to others, too, as a
part of the reparation. In many relationships, a hug is a great reparation.

Often, all we need to do is explain what we are going to do differently
the next time so that we don't repeat the offending action or behavior. This
helps us rebuild trust and repair the relationship. If you aren't sure how to
make it right, just ask, "Is there anything I can do to make this up to you?"

Above all, deliver on any promises you make. When we feel guilty or
embarrassed, sometimes we over-correct in our attempt to gain forgiveness. If the person is asking for something that you can't give, say so, and
say that you will give some thought to what you can give to make it up to
him or her.

Margin notes:
- Step 2 of the process
- Explanations and examples
- Step 3 of the process
- Explanations and examples

Source: Carter, Christine, "The Three Parts of an Effective Apology," *The Greater Good*, November 12, 2015. This article originally appeared on *Greater Good*, the online magazine of the Greater Good Science Center at UC Berkeley. Read more at *greatgood.berkeley.edu*.

A Process Analysis Text: Conclusion

The function of the conclusion paragraph is to add any remaining explanations, to comment on the process, and to end the text.

Conclusion Paragraph from "The Three Parts of an Effective Apology" by Christine Carter

> Knowing how to apologize well is at the top of my priorities. It's a life skill I want my children to practice and master. And it's one that I'm still working on myself.

Source: Carter, Christine, "The Three Parts of an Effective Apology," *The Greater Good*, November 12, 2015. This article originally appeared on *Greater Good*, the online magazine of the Greater Good Science Center at UC Berkeley. Read more at *greatgood.berkeley.edu.*

The simple but effective conclusion emphasizes the importance of knowing how to apologize.

PRACTICE

Analyzing a Process Analysis Text

On a separate sheet, answer the following questions about "The Three Parts of an Effective Apology."

1. What is the writer's purpose? Explain.

2. Think about the 5 W's and 1 H questions (who, where, what, when, why, and how). Which of these questions does the writer answer in the body paragraphs?

3. Imagine this article without the explanations and examples. Would the article be as convincing to you? Explain.

4. Why do you think the writer mentions herself in the conclusion paragraph?

Using Process Analysis in Your Writing

You can use process analysis to structure an essay when you want to guide readers through the steps of a process (such as applying for citizenship) or when you want to describe the stages of an event or phenomenon (such as photosynthesis). The guidelines that follow will help you plan a process analysis essay.

1. Determine whether process analysis will fit your topic and your purpose.
If you believe your topic is appropriate, determine what you hope to accomplish by presenting the process. Is your goal to present a simple overview of the process? Is the purpose of your writing to teach readers to use the process you will describe? Keep your purpose in mind as you select the types of details to include in your paper.

2. Carefully and critically consider your audience and what your audience needs to know as you explain the process. When explanations of processes go wrong, the reason is usually a failure on the part of the writer to think about the needs of the audience. If you can clearly identify your audience, think about the particular knowledge this audience already has. A general audience cannot be expected to have specific knowledge of specialized subjects. For example, while you can expect a general audience to know that refining oil is an industrial process, you cannot expect such readers to know anything specific about the process.

3. Use prewriting to determine the particular steps of the process you will discuss. Prewriting can help you determine the stages, steps, or phases involved in the process. Read through your prewriting critically to decide the best way to arrange your information. For example, determine whether each step needs its own paragraph or whether some steps belong in a paragraph together. Also, make sure you do not leave out any steps. Thinking like a reader will help you anticipate your readers' needs.

4. Write a thesis statement, and create a simple outline. Choose the best order in which to present each step or stage. Usually, steps or stages are presented in chronological order.

5. Have someone read over your rough draft, looking for missing steps. If you are familiar with the process you are describing, you may forget to include small, but important, steps. For example, a chef knows that to make an omelet, she needs to grease an omelet pan; because she is so familiar with the process, she may leave out this step, thinking readers will certainly know to grease the pan. Make sure you include all the necessary steps in your essay.

PRACTICE

Using Process Analysis in Your Writing

Use the preceding steps to write a process analysis essay. Choose one of the following topics, or select your own.

A. Using "The Three Parts of an Effective Apology" as a model, write an essay in which you present steps to another interpersonal task, such as the steps in forgiving someone, the steps involved in making a close friend, or the phases involved in falling in love.

B. Write about a process you have mastered. For example, if you know how to make tamales, you might write an essay explaining the process. If you understand the way an internal combustion engine works, you might write an essay about it. Write with the idea that your essay will be read by someone who knows nothing about the process you are describing.

C. How does online dating work? Describe the process in steps. Alternatively, what is the process many people use to find a life partner?

D. Write an essay in which you discuss how parents can build their children's self-esteem. Alternatively, write an essay about the stages teens go through as they become young men and young women.

Recognizing and Using Mixed Text Patterns

Most professional writers use a mixture of patterns as supporting details in their writing. When you read an essay, mark the types of supporting details you find. If most of the supporting details are one particular type, the essay may be written using a single text pattern. For example, an essay that presents primarily causes and effects is likely to be written using the cause and effect text pattern. If the types of supporting details vary, the writer is probably using a mixture of text patterns to support his thesis statement.

In a mixed pattern essay, a writer may devote a few sentences to offering a definition. She may then discuss a cause or an effect or make a brief comparison. The writer chooses the type of supporting detail to use based on her writing purpose.

To analyze mixed pattern essays, ask yourself what the writer is doing in each body paragraph. More specifically, ask questions such as these:

- Is the writer telling a short *story*?
- Is the writer giving an *example* or providing an *illustration*?
- Is the writer *defining* a term or concept?
- Is the writer putting information into a *category*?
- Is the writer explaining a *cause* or *effect*?
- Is the writer making a *comparison*?
- Is the writer explaining the stages, phases, or steps of a *process*?

In addition to finding these text patterns used as support, you may also find other supporting elements, such as *rhetorical questions* (questions to which the writer knows the answer), the use of facts and data, descriptions, summaries of other people's ideas, and explanations. By analyzing each body paragraph and jotting down the type of support the paragraph contains, you will be able to more easily identify the writer's thesis statement and major supporting points. Additionally, you will recognize how writers use mixed patterns and will be able to emulate the strategy of mixing text patterns in your own essays.

What follows is a humorous essay that includes a variety of types of support. As you read it, notice the annotations about the support the writer uses.

How to Plan a Vacation

My wife and I were brainstorming recently about what our next vacation should involve. As she talked about shopping in little boutiques along a flower-lined road, it became clear to me that her idea of a vacation was nowhere near my idea. I realized then that I needed to put my analytical prowess to good use.   *Anecdote*

First, we had to agree about what *vacation* means. Being the geeky type, I dusted off our ancient dictionary and thumbed my way to the *V* section. "A vacation," I read to my wife as she looked at red purses on a Web site, "is a period of time that a person spends away from home." That was not a very satisfactory definition. After all, shopping in precious boutiques is time away from home. I'd have to do more analysis.   *Definition*

My wife, having happily agreed to spend a vacation "away from home," kept browsing. I decided to add to the definition. "Additionally," I said, "a vacation cannot involve business or work—or the use of computers." I reasoned that not having a computer would make my wife less likely to find those cute boutiques she imagined dragging me to. Again, she happily agreed with my definition.   *Definition*

(continued)

Maybe this wouldn't be such a difficult process after all. The next thing to decide was where to go. I identified the two chief issues that mattered to us: temperature (cold-weather versus warm-weather settings) and activity level (primarily active versus principally relaxed agendas). In analyzing our options, I came up with four possible combinations: cold and active, cold and relaxed, warm and active, warm and relaxed. Now we were getting somewhere!

A "cold active" vacation might involve downhill skiing, snowshoeing, or cross-country skiing. A "cold relaxed" retreat could include reading by a roaring fire, soaking in hot springs or a hot tub outside, chatting and sipping hot drinks while looking out on a beautiful landscape and watching the snow fall. A "warm active" holiday might consist of snorkeling at a coral reef, fishing on a chartered boat, or spending time at a jumbo water park. A "warm relaxed" vacation might entail sunning at a beautiful beach, whale-watching, or taking a cruise. The best part about all of these ideas? They could all be in the countryside, and we wouldn't have to shop!

I wrote down all of the options, and I even did some pricing. Noticing that my wife was no longer looking at red purses on the Internet, I thought maybe it would be a good time to present my ideas. I showed her all of my analysis and described the four types of vacations we might take. Her eyes lit up at the prospect of lying in a hammock on a tropical beach and watching sunsets. "I would feel like a different person if I could just lounge on a beach," she said. She came up with some even better ideas than I had: she suggested we add a few active activities to our otherwise relaxing vacation by going snorkeling and taking a deep-sea fishing trip! That sealed the deal for me. We ultimately decided on the Florida Keys.

Having finally come to a decision, she gave me a quick kiss. "You know that the Keys have some of the most beautiful conch pearl jewelry, don't you?" she asked with a wink.

Annotations (right margin): Process · Classification · Illustrations · Cause and effect · Cause and effect

PRACTICE

Analyzing a Mixed Pattern Essay

On a separate sheet, answer the following questions about "How to Plan a Vacation."

1. The title suggests the essay might present a process. Does it? Explain your answer.

2. The annotations point out some of the major types of support the writer uses. Can you find additional types of support in the essay? If so, explain what they are and where they are used.

3. Could the writer have presented this information using a single text pattern? Why or why not?

4. In what way does the writer use classification? Explain.

Mixing Text Patterns in Your Writing

When you plan an essay, consider whether you can best communicate your main idea by using a single text pattern to organize your thoughts or by using a variety of text patterns as support. We will follow the process used by Marcus as he composes an essay using mixed text patterns.

Marcus is writing an essay for his biology class. The instructor has asked each student to write an informative essay about a particular illness. Each student has been assigned a particular disease and has received an information sheet about it. After students submit their work, the instructor will make copies of each student's essay to distribute to the class: the essays must help students learn enough about each illness to be able to answer questions about it on a test. Thus, Marcus's essay needs to include enough information to give his classmates a thorough understanding of the illness.

What text pattern or patterns should Marcus use in his essay on his assigned subject, mononucleosis? Clearly, he will need to *define* the illness because readers will want to know what the disease is. But readers will have other questions as well. Marcus makes a list of the questions readers may have, and then he jots down the kinds of information that will help him answer those questions.

Readers' Potential Questions about Mononucleosis

1. What is it? *definition*
2. How do people get it? Is it contagious? *cause and effect*
3. How serious is it? *cause and effect*
4. What does it "look" like? Can you see it (like measles)? *description*
5. What does it feel like? *illustration*
6. What are its symptoms? *part of definition, illustration*
7. What parts of the body does the disease affect? *cause and effect*
8. Does the disease have long-lasting effects? *cause and effect*
9. How long does it take to get rid of it? *cause and effect*
10. How is it treated? *process analysis*
11. How can people prevent it? *cause and effect*

Marcus realizes that his essay does not fit into one text pattern. Rather, he will be using a variety of text patterns as supporting details.

What is the logical way to organize these patterns? To answer this question, Marcus determines what readers need to know first: most likely, they need a definition of mononucleosis. A description of the illness and examples of symptoms will enhance the definition, so he places those items together. Next, Marcus plans to talk about the causes and effects of mononucleosis and the process of treating it. Since understanding causes and effects is yet another way of getting a basic idea of what mononucleosis is, Marcus decides to discuss those as the second major supporting point in the essay. The final major supporting point is the treatment process, so he places that last. He also creates a thesis statement that unifies the major supporting points.

> **Thesis statement:** Mononucleosis is a serious illness, but it is fairly common and is very treatable.
>
> **Major supporting point 1:** Definition, description, and examples of symptoms
>
> **Major supporting point 2:** Causes and effects
>
> **Major supporting point 3:** Treatment process

To finish the outline, Marcus needs to include the supporting details he will use in each section of the body of his essay. At this point, Marcus consults the disease information handout his instructor provided. Using it, he finds specific information to plug into his outline. (He will give credit to the source of this information in his essay.) Here is how he organizes the supporting details (shown in italics).

A Simple Outline for a Mixed Pattern Essay

> **Thesis statement:** Mononucleosis is a serious illness, but it is fairly common and is very treatable.
>
> **Major supporting point 1:** Definition, description, and examples of symptoms
>
> *Definition: "Infectious mononucleosis (IM) is a disease that occurs in older children and adolescents when they develop a primary EBV infection" (Pediatrics).*
>
> *Description and symptoms:*
>
> - *Usually appears in teens*
> - *May not look sick but do feel sick*
> - *Those infected may seem to simply be tired or lazy*
> - *A rash can develop*
> - *Pharyngitis*
> - *Fever*
> - *Profound fatigue*
> - *Lymphadenopathy (swollen, enlarged lymph nodes)*
>
> **Major supporting point 2:** Causes and effects
>
> - *What causes it*
> - *What causes it to spread*
> - *What body parts it affects*
> - *What serious damage it can cause*
>   - *Short-term*
>   - *Long-term*
>
> **Major supporting point 3:** Treatment plan (process)
>
> - *Rest (disease resolves on its own)*
> - *No contact sports*
> - *Over-the-counter medicines for pain and symptom relief*

Marcus can use his simple outline to draft paragraphs for his essay. Additionally, by noting the particular details he will use from his source, Marcus can take these details from his outline and integrate them into his essay, taking care to use the appropriate methods for giving credit to the source.

Complete the practice exercise that follows to try your hand at using mixed text patterns in an essay.

PRACTICE

Selecting Text Patterns for a Mixed Text Pattern Essay

Follow these steps to select text patterns and create an outline for an essay responding to the question, what is a "good parent"? Then write an essay in which you answer this question.

1. Use a prewriting process to create ideas about what makes a good parent.

2. Determine which ideas from your prewriting you would like to include in your essay.

3. Identify the best text pattern to use for presenting each idea.

4. Using the outline for the essay on mononucleosis as a model, write an outline for your essay.

5. Using your outline, compose the essay. Refer to the Quick Start Guide to Integrated Reading and Writing Assignments if you need assistance.

The Basic Elements of Argument

The word *argument* has a bad reputation. When we hear the word, we often think of an unpleasant disagreement or confrontation. We might think of a shouting match or an emotionally charged exchange of words between two angry people. Certainly, these kinds of exchanges are indeed arguments.

However, as the term is used academically, an **argument** is simply an opinion supported by evidence. The word is used in the same way that we use the word *viewpoint,* except that by definition, argument rests on supporting reasons whereas a person's viewpoint may not be as clearly supported. Thus, without any unpleasantness or rancor, a college professor may present her argument on an issue and may ask students to present their arguments on that issue.

Identifying the Purpose of Argument Texts

Unlike essays that are written to inform, to analyze, or to evaluate, the goal of an argument essay is to **persuade** a reader to accept a particular position or point of view. In college, you will read many written arguments, and you will also hear many oral arguments. Additionally, you will sometimes be required to write your own argument papers.

As a reader, when you approach argument texts, your goal is to determine the writer's main point and to find the support he uses to back up that point. You should also be able to evaluate the effectiveness of the support the writer uses. For example, a writer claims that Windows-based computers are better than Macs, and he bases that claim on the fact that he had a Mac once and did not like it, whereas he had a Windows-based computer and thought it was great. As a critical reader, you will recognize the weakness of the writer's evidence. He has only one piece of evidence about the quality of Windows-based computers—his own experience! He needs far more evidence to be able to prove persuasively that Windows-based computers are better than Macs. Ultimately, to assess the quality of an argument, you will need to analyze the writer's support and determine the weaknesses and strengths of the writer's argument.

Being able to read arguments critically will help you write better arguments, for you will know where potential weaknesses can lurk in your reasoning and can make sure you present the most convincing case to support your claim. To create a convincing case, you will need to have done enough reading and thinking to form and support a sound argument. Almost always, the grade you receive on an argument paper will be based on the quality of your argument, not on the particular opinion you express. Learning how to construct a sound argument is the aim. Ultimately, the goal of education is for students to think clearly and independently about issues; reading and writing arguments help develop this skill.

Recognizing the Elements of Argument

In an argument text, the thesis statement puts forth a *claim*—the writer's opinion about a debatable issue. For a thesis statement to be a claim, it has to assert an arguable point. In contrast, the thesis statement of an information or evaluation essay may not be a claim.

Thesis statement that is not a claim: Laws about keeping wild animals as domestic pets vary across the United States. *This is a fact, not an arguable issue. An essay on this topic would present information about the laws in question.*

Thesis statement that is a claim: Keeping wild animals as domestic pets should be illegal. *This statement is an opinion; thus, it is a claim.*

As always, a thesis statement must be supported, and in an argument essay, the support usually consists of evidence in the form of reasons. **Reasons,** then, are the major supporting points of an argument essay. The supporting details for reasons consist of all the information, or **evidence,** a writer needs to back up, explain, illustrate, define, or otherwise defend the major supporting points.

An additional element in argument essays is a **counterargument,** the opposing argument. Writers will often include the opposing argument and then attempt to **refute** it, to show where it is weak and flawed.

Structuring an Argument

Imagine you are making the claim that parents should not use physical punishment to discipline their children. The following list shows one *reason* (a major supporting point) you might use to support your claim and the kinds of *evidence* (supporting details) you might use.

> **Claim (thesis statement):** Parents should not use physical punishment to discipline their children.
>
> > **Reason (major supporting point):** Children who experience physical punishment act out in physical ways, such as by hitting or biting their peers.
> >
> > **Support (supporting details):**

- Explain how children learn behaviors by imitating their parents.
- Use a quote from the psychology textbook to support the point about how children learn.
- Explain the results of a psychological study that showed physical punishment resulted in physically aggressive children.

Notice that the supporting details are very specific. In this case, the supporting details consist of an explanation, a quotation, and the results of a study, and they combine to make the reason believable. If we were to outline the rest of this essay, we would see additional reasons and the supporting details the writer would use to back them up.

Identifying Three Types of Appeals in Arguments

Writers generally use three types of support for their claims: logical appeals, ethical appeals, and emotional appeals. An appeal is simply a type of reason.

To support an argument with **logical appeals,** a writer will use reasonable—logical—explanations. For example, if it is raining outside, it is reasonable to argue that your friend should take her umbrella with her when she leaves for work. Another example is to argue that people should avoid getting into debt because debt leads to decreased financial options in life. Logical appeals often make use of text patterns such as cause and effect and comparison-contrast.

In addition to logical appeals, writers also try to assure readers of their good intentions—that they are sincere, honest, and fair and that they have the readers' interests and concerns in mind. They use the testimony of knowledgeable experts to bolster their own credibility and to project self-confidence in their views. An **ethical appeal** consists of support that convinces us of the writer's trustworthiness, impartiality, expert knowledge, and goodwill.

A third type of support appeals to our emotions. Emotions are powerful; they can convince us to believe things and to take actions. For example, advertisements often tap into our emotions to sell products. A pair of name-brand, expensive athletic shoes may be the same quality as a pair of no-name sneakers, but wearing the expensive shoes gives us a *feeling* that the cheap shoes cannot provide. Appealing to our emotions can also mean appealing to our sense of shared values. In a written argument, we might tell the story of a child who is always hungry to make the claim that people should support a government supplemental food program because no child should have to suffer hunger. **Emotional appeals** can provide strong reasons for believing a claim or for taking an action.

PRACTICE ●

Identifying the Elements of Argument

Match the term in the left column with the correct definition or example in the right column.

_____ 1. argument

_____ 2. reason

_____ 3. ethical appeal

_____ 4. emotional appeal

_____ 5. logical appeal

_____ 6. counterargument

_____ 7. claim

a. If we don't get enough contributions, kittens like Sadie will be left to live a miserable, lonely life.

b. The thesis statement in an argument essay.

c. I have been a detective for twenty-five years, and I have never seen a defendant more guilty than Mr. Sellers.

d. A major supporting point for an argument essay's thesis statement.

e. The point of view of the opposing side.

f. You should buy the Chevrolet instead of the Ford because the Chevrolet gets better gas mileage.

g. An opinion supported by reasons.

Recognizing Arguments by Analyzing Topics

One way to recognize an argument essay is to focus on the essay's topic. Some topics are arguable, and some are not. An arguable topic is one that can be stated as a question whose answer is *debatable*—that is, it can be considered from multiple perspectives. Here are some topic questions whose answers are *not* arguable.

Question: What is the H1N1 flu?

Arguable or not? This question is not arguable because the answer is universally agreed on. Medical professionals know what H1N1 flu is. Thus, a paper that answers this question will simply inform, not argue.

Question: What kinds of college financial aid are available for veterans?

Arguable or not? The answer to this question requires some research, but the answer is easily found and is clear-cut. We do not have to
argue about the kinds of financial aid available for veterans because there is an authoritative answer to this question. A paper on this topic will inform, not argue.

Although the questions above are not arguable as they are stated, we can refocus them as arguable issues. To do so, we simply ask, "With what aspects of this topic might people disagree?" Notice how refocusing can result in arguable issues:

Refocus: Should the United States require people to be vaccinated against the H1N1 flu?

Arguable or not? The issue is now arguable. People will disagree on whether the vaccine should be required by law.

Refocus: Should veterans be given more financial aid opportunities than nonveterans?

Arguable or not? Now the issue is arguable. Some people will think the answer is *yes,* and others will disagree.

PRACTICE

Recognizing Arguable Issues

Below, you will find a table that lists questions on different topics. If a topic question is arguable, write "arguable" in the right-hand column next to the question. If it is not arguable, then find an issue related to the question that would be arguable. Write the new, arguable question in the right-hand column next to the question. Two examples are given.

Question	Your Response
Example: Should public schools continue to offer summer vacations, or should schooling be year-round?	Arguable
Example: What is text messaging?	Not arguable. Change to this: Why should text messaging while driving be illegal?
1. Should the first two years of college be free?	
2. What does it mean to "drink responsibly"?	
3. Who was Thomas Jefferson?	
4. What is the history of tattooing?	

Recognizing Argument Texts by Their Characteristics and Key Words

In addition to recognizing argument texts by analyzing their topics, you can also use the characteristics of argument texts and the key words associated with argument as clues.

CHARACTERISTICS OF ARGUMENT TEXTS

- Texts that argue have persuasion as their purpose.
- The subject of argument texts is an arguable issue.
- Arguments present the writer's opinion on the issue.
- Arguments present reasons and supporting details to back up the writer's opinion.
- Arguments often use research and analysis as support.

KEY WORDS OF ARGUMENT TEXTS			
according to	counters	in fact	since
argues	evidence	logic	supports
because	furthermore	reasons	therefore
claims	illogical	refutes	thus

Reading and Annotating an Argument Essay

Bernie Sanders, a US senator from Vermont, wrote the argument you are about to read. His editorial was published in *The Washington Post* in October 2015. As you read, notice the elements of argument that have been annotated. The sentences in body paragraphs that have not been highlighted are the supporting details for the reasons in the paragraphs.

Make College Free for All

By Senator Bernie Sanders

In 1877, Rutherford B. Hayes became the first president to make a strong case for universally available public education. "Universal suffrage should rest upon universal education," he said in his inaugural address, adding that "liberal and permanent provision should be made for the support of free schools." Hayes, a Republican, didn't worry that some poor kid might benefit from access to "free stuff," nor did he believe that the children of wealthy elites should be excluded from the universal nature of the program. For him, education was the basis for full economic and political participation, and full participation was the basis for all prosperity. An education should be available to all regardless of anyone's station.

Historical background

Today, there is universal access to free public schools across the United States for kindergarten through 12th grade. That didn't happen by presidential decree. It took populist pressure from the progressive movement, beginning in the 1890s, to make widespread access to free public

Current situation

(continued)

schools a reality. By 1940, half of all young people were graduating from high school. As of 2013, that number was 81 percent. But that achievement is no longer enough. A college degree is the new high school diploma.

In the 1950s and 1960s, it was possible to graduate from high school and move right into a decent-paying job with good benefits. Strong unions offered apprenticeships, and a large manufacturing sector provided opportunities for those without an advanced degree. A couple with a sole breadwinner could buy a home, raise a family and send their kids to college. That was the American dream. Unfortunately, today, for too many Americans, it's not a possibility.

An important pathway to the middle class now runs through higher education, but rising costs are making it harder and harder for ordinary Americans to get the education they want and need. In 1978, it was possible to earn enough money to pay for a year of college tuition just by working a summer job that paid minimum wage. Today, it would take a minimum wage worker an entire year to earn enough to cover the annual in-state tuition at a public university. And that's why so many bright young people don't go to college, don't finish, or graduate deeply in debt. With $1.3 trillion in student loans, Americans are carrying more student debt than credit card or auto loan debt. That's a tragedy for our young people and for our nation.

In my view, education is essential for personal and national well-being. We live in a highly competitive global economy, and if our economy is to be strong, we need the best-educated workforce in the world. We won't achieve that if, every year, hundreds of thousands of bright young people cannot afford to go to college while millions more leave school deeply in debt. We need to ensure that every young person in this country who wishes to go to college can get the education that he or she desires, without going into debt and regardless of his or her family's income.

It may seem hard to believe, but there was a time when higher education was pretty close to free in this country, at least for many Americans. After World War II, the GI Bill gave free education to more than 2 million veterans, many of whom would otherwise never have been able to go to college. This benefited them, and it was good for the economy and the country, too. In fact, scholars say that this investment was a major reason for the high productivity and economic growth our nation enjoyed during the postwar years. And, in certain states, such as California and New York, tuition was so low that college was practically free for much of the 20th century. That is no longer the case in America, but free college is still a priority in many parts of the world.

In Finland, Denmark, Ireland, Iceland, Norway, Sweden and Mexico, public colleges and universities remain tuition-free. They're free throughout Germany, too, and not just for Germans or Europeans but for international citizens as well. That's why every year, more than 4,600 students leave the United States and enroll in German universities. For a token fee of about $200 per year, an American can earn a degree in math or engineering from one of the premier universities in Europe. Governments in these countries understand

---

Reason 1: a college degree is necessary today.

Supporting details for Reason 1

Reason 2: Rising college costs make the pathway to the middle class less achievable.

Supporting details for Reason 2

Reason 3: Education is essential—both personally and nationally.

Supporting details for Reason 3

Recap of the benefits of a free college education for all

Reason 4: Other countries offer free higher education.

Supporting details for Reason 4

(continued)

what an important investment they are making, not just in the individuals who are able to acquire knowledge and skills but for the societies in which these students will serve as teachers, architects, scientists, entrepreneurs and more.

It is time to build on the progressive movement of the past and make public colleges and universities tuition-free in the United States—a development that will be the driver of a new era of American prosperity. We will have a stronger economy and a stronger democracy when all young people with the ambition and the talent can reach their full potential, regardless of their circumstances at birth.

Claim (thesis statement)

Recap of the benefits of a free college education for all

Source: Sanders, Bernie, "Make College Free for All," *The Washington Post*, October 22, 2015.

PRACTICE

Analyzing an Argument Text

Using a separate sheet, answer the following questions about "Make College Free for All."

1. Why do you think Sanders waited until the last paragraph to fully state his claim?

2. How do historical facts help Sanders support his claim?

3. What is the weakest part of Sanders argument?

4. What does Sanders mean by this phrase in the last sentence: "regardless of their circumstances at birth"?

Using Argument in Your Writing

When you have an assignment to write a persuasive essay, you will need to use the argument text pattern. Follow these guidelines.

1. Make sure your topic is an arguable topic. The primary test is to state the topic in the form of a question and then ask whether the answer to that question is debatable. If the answer is debatable, your topic is probably suitable for an essay employing the argument text pattern.

2. Prewrite to determine what your claim will be, and write a thesis statement. Once you have a thesis statement, you can come up with the best kind of support.

3. Analyze your audience before you construct reasons for your claim. Audience awareness is crucial in determining the kinds of arguments that are likely to persuade an audience and the kinds that are likely to fail. Use these principles to think through your audience's needs and expectations:

- **Write for a diverse audience.** Imagine your audience will contain people who hold a variety of viewpoints, some who agree with you and some who do not.

Imagine your audience to be composed of people from various backgrounds, of various ages, of various ethnicities, and so on. For example, if you are trying to convince your audience that women should not serve in active military combat, you should keep in mind that approximately 50 percent of readers will be female. If your thesis is likely to make your audience defensive, it is especially important to word your thoughts carefully and respectfully. It is never appropriate to include profanity or remarks that are racist or sexist or that show disrespect for those who are older or who have disabilities. Showing respect to your audience is key. The technique used by some radio and television hosts of making provocative and biased statements in the guise of "argument" may earn them high entertainment ratings and income, but it is not appropriate or useful in academic argument or in any argument that seeks to find meaningful solutions to problems.

- **Think about the kinds of evidence your audience might find convincing.** Many types of evidence can be used in argument papers: statistics, stories, analogies, facts, studies, explanations of causes and effects, definitions, and predictions. If you are writing an essay for a history professor, it is probably important to use relevant facts, details, and maybe even stories. If you are writing for a general audience, use research that your audience can easily understand. Evidence such as studies, quotes from authorities in the field, and logical explanations of cause and effect can be effective in supporting your thesis. Remember that you will probably have a lot of evidence to choose from as you write your paper. Select only evidence that you think will be effective for your audience.

- **Always imagine that you are writing for a skeptical audience.** Imagine that as they study your paper, your readers are muttering, "Where's the evidence?" or "I disagree" or "Prove it!" Make sure you anticipate the audience's doubts and address them in your paper. Another way to be mindful of your audience's doubts is to be fully aware of the opposing position. If you are arguing for random drug testing in the workplace, for example, you should be fully aware of all the reasons against workplace drug testing. In your paper, you can address the reasons that opponents would offer and then refute them.

- **Keep in mind that your audience is interested in hearing your thesis and your evidence, but your audience also wants to think that you—as a writer—are credible and believable.** Your readers will be judging not only your argument but also *you*. To come across as knowledgeable and competent to a general audience, you must ensure that your paper is written in standard English, conforms to an acceptable format, and demonstrates that you have done the reading necessary to know what you are talking about. Additionally, your argument should show that you are fair to the opposing side. You can demonstrate this fairness by thoroughly understanding the opposing argument and by showing respect to those who advocate it.

4. Identify the reasons you will use to support your claim. List all the reasons you can think of, and analyze each one. Which ones will the opposing side easily refute? Which ones are the most logical? Which, if any, might elicit a positive emotional response from readers? Determine the best reasons and then work on finding support to explain and develop those reasons fully.

5. Analyze counterarguments, and plan how you will refute them. In many argument essays you will find a counterargument (the opposing viewpoint). To show you understand the argument of the other side, your essay can include the arguments of the opposing side and your objections to those arguments.

In professional essays, writers use counterarguments for a variety of reasons. First, by acknowledging the strengths of the opposing argument, they establish goodwill, the sense that they are fair-minded and are giving credit to the valid points of their opponents. Second, explaining a counterargument shows that a writer has carefully listened to the opposing viewpoint. An argument can be fair only when both parties actually listen to each other and consider each other's point of view. Third, knowing the best points of the counterargument enables writers to craft an argument that is effective because they know the points they need to refute. This strategy is similar to the way football coaches and players think. If you can anticipate the play the opposing team will make, you can construct a good counterstrategy.

One way to use argument successfully is to fully understand the *best* arguments of the opposing position. Suppose you strongly believe that gun control laws should be strengthened. When you feel strongly about an issue, it's easy to not really hear the opposing argument. But hearing the opposing argument is not only important; it's absolutely necessary. If you cannot address the opposing argument, point by point, and show why your position is superior, you will not be able to write a convincing essay.

6. Create a simple outline for your argument essay. Determine the order in which you will present each reason and the supporting details needed to develop each reason. If you plan to include counterarguments and refute them, use your outline to note where these elements will occur in your essay.

Avoiding Common Logical Errors

It is important to use logical reasons when you construct an argument, but it can be easy to make logical errors. Avoid the following logical errors in your writing.

Faulty Causes or Effects

You cannot say that X caused Y without having some proof. Imagine that your town recently elected a new mayor. In the two years she has been in office, the unemployment rate in your city has increased. It is illogical to claim that X (electing the new mayor) caused Y (the increase in unemployment). Maybe these two things were a coincidence. Unless you have additional information to prove that X caused Y, it is unfair and illogical to make that claim.

You cannot say that if we do action X, then Y will happen, unless you have good evidence. Some people create fear-inducing predictions to convince others of a point of view. For example, a parent who wants her son to go to college might say that if he does not go to college (X), he will end up jobless and homeless (Y). Does she have proof for that prediction? No. She says it to scare her son into believing her point that every successful person goes to college. Making a prediction without enough evidence to do so is a logical error.

Faulty Generalizations

A *generalization* is a statement made about an entire group or class, such as "All horses are animals." Generalizations based on evidence can be fair, but unsubstantiated generalizations are often faulty. For example, consider this statement: women are better chefs than men. Such a generalization is simply not logical. Some women may be better chefs than some men, but it does not follow that all women are better chefs than all men.

Almost any broad statement about a racial, ethnic, socioeconomic, or gender group will result in a generalization that is unfair. Generalizations are commonly used incorrectly in two specific ways: making a statement based on small samples and unfairly representing the opponent's viewpoint.

Generalizations Based on Small Samples.   Assume that you had a BXC smartphone and that it performed very poorly. You cannot logically claim that BXC smartphones are low quality because you have only *one* piece of evidence—one phone. Your experience with one sample (one BXC smartphone) is too limited for you to draw conclusions about BXC phones. What if BXC produced two million smartphones and yours was the only one that had problems? Since you do not know the data about the larger group, it is illogical to make a generalization about BXC smartphones.

Unfair Representations of Your Opponent.   Imagine reading an argument against gun control in which the writer says people who want guns to be more widely available do not care about human life and want to be able to kill people. This kind of error is unfair because it relies on a stereotype, rather than evidence, about gun rights proponents. It is also unfair because it misrepresents the argument of the group.

Faulty Analogies

One way that people often make a point is by making a comparison. In the study of argument, comparisons are called *analogies*. Here are some examples of analogies.

- Comparing marijuana to alcohol to support an argument that marijuana should be legal
- Comparing the leader of a country to Hitler to support an argument that war against the leader's country is a good idea
- Comparing a current situation—like a recession—to a situation in the past to support an argument that we need to take X or Y action

Analogies can often clarify ideas for readers. It is acceptable to use analogies as long as the two things being compared are similar enough to support the point being made. By definition, the two things being compared in an analogy are different. The critical question is, how different are they?

It would not be fair, for example, for a professor to expect her freshmen writing students to write like students in a senior-level advanced writing course. The analogy between those two groups would be illogical. Neither is it fair to make a comparison like this: young people can serve in the military at age 18, so they should be able to drink at age 18. The assumption is that serving in the military is similar to drinking alcohol. Is it? In what ways are those two things similar? In the military, 18-year-olds are heavily supervised and trained. They can serve in the military because of this training. Are 18-year-olds who want to drink going to be supervised as they drink and trained in the safety and health principles that govern responsible drinking? Probably not. Thus, the comparison of these two things is not logical.

PRACTICE ●

Using Argument in Your Writing

1. Respond to Bernie Sanders's editorial by writing your own argument about whether or not a college education should be free. If you argue that a college education should be free, come up with reasons that are different from those Sanders uses.

2. Consider the following list of topics for an essay using the argument text pattern. For each one, decide whether it is an arguable issue. If it is not an arguable issue, refocus the topic so that it becomes arguable.

    a. The need to make adoptions more affordable
    b. Why people should be organ donors
    c. What diabetes is and how it is treated
    d. Why a missile defense program is a bad idea for the United States
    e. The history of yoga
    f. How we can improve driver's education programs

3. Choose one of the following questions, and use it as the basis for an essay using the argument text pattern.

    a. Do Americans value entertainment more than education?
    b. What are the principles of socialism? Once you learn what they are, judge for yourself: Is socialism an undesirable form of government? Make an argument to prove your point.
    c. Do group projects constitute an effective method for teaching students? Do they really help students learn?
    d. Should all children be required to learn to read music?
    e. Should airline pilots be allowed to carry guns?
    f. Should public school teachers be allowed to carry guns?
    g. Should parents enter their children in beauty pageants?

Grammar Focus

Passive and Active Voice

Consider this: If you were a prosecutor making the case that a defendant is guilty, which of these sentences would best serve your argument?

A. The defendant <u>threw</u> the woman to the ground and <u>grabbed</u> her purse.

B. The woman <u>was thrown</u> to the ground, and her purse <u>was grabbed.</u>

Sentence A is a direct statement that assigns blame, and it clearly tells us that a particular person (the defendant) did the crime. Sentence B describes the same situation, but it does not tell us *who* did the throwing and grabbing. It does not assign responsibility for the action. Most readers would find sentence A, which is in the active voice, more persuasive than sentence B, which is in the passive voice.

Voice is one way to describe verbs in a sentence. If a verb is in the **active voice,** the verb's subject (underlined in the following example) *performs* the action.

(continued)

Example: <u>Tasha</u> threw the javelin.

Tasha—the subject of the sentence—is clearly the doer of the action; she was the one who did the throwing.

If a verb is in the **passive voice,** its subject (underlined below) *receives* the action.

Example: The <u>javelin</u> was thrown by Tasha.

The subject, *javelin,* is not doing the action; rather, the javelin is being acted upon. It is the recipient of the action. The sentence includes *by Tasha,* so we know who threw the javelin. However, because the doer of the action is not the subject, the sentence has less impact.

Generally, the active voice is best for most writing. Sentences in the active voice are usually more straightforward and lively than those in the passive voice.

There are times, however, when you may want to use passive instead of active voice.

1. USE PASSIVE OR ACTIVE VOICE FOR EMPHASIS

The subject of a sentence is usually the focus of the reader's attention. So, if you want to emphasize a particular element, make that element the subject.

Passive voice: Evidence that hunter-gatherers lived in Texas as far back as 15,500 years ago was recently unearthed by anthropologists.

Emphasizes the newly discovered evidence about prehistory in Texas.

Active voice: Anthropologists recently unearthed evidence that hunter-gatherers lived in Texas as far back as 15,500 years ago.

Emphasizes who discovered the new evidence about prehistory in Texas.

To decide where to put the emphasis in a sentence, imagine that your sentence is answering a question.

Passive voice: Evidence that hunter-gatherers lived in Texas as far back as 15,500 years ago was recently unearthed by anthropologists.

Answers this question: What was recently discovered about prehistory in Texas?

Active voice: Anthropologists recently unearthed evidence that hunter-gatherers lived in Texas as far back as 15,500 years ago.

Answers this question: Who recently discovered new evidence about prehistory in Texas?

2. USE PASSIVE OR ACTIVE VOICE TO EVADE OR INDICATE RESPONSIBILITY

The passive voice can conceal or deemphasize responsibility for an action. For that reason, it is sometimes used in controversial or politically sensitive writing.   *(continued)*

Passive voice: During those decades, many Indian children were forcibly removed from their families.

Active voice: During those decades, the federal government forcibly removed many Indian children from their families.

3. USE THE PASSIVE VOICE WHEN THE DOER IS UNKNOWN OR ASSUMED

When readers will presumably know who the doer is, the passive voice allows you to write a more concise sentence.

Passive voice: The new song was written, arranged, recorded, and produced in a matter of months.

Active voice: In a matter of months, the songwriter wrote the new song, the arranger arranged it, the singer recorded it, and the recording studio produced it.

Because it is not necessary to spell out all the doers of various actions, as in the active voice sentence, the passive voice allows the writer to create a more concise sentence.

A RELATED ISSUE: STARTING SENTENCES WITH *There is/are* AND *It is/was*

When writers are composing a first draft, they often resort to using *There is/are* and *It is/was* to begin sentences. Sometimes using these expressions makes it easy to get thoughts down in sentence form. But with few exceptions, these expressions can diminish the quality of the writing. The revision stage is a good time to rewrite these sentences for greater impact. Consider these examples.

Acceptable: There is evidence that high-quality early childhood programs can have a positive effect on the health of adults years later.

Better: Evidence shows that high-quality early childhood programs can have a positive effect on the health of adults years later.

Better: High-quality early childhood programs can have a positive effect on the health of adults years later, according to some evidence.

When you see a sentence in your writing that begins with *There is/are* or *It is/was,* ask yourself, "What is important in this sentence? What do I want to emphasize?"

Sentences beginning with *There is/are* or *It is/was* are grammatically correct, but they are weak. With some effort they can be transformed into sentences that can more effectively communicate your ideas to readers.

SENTENCE COMBINING

In the example that follows, notice how the short sentences are combined into longer sentences that employ active voice.

(continued)

Ideas to combine:

- That the design was flawed was well known by the company.

- Documentation of the flaw was made before the car seats were manufactured.

- Negligence is what caused the car seats to be manufactured in such a way.

Combined using active voice: The company was negligent when it manufactured the car seats. Even though it knew the design was flawed, the company manufactured the car seats anyway.

EXERCISES

Combine each set of sentences into longer, smoother sentences, and use active voice when appropriate.

1. Ideas to combine:

- The old house was inspected by the landlord.

- It was inspected by him after the flood.

- The flooring had been warped by the floodwaters.

- However, the frame of the house had been spared.

- The house was still in good condition.

   Answer: _____

   _____

2. Ideas to combine:

- Children should be taught problem-solving skills.

- Critical thinking skills can be developed by the teaching of problem solving.

- There is a true sense of accomplishment that can be felt by children who can solve problems.

   Answer: _____

   _____

3. Ideas to combine:

- One serious disease is diabetes.

- An increased risk of heart disease can be a result of diabetes.

- An increase in the risk of stroke can be caused by diabetes.

- Eye problems can be caused by diabetes.

- It is known that nerve damage can occur.

- Foot or leg amputations can be caused by complications of diabetes.

   Answer: _____

   _____

   _____

Organizing, Drafting, and Summarizing

Skill at organizing documents can transfer directly to the skill of organizing the tasks, events, and materials required in a wide range of careers and is essential in fields such as paralegal or bookkeeping work.

Chapter Objectives

After completing this chapter, students will be able to do the following:

- Identify common strategies for ordering information.

- Use information-ordering strategies in writing.

- Use outlines and graphic organizers to analyze a text's organization.

- Use outlines to draft essays.

- Use outlines to write detailed and brief summaries.

- Write paraphrases.

Have you ever watched a movie that presents plot events in a jumbled order? For example, a movie may start with a dramatic scene—such as a standoff between good guys and bad guys—and then loop back in time to provide the backstory, the information that helps viewers understand the standoff. Or perhaps you have seen a movie that *seems* to be taking place in the present, but at the end of the film you learn that the actions were only a dream. Filmmakers make very intentional choices about the order in which they present scenes, and these choices can have dramatic effects on viewers.

Writers also carefully select the order in which they present information. Becoming more aware of the ordering strategies other writers use will help you comprehend the texts you read and will enable you to experiment with these strategies when you write your own essays.

A careful reading of a text can also help you record the writer's ideas in a detailed outline or a graphic organizer, which you can use to write an accurate summary. Many students find that a crucial study skill is to write outlines and summaries of the texts they study. A related skill—writing a paraphrase—also requires a careful, close reading of a text. In this chapter, you will have the opportunity to hone these skills.

Identifying Common Strategies for Ordering Information

As you analyze texts, notice the choices writers make about the order in which they present information. In general, when we talk about the order of information, we are referring to where writers place the thesis statement and the major supporting points. Three common strategies for ordering information are to use order of importance, chronological order, and spatial order.

Order of Importance

Writers use **order of importance** to organize reasons, concepts, and general information. They consider the effect on readers when deciding whether to place the most important item first or last. Presenting the most important major supporting point first immediately alerts readers to the point's significance for the thesis statement. Placing the most important major supporting point last can also be effective because this point will be fresh in the minds of readers as they finish the text.

In the following example, the writer places the most important major supporting point last to emphasize its value. Note also that placing a major supporting point last in the thesis statement gives it more emphasis than the other points.

Order of Importance Organization in an Essay

INTRODUCTION
Introduction paragraph

Thesis statement: Sibling rivalry is good for children because it promotes listening skills, social skills, problem-solving skills, and self-control.

BODY

Topic sentence for major supporting point 1: One good thing about sibling rivalry is that it helps children develop listening skills.

Topic sentence for major supporting point 2: Children who fight with siblings also have better social skills than children who do not.

Topic sentence for major supporting point 3: Even more significantly, sibling rivalry helps children develop problem-solving skills.

Topic sentence for major supporting point 4: Most importantly, children who fight with siblings have greater self-control than children who do not.

CONCLUSION
Conclusion paragraph

Chronological Order

Chronological order uses time or sequence to organize ideas. Events are usually presented in chronological order; steps in a process are presented sequentially. Notice that in the following simple outline, the stages of training for medical doctors are discussed in the order in which they occur—that is, chronologically.

Chronological Order Organization in an Essay

INTRODUCTION
Introduction paragraph

Thesis statement: The three stages of training for medical doctors are medical school, internship, and residency.

BODY

Paragraph 2: Medical school

Paragraph 3: Internship

Paragraph 4: Residency

CONCLUSION
Conclusion paragraph

Spatial Order

Spatial order uses the physical position of objects to organize ideas. Many descriptive passages use spatial organization, as the example on the next page shows. Notice how prepositional phrases (underlined) guide the reader around the cabin's interior.

Spatial Order Organization in a Descriptive Paragraph

The cabin that would be my home for three months needed repair. I walked through the doorway, and to my left I saw an ancient black cookstove. It seemed to be in better condition than anything else in the cabin. Directly above the stove and to the left was a hole in the roof about the size of a tire. Light streamed in and pooled on the rotted floorboards that had fallen victim to rain, snow, and ice. On the right side of the cabin was an old aluminum cot, its canvas clearly suffering from dry rot. A knee-high pile of trash was heaped in the back corner underneath three shelves next to the only window in the cabin. It would be a long winter.

Transitional Terms for Information-Ordering Strategies

The transitions that follow are helpful additions that you can use to identify the order of information in a particular text. You can also use these in your own writing.

TRANSITIONS		
Transitions for Order of Importance	**Transitions for Chronological Order**	**Transitions for Spatial Order**
first, second, third, significantly, more significantly, most significantly, importantly, more importantly, most importantly, above all, of less significance, of less importance	first, second, third, before, to begin, to continue, during, next, while, until, when, afterward, finally, to conclude	to the right, to the left, above, below, inside, outside, under, beneath, behind, around, beside, next to, adjacent, joining, continuing around, in front of, in back of

By being aware of the ordering strategy a writer uses, you can more effectively understand passage, the text pattern or patterns being used, and the organization of the content.

PRACTICE 1

Identifying Ordering Strategies

On the basis of the transitions and content in each passage below, identify the order of arrangement the author has used. Use *OI* for order of importance, *CO* for chronological order, and *SO* for spatial order.

____ **1.** In April 1952, my father lost his job. He became depressed, and the entire summer, he sat on the front porch smoking cigarettes and barely talking. Mother could do little to console him, for he snapped at anyone who dared conversation. In August of that year, I turned six years old.

____ **2.** Perhaps the most significant cause of the war was famine and starvation. The people had reached a point of desperation. There was not even enough food to steal from the wealthy. Disenchantment with the priest's advice—while not as significant as the incessant hunger—was prevalent. The priest's assurances of better days to come were hollow utterances in a world of deprivation and despair.

____ **3.** The top floor of the building was full of windows overlooking the bay. The view was splendid. To the left was the Golden Gate Bridge, **resplendent** in the morning sun. In the distance was Mount Tamalpais's peak.

VCW resplendent

For every Vocabulary Collection Word (VCW), give your in-context idea of the word's meaning and then look up the word's dictionary definition.

Using Information-Ordering Strategies in Your Writing

Making intentional decisions about the order in which you present ideas will help you write more clearly and effectively. Use the following chart to select an information-ordering strategy that fits your purpose.

USES FOR ORGANIZING STRATEGIES		
Order of Importance	**Chronological Order**	**Spatial Order**
• Reasons • Classifications (types) • Comparison-contrast information • Causes and effects	• Historical information • Narratives • Processes • Stages or steps • Causes and effects	• Descriptions

In your essay, be sure to present your points in the same order in which they occur in your thesis statement. For example, earlier in the chapter, an example of chronological order contained this thesis statement:

> The three stages of training for medical doctors are medical school, internship, and residency.

In the body paragraphs, the writer should discuss these stages in the order in which they appear in the thesis statement.

PRACTICE **2**

Using Order of Importance, Chronological Order, and Spatial Order

Complete the following paragraph-writing activities.

1. Order of importance: Write a paragraph in which you present the three most important priorities in your life. Put the most important priority last. Use appropriate transitions.

2. Chronological order: Write a paragraph in which you describe an event, such as what happened during a recent family celebration, or a process that follows a particular sequence, such as how to change a flat tire.

3. Spatial order: Write a paragraph in which you describe your kitchen. Use appropriate transitions.

Using Outlines and Graphic Organizers to Analyze a Text's Organization

An outline can be helpful to you as a reader and as a writer. As a reader, an outline helps you understand the organization of a text and the relationships among ideas in the text. It equips you with everything you need to write a good summary of the reading. As a writer, an outline helps you determine where to place support and how to organize your ideas.

Creating Outlines to Analyze Organization

There is no one-size-fits-all pattern of organization that works for every text. However, most texts do have three components: an introduction, a body, and a conclusion. The number of paragraphs in these three components can vary. Some writers even offer three or four paragraphs of introductory material before getting to the main idea. When you outline a text, be aware that writers do not always place information in the order you expect.

To write an outline for a text you are reading, you need to find the writer's main idea and determine the major supporting points. Sometimes the writer provides clues, such as headings and subheadings. When you see them, notice the differences in size, style, and color. Look at the example that follows. In a textbook on business management and **entrepreneurs**, chapter titles are large and always appear at the top of a page, main headings appear in green, subheadings are smaller than main headings and appear in blue, and sub-subheadings are in black. As you study the example that follows, think about what information each section of the text might present.

VCW entrepreneur

CHAPTER 4 **Starting a Business**

Entrepreneurialism

    Personal Traits of Entrepreneurs

        Entrepreneurs Are Visionary

        Entrepreneurs Are Personable

        Entrepreneurs Are Highly Motivated

        Entrepreneurs Are Researchers

In a text that does not contain headings and subheadings, you can still distinguish the elements of importance and determine their relationship to one another. The annotations in the following essay identify the elements a reader would use to construct an outline.

How Delaying Gratification Predicts Future Success

By Kari Gardner

"I want what I want, and I want it *now*." We live in a world in which instant gratification is not merely desired: it's expected. If Internet access is delayed for even a few seconds, we are frustrated. If our fast food is not fast enough, we are miffed, and so it goes.

What is required in these circumstances is *delayed gratification*, the ability to postpone the fulfillment of an immediate desire in order to obtain a more substantial reward in the future. To put it more informally, delayed gratification means putting off having something now so you can get something better later on.

Educators and psychologists alike say that being able to tolerate delayed gratification is an extremely valuable skill. People who can put off immediate gratification are more likely to have what it takes to be successful in the important things in life. And there is research to support that opinion.

In the late 1960s and early 1970s, psychologists at Stanford University (led by Walter Mischel) performed a series of studies that came to be known as the Marshmallow Experiment. Young children (from four to six years old) were given a large, fluffy marshmallow and were told they could eat the marshmallow now, or they could wait fifteen minutes and get a second marshmallow.

Many of the kids who were able to delay gratification distracted themselves from the marshmallow by covering their eyes with their hands, turning their backs to the treat, kicking the table, and so forth. Other children who successfully delayed eating the marshmallow used their imaginations to reframe the treat as something else. For example, by thinking about the marshmallow as a cloud or by thinking the marshmallow was just a picture of a marshmallow, children were able to resist eating it immediately.

Annotations (margin):

Introduction: examples of how people have trouble delaying gratification

Definition

Thesis statement
Major supporting point 1 (implied): The Marshmallow Experiment shows that delayed gratification skills lead to more success in life.

Details: focus on how the experiment was set up (process analysis)

Details: focus on what happened in the experiment (cause and effect)

(continued)

Of course, a significant number of children simply could not wait. Some nibbled on the marshmallow and eventually popped the whole thing into their mouths, and some ate it almost immediately.

In follow-up studies years later, the psychologists determined that the children who were able to wait longer—to postpone their gratification—tended to do substantially better as adults than those children who were less patient. The psychologists based their assessment on the analysis of the test subjects' levels of behavioral problems, drug and alcohol addiction, educational achievement, SAT scores, and other measures. Although recent studies have suggested that the fundamental issue is more complex than simple self-control, the basic point still stands: it is important to learn to tolerate delayed gratification.

Psychological tests are not the only way to demonstrate the importance of delayed gratification. Proof that it pays to put off pleasure is all around us. People who have the patience and willpower to regularly invest even small amounts of money can easily become very wealthy—if they are willing to wait long enough for their money to multiply. Students who seek college degrees earn them by putting off pleasure today for the reward of a degree tomorrow. And athletes who make it to the top know very well the importance of working hard today so that they can perform well tomorrow.

It will always be easier to eat the marshmallow right away, but doing so may not always be the best choice.

> Details: the conclusion drawn from the experiment (explanation)
>
> Major supporting point 2
> Details: people who delay gratification to pursue success (examples)

To outline a text, list the main idea (whether stated in a thesis statement, as in this case, or implied), the major supporting points, and the supporting details that follow the major supporting points. When writing an outline, always use quotation marks if you use actual phrases and sentences from the text, as shown in the outline that follows. Doing so enables you to remember which words are yours and which came from the source.

Simple Outline of "How Delaying Gratification Predicts Future Success" by Kari Gardner

Thesis statement: "People who can put off immediate gratification are more likely to have what it takes to be successful in the important things in life."

Major supporting point 1 (implied): The Marshmallow Experiment shows that delayed gratification skills lead to more success in life.

Supporting details:
- How the experiment was set up
- What happened in the experiment
- The conclusion drawn from the experiment

(continued)

Major supporting point 2: "Proof that it pays to put off pleasure is all around us."

Supporting details:
- People who invest
- Students who graduate
- Athletes who train

The preceding outline of "How Delaying Gratification Predicts Future Success" is a simple outline. It includes just the minimum amount of information necessary to map the essay. If you need to remember more of the details than a basic outline allows, you can construct an **enhanced** outline by including additional important information, as this example demonstrates (the added information is in *italics*):

 **VCW** enhanced

Enhanced Outline of "How Delaying Gratification Predicts Future Success" by Kari Gardner

Introduction: Provides examples of how people have trouble tolerating delayed gratification. **Definition** *of delayed gratification: "the ability to postpone the fulfillment of an immediate desire in order to obtain a more substantial reward in the future."*

Thesis statement: "People who can put off immediate gratification are more likely to have what it takes to be successful in the important things in life."

Major supporting point 1 (implied): The Marshmallow Experiment shows that delayed gratification skills lead to more success in life.

Supporting details:
- How the experiment was set up: *Children were given the option of one marshmallow now or two later.*
- What happened in the experiment: *Some children waited to eat the marshmallow, and some did not.*
- The conclusion drawn from the experiment: *Children who waited had more success as adults.*
  - *Assessment based on behavioral problems, drug and alcohol addiction, educational achievement, SAT scores*

Major supporting point 2: "Proof that it pays to put off pleasure is all around us."

Supporting details:
- People who invest *(end up wealthy if they wait)*
- Students who graduate *(put off pleasure today for reward tomorrow)*
- Athletes who train *(practice today for performance rewards tomorrow)*

The enhanced outline has more information than the basic outline, particularly in the supporting details.

Some instructors may ask you to submit a formal outline with your essay. The formal outline uses an alphanumeric labeling system, and subordinate items are indented. The items are usually either all phrases or all full sentences.

Formal Outline for "How Delaying Gratification Predicts Future Success" by Kari Gardner

I. Introduction
   A. Examples of how people have trouble tolerating delayed gratification.
   B. Definition of delayed gratification: "The ability to postpone the fulfillment of an immediate desire in order to obtain a more substantial reward in the future."
   C. Thesis statement: "People who can put off immediate gratification are more likely to have what it takes to be successful in the important things in life."
II. The Marshmallow Experiment: Proof that delayed gratification skills lead to more success in life.
   A. How the experiment was set up: Children were given the option of one marshmallow now or two later.
   B. What happened in the experiment:
      1. Some children waited to eat the marshmallow.
      2. Some did not wait.
   C. Conclusion drawn from the experiment: Children who waited had more success as adults.
   D. Assessment based on behavioral problems, drug and alcohol addiction, educational achievement, SAT scores.
III. Conclusion: "Proof that it pays to put off pleasure is all around us."
   A. People who invest (end up wealthy if they wait).
   B. Students who graduate (put off pleasure today for reward tomorrow).
   C. Athletes who train (practice today for performance rewards tomorrow).

PRACTICE 3

Outlining a Brief Reading

Read the following passage, and annotate the thesis statement, major supporting points, and supporting details. Then, on a separate sheet, create a simple outline for the reading.

Achieving Optimum Fitness

Physical activities play an important role in fitness. Many people participate in endurance exercises, such as walking, running, and swimming, but optimum fitness requires more than endurance activities. Strength training and flexibility development are also important. Maximum fitness can be achieved by performing these three types of exercises regularly.

Exercises such as brisk walking, jogging, and swimming help athletes develop endurance. Endurance training is accomplished by participating in aerobic activities for an extended period of time. Biking, dancing, and yard work (for example, pushing a lawnmower or raking leaves) also qualify as endurance training. These activities involve relatively low-intensity actions performed for extended periods

YOUR ANNOTATIONS

(continued)

of time. Twenty minutes of continuous activity is typically considered the minimum length of time necessary for significant improvement in endurance. The intensity should be between 60 and 85 percent of maximum heart rate.

Generally speaking, endurance exercises require repeated movement of the large muscles in the arms, legs, or hips. These movements are required to get one's heart pumping rapidly. The principal positive effects of endurance exercise are to the cardiovascular system. (That's why endurance training is also referred to as *cardio*.) Endurance exercise keeps the heart, lungs, and circulatory system healthy and improves overall fitness. As a result, doing cardio helps delay or prevent many diseases that are common in older adults, such as diabetes and heart disease. In addition, building endurance makes it easier to carry out many everyday activities, such as climbing stairs. A bonus of moderate to intense endurance exercise is that the body releases endorphins, natural painkillers that promote an increased sense of well-being.

Strength training is another important activity for fitness. Sometimes called *resistance training*, strength training involves using muscles against a resistant force. The muscles are said to be "under load." Most often the resistance is the function of gravity and weights, although other methods are available (for example, strong elastic bands, and pneumatic/hydraulic cylinders). "Free weights" include barbells and dumbbells with heavy disks attached. Weight machines operate on the same property of gravity.

Lifting weights actually causes microdamage to muscles, which become stronger when they rebuild themselves. At least one day of rest between exercising any particular muscle group is recommended. When properly performed, strength training provides significant benefits in addition to an increase in muscle strength and mass. The connective tissues of the musculoskeletal system—tendons and ligaments—are also strengthened. That is very significant for joint stability, particularly as people age. Weight training also increases bone strength and density, which is very important in the prevention of osteoporosis. An increase in HDL ("good") cholesterol has been linked to resistance training. Increased muscle mass leads to a higher metabolic rate; that means that a person with a muscular body is burning more calories while resting than a person with less muscle mass.

The aspect of fitness people are less likely to consider is flexibility. **Nonetheless**, flexibility is very important for daily life as well as for professional competition. Flexibility exercises stretch the muscles, ligaments, and tendons. The result is that the body becomes more limber. Being flexible gives a person more freedom of movement for other exercises as well as for everyday activities. Stretching exercises, when done properly, assist with posture by balancing the tension placed across the joint by the muscles that cross it. Proper posture minimizes stress and maximizes the strength of all joint movements. Many cases of chronic lower back pain are actually a function of a lack of limberness in the upper legs and in the lower back.

VCW nonetheless

Perhaps the form of exercise most specifically focused on flexibility is yoga. In addition to yoga's obvious contribution to limberness, many practitioners find that it has a positive psychological effect. (Of course, that can be said for the first two types of exercise as well!) Those who regularly practice yoga report that they experience a reduction in anxiety, stress, depression, chronic pain, and sleep difficulties. Put positively, they report a higher general sense of well-being.

A person who engages regularly in endurance exercises, strength training, and flexibility development will become fit. Adding a healthy diet, adequate water intake, and sound sleeping patterns to these three physical activities will result in an optimum level of health and fitness.

Creating Graphic Organizers to Analyze Organization

A **graphic organizer** is a visual map that displays much of the same information as an outline. Graphic organizers are designed to show relationships among ideas. Some people find that working with graphic organizers is easier than working with outlines.

Many word-processing programs have a feature, like SmartArt in *Microsoft Word,* that offers templates for graphic organizers. However, you can also draw a graphic organizer by hand.

To create a graphic organizer, begin by drawing a box at the top of the page. The box should be as wide as your sheet of paper because it will form the canopy for all the boxes that follow. As you reread your text, find what you think is the main idea or thesis statement, and write it inside the box. Remember to use quotation marks if you are using a direct quote.

> "People who can put off immediate gratification are more likely to have what it takes to be successful in the important things in life."

Next, look for a major supporting point—an idea that directly supports the main point. Draw a narrower box with this information in it, and connect it to the main box, as follows.

> "People who can put off immediate gratification are more likely to have what it takes to be successful in the important things in life."

> The Marshmallow Experiment shows that delayed gratification skills lead to more success in life.

As you come across details, add more boxes, connecting the new boxes to the ideas that they support. When you find new major supporting points that directly prove the main idea, add boxes for those too. Step back and look at the graphic organizer. Does the arrangement of boxes seem logical to you, with lesser ideas supporting greater ideas? If not, rearrange the boxes so that they better reflect a logical organization. As a final step, you might find it helpful to label the boxes that contain the thesis statement and the major supporting point.

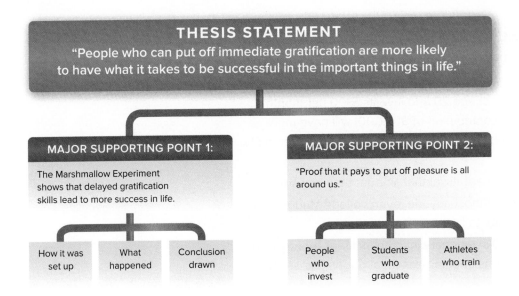

Outlines and graphic organizers illustrate the *logic* of a text. Sometimes, though, a writer will jump around in presenting ideas and information. For example, to arouse readers' interest in what lies ahead, a writer may start an essay with a detail for a point that will come later on in the text. In your graphic organizer, be sure to attach the detail to the point that it supports even if the detail appears out of order in the text.

Using Outlines to Draft Essays

In addition to serving as a tool to help you understand readings, outlines also make drafting your essay easier. The best kind of outline to use for writing is an enhanced outline. It should contain your thesis statement, your main supporting points, and the supporting details you will use to develop each main supporting point. We will follow the process of Ian, a writing student, as he uses an enhanced outline to draft his essay.

Ian is writing an essay to convince his classmates that investing at an early age is wise. He has already used prewriting to generate ideas, has written a thesis statement, has determined his major supporting points, and has developed the supporting details he will use to develop his ideas. Here is the enhanced outline Ian has created for his essay. Notice that he has indicated the source for each quote he uses—an article entitled "Six Misconceptions about Investing Young" by Jean Folger (www.investopedia.com) and a personal communication from Sean Williams, an investment banker he contacted.

Ian's Enhanced Outline

Title: Start with a Penny

Introduction: I'll tell the story of my grandparents, who came to the United States with nothing and ended up having over a million dollars, simply because they made small deposits into their investment account each week since they were young.

Thesis statement: One of the most important preparations college students can make for the future is to start investing immediately.

(continued)

Major supporting point 1: Accruing wealth comes from making small investments over a long period of time.

> **Support:** Explanation of mathematics
> - "A person who starts at age 20 and invests $100 per month until age 65 (a total contribution of $54,000) will have more than $200,000 when he or she reaches age 65 assuming a 5% return" (Folger).
> - Example of my grandparents (actual amount they invested)

Major supporting point 2: Almost anyone, even college students, can find small amounts of money to invest.

> **Support:** Definition—"Discretionary income includes money spent on luxury items, vacations and non-essential goods and services" (Folger).
> - How to find discretionary income
> - How discretionary income adds up (provide explanation)
> - Provide examples

Major supporting point 3: Additionally, investing is easy, and starting to invest at a young age will help you get into the habit of investing.

> **Support:** Explanation about how easy it is to invest
> - Example of setting up an investment account
> - Example of buying bonds
> - Quote from investment company: "Many people have the idea that investing requires a lot of technical knowledge, but it doesn't. All you need to do is come in and talk with an adviser. The process is similar to setting up a savings account" (Williams).

Major supporting point 4: Finally, college students should start investing because they will most likely need the money.

> **Support:** Social security and retirement plans may not work.
> - Quote: "It is difficult to predict where social security will be in future years, and many investors learned the hard way in the last decade that employee-sponsored retirement plans don't always work out" (Folger).
> - As you age, expenses increase.
> - Examples of expenses

Conclusion: End by telling readers about the relaxing life my grandparents now enjoy (their travels, nice home, etc.) because of their investments.

Because Ian has a wealth of information in his outline—including quotes, stories, and examples—he can start drafting the body paragraphs by writing sentences for each item on his outline. Using an outline to guide you will make the drafting process easier, but you may still find that your outline is incomplete. Once you start drafting, you may think of additional ideas that would make your essay better. You can always add these ideas to your outline and make sure they fit.

The two columns below demonstrate how Ian uses his outline to draft the sentences in the first body paragraph. Ian had planned to devote only one paragraph for each major supporting point. However, as he began writing, he realized that the explanation of how the math of investing works was requiring a lot of space. Thus, he decided to create a new paragraph for the remaining support he wished to discuss.

Ian's First Draft   **Ian's Enhanced Outline**

Accruing wealth comes from making small investments over a long period of time. My grandfather explained the process so that it was very easy to understand. He told me to imagine loaning a friend $10. Because you loaned him the money, he gives you a 10 percent fee ($1) when he repays the loan. Now you have $11 to loan. Your friend borrows the $11, again paying a 10 percent fee. This time the fee is $1.10. When your friend repays the money, you have $12.10. You haven't done anything but loan money to earn the extra $2.10! Now, imagine you keep doing this until you have $200. When you loan out the $200, you get 10 percent, which is $20. You then have $220 to loan. When you loan it out, you earn $22. The amount of interest goes up as the amount of money you have to loan increases.

The reason to invest at a young age is that if you keep reinvesting your profits, you can accumulate a great deal of wealth over a long time. In fact, "a person who starts at age 20 and invests $100 per month until age 65 (a total contribution of $54,000) will have more than $200,000 when he or she reaches age 65 assuming a 5% return" (Folger). As in Folger's example, my grandparents started by investing $20 a month. They probably never thought they would be millionaires in retirement!

Major supporting point 1: Accruing wealth comes from making small investments over a long period of time.

Support: Explanation of mathematics

[Explanation of mathematics continues]

- "A person who starts at age 20 and invests $100 per month until age 65 (a total contribution of $54,000) will have more than $200,000 when he or she reaches age 65 assuming a 5% return" (Folger).

- Example of my grandparents (actual amount they invested)

As Ian continues to write body paragraphs, he will make decisions like the one he made regarding creating a new paragraph. Good writers constantly review, revise, and rethink their outlines during the drafting process. Don't be afraid to make changes when you believe those changes would make your essay better. Consider the checklist that follows as you draft your own essays:

- Am I using enough support to fully develop the idea?
- Should I break paragraphs (or combine paragraphs)?
- Should I change the order in which I present information?
- When I reread my essay from the beginning, are there places where the ideas seem not to fit together?
- Are there places where I repeat ideas?

These are only some of the considerations to keep in mind during the drafting process. You will analyze your paper in even more depth as you revise it.

PRACTICE 4

Drafting Body Paragraphs from an Outline

Ian's second major supporting point is that college students can find discretionary income—extra money—to invest. Using Ian's prewriting and outline (both below), draft a paragraph or more for this major supporting point. Use a separate sheet for your draft.

IAN'S PREWRITING

Where college students can find extra money:

- Part-time work

- Not having a cell phone (or having only a basic cell phone)

- Not buying cable TV

- Avoiding debt

- Donating plasma

- Using a portion of birthday gifts to invest

IAN'S ENHANCED OUTLINE

Major supporting point 2: Almost anyone, even college students, can find small amounts of money to invest.

Support: Definition—"Discretionary income includes money spent on luxury items, vacations and non-essential goods and services" (Folger).

- How to find discretionary income

- How discretionary income adds up (provide explanation)

- Provide examples

Using Outlines to Write Detailed and Brief Summaries

In addition to being a tool for understanding texts and for drafting, outlining assists in writing summaries. In both workplace and academic writing, summarizing is an important skill. As an employee, you may be called on to read a work-related report and summarize it for your boss or coworkers. Or you may be given a thick booklet of guidelines and be expected to follow them. Being able to summarize the booklet and extract the most important information will help you follow the guidelines. In college, you will often summarize textbook chapters and other materials.

The Purpose of a Summary

A **summary** is a shortened version of a source. In a summary, you present the main idea and major supporting points of the source in your own words. A summary must be accurate, appropriately focused, and objective. To ensure the accuracy of your summary, you must correctly understand the text you are summarizing. Thus, it is vital that you read, annotate, analyze, and reread the source until you feel confident you understand it.

To give your summary an appropriate focus, you must carefully choose the points from the original source that you wish to emphasize. Specifically, you need to focus on the main idea (or thesis), the major supporting points for the main idea, and any other important ideas presented after—or in conjunction with—the central idea.

Finally, summaries must be objective. Being objective means that you do not express an opinion on the text you are summarizing. Whether you agree or disagree with the source does not matter in a summary: your goal is to simply present the source's ideas in a brief way.

Steps for Writing Summaries

The ten steps listed here will help you write an effective summary. You may occasionally quote directly from the text, but most of the summary should be in your own words.

Step 1: Read and annotate the source.

Spend sufficient time reading and annotating the source material. As always, mark the main idea and major supporting details. Look for the information that supports the major supporting details.

Step 2: Create an enhanced outline.

By creating an enhanced outline, such as the one presented earlier in this chapter on "How Delaying Gratification Predicts Future Success," you will have most of the information you will need to write a summary.

Step 3: Start with bibliographic information.

A helpful way to start a summary is to provide bibliographic information about the source. Bibliographic information includes the following:

- Author's name and credentials, if available
- Title of the source (use quotation marks for an article title; italics for a book title)
- Type of publication (specify *book* or *journal;* use italics for titles)
- Publisher and place of publication for a book
- Date of publication (add volume and issue numbers for a journal, if available)

We will follow the process that Jason, a college student, follows to write a summary based on the enhanced outline for "How Delaying Gratification Predicts Future Success," which appears earlier in this chapter.

In 2005, *Prescott Journal of Ideas* published a brief essay called "How Delaying Gratification Predicts Future Success" by Kari Gardner, a professor of education at Hinton University's Graduate School of Education.

The bibliographic information includes the date, the name of the journal (in italics), the title of the article (in quotation marks), and the author's name and credentials.

Jason could have worded the bibliographic information differently. Following are two alternative opening statements:

In 2005, Kari Gardner, a professor of education at Hinton University's Graduate School of Education, published a brief essay, "How Delaying Gratification Predicts Future Success," in *Prescott Journal of Ideas*.

"How Delaying Gratification Predicts Future Success," by Kari Gardner, a professor of education at Hinton University's Graduate School of Education, was published in *Prescott Journal of Ideas* in 2005.

Step 4: Write a sentence that tells the reader the topic of the source.

After you read the source, you should have a clear idea of the topic being addressed. Express this topic in one sentence, as Jason did here.

Gardner's essay concerns the issue of delayed gratification.	Source's topic

Step 5: Tell the reader the main idea of the text.

If the thesis statement is explicitly stated in the source, you can quote it directly. If you quote the author's words from the original published source, be sure to note the page on which the words appear. For a source you obtained electronically—such as through your library's online **databases**—you will usually need only the writer's name. Do not use page numbers from a printout of a source, unless the printout shows an exact replica of the article's pages.

VCW database

If the writer's thesis statement is implied—not stated directly—you will need to write a sentence that accurately reflects the thesis statement. In her essay, Gardner includes a thesis statement, so Jason quoted the statement directly.

The essay's thesis statement is clear: "People who can put off immediate gratification are more likely to have what it takes to be successful in the important things in life" (Gardner).	Source's thesis. The author's name is included in parentheses after the quote. Notice where the punctuation is placed.

Step 6: Use the writer's major supporting points and supporting details to summarize the body of the text.

This section will probably be the lengthiest part of your summary. Put all of these ideas in your own words. Here is the main part of Jason's summary.

Gardner proves that people who can delay gratification seem to be more successful in life. She discusses the Marshmallow Experiment in which children were given the option of eating one marshmallow immediately or waiting fifteen minutes and getting a second marshmallow. The children who waited for the second marshmallow ended up becoming more successful adults. Another point Gardner makes about delaying gratification is that people who are able to wait sometimes end up getting benefits. As examples, Gardner shows that people who invest and are patient can become wealthy. Students who work hard in college can graduate, and athletes who train hard can succeed in their sports.	Topic sentence Source's first major supporting point Summary of supporting details Source's second major supporting point Summary of supporting details

Step 7: If any of the points need more explanation, add a sentence or two to provide it.

If your reader might not understand a particular supporting point without an explanation, then you must provide it. Read your summary as if you had never read the original source. Are there places where the supporting details need to be explained in more depth? Keep in mind that a summary should be short, so provide explanations only if they are really needed. Jason added following information to one of the paragraphs in his summary to explain points that might be unclear to the reader.

She discusses the Marshmallow Experiment in which children were given the option of eating one marshmallow immediately or waiting fifteen minutes and getting a second marshmallow. The children who waited for the second marshmallow ended up becoming more successful adults. They had fewer behavioral problems, less drug and alcohol addiction, greater educational success, and higher SAT scores.	Additional information

Step 8: Discuss any other important points the author makes.

Sometimes sources will include important points that fall outside the main idea and the major supporting points for the main idea. For example, some sources begin by discussing the background of the issue being discussed. Writers sometimes include definitions, alternative points of view, or additional considerations about the topic. If the additional points in a source are important to readers' understanding to the text, include them. In her essay, Gardner provides a definition of *delayed gratification*. Jason decided to include this definition in his summary since understanding this concept is important to the meaning of the text.

Gardner defines *delayed gratification* as "the ability to postpone the fulfillment of an immediate desire in order to obtain a more substantial reward in the future."	Additional information needed for understanding

Step 9: Tell the reader how the source ends.

A simple but effective way to end a summary is to briefly tell the reader how the writer ends his or her article. Here is the end of Jason's summary.

Gardner ends her essay with some advice. "It will always be easier to eat the marshmallow right away, but doing so may not always be the best choice."	End of summary

Step 10: Once you have determined the content of your summary, you are ready to write a draft.

Read Jason's completed **detailed summary** on the next page. Notice not only the content but also the formatting. The summary follows MLA style guidelines.

Model Student Paper: "A Summary of 'How Delaying Gratification Predicts Future Success'" by Jason Alameda

Alameda 1

Jason Alameda

Dr. Hall

ENGL 1301.33

12 October 2017

A Summary of "How Delaying Gratification Predicts
Future Success"

In 2005, *Prescott Journal of Ideas* published a brief essay called "How Delaying Gratification Predicts Future Success" by Kari Gardner, a professor of education at Hinton University's Graduate School of Education.

Gardner's essay concerns the issue of delayed gratification. The essay's thesis statement is clear: "People who can put off immediate gratification are more likely to have what it takes to be successful in the important things in life" (Gardner).

Gardner proves that people who can delay gratification seem to be more successful in life. She discusses the Marshmallow Experiment in which children were given the option of eating one marshmallow immediately or waiting fifteen minutes and getting a second marshmallow. The children who waited for the second marshmallow ended up becoming more successful adults. They had fewer behavioral problems, less drug and alcohol addiction, greater educational success, and higher SAT scores.

Another point Gardner makes about delaying gratification is that people who are able to wait sometimes end up getting benefits. For example, people who invest and are patient can become wealthy. Students who work hard in college can graduate, and athletes who train hard can succeed in their sports.

Gardner defines *delayed gratification* as "the ability to postpone the fulfillment of an immediate desire in order to obtain a more substantial reward in the future."

Gardner ends her essay with some advice. "It will always be easier to eat the marshmallow right away, but doing so may not always be the best choice."

MLA-style heading

Title, centered

Bibliographic information

Source's topic and thesis

Source's first major supporting point and supporting details

Source's second major supporting point and supporting details

Additional background information: definition

End of summary

Jason's detailed summary above is about half the length of the original text. Sometimes you will want to write summaries that are much shorter. For example, if you need only a brief reference to Gardner's essay in a paper you are writing, you might want only a few lines of summary. In such cases, it is sufficient to include brief bibliographic data and the writer's main point. Here is an example of a **brief summary.**

Example of a Brief Summary

> In her essay entitled "How Delaying Gratification Predicts Future Success," Kari Gardner shows that people who can delay gratification end up more successful than those who cannot.

Whether you write a detailed summary or a brief one, your most important task is to provide an accurate representation of the ideas in the text you are summarizing. Try your hand at writing summaries by completing the following exercise.

PRACTICE ⑤

Writing Detailed and Brief Summaries

In Practice 3, you created an outline for "Achieving Optimum Fitness." Use your outline to write a detailed summary for the reading. When you are finished with the detailed summary, write a brief summary.

Writing Paraphrases

A **paraphrase** is a rewording of a *portion* of a text in your own words to make the meaning of the original text more clear. Paraphrases help you integrate a source's ideas smoothly into your own writing without overusing direct quotations.

COMPARING SUMMARIES AND PARAPHRASES	
Summary	**Paraphrase**
• Presents the main idea and major points • Usually concerns a whole text • Helps readers to understand an entire text • Ends up being shorter than the original text • Gives credit to the original source and uses quotation marks for any direct quotes	• Presents a sentence-by-sentence rewording • Usually concerns only part of a text • Helps to clarify complex ideas in a text • Ends up being longer than or as long as the original text • Gives credit to the original source and uses quotation marks for any direct quotes

To write a paraphrase, follow these steps.

1. Read the first sentence or two from the original source, and then put the source aside.
2. Put the ideas you just read into your own words and write your own sentence.
3. Check your paraphrase to make sure that it reflects the meaning of the original text.
4. If you use phrases from the original text, put quotation marks around them. (Make sure that passages in quotation marks are quoted **verbatim**—word for word.)   **VCW** verbatim
5. Use attributive tags such as "the author says" or "the author explains" to let readers know you are paraphrasing another person's ideas.

The example that follows shows how a student writer created a paraphrase of an excerpt from *Selecting a Career in Mental Health.*

Original from *Selecting a Career in Mental Health* by Camille Roberts	Student's Paraphrase
Psychology is both a science and a profession. As a science, psychology is the study of how people perceive, think, feel, and act; as a profession, it is concerned with predicting how people will act, helping people modify their behavior, and helping organizations, communities, and societies change. Some psychologists focus on research. These professionals conduct experiments and observe human behavior to add to our knowledge about how the mind works. Other psychologists focus on helping people and institutions change their behavior, structure, or functions. They spend time working with individuals and groups of people by analyzing their behaviors and helping them learn to modify their behaviors.	Roberts points out that psychology is a science as well as a profession. The science of psychology covers "how people perceive, think, feel, and act," and the profession focuses on predicting and changing behaviors. Roberts identifies two kinds of psychologists. First, some psychologists are researchers who spend their time doing experiments and observing people. These psychologists help create information and add to what we already know about how the mind works. The other type of psychologist works directly with people to help them change behaviors that are not working well. This type of psychologist may also work with groups of people to help them change their behaviors.

Remember that you cannot use paraphrased ideas without citing the source. Additionally, if you use any of the source's original language in your paraphrase, you must treat the language as a direct quote and use quotation marks. For example, in the preceding paraphrase, notice that the student includes a direct quotation from the source—in quotation marks—in her second sentence.

PRACTICE 6

Writing a Paraphrase

The following reading about antibiotic resistance is from the Centers for Disease Control and Prevention. Write a paraphrase of this reading.

Antibiotic resistance is a quickly growing, extremely dangerous problem. World health leaders have described antibiotic-resistant bacteria as "nightmare bacteria" that "pose a catastrophic threat" to people in every country in the world. Each year in the United States, at least 2 million people become infected with bacteria that are resistant to antibiotics, and at least 23,000 people die each year as a direct result of these infections. Many more people die from other conditions that were complicated by an antibiotic-resistant infection.

CHAPTER ACTIVITIES

➔ READING AND ANNOTATING

The following passage is from *Mirror for Humanity,* an anthropology textbook by Conrad Phillip Kottak published in 2014. Read and annotate the passage. In particular, identify the thesis statement, the major supporting points, the supporting details, and any other information that would be suitable for an outline, graphic organizer, or summary. If the thesis statement is implied rather than explicit, write it in your own words. When you are finished, answer the questions that follow.

Experiencing Culture: Personal Space and Displays of Affection

By Conrad Phillip Kottak

A few years ago I created and taught a course called Experiencing Culture to American college students in Italy. Students wrote biweekly journals reflecting on the cultural differences they observed between Europeans and Americans. One thing that really struck them was the greater frequency and intensity of PDAs—public displays of affection—between romantic couples in Italy, compared with the United States.

The world's nations and cultures have strikingly different notions about displays of affection and personal space. Cocktail parties in international meeting places such as the United Nations can resemble an elaborate insect mating ritual as diplomats from different countries advance, withdraw, and sidestep. When Americans talk, walk, and dance, they maintain a certain distance from others. Italians or Brazilians, who need less personal space, may interpret such "standoffishness" as a sign of coldness. In conversational pairs, the Italian or Brazilian typically moves in, while the American "instinctively" retreats from a "close talker." Such bodily movements illustrate not instinct, but culture—behavior programmed by years of exposure to a particular cultural tradition.

To what extent are you a product of your particular culture? How much does, and should, your cultural background influence your actions and decisions? Americans may not fully appreciate the power of culture because of the value their culture places on the individual. We have seen that individualism is a distinctive shared value, a feature of American culture, transmitted constantly in our daily lives. In the media, count how many stories focus on individuals versus groups. . . . Certainly we have distinctive features because we are individuals, but we have other distinct **attributes** because we belong to cultural groups.

VCW attribute

To return to the cultural contrast that so impressed my American students in Italy, there are striking contrasts between a national culture (American) that tends to be reserved about displays of physical affection and national cultures in which the opposite is true. Brazilians approach, touch, and kiss one another much more frequently than North Americans do. Middle-class Brazilians teach their kids—both boys and girls—to kiss (on the cheek, two or three times, coming and going) every adult relative they ever see. Given the size of Brazilian extended families, this can mean hundreds of people. Women continue kissing all those people throughout their lives. Until they are adolescents, boys kiss all adult relatives. Men typically continue to kiss female relatives and friends, as well as their fathers and uncles throughout their lives.

Do you kiss your father? Your uncle? Your grandfather? How about your mother, aunt, or grandmother? The answer to these questions may differ between men and women, and for male and female relatives. Culture can help us to make sense of these differences. In America, a cultural homophobia (fear of homosexuality) may prevent American men from engaging in displays of affection with other men. Similarly, American girls typically are encouraged to show affection; this is less true for boys.

However, culture is not static. Sarah Kershaw (2009) describes a recent surge of teenage hugging behavior in American schools. Concerned about potential sexual

(continued)

harassment issues, parents and school officials remain suspicious of such PDAs, even if the younger generation is more tolerant. Even American boys appear to be more likely nowadays to share nonromantic hugs, as such expressions as "bromance" and "man crush" enter our vocabulary. Hugging also has migrated online, where Facebook applications allowing friends to send hugs have tens of thousands of fans.

It's important to note that cultural traits exist because they are learned, not because they are natural or **inherently** right. Ethnocentrism is the error of viewing one's own culture as superior and applying one's own cultural values in judging people from other cultures. How easy is it for you to see beyond the ethnocentric blinders of your own experience? Do you have an ethnocentric position regarding displays of affection?

VCW inherently

Questions for Consideration

1. What is the author's thesis statement? If the author expresses it in a sentence, copy the sentence. If not, put the thesis statement in your own words.

2. What are the chief differences between displays of public affection in the United States and Brazil?

3. What does the author identify as some reasons for American attitudes about public affection?

4. Does the author present this information in an unbiased way, or does he present his own opinion?

5. What is ethnocentrism?

⊘ USING MODELS TO PRACTICE COMPOSING

Earlier in this chapter, you studied a detailed summary of "How Delaying Gratification Predicts Future Success," which you will use as a model for writing your own summary of Conrad Phillip Kottak's "Experiencing Culture: Personal Space and Displays of Affection."

1. On a separate sheet, construct an enhanced outline or graphic organizer of Kottak's text.
2. Follow your outline and the steps below to write a detailed summary of "Experiencing Culture." Use the detailed summary of "How Delaying Gratification Predicts Future Success" shown earlier in this chapter as a model.
   - Write a title for your summary.
   - Write an introduction paragraph that provides bibliographic information for the reading. Start with the date, the publication, and the title.
   - Write a paragraph in which you provide the topic and the writer's main idea.
   - Write a paragraph about the first major supporting point the writer uses. Include information about the support used to back up this major supporting point.
   - Write a paragraph for each additional major supporting point the writer uses. Include information about the support used to back up each major supporting point.
   - Provide any additional information needed to understand the reading.
   - Write a brief ending for your summary by telling readers how the writer ended the text.

➡ A READING AND WRITING ASSIGNMENT

Conrad Phillip Kottak writes about the cultural preferences of most North Americans regarding displays of affection. As Kottak notes, cultural preferences change over time. Write an essay in which you discuss three or four cultural preferences, rules, or traditions that have changed over time. For example, at the beginning of the twentieth century, most middle-class American women did not work outside the home. However, this tradition has changed, and now a majority of women work outside the home. What other preferences, rules, or traditions can you think of that have changed? Here are some areas to consider:

- Child care and child rearing
- Roles of fathers, mothers, grandparents, children
- Rules of etiquette, such as table manners, greetings, rules of politeness
- Traditional activities, such as those involving holiday customs, family meals, birthday parties

Use the Quick Start Guide to Integrated Reading and Writing Assignments to help you with this process.

➡ ADDING TO YOUR VOCABULARY

This chapter's vocabulary words appear below.

attribute	enhanced	inherently	resplendent
database	entrepreneur	nonetheless	verbatim

Choose five of the vocabulary words from this chapter that you would like to add to your vocabulary, and think about how you can use them this week. For example, one of this chapter's words is *nonetheless*. You can often substitute *nonetheless* for *but,* as in the example that follows.

> **Example:** I put bread on my shopping list, *but* I forgot to buy it at the store.
>
> I put bread on my shopping list. *Nonetheless,* I forgot to buy it at the store.

List each of the five words you plan to use this week, and make note of a context in which you could use each word.

> **Example:** *Nonetheless.* I can use this in ordinary conversation with my spouse.

➡ ADDITIONAL ASSIGNMENTS

1. Earlier in this chapter you read about how children in the Marshmallow Experiment who were able to delay gratification turned out to have more successes in life than the children who could not resist temptation. Write three or four paragraphs about times in your life when you decided to either delay gratification or not. What were the circumstances? As you look back, do you think you made the right choice? Explain these situations and reflect on them in your writing.

2. Create a graphic organizer for the essay you wrote in response to "Experiencing Culture: Personal Space and Displays of Affection."

3. Do an Internet search to find information about one of the cultures to which you belong. For example, if you are a horse lover, search for information about equestrian (horse) culture. List some of the cultural beliefs, behaviors, or attributes you find online. Make sure you reference the Web site on which you find the information. Write an essay in which you respond to these attributes by either agreeing that they are part of your culture or disputing them. Explain your reasoning.

4. *Ethnocentrism* results in our believing that our cultural practices are the best ones. What is the problem with ethnocentric thinking? Explain. Think of an example in history when ethnocentrism led to tragedy. Write a paragraph about the tragedy and how it resulted from ethnocentrism.

EMOTIONAL INTELLIGENCE

An important part of emotional intelligence is the ability to understand and deal with your feelings. To be able to do that, you must be able to *name* your feelings.

Sounds easy, right? It's surprisingly difficult sometimes. For example, many people experience periods of unhappiness but cannot quite name what they are feeling. They may feel sad, angry, hopeless, helpless, fearful, or any number of other emotions. By being able to accurately name what you are feeling, you can then find ways to deal with your emotions.

Think of a time you felt very upset. What was the emotion that caused you to be upset? For example, if you have ever come close to being in a car accident caused by another driver, you have probably experienced anger. Underneath that anger, however, would be fear. Write a paragraph about a time you were very upset. What were the emotions responsible for your condition? Work on naming your emotions, and consider writing about your emotions when you experience upsetting (or even joyous) occasions.

METACOGNITION

Look back at the last few years of your life and assess the major decisions you have made. Now, consider your ability to make good predictions. Think about times when you made predictions that turned out to be accurate. Perhaps you predicted you would really like a particular job, so you took the position and you did, indeed, really like the job. Why do you think you made a good prediction in that scenario? Explain.

Now think about a time when you made a bad prediction. Perhaps you were in a failed relationship or did not prepare well enough for a test or assignment. Why do you think you made a poor prediction in that scenario?

On the whole, have you been good at making accurate predictions? Think through your past experiences and reflect on them. How can you make better predictions in the future?

Text Credits

Page 252: Source: *Antibiotic Resistance Threats in the US.* Atlanta, GA: Centers for Disease Control and Prevention, September 16, 2013. www.cdc.gov; Pages 253–54: Kottak, Conrad Phillip, *Mirror for Humanity*, 9th ed. 36–37. Copyright ©2014 by McGraw-Hill Education. Used with permission of McGraw-Hill Education.

Titles, Introductions, and Conclusions

After completing this chapter, students will be able to do the following:

- Analyze and create titles.

- Read, analyze, and create introductions.

- Read, analyze, and create conclusions.

©Felix Behnke/Getty Images RF

The beginning of a path should be inviting, and the end should make the journey worthwhile. In the same way, as readers we expect texts to invite us in and then end agreeably. In addition, as writers we need to focus on composing engaging introductions and satisfying conclusions.

Have you ever picked up a magazine, perhaps while waiting in line at the grocery store, because something on the cover caught your eye? Sometimes a photo makes us curious, or perhaps a title or a description on the cover arouses our interest. Magazine editors depend on intriguing titles and introductions to sell their products. In the same way, good writers create titles and introductions that entice readers.

Titles, introductions, and conclusions frame a text and help readers understand its structure and content. The title is the first clue about a text's content. The introduction often provides background information or uses another method to invite readers to continue reading. The conclusion serves an important function, too. It provides **closure** for readers—the sense that the essay has reached its end.

Mastering the creation of effective titles, introductions, and conclusions is part of writing well. One way to achieve this mastery is to use your reading and analysis skills to determine how successful writers construct these elements.

Analyzing and Creating Titles

The primary purpose of a title is to give readers an idea about the contents of the essay or to make readers curious about it. Many essays have straightforward titles, as the following examples show.

Essay Content	Straightforward Title
An essay explaining ikebana—the Japanese art of flower arranging	"What Is Ikebana?"
An essay comparing and contrasting nuclear energy and geothermal energy	"A Comparison of Nuclear and Geothermal Energy"
An essay arguing that medicinal marijuana should be legal	"Why Medicinal Marijuana Should Be Legal"

Titles should be short—ideally, just a few words—although there are no set rules about how many words to use. Here are some examples of titles that are unnecessarily long.

- "A Brief Explanation of Ikebana, the Japanese Art of Flower Arranging"
- "A Comparison and Contrast Essay Concerning the Differences between Nuclear Energy and Geothermal Energy"
- "The Debate about Medicinal Marijuana: Why Marijuana Should Be Legal for Medicinal Purposes"

Some titles are creative; they provide more than a straightforward glimpse into the text's content. Consider these titles.

Essay Content	Creative Title
An essay explaining ikebana—the Japanese art of flower arranging	"Ikebana: It's Not Just for Japanese Florists"
An essay comparing and contrasting nuclear energy and geothermal energy	"Geothermal: An Alternative to the Nuclear Option"
An essay arguing that medicinal marijuana should be legal	"Marijuana Is Good Medicine"

These titles do not explicitly announce what the essay is about. Rather, they give the reader an idea of the topic.

Another feature of two of these titles is the colon (:). Colons introduce lists or explanations. In the examples given above, the colon separates a word (the main part of the title) from a brief phrase that provides more information (the subtitle). In "Ikebana: It's Not Just for Japanese Florists," the phrase after the colon explains a bit about the topic, ikebana. The same occurs with this title: "Geothermal: An Alternative to the Nuclear Option." In titles, a colon generally introduces an explanation.

Titles that are not straightforward generally require more creativity to compose. Consider documentary film titles, for instance. Like a written essay, a documentary film has a point to make. A film may have a political message, or it may seek to explain important concepts such as nuclear proliferation or the health-care crisis, or it may simply document historical events.

Think about some of the documentary films you have seen lately. Did their titles entice you? The documentary film about former Vice President Al Gore's attempts to educate Americans about destructive global climate change is called *An Inconvenient Truth.* The title does not announce the film's subject but rather calls attention to the importance of the film's content. On the other hand, the title of Ken Burns's documentary *The National Parks: America's Best Idea* reveals not only the film's subject but also the filmmaker's view of the subject. In fact, many titles present the main idea directly or provide important clues, so analyzing titles is an important reading strategy.

Be aware of titles you encounter. Think about how well they accomplish the tasks of indicating the content of the work and making you want to read (or view) it.

PRACTICE 1

Analyzing Titles

Read each of the titles that follow, and indicate whether it is a straightforward title or a creative title. Then make a prediction about the text's content.

Title	Straightforward or Creative?	Predicted Content of Text
1. Keys to Passing Algebra		
2. Waking Up to Happiness		
3. Old McDonald Had a Heart Attack: Fast-Food Perils		
4. How to Reform Immigration Laws		

PRACTICE 2

Choosing Titles

Each item below describes an essay. Choose an appropriate title for each essay, and label the title as either "straightforward" or "creative." Construct at least two creative titles.

1. In this essay, the writer argues that race should not be a factor in adoptions.

    Title: _____

    Type of title: _____

2. This personal essay, by a journalist who survived Hurricane Katrina in New Orleans, concerns his struggle with depression afterward.

    Title: _____

    Type of title: _____

3. The writer of this essay argues that migrant farmworkers live in terrible conditions.

    Title: _____

    Type of title: _____

(continued)

4. In this essay, the writer explains how scientists develop flu vaccines.

Title: _____

Type of title: _____

Reading, Analyzing, and Creating Introductions

An introduction serves two functions: it attempts to engage readers, and it offers hints about what the text will concern. Most readers expect an introduction to give them a sense of where the essay will go and what they will learn or experience by reading it. Good readers use the introduction of an essay to develop a set of expectations about what the text will concern.

How Introductions Function

An introduction can consist of one paragraph, or it can have several paragraphs. In the introduction paragraphs, we will often find the essay's thesis statement, but not always. Writers decide where to place the thesis statement based on the content of the essay and on the audience.

Like a first impression at a job interview, an introductory paragraph carries a great deal of weight. It may not be fair to judge an essay by its introduction, but as readers, we all do. The time and effort spent crafting a carefully written, engaging introduction will be worthwhile.

"Once upon a time . . ." is a famous introductory phrase. What does it tell the reader? How do beginnings help us anticipate the content to come?

Strategies for Introductions

Writers often use one of seven strategies to compose introduction paragraphs. The strategies are summarized in the following table and discussed below.

STRATEGIES FOR INTRODUCTIONS	
Starting with a question	Ask one or more questions that you answer later on in the essay.
Starting with a story	Tell one or more anecdotes, or start a story that you finish later on in the essay.
Starting with background information	Give information about the topic that readers might need—for example, history or definitions.
Starting with a surprise	Begin with one point of view on the topic, and then switch unexpectedly.
Starting with data	Provide relevant statistics on the topic.
Starting with a quotation or adage	Offer a quotation, perhaps from an expert, or an appropriate saying.
Starting with an objective overview	Give both sides of an argument in neutral language before proceeding to focus on a particular point of view.

Each of these strategies is described in more detail below and is illustrated by a professional selection. In addition, an example shows how each strategy could be used to introduce an essay about the benefits of walking. As you study the examples, pay attention to the hints that the introduction paragraphs give regarding the essay content. Also, think about how you can use these strategies in your own writing.

Starting with a Question. Sometimes writers use a question or a set of questions to introduce a topic. The question often presents the topic and leads to the writer's main point. Notice how starting with questions works in the following example.

Introduction from "Campus Diversity and Student Self-Segregation: Separating Myths from Facts" by Debra Humphreys

> When students went off to college this fall, they entered more diverse campuses than ever before. For many students, in fact, their college community is the most diverse they have ever encountered. Most students entering college today come from high schools that are predominantly or exclusively one racial or ethnic group. Given this reality, how are students interacting with one another educationally and socially in college? How socially segregated are college campuses? Is campus diversity leading to educational benefits for today's college students or are students too separated into enclaves on campus to benefit from campus diversity?

Three questions introduce the topic. The writer answers these questions later in the text.

Humphreys does not immediately answer the questions she raises in the introduction paragraph. Rather, she uses the questions to focus attention on the issue of self-segregation in colleges. Later in her essay, she answers the questions raised in the introduction.

In texts that start with a question, the *answer* to the question is often the main idea of the reading. Sometimes, though, a question is used simply to get the audience to think about the topic rather than to introduce a specific thesis statement.

Using This Strategy in Your Writing. One way to use this strategy is to make the first sentence of your introduction paragraph a question. If you create a question whose answer will be your thesis statement, you can discuss **conceivable** answers to this question but save *your* answer for last. Your answer to the question will be your thesis statement.

(Make sure to check your instructor's preferences before using the second-person pronoun *you*. While the use of second person is appropriate for *informal* writing, it is generally not acceptable in formal, academic writing.)

Here is an example of an introduction that uses a question at the beginning of the paragraph.

VCW conceivable

For every Vocabulary Collection Word (VCW), give your in-context idea of the word's meaning and then look up the word's dictionary definition.

Example: Starting with a Question

> Is walking really a legitimate form of exercise? Many people think walking is not strenuous enough to have health benefits. They think that to get in good shape, people must run, do aerobics, kickbox, or participate in another high-intensity exercise. While all of those are good exercises, the reality is that strenuous exercise is not the only way to work out productively. Millions of people who walk for exercise can attest to the power of walking. The truth is simple: walking for exercise results in a variety of health benefits.

A question suggests that the topic is walking for exercise. The question is followed by possible answers.

The writer transitions away from what others think.

The writer ends with a thesis statement that answers the opening question.

PRACTICE 3

Writing an Introduction That Uses a Question

Imagine you are writing an essay in which you discuss qualities needed in a successful manager. You have decided to use this thesis statement:

> Successful managers must be able to work well with others, solve problems, and manage their time wisely.

On a separate sheet, write an introduction paragraph using this thesis statement. Use the strategy of *starting with a question*.

Starting with a Story.   Writers know that everyone likes a good story. One way to create interest is to begin a text with a story. If a writer knows of an anecdote that fits the topic and her point, she may use that story as a starting point. Sometimes writers use **hypothetical stories**—stories that are made up but are realistic enough to be **credible** and likely. A hypothetical story will work only if it relates to your point and comes across as believable to a reasonable audience.

VCW credible

Look at the beginning paragraph of "Bouncing Back" by Melissa Balmain. After a brief introductory sentence, Balmain starts with an anecdote (a true story) about Truong, a postwar Vietnamese man who fled his country with his wife and child. The writer comments on Truong's story and then presents her thesis statement.

Introduction Paragraphs from "Bouncing Back" by Melissa Balmain

No matter what troubles you face, at work or at home, it's worth asking yourself one question: What would Howie Truong do?

In 1977, as Truong fled postwar Vietnam with his wife, baby son and several other people, their motorboat was captured by pirates. The pirates forced everyone to board their own boat; although brusque toward the adults, they doted on the baby and tried to buy him. After a few days, they shoved Truong into the sea. He nearly drowned before he was rescued by fishermen. Weeks later, in Thailand, he learned that his wife's body had washed ashore; he would spend 34 years wondering what had happened to his son.

Brief story

How in the world did Truong survive the grief that followed his ordeal? How did he move to America, become an expert metalworker, remarry, raise four more children, and eventually find his firstborn? Truong, handsome and dark-haired at 54, smiles in his living room in West Henrietta, N.Y. "I told myself, 'Get going,'" he replies emphatically. "'Life has to go on.'"

Transition from story to thesis statement

If you think Truong's story has little to do with your own, think again. Resilience like his can be learned, experts say. And it can help you through just about any setback—a blow to your business or health, for instance; a death, a divorce, a disaster.

Thesis statement

The story about Truong is much more interesting than a definition of resilience. Be aware as a reader that while some texts *are* primarily about a story, others will simply use stories to make a point or to begin the text, as "Bouncing Back" does. When you read a text that begins with a story, first determine whether the story is what the entire essay will be about. If it is not, ask yourself, "What point is the writer making with this story?"

Using This Strategy in Your Writing.   Most people like reading a good story, so they will tune in right away. The key is finding a story that is appropriate for your point. For example, if you want to make the point that insomnia is a disorder that affects the quality of life for those who suffer from it, then including a story about a person's experience with insomnia might be a good way to start an introduction. The example that follows shows how you can use a story to introduce an essay.

Example: Starting with a Story

> In 2007, Felicity Martinez was twenty-four, and she was dying. She had been diagnosed with melanoma not long after she found a suspicious-looking mole on her right shoulder. Felicity got depressed. She knew that depression would not help her put up the strongest fight she could against cancer. Her doctor prescribed a variety of treatments for depression, and they worked. Felicity believes that one of the treatments that especially helped her take control of her life and feel empowered was a **therapeutic** walking routine. Walking helped her become more centered and more determined as she fought and eventually beat the disease. As Felicity's story shows, walking for exercise can result in a variety of positive effects.

The writer starts with a story (narrative) about Felicity Martinez.

VCW therapeutic
The writer uses a transition to move from the specifics of the story to the thesis statement about walking.

Notice that the writer did not abruptly stop Felicity's story. Instead, after giving Felicity's thoughts about her experience, the writer used a transition ("As Felicity's story shows") to gracefully move to the thesis statement.

When you use a story in an introduction, make sure the story is *entirely* related to your point. In this example, if Felicity had survived cancer and then incidentally became a walker, her story would not really show that walking can be a life-changing activity.

PRACTICE **4**

Writing an Introduction That Uses a Story

Imagine you are writing an essay in which you discuss qualities needed in a successful manager. You have decided to use this thesis statement:

Successful managers must be able to work well with others, solve problems, and manage their time wisely.

On a separate sheet, write an introduction paragraph using this thesis statement. Use the strategy of *starting with a story*. Consider telling a story about a work experience you had with a good or bad manager.

Starting with Background Information.   Some topics are complex enough that audiences need background information. Thus, using background information to lead up to the main point is one way to write an introduction. Notice the annotations in the following example, "Using Media to Make a Difference," from *Introduction to Mass Communication: Media Literacy and Culture* by Stanley J. Baran.

Introduction from "Using Media to Make a Difference: Social Media and the Middle East Democracy Movement" by Stanley J. Baran

Tens of thousands of Iranians from all walks of life took to the streets in the summer of 2009 to protest what they saw as the illegitimate reelection of President Mahmoud Ahmadinejad. The government, already skilled at slowing the Internet and shutting down opposition websites, immediately expelled or placed under house arrest all foreign journalists, closed opposition newspapers, and used its own state-run radio and television stations to first ignore the protests and then blame them on outside Western agitators hostile to Iran. The protesters responded by using the Internet and social media to make a difference for their Green Revolution and democracy.

> Topic: using social media for political change
>
> The entire introduction paragraph consists of background information about the protest in 2009.
>
> The writer reveals his thesis statement in the first paragraph.

As a reader, be careful not to confuse background information with the writer's main idea. As you read an introduction paragraph, ask yourself, "Will the information being presented help me understand this concept or issue more clearly?" When introductory paragraphs provide *a summary of an event* that happened or *a definition of a concept,* that information may be background material.

Using This Strategy in Your Writing.   Sometimes, providing background information in the introduction paragraph can help readers more fully understand the context of your thesis statement. Present the background information logically so that it leads to the thesis statement.

Example: Starting with Background Information

Americans have a problem with obesity. According to the Centers for Disease Control and Prevention, to be obese means having a body mass index (BMI) of 30 or higher. Another category of weight management is *morbid obesity.* People who are morbidly obese are at high risk for breathing and walking problems, as well as premature death. We are a nation that has a high obesity rate, and our children are included in the problem. However, there is something we can do to start making changes: we can walk. If we all began to walk every day, obesity rates in our country would drop dramatically.

> The writer starts with background information about obesity.
>
> The sentence forms a transition from the background information to the thesis statement.

In the example above, the background information defines obesity and gives some of its consequences. The writer ends the paragraph with the thesis statement—a solution to the problem.

Be aware that any background information you provide must be true and accurate. Never make up data or statistics. If your instructor allows you to use source material for an assignment, be sure to credit the source properly and provide complete bibliographic information.

PRACTICE 5

Writing an Introduction That Uses Background Information

Imagine you are writing an essay in which you discuss qualities needed in a successful manager. You have decided to use this thesis statement:

> Successful managers must be able to work well with others, solve problems, and manage their time wisely.

On a separate sheet, write an introduction paragraph using this thesis statement. Use the strategy of *starting with background information.*

Starting with a Surprise.   Startling a reader with a shocking statement or by using **irony** can be an effective technique in an introduction. Irony can be interesting, amusing, or shocking.

VCW irony

If a police officer gets a ticket for speeding, we would call the situation ironic. If you get into an accident that wrecks your car the day after you pay off your car loan, the situation would be ironic. The use of irony is one type of surprise that can introduce an essay. Notice how an element of surprise is used in the following example, "Love as a Story," from the textbook *Understanding Human Sexuality* by Janet Shibley Hyde and John D. DeLamater.

Introduction from "Love as a Story" by Janet Shibley Hyde and John D. DeLamater

When we think of love, our thoughts often turn to the great love stories: Romeo and Juliet, Cinderella and the Prince (Julia Roberts and Richard Gere), King Edward VIII and Wallis Simpson, and *Pygmalion/My Fair Lady.* According to Sternberg, these stories are much more than entertainment. They shape our beliefs about love and relationships, and our beliefs in turn influence our behavior.

The writers explain the effects of love stories.

Zach and Tammy have been married 28 years. Their friends have been predicting divorce since the day they were married. They fight almost constantly. Tammy threatens to leave Zach; he tells her that nothing would make him happier. They lived happily ever after.

The writers give examples of two love stories that are ironic.

Valerie and Leonard had a perfect marriage. They told each other and all of their friends that they did. Their children say they never fought. Leonard met someone at his office, and left Valerie. They are divorced.

Wait a minute! Aren't those endings reversed? Zach and Tammy should be divorced, and Valerie and Leonard should be living happily ever after. If love is merely the interaction between two people, how they communicate and behave, you're right—the stories have the wrong endings. But there is more to love than interaction. What matters is how each partner interprets the interaction. To make sense out of what happens in our relationships, we rely on our love stories. A love story is a story about what love should be like, and it has characters, a plot, and a theme.

The text makes a transition from the surprise of the stories to the writers' thesis statement.

The thesis statement appears at the end.

Notice that the writers of this selection use the ironic stories to introduce their thesis statement. The stories clearly serve a function. Sometimes, writers will use facts that are surprising or will make shocking statements as a way to catch the attention of their readers.

Using This Strategy in Your Writing.   One way to use surprise is to employ irony, as the writers of "Love as a Story" do. Another way is to start by offering commonly believed information and to then show that this information is wrong.

Imagine you are writing an essay to argue that homework is *not* a good learning tool for school children. You might begin your essay with all of the common assumptions about homework: that it helps kids learn, that doing homework shows independent thinking, that it fosters discipline, and so on. Close to the end of the paragraph, however, you could tell your readers that this **conventional** wisdom is actually *wrong*. By making readers think they know what you are going to say, you provide a mild shock when you actually say the opposite. As a result, you may make readers want to know more about your unexpected thesis statement.

VCW conventional

This method is tricky to master, but it can be an effective introduction for some essays. Notice how it works in the following example.

Example: Starting with a Surprise

Walking is a ridiculous form of exercise. How can people who take leisurely strolls around town call themselves exercise enthusiasts—as if walking counts as a legitimate exercise? We all walk, every day, all the time, yet a large percentage of Americans are still overweight. If people really want to exercise, they need to get serious and train like professional athletes. Does this kind of thinking sound familiar? Anyone who believes such foolish ideas has never tried walking for exercise. People who do walk for exercise tell a different story about walking. They talk about how walking has changed their health, has sharpened their thinking, and has helped them sleep better at night, among other benefits. Anyone who walks regularly knows that walking for exercise results in a variety of positive effects.

The first sentences present misconceptions about walking. The sentences are italicized to represent overheard speech.

The question serves as a transition. Then the writer contradicts the italicized ideas.

The thesis statement makes the *opposite* case from the earlier italicized point of view.

As a reader, notice the important shift from the italicized thoughts to the nonitalicized writer's voice. This is the place where the writer leads to her thesis statement. Not all writers will use italics in this way, but there will likely be a transition between the initial ideas presented and the writer's opposite ideas.

Surprise introductions can be difficult to write. Readers need to "get" the surprise. If you use irony, for instance, readers must be able to identify the irony. If you find surprise introductions too difficult to write well, then choose a more straightforward method.

PRACTICE 6

Writing an Introduction That Uses a Surprise

Imagine you are writing an essay in which you discuss qualities needed in a successful manager. You have decided to use this thesis statement:

Successful managers must be able to work well with others, solve problems, and manage their time wisely.

On a separate sheet, write an introduction paragraph using this thesis statement. Use the strategy of *starting with a surprise*.

Starting with Data.   Data—statistics, percentages, studies, and other types of information—can be incredibly powerful, but this kind of information can also be mind-numbing. Before you consider using data, be sure to check with your instructor about whether source materials can be used for your assignment. Data always come from a source, and you will always need to cite the source if you use data.

Notice the annotations in the following introduction to "Driven to Distraction: Our Wired Generation" by Larry Rosen.

Introduction from "Driven to Distraction: Our Wired Generation" by Larry Rosen

> A recent Pew Internet & American Life Project report surveyed 2,462 middle school and high school advanced placement and national writing project teachers and concluded that: "Overwhelming majorities agree with the assertions that today's digital technologies are creating an easily distracted generation with short attention spans and today's students are too 'plugged in' and need more time away from their digital technologies." Two-thirds of the respondents agree with the notion that today's digital technologies do more to distract students than to help them academically.

The source of the data is given, together with details.

A quotation is followed by more data.

In this example, the writer does not place his thesis statement in the first paragraph. Rather, the first paragraph gives us data to get us thinking about the effects of digital technologies on students.

Using This Strategy in Your Writing.   If you find data that are truly interesting and perhaps even surprising, presenting some of that information can be an effective way to introduce your topic. Keep in mind that any data you use must come from a reputable source and that making readers aware of the source is also crucial. Also, remember to ask your instructor whether using a source is acceptable for the assignment. The following example shows how you might use data as a way to introduce a topic.

> Sometimes we forget that walking can have powerful effects on health. According to the Centers for Disease Control, (CDC), "Physical activity such as walking can help improve health even without weight loss. People who are physically active live longer and have a lower risk for heart disease, stroke, type 2 diabetes, depression, and some cancers." People are getting the message. The CDC points out that "about 6 in 10" adults walk for exercise, and the percentage of adults who walk increased by 6 percent in 5 years. Far from being a useless activity, walking for exercise results in a variety of positive effects.

The introduction provides a source of data, the CDC, and then presents quotes and a summary of the data.

The thesis statement is a logical conclusion of the data presented earlier.

Notice that statistical information is always used to support a point. The information itself is rarely, if ever, the main point of a text.

PRACTICE 7

Writing an Introduction That Uses Data

Imagine you are writing an essay in which you argue that the minimum wage should be raised. You have decided to use this thesis statement:

> The minimum wage in the United States should be raised so that every worker has a chance to escape poverty.

On a separate sheet, write an introduction paragraph using this thesis statement. Use the strategy of *starting with data*. Choose from the data given below to write your introduction.

> Quotation: "Today, the real value of the minimum wage has fallen by nearly one-third since its peak in 1968. And right now, a full-time minimum wage worker makes $14,500 a year, which leaves too many families struggling to make ends meet."
>
> *Source:* The White House Web site at www.whitehouse.gov.

> Quotation: "President Obama took action to lift more workers' wages by requiring that federal contractors pay their employees a fair wage of at least $10.10 an hour."
>
> *Source:* The White House Web site at www.whitehouse.gov.

Starting with a Quotation or Adage.   Sometimes, as a writer, you think of the *perfect* quotation or adage (a common saying that states something most people believe to be true). Using a quotation or an adage to start an introduction can be effective.

Since a quotation or an adage is likely to be a single sentence, using this method of introduction requires writers to add either an explanation or additional information. In the introduction that follows, Jian Cass uses an adage to begin his essay, "Telepathic Inventions Are Changing the World." Notice the information that follows the adage and where Cass places his thesis statement.

Introduction from "Telepathic Inventions Are Changing the World" by Jian Cass

Necessity is the mother of invention. And thank goodness for necessity because it has brought us some revolutionary inventions in the last few years. Inventions such as 3D printing have made possible a host of new wares, including even homes created by 3D printers. Robotics technology has rendered some pretty amazing products, such as microscopic robots that might be able to fight cancer in the human body. But perhaps the coolest inventions in recent years are those that actually enable telepathy, the ability to control an external object just by thinking about it. Today, telepathic technology is making everyday tasks more convenient, helping people with disabilities, and even fighting terrorism.

Adage

Examples

Thesis statement

Using This Strategy in Your Writing.   If you find a striking quotation, saying, short song lyric, poem, or any other such item, you can use it to start your introduction paragraph. You must be sure that the item you are using fits the topic *exactly*. If you choose a quote that "kind of" fits, your reader will simply think the introduction paragraph is odd. Notice that the writer of the example below did not have a perfect adage for her thesis. Instead, she chose to adapt a well-known adage.

Example: Starting with a Quotation or Adage

We all know that an apple a day is supposed to keep the doctor away, but eating apples will not necessarily make you fit. A healthier version of the old adage might be "A walk every day keeps illness away." While diet is important for health, exercise is also crucial for maintaining physical well-being. A daily walk for exercise results in a variety of positive effects.	The writer starts with a well-known adage and then critiques it. The writer suggests a new adage that acts as a transition to the thesis statement. The thesis statement appears at the end.

As a reader, any time you see an adage, ask yourself, "What is the general truth the adage presents?" Use the answer to gain understanding about the writer's point.

PRACTICE (8)

Writing an Introduction That Uses a Quotation or Adage

Imagine you are writing an essay in which you discuss qualities needed in a successful manager. You have decided to use this thesis statement:

> Successful managers must be able to work well with others, solve problems, and manage their time wisely.

On a separate sheet, write an introduction paragraph using this thesis statement. Use the strategy of *starting with a quote or an adage*.

Starting with an Objective Overview.   Some essays begin with a simple overview of the issue being discussed. If the issue is controversial, an objective overview requires both sides of the issue to be presented. An objective overview can be used to introduce an informative article about the issue, or it can be used at the beginning of a persuasive essay to show that the writer is aware of both sides of the issue.

The following paragraph shows an objective overview used as an introduction to an informative article, "Wal-Mart and the Local Economy," by Mitch Renkow.

Introduction from "Wal-Mart and the Local Economy" by Mitch Renkow

With total revenues in excess of $250 billion per year and more than 1.3 million employees worldwide, Wal-Mart Stores, Inc., is the largest corporation in the world. Wal-Mart's staggering—and continuing—growth traces directly to its pioneering of an innovative business model that features sophisticated supply chain management and aggressive cost-cutting. That model, as revolutionary as was that of the Sears & Roebuck Co.	Pro position: The writer starts with positive info about Wal-Mart and its successes. *(continued)*

in the late 1800s, has profoundly altered patterns of local retail and whole-sale trade, as well as the logistics of the transportation and distribution of goods. Wal-Mart sells a wide array of products at lower prices than competing retail outlets. It also hires large numbers of local workers, as well as generating substantial property tax and sales tax revenues for local communities. Nonetheless, Wal-Mart is a frequent target of hostile sentiment, and announcements of plans to build a new Wal-Mart in a given community are often met with considerable protest. Much of the antagonism toward Wal-Mart is rooted in the perceived dislocating effects that new Wal-Mart stores have on competing "mom-and-pop" retail stores.

The writer goes on to give historical info about Wal-Mart's business practices.

Con position: The writer gives "the other side": hostility toward Wal-Mart.

In this article, the writer will not take a position on whether Wal-Mart is good for society or the economy. Rather, as the introduction indicates, he will discuss both sides. The objective overview in the introduction paragraph forecasts the discussion to come.

Not much information is provided about either side of the issue in Renkow's introduction paragraph. He will provide more details in the article itself. This is one way to present a very basic overview of the two sides of an issue. Another way is to write one paragraph presenting one viewpoint and a second paragraph for the opposite viewpoint. The writer might then present her thesis statement in a third paragraph.

Using This Strategy in Your Writing. To use this strategy in your own writing, be sure that you clearly understand both sides of the issue. Provide an overview of both sides, and then present your thesis statement. If you are writing an argument essay, be sure to word your introduction and thesis statement in such a way that readers understand which point of view you are **advocating.**

VCW advocate

Example: Starting with an Objective Overview

Although we know that exercise is important, very few Americans participate in regular exercise. Realizing this, several national companies have begun to offer their employees 20 minutes per day—in addition to regular breaks and lunch time—to simply take a walk. These employers argue that their companies save money by encouraging daily walks since walkers have lower health-care expenses and higher morale. Some executives, however, say their companies will lose valuable productive time by providing time for daily walks. They believe their employees already have enough time—through scheduled breaks and lunch—to exercise if they really want to. Although both sides make valuable points, companies who have implemented walking programs are beginning to see real benefits from them. A close examination of this issue will show that the potential benefits of giving employees time to walk each day far outweigh any negative consequences.

Pro argument in favor of time off for exercise at work

Con argument against time off for exercise at work

Transition moves from the two points of view to the writer's thesis statement

Thesis statement

Notice that even though both sides of the issue are briefly mentioned, the writer ends with a thesis statement that shows the position he supports.

PRACTICE 9

Reading, Annotating, and Analyzing Introductions

The introductions from two essays follow. Read and annotate each introduction, and then answer the analysis questions that follow each one.

Passage A: Introduction from "Probing Question: Is 'Just Say No' an Effective Anti-Drug Approach?" by Tom Fitzgerald

Many people remember the famous anti-drug slogan coined by former first lady Nancy Reagan: "Just Say No." Critiqued by some for reducing a complex issue to a catch phrase, Reagan's campaign is generally considered to have been unsuccessful, and the phrase "just say no" has become a pop-culture joke.

YOUR ANNOTATIONS

1. What strategy did the writer use to write this introduction paragraph?

2. What do you predict the essay will be about, based on the introduction and the title?

Passage B: Introduction from "Mark Lepper: Intrinsic Motivation, Extrinsic Motivation and the Process of Learning" by Christine Vandevelde

Some years ago, after a lecture, Professor Mark Lepper was approached by a couple who told him about a system of rewards they had set up for their son, which had produced much improved behavior at the dinner table. "He sits up straight and eats his peas and the Brussels sprouts and he is really very well behaved," they reported. Until, that is, the first time the family dined at a nice restaurant. The child looked around, picked up a crystal glass from the table and asked, "How many points not to drop this?" A fine example, says Dr. Lepper, of the detrimental effects of over-reliance on rewards to shape children's behavior.

YOUR ANNOTATIONS

1. What strategy did the writer use to write this introduction paragraph?

2. Did the writer include his thesis statement in this paragraph?

3. What do you predict the essay will be about, based on the introduction and the title?

PRACTICE 10

Choosing Introduction Strategies

Below are three thesis statements. If you were writing an essay for the following thesis statements, which type of introduction paragraph might you use for each one? Why? Explain in one or two sentences.

1. Thesis statement: We need to take action to save our beaches.

(continued)

2. Thesis statement: Instead of punishing students who use smartphones in class, instructors should integrate smartphone technology into their teaching.

_____

_____

3. Thesis statement: If you believe a person is having a stroke, there are four actions you can and must take.

_____

_____

Reading, Analyzing, and Creating Conclusions

We have all seen movies that end poorly, leaving us with a sense that the movie should not have ended just yet or should have had a different ending. Texts can also suffer from poor endings. The examples that follow will help you understand the function of conclusions and learn how to craft effective endings for your own writing.

How Conclusions Function

The main purpose of a conclusion is to help the reader gain a sense of *closure*—a feeling that it is the right time to bring the writing to an end—and a sense that something has been accomplished, a point has been made, or an idea has been shared.

To **impart** closure, conclusions often re-emphasize the purpose of the essay. Conclusions may also make predictions, emphasize the importance of the issue being discussed, or provide the end of a story that was started in the introduction paragraph.

VCW impart

By analyzing a conclusion, you can sometimes tell whether you fully understand the writer's main point. For example, if the essay is intended to persuade, then the conclusion can serve as a last attempt to get readers to do or believe what the writer is advocating. If the essay presents an analysis and draws a conclusion, the conclusion paragraph is a good place to reiterate the results or findings. While conclusions do not always restate the main point, the content in them should be consistent with the main idea of the essay.

Strategies for Conclusions

Four strategies, summarized in the table below and illustrated in the examples that follow, are commonly used to conclude essays. Keep in mind that regardless of the conclusion strategy employed, an essay can also end with a **proposal**—a suggestion that readers take particular actions in response to what the writer is saying in the essay.

As you read each example, think about whether the conclusion produces a sense of closure. You may notice that conclusion paragraphs often make use of more than one strategy, as the annotations will show. Notice also that the writers do not use "in conclusion" or "to conclude." A good conclusion does not have to announce itself.

In a fairy tale, "happily ever after" tells us the story has come to an end. What do you think readers expect from a satisfying conclusion?

©Comstock Images/Getty Images RF

STRATEGIES FOR CONCLUSION PARAGRAPHS

Concluding by restating and summarizing	Emphasize the thesis or the key points in the essay by restating them in different words.
Concluding by answering an earlier question	Answer a question you asked in the introduction to the essay.
Concluding by finishing a story	Tell the end of a story that you began in the introduction to the essay.
Concluding by speculating	Explain some results, events, or other consequences that *might* occur.

Concluding by Restating and Summarizing.   A common method of concluding an essay is to emphasize the thesis statement by restating it. You have read the introduction paragraph Mitch Renkow uses to start his informative essay on Wal-Mart. Now read the conclusion paragraph, and notice how he sums up his informative essay.

Conclusion from "Wal-Mart and the Local Economy" by Mitch Renkow

> As is commonly the case with any large shock to the economic system, the coming of a new Wal-Mart to a given community is accompanied by a multitude of different impacts on different individuals and on the local government. Some of these impacts are unambiguously positive for certain groups—lower prices for consumers being an example. Some are unambiguously negative for other groups, such as the loss of business experienced by competing retail outlets. And still others will vary on a case-by-case basis, such as the impacts on local employment and the local government's budget. To a very large extent, whether a new Wal-Mart is a "good" or "bad" thing for an individual depends on which of these varied impacts are most strongly relevant to that individual.

The writer summarizes positive effects.

The writer summarizes negative effects.

The writer restates the thesis statement.

As a reader, pay particular attention to the conclusion paragraphs. Often, if the writer reiterates a point in the conclusion, that point will be the text's thesis statement. You can sometimes check your knowledge of the thesis statement by studying the writer's closing words.

Using This Strategy in Your Writing.   When you use this method for concluding your writing, be sure to continue composing *new* sentences. It may be tempting to simply insert the thesis statement word for word, but avoid doing so. In the following example, notice that the last sentence adds emphasis to the writer's thesis statement by calling walking "the perfect exercise." Make sure your final sentence wraps up the essay and gives readers a sense of closure.

Example: Concluding by Restating and Summarizing

> Walking is clearly an effective form of exercise. Anyone can walk, and very little special gear is needed to participate in a walking program. It is an economical way to exercise, and it pays off in both mental and physical benefits. Walking may just be the perfect exercise.

The thesis statement is reworded.

The support is briefly summarized.

The short final sentence provides a simple ending for the essay.

PRACTICE (11)

Writing a Conclusion by Restating and Summarizing

Read the following student essay on the topic of divorce. Then, on a separate sheet, write a conclusion paragraph for it that uses the strategy of *restating or summarizing*. You will use this essay again for Practices 12 and 14.

What Causes Divorce?

Most people enter marriage with the thought that they will never divorce. Since about half of all marriages *do* end in divorce, it is important to understand just what causes marriages to fall apart. Just what goes wrong?

Why do so many marriages end in divorce? While no two marriages are alike, three causes seem to be at the root of many divorces: lack of faithfulness, lack of respect, and lack of communication.

One of the most common reasons for divorce is infidelity. For many people, an affair means the end of their marriage. The reason an affair often causes divorce is that it makes one partner lose trust in the other. The only way to be really open and truthful with one's spouse is to be able to trust him or her. Without trust, the closeness and unity that should be in a marriage disappear. For example, after Meredith's husband had an affair, she found herself constantly worrying about whether her husband was lying to her. This worry caused their marriage to erode further. Meredith began to confide to her friends when she needed someone to lean on, and she felt that her marriage was a failure. Once a partner has an affair, it may be impossible to regain the spouse's trust. This can be the death knell for a marriage.

Another cause of divorce is having a lack of respect for one's partner. Most people start their relationships with respect for their partners. Over time, however, couples begin to notice each other's flaws. Focusing on these flaws can lead to disrespect. One partner may begin to think negative thoughts about the other. The marriage will begin to suffer when the spouses begin to point out each other's flaws. Also, if one partner shows disrespect for the ideas or opinions of the other, the couple will begin to feel divided, not unified. For example, it would be difficult for a Democrat to be married to a Republican if each of the partners showed disrespect for the other's viewpoints. This kind of disrespect is not only damaging; it can be very hurtful. Everyone wants to be loved and respected, and if one's spouse is not respectful, it is difficult to stay married.

Good communication is another requirement for a happy marriage. Not having good communication is another reason for divorce. All couples will have occasional problems. Talking is really the only way to bring resolution to these problems. Couples who bury their feelings or who do not want to fight because they think fighting is destructive can end up with communication problems. No one likes to fight, but sometimes people have honest disagreements. When people don't voice their anger, that anger can intensify. The result may be that one partner makes false assumptions about the other, and that can cause in a miserable situation. If this misery lasts for very long, the couple will consider divorce as a way to ease their pain.

Concluding by Answering an Earlier Question. Essays that begin with questions can neatly conclude by going back to the question and reminding readers of its answer. Review Debra Humphreys's introduction, which appears earlier in this chapter. She began her essay by asking questions, and she ends it with a summary of the answers. She uses two paragraphs to bring her essay to a conclusion.

Conclusion from "Campus Diversity and Student Self-Segregation: Separating Myths from Facts" by Debra Humphreys

There is little cause for alarm, some cause for celebration and much hope for what lies ahead. The reality is that while there is still a long way to go before American higher education will truly reflect the full diversity of American society, college campuses are becoming much more diverse and their diverse campus environments are having a significant positive effect on this generation of students.

College campuses are not dominated by widespread racial/ethnic segregation and the racial/ethnic clustering that does occur isn't impeding intergroup contact. In fact, the existence of racial/ethnic groups and activities, along with other comprehensive campus diversity initiatives, is contributing to the success of today's college students and preparing them to help build a healthier multicultural America for the future.

> The essay answers some of the questions posed in the introduction paragraph, and the conclusion sums up the answers.
>
> Answer to "How socially segregated are college campuses?"
>
> Answer to "Is diversity leading to educational benefits?"

Using This Strategy in Your Writing. To use this strategy, find new words to repeat the question asked in the introduction. In the example of writing introductions with questions earlier in the chapter, we asked, "Is walking really a legitimate form of exercise?" While the thesis statement provides an answer to the question, the writer can emphasize the answer by repeating the question-and-answer strategy in the conclusion, as shown in the following example.

Notice also that the last sentence is a lighthearted imitation of a television infomercial. This kind of encouragement can be a pleasing way to end an informal essay that advocates an action.

Example: Concluding by Answering an Earlier Question

Is something as simple as taking a daily walk really going to improve your health? The answer is a resounding "Yes!" Not only will walking improve your health and your mood, but it will also make your commitment to an exercise program easier since it requires so little and costs next to nothing. So lace up your sneakers and start your no-risk free trial today!

> The introduction question is reworded here.
>
> The answer repeats the reasoning used in the essay.
>
> The last sentence is a proposal—a call to action for readers.

Notice that both the question and the answer have been reworded for the conclusion paragraph. Never repeat an idea without rewording it.

PRACTICE 12

Writing a Conclusion Paragraph by Answering an Earlier Question

Reread the essay "What Causes Divorce?" in Practice 11. The writer uses these questions in the introduction:

(continued)

- Just what goes wrong?
- Why do so many marriages end in divorce?

On a separate sheet, write a conclusion paragraph for the essay that uses the strategy of *answering an earlier question.*

Concluding by Finishing a Story.   Like returning to an earlier question, another method of concluding is to return to an earlier story. When using stories to introduce essays, writers will sometimes give only a portion of the story and save the story's ending to wrap up the essay. Earlier in this chapter, you read the introduction to "Bouncing Back," an essay that began with a short anecdote about Truong, a Vietnamese refugee. In the body paragraphs, Melissa Balmain, the writer, discusses how some people manage to deal with very difficult situations. When she is ready to conclude, she goes back to Truong's story to tell readers how it ends.

Conclusion from "Bouncing Back" by Melissa Balmain

And here, again, we look to Howie Truong.

As the decades passed, he couldn't shake the feeling that his stolen child, Khai, was still alive. The pirates had been too fond of the boy to have killed him, he believed. Last summer, after years of fruitless attempts to find him long-distance, Truong got his family's blessing to take an extended trip to Thailand. Incredibly, thanks in large part to his dogged questioning of strangers and help from Thai officials and media, he found Khai in a month. He turned out to be a father of two known as Samart Khumkhaw, who worked on a rubber plantation near the home of the couple who—apparently ignorant of his kidnapping—had adopted him when he was a baby.

Now Khumkhaw, on his first visit to the United States, sits with Truong in his living room. Father and son have matching eyes, matching mustaches, and, above all, matching infectious grins. Truong, the only one adept at English, does most of the talking.

One thing he realized during his trip to Thailand, he says, is that he could easily track down the pirates and press charges against them. But he won't. "I figure if I forgive them now," he says, "later somebody will forgive me for something." He glances at his recovered son, eyes widening as if he still can't believe he is right beside him. "He was lost for 34 years. It's time for me to make up for that."

> The writer finishes the story begun in the introduction.

Using This Strategy in Your Writing.   To use this method of concluding, make sure your introduction presents a story. If you have already given readers the ending, you can provide an "update" that bring the readers' attention back to the story.

The example below provides an ending to the story of Felicity Martinez, which was used earlier in this text to start an essay about walking. Notice how the ending provides an update of Felicity's situation.

Example: Concluding by Finishing a Story

Felicity Martinez credits walking with transforming her life during her battle with cancer, but her story does not end there. Today, Felicity is a fitness and wellness instructor at Lombardy Health Institute. She specializes in exercise therapy for cancer recovery and prevention. Felicity believes, as do many others, that the benefits of a simple activity like walking are not easily grasped, and she is determined to give to others what walking gave to her.

The writer returns to the story begun in the introduction.

The writer gives an update or provides the ending of the story. The writer uses the end of the story to emphasize the thesis statement.

Going back to Felicity's story helps readers feel that not only has the writer made her point, but also that Felicity's story has been thoroughly told.

PRACTICE 13

Writing a Conclusion Paragraph by Finishing a Story

For Practice 4, you used a story to write an introduction to an essay. Return to that introduction. On a separate sheet, write a conclusion paragraph for the same essay that uses the strategy of *finishing a story*.

Concluding by Speculating.   After thinking about an issue, we often speculate about what that issue means to us personally or to the larger world. To *speculate* is to wonder. For example, when we consider how easy it is to take a walk every day and the healthful effects of walking, we may wonder why more people do not walk daily. We may, in addition, speculate about what life would be like if everyone began to walk more. This speculation might lead to a prediction. Perhaps if more people walked regularly, our health insurance costs would go down. Or perhaps cities would begin to develop more pedestrian-friendly transit routes.

Speculations that predict or that ask "what if" can also be used to forecast dire consequences so that readers will understand the seriousness of an issue or will take action. In "Homo Sapiens RIP," Andrew Gumbel writes about how some people see artificial intelligence used in robots as a serious threat. Notice how Gumbel uses speculation to conclude his essay. (Note: In his conclusion, Gumbel quotes Bill Joy, a computer expert.)

Conclusion from "Homo Sapiens RIP" by Andrew Gumbel

"We have yet to come to terms with the fact that the most compelling 21st-century technologies . . . pose a different threat than the technologies that have come before," Joy writes. "Specifically, robots, engineered organisms, and nanobots share a dangerous amplifying factor: they can self-replicate. A bomb is blown up only once—but one bot can become many, and quickly get out of control. . . .

"I think it is no exaggeration to say we are on the cusp of the further perfection of extreme evil, an evil whose possibility spreads well beyond that which weapons of mass destruction bequeathed to the nation-states, on to a surprising and terrible empowerment of extreme individuals."

The writer repeats the problem by quoting Bill Joy, an expert.

The writer ends by quoting Joy's speculations about the future.

Using This Strategy in Your Writing.   Carefully consider your thesis statement. If your thesis statement and essay lead you to make speculations and predictions, consider using this strategy. Be careful that these predictions tie directly into your thesis statement's point. Word your predictions in such a way so that your audience understands these things *might* occur, not that they *will* occur.

The following example shows how we might conclude the essay on the benefits of walking with an ending that uses speculation.

Example: Concluding by Speculating

If more people began to walk for exercise, we might see significant changes in the health of our country. These changes might result in lower costs for health insurance, longer lives, and happier people. Cities might begin to accommodate walkers by creating pedestrian-friendly transit routes, thus reducing traffic. The benefits of walking are worth giving it a try.	The first three sentences speculate about how walking could change the future. The final sentence proposes an action ("giving it a try").

Note that these predictions or speculations are not part of the writer's support for his thesis statement. They are merely encouragements inserted at the end to motivate readers to try walking. The writer is careful to use the word *might* to avoid saying or implying that these results will definitely occur.

PRACTICE 14

Writing a Conclusion Paragraph by Speculating

Reread the essay "What Causes Divorce?" in Practice 11. On a separate sheet, write a conclusion paragraph for the essay that uses the strategy of *concluding by speculating*.

CHAPTER ACTIVITIES

→ READING AND ANNOTATING

The following article, by Jenny Williams, was originally published on the blog "A Fine Parent" (www.afineparent.com). Read and annotate the article. Make annotations about the methods used to introduce and conclude the essay.

What Is Grit, Why Kids Need It, and How You Can Foster It

By Jenny S. Williams

You've probably heard the word *grit* mentioned several times in recent years in the context of raising kids who go on to fulfill their potential. While the word *grit* may conjure up images of Rocky Balboa or Dirty Harry, in the past decade or so it

YOUR ANNOTATIONS

(continued)

has taken on a whole new meaning that has stolen the attention of parents and educators alike. That's because according to University of Pennsylvania psychologist and MacArthur "genius" Angela Duckworth, *grit*, defined as a child's "**perseverance** and passion for long-term goals," is a better indicator of future earnings and happiness than either IQ or talent. Today's mounting research on *grit* suggests that your child's ability to work hard, endure struggle, fail, and try again may be the key to determining his or her long-term success and happiness.

VCW perseverance

When we are in pursuit of a lofty goal, we don't know when or even *whether* we will succeed. Grit is a distinct combination of passion, resilience, determination, and focus that allows a person to maintain the discipline and optimism to persevere in their goals even in the face of discomfort, rejection, and a lack of visible progress for years, or even decades. Through extensive research, Angela Duckworth and her team have proven that the common denominator among spelling bee finalists, successful West Point cadets, salespeople, and teachers who not only stick with, but improve in, their performance is *grit*. And according to study after study, people who are smart, talented, kind, curious, and come from stable, loving homes, generally don't succeed if they don't know how to work hard, remain committed to their goals, and persevere through struggles and failure.

My husband tells the story of his qualification to attend the U.S. Army's Ranger School, its premier small-unit leadership course. In the final exercise before soldiers were chosen to attend the school, he and his fellow soldiers were told to "ruck up" with 35-pound packs and start walking. The instruction was something like, "We're not going to tell you how far you have to walk or what the cut-off time is, but if you don't finish under time, you're going home." The would-be Rangers started walking, fast.

Finally, after hours of walking, the soldiers came to the spot where they had begun. From a distance, it looked like the finish. But as each man approached, the sergeant yelled out a time and then said, "Good work. One lap down." More than one soldier crumbled there, dropping his pack and surrendering his spot in Ranger School. But those who continued walking found that the real finish was just around the corner, a few hundred yards away.

"*Never quit in a valley,*" says Angela Duckworth. Indeed, had those soldiers who quit maintained the fortitude to go on and move past that low-point they would have secured their spots in Ranger School.

So as parents, what can we do to provide that support? How do we teach our kids to push themselves? What can we do to help our kids be receptive to these tough lessons? Here are few ideas gleaned from the "grit" experts about how to be intentional in our quest to build grit.

Find a Passion (or At Least an Engaging Activity)

As children grow older, pursuing a particular interest of their own choosing can help them to identify a passion and understand that practice, hard work, and perseverance are surest way to achievement. One of the characteristics of "gritty" people is that they are "especially motivated to seek happiness through focused engagement and a sense of meaning or purpose" (according to the Duckworth Lab Research Statement), so letting a child find his or her own passion is necessary in the long term.

(continued)

At the Duckworth house, they have implemented a "Hard Thing Rule," which says that every member of the family has to be working on something difficult at any given time. Each person can choose his or her "thing," but it should both be both interesting and require "deliberate practice almost daily." And everyone has to stick with his or her selected activity for a set period of time. Be it ballet, soccer, violin, or karate, allowing a child to choose an activity and work at it for a whole season (or longer for older children) not only helps children find and cultivate a passion; it also teaches self-discipline and reinforces the idea that practice begets skill. The learning process is not always fun, and improvement does not come without effort. But if a child is motivated to improve at something because she likes it, then the struggle will seem worthwhile and success will be its own reward.

Recognize That Frustration, Confusion and Practice Are Par for the Course

According to the Duckworth lab, those who believe that diligence and perseverance pay off beat out their less optimistic, and often more talented, counterparts nearly every time. In a 2013 TED Talk, Duckworth said the "best idea" she has heard about how to increase grit in children is to teach what Stanford professor and author of the highly acclaimed book *Mindset: The New Psychology of Success*, Carol Dweck, calls a "growth mindset." Dweck has found that people with "growth mindsets" are more resilient and tend to push through struggle because they believe that hard work is part of the process and they understand that failure is not a permanent condition. Those with "fixed mindsets" on the other hand, believe that success stems from innate talent and tend to give up easily— why work hard at something if you don't believe you can change anything?

The Duckworth lab's recent research, undertaken in partnership with classroom teachers, shows that students become less frustrated with the learning process and put forth more effort when they understand that even experts struggle to learn their craft. First-hand accounts of the obstacles that experts have to overcome to "make it" have a real impact on helping kids manage frustration. Duckworth is fond of quoting world-class dancer Martha Graham who said, "Dancing appears glamorous, easy, delightful. But the path to the paradise of achievement is not easier than any other. There is fatigue so great that the body cries, even in its sleep. There are times of complete frustration, there are daily small deaths."

Take Risks (and Tell Your Kids about Them)

Grit demands risk taking. Successful people are willing to step out of their comfort zones and risk failure in order to learn something new or pursue a long-term goal. And while, by definition, a risk may end in failure, successful adults don't give up.

The Summers boys were 9, 11, and 13 when the late Dr. Robert Summers, an economist at the University of Pennsylvania, applied for a Ford Foundation grant that would allow the family to spend a year in England. As his wife, Dr. Anita Summers, tells it, the Summers decided to share their risk-taking with their children by telling the boys about the application months before they knew the outcome. In addition to wanting the boys to "get their arms around the possibility of being away for the year," Dr. Summers says they wanted their sons to see that if their father didn't win the fellowship, they "would be very disappointed, but [that] life goes on." Either way, the boys would gain valuable insights from feeling the anticipation and excitement that accompanies risk-taking.

(continued)

On the day that Dr. Summers finally received his letter, the family waited for him to come home and deliver the news. And when he produced the acceptance letter, the boys were able to celebrate with their parents in a way that they could not have if they hadn't felt the apprehension and excitement that preceded the acceptance. Further, if the boys hadn't been privy to the discomfort of not knowing the outcome, they might have been left with the impression that winning a prestigious fellowship simply falls into one's lap rather than being sought after and hard won.

Teach That Failure Is Not the End

Guess how many failed vacuum prototypes were created by James Dyson before he came out with the Dual Cyclone bagless vacuum cleaner that made him a billionaire? Four? Five? No, the actual answer is 5,127. And how many rejections had Stephen King received before his first novel, *Carrie*, was finally accepted by a publisher? Thirty. How many dollars were lost on GoPro inventor Nick Woodman's first company? Four million. Yet all three men succeeded in the long run because of their grit, their determination to see their dreams through to realization.

According to the Duckworth lab statement, gritty people have "cognitive dispositions that incline [them] to look for changeable causes of their current problems." Grit means maintaining the hope and vision to change even under the most challenging circumstances. In order to teach children to be resilient, we need to show them real examples of how failures and setbacks can lead to success—by talking about them regularly, sharing our own experiences, and most importantly *allowing them to fail*. In his *New York Times* article "The Secret to Success Is Failure," Paul Tough says,

> We have an acute, almost biological impulse to provide for our children, to give them everything they want and need, to protect them from dangers and discomforts both large and small. And yet we all know—on some level, at least—that what kids need more than anything is a little hardship: some challenge, some deprivation that they can overcome, even if just to prove to themselves that they can.

Failure is painful and humbling, and as parents it is difficult to admit to our kids that it happens to us too. Yet exposing them to failure may be the very thing to inoculate them against giving up when they come face-to-face with failure themselves. They need to know that frustrating and painful moments are not the end of something but a natural part of the journey toward achievement.

By teaching our children grit, we may be equipping them with the key to deal with the failures and disappointments that inevitably come in life. And that same key may be the one that helps them unlock their personal potential and realize even their most lofty dreams.

Questions for Consideration

1. In your own words, explain what *grit* is and why the author thinks it is so important.

2. Write a paraphrase of this sentence: "According to the Duckworth lab statement, gritty people have 'cognitive dispositions that incline [them] to look for changeable causes of their current problems.'"

3. How does Duckworth help her children to develop grit?

4. What are Carol Dweck's ideas, and why does Duckworth discuss them?

5. What method does the writer use to introduce this essay? Do you find this method effective? Explain why or why not.

6. What method does the writer use to conclude this essay? Do you find this method effective? Explain why or why not.

➲ USING MODELS TO PRACTICE COMPOSING

Reggie, a student in an English class, has been given a reading and writing assignment. Here are Reggie's annotations of his assignment.

Reggie's Annotated Assignment

Read, annotate, and analyze "What Is Grit, Why Kids Need It, and How You Can Foster It."

Write an essay in which you answer this question: Why is grit particularly important for college students? Write a thesis statement that answers this question. Provide at least three reasons for your thesis statement. Consider creating hypothetical or real world examples for your reasons. You may use Jenny Williams's article as a resource. Be sure to give credit to Williams if you use any of the ideas that come from her article.

Read, annotate, and analyze the article
Write an essay
Write a thesis statement
Provide at least 3 reasons and provide examples
Give credit to article when necessary

Reggie starts prewriting for his assignment by making a list of reasons why grit is important for college students. He then puts a checkmark (✓) next to the three reasons he will use in his essay.

Why is grit important for college students?

✓ A degree takes a long time to achieve, so you have to stick with it.

✓ Some of the skills you have to learn are very hard.

When you're a young adult, you have lots of things other than school that you want to do.

✓ You have to spend a lot of time studying, and that's not fun, so it takes grit.

Sometimes even sticking with a class for the whole semester takes grit; I get really tired of the same class for fifteen weeks.

Takes grit to write lots of drafts for a paper; I get sick of writing on the same topic and going over and over my work.

Takes grit to study math. I hate math.

Reggie is now ready to create an outline for his essay on his computer. Notice that Reggie has slightly changed the wording of the reasons he is going to use in his paper. He arranges his reasons in order of importance, giving the most significant, and least obvious, reason last. He has also added transitions, and he has added the examples he will use to support each reason.

Reggie's Outline

<u>Topic</u>: Why grit is important for college students

<u>Thesis statement</u>: College students need grit because attaining a college degree takes time, demands a commitment to studying, and requires the development of difficult skills.

<u>Idea for introduction</u>: Provide a definition of grit: "a distinct combination of passion, resilience, determination, and focus that allows a person to maintain the discipline and optimism to persevere in their goals even in the face of discomfort, rejection, and a lack of visible progress for years, or even decades" (Williams).

<u>Major Supporting Point 1</u>: Obviously, since earning a college degree takes time, college students need grit just to stay in school.

<u>Support</u>: Examples
- How semesters work
- Years required for an AA and a bachelor's degree

<u>Major Supporting Point 2</u>: Another reason college students need to have grit is that studying demands time and effort.

<u>Support</u>: Examples
- A typical study schedule
- Potential distractions that must be managed

<u>Major Supporting Point 3</u>: Finally, college students need grit to develop difficult college-level skills.

<u>Support</u>: Examples
- Writing a paper with multiple drafts
- Mastering a musical instrument

Now that Reggie has an outline, he uses the remaining steps in the writing process to draft his essay, revise it, and edit it. What follows is Reggie's final draft. Annotate Reggie's draft for the thesis statement, major supporting points, and other important elements. Also, determine the introduction and conclusion strategies Reggie uses.

Model Student Paper: "Why College Students Need Grit" by Reggie Chambers

Reggie Chambers

Mr. Roberts

ENGL 0402

25 February 2018

Why College Students Need Grit

Since most people agree that having a college education is important, why do so few people finish college? Several reasons may come to mind. College is expensive. It takes time. It is not easy. Family life may interfere, and work requirements may make college impossible. These are all good reasons, but another reason why so few people finish college is summed up in one word: grit. Grit can be defined as "a distinct combination of passion, resilience, determination, and focus that allows a person to maintain the discipline and optimism to persevere in their goals even in the face of discomfort, rejection, and a lack of visible progress for years, or even decades" (Williams). College students need grit because attaining a college degree takes time, demands a commitment to studying, and requires the development of difficult skills.

Obviously, since earning a college degree takes time, college students need grit just to stay in school. A typical semester lasts 15–16 weeks, approximately four months. That is a long time to stay focused on one thing. Cecelia French, a professor of English at a community college, explained that most students get tired of the work load around mid-semester. She said, "Two-thirds of the way through the long semester, I have lost a lot of students. They give up because they get tired of coming to class and working hard." Semesters are long, but the time it takes to earn an actual degree is even longer. Most students take at least two years to earn an associate's degree, and a bachelor's degree takes at least four years. Without grit, students will drop out of school because they become tired of the effort.

Another reason college students need to have grit is that studying demands time and effort. Going to class takes effort, but taking the time to study properly takes even more effort. At least going to class does not require much more than sitting and listening. Studying requires actively trying to learn. John Hess, a professor of speech, explains that the general rule of thumb for study time is to study 2–3 hours for each credit hour. This means a 3-credit hour course requires 6–9 hours of study outside of class. Students who are taking fifteen hours would need to study 30–45 hours per week according to this rule. Without grit, a student simply will not be able to stick to such a schedule. In addition, students have to have grit during those study sessions. With potential distractions such as social media, college activities, and family needs, students need grit to keep their attention focused on their studies.

Finally, college students need grit to develop difficult college-level skills. The skills needed to survive college are often hard to develop. Many students go to college thinking that they have good writing skills only to learn that the standards for college writing are quite high. To write a good paper, a student will need the grit to write multiple drafts. And between drafts, students need the grit required to learn how to improve their writing. The same is true for learning other skills, such as mastering an instrument. Margaret Benson, a college flute instructor, explains, "A student who is a music major may have to spend up to five hours a day practicing his or her instrument. This may be far more time than the student is used to practicing, and many music majors drop out because of the practice required." Mastering college-level skills requires grit because those skills demand effort

Chambers 3

and practice. Skills usually take time to develop, and being willing to invest that time takes grit.

Since so much grit is required to achieve a college degree, maybe a good question to ask is how so many students actually *do* manage to get through college. Of course, having grit is only one of many requirements. Keeping one's eyes on the goal is also important. Sarah Blount graduated with her bachelor's degree last year. When asked how she managed to stay motivated during the five years it took for her to finish, Blount said, "I never wanted to give up my dream of being a teacher." Today, she teaches her own classroom of third-grade children, and she hopes that one of the lessons those students learn is the importance of the ingredient that helped their teacher so much: grit.

Chambers 4

Works Cited

Benson, Margaret. Personal interview. 16 Feb. 2018.

Blount, Sarah. Personal interview. 16 Feb. 2018.

French, Cecelia. Personal interview. 18 Feb. 2018.

Hess, John. Personal interview. 18 Feb. 2018.

Williams, Jenny. "What Is Grit, Why Kids Need It, and How You Can Foster It." *A Fine Parent*, afineparent.com/author/jenny-williams. Accessed 16 Feb. 2018.

➔ A READING AND WRITING ASSIGNMENT

Now that you have analyzed Reggie's process for completing his essay assignment, write an essay of your own in response to the reading. Use the following assignment.

> Read, annotate, and analyze "What Is Grit, Why Kids Need It, and How You Can Foster It."
>
> Write an essay in which you answer this question: In what life situations is grit especially important? Write a thesis statement that answers this question. Discuss at least three life situations that demand grit. Consider creating hypothetical or real world examples for your reasons. You may use Jenny Williams's article as a resource. Be sure to give credit to Williams if you use any of the ideas that come from her article.

YOUR ANNOTATIONS

Use the Quick Start Guide to Integrated Reading and Writing Assignments to assist you in the writing process.

➔ ADDING TO YOUR VOCABULARY

This chapter's vocabulary words appear below.

advocate	conventional	irony	resilient
conceivable	credible	perseverance	therapeutic

Choose five of the vocabulary words from this chapter that you would like to add to your vocabulary, and think about how you can use them this week. For example, one of this chapter's words is *advocate*. You can often easily substitute *advocate* for *suggest* or sometimes *say,* as in the example that follows.

> **Example:** I am *saying* that you should obey speed limit laws.
>
> I am *advocating* that you obey speed limit laws.

List each of the five words you plan to use this week, and make note of a context in which you could use each word.

> **Example:** *Advocating.* I can use this word when I give advice to a family member.

⊙ ADDITIONAL ASSIGNMENTS

1. Imagine you are writing an essay with this thesis statement: *Six steps can help you be a more organized person.* The six steps you will discuss are these:

   - Make and use lists.

   - Keep a neat desk.

   - Organize paperwork effectively and daily.

   - Use your smartphone's organizational tools.

   - Identify the obstacles that keep you from being organized, and make a plan to deal with them.

   - Hire help when it is necessary.

   Write an introduction paragraph, a conclusion paragraph, and a title for this essay.

2. Find an essay in this textbook or an essay you wrote that could benefit from a new introduction paragraph or conclusion paragraph, and write the paragraph.

3. a. Scan magazines, textbooks, or other texts. Choose a text with an interesting title. Explain in a paragraph what makes the title interesting.

   b. Find a text that contains a well-written introduction. Write a paragraph explaining why you find the introduction well written.

   c. Follow this same procedure for a conclusion paragraph. Be sure to write down the name of the essay (or textbook chapter) in which you found the interesting or well-written introduction and conclusion.

4. Take out an essay you wrote for this course or for another course. Rewrite the title, introduction, and conclusion using strategies from this chapter. Work on improving the interest and quality of all three elements.

EMOTIONAL INTELLIGENCE

Two types of motivation exist. First, there is *extrinsic motivation.* Something that motivates us extrinsically is something that is outside of us. For example, if a person stands over me with a stun gun and commands me to move rocks, I will move the rocks—not because I want to move rocks, but because I am being forced to move them. *Intrinsic motivation* is motivation that comes from inside. If I am building an outdoor fire pit with rocks, I will move the rocks because I want to build the fire pit.

Studies show that students who do work because they are intrinsically motivated to succeed in college *always* do better work than students who do work because they are being forced to. Think of a time when you did a college assignment that you *wanted* to do, not because you were forced to. Now think of an assignment you did because you had to. What was the difference in the quality of those assignments? Explain your answer in a paragraph.

Think about how you can be intrinsically motivated to do college assignments in which you are not personally interested. How can you transform extrinsic motivation to intrinsic motivation—even when the assignments are not ones you long to do? Write a paragraph explaining your ideas.

METACOGNITION

Metacognitive ability means you can see yourself from the outside. Answer the following questions from a metacognitive point of view. Are you an ethnocentric thinker? (An ethnocentric thinker is unable to see things from a different cultural perspective.) Is this something you can change? Explain.

Text Credits

Inferences and Tone

©Terry J Alcorn/Getty Images RF

An inference is an educated guess. By examining the details of this photo, what inferences can you make? Readers and writers work with inferences in texts as well as in illustrations.

- Use details and common knowledge to make sound inferences.

- Draw accurate inferences from visuals.

- Analyze tone in texts.

- Recognize first, second, and third person in readings, and make appropriate writing choices concerning person.

- Choose an appropriate tone for writing assignments.

- Analyze figurative language to make accurate inferences.

- Use figurative language in writing.

An inference is a conclusion a person draws based on evidence. When we read, we **infer** by examining the information the writer provides. On the other hand, when we speak or write, we can **imply** meanings without stating them outright. For instance, when we need to finish a conversation, we might say something such as "It's getting late." Our words *imply* a deeper meaning—"We need to end this conversation"—and we hope our listeners will *infer* this meaning from what they hear us say.

As readers and observers, we make inferences every day. We might see a restaurant with a paint-worn and disheveled appearance and infer that the food must not be good. Or perhaps we find ourselves in stop-and-go traffic and infer that the freeway will be clogged for a long time, so we take an exit and find an alternative route.

Sometimes our inferences are correct, and sometimes they are totally mistaken. We may learn that the "rundown" restaurant is a fabulous eatery that has been featured on a televised food program, or we may learn that the freeway was not clogged: debris from a tire blowout had simply slowed down traffic temporarily. Being able to make accurate inferences is crucial for good communication.

Using Details and Common Knowledge to Make Sound Inferences

One way to make accurate inferences is to consider details. To be sound, an inference must be based on the actual information in a text. Read the following passage, and notice the details that are underlined.

As I walked to my trigonometry class on the first day of the semester, I felt full of hope. Math had never been an easy subject for me, but I knew that with determination, I could do anything. I really believed that.

I found a seat in the middle of the classroom and glanced at the people around me. Most looked **nonchalant**, as if taking a class in trig were not a big deal. No one spoke.

Five minutes after the class was supposed to begin, a man who looked too young to be a professor walked into the class, slung his gray, worn backpack on the professor's table, and started writing an equation on the board. He muttered something about page 33, so I fumbled through my textbook to find the page. Nothing on the page looked remotely like what the professor had written on the board.

He kept explaining. Something.

"You understand?" he asked the class, turning back to the board before anyone could answer.

I felt that sinking feeling in my stomach that I have felt in so many math classes before. It would be a long semester after all.

VCW nonchalant

To make a sound inference, read the text and pay attention to details. Think about ideas that the details suggest. Write a sentence that expresses an inference. The illustration "Drawing Inferences from Details" on the next page shows the process for drawing sound inferences and a few examples.

For a conclusion to be considered a sound inference, you must always be able to support the inference with details from the text.

Inaccurate Inferences

When you read a text, all kinds of ideas come to mind. For example, if you once experienced a math class that was similar to the one described in the text, your personal experience might pop into your mind. If it did, you might be tempted to take some of the details from your experience and apply them to what you are reading. Doing so could lead you to create unsupported inferences. The illustration "Making Inaccurate Inferences" on the next page gives some examples.

DRAWING INFERENCES FROM DETAILS

THESE DETAILS FROM THE TEXT . . .	. . . SUGGEST THAT . . .	. . . THESE INFERENCES ARE SOUND.
1 **Detail:** ". . . a man who looked too young to be a professor walked into the class."	*suggests that . . .*	**Inference:** The instructor is young. *This inference is sound because the detail from the text supports it.*
2 **Detail 1:** "I fumbled through my textbook to find the page. Nothing on the page looked remotely like what the professor had written on the board." **Detail 2:** "I felt that sinking feeling in my stomach that I have felt in so many math classes before. It would be a long semester after all."	*suggests that . . .*	**Inference:** The narrator does not feel optimistic about his ability to pass the class. *This inference is sound because the detail from the text supports it.*

MAKING INACCURATE INFERENCES

THESE DETAILS FROM THE TEXT . . .	. . . COMBINED WITH IRRELEVANT IDEAS . . .	. . . MAKE FOR INACCURATE INFERENCES.
1 **Detail:** ". . . a man who looked too young to be a professor walked into the class."	I once had a young teacher, and he was very arrogant.	**Inaccurate inference:** The instructor is arrogant. *The text does not have evidence to support this inference.*
2 **Detail:** "I fumbled through my textbook to find the page. Nothing on the page looked remotely like what the professor had written on the board."	Whenever I fumble through a textbook, it is usually because the instructor is going too fast.	**Inaccurate inference:** The instructor speaks too quickly. *The text does not have evidence to support this inference.*

Be careful about using your personal experiences and ideas to draw inferences. Stick to the details in the text, and you will be able to draw inferences that are sound and reasonable.

Common Knowledge

Common knowledge refers to information that most people have or ideas that most people would easily and readily believe or accept. For instance, it is common knowledge that Barack Obama was the first African American president of the United States, that lightning and thunder signal rain, and that children need supervision. You can use common knowledge to help make inferences.

Now we will look at a text that is a bit more complex and use it to judge inferences. Some of the inferences will rely on details as well as common knowledge. Read and carefully annotate the following selection from *A First Look at Communication Theory* by Em Griffin. Pay special attention to the details it offers.

What We Can Learn from the *Challenger* Disaster

By Em Griffin

YOUR ANNOTATIONS

[1]On the morning of January 28, 1986, the space shuttle *Challenger* blasted off from the Kennedy Space Center in Florida. [2]Seventy-three seconds later, millions of adults and school children watched on television as the rocket disintegrated in a fiery explosion, and the capsule plunged into the Atlantic Ocean. [3]The death of all seven crew members, and particularly teacher Christa McAuliffe, shocked the nation. [4]For many Americans, the *Challenger* disaster marked the end of a love affair with space. [5]As they learned in the months that followed, the tragedy could have been—should have been—avoided.

[6]President Reagan immediately appointed a select commission to determine the probable cause(s) of the accident. [7]The panel heard four months of testimony from NASA officials, rocket engineers, astronauts, and anyone else who might have knowledge about the failed mission. [8]In a five-volume published report, the presidential **commission** identified the primary cause of the accident as a failure in the joint between two stages of the rocket that allowed hot gases to escape during the "burn." [9]Volatile rocket fuel spewed out when a rubber O-ring failed to seal the joint.

VCW commission

[10]The average citizen could understand the mechanics of the commission's finding. [11]After all, everyone knows what happens when you pour gasoline on an open flame. [12]What people found difficult to **fathom** was why NASA had launched the *Challenger* when there was good reason to believe the conditions weren't safe. [13]In addition to the defective seal, the commission also concluded that a highly flawed decision process was an important contributing cause of the disaster. [14]Communication, as well as combustion, was responsible for the tragedy.

VCW fathom

After you read the passage, notice in the illustration "Inferences Supported by Details and Common Knowledge" on the next page how we can use the details to draw a sound inference when we apply some common knowledge to the details.

INFERENCES SUPPORTED BY DETAILS AND COMMON KNOWLEDGE

THESE DETAILS FROM THE TEXT . . .	. . . COMBINED WITH COMMON KNOWLEDGE . . .	. . . MAKE FOR A SOUND INFERENCE.
Detail 1: "Millions of adults and school children watched on television as the rocket disintegrated in a fiery explosion" **Detail 2:** "The death of all seven crew members, and particularly teacher Christa McAuliffe, shocked the nation."	**Common knowledge:** Watching people die is traumatizing for most people. Also, events that are shocking can be traumatizing.	**Inference:** The *Challenger* explosion was an especially traumatic event for teachers and school children. *This inference is sound because the details from the text, as well as common knowledge, support it.*

Unsupported Inferences

Now let's consider some unsupported inferences. The example in the illustration "Unsupported Inferences," which follows, is not based on details from the text. Notice how easy it is to make conclusions, especially judgments, that are not supported by the information in the text.

As you look for inferences in texts, make sure you use the actual details that the text supplies, not ideas you bring to the text. Be sure you can point to the details that make your inferences sound.

UNSUPPORTED INFERENCES

THIS DETAIL FROM THE TEXT . . .	. . . IS NOT ENOUGH FOR . . .	. . . THIS UNSUPPORTED INFERENCE.
Detail: "Volatile rocket fuel spewed out when a rubber O-ring failed to seal the joint."	*. . . is not enough for . . .*	**Unsupported inference:** NASA engineers did not know how to design flawless O-rings. *This inference is not sound because there are no details to support it. The O-ring failed, and communication contributed to this failure. But the text does not say the engineers lacked knowledge. Sentence 5 says that "the tragedy could have been—should have been—avoided." This line suggests the engineers could make flawless O-rings.*

PRACTICE **1**

Drawing Inferences Based on a Text's Details

Use the passage from *A First Look at Communication Theory* to determine whether the inferences that follow are sound. Write *S* for inferences that are sound and *NS* for those that are not sound. Write a sentence explaining your reasoning for each answer.

_____ 1. President Ronald Reagan was very concerned about the *Challenger* explosion.

_____

_____

_____ 2. The writer believes that school children should not be allowed to watch rocket launches.

_____

_____

_____ 3. Some people at NASA were probably worried about something going wrong with the launch.

_____

_____

_____

_____ 4. The panel investigating may not have been qualified to make the investigation.

_____

_____ 5. Some people involved in the launch knew the shuttle was going to blow up during liftoff.

_____

_____ 6. Even the most minor details of space flight must be considered for the flight to be safe.

_____

PRACTICE **2**

Drawing Your Own Inferences

Read "Nelson Mandela and Apartheid," below, which is followed by a blank chart. Draw two accurate inferences from the passage. Write your inference in the right-hand column of the chart, and write the details that support your inference in the left-hand column.

Nelson Mandela and Apartheid

Apartheid was a legal system of segregation and institutionalized racism in South Africa. It began officially in 1948, although South Africa had discriminated against people of color since the Dutch colonial period.

One of the most prominent and influential critics of apartheid was Nelson Mandela. Born in 1918, Mandela came of age during the institutionalization of apartheid. Mandela practiced nonviolent resistance to apartheid. He was a natural leader.

Although he spent twenty-seven years in prison for an alleged plot to overthrow the racist government, he eventually became president of South Africa in 1994. Nelson Mandela was instrumental in ending apartheid in South Africa.

(continued)

These details . . .	. . . support . . .	. . . this inference.
_____ _____ _____ _____ _____ _____	. . . support . . .	1.
_____ _____ _____ _____ _____	. . . support . . .	2.

Drawing Accurate Inferences from Visuals

Many texts are accompanied by visuals, such as charts, graphs, artwork, cartoons, and photos. Often visuals are not explained: they are simply presented alongside other information. Thus, readers must infer their meanings.

General Guidelines for Reading Graphics

You can make accurate inferences from graphics by following these guidelines.

Step 1: Read the Graphic's Title.   Because charts, graphs, and illustrations contain so few words, it is crucial to start by reading the title. From the title you can often determine the type of information offered. In the graphic below, for example, the title helps us understand the three elements that make up the graph: unemployment, weekly earnings, and education.

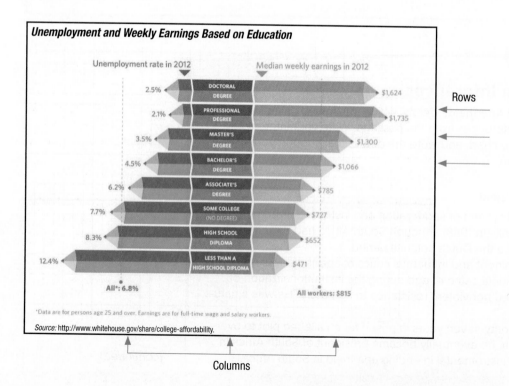

Step 2: Read the Descriptions in the Graphic.   Often, graphics use colors to code particular pieces of information. In the graph shown above, red depicts the unemployment rate in 2012. Gray presents education level, and yellow depicts median weekly earnings in 2012. Like tables, graphs often present information in columns and rows. Rows are always horizontal, and columns are vertical.

Step 3: Write Sentences Based on a Graph's Details.   By putting graphic information into your own words, you can more easily understand the meaning of the information. For example, start with the bottom row of information in the preceding graphic. It tells us that in 2012, the people who had less than a high school diploma (gray) experienced an unemployment rate of 12.4 percent (red) and made approximately $471 a week (yellow). We can write sentences expressing the data for each row in the graph. Here are two of the sentences we can construct.

- People who had a bachelor's degree had an unemployment rate of 4.5 percent and earned approximately $1,066 a week.
- People who had a doctoral degree had an unemployment rate of 2.5 percent and earned approximately $1,624 a week.

Step 4: Draw Inferences from Your Sentences.   What conclusions can you draw from the content of your sentences? In the case of the preceding graph, we can analyze the sentences listed above. From these sentences, we can infer the following.

Inference: In general, the more education a person has, the less likely he or she is to be unemployed and the more money per week the person will make.

Note that there is one exception. People with doctoral degrees had slightly more unemployment and made slightly less money per week than people with professional degrees. Notice how the inference contains the phrase *in general.* When wording inferences, be careful to use **qualifiers** such as *most, some, on the whole,* and *usually.*

VCW qualifier

PRACTICE 3

Drawing Inferences from Graphics

The following graphic is from the Food and Drug Administration. On a separate sheet, use the four-step process to analyze the graphic. After completing your analysis, make two inferences. Use a separate sheet for your response.

(continued)

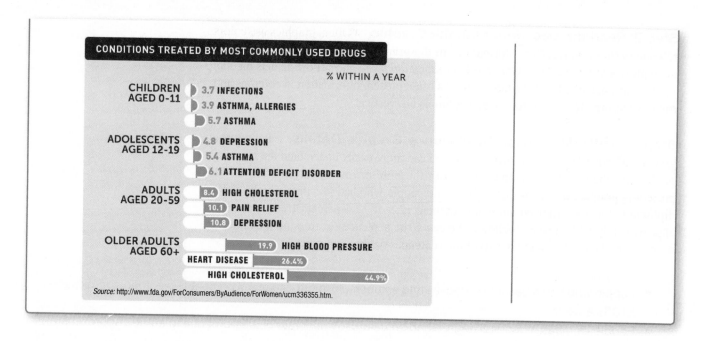

Special Considerations for Reading Line Graphs, Pie Charts, and Maps

A **line graph** shows relationships between data by plotting points. You may be familiar with line graphs from math courses. A line graph has a vertical axis and a horizontal axis. Each axis represents different values—such as years, amounts, and so on. In the example that follows, the horizontal axis indicates years, and the vertical axis indicates the percentage of increase. The graph presents two types of information: the increase in the miles people travel and the increase in population. The legend indicates what the different-colored lines represent.

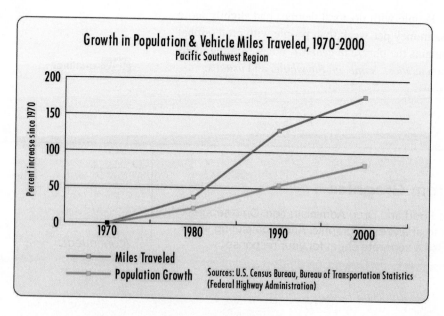

Notice that the distance traveled (depicted by the purple line) increases at a faster rate than the population (green line). One inference we can make from this data is that people are traveling more than they used to.

In addition to line graphs, you will encounter graphs that are round—often called **pie charts.** These graphs divide data into groups, and each group is represented by a "slice" of the pie chart. The size of each slice indicates the percentage of the pie that it constitutes. Added together, they generally total 100 percent. The title, given in the middle of the pie chart that follows, indicates that the chart is displaying greenhouse gas emissions categorized by economic sector. If you are not sure what economic sectors are, you can look at the pie pieces and see that there are five sectors: electricity, agriculture, commercial and residential, industry, and transportation. Which sector produces the most greenhouse gas emissions? The chart shows that the greatest quantity of emissions comes from the production of electricity because its share of the pie is 33 percent, larger than the share of any other sector.

By analyzing this chart, you can make some inferences. For one, it is accurate to infer that if we want to substantially reduce greenhouse gas emissions, we need to put more emphasis on transforming sectors like electricity, which accounts for a high percentage of total emissions, rather than sectors like agriculture, which accounts for a low percentage. By addressing electricity emissions, we would be focusing on one-third of the greenhouse gas emissions in the country.

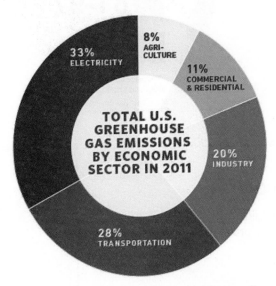

Source: http://www.whitehouse.gov/share/climate-action-plan.

Maps are another way to present information. The map of the United States shown on the next page depicts the hours per week a person would need to work at minimum wage to afford an apartment in each state. Notice how the graphic uses color to depict data.

From this map, we can infer that the least expensive states to live in are in the southern and middle United States. Living on the East Coast is expensive, as is living in California, Florida, Alaska, and Hawaii. What other inferences can you draw from this graphic?

Another thing to remember about interpreting graphics is that most of the time, graphics are comparative. That is, they provide data that allow readers to make comparisons and to create inferences from those comparisons. For example, the map enables readers to compare the affordability of living in particular states. The comparison of data makes the graphic meaningful because it allows readers to use the data to make inferences and decisions.

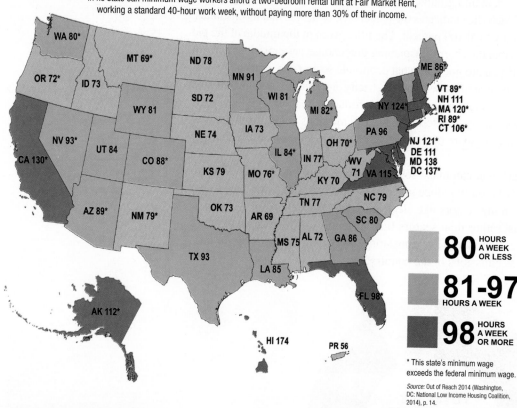

2014 HOURS AT MINIMUM WAGE NEEDED TO AFFORD RENT

In no state can minimum wage workers afford a two-bedroom rental unit at Fair Market Rent, working a standard 40-hour work week, without paying more than 30% of their income.

80 HOURS A WEEK OR LESS

81-97 HOURS A WEEK

98 HOURS A WEEK OR MORE

* This state's minimum wage exceeds the federal minimum wage.

Source: Out of Reach 2014 (Washington, DC: National Low Income Housing Coalition, 2014), p. 14.

PRACTICE 4

Analyzing Inferences Drawn from Graphics

Following the line graph are six statements. Study the line graph, and then determine whether the statements and inferences are accurate.

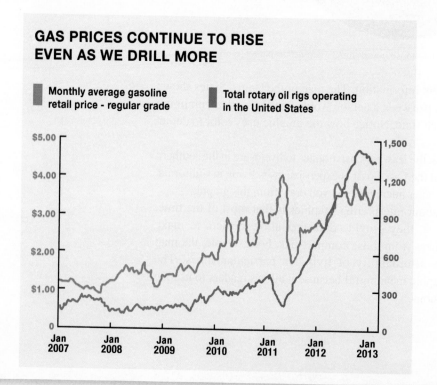

GAS PRICES CONTINUE TO RISE EVEN AS WE DRILL MORE

Monthly average gasoline retail price - regular grade

Total rotary oil rigs operating in the United States

(continued)

Accurate or inaccurate?

_____ 1. Statement: In January 2008, fewer than three hundred rigs were operating in the United States, and the price of gas was a little more than $1.00.

_____ 2. Statement: In 2011, gas prices reached their highest point.

_____ 3. Statement: Every time the number of rigs operating is increased, gas prices increase.

_____ 4. Inference: For the most part, gas prices have increased over time, even though the number of oil rigs has generally increased during the same period.

_____ 5. Inference: A dramatic increase in the number of oil rigs will result in a dramatic decrease in the cost of gasoline.

_____ 6. Inference: Factors other than the amount of drilling we do in the United States affect the cost of gasoline.

Drawing Inferences from Photos

When we observe an image such as a photograph, the details in the photo help us draw inferences. Study the picture shown here. What inferences can you draw from the details in the photo?

©Fuse/Getty Images RF

Perhaps you noticed the girl in the forefront and the three children in the background. The girl gazing out the window does not have a smile on her face, and her eyebrow is slightly raised. Her intense gaze suggests worry. The children in the background, meanwhile, are running barefoot. All the children have on similar clothing. We might infer that these children are in school because they seem to be wearing school uniforms. We might also infer that the girl looking out the window is not part of the group or that she is not in a playful mood. We may infer that she is lonely or worried or that she wants to be somewhere other than school. These are sound inferences because we can support them with the details in the photo.

What would you say to a person who looks at the photo and thinks the girl is nervous and unhappy because she is a new student at the school and misses her old friends? We can see that she is unhappy, but we really cannot see why. The fact that she is not playing with the other children does not give us enough information on which to base the inference that the school is new to her and that she misses her friends. While it would be easy to imagine many different reasons for the girl's posture and facial expression, we can use only the reasons that are supported by evidence to draw correct inferences.

PRACTICE **5**

Making Inferences from Photos

Analyze the details in each photo below. Using the details, write a sound inference for each photo. Make a list of the details in the sentence that support your inference.

Photo A

©McGraw-Hill Education/John Flournoy, photographer

1. Your inference: _____
    _____

2. Details that support your inference:

    • _____

    • _____

    • _____

(continued)

Photo B

©Johannes Mann/Corbis/Getty Images

1. Your inference: _____

_____

2. Details that support your inference:

- _____

- _____

- _____

Analyzing Tone in Texts

If you have ever spent time around children, you know a disrespectful tone when you hear one. To such a tone, a parent may reply, "Don't take that tone with me!" So, what exactly is tone?

Tone is the attitude with which a message is conveyed. We might use a tone of respect when we speak, or we might use a tone that reveals frustration, anger, or impatience. Both voice and body language help us discern tone in face-to-face communication. In texts, however, we depend on textual clues to help us identify tone.

Have you ever noticed how difficult it is to determine the tone of a text message or an e-mail? Read the e-mail message that follows. What is its tone?

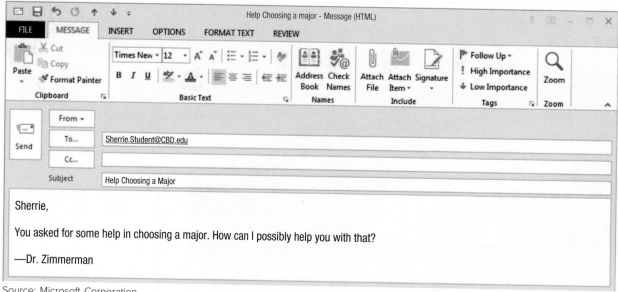

Source: Microsoft Corporation

As you read the e-mail message, did you hear a helpful tone in the last sentence, or did you hear a sarcastic tone? Because readers could infer a sarcastic tone, it would be better to write a reply that leaves no room to wonder about the writer's attitude. Compare the following message. Notice how adding a few extra details and making intentional choices about wording help the writer convey a tone that is decidedly positive. Writers must carefully select their words to help readers understand the tone they hope to establish.

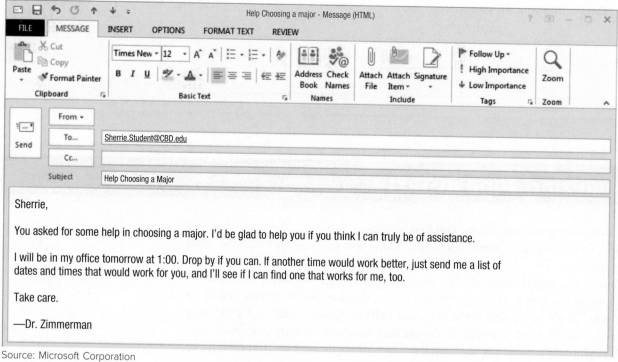

Source: Microsoft Corporation

Objective Tone

One way to understand tone is to consider two types: objective and subjective. When a writer attempts to write a text *without* tone or with a neutral tone, we say that the writer uses an **objective tone.** Imagine a news anchor reading the evening news. The anchor's job is to minimize the tone in her voice so that she presents the news in a nonbiased, or objective, manner. The anchor is speaking as a reader, not as an individual. Thus, we are not supposed to focus on the anchor and her particular views. Read the following text for an example of objective tone.

Example of Objective Tone

People who are regularly late for meetings or other appointments can eventually develop a reputation for being less dependable than others. Coworkers and acquaintances rarely know or understand the situations that cause a person to be habitually late, and even if they are aware of such circumstances, they may still come to view the late person as unreliable. In turn, having a reputation as an unreliable person makes it more difficult to receive promotions or be entrusted with high-level tasks.

The illustration "Characteristics of Objective Tone" provides help in identifying an objective tone.

CHARACTERISTICS OF OBJECTIVE TONE
An Objective Tone ...

Avoids emotionally charged terms	• In Example of Objective Tone, the term "unreliable person" is far less emotionally charged than the term "loser" or "slacker" would be.
Uses impartial, unbiased language	• The writer of "Example of Objective Tone" does not judge habitually late people with a term like "poor employees." She just explains a possible effect of being consistently late.
Is used in formal (professional and academic) writing	• Not only does slang (such as the word "loser") convey an emotional and biased tone, it also makes a text informal.

When a writer uses an objective tone, we are more likely to infer that the information is reliable. We may not be correct, of course, but we expect reliable information to be delivered in an impersonal, objective way. Thus, when we see the use of an objective tone, we can use it as a clue for making inferences. For example, in the paragraph about people who are habitually late, it would be wrong to make the inference that the writer has **disdain** for such people. The writer does not reveal her own attitude toward the subject.

 disdain

We would also be wrong to infer that the writer is never late for her own appointments. She reveals nothing about her behaviors or her attitudes. For all we know, the writer might be a habitually late person herself! Thus, when you identify an objective tone, you cannot make inferences about the writer's attitude toward the topic.

Subjective Tone

A **subjective tone** is used when a writer is not trying to present information in a neutral way. We have shown how news anchors attempt to use an objective tone so that they do not reveal their personal biases about issues. Political commentators, on the other hand, discuss news events but do so in a subjective, biased way. They are paid to offer their opinions on current events, so using a subjective tone is appropriate.

The use of a subjective tone is intentional: writers hope readers will come to share the same emotions or opinions as they do. Read the following example to become familiar with subjective tone.

Example of Subjective Tone

I work with a poor colleague who is always late. He's not only late to meetings, but he's late to work every single day. The variety of excuses he uses when he stumbles through the door each morning is always amusing. He cannot help but utter some lame excuse. "I was caught in traffic. Darn freeway!" or "I can't believe my alarm clock failed me again!" It would be so much better—and so much more appropriate—for him to creep over to his office and slink into his chair like the clueless **buffoon** he is.

VCW buffoon

CHARACTERISTICS OF SUBJECTIVE TONE
A Subjective Tone ...

Uses emotional clues	• In "Example of Subjective Tone," the term *poor colleague* is an emotional clue. The speaker either feels sorry for the worker or, worse, has disrespect for the worker.

Can express bias —a person's preferences or particular point of view	• In "Example of Subjective Tone," these phrases show the writer's bias against his colleague:
	  • "Stumbles through the door" implies that the person is clumsy.
	  • "Creep over to his office and slink into his chair" implies that the person moves like an animal and thus is less than human.
	  • "Clueless buffoon" shows the writer engaging in name-calling, which ensures that the tone is not objective.

Is often used in informal writing	• In "Example of Subjective Tone," the writer uses "I" (first person) and contractions, which are characteristics of informal writing.

One element of subjective texts is that they reveal a writer's bias. Sometimes we hear the term *biased* and think it means "unfair." However, a person who is biased about a subject is not necessarily unfair. When you write an essay on a controversial topic, such as immigration reform, and submit it for grading, you can expect that your instructor will be biased about the issue, but he or she can still grade your paper fairly.

We see bias in texts when writers reveal their personal opinions or points of view. Writers seeking to be objective try to present a topic in a neutral manner. The use of a subjective tone is appropriate when writers want to present their personal views or reveal information about themselves. A subjective tone will often allow readers to infer the writer's bias or attitudes toward a subject. It can also reveal the writer's emotions about the subject.

Because a subjective tone reveals a great deal about the writer's thoughts and attitudes, you can create accurate inferences by analyzing the tone. Notice how the inferences that follow are based on the writer's subjective, **condescending** tone.

 condescending

Accurate inference: The writer has disrespect for his colleague.

Accurate inference: The writer does not think his colleague's reasons for being late are legitimate.

Accurate inference: The writer feels superior to his colleague.

Complete the following exercise to try your hand at distinguishing between objective and subjective tones, and then use your analysis of tone to make accurate inferences.

PRACTICE 6

Identifying Tone to Make Accurate Inferences

Read each of the following passages, and answer the corresponding questions.

Passage A: Excerpt from *Business Now* by Amit Shah

An entrepreneur has several potential sources of capital: personal savings, relatives, former employers, banks, finance companies, venture capitalists (a person or investment company that loans money to businesses), and government agencies such as the SBA [Small Business Administration], the Farmers Home Administration, and the Economic Development Authority. Isabella Capital, LLC, is a venture capital firm that focuses on woman-owned businesses.

There are also angel investors, usually wealthy people who invest their own money in a business in return for a share of the company. Angel investors are different from venture capitalists, in that venture capitalists usually invest other people's money, while angel investors invest their own funds. The Angel Capital Association operates in North America and works to bring together angel investors and entrepreneurs.

1. What is the tone of this passage?

   _____

2. On the basis of the tone, is it accurate to infer that the writer approves more highly of angel investors than the other kinds of investors mentioned in the paragraph? Explain your answer.

   _____
   _____
   _____

Passage B

So-called authorities urge everyone, every year, to get the flu shot. Almost all the people I know seem to go for the hype and rush to the local clinic or local drugstore, stand in line, and pay for this vaccination. What they don't realize is that they're paying for a mixture of vaccine and toxic chemicals—such as mercury and thimerosal—that is not even guaranteed to work. In fact, when my neighbor got a flu shot, she became so ill with a flu-like sickness that she could barely get out of bed. When ignorance meets fear, people make extremely bad decisions. You won't see me in line for a flu shot, and I've never had the flu yet!

1. What is the tone of this passage?

   _____

2. On the basis of the tone, is it accurate to infer that the writer thinks she is smarter than people who get flu shots? Explain your answer.

   _____
   _____
   _____
   _____

Formal Writing

The kind of writing you will do for college assignments is formal writing. Business reports, letters, legal documents, and many other professional texts consist of formal writing. The characteristics of formal writing include the following:

- Use of third person (*one*); avoidance of first person (*I*) and second person (*you*)
- Avoidance of slang
- Avoidance of contractions
- Use of proper grammar
- Use of higher-level sentence structure (more complex sentences) and vocabulary

Save informal writing for correspondence—such as e-mail and text messages—between friends and for other informal occasions. Do not use it in your academic writing. Even though many people think of e-mail as an informal mode of expression, it is better to use formal rather than informal writing for e-mail messages to employers and professors. Above all, do not use the informal language of text messaging in academic or job-related e-mail messages.

Grammar Focus

Point of View

Writers have the choice of using first-, second-, or third-person point of view. The point of view is conveyed by the pronouns a writer uses.

First-person pronouns: I, me, my, mine, myself; we, us, our, ours, ourselves

Second-person pronouns: you, your, yours, yourself

Third-person pronouns: he, him, his, himself; she, her, hers, herself; they, them, their, theirs, themselves; it, its, itself; one's, oneself

The point of view a writer uses contributes to establishing a subjective or objective tone. The key is to choose the correct point of view for your writing purpose.

1. USE FIRST-PERSON POINT OF VIEW FOR A SUBJECTIVE TONE

First-person point of view is the writer's voice, so it draws attention to the writer and conveys a more intimate and subjective tone than second- or third-person point of view. Sometimes such a tone is desirable, as in a narrative essay, autobiography, or personal letter. At other times, using first person may detract from the authority of your voice. Consider the difference in these two statements.

Uses first person: <u>In my opinion,</u> using physical punishment to teach children lessons is not wise.

Does *not* use first person: Using physical punishment to teach children lessons is not wise.

(continued)

The example using first person (*In my opinion*) weakens the impact of the idea that is presented by implying that it is simply a matter of the writer's belief. While the second example is still an assertion of a belief, it sounds more confident and objective and therefore seems to be universally true.

2. USE SECOND-PERSON POINT OF VIEW TO GIVE INSTRUCTIONS

Second-person point of view addresses readers directly, so it can convey a personal tone. However, statements in second person can sound demanding. At its worst, the use of second person can result in writing that is the equivalent of wagging one's forefinger, as these examples show.

Uses second person: <u>You</u> need to stop playing on <u>your</u> cell phone and start listening in class.

Does *not* use second person: Students need to stop playing on their cell phones and start listening in class.

Notice how the first example (*You . . . your*) sounds like a personal scolding. The second example gets across the same idea without scolding the reader.

Second-person writing can be used effectively in business letters, in instructions and how-to or process texts, and in speeches. For example, in a how-to text, a writer may use second person to personalize instructions, as follows.

Uses second person: When <u>you</u> calculate <u>your</u> income taxes, <u>you</u> will need <u>your</u> W-2 forms from the previous year, as well as any other forms that show the income <u>you</u> earned during the tax year.

Remember also that command statements are implicitly in second person.

Uses a command: To calculate your income taxes, <u>use</u> your W-2 forms from the previous year, as well as any other forms that show the income you earned during the tax year.

The word *you* is implied as the subject of *use* (*To calculate your income taxes, [you] use . . .*). Notice how terse a command can be; because of their no-nonsense tone, commands are best employed sparingly.

3. USE THIRD-PERSON POINT OF VIEW FOR ACADEMIC WORK AND OTHER FORMAL WRITING

Third person helps create an objective tone. The writing sounds more authoritative because the information in the text is not tied to the writer's voice. Note the following example.

Uses third person: <u>Several educators</u> have studied issues associated with higher education. <u>They</u> believe that the most significant problem in higher education is affordability.

(continued)

Compare this with the following example, which uses first person.

Uses first person: I believe that the most significant problem in higher education is affordability.

Using third person—and avoiding *I think* or *I believe*—de-emphasizes the writer and puts the focus on the idea, which is presented as a significant view that can be supported by evidence, and not just as the writer's personal opinion.

As a general rule, use third person for all academic writing. Formal business writing and government reports also require third-person point of view.

SENTENCE COMBINING

The examples that follow show how to take ideas expressed in one point of view, combine them, and change them into third-person point of view.

Ideas to combine and express in third person:

- I believe we should allow casino gambling in Texas.

- It should be legal.

- You may think casinos create addictions to gambling.

- That is simply not true.

- I have not gotten addicted even though I've gambled for years.

Combined sentences using third person: Casino gambling should be legal in Texas. Although some people believe casinos create gambling addictions, that is simply not the truth. People can gamble for years without becoming addicted to it.

Try your hand at converting first and second person into third-person texts.

EXERCISES

You will find three sets of sentences below. Combine the sentences to make smoother, longer ones, and change all first- and second-person pronouns into third person. You may change the wording as much as you like as long as you communicate the same ideas.

1. Ideas to combine and express in third person:
   - You should use three guidelines to control credit card spending.
   - You will avoid getting into financial difficulty if you do.
   - You should not charge more than you can afford.
   - You should always pay more than the minimum amount due each month.
   - You should use cash for luxury items.
   - Luxury items are things like iPads, expensive purses, and car stereos.

Answer: _____

_____

_____

_____

(continued)

2. Ideas to combine and express in third person:

- One education law is called the No Child Left Behind Act.
- Under this act, you have more options for your children's education.
- You can choose a public school other than the one in your district.
- You can do this if the school in your area is not performing well.
- You can do this if your local school is unsafe.

Answer: _____

_____

_____

3. Ideas to combine and express in third person:

- The flu and the common cold have symptoms.
- These symptoms are similar.
- I can tell you that the flu is worse than the common cold.
- You have symptoms such as fever, body aches, tiredness, and cough.
- Your flu symptoms are more intense than your cold symptoms.

Answer: _____

_____

_____

Choosing an Appropriate Tone for Your Writing Assignments

If your purpose in writing is to inform, you should strive to create an objective tone. Doing so will help readers understand that you are writing to inform them, not persuade them. To create an objective tone, write on a formal level by avoiding contractions, slang, and conversational-style language. Avoid emotional language and bias, also. Notice the differences between the two examples that follow:

Subjective tone: People who make the mistake of getting the flu shot aren't the sharpest tools in the shed.

↑ contraction

↑
cliché used in conversational-style language

Objective tone: People who choose to get the flu shot may not be properly informed about the dangers and **efficacy** of the vaccine.

VCW efficacy

When you are writing a text in which you want to reveal your own opinion or set a particular tone, be sure to choose language carefully to reveal the *type* of subjective tone you wish to communicate. For example, a text written with a subjective tone can be worded in such a way as to communicate different feelings.

Subjective tone communicating anger: People who avoid the flu shot are ignorant fools. They are so selfish that they don't care that their choice might result in a major flu epidemic.

Potential inference: *The writer is angry and feels threatened by those who resist the flu shot.*

Subjective tone communicating compassion: People who avoid the flu shot are simply unaware of the tragic results that can follow their decision. They want the best for their families, but their lack of information leads them to make choices that, sadly, may result in more harm than good.

Potential inference: *The writer feels sorry for people who resist the flu shot and thinks they are simply misinformed.*

If you choose an appropriate tone for your writing, your potential readers will be more likely to make correct inferences about the content you are communicating.

PRACTICE 7

Writing to Convey a Particular Tone

Write three paragraphs, each with a different tone. In each paragraph, explain the same content: one reason why some people make the decision to drive when they are legally intoxicated. In the first paragraph, convey your idea using an objective tone. In the second, use a subjective tone that communicates anger. For the third paragraph, use a subjective tone that communicates compassion. Use a separate sheet.

Analyzing Figurative Language to Make Accurate Inferences

Figurative language is language that creatively suggests meanings beyond the literal meanings of the words. A word's **literal** meaning is its *actual* meaning. For example, the literal meaning of the word *star* is a celestial body made of gases. However, we also use the word *star* in a figurative way to suggest a person who is a celebrity. Similarly, we frequently use adjectives in nonliteral ways: a *sweet* car is not one made of sugar; a *crabby* customer does not have an exoskeleton and pincers; and a *chilling* reminder does not change a room's temperature. These adjectives are used figuratively: they convey meanings that are not literal.

One way figurative language works is by tapping into the connotations of words. Words have both connotations and denotations. The **denotation** of *rock*, for instance, is a mass of solid material from the earth. A husband who says that his wife is "his rock" does not mean she is a mass of solid material. He is using the qualities of a rock to describe his wife: she is unchanging, dependable, and solid. These positive qualities are **connotations:** they are ideas that go beyond the word's denotation to suggest additional meanings.

Similes and Metaphors

Metaphors and similes are commonly used types of figurative language. A **metaphor** is the use of a word in a nonliteral way to suggest a comparison. Here are some examples of metaphors.

Metaphor: Our copy machine is a *fossil* that, surprisingly, still functions.

This metaphor works by transferring a characteristic of a fossil—its old age—to the copy machine. We can infer that the copy machine is old.

Metaphor: I found a *gem* at the garage sale—a signed photograph of Martin Luther King, Jr.

A photograph is not a gem, but in the same way that a gem is rare and valuable, the signed photograph is also. We can infer that the signed photograph may be worth significant money.

A **simile** also suggests a comparison but does so by using the words *like* or *as.* Here are a few examples of similes:

Simile: When I opened the dishwasher door, water gushed out *like a tidal wave.*

By comparing the water to a tidal wave, the writer leads readers to infer that a large quantity of water quickly rushed out of the dishwasher.

Simile: The policy was *as clear as mud.*

Since mud is not clear, we can infer that the policy was not clear either.

Recognizing similes and metaphors can help you make correct inferences. For example, consider the following passage from sports reporter Tom Orsborn's blog on the Web site of the *San Antonio Express-News*. Note especially the figurative language, some of which is underlined.

> Nicknamed "The Brick Layer" by defensive line coach Rod Marinelli, Dallas Cowboys end George Selvie is ready to do some heavy lifting with Anthony Spencer out for the year.
>
> "It's just going out there and working hard every day, <u>just laying bricks</u>," Selvie said, when asked about his **moniker**. "That's what we say, '<u>Brick layer, go lay some bricks today.</u>' I just go out there and do my job and, hopefully, a couple of times I get <u>thrown a bone</u> and <u>get a sack</u>."

VCW moniker

You probably figured out that George Selvie is a football player, not a brick layer. Using the brick layer metaphor, however, adds meaning to Selvie's role on the team. Laying bricks, in this context, is an ordinary kind of job that takes a particular skill. Readers can infer that Selvie is not playing a flashy role in his position. They can also infer that being a brick layer is a positive thing. The coach's instruction to "go lay some bricks today" is matter-of-fact and reveals that this activity is a necessary element for team success.

We can find additional figurative expressions in the passage. For example, Selvie says he will occasionally get "thrown a bone." Obviously, no one really throws bones to him, but just as getting a bone is a treat for a dog, getting "a bone" is a metaphorical treat for Selvie.

Also, "sacking" a quarterback does not mean putting the guy in a big bag; it means tackling him to prevent a pass or a play. The word *sacking* is used metaphorically.

Personification

A third type of figurative language is personification, the use of human (and sometimes animal) qualities to describe an inanimate object. Notice how personification works by studying the examples that follow.

Personification: The table groaned with the weight of years of unopened mail, packed boxes, and old office supplies.

A table cannot groan, but a human or an animal can. Using the term groan *to describe the table helps readers think of the table as a person under too much stress.*

Personification: My old iPod drew its last breath yesterday. I will be shopping for another one today.

The personification of the iPod as a kind of living creature is a creative way to imply that the iPod is irreparably broken.

Irony and Sarcasm

Two other types of figurative language are irony and sarcasm. **Verbal irony** occurs when a writer uses language to express a meaning that is opposite of what the words literally express. Here is an example.

Verbal irony: We spent the morning busting out the old sidewalk, and <u>for a bit of relaxation</u>, in the afternoon we dug a drainage ditch.

Since the underlined passage clearly says the opposite of what the writer means, it constitutes verbal irony.

   Situational irony occurs when something happens that is the opposite of what one would expect. Here are some examples:

Situational irony: The doctor treating Devin's lung cancer stepped outside and had a cigarette.

We would not expect a doctor, who knows the dangers of smoking, to be a smoker.

Situational irony: Most of the poor residents in the county voted for Candidate X. Candidate X got into office and immediately raised taxes on the poor and cut taxes for the wealthy.

We would expect officeholders to advance their constituents' interests, not work against those interests.

   Dramatic irony usually happens in the context of a story or plot line. Here are some examples.

Dramatic irony: A young man meets his best friend's parents for the first time. The audience knows that his friend's parents are lawyers, but the young man does not know this. At dinner, the young man talks about how corrupt lawyers are and rails against the legal profession.

Because the audience knows the parents are lawyers but the young man does not, the plot is using dramatic irony.

Dramatic irony: Sally goes to a hardware store to buy new locks and keys for her home so she will be safe. The clerk—whom the audience knows to be a homicidal villain—makes an extra key for himself so that he can sneak into her house and murder her.

Because the audience knows the clerk's homicidal disposition but the customer does not, the plot is employing dramatic irony.

In addition to irony, writers sometimes use sarcasm. Sarcasm is a special use of irony. Sarcastic comments are meant to ridicule or to express an attitude such as anger or contempt. Here are some examples.

Sarcasm: In response to being given a new task to complete at work, an employee mutters, "I am so happy to do two jobs and get paid for one."

Since no one is happy to do more work without getting more pay, the underlined passage is sarcasm.

Sarcasm: Mom says to a teenage son who slept all day Saturday, "I'm glad you got caught up on sleep. Sleeping all day is an especially effective way to pass your midterms."

Obviously, sleeping is not the way to study for a midterm, so the underlined passage demonstrates sarcasm.

Carefully analyzing the figurative language in readings can help you gain a better understanding of the writer's point, the writer's attitude toward that point, and the inferences you can draw from the text.

PRACTICE 8

Drawing Inferences from Figurative Language

Analyze each of the following passages. Underline each of the figurative words or phrases you find, and answer the questions that follow.

Passage A

Alaska is a land of extremes. There is no other way to say it. It's extreme in temperature—from 50° below zero to close to 100°F within a single year. It's extreme in landscape—from valleys so wide that you can't see across them to mountains that reach to the sky. It's extreme in population density—from Anchorage with its bustling 300,000 people to the hundreds (or perhaps thousands) of people who live alone in cabins as isolated as polar bears' dens. It's extreme in the amount of sunlight it receives. Above the Arctic Circle, the sun hides in winter, peeking out only occasionally. But in the summer, the sun is a constant companion, sometimes brightening the sky for twenty-four hours at a time. Regardless of these extremes—or perhaps because of them—Alaska is irresistible to many.

(continued)

1. Where is personification used in this paragraph?

_____

_____

2. Based on the figurative language in this passage, what can you infer about Alaska?

_____

_____

3. Find a simile or metaphor in this reading and explain how it works.

_____

_____

Passage B

This passage is from Mark Twain's novel *Huckleberry Finn.* "The men" mentioned in sentence 2 are in a feud with "The Shepherdsons," who are mentioned in sentence 3.

[1]Next Sunday we all went to church, about three mile, everybody a-horseback. [2]The men took their guns along, so did Buck, and kept them between their knees or stood them handy against the wall. [3]The Shepherdsons done the same. [4]It was pretty ornery preaching—all about brotherly love, and such-like tiresomeness; but everybody said it was a good sermon, and they all talked it over going home, and had such a powerful lot to say about faith and good works and free grace and preforeordestination, and I don't know what all, that it did seem to me to be one of the roughest Sundays I had run across yet.

1. Is any irony used in this passage? Is so, what kind, and how does the irony work? Explain your answer.

_____

_____

_____

2. Is any sarcasm used in this passage? Explain your answer. There is no sarcasm in this passage.

_____

_____

_____

Using Figurative Language in Your Writing

One of the functions of figurative language is to suggest meanings. By suggesting meanings, figurative language adds to how readers understand texts. For example, a writer could describe a restaurant in a literal way.

Literal description: My Bánh Mì is a Vietnamese restaurant that features freshly baked bread and traditional bánh mì sandwiches.

But the use of figurative language to describe the restaurant helps readers infer what makes the restaurant special.

Figurative description using a simile: Stepping into My Bánh Mì *is like* stepping into a bakery tucked away on a side street in Saigon.

While both sentences are well written, the use of figurative language in the second sentence suggests that the restaurant has a certain **ambience**; the first sentence does not make the same suggestion.

VCW ambience

In the following sentences, notice how the figurative description suggests meanings that the literal description does not.

Literal description: The neglected lodge had old carpeting and smoke-stained wallpaper. It was not a good location for the reception.

Figurative description using sarcasm: The lodge would be a perfect place for a wedding reception if you like tired and peeling wallpaper, thick shag carpet, and the smell of cigarettes.

While the literal description may be accurate, it does not provide the reader with the details needed to really visualize the lodge. The figurative description, on the other hand, helps the reader understand not only the state of the lounge, but also the writer's attitude about it. Thus, the second description allows the reader to make accurate inferences.

When possible, use figurative language to suggest meanings. Instead of *telling* readers what things are like, use figurative language so that readers will have a more active role in imagining and making correct inferences. When you use figurative language, readers may find your writing more enjoyable and richer in meaning than they would otherwise.

Be careful about overusing figurative language. A text with too many metaphors or too much personification may end up sounding silly. Also, be careful about mixing metaphors. A **mixed metaphor** is a sentence or set of sentences that makes use of more than one metaphor and, as a consequence, results in confusion (or laughter), as these examples show:

I'm grasping at the last straw. (*Grasping at straws* is combined with *the last straw.*)

I was out on a limb without a leg to stand on. (*Out on a limb* and *without a leg to stand on* are both metaphors, but they don't belong together.)

We'll burn that bridge when we come to it. (Combines *Don't burn your bridges* and *We'll cross that bridge when we come to it.*)

PRACTICE 9

Experimenting with Figurative Language to Suggest Meanings

Use figurative language—metaphors, similes, personification, irony, and sarcasm—to complete each writing task. When you finish writing each description, reread your writing and ask yourself, "What inference could a person make from this writing?" Use at least three different types of figurative language. Use a separate sheet.

(continued)

1. Write two or three sentences in which you use figurative language to describe a dog that looks vicious.

2. Write two or three sentences in which you use figurative language to describe a memorable meal.

3. Write two or three sentences in which you use figurative language to describe a particular quality of a boss, a friend, a coworker, or a family member. For example, you could describe a friend's constantly positive attitude.

CHAPTER ACTIVITIES

→ READING AND ANNOTATING

The following explanation of unwarranted assumptions is excerpted from a critical thinking textbook, *Beyond Feelings: A Guide to Critical Thinking,* 9th edition, by Vincent Ruggiero. Read and annotate the text, and then answer the questions that follow.

Unwarranted Assumptions

By Vincent Ruggiero

YOUR ANNOTATIONS

Assumptions are ideas that are merely taken for granted rather than produced by conscious thought. Making assumptions is natural enough, and many assumptions are not only harmless but helpful. When you get up in the morning and head out for class, you assume your watch is working, the car will start, and the professor will be there to teach. You may occasionally encounter a surprise—a broken watch, a dead car battery—but that won't invalidate the assumption or diminish the time it saves you. (You wouldn't get much accomplished if you had to ponder every move you made each day.)

When are assumptions unwarranted? Whenever you take too much for granted—that is, more than is justified by your experience or the particular circumstance. Smokers who assume that because the habit hasn't caused them noticeable physical harm already it never will are making an unwarranted assumption. So are sunbathers who assume that their skin is **impervious** to solar radiation and investors who assume a stock tip they found on an Internet bulletin board is reliable.

VCW impervious

Many people who hold a pro-choice position on abortion assume that the right to an abortion is expressed in the U.S. Constitution, that the *Roe v. Wade* Supreme Court decision is logically unassailable, and that the pro-life position is held only by conservative Christians. All three assumptions are unwarranted. Justice Byron White, in his *Roe v. Wade* dissent, rejected any constitutional basis for the majority decision, terming it an "exercise of raw judicial power." The argument that life begins when the genetic "blueprint" is established at conception and that a human being is present from that moment on, though unfashionable, is not illogical. And abortion is opposed not only by conservative Christians but also, for example, by Mennonites, Muslims, Buddhists, and Hindus. Although

(continued)

Jews remain divided on the issue, many oppose abortion. . . . Nonreligious groups opposing abortion include the Atheist and Agnostic Pro-Life League, Pagans for Life, Libertarians for Life, Feminists for Life, and the Pro-Life Alliance of Gays and Lesbians. (All of these groups have Web sites.)

The most common unwarranted assumptions include the following:

The assumption that people's senses are always trustworthy. The fact is that beliefs and desires can distort perception, causing people to see and hear selectively or inaccurately.

The assumption that if an idea is widely reported, it must be true. Fiction can be disseminated as far and as widely as truth.

The assumption that having reasons proves that we have reasoned logically. Reasons may be borrowed uncritically from others, and even if they have been thought out, they may still be illogical.

The assumption that familiar ideas are more valid than unfamiliar ones. Familiarity merely indicates having heard or read the idea before; it provides no guarantee that what we have heard or read is correct.

The assumption that if one event follows another in time, it must have been caused by the other. The order of and closeness in time between two events could have been accidental.

The assumption that every event or phenomenon has a single cause. Some events have multiple causes. For example, in medicine it is well known that numerous risk factors may contribute to a person's contracting a disease.

The assumption that the majority view is the correct view. Majorities have been wrong—for example, in supporting the execution of witches and in condoning slavery.

The assumption that the way things are is the way they should be. Humans are imperfect, and their inventions, including ideas, always allow room for improvement.

The assumption that change is always for the better. In some cases, change improves matters; in others, it makes matters worse. For example, when the government has sought to gain revenue by increasing tax rates, the net effect usually has been a decline in revenue. (For numerous examples of the error of this assumption, do a Google search using the search term "unintended consequences.")

The assumption that appearances are trustworthy. Appearances can be mistaken. For example, American novelist Sinclair Lewis was traveling on an ocean liner to England. As he and a friend were walking on the deck, he noticed a woman sitting on a deck chair reading one of his novels. Filled with pride, he remarked to his friend what a good feeling it was to see someone so absorbed in his work. At that very moment, the woman threw the book overboard.

The assumption that if an idea is in our mind it is our own idea and deserves to be defended. Some, ideally most, ideas in our mind are the result of our careful analysis. Others, in some cases an embarrassingly large number, are uncritically absorbed from other people and therefore are not "our own" in any meaningful sense.

The assumption that the stronger our conviction about an idea, the more valid the idea. An idea's validity is determined by the amount and quality of the evidence that supports it. The strength of our conviction is irrelevant. In other words, it is possible to be absolutely convinced and still be wrong.

The assumption that if we find an error in someone's argument, we have disproved the argument. An argument can contain minor flaws yet be sound.

(continued)

For example, one or two items of evidence may be flawed, yet the remaining evidence may be sufficient to support the argument. Simply said, it takes more than nitpicking to disprove an argument.

Remember that assumptions are usually implied rather than expressed directly, much like the hidden premises in arguments. To identify them, develop the habit of reading (and listening) between the lines for ideas that are unexpressed but nevertheless clearly implied. Once you have identified an assumption, evaluate it and decide whether it is warranted.

Questions for Consideration

1. What is the difference between a warranted assumption and an unwarranted assumption? Offer examples of each, and explain in a paragraph.

2. The writer includes a long paragraph about the abortion controversy. What is the writer's main point about abortion opinions? In other words, in what way does the abortion controversy help the writer make his point about assumptions? Explain in a paragraph or two.

3. Is the paragraph about abortion written with an objective or subjective tone? Explain your answer in a paragraph.

4. Choose one of the assumptions the writer discusses, and provide an example of a time when you held that assumption and learned that it was wrong. How did you come to understand that the assumption you held was wrong?

5. Imagine that a friend or family member tells you, "I would never live near a nuclear power plant." What assumption is the speaker making? Is the assumption warranted or unwarranted? Explain.

➔ USING MODELS TO PRACTICE COMPOSING

Leticia is a student in a writing class. She has been given a writing assignment, which she has annotated. Read through the assignment instructions Leticia's professor provided, and note how Leticia annotated the assignment. Did she neglect to annotate a key point? If so, add your own annotation.

Leticia's Annotated Assignment

Read and annotate "Unwarranted Assumptions," paying particular attention to the various types of assumption errors people commonly make. Select three or four assumptions that can have disastrous results in the context of college. For example, consider the effects of believing this assumption: *If an idea is widely reported, it must be true.* Perhaps you have heard from several students that to pass Dr. B's essay exam, all you have to do is find a way to talk about global warming in each of the essay questions. These students explain that because Dr. B is passionate about global warming, she gives high grades to students who discuss it. You are tempted to believe these students because *so many* students have told you the same thing. Believing them, however, could be a disastrous decision.

Read and annotate article

Select 3 or 4 assumptions

Example

Prewrite

Present assumptions, use examples to show assumptions aren't true, and present the negative effects of making these assumptions.

(continued)

After you select three or four assumptions to analyze, use a method of prewriting to think about how using the assumptions to make decisions in college can have tragic consequences. Write an essay in which you present each of these assumptions and the examples you have found or created. (You may use hypothetical examples.) Use your examples to show how the assumption is not true. Be sure to discuss the potential negative effects of using the assumption to make college-related decisions. Your essay should be written in formal language and have an objective tone.

Figure out how using the assumption leads to tragic consequences.

Formal language, objective tone

After annotating her assignment, Leticia was ready for prewriting. She started by selecting several assumptions and using freewriting—writing without stopping for 15 minutes—to think about how each assumption might lead to disastrous results in college. Here's Leticia's freewriting—done on a computer—on one of the assumptions.

Leticia's Freewriting

Assumption 1: The stronger our conviction about an idea, the more valid the idea.

OK, let's say I really, really believe algebra is stupid. I don't even question my belief because I believe it so strongly. So I may not study hard for algebra, or I may have a bad attitude in the class or be angry about having to take it. That might result in failing the class or being miserable. OK, another thing I might believe ... So let's say I'm in a class and we're talking about something controversial, like abortion, and I have my strong beliefs about it. Just because my beliefs are really strong, I might not think any other person's ideas are valid. So I'd be closed off to learning about what other people think, and that might mean I wouldn't learn much. I'd be stuck with my own views and not learn or grow.

After freewriting about several assumptions, Leticia chose three assumptions as the topic to be discussed in her essay. She created a thesis statement and a simple outline.

Leticia's Simple Outline

INTRODUCTION PARAGRAPH

Thesis statement: In college, making decisions based on false assumptions can have disastrous effects.

Body paragraph 1: One assumption that can have negative effects in college is believing that our senses are always trustworthy.

Body paragraph 2: Another assumption that can get college students into trouble is the belief that if an idea is widely believed, it must be true.

Body paragraph 3: Finally, negative effects can result from believing that because we have reasons for a position, we have reasoned logically.

CONCLUSION PARAGRAPH

At this point, Leticia started drafting her essay. What follows is one of the body paragraphs from her essay. Read and annotate the paragraph to identify the assumption she is discussing and the negative effects she identifies. Annotate passages that help you identify the tone Leticia is using.

Leticia's Paragraph

One assumption that can have negative effects in college is believing that our senses are always trustworthy. For example, many students rely on only one sense—such as hearing—to learn material. They assume that they can trust their hearing to prepare them for tests and to help them learn. However, no one hears everything. It is impossible to listen to every single thing an instructor says, even if the instructor speaks loudly and clearly. In addition, people can hear things differently. One student may say that the professor said the homework is due on Tuesday, and another may say the professor said the homework is due on Thursday. These kinds of disagreements are common because our senses really are not perfect. Depending on one sense—hearing, for example—can cause a student to get the facts wrong and to not understand course information. It would be much better to assume our senses are flawed and to use more than one sense to understand course material. Listening to a lecture is fine, but because our senses can be wrong, it is wise to also read the course material.

YOUR ANNOTATIONS

➲ A READING AND WRITING ASSIGNMENT

Now it is your turn to write an essay about assumptions in response to the assignment Leticia's instructor gave her (see "Leticia's Annotated Assignment"). Follow these steps, using Leticia's work as a model. Do your work on a separate sheet.

1. Reread Leticia's assignment and any additional annotations you made.
2. Use freewriting to think about how different assumptions can have negative effects when used to make decisions in college.
3. Choose three assumptions; if you need to, use additional prewriting to develop more ideas about the negative consequences of the assumptions.
4. Write a thesis statement.
5. Create a simple outline that contains your thesis statement and topic sentences for your body paragraphs. Write as many body paragraphs as you need to support your thesis statement.
6. Using your outline, draft the introduction, body paragraphs, and conclusion for your essay.
7. As you revise and edit your writing, look for words and phrases that express the tone of your essay. Make any necessary changes to achieve an objective tone.

Use the Quick Start Guide to Integrated Reading and Writing Assignments for assistance.

➡ ADDING TO YOUR VOCABULARY

This chapter's vocabulary words appear below.

ambiance	commission	fathom	moniker	qualifier
buffoon	condescending	imprevious	nonchalant	

Choose five of the vocabulary words from this chapter that you would like to add to your vocabulary, and think about how you can use them this week. For example, one of this chapter's words is *buffoon*. You can often substitute *buffoon* for *clown* or *joker*, as in the example that follows.

> **Example:** Some *joker* thought it would be funny to push all of the buttons on the elevator.
>
> Some *buffoon* thought it would be funny to push all of the buttons on the elevator.

List each of the five words you plan to use this week, and make note of a context in which you could use each word.

> **Example:** *Buffoon*. When someone is acting silly at an inappropriate time, I can call him a buffoon.

➡ ADDITIONAL ASSIGNMENTS

1. Write an essay in which you analyze how social cues lead us to form inferences. For example, if you are in a conversation with someone and the person starts looking away, nodding, and saying "uh-huh" but is obviously not listening to you, you are likely to infer that the person is not interested in talking to you. In your essay, discuss four or five inferences we can make from social cues.

2. Write a paragraph in which you explain how people use assumptions to draw inferences.

3. Write a list of inferences you can draw from the infographic "Save Water in the Yard This Summer," which appears on the next page. The infographic is taken from the Environmental Protection Agency's Web site.

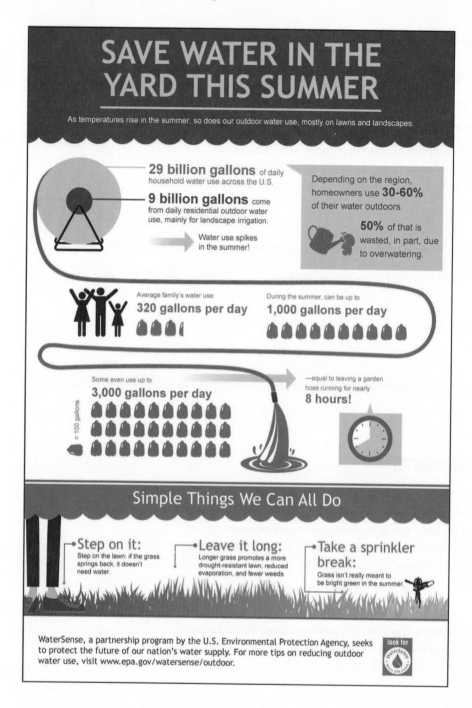

4. Write an essay in which you discuss a time when you used an unwarranted assumption and made a serious mistake. Explain why you held the assumption, why you did not question it, the decision you made, and why the decision was a mistake. Explain the consequences of this mistake and what you could have done to prevent it.

EMOTIONAL INTELLIGENCE

Good emotional intelligence requires that we make sound inferences about other people and about social situations. Have you ever misinterpreted another person's actions? If so, you have made an incorrect *social* inference. For example, we might infer that a quiet person is a snob. After getting to know the person, however, we may discover the person is not a snob at all but is shy. Think of a time when you made an incorrect social inference. What caused you to make this mistake? What can you learn from the experience? Explain in a paragraph.

METACOGNITION

One way to have more metacognitive awareness is to think about *how your thinking* is affected by your assumptions. To do this, spend a moment considering how your life would be different if you held each of the assumptions below. Write a sentence or two explaining how your thoughts and actions might change if you really believed each assumption.

- Everyone you meet will like you and will treat you kindly.
- Your instructors really care about you and your success.
- Most of the people in your city are criminals.
- You will someday have a college degree and a great job.

Text Credits

Page 293: Source: Griffin, Emory A., *A First Look at Communication Theory*, 1st ed. New York: McGraw-Hill, 1991; Page 296: Source: www.whitehouse.gov/share/college-affordability; Page 307: Source: Shah, Amit, *Business Now*. New York: McGraw-Hill, 2011. 79; Page 313: Source: Orsborn, Tom, "'Brick Layer' Ready to Replace Spencer Full-Time," *MySanAntonio.com*, September 25, 2013; Page 300: Map from Arnold, Althea, et al., *Out of Reach 2014*. Washington, DC: National Low Income Housing Coalition.14. © 2014 National Low Income Housing Coalition. Reprinted with permission; Page 300: Source: "The Obama Energy Agenda: Gas Prices" April 3, 2013. www.whitehouse.gov/energy/gasprices; Page 318: Ruggiero, Vincent Ryan, *Beyond Feelings: A Guide to Critical Thinking*, 9th ed. 103–05. Copyright © 2012 by McGraw-Hill Education. Used with permission of McGraw-Hill Education.

Revising and Editing

©Aaron Lindberg/Getty Images RF

Making a clay pot involves a series of modifications. Sometimes the potter even has to start anew. Writing is a similar craft: successful essays require thoughtful reshaping and revising.

Chapter Objectives

After completing this chapter, students will be able to do the following:

- Revise essays for better organization and unity.

- Revise paragraphs for better organization and unity.

- Revise for better development.

- Revise for better clarity.

- Connect pronouns to unambiguous antecedents.

- Make revisions during drafting.

- Make revisions after drafting.

- Use reader-based suggestions to revise.

- Use listening skills to revise.

- Edit and format an essay.

- Create agreement between subjects and verbs.

Have you ever painted a room in your house or apartment? If so, you know that while painting can start out as an enjoyable project, it quickly becomes hard work. As you get closer and closer to finishing the painting job, you begin to long for the moment when you can stand back and look at what you have accomplished. What happens if you stand back, sighing in relief, only to notice that one half of the room needs another coat, and paint dripped onto the baseboard, and you see a spot on the ceiling? Even worse, what happens if you realize that the color is just not right?

If you really want the room to look perfect, you will have to make some revisions. Some revisions will be major, such as changing the color of the paint. Other revisions may be less difficult, such as adding another coat or cleaning up areas where the paint went out of bounds. In writing, too, you will find that you must make revisions even after you thought you were done. How well you focus on making minor as well as major changes will determine the quality of your finished work.

The purpose of revising is to make sure your writing communicates its message as well as it can. For a text to communicate successfully, it must be well organized and unified, well developed, and clearly presented. Additionally, writing should be edited so that it is free from grammatical and mechanical errors.

Revising Essays for Organization and Unity

Organization refers to the order in which you present information in your essay. You achieve **unity** in paragraphs when all the content in the paragraph is related to the topic sentence and appropriate for the paragraph. Let's look at how to check your paper for both qualities.

After you finish writing a paper, it is difficult to *see* the organization of ideas unless you look at your paper analytically. You can do this by reverse outlining your paper.

Using Reverse Outlining

Most people use outlines *before* they write, and that is a good strategy. Reverse outlining occurs after you write, and it enables you to pull out the organizational strategy in your paper. You will also be able to see if the paragraphs are unified—that is, if they all support the thesis statement.

To reverse outline, read over your paper, and in the margin, write a very short summary of the paragraph's main idea and support. Here is an example of how one student, Ricky, uses reverse outlining on a draft.

Ricky's Annotation of His Draft

Life with Asperger's Syndrome

Eleven-year-old Paul paced nervously back and forth at the bus stop. His school bus is supposed to arrive every morning at 7:04. Usually Paul could see the bus coming down the street at 7:03, but this morning, at 7:03, there was no bus. A feeling of panic washed over him. When his watch said 7:04, tears began to stream down his face. The bus was not on time. By 7:05, he could not stand it any longer and ran home. If Paul had not been diagnosed with Asperger's syndrome, his mother would probably have been puzzled by this behavior, but she was not shocked. Because he has Asperger's syndrome, Paul is not like other children. — *Introduction story*

Asperger's syndrome is a type of autism. Many people have heard of autism before, but not many know about Asperger's syndrome. Autism comes in many forms, some very severe and some quite mild. People who have Asperger's are on the mild "high functioning" side of the autism range. People with classic autism are often unable to talk and do not like being touched, while many of those with Asperger's can function well in these areas. However, there are some challenges for those who have Asperger's syndrome, and some of these challenges are significant. — *Definition and thesis statement*

First, those who have Asperger's have a hard time interacting with other people. While most people can read body language, those with Asperger's — *People with AS have a hard time interacting with others. Examples support the idea.*

(continued)

("Aspies," as they are sometimes called) cannot. For example, when people are exasperated, they might roll their eyes, cross their arms, or smirk. These body language clues convey a sense of aggravation. When people use this kind of body language, they expect others to step back and proceed with caution. Aspies are often not able to read such body language. Thus, they may respond inappropriately in social situations. Another problem is being able to use body language themselves. One mother recounts how her daughter Chrissy wanted to learn to roll her eyes. Unable to master the eye roll, and unaware of when eye rolling is an appropriate gesture, Chrissy finally (to her mother's relief) stopped trying to do it. Aspies may cross their arms and impatiently tap their feet, not being aware of the message they are sending. Those with Asperger's can be taught how to read body language; however, social interactions are still often difficult because of this aspect of Asperger's syndrome.

Another tendency shared by those with Asperger's is literal thinking. Language meant to be understood literally should be interpreted to mean exactly what the words denote. For example, interpreted literally, the phrase "money talks" would mean that money has a voice and audibly speaks. Much of our language is not meant to be interpreted literally. Kevin Leary recounts a moment when Ryan, his eight-year-old son with Asperger's, was playing with cousins. An adult in the family said to one of the children, "You have ants in your pants!" Ryan ran to the boy and started helping him take off his pants, unaware of the non-literal nature of the comment. Young Aspies are especially literal-minded because they have not had enough experience with the world to understand which phrases are meant figuratively. For example, if a person were to tell Ryan that he will get a popsicle "in a minute," Ryan may watch the clock and be upset if he does not receive his treat in 60 seconds. It is a challenge for Asperger's children to learn to be less literal-minded.

No one knows what causes this kind of autism. Children with Asperger's do not have any symptoms for the first eighteen months to two years of life. Around the age of two, issues arise because of inflexibility. Toddlers with this form of autism may seem to be going through the "terrible twos," but their tantrums are often more frequent and more prolonged than tantrums of neurotypical children. Researchers are continuing to look for the causes of autism and Asperger's syndrome.

A third characteristic of those with Asperger's is inflexibility. They find it extremely agitating when the rules change or when routines must shift. If a tantrum results, the child is not being bratty. Rather, the Asperger's brain sends distress signals when routines are broken or change occurs. Not all changes elicit the same reaction, so parents must learn what sets off their child. Learning to be flexible is another of the major challenges that those with Asperger's face.

People with AS tend to think literally. Supported by examples.

No one knows what causes autism; it appears around 2 yrs old.

People with AS deal with inflexibility. Supported with explanations.

(continued)

While Asperger's syndrome makes life different and sometimes difficult for those who have it, there are several coping mechanisms those with the syndrome can develop to function well. Therapists and physicians are becoming more familiar with Asperger's syndrome now as increasing numbers of diagnoses have been made in the last twenty years. Many people with Asperger's syndrome live typical lives. However, being able to adjust to the way neurotypical people think—especially about social interaction—requires effort and diligence.

Conclusion

Once Ricky annotates his paper, on a separate sheet, he writes his thesis statement and makes a list of his annotations. Next, he examines each paragraph's ideas. He uses "Reverse Outlining Questions" as a guide.

REVERSE OUTLINING QUESTIONS

Do all paragraphs support the thesis statement?	If not, plan to remove paragraphs that do not fit.
Does the order of the paragraphs make sense?	If not, plan to re-order the paragraphs.
Do any paragraphs repeat information?	If so, plan to combine the ideas into one paragraph.
Do any paragraphs present more than one topic?	If so, plan to write separate paragraphs for each idea.

You have a revision plan for your draft.

Here is Ricky's reverse outline for his paper "Life with Asperger's Syndrome." Ricky notices that in terms of unity, one of the paragraphs does not fit because it does not support the thesis statement. He will need to remove this paragraph. He also notices that while two of the paragraphs are supported with examples, one paragraph is not. When Ricky revises later for paragraph development, he can add examples to this paragraph.

Ricky's Reverse Outline

1. Introduction story
2. Definition and thesis statement: *However, there are some challenges for those who have Asperger's syndrome, and some of these challenges are significant.*
3. People with AS have a hard time interacting with others. Examples support the idea.

(continued)

4. People with AS tend to think literally. Supported by examples.

5. No one knows what causes autism; it appears around 2 yrs old. *does not fit*

6. People with AS deal with inflexibility. Supported with explanations. *add examples*

7. Conclusion

PRACTICE ❶

Creating a Reverse Outline to Check for Organization and Unity

Select an essay you have written for this class. Create a reverse outline by following the instructions in this chapter. Next, write a paragraph in which you answer these questions on a separate sheet of paper.

1. Did the reverse outline you created reveal any errors in *unity*? If so, what were they, and how could you revise the paper to eliminate these errors?

2. Did the reverse outline you created reveal any errors in *organization*? If so, what were they, and how could you revise the paper to eliminate these errors?

Revising Paragraphs for Organization and Unity

In the same way that essays need to be organized and unified, paragraphs also need these qualities. Paragraphs are organized well when the order of sentences makes sense. Paragraphs have unity when the sentences within them are related to the paragraph's topic sentence. No random thoughts or "stray" ideas occur in unified writing.

To check for unity, answer these questions:

- Do all the sentences in the paragraph support the paragraph's topic sentence?

- Do any sentences present information that is unrelated to the main idea of the paragraph?

If you see a sentence that does not fit, either revise it so that it supports the information in the paragraph or omit the sentence altogether.

To check for organization, answer these questions:

- Does the order of sentences in the paragraphs make sense?

- Would a different order help readers understand the content more easily?

With these questions about organization and unity in mind, read the following paragraph.

[1]One of the most demanding parts of owning a bakery is cleaning up. [2]Most bakeries are small operations, and their owners cannot afford to hire custodial staff. [3]Thus, the bakers themselves are responsible for

Sentence 1: topic sentence

(continued)

cleanup duties. ⁴Whenever flour, sugar, cocoa, and other powdery foods are used in a kitchen, there will be a mess, regardless of how careful kitchen staff are. ⁵Cleaning up requires a great deal of time, and the process is physically demanding. ⁶Potential bakery owners should be aware of the time and effort that must be expended to simply keep the kitchen clean. ⁷Perhaps the most important part of cleanup is keeping the floor clean. ⁸Oils are always involved in the baking process and present a true hazard if they end up on the floor. ⁹And because oil is an expensive ingredient, bakers should be especially careful with it.

Sentence 4: examples of foods that make a mess

Sentences 5 and 6: details about time and effort needed for cleaning up

Sentences 7 and 8: details about keeping floors clean and hazards of oil

Sentence 9: detail about cost of oil

One sentence is out of place. Can you tell which one? Most of the sentences support the topic sentence. They give examples of messy foods, discuss the time and effort needed for cleaning up, and point out the importance of dealing with spilled oil.

Sentence 9, however, does not belong in the paragraph. Although the sentence deals with oil, which is discussed in the paragraph, the information it gives—the high cost of oil—has nothing to do with the task of cleaning up a bakery kitchen. We can see why the writer included the sentence while drafting the paragraph; it seems to be linked to the discussion of oil. But if the writer takes the time to revise, she will see that the cost of oil is not really important to the point she is making in the topic sentence.

The writer had planned to end her paragraph with the most **precarious** aspect of a messy kitchen—the floor. However, by ending her paragraph with a discussion of the hazards of oil, she has separated the mess caused by oil from the messes caused by powdery foods. It would be more logical to put the specific *causes* of a messy kitchen together. Thus, the paragraph would be improved if sentences 7 and 8 were nearer to the sentences about powdery foods. Here is the revised paragraph.

VCW precarious
For every Vocabulary Collection Word (VCW), give your in-context idea of the word's meaning and then look up the word's dictionary definition.

One of the most demanding parts of owning a bakery is cleaning up. Most bakeries are small operations, and their owners cannot afford to hire custodial staff. Thus, the bakers themselves are responsible for cleanup duties. Whenever flour, sugar, cocoa, and other powdery foods are used in a kitchen, there will be a mess, regardless of how careful kitchen staff are. Perhaps the most important part of cleanup is keeping the floor clean. Oils are always involved in the baking process and present a true hazard if they end up on the floor. Cleaning up requires a great deal of time, and the process is physically demanding. Potential bakery owners should be aware of the time and effort that must be expended to simply keep the kitchen clean.

Topic sentence

Cause: powdery foods

Cause: oils

Complete the practice exercise that follows to improve the organization and unity of a paragraph.

PRACTICE ②

Improving the Organization and Unity of a Paragraph

Read the paragraph that follows, annotating it to determine how its organization can be improved. Using sentence numbers, note the order in which you would place the sentences. If any sentences detract from the paragraph's unity, reword or delete them. Next, revise the paragraph on a separate sheet. Reword sentences, if necessary, to write a clearer, more organized paragraph.

YOUR ANNOTATIONS

[1]While a wide variety of majors and minors exist for college degrees, four primary types of degrees are common. [2]The associate's degree requires roughly sixty hours of college credit, approximately two years of full-time college course work. [3]The doctorate requires approximately four years of course work beyond the master's degree. [4]Not many people wish to be in college long enough to earn doctorate degrees. [5]A master's degree requires two years of course work beyond a bachelor's degree, approximately six years of course work from the start of college. [6]The time spent on a master's degree usually pays off. [7]A bachelor's degree requires approximately four years of college: two years to earn an associate's degree plus two more years to obtain the bachelor's degree.

Revising for Better Development

Development refers to the quantity and the quality of supporting details you use to back up your ideas. To judge the development of your writing, first think about the main idea you are communicating. Without looking at your draft, make a list of the questions your audience would need to have answered in order to fully understand or accept your main idea. Next, read your paper. Have you included enough information for readers to understand or accept the main idea? Is the information the *right kind* of information?

In the following paragraph, the writer's main idea is to explain one method for financial decision making. Read the annotations to see the kind of development this paragraph needs.

[1]One way to make smart fiscal decisions is to use the Internet for research. [2]Almost any topic can be thoroughly researched with an Internet search. [3]Many consumers have questions about their finances. [4]Using Internet sources can help consumers make smarter decisions.

Sentence 1 is the topic sentence.

Sentences 2 and 3 provide no new information.

Sentence 4 repeats the information in the topic sentence.

A reader interested in learning how to use the Internet for financial research will need more specific information than the writer offers. Notice that sentences 2 and 3 do not contribute new information to develop the idea of using an Internet search. Also, sentence 4 simply repeats the information in the topic sentence. Repeated information detracts from a paragraph's development and takes up space that should be given to useful information.

By thinking of some of the questions readers may have, the writer can revise the paragraph to make it much more detailed and helpful. Here are some questions the writer could answer:

- *For what kinds of financial decision making is the Internet helpful?* The Internet provides advice for getting a mortgage, figuring out the most economical transportation options, and finding the credit cards with the lowest interest rates, as well as information on many other financial topics.

- *Can you give me an example of how a financial Web site might help me?* For example, www.bestccsaround.com offers information to help consumers find credit cards with low interest rates.

- *How can I put the knowledge I gain from such Web sites to use?* Many of the Web sites even contain links that will take consumers to sites where they can apply for low-interest financial products. For example, www.creditcarddreams.com links consumers to credit cards that fit their needs.

Thinking through readers' potential questions allows the writer to revise the paragraph so that it is much more fully developed. Notice how the writer has used the answers to these questions to revise the paragraph, providing major supporting points and details that improve its development.

One way to make smart fiscal decisions is to use the Internet for research. Web sites provide advice for getting a mortgage, figuring out the most economical transportation options, and finding the credit cards with the lowest interest rates, as well as information on many other financial topics. For example, *Best Credit Cards Around* (www.bestccsaround.com) offers information on the interest rates of loans and credit cards available to consumers. Many of the Web sites even contain links that will take consumers to sites where they can apply for low-interest financial products. For example, *Credit Card Dreams* (www.creditcarddreams.com) links consumers to credit cards that fit their needs.	Topic sentence Major supporting point 1 Supporting details Major supporting point 2 Supporting details

Complete the practice exercise that follows to improve the development of a paragraph. As you complete the exercise, try to think like a reader. What information would a fully developed paragraph give readers?

PRACTICE 3

Improving the Development of a Paragraph

The following paragraph's main idea needs better development. List questions readers might ask, and use the answers to make changes to the paragraph. Rewrite the paragraph on a separate sheet.

Some people opt to purchase smartphones instead of laptop computers because the apps on smartphones can do almost everything one expects from a computer. While reading the screen may be a bit more difficult with a smartphone, the computer capabilities are quite amazing.

(continued)

Readers' questions:

_____

_____

_____

_____

_____

_____

Revising for Better Clarity

Writing clearly starts at the level of word selection. It is important to choose the very best word to communicate a thought. The suggestions in this section will help you express your ideas clearly.

Look for Awkward or Vague Expressions

In an essay about whether college education should be free, a student, Sandra, wrote this sentence:

> Some teens have immaturity and may turn to certain illegal things to gain what they could have from college.

Can you spot places where the student's expression could be clearer? Think about these points:

- The expression "teens have immaturity" is awkward. The more standard expression is to say "teens are immature."

- "Turn to" is not exactly what the writer means. Perhaps she is trying to say that some teens may *resort to* certain illegal things.

- The phrase "certain illegal things" is vague. Why not be concrete and specific? This unclear wording leaves readers wondering what those *certain illegal things* might be. Her sentence would be improved if she substituted "selling drugs or engaging in crime" for "certain illegal things."

- Finally, she says teens might turn to crime to "gain what they could have from college." Being more specific helps clear up any **ambiguity**, so a better sentence ending would be "have the kind of money a college education would have provided."

VCW ambiguity

Here is Sandra's sentence revised for clarity:

> Some teens are immature and may resort to selling drugs or engaging in crime to have the kind of money a college education would have provided.

Restate Complicated Ideas Out Loud

Later in her paper, Sandra wrote this passage:

> Everyone deserves the **incentive** to go to college free, so to make Americans fine with using taxes on college, you can put in certain rules such as making a certain amount of tries at one class before you have to pay and things like that to push them even more would be in place.

VCW incentive

Sometimes when students write sentences like these, if an instructor asks them to explain their ideas aloud in their own words, they will construct much clearer sentences. Consider this exchange.

INSTRUCTOR: Sandra, you wrote, "You can put in certain rules such as making a certain amount of tries at one class before you have to pay and things like that to push them even more would be in place." What did you mean by that?

SANDRA: Oh, I just meant that we could put certain rules in place. For example, students would have a specific number of attempts to pass a class. Once they reached the maximum attempts, they would have to pay for the class themselves.

INSTRUCTOR: Beautiful! Now write down what you just said, and you will have a very clear explanation of your point!

Speaking your ideas out loud can help you revise sentences in more easily understood language.

Write Complete Sentences for Every Idea

Another tip is to revise a long passage by writing complete sentences for every idea. First, break the passage into parts that reflect different ideas. Then write at least one full sentence for each idea that you have identified. In the following example, each idea from Sandra's original statement (in the left column) is rephrased as at least one sentence (in the right column).

Instead of . . .	Try . . .
Everyone deserves the incentive to go to college	Everyone deserves an incentive to go to college.
free,	One incentive would be to make college free.
so to make Americans fine with using taxes on college,	Americans may not want their tax money to pay for free college education. They may be afraid students will abuse the new system.
you can put in certain rules	To help Americans accept the idea of free college, we could make rules.
such as making a certain amount of tries at one class	One rule could be to limit the number of times students can take a class.
before you have to pay and things like that to push them even more would be in place.	We could say that students could take a class only so many times before they would have to pay for it themselves.

Imagine a Younger Audience

Finally, you can improve the clarity of your sentences sometimes by imagining you are writing for a younger audience. Writers often tend to explain things more clearly to young people. For example, Sandra wrote the following sentence:

> The way to education for most individuals in our society is unknown.

The sentence is vague and uninformative. To understand how to improve it, Sandra imagined a child asking for clarification.

CHILD: What does *that* mean?

SANDRA: Most people don't know how they are going to pay for college.

Sandra's simpler and clearer rewording would greatly improve the quality of her writing. Contrary to what some students think, a long and complex sentence that is difficult to understand is *not* good writing. Aim for clear sentences, even if that means making them very simple.

PRACTICE 4

Revising for Clarity

The following paragraph is from a student's essay. First, annotate the passage, identifying any words, phrases, or sentences that could be expressed more clearly. Next, use one of the methods described above to revise each unclear item. Write your revised paragraph on a separate sheet. At least four items need to be revised.

> Gambling would not damage the state of Texas in any way but would actually see development through it. Once Texas decided to make gambling legal, that in itself would be a general improvement because a casino and other gambling essentials would make for great tourist arenas, and those attractions could cause more hotels, restaurants, and even other attractions to be built along the state. People would definitely want to move here, so our state would be expanded that much more.

YOUR ANNOTATIONS

Grammar Focus

Clarity in Pronoun Reference and Agreement

Using pronouns correctly can help you write more clearly. Pronouns are words that take the place of nouns, and they include words such as *he, she, it, they, that, one,* and *everyone.* Writers use pronouns to avoid unnecessary repetition and to keep sentences short. Note the unnecessary, and uninteresting, repetition in the following example.

Noun repeated:

<u>The water shortage</u> caught citizens by surprise, but the city was prepared for <u>the water shortage.</u>
   noun phrase   noun phrase

(continued)

To use a pronoun effectively, readers must be able to identify the pronoun's **antecedent,** the noun or noun phrase to which the pronoun refers. In the following example, the pronoun *it* replaces *the water shortage*.

Clear antecedent:

<u>The water shortage</u> caught citizens by surprise, but the city was prepared for <u>it</u>.
    antecedent   pronoun

Using a pronoun instead of repeating the noun phrase makes the sentence more concise without sacrificing clarity. You can follow these guidelines to use pronouns and antecedents correctly.

1. USE SINGULAR PRONOUNS FOR SINGULAR ANTECEDENTS AND PLURAL PRONOUNS FOR PLURAL ANTECEDENTS

Most antecedents are clearly either singular or plural. Make sure the pronoun matches, or agrees with, its antecedent.

Faulty: <u>The city council</u> was prepared for the water shortage. <u>They</u> had made sure adequate supplies were on hand.

In the preceding example, the pronoun *they* is plural, but the antecedent (*the city council*) is singular. Consequently, the pronoun and the antecedent do not agree. We can correct the sentence by making the antecedent and the pronoun both plural.

Corrected: <u>The city council members</u> were prepared for the water shortage. <u>They</u> had made sure adequate supplies were on hand.

When a pronoun takes the place of another, different pronoun, make sure the two pronouns are both either plural or singular.

Faulty: <u>Everyone</u> in the city tried to conserve water. For example, <u>they</u> watered <u>their</u> lawns less frequently than usual.

The pronouns *they* and *their* are plural, but the antecedent *everyone* is singular. One way to correct the sentence is to replace *everyone* with a plural antecedent.

Corrected: <u>Residents</u> in the city tried to conserve water. For example, <u>they</u> watered <u>their</u> lawns less frequently than usual.

Writers need to pay special attention to words like *anyone, everyone, no one,* and *someone* when they are used as antecedents. Pronouns that refer to these words must be singular.

(continued)

2. MAKE SURE THE PRONOUN CAN REFER TO ONLY ONE ANTECEDENT

Sometimes a pronoun reference is vague or unclear. If the pronoun can refer to more than one antecedent, readers will be confused.

> **Unclear antecedent:** The <u>drought</u> and <u>water shortage</u> caught citizens by surprise, but the city was prepared for <u>it</u>.
>
> Is *drought* the antecedent, or is *water shortage* the antecedent? What happens if we change *it* to *them*?
>
> **Unclear antecedent:** <u>The drought and water shortage</u> caught <u>citizens</u> by surprise, but the city was prepared for <u>them</u>.
>
> This sentence is also confusing! What does the word *them* refer to—*the drought and water shortage* or *citizens*? Notice how the corrected version of the sentence clears up any potential confusion.
>
> **Corrected:** <u>The drought and water shortage</u> caught citizens by surprise, but the city was prepared for <u>both events</u>.

In the final version, the writer chooses to use a synonym (*both events*) rather than a pronoun because using a pronoun would cause confusion.

3. PLACE PRONOUNS CLOSE TO THEIR ANTECEDENTS

Sometimes in paragraphs the pronoun gets separated too far from the antecedent, and the separation can result in confusion. The reader may forget what antecedent the pronoun is referring to.

> **Faulty:** Citizens had hoped <u>the water shortage</u> in July would last only briefly. They began to water their lawns less frequently than usual, conserve water in their homes, and comply with the city's additional conservation guidelines. But <u>it</u> did not.

The pronoun *it* is so far away from the antecedent, *the water shortage,* that readers may experience confusion.

> **Corrected:** Citizens had hoped <u>the water shortage</u> in July would last only briefly. They began to water their lawns less frequently than usual, conserve water in their homes, and comply with the city's additional conservation guidelines. But <u>the water shortage</u> did not last briefly. <u>It</u> continued for another six weeks.

Use a pronoun only if the antecedent is nearby. Notice that the last sentence uses *it,* but because *the water shortage* is nearby, the reference for *it* is easily identified.

4. PROVIDE ANY MISSING ANTECEDENTS

Sometimes an antecedent is missing altogether. In some cases, the writer may believe he has provided an antecedent but actually has not.

(continued)

Faulty: The citizens conserved water in a number of ways. They saw <u>it</u> as a serious responsibility.

This passage has a pronoun—*it*. But what noun or noun phrase is the antecedent for the pronoun? The writer may mean to say that "conserving water" was seen as a serious responsibility. Notice, however, that the phrase *conserving water* does not appear in the first sentence. Thus, there is no antecedent for the pronoun.

Corrected: The citizens conserved water in a number of ways. They saw <u>conserving water</u> as a serious responsibility.

In the corrected sentence *it* is replaced with *conserving water*.

SENTENCE COMBINING

The following example achieves clarity while using pronouns. Notice that the sentences to combine use the same nouns repeatedly. In the revision, the short sentences are combined and some nouns are replaced with pronouns, but the antecedents are always nearby and easily identifiable.

Ideas to combine:

- There is a Northern Rio Grande National Heritage Area in New Mexico.
- Different cultures coexist in the Northern Rio Grande National Heritage Area.
- The cultures' languages, crafts, and architecture coexist.
- The Northern Rio Grande National Heritage Area includes impressive natural resources.
- The Northern Rio Grande National Heritage Area includes breathtaking scenery.
- The Northern Rio Grande National Heritage Area includes abundant recreational resources.

Revised using pronouns and antecedents: The Northern Rio Grande National Heritage Area in New Mexico is a place where different cultures—with their languages, crafts, and architecture—coexist. It includes impressive natural resources, breathtaking scenery, and abundant recreational resources.

Try your hand at using pronouns clearly by completing the following exercises.

EXERCISES

You will find three sets of sentences below. Combine the sentences to make smoother, longer ones, and use at least two pronouns to avoid repeating nouns excessively. Make sure you use pronouns in such a way that their antecedents are clearly identifiable.

1. Ideas to combine:

- One highly contagious disease is chicken pox (varicella).
- The most common symptoms are rash, fever, headache, sore throat, and cough.

(continued)

- Chicken pox can also lead to very serious complications for vulnerable people.
- The best protection against chicken pox is the chicken pox vaccine.
- The chicken pox vaccine has been used widely in the United States since 1995.

Answer: _____

_____

_____

_____

2. Ideas to combine:

- Older people may have more difficulty falling asleep.
- People may have insomnia or awaken more often.
- People may awaken three or more times a night.
- Medical conditions may interfere with peaceful sleep.
- Older people get about the same number of hours of sleep.
- Older people may spend more time awake in bed than they used to.

Answer: _____

_____

_____

_____

3. Ideas to combine:

- The Florissant Valley lies thirty-five miles west of Colorado Springs.
- Visitors can see the Rocky Mountains.
- The Rocky Mountains are to the north.
- The Rocky Mountains are to the east.
- The meadows in the Florissant Valley are filled with native grasses and wildflowers.
- The native grasses and wildflowers wave in the breeze.
- The meadows are a beautiful sight.

Answer: _____

_____

_____

_____

Making Revisions during Drafting

You are ready to begin drafting after you have selected and narrowed your topic, used prewriting to generate ideas, written a thesis statement and topic sentences, and constructed an outline. At this point, you have already accomplished much of the hard work of writing. Drafting is simply putting into words all of the ideas you have generated.

As you draft your paper, plan on using a writing process that is recursive. Something is recursive if it occurs again and again. In writing, a recursive process involves moving forward in the following way:

- Writing sentences and paragraphs

- Stopping occasionally to reread everything you have written

- Going back to previous stages of the writing process.

- Revising what you have written before moving forward

Many good writers use a recursive writing process.

Some student writers hesitate to use a recursive process because it takes more time than just plodding ahead without revising. While this method does take more time, it also results in *much* better writing!

Another tip is to read your work out loud when you are rereading your draft. Sometimes you will hear passages that need to be worded more clearly, paragraphs that lack unity, or sentences that need to be combined or separated.

Try using this recursive writing process by completing the following exercise.

PRACTICE 5

Using the Recursive Writing Process

On a separate sheet, write a paragraph on one reason why the minimum wage should or should not be raised. First, use a prewriting activity to generate ideas for the paragraph, then write a topic sentence and outline for the paragraph, and finally use the recursive writing process to compose the paragraph. Specifically, after each sentence you write, go back to the beginning of the paragraph and read it again, making any changes you feel are needed.

Making Revisions after Drafting

To revise well requires a heightened awareness of the audience. Because you are usually not near readers when they read your text, you cannot clear up confusion, add missing information, or explain the tone of the message. Your readers must infer your meaning from only one thing: the words you have chosen to use.

For college writing assignments, your audience is usually your instructor but can sometimes include your peers, depending on the purpose of the assignment. Keeping in mind your audience's values, expectations, needs, assumptions, and abilities will help you write a paper that communicates your ideas clearly to that audience. If you revise with a reader in mind, you will almost always find opportunities to make changes.

Using the questions in the chart on the next page will help you find the parts of your writing that need to be revised.

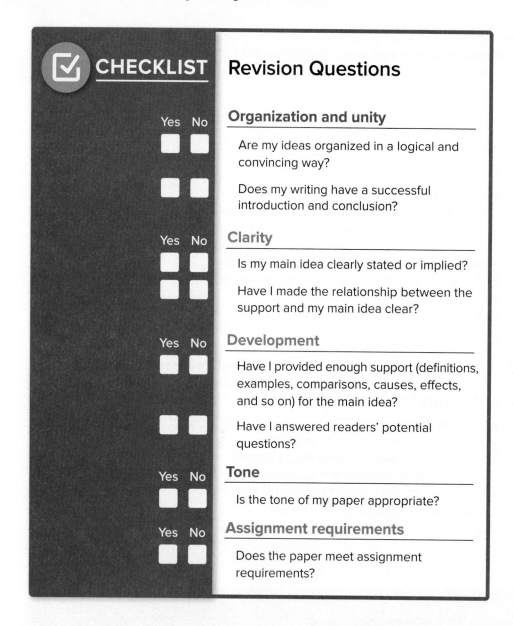

Student Example of Preparing to Revise a Draft

To demonstrate the essay revision process, we will observe the revision process used by Maria, a student in a college reading and writing class. Maria has drafted an essay for her English class. To begin the revision process, she reviews the assignment instructions, which she had annotated at the start of the assignment.

Maria's Annotated Assignment

Write an essay to be published in our college newspaper. (You do not really have to publish your essay, but imagine that your audience will be the student body and anyone else who reads our newspaper.) Your topic is this: Should instructors assign group projects? Some students dislike group projects because not everyone in the group does the work, so

Write a college newspaper essay.

Audience = student body

Topic

(continued)

these projects unfairly reward slackers. Other students love group projects because they learn from their peers and enjoy working with them. What is your point of view on this topic? <u>Select one of these views:</u>

Provide my opinion

- Group projects are good assignments.
- Group projects are good assignments only if they include certain conditions.
- Group projects should not be assigned.

Looks good! <mark>Use this.</mark>

Discuss at least <u>three reasons</u> for your position.

Need 3 reasons.

<u>I have to tell her what I think about group projects.</u> *I did that—I think. Will check and make sure.*

<u>Correct grammar and spelling.</u> *I need to look over grammar and run a spell-checker, and then I need to read it myself to check for misspellings and other obvious errors.*

<u>I need a thesis statement.</u> *I have that.*

<u>She told me that my last paper was not "developed" enough.</u> *I need to make sure that the body paragraphs are as full as I can make them so that she is convinced of my thesis.*

<u>I have to provide three reasons to back up my point of view.</u> *OK, I did that.*

<u>I know that I am supposed to have an introduction paragraph, a body, and a conclusion.</u> *I do have those, but some of them are not very good.*

<u>Write for a particular audience: the student body.</u> *I did not really think about how different students might react to my essay.*

After rereading the assignment instructions, Maria thinks about each particular assignment element:

- Write for a student audience.
- Choose one point of view.
- Give three reasons.

Maria also figures out her instructor's unstated expectations:

- Write a thesis statement.
- Write an introduction, body, and conclusion.
- Make sure the paper is developed enough.
- Use correct grammar and spelling.

Student Example of a Draft Annotated for Revision

Now that Maria has reviewed the assignment, she can start the revision process. She begins by printing out a copy of her draft. Having a paper copy to write on is the best way to revise. It is easier to skip over mistakes when you read a computer screen, so revise with a pen in your hand.

To begin, Maria consciously shifts her thinking so that she is reading her paper not as herself but as her readers—the student body and others who read the newspaper. As she reads, she makes notes about what her readers might think. She looks for places where organization and unity, clarity, and tone can be improved.

Maria's Annotated Draft

Intro is too short.

I do not understand why every instructor at Marquez College seems to love group projects. Group projects are truly a waste of time, to be honest.

Sounds rude.

I didn't state my thesis: Group projects should not be assigned.

I clearly remember my speech class here at Marquez College. The most difficult assignment I ever did in my life was in that class, and it was a group assignment in which we had to choose a controversial issue, find the best research we could on that issue, and use that research to make an argument for or against the issue. It was a horrible experience.

This sentence is too long!!!

I didn't explain why it was so horrible. Need more details.

This para is all negative. Need a more positive tone.

In my speech class, our professor sat at her desk and read a book while we struggled to make sense of the assignment in groups. Instead of reading, she could have been really teaching us. I want to learn from my professor, not my classmates.

A bit rude. Need to say how great that prof's lectures actually were!

Reorganize this para so it doesn't start with the example.

Readers may not get what I mean by "terrible decisions." Needs more explanation.
Seems random—cut.

In another class, the professor assigned the group project and made some terrible decisions about due dates and announcements. Most of the groups were scrambling at the last minute to throw something together for a grade. ~~The topic was global warming.~~

But not all instructors handle group projects in this way. I should say that.

(continued)

Another reason to not assign group work is the issue of time. Groups spend so much time just figuring out how to work together that little time is available for the project. It is usually impossible for all group members to meet at the same time, so there are lots of e-mails and texts we have to send. And even wasted time in personal meetings make group projects unpleasant. People feel awkward, so we end up talking about our lives and getting to know each other. Getting to know my classmates is fine, but it's not why I enrolled in the course.

Grammar? Revise.

Maybe profs could tell us how to get to know one another quickly and then move on to the assignment.

An instructor might say the purpose of a group project is to teach time management. If they would give some guidelines or ideas about time management, maybe group projects wouldn't be so horrible.

The way group projects are graded is simply unfair. For example, I did most of the work in my group, but the other group members got the same grade I did. A (slacker) got the very same grade I got. ~~He was actually a jerk I knew from high school.~~ What did he learn from this project? He learned that he can get away with being a slacker.

Give more details about the slacker. Use term "slacker"?

Unrelated-delete.

Sounds so snobby!

Maybe this is a rude tone.

Sounds whiny.

I can tolerate working with students, but do not base my grade on that work. Instructors can assign group projects, but they should also teach students how to work in groups.

Last sentence doesn't fit thesis statement. Do I want to say group projects are OK if instructors do certain things, or do I want to stick with idea that group projects should never be assigned? Revise.

Maybe give an idea about how projects could be graded more fairly?

Student Example of a Revised Draft

Maria has come up with a variety of ideas for improving her paper when she revises. What follows is Maria's revised essay. Notice that Maria changed her point of view from the one she initially highlighted in the assignment. So she changed her thesis statement to reflect her new point of view. As you read it, annotate the areas where you see other changes. Do you see any other places where Maria could make more improvements?

**Model Student Essay: "Professors: Just Say 'No' to Group Projects"
by Maria Colonio**

Colonio 1

Maria Colonio

Prof. Liu

English 110

4 April 2017

Professors: Just Say "No" to Group Projects

Group projects are popular assignments at Marquez College and

probably at many other colleges. I understand why teachers use group projects. They want students to learn to work together, and they want us to help one another in the learning process. However, I do not think these goals are met very well by group projects as most instructors assign them. For group projects to really work, professors need to include specific information about how the groups should function and how individual student grades will be determined.

I clearly remember my speech class here at Marquez College. The most difficult assignment I ever did in my life was in that class. It was a group assignment. We had to choose a controversial issue, find the best research we could on that issue, and use that research to make an argument for or against the issue. It was not a good experience. My group was dysfunctional. As a student concerned about grades, I was the one who did the calling and e-mailing to beg group members to contribute to the project. In the end, I alone did the work. I learned quite a bit, but it simply was not fair that the other group members received the same grade of "A" that I did.

One reason to not assign group work is the issue of time. Groups spend so much time just figuring out how to work together that little time is available for the project. It is usually impossible for all group members to meet at the same time, so there are lots of e-mails and texts we have to send. This could be time we spent on the task, not on coordinating meetings with our fellow students. And even meetings include a lot of wasted time. People feel awkward, so we end up talking about our lives and getting to know one another. That is fun, but it is not exactly the kind of learning I want to be doing in college. If instructors would give groups instructions to spend five minutes on introductions, five minutes to exchange information, and so on, groups would function better.

The second reason group projects should not be assigned is that the way they are graded is sometimes seen as unfair by students. I am sure my professors all try to be fair, but group projects sometimes make it

Colonio 3

impossible. For example, I did most of the work in my group, but the other group members got the same grade I did. I researched the issue along with another student, while three of our classmates sat in the library and talked. One guy never attended the group meetings, and he only did a small portion of what he was assigned to do. He turned in a paragraph the day before our paper was due, but he got the very same grade I got. What did he learn from this project? He learned that he can get away with being a slacker. That is not the kind of message professors are trying to send to their students. A better way to grade group projects would be to give students individual grades based on the quality of the project and the participation level of the student. That way, even if the project is an "F," the student who worked the hardest has a chance to pass.

Another reason why I dislike group projects and think they should not be assigned is that I want to learn from my professor, not my fellow students. No offense, fellow students, but you guys do not have the master's degree or doctorate that our professors have. I get much more out of a good discussion or lecture than a group project. Teachers have lots of knowledge and expertise. Finding a way to share this knowledge would be much more valuable than assigning a group project.

I know that some professors value group projects because of the cooperation required to do them. I do not mind working with my fellow students, but please do not base my grade on the classmates in my group. If Marquez College faculty use group projects, I hope they will consider helping the groups function better and assigning individual grades to individual students. These steps will make group work something students can really use for learning.

Maria's essay changed dramatically through the revision process. Examine the important changes Maria made by completing the following exercise.

PRACTICE (6)

Analyzing a Student's Revision

List three changes Maria made in her revised draft on the previous three pages, and explain the effect the change might have on the reader.

1. _____
   _____
   _____

2. _____
   _____
   _____

3. _____
   _____
   _____
   _____

Using Reader-Based Suggestions to Revise

One of the best ways to revise is to have someone read your paper and to respond to his or her criticisms. Finding the right person to read your paper is important. Here are some suggestions for finding readers.

Instructors

Start by asking whether your instructor looks at drafts and offers comments. If your instructor wants you to work on drafts without his or her suggestions, ask if there is a writing lab or other resource on campus where you can get help with your papers.

Writing Labs

Most campuses have writing labs where tutors will sit with students, read their papers, and offer suggestions for improvement. If you use a writing lab, plan on spending enough time in the lab to work on your paper after a tutor offers suggestions. You can go back and forth from the tutor to your desk as you work. You will learn a lot about writing during this process, and you will almost certainly produce a better draft by having someone read your work.

Peer Editing

Many writing instructors have their students use peer editing, a process that involves reading classmates' papers and offering suggestions for improvement. To get the most out of peer editing, talk to the classmate who reads your paper. Ask that person for explanations and suggestions. If you disagree with a suggestion, take the paper to a tutor in your writing lab and discuss the suggestion to see what the tutor thinks. Take each suggestion seriously, but since these suggestions have been made by classmates, realize that you have to decide whether the suggestions are worth using or not.

Peer editors are more helpful finding certain errors than others. If your instructor does not give you a list of questions to use while peer editing, ask your peer editor to look at these questions and consider these issues:

- Can you tell what the main idea of the essay is?

- Do all the body paragraphs support this idea?

- Do any of the body paragraphs need more explanation, examples, or support?

- Are any ideas in the essay unclear?

- Are any sentences unclear? (If so, mark them.)

- Does the introduction help you to understand the topic and lead to the thesis statement?

- Does the conclusion provide a sense of closure—the idea that the essay is over?

Being a peer editor yourself can help you sharpen your own editing skills. If you become a peer editor of a classmate's work, you can use these questions to guide your own evaluation. In addition, remember to respect the writer's work. Use polite, neutral language; use comments, suggestions, and questions, not commands. For instance, instead of writing "You should add more examples here," explain your observation and offer a suggestion: "This point lacks support. Do you have more examples to add?"

Family and Friends

Ask a family member or friend to read your paper. Have the person use the same questions as you would use for peer review. In the same way that you must decide whether the suggestions made by peers are worth implementing, you must be careful about using the suggestions of family and friends.

Using Listening Skills to Revise

Have you ever listened to someone read your paper, only to find that you have left out words or made mistakes? Hearing your paper read aloud can help you find errors that you may not see as you revise. To use listening skills to revise, consider one of these methods:

- Use your smartphone's recording capability. Turn on your recorder, and read your paper into it. Read word for word. You will probably not be able to read the entire paper without stopping to fix errors!

- Ask a friend to read your paper aloud to you.

- Use a software program that reads text aloud. Several programs enable computers to read text.

As you listen to your paper being read, have a copy in front of you and have a pen handy. Mark the areas where you need to make changes, and when you are finished listening, do the necessary revising and editing.

Editing and Formatting an Essay

The best way to distinguish editing from revising is to think of revising as re-visioning ideas, and editing as finding mistakes in specific grammatical and stylistic details. Editing helps you prepare your revised text for submission.

People who are employed as editors are trained to find *every* error in a text. The range of errors one could look for is very wide. When you edit, it is important to focus on the most common areas of difficulty that you have in writing. If you know that you have particular trouble with a certain grammatical concept, such as subject-verb agreement, make sure that you take extra time during the editing stage to check the agreement of each subject and verb.

Using SMART TRACS to Edit Your Essay

In addition to checking for the specific errors you tend to make, use the **acronym** SMART TRACS to remember ten issues to check for in your paper.

 acronym

SMART TRACS EDITING PLAN

S Spelling
- Always check spelling before handing in a paper.
- Use your computer's spell-checker. If you do not know how to use the spell-checker, ask for help.
- If you come to an unfamiliar word, guess at its spelling and then look up the word in a dictionary.

M Mechanics
- Check for mechanical correctness by making sure you have used capitalization, underlining, abbreviations, and numbers correctly.

A Accurate Punctuation
- Make sure you do not use a comma alone to join two complete sentences. Use a coordinating conjunction (*for, and, nor, but, or, yet, so*) plus a comma, use a semicolon, or create two separate sentences.
- Check all commas to make sure you are using them correctly.
- Check all semicolons to make sure you are using them correctly.
- Make sure you are using quotation marks, hyphens, dashes, and colons accurately.

R Repeated or Missing Words
- Read your paper word-for-word out loud to find missing words.
- Have a friend read your paper aloud to you.
- Read your paper out loud to catch repeated words.
- Use synonyms to avoid repetition.

T Terminal Punctuation
- Check every sentence for the appropriate end punctuation.
- Make sure you use a period only with a complete sentence.
- Do not use a comma to end a sentence and start another one.

(continued)

SMART TRACS EDITING PLAN *(continued)*

T — Tense & Verb Issues
- If you start your paragraph in past tense, stay in past tense.
- If you start in present tense, stay in present tense, but shift tenses when you refer to something in the past.
- Circle each verb and check it for the appropriate tense.
- Make sure each verb agrees with its subject.

R — Reference of Pronouns
- Check to make sure that the antecedent for each pronoun you use is immediately clear to readers.
- If an antecedent is missing, revise so that the antecedent is included.

A — Apostrophe Use
- Find each possessive noun and make sure apostrophes are used correctly.
- Find each contraction and revise so that contractions are eliminated.

C — Confusing Words
- Check for commonly misused words such as *their, they're, there; its, it's; two, too, to; affect, effect; loose, lose;* and *desert, dessert.*
- On a list of commonly confused words, mark those that you have trouble with.
- Make note cards for your "trouble" words with their meanings and rules for use.
- As you read and write, refer to your note cards.
- When you revise, look for your "trouble" words by using the computer's "find" function.
- Check each word to make sure you have used it correctly, and make changes where necessary.

S — Sources
- If your writing contains sources, make sure you give credit to those sources in your paper.
- Ask your instructors how they want you to give credit to source materials.

In the exercise that follows, you will use the SMART TRACS editing plan to make changes to the first two paragraphs of a student's essay.

PRACTICE 7

Editing a Text

Read the two paragraphs that follow from a student's essay on how to raise healthier children. Use SMART TRACS to look for specific types of errors. When you find errors, annotate them. When you finish, rewrite the student's paragraphs on a separate sheet to correct the errors.

Parents do want the best for their children. To have a good education, strong morals, respectful to others, and to grow up to be strong and healthy. So parents always thinking of ways to protect the future of their kids and to do that is making sure they're healthy.

First, parents need to consider the healthy foods they will feed their children. When their toddlers parents shouldn't give up them alot of sweets try to balance it out by giving them plenty of healthy fruits and vegetables. For instance healthy foods like carrots, apples, grapes, sweet peppers, and oranges should be given to the children. These healthy foods are much healthier than

(continued)

the junkfood most children crave. Even though its hard to get kids to eat healthy vegtables. The best kinds of vegtables are the healthy leafy green vegtables like collard greens, spinach, and green beans These are the foods that have positive health affects. As far as healthy snacks for them I would give them gram crackers, yogurt and popcorn but not soda, you could switch that out with a healthier drink such as natural juice, milk or some water.

Grammar Focus

Subject-Verb Agreement

A common and significant error is a lack of agreement between a subject and its verb. If you know that you are prone to make this error, focus on it while editing, and take a moment to review the basics of subject-verb agreement.

A singular subject must be matched with a singular verb, and a plural subject must be paired with a plural verb. In the following examples, the sentence's subject is in italics, and the sentence's verb is underlined.

> **Examples:**   An *animal* <u>releases</u> hormones as a response to stress.
> *Animals* <u>release</u> hormones as a response to stress.

You may notice that nouns ending in -s (plural nouns) often agree with verbs that *do not* end in -s. While there are exceptions, it can be helpful to check subject nouns and verbs for their -s endings and to make sure the subject and verb agree.

> **Examples:**   hawk flie<u>s</u> (singular)   hawk<u>s</u> fly (plural)
>
> psychologist listen<u>s</u> (singular)   psychologist<u>s</u> listen (plural)
>
> she i<u>s</u>   they are

As the last example above shows, even irregular verbs (*is*) have an -s ending in the singular.

The guidelines that follow show how to think about particular subject-verb agreement situations that can be confusing.

1. IF A SUBJECT CONTAINS TWO OR MORE NOUNS OR PRONOUNS JOINED BY *AND,* USE A PLURAL VERB

Often a subject contains two or more nouns or pronouns joined together. If *and* is used to connect the parts of the subject, then the verb should usually be plural.

(continued)

> **Example: An** *evaluation* **and an** *analysis* <u>**are**</u> **included in the report.**

A rare exception occurs when the two nouns are typically thought of as a single unit.

> **Example:**   *Steak* and *eggs* <u>is</u> my favorite breakfast.

2. IF A SUBJECT CONTAINS *OR* OR *NOR*, MAKE THE VERB AGREE WITH THE PART OF THE SUBJECT CLOSEST TO THE VERB

If two nouns or pronouns in a subject are joined by *or* or *nor*, the subject is not necessarily plural. The part of the subject that is nearest to the verb determines whether the verb is singular or plural. When a singular subject noun is connected by *or* or *nor* to a plural subject noun, place the plural noun closer to the verb, and use a plural verb, as in the following examples.

> **Examples:**   The *awl* [singular noun] **or** the *bits* [plural noun] <u>belong</u> in the bin.
>
> <u>Do</u> the *bits* **or** the *awl* <u>belong</u> in the bin?

In the question example above, the helping verb (*do*) shows that the verb is plural.

3. WATCH OUT FOR WORDS THAT COME BETWEEN THE SUBJECT AND THE VERB

Sometimes a phrase or a clause that comes between the subject and the verb can cause confusion about subject-verb agreement. Remember that the verb should agree with the subject, not with a noun or pronoun in the phrase or clause.

> **Examples:**   The *computers* **in the new lab** <u>are</u> easy to use.
>
> The *diagram* **that came with the instructions** <u>identifies</u> the parts.

To determine the right agreement, mentally strike through intervening words to identify the correct subject.

4. DETERMINE WHETHER SUBJECTS INDICATING QUANTITIES ARE SINGULAR OR PLURAL

Words such as *fraction, majority, part,* and *percent* are typically followed by a prepositional phrase. In those cases, the **object of the preposition** determines

(continued)

whether you should use a singular or plural verb. If the object of the preposition is singular, use a singular verb. Likewise, if the object of the preposition is plural, use a plural verb.

> **Examples:**   Forty percent **of the hay** has been distributed.
>
> Forty percent **of the bales** have been distributed.

5. FOR NOUNS THAT CAN BE PLURAL OR SINGULAR, USE THE VERB FORM THAT REFLECTS THE MEANING OF THE SENTENCE

Many nouns that refer to groups of people can be either singular or plural. Some examples are *audience, board, committee, council, family, group, set,* and *team.* In a sentence describing the action of the entire group, a singular verb is needed. In a sentence describing the actions of individuals in a group, a plural verb is logical.

> **Examples:**   The *committee* has voted in favor of the proposal.
>
> The *committee* have different views on the proposal.

If a plural verb sounds awkward, try inserting a plural noun into the subject, as follows.

> **Example:**   The *committee members* have different views on the proposal.

6. DETERMINE WHETHER PRONOUN SUBJECTS ARE SINGULAR OR PLURAL

Pronouns that include the word *one* or *body* are singular and need singular verbs. Some pronouns—for example, *both, few, many,* and *several*—are plural and need plural verbs. A few pronouns—*all, any, more, most, some*—can be singular or plural depending on the meaning of the sentence. As with nouns indicating quantities, a prepositional phrase may determine whether the pronoun is singular or plural.

> **Examples:**   More is known today about effective urban planning strategies.
>
> More [strategies] are used by planners to resolve overcrowding issues.
>
> All of the study **participants** have been paid a nominal fee.
>
> All of the study's **cost** has been covered by a grant.

(continued)

7. USE SINGULAR VERBS FOR MONEY, TIME, AND TITLES

A sum of money, a period of time, or a title of a work is thought of as a single unit and so takes a singular verb.

> **Examples:**   *Twenty years* <u>is</u> a long time to spend in college.
>
> *Seventy-five* dollars <u>is</u> the price of the ticket.
>
> *Bury My Heart at Wounded Knee* <u>is</u> the assigned reading.

SENTENCE COMBINING

The examples that follow show how to combine sentences and select the appropriate verb to create subject-verb agreement.

Ideas to combine using correct subject-verb agreement:

- Nearly half the electricity created in the United States results from burning coal.
- Soot is a by-product of burning coal.
- Toxic air emissions are a by-product of burning coal.
- There are other by-products of burning coal.
- These by-products include acid rain.
- They include smog.

Combined sentences with subject-verb agreement: Nearly half the electricity created in the United States results from burning coal. Soot and toxic air emissions are by-products of burning coal. Other by-products include acid rain and smog.

Try your hand at combining sentences and selecting the appropriate verbs to create subject-verb agreement.

EXERCISES

You will find three sets of sentences below. Combine the sentences to make smoother, longer ones, and make sure subjects and verbs agree.

1. Ideas to combine:
- Genes probably influence the development of autism spectrum disorders.
- The environment seems to influence the development of autism spectrum disorders.
- The disorders are usually diagnosed in children rather than adults.
- The cause is being researched.
- Methods for treating autism spectrum disorders are being researched.

Answer: _____

_____

_____

(continued)

2. Ideas to combine:
- Contracts are signed by people.
- The people who sign them are called "parties" to the contract.
- One party signs the contract.
- Another party signs the contract.
- The agreement is between both parties.

Answer: _____

_____

3. Ideas to combine:
- Nanoscience is a relatively new scientific interest.
- Nanoscience is the study of very small things, such as atoms.
- Nanoscience involves using small things for inventions.
- Agricultural practices are affected by nanoscience.
- Computer technology is affected by nanoscience.
- Certain fields of study use nanoscience.
- One field is chemistry.
- Another field is physics.

Answer: _____

_____

_____

_____

Formatting Your Essay

In addition to being revised and edited, the final draft of your paper should meet the formatting requirements specified by your instructor. If your instructor has not given you specific information about how to format your paper, use the formatting specifications from the Modern Language Association.

Important formatting considerations include these:

- Setting the correct margins and tabs
- Using a correct header and page number system
- Using an appropriate heading
- Knowing whether to use a cover sheet, binder, staple, or paper clip for submitting your paper
- Using appropriate line spacing
- Using the appropriate font and font size
- Using the appropriate method for documenting sources

Using the correct format for setting up and submitting your paper is one of the easiest parts of writing. Make sure you get credit for this easy task by following instructions perfectly.

CHAPTER ACTIVITIES

→ READING AND ANNOTATING

Read and annotate "Troubleshooting a Fail," a personal essay written by a college English professor. As you read, think about experiences you have had with failure. What have your reactions been?

Troubleshooting a "Fail"

By Lyndie Connell

YOUR ANNOTATIONS

It's Saturday morning. I'm awake, coffee in hand, blinds open, feet propped up, laptop situated just perfectly for optimal viewing, ready for some long-awaited free time cruising the Internet and looking at stuff that interests me. I want to do fun stuff—no work involved this morning. I click. And wait. And wait. Then the dreaded icon appears, and I read, "Server not found."

Unless you are an IT wizard, you are probably like most of us who try any manner of random fixes that worked in the past. Sometimes it takes a click; other times it takes hours of grappling with cable modems, wireless routers, and internal settings. I put my troubleshooting skills to work and start wondering why troubleshooting is so bothersome.

Reflecting on this process, I began to think about my students. *What do they do when they lose their Internet connections?* I wondered.

Earlier in the week, I had handed back essays to my freshman writing students. I hate giving Fs. I don't like the look of failure on the faces of otherwise bright and hopeful students. And having received an F or two in my own college work long ago, I remember the shoulder droop and the stomach churn that accompanies receiving such bad news.

Yet even with the pain of failing, I know that some of the same students are likely to receive Fs on their next papers, too. A few of them quickly cram their papers into their backpacks, and some walk straight to the trash can and drop in their work.

As I reflect on their reactions, I think about troubleshooting. If they lost their Internet connections, would they put their computers down and find something else to do? I cannot imagine they would. Maybe they don't realize that the very same skill set required for getting back online can be used for making higher grades. Maybe they simply don't know how to troubleshoot an F.

So instead of troubleshooting my online problem, I have decided to write a primer on how to do exactly that.

* * *

(continued)

What do you do when you receive an F on a college assignment? Your reaction to the problem is crucial, and there are several types of reactions you can have. One type of reaction is the "out of sight, out of mind" game plan. The student who throws away her paper or crams it somewhere never to look at it again will simply make the same mistakes next time. (Yet she would probably not throw away her computer if she couldn't get online!)

Another type of reaction is the **existential** crisis. Students with this reaction make the mistaken assumption that the "F" means *they*—not their work—are flawed. Their self-esteem plummets, and they can barely make eye contact with me. Because they see the paper as a measure of their personal worth, it is too painful to take out the paper and troubleshoot. Result: A failing grade again, next time, followed by even more loss of self-esteem.

A third reaction is the **indignant** response. The indignant group uses anger to deal with frustration. They see the grade as unjust—often before they even know why they received the failing grade—and put the blame on their instructors. Psychologists tell us that anger is often a reaction to fear. A failing grade can cause fear deep down in the psyche: we start to fear failing the class, or we may fear that we are inadequate. Responding with anger allows us to temporarily outdistance those fears. The problem is, anger doesn't get anything done. In actuality, it makes troubleshooting an even more difficult task. If I throw my cable modem across the room and break it into a million pieces, I may temporarily feel better, but my problem will be compounded.

The best type of response to a "fail" is the "turning point" reaction. This response happens when students see an F as a troubleshooting opportunity. Instead of anger, these students have determination. Instead of self-loathing, these students *know* they can figure out the problem. Instead of thinking the grade is unjust, they are open to figuring out why they received the grade in the first place. This self-confidence does not always come naturally. Such people (and I include myself in this group) have to fight down the negative voices that say "See, you're not college material" or "Drop this class. You can't do it!" Students in this group are successful at blocking out the negative thoughts, keeping an open mind, and remaining optimistic.

Part of successful troubleshooting is *willing* yourself into participating in the process. It's the same with getting back online. I must first become more **amenable** to investing time in fixing the problem. I must resolve that, okay, this is going to take some work. I won't immediately be able to fix the problem. So I have to calm myself down, adjust my plans, and come to peace with the realization that my day's agenda is going to change. The same is true with figuring out the F. It will take time. It will require changing plans. It will make the semester more difficult. Calming down and not being resentful about the extra time required is the first step. To learn something, you must invest in it.

Second, I know from my own experience with troubleshooting that figuring out where to start and which resources to use is crucial. A student who decides to read his textbook to see what went wrong with his paper is making a start, but that is not the best start. The best start is to go to the source: the instructor. Ask for help. Your instructor knows *exactly* what you need to do to improve. Let her guide you to the resources that will work best.

VCW existential

VCW indignant

VCW amenable

(continued)

Third, you must follow through. This is the hard part. For me, it sometimes means sitting all day in my study trying to figure out how to get back online, or making three calls to the cable Internet folks for their assistance. It has even meant using another person's computer and Internet connection to figure out what was wrong with mine.

The follow-through for students means doing the hard work of learning. But this is where the real progress is made. Whether you work with a tutor, your instructor, or a lab teacher, the work these knowledgeable people guide you through will be what makes the difference between your failing paper and your next paper. True, this is the hard part, but it is also the empowering part. Slowly you realize that the material is learnable. You start to gain understanding, and with that understanding comes a bit of amazement. The tasks that used to be so puzzling become easy. Instead of confusion, you have clarity. Terms become more meaningful, processes start to develop, and you begin to feel that you truly can fix the problem.

The last part of troubleshooting is the next "moment of truth." After I have spent an hour reading about Internet connectivity, fumbling through computer lingo, and changing settings, the moment of truth occurs when I click the "Connect" button. I either connect or do not. If I don't, it's back to the drawing board. And going *back* to troubleshooting certainly takes a great deal of energy. But even if I fail again, I've made progress. I have learned new terms, I have learned what doesn't work, and I have gained a better understanding by spending the time working on the problem.

The same thing *should* happen when troubleshooting an F. The next moment of truth is the next paper. If the paper comes back with yet another F, the process repeats. And yes, troubleshooting is frustrating. It takes time. It takes a major amount of energy. But this is the process we use when things don't work. It's not a process reserved exclusively for college students who make occasional Fs: it's what we all do to succeed in tasks that are important to us.

* * *

I have finally figured out the Internet connection problem. Now, with my Internet connection restored, I can sit back and mindlessly visit all the frivolous Web sites I've yearned for during the work week. I also feel some pride—just a bit—in knowing that I can do something that computer geeks can do. I can wade through their lingo and figure out how to fix my own problem.

My coffee is cold, but I'm back on track. And I have a bit more confidence now that if my connection goes down again, I can handle it.

Questions for Consideration

1. What are the four responses to "a fail" that the writer presents?

   _____

2. Which of these four responses have you had to a failing grade? Which response is the one you are most likely to have? Explain.

   _____

3. What are the three steps the writer suggests for responding to "a fail"?

   _____

4. According to this essay, how might a student see "a fail" as an opportunity?

_____

_____

➜ USING MODELS TO PRACTICE REVISING AND EDITING

Below you will find a list of specific revision and editing strategies, followed by a student paragraph, "Tattoos on Children." As you read the paragraph, look for opportunities to make the changes listed, and then revise or edit as appropriate.

Revision and Editing Strategies

1. Find two short sentences, and combine them to make a longer sentence.

_____

2. Find a sentence that could be followed with an example. Write a sentence providing the example.

_____

3. Consider how the order of the sentences could be improved. List the sentence numbers in the order in which you would place them.

_____

4. Find an error in word choice by considering commonly confused words. Change the misused word to the appropriate one.

_____

5. Find a phrase that is vague. Revise it so that its meaning is clear by using more specific, concrete terms.

_____

Tattoos on Children

[1]Should parents be allowed to get their children tattooed? [2]What if a parent of a two-year-old child decides to put a "tramp stamp" on the child's back? [3]Should this be legal? [4]Modifying a child's body can have various affects. [5]These are some of the questions state legislators have to consider in this new era of body art. [6]The argument against allowing parents to tattoo their children is the fact that tattoos are permanent. [7]The interesting counterargument is that we have not questioned other practices that modify a child's body. [8]Circumcision, for example, is perfectly legal. [9]It significantly changes a child's body.

➜ A READING AND WRITING ASSIGNMENT

Below, you will find an essay assignment and a rough draft written by Jalyn Martin, a student in an English class. First, read and annotate the assignment, and then read through Jalyn's rough draft. Revise his rough draft, and use SMART TRACS to edit it. Produce a final copy of Jalyn's paper in a correctly formatted document.

Essay Assignment for English 1301

Write an essay in which you provide a single change or a variety of changes parents can make to help their children be healthier. Imagine you are writing to have your essay published in a parenting magazine. Be sure to take the audience into consideration as you write. In addition, follow these instructions:

- Offer at least three reasons for your position.
- Include topic sentences for each of the body paragraphs.
- Make sure that each body paragraph is well supported.
- Use standard English grammar, correct spelling, and appropriate punctuation.
- Do not include the use of any sources.
- Format your essay using MLA style.

Jalyn's Draft

An old saying is *the work of a child is to play*. This adage is absolutely true, but it does not specify the type of play children need. More and more, children are abandoning the good, wholesome play that occurs in backyards and on sidewalks. Play is becoming an inside activity, and it is becoming solitary. Is sitting in front of a video game really the kind of play that should be *children's work*? There is nothing wrong with inside play, but children need more outside play than they get. Parents can help their children be healthier by making them play outside.

First, Children need sunshine. Playing outside means children will get the Vitamin D they need. Our bodies need vitamin D. You may know that vitamin D comes from milk, but it also comes from being in the sun. Without it, children are more susceptible to diseases. Additionally, being in

©John Lund/Sam Diephuis/Getty Images RF

(continued)

the sun seems to have an affect on your mood. Who can be sad or grumpy on a beautiful sunny day?

Second, Video games make our kids lazy, so people need to send their kids outside. People debate whether violent video games make children more violent. Too much staring into a tv screen can't be a good habit. Besides, when you are playing video games, they are sitting down all day. Everybody needs to play some video games, but playing too much can turn you into a couch potato.

Third, There are things kids can do outdoors that they can never do indoors. Exploring nature, building forts, doing mischievous things like graffiti, getting to know the kids that live around them. Outdoor play makes kids be more creative. They have to come up with their own games. They can also get to know the children who live around them. They can ride bikes. They can explore parts of their neighborhood they would never see if they were in front of a tv all day.

Parents who care about their children's health need to consider sending their kids outside, a healthy kid is a kid who comes in totally wiped out and filthy from a wonderful day playing cowboys and Indians or hiking through the woods with their buddies. If we want our children to not be overweight and to get the vitamins they need, we should encourage them to play outside. The way we all did when we were children.

➲ ADDING TO YOUR VOCABULARY

This chapter's vocabulary words appear below.

acronym	amenable	incentive	precarious
ambiguity	existential	indignant	

Choose five of the vocabulary words from this chapter that you would like to add to your vocabulary, and think about how you can use them this week. For example, one of this chapter's words is *amenable.* You can often substitute *amenable* for *open to* or *OK with,* as in the example that follows.

> **Example:**   Marcus is *OK with* having the party at his house.
>
> Marcus is *amenable to* having the party at his house.

List each of the five words you plan to use this week, and make note of a context in which you could use each word.

> **Example:**   *Amenable.* I can use this with my kids when they propose going somewhere or doing something.

➡ ADDITIONAL ASSIGNMENTS

Source: The Jon B. Lovelace Collection of California Photographs in Carol M. Highsmith's America Project, LOC

©Radius Images/Getty Images RF

1. Revising and editing enable you to improve your writing. People who restore automobiles or houses participate in a kind of revision process. Even cooking makes use of revision. Chefs, for example, might alter a recipe five or six times before they consider it perfect. Write an essay in which you compare the process of revising a text to the revision process of some other creative activity. In what ways are the processes similar?

2. Write an essay about a time when you "revised" a product or a process repeatedly. Describe the process you used. Explain what motivated you to keep revising until the product was nearly perfect.

3. Write an essay in response to "Troubleshooting a Fail." In your essay, compare and contrast two different responses you have had to failures. How did your response to the situation affect the ultimate outcome?

4. The word *revision* includes two word parts with which you are familiar: *re* (again) and *visi* (to see or view). *Revision,* then, means "to see again." To the right are two photographs. Choose one photograph. Imagine you are an artist and a client has asked you to revise her house or her old truck. Envision what the house or truck *could* look like. What particular features would you change to make it more beautiful or more appealing? Explain your vision in one or two paragraphs. Revise and edit your paragraphs when you are finished.

5. Find an essay you wrote for this writing class or for another college course, and print out a copy. Read your paper out loud, imagining yourself reading it for the first time. Use the processes in this chapter to revise and edit your paper. When you are finished with your revision, repeat this entire process. See if revising the paper a second time makes a difference in the quality (and quantity) of your writing.

EMOTIONAL INTELLIGENCE

What is *netiquette*? If you are unsure, do an Internet search, and read about the topic. Write two or three paragraphs in which you define *netiquette* and explain some common netiquette guidelines. Be sure to give credit to any sources you use.

METACOGNITION

Think back to a group project in which you participated. Imagine that you can see yourself—and all of the other group members—from the outside. Evaluate your role in the group. Did you contribute in a positive way? Were you the leader? How important a role did you play? If you were an instructor, how would you evaluate the role you played in the group project? Explain in one or two paragraphs.

©Doug Sherman/Geofile RF

Step-by-Step Guidance for Integrated Reading and Writing Projects: A Student Example

Project 1
Working with a Text to Create a Summary

Project 2
Working with Informative Texts

Project 3
Completing an Argument Project

AVAILABLE ONLY IN

Project 4
Working with Analysis and Evaluation Texts

Three Integrated Reading and Writing Projects

Writing topics can be wide-ranging and thought-provoking—from ideas in psychology, to the effects of social media, to attitudes toward businesses like Walmart. Whatever topic stirs your interest, you will find that following an integrated reading and writing process will help you successfully complete your assignment.

Chapter Objectives

After completing this chapter, students will be able to do the following:

- Use a complete integrated reading and writing process to finish a reading and writing project.

- Read an article and write a complete summary (Project 1).

- Read four articles and write an informative essay (Project 2).

- Read five articles and write a persuasive essay (Project 3).

In many college courses, you will be expected to use both reading and writing skills to demonstrate your learning. For example, in an economics class, you may be assigned a chapter to read on the ten laws of economics. To demonstrate your understanding of the chapter, your instructor may require you to write a paper explaining one of the laws and providing examples of how the law works.

In this chapter, you will learn how to complete a reading and writing project. Your project will start with assignment instructions that will help you read in a focused way so that you can accomplish the assignment's purpose. Here is an overview of the three projects in this chapter:

Project 1. Working with a Text to Create a Summary

Purpose: to read a text and write a summary of the text

Project 2. Working with Informative Texts

Purpose: to read several texts and use the information to write an informative essay

Project 3. Completing an Argument Project

Purpose: to read texts on an arguable issue, figure out your position on the issue, and write a persuasive essay in which you present your position and the reasons for it

Even though these three projects have different purposes, you can use a similar process to complete each assignment. Here, we will follow a student, Alex, to see the process he uses to complete an integrated reading and writing project.

Step-by-Step Guidance for Integrated Reading and Writing Projects: A Student Example

Alex is a student in an integrated reading and writing class. Alex has studied the individual tasks in reading and writing processes. Now he is ready to complete an assignment that involves reading some texts and writing a paper based on what he has read. Let's follow Alex as he goes step-by-step through an integrated reading and writing project. When you complete your own project, you will use the same steps Alex has used.

Getting Started

Before he launches into reading or writing, Alex uses pre-reading and prewriting strategies. He begins by making sure he fully understands what he is supposed to be doing.

1. Analyze Your Assignment

Alex reads the assignment instructions carefully. He analyzes the assignment by highlighting the significant verbs and making notes in the margin. Alex's assignment appears below. Notice his annotations.

Alex's Assignment

Select one of four articles on the topic of generational differences. Read and annotate the article you choose. Next, create an outline of the article, and write a complete summary. Submit your summary to be graded. Then, read and annotate the remaining three articles.

Next, write an informative essay in which you use the information from at least one of the sources you have read. In your essay, discuss three ways in which two of the generations you have read about might conflict. Limit your discussion to how they may conflict in a certain environment: at home, in the workplace, or in college. Give credit to the source when you use its ideas or when you use quotations from it.

Use a complete writing process to generate drafts and to revise and edit your work. Format your paper correctly and submit it.

ALEX'S ANNOTATIONS

Select an article.
Read and annotate the article.
Create an outline.
Write and submit complete summary of the outlined article.
Read remaining three articles.
Write an essay.
Use one article's information to discuss three ways generations might conflict.
Limit to a certain environment.
Give credit to article's author.
Use complete writing process.
Format paper correctly.

2. Identify Your Purpose

Having read and annotated the assignment, Alex is able to clarify his purpose for reading the articles. One purpose is to write a summary. He knows that to write a summary, he will need to figure out the article's main ideas and its major supporting points. As he annotates the reading, he will mark these elements.

Another purpose is to write an information essay. To write this essay, Alex will need to understand the information the article presents. He will also need to apply the knowledge he gains about generations to figure out how two generations might conflict in a particular environment. With these thoughts in mind, Alex starts the pre-reading process.

Working with Readings

Before he starts reading, Alex needs a plan for getting the most out of the reading process. He follows these steps.

1. Preview the Reading and Think about the Topic

Alex selects one of the four texts to read, and he starts previewing the reading and thinking about its topic. He takes out a sheet of paper and writes notes as he previews, predicts, recalls, and asks questions.

PREVIEW

What do you notice when you preview the text?

- Author: Ken Culp, III
- Title: Understanding Generational Differences
  Publisher: U of Kentucky Cooperative Extension
- Date of publication: Mar. 2011

PREDICT

What do you predict the topic will be?

Topic: generations and how they differ

Looks like the article text will talk about five generations because there are five sub-headings.

RECALL

What do you already know about this topic?

I'm a Millennial. I know that sometimes people believe Millennials think they are "entitled." I know my generation differs from my parents' generation!

ASK

What questions do you have about the text or the topic?

- What are the characteristics of each generation?
- Which generation are my parents in? Do my parents fit the descriptions?
- What is this article's thesis statement? What are the major supporting points for the thesis statement?

2. Read and Annotate the Text

Before Alex reads the text, he decides what he will annotate. The illustration "Alex's Annotation Plan" shows how Alex prepares to read actively.

ALEX'S ANNOTATION PLAN

Now Alex can read the text and use his annotation plan to mark it. The original text is a pamphlet entitled *Understanding Generational Differences*. What follows is the text with Alex's annotations. He highlights possible thesis statements and major supporting points in yellow and other interesting information in green. He underlines words that he will look up in a dictionary, and he puts check marks next to important details.

About the Author.   Dr. Ken Culp, III, is Principal Extension Specialist for Volunteerism in the Department of 4-H Youth Development and Adjunct Associate Professor in the Department of Family Sciences at the University of Kentucky in Lexington. His research interests include volunteer recruitment, motivation, recognition, and retention; generational differences; gender differences in volunteerism; trends in volunteerism; volunteer competencies; volunteer program effectiveness; and leadership development. *Understanding Generational Differences* was published by the University of Kentucky Cooperative Extension in March 2011.

Understanding Generational Differences

By Ken Culp, III

The study of generational differences is an inexact science. Any time we try to characterize an entire group of people, we are bound to make some generalizations that do not fit everyone in that group. Nonetheless, it is possible to see some similarities that we can use to try to define the generations. Beginning with the dawn of the 20th century, we can examine the five American generations and the factors that make them different from one another.

The Civic Generation

This generation was born from 1901 through 1929. Civics are motivated by altruism and community needs; they want to be useful. Reputation is extremely important to Civics. They grew up with expressions such as "A man's word is his bond," "We have a handshake agreement," and "Give an honest day for an honest wage."

The breaking points for this generation were the dawn of the 20th century and the Stock Market Crash of 1929, which signaled the onset of the Great Depression. This is a generation of survivors. They survived both world wars and the Great Depression. Due largely to their experiences growing up during the Great Depression, this generation learned to be frugal, to "make do" or to do without. Conserving, efficiency, and economizing are a way of life. There was no welfare system. Debt was a crime. People who couldn't pay their bills went to "Debtor's Prison." People who were destitute went to live at the "County Farm" and worked for their keep.

The Meditating or Silent Generation

This generation was born from 1929 through 1946. This generation gets its name from their habit of thinking about (meditating on) or considering things before taking action. This is a generation of "watchers" (unlike the previous or following generations). Meditators focus on stability, being helpful, serving the community and contributing to the greater good.

The breaking point for this generation was the Stock Market Crash, which signaled the onset of the Great Depression. Defining moments for this generation included WW II (1939–1946), the Japanese attack on Pearl Harbor (Dec. 7, 1941), and the end of WW II (V-E Day, May 8, 1945). As a generation, their formative years were spent growing up during difficult times. Meditators learned to share, make do with the resources that were available to them, or do without. Stability is important to this generation because of the upheaval and instability they experienced during the Great Depression and WW II.

The Baby Boomers

The largest and most well-known generation, the Baby Boomers, were born between 1946 and 1964. Following World War II, there was a great increase in the birth rate; thus, the term "Baby Boomers" is used to describe this generation. A time of great unrest, defining events of this generation included the Civil Rights Movement, the assassinations of JFK, RFK, and MLK; the Vietnam War, Woodstock, the Cold War, and the Supreme Court case *Roe vs. Wade*. In 1960,

---

ALEX'S ANNOTATIONS

Thesis?

MSP 1: Civics

*-IMP: altruism, useful, reputation,
honesty*

-dealt with Stock Market Crash, Great Depression
-IMP: Were survivors
-Learned to be frugal, make-do, conserve, be efficient, economize

-INT: debtor's prison!

MSP 2: Meditating Gen.

-watchers
-IMP: want stability, offer service

-Stock mkt crash, Great Depression
-suffered through WWII

-share, make do, do without

MSP 3: Baby Boomers
-named for increase in birth rate after WW2

(continued)

Rockwell painted "The Problem We All Live With," which appeared in 1964 on the cover of *LOOK* magazine. The painting depicted Ruby Bridges, the first African American child to attend a white school in New Orleans. Famous Baby Boomers include George W. Bush (1946), Bill Clinton (1946), Oprah Winfrey (1954), and Bill Gates (1955).

The educational system was unprepared for the rapid increase in the number of children attending school. The result was that class sizes increased exponentially. To serve such large classrooms, teachers assigned group projects to reduce the amount of time spent grading papers and projects. Boomers were raised in big families, were educated in big classrooms, and learned to be a part of teams. Boomers are goal oriented, and their jobs are often their first priority, with their personal lives trailing behind in importance.

Generation X

Born from 1965 through 1981, Generation X is known as the 13th generation born in America. Known as "the ME Generation," Xers are intensely private, individualistic, are highly educated and often underemployed. Xer males are the first group to earn less than their fathers did at the same age (salaries adjusted for inflation). Xers were the first generation born to two-income families.

One of the primary differences between Xer and Boomer babies was that Boomer mothers stayed home to raise their children until they started school. Conversely, Xer babies were born to working mothers who took six to eight weeks of maternity leave prior to returning to their employment. Gen Xers were the first cohort to spend their pre-school years in childcare. In addition, the term "latch-key kids" was coined to describe this generation. Originally, this generation was unkindly defined as "slackers," unmotivated, lethargic, sarcastic, and irreverent. This could largely be due to their lack of supervision and parenting by their workaholic parents.

Gen Xers are strongly individualistic and are motivated by personal benefits. They ask the question "How will this help me?" or "What's in it for me?" or "Why do I need to know that?" Due largely to their smaller family size and the independence developed during the latch-key years, this generation is not motivated by working with other people. Unlike in the previous generation, the words "committee" and "teamwork" have strong negative connotations. Xers value fun and know how to have a good time. Unlike previous generations, they place a higher priority on family time. They value independence and individuality. Xers value balance in their lives.

Millennials

The second largest generation in history, Millennials, were born from 1982 through 2001. They were so named because they are the first generation to grow up during the third millennium. The ending point for this generation was the attack on the World Trade Center on 9/11. Also known as "Generation Why?" they are a cynical, questioning group that has never lived in a world without terror. This generation has experienced less prejudice and a greater emphasis on multiculturalism, globalism, and diversity than any other.

They are collaborative, open-minded, and influential and are very achievement-oriented. Millennials are sociable, optimistic, talented, and

---

-IMP: lived during unrest
-lived during Civil Rights Movement

-INT: a lot was going on

-Examples: GW Bush, Bill Clinton, Winfrey, Gates
-class sizes increased
-used to big families
-used to teamwork
-IMP: jobs first priority
-personal lives trailed behind

MSP 4: Generation X
-"ME" generation
-private, individualistic, highly educated, underemployed

-first gen from 2-income families

-had working mothers

-childcare
-latch-key kids
INT: slackers? Parents were workaholics—sounds opposite of Gen X

-IMP: wanted personal benefits
-smaller families
-not motivated to work w/others

-IMP: high priority on family time, independence, balance

MSP 5: Millennials
-second largest gen.
-grew up during World Trade Center attack
-IMP: cynical and questioning
-INT: less prejudice, more diversity, globalism, multiculturalism.

-collaborative, open-minded,
(continued)

well-educated. They've always felt sought after, needed, and indispensable. This generation was born in homes and educated in classrooms with computers, Internet, and unlimited connectivity and accessibility. Parents of Millennials took the sides of their children and battled teachers and school administrators. Grading standards changed dramatically. Competition was no longer seen as being healthy for the development of youth. Children were nurtured and encouraged to find something at which they excelled.

Millennials are extremely time conscious, ambitious, civic-minded, and socially engaged, and are motivated by a desire to change the world. Millennials focus on children and families and are strong parent advocates.

Each generation is significantly different than those that preceded and followed it because each generation was shaped and molded by markedly different societal influences during its developmental years. Each generation has marked strengths as well as specific challenges.

Source: Culp III, Ken, *Understanding Generational Differences*, Kentucky Extension Leadership Development (KELD), Cooperative Extension Service, University of Kentucky College of Agriculture. Used by permission of Ken Culp III.

(margin annotations:)
influential, achievement-oriented.
-IMP: felt sought after
-access to computers, internet
-grading standards changed
-competition bad
-IMP: everyone nurtured

-social engagement: desire to change the world
Thesis?

3. Outline and Summarize the Reading

One part of Alex's assignment is to write a summary of the reading. He will use the process shown in the illustration "Writing a Complete Summary."

WRITING A COMPLETE SUMMARY

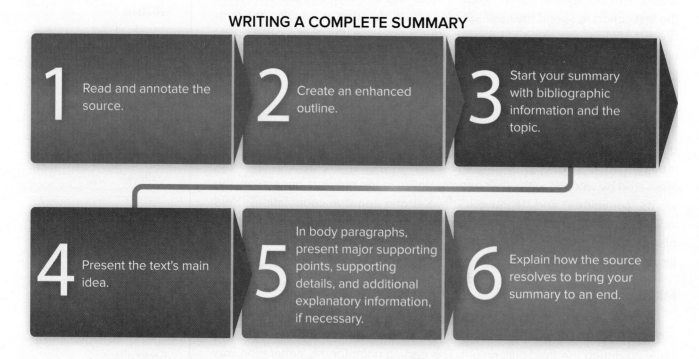

1 Read and annotate the source.

2 Create an enhanced outline.

3 Start your summary with bibliographic information and the topic.

4 Present the text's main idea.

5 In body paragraphs, present major supporting points, supporting details, and additional explanatory information, if necessary.

6 Explain how the source resolves to bring your summary to an end.

Since he has already read and annotated the reading, Alex is ready to write an enhanced outline, an outline that lists the writer's thesis statement, major supporting points, and supporting details.

To demonstrate his understanding of the thesis statement and major supporting points, he puts them in his own words. Many instructors expect students to use their own words when writing a summary, so if Alex uses his own words for his outline, he will be able to transfer some of the same sentences from his outline when he drafts his summary.

Notice how Alex uses his annotations to figure out which supporting details to put on his outline.

Alex's Enhanced Outline of a Source

Enhanced Source Outline

Author: Ken Culp, III

Title: *Understanding Generational Differences*

Thesis Statement: Starting in 1901, there have been five American generation groups. Each one is different because of the social influences that shaped it.

Major Supporting Point 1: The Civics, born between 1901 and 1929, survived the Great Depression and have values such as honesty and frugality.

- valued altruism, reputation, honesty, being useful
- dealt with stock market crash, Great Depression
- were "survivors"
- learned to be frugal, make-do, conserve, be efficient, economize

Major Supporting Point 2: The Meditating, or Silent, Generation, born between 1929 and 1946, experienced scarcity and valued stability.

- valued stability (were careful, "watchers")
- offered service (lived during WWII)
- dealt with aftereffects of stock market crash and Great Depression
- learned to share, make do, do without

Major Supporting Point 3: The Baby Boomers, born between 1946 and 1964, is a large generation that learned to work together and valued work, sometimes over family.

- very large generation because of birth rate after WWII
- lived during unrest (Civil Rights, *Roe vs. Wade*, assassinations)
- include GW Bush, Bill Clinton, Winfrey, Gates
- experienced big classes, big families, and teamwork
- prioritized the importance of jobs (are workaholics)

Major Supporting Point 4: Generation X, born between 1965 and 1981, value independence, family, and balance.

- value privacy, individualism, independence
- had working mothers; some were latch-key kids; went to childcare

(continued)

- value personal benefits from work; value balance and family time
- had smaller families

Major Supporting Point 5: Millennials, born from 1982 to 2001, experienced less prejudice and more nurturing, and they value social engagement.

- second-largest generation
- cynical, questioning, less prejudiced, more global
- value collaboration, open-mindedness, achievements
- a computer generation
- experienced more nurture and less competition
- want to change the world; are socially conscious

Now that Alex has created an enhanced outline, he can use the remaining summary writing steps to write a draft of his summary. After Alex drafted his summary, he revised and edited it. This is Alex's final draft.

Model Student Paper: "A Summary of *Understanding Generational Differences*" by Alex Martin

Martin 1

Alex Martin

Mrs. Sutter

English 0300

15 November 2017

A Summary of *Understanding Generational Differences*

Ken Culp, III, is an adjunct associate professor in the Department of Family Sciences at the University of Kentucky in Lexington. In his informational pamphlet *Understanding Generational Differences*, Culp says that starting in 1901, there have been five American generation groups. Culp shows that each generation is different because of the social influences that shaped it.

The first generation Culp presents is the Civics. The Civics, born between 1901 and 1929, survived the Great Depression and value honesty and frugality. Culp points out that altruism and usefulness, as well as possessing a good reputation, were important to the Civics. Because they witnessed the 1929 stock market collapse and Great Depression, Civics learned to be frugal, to make-do, and to conserve. Culp points out that Civics were survivors in a time when resources were scarce.

Culp next presents the Meditating, or Silent, Generation. Members of this generation were born between 1929 and 1946. They experienced scarcity and valued stability. As Culp explains, one reason they are described as "meditating" and "silent" is that they were very careful. They were watchful because they had grown up in the years after the stock market crash and Great Depression, and they were aware that calamities could happen at any time. Culp notes that World War II was a defining experience in their lives, so they learned that offering service was important, as well as sharing, making do, or doing without.

The third generation Culp presents is the Baby Boomers. A large generation, the Baby Boomers, born between 1946 and 1964, learned to work together and valued work, sometimes over family, Culp explains. This generation was large because of a surge in the birth rate after WWII. Baby Boomers experienced social unrest, such as the Civil Rights Movement, the *Roe vs. Wade* Supreme Court decision, and the assassinations of American leaders according to Culp. Boomers were educated in classes with large numbers of students, and they came from big families. As such, they valued teamwork. Additionally, Culp notes that Baby Boomers often valued work and could be workaholics, sometimes sacrificing family time.

Generation X, born between 1965 and 1981, is the next generation described by Culp. Generation X values independence, family, and balance. As Culp explains, many of the children in this generation were "latch-key" kids. Because both parents were working,

Martin 3

the children went home to empty houses and were unsupervised.
These children, as a generation, grew to value individualism, privacy,
and doing what is best for themselves as individuals. Culp notes that
as parents, they had smaller families and tended to value a balance
between family time and work time.

The final generation Culp discusses is the Millennials. Born
between 1982 and 2001, Millennials experienced less prejudice and
more nurturing, and they value social engagement, according to Culp.
Millennials were children during the 2001 attacks on the World Trade
Center and the Pentagon. They are cynical, questioning, less
prejudiced, and more global in their thinking. Culp says that Millennials
value collaboration and open-mindedness, and they are high
achievers. This generation was born into households that had
computers and Internet connections. Additionally, Millennials were
nurtured in a less competitive environment than previous generations.
Culp claims that Millennials are socially conscious and want to make a
difference in the world.

Each of the five generations Culp presents is unique because of
the particular events that shaped it.

Alex has finished the first part of his assignment: writing a summary of one of the articles he has read. He can submit his summary and go on to the steps that will help him write his essay.

4. Prepare an Information Sheet for the Reading

An important step in the process of writing about a reading is to prepare an information sheet about the reading. Alex has already created an outline and a summary for one article, so he knows a great deal about that particular source. If writing a summary had not been part of Alex's assignment, Alex would have skipped over the summary steps and started immediately preparing his information sheet. What follows is Alex's information sheet for the first reading. Notice how it is constructed. You can use it as a model for your own information sheets.

Alex's Information Sheet for a Source

Information Sheet

Author: Dr. Ken Culp, III, adjunct associate professor in the Department of Family Sciences at the University of Kentucky.

Title: *Understanding Generational Differences*

Publication Information: U of Kentucky Cooperative Extension, Mar. 2011

How I Might Use This Source:

- might compare how Boomers and Millennials would get along in a work environment
- might compare how Gen Xers and Millennials would do classwork for a college course
- might compare how Silent Generation members would differ from Gen Xers in their spending habits.

Brief Outline:

Thesis Statement: Starting in 1901, there have been five American generation groups. Each one is different because of the social influences that shaped it.

Major Supporting Point 1: presents Civic Generation

Major Supporting Point 2: presents Silent Generation

Major Supporting Point 3: presents Baby Boomer Generation

Major Supporting Point 4: presents Generation X

Major Supporting Point 5: presents Millennials

Brief Summary: Ken Culp writes that starting in 1901, there have been five American generation groups. Each one is different because of the social influences that shaped it. The Civics, born between 1901 and 1929, survived the Great Depression and have values such as honesty and frugality. The Meditating, or Silent, Generation, born between 1929 and 1946, experienced scarcity and valued stability. The Baby Boomers, born between 1946 and 1964, is a large generation that learned to work together and valued work, sometimes over family. Generation X, born between 1965 and 1981, valued independence, family, and balance. Millennials, born between 1982 and 2001, experienced less prejudice and more nurturing, and they value social engagement.

Issues: generational differences, generational values, social events that shape generations

Key Words: Civics, Silent Generation, Baby Boomers, Generation X, Millennials, frugality, stability, social events, family

(continued)

Potential Quotes:

1. According to Culp, "People who couldn't pay their bills went to 'Debtor's Prison.' People who were destitute went to live at the 'County Farm' and worked for their keep."

2. Culp points out that "Meditators learned to share, make do with the resources that were available to them, or do without. Stability is important to this generation because of the upheaval and instability that were experienced during the Great Depression and WW II."

3. Culp notes, "Boomers were raised in big families, were educated in big classrooms, and learned to be a part of teams."

4. As Culp points out, "Due largely to their smaller family size and the independence developed during the latch-key years, this generation [Generation X] is not motivated by working with other people."

5. Culp claims that "Millennials are sociable, optimistic, talented, and well-educated. They've always felt sought after, needed, and indispensable."

Alex reads three more articles and prepares an information sheet for each of the articles he reads. These sheets will help him remember the key information from the articles as he prepares his essay. (Those information sheets are not shown here.)

Developing Your Essay

After reading his sources and completing information sheets, Alex is ready to start the writing process. The following steps guide him through the process of using the reading as a springboard for planning and composing his own essay.

1. Synthesize Your Sources

For many college reading and writing assignments, you will have to use more than one source. One way to compare sources is to create an **issues chart**—a chart that lists all the problems or concerns about the topic raised in a source. Issues are generally phrased as questions. Alex first identifies the issues posed in the four articles he has read and then creates a chart to compare them.

Identifying Issues.   As Alex reads and annotates the articles, he thinks about the issues the writers discuss. For example, Alex notices that for each generation being discussed, Culp mentions the issue of teamwork versus individualized work. Thus, one issue Alex writes down is "teamwork." He also notices that each generation's values are discussed, so he will include "values" as one of the issues that is important in this article. He turns each issue into a question:

- Teamwork: How do members of a generation view teamwork?

- Values: What does the generation value?

Eventually, Alex identifies four issues in all his source texts.

Completing the Issues Chart. One way to make an issues chart is to follow Alex's example:

- On paper or on your computer, create a table. Include enough rows for all the issues you have identified and a column for each source.
- List the issues in the first column at the far left. State each issue as a question.
- List one source at the top of each remaining column.
- In the body of the chart, make a note about whether the issue was "covered" or "not covered" in the source. Not all sources will cover all issues.

Alex's chart shows the issues he discovered in all four of the readings. (You will be familiar with only those from the first reading, since we have not seen the other articles Alex has read.) Look at Alex's issues chart to see how he listed all the issues and then noted the articles that address each issue.

Once he finishes his chart, Alex can tell which sources deal with which issues. He can use this information to find sources for his essay.

ALEX'S ISSUES CHART				
Issues	**Source 1**	**Source 2**	**Source 3**	**Source 4**
	"Understanding Generational Differences" by Ken Culp, III	"Generation X and Baby Boomers Conflict over Money" by Macy K. Levine	"Was There a 'Greatest Generation?'" by Jack Wright-Bartberry	"Millennials in the Work Place" by Brenda Kimkillen
Teamwork: How do members of this generation view teamwork?	covered	covered	not covered	covered
Values: What does the generation value?	covered	covered	not covered	not covered
Conflicts: What conflicts can arise when the generations come together?	not covered	covered	not covered	covered
Events: What historical events shape generations?	covered	not covered	covered	not covered

Let's say that Alex is going to write about the first issue—teamwork. He has identified three articles that cover this information, so he can go to those three articles and use them in his essay.

When you are working with more than one source, it is easy to forget what issues each source covers. An issues chart will help you keep the ideas straight.

2. Prewrite to Develop Your Ideas

Even if you think you know what you want to write about, use a prewriting process to make sure your ideas meet the assignment's instructions. Follow these steps.

Review the Assignment.   To make sure his essay meets assignment requirements, Alex goes back to the assignment. He annotates additional information in his assignment. Using the assignment instructions and his annotations, Alex creates a "self-assessment list," a column of questions he can use to make sure his essay meets the assignment requirements.

Alex's Self-Assessment List

Alex's Assignment

Next, write an original, informative essay in which you use the information from at least one of the sources you have read. In your essay, discuss three ways in which two of the generations might conflict. Limit your discussion to how they may conflict in a certain environment: at home, in the workplace, or in college. Give credit to the source when you use its ideas or when you use quotations from it.

Use a complete writing process to generate drafts and to revise and edit your work. Format your paper correctly and submit it.

-Do I give credit to the article when I use its ideas or quote from it?

-Do I use a complete writing process?

-Have I formatted my paper correctly and submitted it?

Essay Self-Assessment List

-Is the essay original?

-Is the essay informative?

-Do I use at least one reading's information in my essay?

-Do I discuss three ways these generations might conflict?

-Do I limit the discussion to a certain environment?

Select a Topic.   To select a topic, Alex uses the issues chart he created. He asks himself, *What environment would show conflicts in the generations' approaches to teamwork and values?* He lists the environments and decides on one, which he circles.

Family life?   Politics?

School?   Sports?

Social settings?   Arts?

(Workplace?)

Alex must also identify two generations to compare. To narrow the list of generations discussed in the readings, Alex does some additional listing:

Civics - interesting from a historical point of view, but I don't know anyone personally in this generation.

Meditating, or Silent, Generation - My grandparents weren't born in the U.S., so I'm not sure how much they have in common with others in their generation. There probably aren't many of these people left in the workforce.

(continued)

> Baby Boomers - My parents' generation, so I've seen how they act socially.
> Don't know many details about their work lives. Most of their friends are
> retiring by now.
>
> Generation X - My sister is Gen-X, so I know a lot about how she and her
> friends view teamwork. Also, I have to work with a lot of Gen-Xers.
>
> Millennials - I'm a Millennial, and I know a lot of stories about how people
> my age work together.

Alex decides that since he knows Millennials and Generation Xers the best, he would like to write on the possible conflicts between those generations in the workplace.

Use a Prewriting Method to Generate Ideas.   Once he selects a topic—Gen-Xers and Millennials in the workplace—Alex uses a simple list to jot down as many ideas about the topic as he can. Without censoring his thoughts, Alex writes down as many ideas as he can. Alex first lists workplace issues and circles some items to explore:

> Gen-Xers and Millennials in the workplace
>
> (Teamwork)   (Decision making)
>
> Punctuality   Learning new skills
>
> Taking responsibility   Flexibility
>
> (Dealing with those in authority)   Communication skills
>
>   Problem solving

For your project, you can use any of these methods shown in "Prewriting Strategies" to come up with ideas.

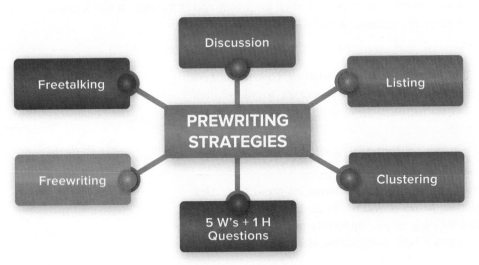

3. Construct a Thesis Statement

After Alex generates ideas, he determines what his main idea will be. He asks, *What is the main point I wish to communicate to my readers?*

To express his main point, he composes a thesis statement. He makes sure his thesis statement is a complete sentence that combines his topic and his point of view about the topic. This statement will help readers accurately predict the content of his essay.

When he composes his thesis statement, he keeps in mind the features listed in "Characteristics of a Thesis Statement."

CHARACTERISTICS OF A THESIS STATEMENT
A Thesis Statement ...

Expresses the most important point in an essay.	• The thesis statement tells readers the exact point the writer hopes readers will remember or believe.
Presents an idea that requires support.	• The thesis statement makes a point that needs to be explained further or backed up with evidence.
Expresses the broadest idea in the essay.	• The thesis sentence includes the ideas presented in the essay's paragraphs.
Is a statement, not a question.	• The idea or opinion in the thesis statement demands explanation, evidence, or discussion in the essay.

Alex thinks about whether his thesis statement will be open or closed. A closed thesis lists the major supporting points. Here are two examples for an essay on an environmental issue.

Open thesis statement: The environmental issue that must be prioritized is the global water crisis.

Closed thesis statement: The environmental issue that must be prioritized is the global water crisis because of the effects water has on the economy, our lifestyles, and our health.

Alex decides to write a closed thesis statement: *In the workplace, Generation Xers and Millennials may have conflicts over decision-making processes, teamwork, and accepting authority.*

4. Develop Support for Your Thesis Statement

Alex's thesis statement lists the main issues he identified during his prewriting. Alex makes these issues the major supporting points he will use to structure his essay.

He writes a complete sentence for each major supporting point. These are the topic sentences he will use for his essay's body paragraphs. Here are Alex's major supporting points.

- One area in which Generation Xers and Millennials might experience conflict is the decision-making processes used in the workplace.
- Another area that might be a problem for Generation Xers and Millennials in the workplace is teamwork.
- Finally, these two generations may differ in the way they view and accept authority.

Now that Alex has major supporting points, he can go on to identify details that he can use to support these points.

Think about Text Patterns You Can Use. Alex thinks about which *text patterns* might work to communicate the information. He considers each text pattern and fills in the following chart as he thinks of ideas.

Text Pattern	Examples
Narration	I could tell stories (short anecdotes) to illustrate how these two generations may come into conflict.
Definition	I will need to define each generation. I might do this in the introduction paragraph.
Illustration	I could present examples to show how these generations differ in the three areas in my thesis statement.
Classification	I will use classification when I discuss the characteristics of each generation.
Comparison-contrast	In the body paragraphs, I will need to compare and contrast how each generation reacts to the three areas in my thesis statement.
Cause and effect	The body paragraphs will be explaining why (the causes) these generations come into conflict.
Process analysis	I probably won't use this text pattern, but I could try to discuss the thinking processes of each generation and how those processes may lead to conflicts.

Determine How You Will Use Information from Your Sources. Some of the information Alex presents to readers will come from the sources he read and the information sheets he created. You can use source information in a few ways.

- **Summaries.** If summarizing a source or a part of a source is an appropriate way to support one of your ideas, you can use the brief source summaries you wrote.
- **Quotations.** Take a look at the quotes you copied onto your information sheets. If these quotes are not the best ones to use, go back to the sources and look at your annotations. You will probably find source material easily if you have made good annotations. Be sure to follow the rules for integrating quoted material.
- **Paraphrased ideas.** You can use ideas from sources rewritten in your own words as long as you give credit to the source's author. Follow the rules discussed later in this chapter for giving credit to sources.

5. Create an Outline to Organize Your Essay

Alex first determines the order in which he will present his ideas. Writers often choose from these three possibilities.

- **Order of importance.** Present the most important major supporting point first—or last.

- **Chronological or sequential order.** Present what happened first, second, and so on in order.

- **Spatial order.** Start with one location, say, the home, and move to locations that are farther away—the neighborhood, the school, the city.

Next, Alex makes an enhanced outline that lists the most important parts of his essay: the thesis statement, major supporting points, and supporting details. He uses complete sentences for the thesis statement and the major supporting points. Alex places his ideas in the outline in the order that he has chosen for his essay.

Notice Alex's outline. You can use the same format when you create an outline, varying the number of paragraphs to accommodate your supporting points.

Alex's Enhanced Outline of His Essay

Enhanced Essay Outline

Topic: Generation X and Millennials in the Workplace

Thesis statement: In the workplace, Generation Xers and Millennials may have conflicts over decision-making processes, teamwork, and accepting authority.

Introduction *(Put thesis statement in introduction.)*

Paragraph 1: Introduction ideas: In the intro, I'll define these two generations before getting to my thesis statement.

Body

Paragraph 2: First major supporting point. One area in which Generation Xers and Millennials might experience conflict is the decision-making processes used in the workplace.

- Supporting detail: Gen X reaction to decisions that come from authorities (not collaborative)
- Supporting detail: Millennial reaction to decisions that come from authorities
- Supporting detail: quote from Culp
- Supporting detail: hypothetical example

Paragraph 3: Second major supporting point. Another area that might be a problem for Generation Xers and Millennials in the workplace is teamwork.

- Supporting detail: Gen Xer reaction to teamwork
- Supporting detail: Millennial reaction to teamwork
- Supporting detail: real-life example from my workplace
- Supporting detail: quote: "Unlike the previous generation, the words 'committee' and 'teamwork' have strong negative connotations' (Culp).

Paragraph 4: Third major supporting point. Finally, these two generations may differ in the way they view and accept authority.

- Supporting detail: Real world example of how Gen Xers view authority (from source)
- Supporting detail: How Gen Xers view authority

(continued)

- Supporting detail: *How Millennials view authority*
- Supporting detail: *Explain the thinking processes for both groups*

Conclusion

Paragraph 5: *I want to end my essay talking about how these two generations can get along. They have some things in common.*

6. Add Source Materials to Your Outline

Notice that Alex has added source materials to his outline. He decided where to use ideas from his sources and made notes on his outline. When he copied and pasted a quote into his outline, he made sure to include the writer's name in parentheses.

Alex also included MLA style citations. If he were using APA style, he would also need to know the date of the source and the page number, if available, like this: (Williams, 2006, p. 15).

7. Write a Complete Draft of Your Essay

At this point in the writing process, Alex has done a substantial amount of work. Now he is ready to follow these steps to draft his actual essay.

Keep the Audience in Mind.   A writer's best tool is to imagine having a conversation with a smart person who disagrees with—or does not understand—the writer's ideas. Alex tries to word his essay so that any reader could understand his thoughts.

Alex also keeps an audience in mind so that he knows how much explanation he should offer. For example, since readers may not know the defining features of Generation X or the Millennials, he will provide that information.

Write an Introduction Paragraph.   The introduction can be a great place to provide background information. Alex, like many students, finds it comfortable to use a single paragraph to introduce the topic and to present the thesis statement. This method is fine, and in fact many professors prefer that you organize your essay in this way.

He can start his introduction with any of the methods shown in "Strategies for Essay Introductions."

STRATEGIES FOR ESSAY INTRODUCTIONS

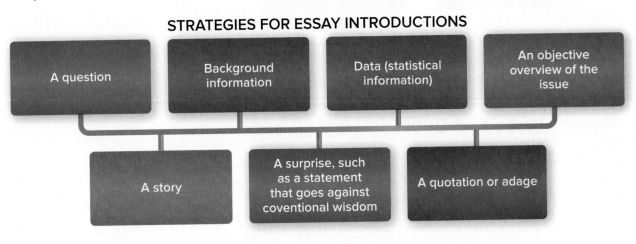

Alex chooses an introduction method and starts to write the first paragraph. He knows that if he feels stuck, he can skip the introduction, write his body paragraphs, and then write the introduction afterward. Sometimes writers find it easier to write the introduction after they have already composed the body of an essay.

Write Body Paragraphs According to Your Outline.   Alex now starts to write his body paragraphs in carefully constructed sentences. As he drafts his essay, he uses the following strategies.

- **He follows his outline, but he is also flexible.** For example, suppose he plans to use only one sentence to present an explanation, but once he starts writing, he finds that it would be easier for readers to understand if he uses two sentences. He can decide to use two sentences.
- **He rereads his work frequently.** When Alex finishes a paragraph or reaches a spot where the ideas stop flowing, he returns to the beginning of his essay or to a previous paragraph and rereads what he has written. A good writing strategy is to constantly reread your writing, not always from the very beginning, but at least from the last paragraph you wrote. Writers find many opportunities to revise by doing this, and they also find grammatical and mechanical mistakes to fix along the way.
- **When he gets stuck, he takes a break or tries something different.** Some strategies that can help are to write paragraphs out of order, reread your outline or prewriting, get feedback from a friend, or read your work aloud.

End with an Effective Conclusion.   Alex wants to makes sure his conclusion paragraph gives readers a sense of closure. He knows he can choose from several approaches, as shown in "Strategies for Essay Conclusions."

STRATEGIES FOR ESSAY CONCLUSIONS

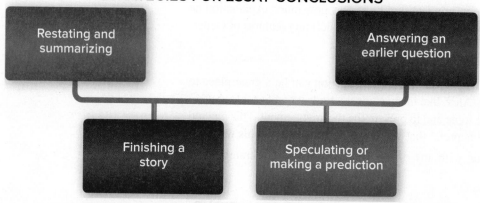

Create a Title.   After writing his conclusion, Alex chooses a short, descriptive title for his essay—"Generation X and Millennials in the Workplace." His title is short and straightforward; it tells the reader what his essay is about.

8. Integrate Ideas and Quotes from Sources Correctly

Since Alex took careful notes, he can easily distinguish his ideas from the ideas he found in sources. He knows that to use sources ethically, he must let readers know which information came from him and which came from source materials. When Alex is unsure whether to reference a source, he always gives credit. The following paragraph illustrates the guidelines for correctly integrating ideas from sources.

The first sentence is the student's words and ideas. When the student uses a direct quote, he gives credit to the source (Culp).	Finally, these two generations may differ in the way they view and accept authority. For example, a newly hired Millennial was working at a law firm when upper management released a new, strict dress code memo. The young employee did not agree with the ideas in the dress code and believed she had a right to be heard. She voiced her complaints and said she refused to comply with the dress code. The next day, her Generation X boss fired her (Levine). This story illustrates a difference in the way Generation Xers and Millennials view authority. Because Generation Xers are "motivated by personal benefits" according to Culp, Xers may be less likely to question authority if doing so could put their jobs in jeopardy. Millennials, on the other hand, are called "Generation 'Why?'" because they want to know the rationale behind decisions (Culp). As a result, they may be more likely to question authority.	The example comes from a source. The student puts the example in his own words, so he does not use quotation marks. He gives credit to the source (an article by Macy K. Levine) at the end of the sentence. The last piece of information also comes from Culp, so the student uses a parenthetical reference to give credit.

When you use source materials, integrate them grammatically so that they work with your words to form complete sentences. The improper integration of quotations can result in a comma splice or run-on sentence. Remember that a comma cannot join a sentence in quotation marks to another sentence.

Comma splice error: Mark Miller explains that the struggle to find clean water will be the issue that defines the next twenty years, "We are focused on energy production, but water will be the issue on which our lives will depend."

Correct: Mark Miller explains that the struggle to find clean water will be the issue that defines the next twenty years: "We are focused on energy production, but water will be the issue on which our lives will depend."

Run-on error: Mark Miller explains that the struggle to find clean water will be the issue that defines the next twenty years "We are focused on energy production, but water will be the issue on which our lives will depend."

Correct: Mark Miller explains that the struggle to find clean water will be the issue that defines the next twenty years: "We are focused on energy production, but water will be the issue on which our lives will depend."

In addition to avoiding comma splice and run-on errors, when possible, use short attributive tags such as "Miller says" or "Miller notes" to show where the quotes came from.

Quotation lacking an introduction: It is dangerous for people to merely hope the water problem will go away. "Not everyone is ready to face the issue" (Miller).

Better: It is dangerous for people to merely hope the water problem will go away. As Miller notes, "Not everyone is ready to face the issue."

To introduce quotations and the ideas of others, use key words such as these:

argues	notes	says	suggests
contends	points out	states	writes
explains	replies		

As always, make sure you give credit to any idea or quote you have used from a source.

Finishing Your Assignment

Because Alex allowed himself enough time for this project, he has several days to set his essay aside and let it rest. Writers find that after setting aside their work several days, they can read it more objectively and find areas to improve.

Alex takes the time to print a copy of his essay. Many writers find that reading and marking their essays on a paper copy helps them to see errors or problems that would not otherwise be obvious. When Alex rereads his work, he sees ideas that need revision and grammatical errors that must be corrected. He follows these steps to revise and edit his essay.

1. Check That You Have Met Assignment Requirements

Before doing anything else, Alex takes out his assignment, his notes, and his self-assessment list. He checks to make sure his essay meets every requirement and revises it as needed.

2. Revise for Organization and Unity

Sometimes in the process of revising a draft, writers realize that the elements should be rearranged. As he rereads his essay, Alex notes how and where his essay may need organizational changes. He makes sure each part of his essay is in its proper place.

A unified essay is one whose ideas all fit together to support the thesis statement. Alex asks himself the questions in "Checklist: Revising for Unity."

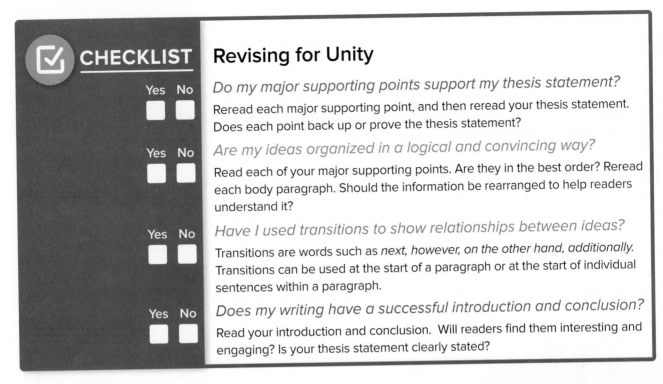

CHECKLIST

Revising for Unity

Do my major supporting points support my thesis statement?

Yes ☐ No ☐

Reread each major supporting point, and then reread your thesis statement. Does each point back up or prove the thesis statement?

Are my ideas organized in a logical and convincing way?

Yes ☐ No ☐

Read each of your major supporting points. Are they in the best order? Reread each body paragraph. Should the information be rearranged to help readers understand it?

Have I used transitions to show relationships between ideas?

Yes ☐ No ☐

Transitions are words such as *next, however, on the other hand, additionally.* Transitions can be used at the start of a paragraph or at the start of individual sentences within a paragraph.

Does my writing have a successful introduction and conclusion?

Yes ☐ No ☐

Read your introduction and conclusion. Will readers find them interesting and engaging? Is your thesis statement clearly stated?

Alex rereads his essay to see if adding transitions or rearranging paragraphs will help create more unity in his writing and more effective organization of his ideas.

3. Revise for Development

Effective writers revise with their readers in mind. Alex makes sure his essay includes all the information his readers need to fully understand his ideas. He imagines that readers have never studied the ideas he is presenting. Then he asks himself the questions in "Checklist: Revising for Development."

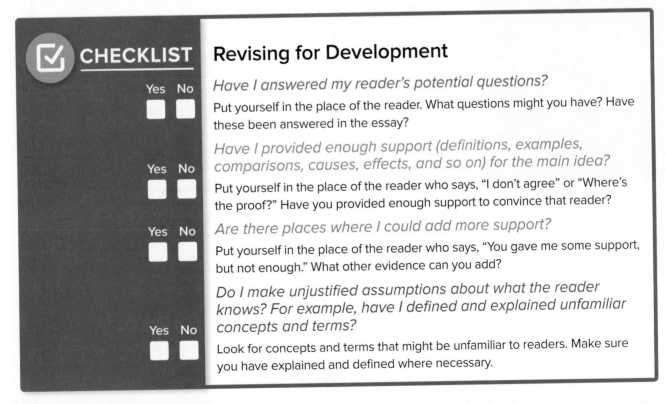

CHECKLIST

Revising for Development

Have I answered my reader's potential questions?

Yes ☐ No ☐

Put yourself in the place of the reader. What questions might you have? Have these been answered in the essay?

Have I provided enough support (definitions, examples, comparisons, causes, effects, and so on) for the main idea?

Yes ☐ No ☐

Put yourself in the place of the reader who says, "I don't agree" or "Where's the proof?" Have you provided enough support to convince that reader?

Are there places where I could add more support?

Yes ☐ No ☐

Put yourself in the place of the reader who says, "You gave me some support, but not enough." What other evidence can you add?

Do I make unjustified assumptions about what the reader knows? For example, have I defined and explained unfamiliar concepts and terms?

Yes ☐ No ☐

Look for concepts and terms that might be unfamiliar to readers. Make sure you have explained and defined where necessary.

If Alex finds areas that might need more explanation, he adds the explanation. For example, suppose an essay mentions *Flickr*. The writer may think readers know what *Flickr* is, but not everyone does. Providing an explanation for readers shows that the writer is aware of the audience's potential needs.

> **Example:** The use of *Flickr*, a Web site for uploading and sharing photos, can lead to some unintended consequences.

Many students ask classmates, lab instructors, tutors, or family members to read their papers and to write questions in the margin where they need more information. Students can then revise their papers to answer important questions that their readers identify.

4. Revise for Clarity

Often, sentences are unclear because writers do not fully figure out what they are trying to say before they write. Alex uses the revision strategy of reading each sentence out loud and asking himself the questions in "Checklist: Revising for Clarity."

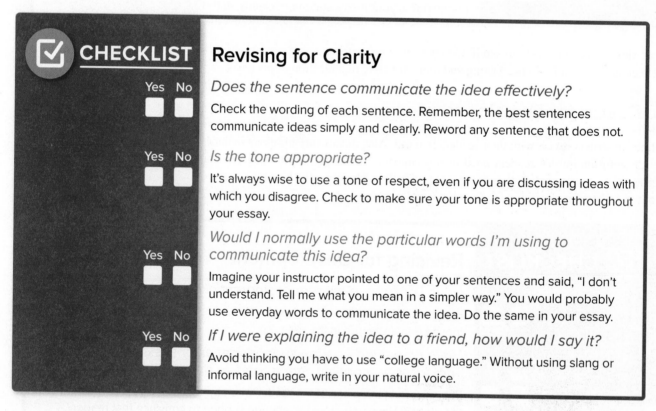

☑ CHECKLIST — Revising for Clarity

Yes No

Does the sentence communicate the idea effectively?

Check the wording of each sentence. Remember, the best sentences communicate ideas simply and clearly. Reword any sentence that does not.

Yes No

Is the tone appropriate?

It's always wise to use a tone of respect, even if you are discussing ideas with which you disagree. Check to make sure your tone is appropriate throughout your essay.

Yes No

Would I normally use the particular words I'm using to communicate this idea?

Imagine your instructor pointed to one of your sentences and said, "I don't understand. Tell me what you mean in a simpler way." You would probably use everyday words to communicate the idea. Do the same in your essay.

Yes No

If I were explaining the idea to a friend, how would I say it?

Avoid thinking you have to use "college language." Without using slang or informal language, write in your natural voice.

Another strategy is to find long, complex sentences and see if revising them makes the ideas clearer. To do this, list each separate on a sheet of paper. Once you know the ideas you wish to express, you can decide whether to use a single sentence for each idea or to use a variety of sentence types.

Unclear: Internet advertising is on some *Google* searches making them hard to understand what's the advertisement and what's the real link.

The ideas being expressed:

- Advertisements appear on *Google*.

- When a person searches, these ads come up.

- It can be hard to understand the search results because of these ads.

- It is difficult to figure out which information is a search result and which is an advertisement.

Once you have figured out the ideas you wish to express, you can combine sentences in an intentional way so that your idea is stated clearly.

Clear: When a person does a search on *Google*, Internet ads appear. Distinguishing the ads from the actual search results can be difficult.

Remember that a writer's first job is to communicate clearly. If a short sentence with simple words helps to communicate an idea clearly, use it! Do not make sentences overly complex or include words from a thesaurus to impress readers.

5. Create a Works Cited or References List

Since Alex uses sources in his essay, he must create documentation for his sources. He goes through his essay and lists all the sources he uses. Alex's assignment specifies MLA (Modern Language Association) format, so Alex creates a works cited list of his sources. If his assignment had called for APA (American Psychological Association) format, he would have created a list of references for his sources.

6. Check for Plagiarism

Alex is aware that every time he uses an idea from someone else—whether he puts the idea into his own words or quotes directly—he must give credit to the source, both in the text of his essay and in a works cited or references list. If he does not give credit properly, he will be plagiarizing.

Double-check your paper to make sure you have avoided plagiarism. Print a copy of your essay and follow these steps to check whether you have integrated and credited sources correctly:

1. Highlight each idea in your paper that came from a source, whether you put the idea in your own words or quoted it.
2. Check to see that you have given credit to the source, either by mentioning the source in the sentence or by using a parenthetical reference.
3. Check that each source appears as a properly formatted entry in your works cited or references list.
4. Make sure that each time you used a quote or an attributive tag (for example, ". . . said Wilson"), you did so in a way that is grammatically correct. If you do not integrate quotes correctly, you can end up with comma splices, run-on sentences, or sentence fragments.

7. Edit Your Essay Using SMART TRACS

Editing consists of checking written work for grammatical and mechanical errors. Alex uses the spell-checker on his computer, and he also uses a grammar-checker. He is aware, though, that both grammar-checkers and spell-checkers have their limitations; he is ultimately responsible for the correctness of his paper.

Many students know their grammatical and mechanical strengths and weaknesses. If you know you tend to confuse *affect* and *effect*, take the time to go back through your paper and check each usage of those words. If you have a tendency to make subject-verb agreement errors, check each and every subject-verb relationship and make changes where necessary. If you are not sure whether your paper is grammatically and mechanically sound, spend time with a lab instructor or tutor. While this person may not show you every error in your paper, he or she can tell you whether your paper needs significant editing and can help you identify the types of errors you are making. Taking the time to enlist the help of others can make a difference in the grade you earn.

Alex uses "SMART TRACS" guidelines to edit his paper. He consults with a tutor or writing center instructor when he has questions.

BRIEF GUIDE TO SMART TRACS

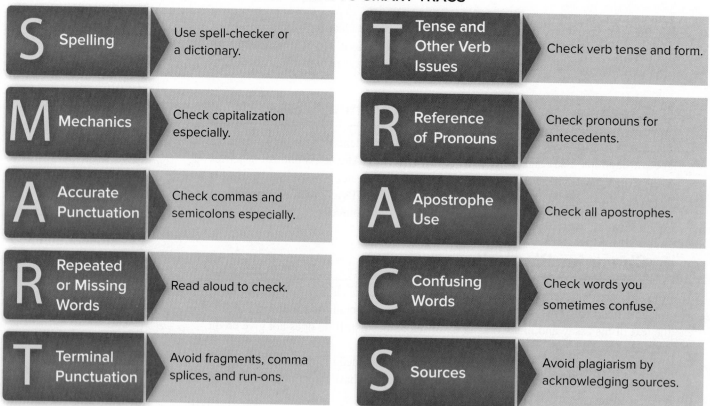

S Spelling — Use spell-checker or a dictionary.

M Mechanics — Check capitalization especially.

A Accurate Punctuation — Check commas and semicolons especially.

R Repeated or Missing Words — Read aloud to check.

T Terminal Punctuation — Avoid fragments, comma splices, and run-ons.

T Tense and Other Verb Issues — Check verb tense and form.

R Reference of Pronouns — Check pronouns for antecedents.

A Apostrophe Use — Check all apostrophes.

C Confusing Words — Check words you sometimes confuse.

S Sources — Avoid plagiarism by acknowledging sources.

8. Put Your Essay in the Proper Format

For this assignment, Alex's instructor wants him to follow MLA publication style for his essay. Alex makes sure his paper layout, heading, header, font type and size, and spacing all conform to this instructor's requirements. (Other instructors sometimes ask for APA publication style.)

If you are not sure about the style requirements, ask. Do not use a binder for your paper unless your instructor tells you to do so.

You have probably been saving your work throughout this process, but as you finish your work, be certain to save a digital copy of your corrected paper. Use a filename you will recognize if you need to search for your paper again. One of the most secure ways to save an electronic file is to use a free "cloud" account from a site such as *Dropbox* or *Google*. You can save your paper to your account and access it from anywhere. Always keep both a saved electronic copy and a hard copy (printout) of your work.

Here is Alex's completed essay.

Model Student Paper: "Generation X and Millennials in the Workplace" by Alex Martin

Martin 1

Alex Martin

Mrs. Sutter

English 0300

7 November 2017

Generation X and Millennials in the Workplace

In today's workplace, it is common to find two generations working alongside each other. Members of Generation X (sometimes called "Gen Xers" or just "Xers") were born between 1965 and 1981, according to Ken Culp. Members of the Millennial generation, explains Culp, were born between 1982 and 2001. Xers are in their prime working years, and Millennials have now entered the workplace and must work alongside Xers. Culp points out that Generation X values independence, family, and balance. As a generation, Xers grew to value individualism, privacy, and doing what is best for themselves as individuals (Culp). Millennials are cynical, questioning, less prejudiced, and more global in their thinking. Millennials value collaboration and open-mindedness, and they are high-achievers (Culp). These generational differences may cause some conflicts to arise. In the workplace, Generation Xers and Millennials may have conflicts over decision-making processes, teamwork, and accepting authority.

One area in which Generation Xers and Millennials might experience conflict is the decision-making processes used in the workplace. Bosses and managers make decisions, and the people who report to them do not question these decisions. Xers may be more used to this kind of decision-making process than Millennials, according to Macy K. Levine. Millennials are used to working collaboratively, and they are used to having their voices heard. As Culp points out, Millennials have "always felt sought after, needed, and indispensable." Millennials may not like accepting decisions from on high without having a chance to offer their input. For example, Sarah, a twenty-five-year-old sales manager, was outraged when upper management sent out a memo specifying a new dress code. Since the dress code would directly affect her, she believed that she had a right to express her opinion on it. Her Generation X supervisor disagreed and said, "You don't get to make the decisions around here. When you've paid your dues and climbed the ladder, then you may get a say in how things go." This kind of conflict can be explained by generational differences in thinking.

Another area that might be a problem for Generation Xers and Millennials in the workplace is teamwork. "Unlike the previous generation, the words 'committee' and 'teamwork' have strong negative connotations" for Gen Xers (Culp). Millennials, on the other hand, like to work collaboratively, Culp notes. They were raised in a time when "competition was no longer seen as being healthy for the development of youth" (Culp). These two ways of thinking about teamwork recently resulted in conflict for the employees of an upscale restaurant. Gen X waiters wanted to keep the tips they individually earned; Millennial waiters wanted everyone to pool the tips and split them equally. The Millennial waiters said they would be motivated to provide good service if they knew the wait staff were working as a team, whereas Xers were more motivated to work competitively. Again, this kind of conflict can be traced to generational differences.

Finally, these two generations may differ in the way they view and accept authority. Generation Xers may more easily accept authority if doing so helps them to achieve their personal agendas. Culp writes, "Gen Xers are strongly individualistic and are motivated by personal benefits."

Martin 3

On the other hand, Millennials may have more direct conflicts with authority because they are "civic-minded and socially engaged, and are motivated by a desire to change the world" (Culp). Since they are motivated by social change, Millennials may be more likely to question authority if they disagree with the authority's values (Levine). For example, if a company makes a decision that conflicts with a Millennial's value, the Millennial may feel compelled to speak up and voice disagreement. A Gen Xer may reason that what the company does is its problem, not his. An Xer may not feel as socially compelled to disagree as a Millennial.

Of course, within any generation there are people who do not fit the stereotypes of their generation. Nevertheless, studying generational differences can help employers and employees work out solutions to conflicts. By thinking carefully about how someone in a different generation might react to a new policy or a collaborative assignment, workers can come up with creative solutions to help generations get along. After all, although the generations are all different, as human beings, they also share many similar values, such as the desire for a happy and productive workplace. Focusing on these shared values can help employees make sacrifices and get along better.

Martin 4

Works Cited

Culp, Ken, III. *Understanding Generational Differences.* U of Kentucky
    Cooperative Extension, Mar. 2011.

Levine, Macy K. "Generation X and Baby Boomers Conflict over
    Money." *Trinity-Mason News*, 13 May 2017, p. A15.

Project 1: Working with a Text to Create a Summary

Mindsets

Now that you've followed Alex step-by-step through his integrated reading and writing project, here is an integrated reading and writing project for you to complete. If you have trouble with any particular step, you can review Alex's example in "Step-by-Step Guidance for Integrated Reading and Writing Projects" for help.

If you have ever studied a long chapter in a textbook, you know how difficult it is to remember everything in the chapter at test time. One method students use to learn the information in long chapters is to make lists of important terms, dates, definitions, and so on, and to memorize those elements. This is a good strategy for learning about the particular details in a text.

But what about the major themes and ideas? What if your instructor asks you to compare an idea at the beginning of the chapter with an idea at the end of the chapter? For example, a chapter in an environmental science book may begin with a presentation of the water cycle—the way water evaporates and eventually becomes rain, falling to the earth again. The same chapter may end with a discussion of the effects of global warming. An exam may ask students to explain the connections between the water cycle and global warming. To be able to explain the connections, you will need to have studied both particular details and the major ideas presented in the text.

©Ion Chiosea/123RF RF

Psychologists study the mind, especially human behaviors. What can we learn about ourselves from the work of psychologists?

To understand how the details connect to the major ideas in a text, you might find it helpful to write a summary. A summary is a shortened version of the source. It contains, in your own words, the main idea of the text—its thesis statement —and the major supporting points that develop the thesis statement. A summary also includes some of the important supporting details used to develop the major supporting points. Because the purpose of a summary is to provide a brief, objective overview of a text, when you write a summary, resist the temptation to add your own views on the topic or text.

For this project, you will read a text carefully and write an accurate summary. The readings in this project will concern mindsets—the beliefs we have about ourselves and our abilities—and their effects on our lives.

Getting Started

Follow these steps to get started on your reading and writing assignment.

1. Analyze Your Assignment

Read and annotate your assignment.

A Reading and Writing Assignment	YOUR ANNOTATIONS
Your assignment is to use an effective reading and writing process to write an accurate summary of a selection about psychological constraints. Your summary should include the reading's main idea (thesis statement), its major supporting points, and any significant supporting details. Your summary should be based on an enhanced outline you prepare for the reading. Finally, your summary should be written in standard English, be free from grammatical, spelling, and formatting errors, and conform to MLA or APA style.	

2. Identify Your Purpose

Recognize why you are reading the project texts. Write your purpose here.

My purpose: _____

Working with Readings

Use the steps that follow to read the source carefully and critically.

SOURCE "Psychological Constraints"

1. Preview the Reading and Think about the Topic

Jot down your notes for the Preview, Predict, Recall, and Ask strategies. For help, with these strategies, see "Step-by-Step Guidance for Integrated Reading and Writing Projects."

2. Read and Annotate the Text

Read "About the Author." Then read and annotate the reading selection. You may need to read the selection more than once.

About the Author. Laura King, who has a PhD in psychology, holds the Frederick A. Middlebush chair in psychology at the University of Missouri–Columbia. She teaches seminars in social psychology, personality psychology, and the development of character. Her research has been published in a number of journals, including *American Psychologist,* the *Journal of Personality and Social Psychology, Personality and Social Psychology Bulletin, Cognition and Emotion,* and the *Journal of Personality.* "Psychological Constraints" is taken from Laura King's text *Experience Psychology* (McGraw-Hill, 2013, pp. 196–98).

Psychological Constraints

By Laura King

YOUR ANNOTATIONS

Are there psychological constraints on learning? For animals, the answer is probably no. For humans, the answer may well be yes. Consider the claim that fish cannot ski. The truth of this statement is clear. Biological circumstances make it impossible. If we put biological considerations aside, we might ask ourselves about times in our lives when we felt like fish trying to ski—when we felt that we just do not have what it takes to learn a skill or master a task.

Carol Dweck uses the term *mindset* to describe why our beliefs about ability dictate what goals we set for ourselves, what we think we can learn, and ultimately what we do learn. Individuals have one of two mindsets: a fixed mindset, in which they believe that their qualities are carved in stone and cannot change; or a growth mindset, in which they believe their qualities can change and improve through effort. These two mindsets have implications for the meaning of failure. From a fixed mindset, failure means lack of ability. From a growth mindset, however, failure tells the person what he or she still needs to learn. Your mindset influences whether you will be optimistic or pessimistic, what your goals will be, how hard you will strive to reach those goals, and how successful you are in college and after.

Dweck studied first-year pre-med majors taking their first chemistry class in college. Students with a growth mindset got higher grades than those with a fixed mindset. Even when they did not do well on a test, the growth-mindset students bounced back on the next test. Fixed-mindset students typically read and re-read the text and class notes or tried to memorize everything verbatim. The fixed-mindset students who did poorly on tests concluded that chemistry and maybe pre-med were not for them. By contrast, growth-mindset students took charge of their motivation and learning, searching for themes and principles in the course and going over mistakes until they understood why they made them. In Dweck's analysis, "They were studying to learn, not just ace the test. And, actually, this is why they got higher grades—not because they were smarter or had a better background in science."

(continued)

Following are some effective strategies [from Dweck] for developing a growth mindset:

- Understand that your intelligence and thinking skills are not fixed but can change. Even if you are extremely bright, with effort you can increase your intelligence.

- Become passionate about learning and stretch your mind in challenging situations. It is easy to withdraw into a fixed mindset when the going gets tough; but as you bump up against obstacles, keep growing, work harder, stay the course, and improve your strategies; you will become a more successful person.

- Think about the growth mindsets of people you admire. Possibly you have a hero, someone who has achieved something extraordinary. You may have thought his or her accomplishments came easily because the person is so talented. However, find out more about this person and how he or she works and thinks. You likely will discover that much hard work and effort over a long period of time were responsible for his or her achievements.

- Begin now. If you have a fixed mindset, commit to changing now. Think about when, where, and how you will begin using your new growth mindset.

An early study on 5- to 7-year-old children demonstrated the power of these mindsets. When faced with math problems that were beyond their age level, the children responded quite differently, depending on their mindset. Children whose views reflected a fixed mindset were threatened by the difficult task, withdrew from it, and were more likely to criticize the task and put themselves down. In contrast, the children who revealed a growth mindset seemed energized by the challenging task. They remained focused and persisted in trying to solve the "impossible" problems.

Amazingly, some of them actually did—they achieved the impossible.

Dweck's work challenges us to consider the limits we place on our own learning. When we think of the relative absence of women and minorities in the math and science professions, we might consider the messages these groups have received about whether they have what it takes to succeed in these domains. Our beliefs about ability profoundly influence what we try to learn. As any 7-year-old with a growth mindset would tell you, you never know what you can do until you try.

Source: King, Laura A., *Experience Psychology*, 1st Edition. Copyright © 2010 McGraw-Hill Education. Used with permission of McGraw-Hill Education.

Check Your Comprehension of the Reading

Review your comprehension of the reading selection by answering the questions below. Use a separate sheet.

1. What is the difference between a fixed mindset and a growth mindset?

2. How does a person with a growth mindset deal with failure?

3. How important is this topic for general readers? How important is it for college students? Explain your answer.

4. Do most students already know what the writer has explained in this essay, or do you believe this would be new information for many students? Explain your answer.

5. Think about your mindset. Do you tend to have more of a fixed mindset or a growth mindset? Explain your answer.

3. Outline and Summarize the Reading

You will use the steps for writing a complete summary to summarize the reading: (1) Read and annotate the source. (2) Create an enhanced outline. (3) Start your summary with bibliographic information and the topic. (4) Present the text's main idea. (5) In body paragraphs, present major supporting points, supporting details, and additional explanatory information, if necessary. (6) Explain how the source resolves to bring your summary to an end.

Create an Enhanced Outline.   Since you have already read and annotated the reading selection, go on to the next step—creating an enhanced outline, using a separate sheet or computer document.

Your outline should follow the format shown in "Step-by-Step Guidance for Integrated Reading and Writing Projects." It should include your topic, your thesis statement, and major supporting points and supporting details for your introduction, body, and conclusion paragraphs.

Start Your Summary with Bibliographic Information and the Topic.
Write your introductory paragraph by starting with bibliographic information. Compose one to three sentences in which you provide information about the text you are summarizing. At the very least, provide the title of the article and the author's name. You may also include additional information that you believe will help readers gain a better understanding of the reading. Additional information might include that author's background, the type of source you are summarizing (book, article, editorial, etc.), and the date of its publication. Write your sentences here. Use additional sheets if necessary.

My introductory sentences:

_____

_____

Present the Text's Main Idea.   At the end of your introductory paragraph, write the text's main idea—its thesis statement—in your own words. When you put together your draft, this will be the last sentence of your introduction paragraph.

Text's main idea:

_____

_____

In Body Paragraphs, Present Major Supporting Points, Supporting Details and Additional Explanatory Information, If Necessary.

On your own paper or computer document, draft body paragraphs. Use these three steps to draft each body paragraph:

- **Present the writer's major supporting points.**
  Each body paragraph of your summary should present a single major supporting point. Put each major supporting point into your own words and use it as your topic sentence for a body paragraph. Be sure to signal to readers that you are writing a summary by using signal phrases like these:

  - Smith says that one reason for...

  - According to Smith, ...

- **Summarize supporting details for each major supporting point.**
  Look back at your enhanced outline and write about the supporting details the writer uses for each major supporting point. Always put the information into your own words.

- **Write additional sentences, if necessary, to explain the author's support.**
  Read over each paragraph. Add information such as explanations or definitions where readers may be confused.

Explain How the Source Ends to Bring Your Summary to an End.

Write a conclusion paragraph in which you bring the summary to an end by explaining how the original source ends. Use the space below to draft your conclusion paragraph.

My conclusion paragraph:

_____

_____

_____

_____

_____

_____

_____

_____

_____

4. Write a Complete Draft of Your Summary

Write a complete draft of your paper, using a word processor. Combine all of the parts of your summary—your introduction, body paragraphs, and conclusion—into a single document. Save your document, and then you can begin the final stages of the writing process.

Finishing Your Assignment

Use the remaining steps to finish your integrated reading and writing assignment.

1. Check That You Have Met Assignment Requirements

Reread your annotated assignment and create a self-assessment list. See Alex's example in "Step-by-Step Guidance for Integrated Reading and Writing Projects" if you need a refresher on how to do this.

A Reading and Writing Assignment	SELF-ASSESSMENT LIST
Your assignment is to use an effective reading and writing process to write an accurate summary of a reading about psychological constraints. Your summary should include the reading's main idea (thesis statement), its major supporting points, and any significant supporting details. Your summary should be based on an enhanced outline you prepare for the reading. Finally, your summary should be written in standard English, be free from grammatical, spelling, and formatting errors, and conform to MLA or APA style.	

Answer each question that you wrote about your assignment and then answer the following:

Have I met my assignment requirements?

Yes or no? _____

If your answer is no, make the necessary corrections to your draft.

2. Revise for Organization and Unity

As your read your draft, answer these questions: (1) Do my major supporting points support my thesis statement? (2) Are my ideas organized in a logical and convincing way? (3) Have I used transitions to show relationships between ideas? (4) Does my writing have a successful introduction and conclusion? See "Checklist: Revising for Unity" in "Step-by-Step Guidance for Integrated Reading and Writing Projects" for more help.

3. Revise for Development

As your read your draft, answer these questions: (1) Have I answered my reader's potential questions? (2) Have I provided enough support (definitions, examples, comparisons, causes, effects, and so on) for the main idea? (3) Are there places where I could add more support? (4) Do I make unjustified assumptions about what the reader knows? See "Checklist: Revising for Development" in "Step-by-Step Guidance for Integrated Reading and Writing Projects" for more help.

4. Revise for Clarity

As your read your draft aloud, answer these questions: (1) Does the sentence communicate the idea effectively? (2) Is the tone appropriate? (3) Would I normally use the particular words I'm using to communicate this idea? (4) If I were explaining the idea to a friend, how would I say it? See "Checklist: Revising for Clarity" in "Step-by-Step Guidance for Integrated Reading and Writing Projects" for more help.

5. Create a Works Cited or References List

Create a works cited or references list, and answer this question:

> *Is my documentation list correctly formatted?*

Yes or no? _____

If you are unsure or you answer no, ask your instructor or tutor for help.

6. Check for Plagiarism

Since you are summarizing a source, you must be sure to regularly give credit to the writer for the ideas in your summary. You can do this easily by using signal phrases such as "Smith says" and "According to Smith." Signal phrases remind the reader that the ideas are the source's, not yours. Double-check your essay and answer this question:

> *Have I used signal phrases often enough so that readers can tell they are reading a summary?*

Yes or no? _____

Add signal phrases where they are needed.

7. Edit Your Essay Using SMART TRACS

Use the "SMART TRACS" guidelines—**S**pelling, **M**echanics, **A**ccurate punctuation, **R**epeated or missing words, **T**erminal punctuation, **T**ense and other verb issues, **R**eference of pronouns, **A**postrophe use, **C**onfusing words, **S**ources—to edit your essay. See "Guidance for Integrated Reading and Writing Projects" for more help.

Correct any errors. List the types of errors that appear more than once in your essay.

Types of errors in my essay:

_____

_____

Make a point of learning how to correct these recurring errors.

Incorporate all of the changes you have made and write a final draft of your essay. Answer the following question:

Does this essay present my best work?

Yes or no? _____

If you answered no, do not stop working on your essay. Go back and work on it until you have created an essay you are proud of.

8. Put Your Essay in the Proper Format

Review your essay to make sure the following elements are correctly formatted: heading, header (and page numbers), spacing, margins, title, font type and size, quotations, and works cited or references list. Answer the following question:

Is my essay correctly formatted?

Yes or no? _____

If you answered no, make any needed corrections.

Turn In Your Completed Assignment

Congratulations! You have completed your integrated reading and writing assignment. Follow your instructor's guidelines for submitting your finished essay.

Project 2: Working with Informative Texts
Social Media—For Better or Worse

Many texts you encounter in college and in your career will be informative texts: they will provide important information about a subject or a task. As with all types of writing, to get the most from informative texts, you need to use critical reading skills. As a writer, you will sometimes be called on to create informative texts, and what you learn from your critical reading of informative sources will help you with that task.

For this project, you will examine four readings that present issues related to social media. Most people know about or have used *Facebook*, *Twitter*, *Flickr*, or another type of social media. Our culture has so quickly embraced social media that many users have not had time to think through the potential dangers of these forms of communication. Policy makers are scrambling to write privacy laws to protect the public, and advertisers are rushing to take advantage of the marketing opportunities afforded by *Facebook*, *YouTube*, and the like. Average users, meanwhile, are experimenting with these new communication technologies in a variety of ways—from finding romantic partners to sparking political protests—and quickly discovering new uses for them.

As you read the articles in this project, you will be prompted to learn about the positive and negative aspects of social media. Some of the issues you will read about may be new to you; others may be familiar. As you read, concentrate on gaining a broad understanding of why social media issues are worthy of our attention. After you have read the sources, you will have the opportunity to focus on a social media issue in an essay of your own.

Social media are a fact of life today. What impact are they having on society?

Getting Started

Follow these steps to get started on your reading and writing assignment.

1. Analyze Your Assignment

Read and annotate your assignment.

An Informative Reading and Writing Assignment	YOUR ANNOTATIONS
The primary purpose of informative writing is to provide readers with information in a clear and organized way. Your assignment is to find an aspect of social media about which readers need more information and to write an informative essay on that aspect.	

The primary purpose of informative writing is to provide readers with information in a clear and organized way. Your assignment is to find an aspect of social media about which readers need more information and to write an informative essay on that aspect.

You will select a social media concern you wish to communicate to readers. Keep in mind that the purpose of your essay is to present information, not to persuade readers about a particular point of view. You will not be writing your own argument about why we should take privacy more seriously, for example. Rather, your essay will simply present the major points readers should consider about the social media issue you select. Your essay will provide the information readers need to know about an issue and, if applicable, what some writers have suggested be done about it.

Finally, your essay should be written in standard English, be free from grammatical, spelling, and formatting errors, and conform to MLA or APA style.

2. Identify Your Purpose

Recognize why you are reading the project texts. Write your purpose here.

My purpose: _____

Working with Readings

Use the steps that follow to read the source carefully and critically.

SOURCE "Driven to Distraction: Our Wired Generation"

1. Preview the Reading and Think about the Topic

Preview the reading by looking over it and noticing the title, bold-faced words, repeated words, and headings. After you have previewed the reading, jot down your notes for the Preview, Predict, Recall, and Ask strategies. For help with these strategies, see "Step-by-Step Guidance for Integrated Reading and Writing Projects."

2. Read and Annotate the Text

Read "About the Author." Then read and annotate the reading selection. You may need to read the selection more than once.

About the Author. Larry Rosen is a professor of psychology at California State University and the author of five books on the "psychology of technology." He wrote *TechnoStress: Coping with Technology @WORK @HOME @PLAY* (1998); *Me, MySpace, and I: Parenting the Net Generation* (2007); and *The Mental Health Technology Bible* (1997).

"Driven to Distraction" was published in the *St. Paul Pioneer Press*, a newspaper in St. Paul, Minnesota, on November 12, 2012.

Driven to Distraction: Our Wired Generation

By Larry Rosen

A recent Pew Internet & American Life Project report surveyed 2,462 middle school and high school advanced placement and national writing project teachers and concluded that: "Overwhelming majorities agree with the assertions that today's digital technologies are creating an easily distracted generation with short attention spans and today's students are too 'plugged in' and need more time away from their digital technologies." Two-thirds of the respondents agree with the notion that today's digital technologies do more to distract students than to help them academically.

Mind you, we are talking about teachers who typically teach . . . students . . . we would generally think of as [not] highly distractible.

Recently my research team observed 263 middle school, high school and university students studying for a mere 15 minutes in their homes. We were interested in whether students could maintain focus and, if not, what might be distracting them. Every minute we noted exactly what they were doing, whether they were studying, if they were texting or listening to music or watching television in the background, and if they had a computer screen in front of them and what websites were being visited.

The results were startling considering that the students knew we were watching them and most likely assumed we were observing how well they were able to study. First, these students were only able to stay on task for an average of three to five minutes before losing their focus. Universally, their distractions came from technology, including: (1) having more devices available in their studying environment such as iPods, laptops and smartphones; (2) texting; and (3) accessing Facebook.

Other researchers have found similar attention spans among computer programmers and medical students, and in those studies technology provided the major sources of distraction.

We also looked at whether these distractors might predict who was a better student in general. Not surprisingly those who stayed on task longer and had well-developed study strategies were better students. The worst students were those who consumed more media each day and had a preference for switching back and forth between several tasks at the same time.

YOUR ANNOTATIONS

(continued)

One additional result stunned us: If the students checked Facebook just once during the 15-minute study period, they had a lower grade-point average. It didn't matter how many times they looked at Facebook; once was enough. Not only did social media negatively impact their temporary focus and attention, but it ultimately impacted their entire school performance.

So, what was going on with these students? We have asked thousands of students this exact question and they tell us that when alerted by a beep, a vibration, or a flashing image they feel compelled or drawn to attend to that stimulus. However, they also tell us that even without the sensory intrusions they are constantly being distracted internally by thoughts such as, "I wonder if anyone commented on my Facebook post" or "I wonder if my friend responded to the text message I sent five minutes ago" or even "I wonder what interesting new YouTube videos my friends have liked." Three-fourths of teens and young adults check their devices every 15 minutes or less and if not allowed to do so get highly anxious. And anxiety inhibits learning.

I am convinced that learning to live with both internal and external distractions is all about teaching the concept of focus. In psychology we refer to the ability to understand when you need to focus and when it is not necessary to do so as "metacognition," or knowing how your brain functions. In one recent study we found a perfect demonstration of metacognition, albeit totally by accident. In this study we showed a video in several psychology courses, which was followed by a graded test.

Students were told that we might be texting them during the videotape and to answer our text messages. In fact, one-third did not get a text message, one-third got four texts during the 30-minute video, and the other third got eight texts, enough, we guessed, to distract them and make them unable to concentrate on the video. One other wrinkle was that we timed the text messages to occur when important material was being shown on the videotape that was going to be tested later.

We were right that the students who got eight texts did worse—they averaged a "D" on the test—but the students who received four texts and the students who did not receive a text message during the video got a "C" on our test. However, a mistake in our instructions told us more about what was going on inside the students' heads when the text arrived. We told students to reply to our text messages, but we did not tell them when to reply. Those students who manifested a knee-jerk reaction to their vibrating phone and answered our texts immediately were the ones who got the lower test grades. Those few students who opted to wait a few minutes to respond got the highest scores in the class.

After the study, when asked why they did not respond immediately they told us that they were waiting for a time when the videotape material seemed less important and not likely to be on the test. Those students were using their metacognitive skills to decide when was a good time to be distracted and when it was important to focus.

How do we teach focus in a world that is constantly drawing our attention elsewhere? One strategy that we are using in classrooms around the world is called "technology breaks." Here's how it works: In many classrooms students are allowed to use their smartphones, tablets, or laptops as tools to search the Web, access social media, or perform other activities that promote learning. In

(continued)

such classrooms teachers often report that in between times that students are using their devices for schoolwork, they are checking their email and text messages, tweeting, or accessing social media.

A tech break starts with the teacher asking all students to check their texts, the Web, Facebook, whatever, for a minute and then turn the device on silent and place it upside down on the desk in plain sight and "focus" on classroom work for 15 minutes. The upside down device prohibits external distractions from vibrations and flashing alerts and provides a signal to the brain that there is no need to be internally distracted since an opportunity to "check in" will be coming soon.

At the end of the 15-minute focus time the teacher declares a tech break and the students take another minute to check in with their virtual worlds followed by more focus times and more tech breaks. The trick is to gradually lengthen the time between tech breaks to teach students how to focus for longer periods of time without being distracted. I have teachers using this in classrooms, parents using it at the dinner table or at a restaurant, and bosses using tech breaks during meetings with great success. So far, though, the best we can get is about 30 minutes of focus thanks to Steve Jobs (and others) for making such alluring, distracting technologies.

Technology is not going to disappear from our world and, in fact, it is only going to get more appealing as screens become sharper, video become clearer, and touch screens become the norm, all of which attract our sensory system and beckon us to pay attention to them rather than schoolwork or the people in front of us.

With more electronic social connections in our lives internal distractors are also increasing and tech breaks can be used to train the brain to focus without the worry and anxiety about what we might be missing in our virtual social world.

Source: Rosen, Larry D., "Driven to Distraction: Our Wired Generation." © 2012 Larry D. Rosen, Ph.D. Reprinted by permission of the author. From *St. Paul Pioneer Press*, November 12, 2012.

Check Your Comprehension of the Reading

Review your comprehension of the reading selection by answering the questions below. Use a separate sheet if necessary.

1. Rosen cites research in his article. Why does he cite this research? What role does it play in the article?

2. Who do you think is the intended audience? What does Rosen want readers to do after they read the article?

3. How important is this topic for general readers? How important is it for college students? Do you think people know enough about the effect of technology use on students? Explain your answer.

4. Do most students already know what the writer has explained in this essay, or do you believe this would be new information for many students? Explain your answer.

5. What does the writer imply about multitasking—doing more than one thing at the same time? Have you found the writer's point about multitasking to be true in your own life? Explain.

3. Outline and Summarize the Reading

On a separate sheet, outline the reading's main ideas, and write a brief summary of the reading.

4. Prepare an Information Sheet for the Reading

Using your annotations and the outline and summary you prepared for step 3, create an information sheet for this article that includes the following headings: *Author, Title, Publication Information, How I Might Use This Source, Brief Outline, Brief Summary, Key Words,* and *Potential Quotes.* See "Step-by-Step Guidance for Integrated Reading and Writing Projects" for more help.

SOURCE 2 "A Harsh Truth about Fake News: Some People Are Super Gullible"

1. Preview the Reading and Think about the Topic

Preview the reading by looking over it and noticing the title, words in bold type, repeated words, and headings. After you have previewed the reading, jot down your notes for the Preview, Predict, Recall, and Ask strategies. For help with these strategies, see "Step-by-Step Guidance for Integrated Reading and Writing Projects."

2. Read and Annotate the Text

Read "About the Author." Then read and annotate the reading selection. You may need to read the selection more than once.

About the Author.   Callum Borchers is part of *The Washington Post*'s news team that explores politics and media. Borchers has reported for *The Boston Globe* and was part of a team that earned a Pulitzer Prize for coverage of the Boston Marathon bombings. He is a graduate of Ithaca College and Northeastern University. "A Harsh Truth about Fake News: Some People Are Super Gullible" appeared in *The Washington Post* on December 5, 2016.

A Harsh Truth about Fake News: Some People Are Super Gullible

By Callum Borchers

YOUR ANNOTATIONS

Fake news is bad because lying is bad. But fake news is a *problem* because people believe it—or, at least, want to.

After all, it is wrong (factually and ethically) to publish false reports that Donald Trump earned Denzel Washington's endorsement and won the popular vote in the presidential election, but that kind of garbage wouldn't matter very much if everyone could recognize what rotting trash smells like—or, if they did, wanted to avoid it. Clearly they can't, or don't.

(continued)

A Stanford University study published Tuesday concluded that many students, from middle school through college, struggle to discern what is legitimate reporting and what is not. *The Wall Street Journal* summarized some of the most alarming findings:

> Some 82 percent of middle-schoolers couldn't distinguish between an ad labeled "sponsored content" and a real news story on a website. . . . More than two out of three middle-schoolers couldn't see any valid reason to mistrust a post written by a bank executive arguing that young adults need more financial-planning help.
>
> And nearly four in 10 high-school students believed, based on the headline, that a photo of deformed daisies on a photo-sharing site provided strong evidence of toxic conditions near the Fukushima Daiichi nuclear plant in Japan, even though no source or location was given for the photo.

Lest you think this kind of naiveté is unique to millennials, consider some of the fake news stories that have caught on in the general population recently. In October, a Twitter joke about an Ohio postal worker who was supposedly tearing up pro-Trump absentee ballots fooled Rush Limbaugh, Matt Drudge and Jim Hoft. A week before the election, Sean Hannity got taken in by a made-up report that President Obama, Michelle Obama and Elizabeth Warren had unfollowed Hillary Clinton on Twitter.

Some fabricated stories have been truly bizarre and wildly far-fetched yet have still duped people who read them—or at least, been embraced and used by some readers. *The New York Times* unspooled the way "dozens of made-up articles about Mrs. Clinton kidnapping, molesting and trafficking children" in the back rooms of a D.C. pizzeria called Comet Ping Pong gained traction.

> The misinformation campaign began when John Podesta's email account was hacked and his emails were published by WikiLeaks during the presidential campaign. Days before the election, users on the online message board 4Chan noticed that one of Mr. Podesta's leaked emails contained communications with [Comet Ping Pong owner James] Alefantis discussing a fund-raiser for Mrs. Clinton.
>
> The 4Chan users immediately speculated about the links between Comet Ping Pong and the Democratic Party. Some posited the restaurant was part of a larger Democratic child trafficking ring, which was a theory long held by some conservative blogs. That idea jumped to other social media services such as Twitter and Reddit, where it gained momentum on the page "The_Donald." A new Reddit discussion thread called "Pizzagate" quickly attracted 20,000 subscribers. . . .
>
> Soon, dozens of fake news articles on sites such as Facebook, Planet Free Will and Living Resistance emerged. Readers shared the stories in Saudi Arabia and on Turkish and other foreign language sites.

Some of the people who share fake news stories on social media surely know they are spreading fiction. They just like to imagine a world that conforms to their views. Or something.

(continued)

Others are genuinely conned, either because they don't know how to tell the difference between real and fake news or because they don't care to try. Deception may drive the creation of fake news; gullibility helps create a market for it.

Check Your Comprehension of the Reading

Review your comprehension of the reading selection by answering the questions below. Use a separate sheet.

1. What are the reasons the author gives for people believing fake news?

2. What was "pizzagate"?

3. How important is this topic for general readers? Explain your answer.

4. Why is fake news dangerous? Explain your answer.

5. What are some ways you can tell the difference between fake news and legitimate news? Explain your answer.

3. Outline and Summarize the Reading

On a separate sheet, outline the reading's main ideas, and write a brief summary of the reading.

4. Prepare an Information Sheet for the Reading

Using your annotations, the outline and summary you created in step 3, and the format shown for the first reading, create an information sheet for this article. Your information sheet should include the following headings: *Author, Title, Publication Information, How I Might Use This Source, Brief Outline, Brief Summary, Key Words,* and *Potential Quotes.* See "Step-by-Step Guidance for Integrated Reading and Writing Projects" for more help.

SOURCE 3 "The Bad, the Ugly, and the Good of Kids' Use of Social Media"

1. Preview the Reading and Think about the Topic

Jot down your notes for the Preview, Predict, Recall, and Ask strategies. For help with these strategies, see "Step-by-Step Guidance for Integrated Reading and Writing Projects."

2. Read and Annotate the Text

Read "About the Author." Then read and annotate the reading selection. You may need to read the selection more than once.

About the Author.   Jim Taylor holds a PhD in psychology and is an adjunct professor at the University of San Francisco. He has published twelve books and more than seven hundred articles and has appeared on NBC's *Today Show* and ABC's *World News This Weekend*, as well as on the Fox News Channel and a number of radio shows. His specialty is the psychology of business, sports, and parenting.

The following article appeared on May 28, 2013, in *The Power of Prime*, a blog written by Jim Taylor, on *Psychology Today*'s Web site.

The Bad, the Ugly, and the Good of Kids' Use of Social Media

By Jim Taylor

YOUR ANNOTATIONS

Whether we like it or not, the Internet, social media, and all of the related technology are here to stay. As evidenced every day in so many ways, this new technological landscape brings many wonderful benefits to our family's lives and relationships. At the same time, as with any new innovations, this impact has a dark side.

Though the study of the effects of social media on children is still relatively new, there is a growing body of evidence demonstrating what I will call the bad, the ugly, and the good (because I prefer to conclude this post on a positive note). I will describe some recent findings that are worth considering as you increasingly expose your children to different types of technology.

The Bad: Facebook Depression

There's no doubt that Facebook is one of the most powerful forms of media for communication today. More than a billion users chat, share photos, and keep their friends and family up to date on their lives regularly. Yet, there is a dark side to its use, along with other forms of social media, that has been labeled Facebook Depression, though this phenomenon also includes anxiety, other psychiatric disorders, and a range of unhealthy behaviors.

Perhaps the most comprehensive study to date found that Facebook overuse among teens was significantly correlated with narcissism. Among young adults, Facebook overuse was also associated with histrionic personality disorder, antisocial personality disorder, bipolar disorder, and sadistic, passive-aggressive, borderline, paranoid, and somatoform personality disorders. This study also explored the strength of Facebook use as a predictor of these psychiatric disorders and found that, even when demographics, such as age, gender, median income, ethnicity, and education were controlled, Facebook use was one of the three strongest predictors.

An analysis of 15 studies found that increased media exposure, including television, movies, video games, and the Internet, was associated with violent behavior and isolation. It reported that children who watched violent shows were not only more likely to be more aggressive, but also to have fewer friends and to be more secluded socially. The researchers concluded that children who are aggressive will have fewer friends and be more likely to be bullies (because they are more aggressive) or victims of bullying (because they are isolated).

Another study of adolescent girls found that the more they used texting, instant messaging and other social media to discuss their problems, particularly

(continued)

romantic difficulties, the more depressive symptoms they presented. The researchers argued that the ease and frequency that technology affords children to communicate allows them to "co-ruminate," that is, dwell on their problems without providing any solutions.

The Ugly: Internet Addiction

Addiction was the most widely used descriptor of the one-day moratorium on technology in the research I just described in a recent post. Internet addiction is commonly characterized as excessive use of the Internet that interferes with daily functioning and that can lead to distress or harm.

A review of research from the past decade has found that adolescents who demonstrated Internet addiction scored higher for obsessive–compulsive behavior, depression, generalized and social anxiety, attention deficit hyperactivity disorder, introversion, and other maladaptive behaviors. This research also revealed an interesting pattern of parental involvement. Those youth who were judged to have an Internet addiction rated their parents as lacking in love and nurturance, being over-invested, unresponsive, angry, and severe disciplinarians.

There is considerable debate within the mental-health field about whether dependence on technology is a true addiction, like alcohol, drugs, or gambling. In fact, the American Psychiatric Association, which produces the *Diagnostic and Statistical Manual* (think "shrinks' bible"), decided not to include Internet addiction in their latest revision. Some experts in the field argue that the unhealthy dependence on technology may be a symptom of some more fundamental pathology, such as depression or anxiety, and that so-called Internet addicts use technology to self-medicate and relieve their symptoms. Plus, unlike alcohol and drugs, Internet use doesn't cause any direct physiological or psychological harm.

Despite this uncertainty in the psychological community, the students in [one] survey . . . made it clear that they believe Internet addiction is very real. It certainly passes the "duck test" (if it looks like a duck and sounds like a duck, it's probably a duck). Not only did the students miss the functions that the technology offered, for example, texting, surfing the Web, and listening to music, but they actually craved the devices themselves. Said an English student, "Media is my drug; without it I was lost. I am an addict. How could I survive 24 hours without it?" Added an American student, "After experiencing this dreadful 24-hours, I realized that our obsession with media is almost scary. I could not even begin to imagine the world if it was media-free."

So what specifically does Internet use provide to people such that it gets to the point of unhealthy behavior often associated with addiction? One study examined the types of gratification that people gain from the Internet and found that four specific forms of gratification were, cumulatively, most predictive of the tendency toward Internet addiction: virtual community (feeling connected to a group), monetary compensation (money they earned through various Web-based activities), diversion (distraction from their lives), and personal status (the feeling of individual standing they gained from Internet use). These types of gratification are normal for children, yet there is something about the Internet that morphs them into unhealthy needs that appear to become addicting.

This so-called addiction appears to go deeper than just psychological dependence. There is emerging evidence indicating that, for example, our

(continued)

interaction with technology produces the same neurochemical reaction—a burst of dopamine—as that found with alcohol, drug, sex, and gambling addictions. Persistent exposure to technology-related cues, such as the vibration from a smartphone announcing the arrival of a new text message or the ping of an incoming tweet, can cause people to get caught in a vicious cycle of dopamine stimulation and deprivation. Moreover, the brevity of technology, for example, 140-character text messages, lends itself to this vicious cycle because the information received isn't completely satisfying, so people are driven to seek out more information for their next shot of dopamine. Imagine your children growing up with this relationship with technology and the strength of its grip on them if they are allowed ungoverned and unguided use of technology.

The Good: Social Media Can Help

Certainly, the research I've just described doesn't paint a very rosy picture of the influence of technology on children. It's not all bad though. Studies have shown that more time spent with social media is related to increased "virtual empathy," meaning that expressed through technology, and "real-world empathy" (considered a related, but separate factor). The best predictor of virtual empathy was the time spent on Facebook and the use of instant messaging. More of both forms of empathy means more social support, always a good thing for children.

Social media can also help those young people who experience shyness or social anxiety. Introverted young people can gain comfort and confidence in social interactions in several ways. Shy children can use social media to overcome what is perhaps their most difficult challenge, namely, initiating new relationships, in a low-risk environment. They can avoid awkwardness that is endemic to making friends by allowing them to gain familiarity with others and build friendships online. Introverted children can also practice social skills with the relative distance and safety afforded by social media.

Technology may improve family relationships and encourage feelings of connectedness. First, technology can be used as a point of entry into children's lives and create opportunities for sharing. Second, they enable families to have quality time and pursue activities of shared interest.

Social media can have educational benefits for children as well. They are learning practical skills that are necessary for success in today's wired world. Specifically, children are learning how to use and become proficient with technology, developing their creative abilities, appreciating new and different perspectives, and enhancing their communication skills.

One study indicated that prosocial video games encourage helping behavior. The researchers found that young people were more likely to help others after playing a prosocial as compared to a neutral video game. In a related study, they observed a similar effect when given the opportunity to protect a stranger who was being harassed.

Technology may even help children to better cope with stress in their lives. Technology can potentially mitigate stress in a number of ways. First, technology provides children with more outlets through which to express their feelings of stress, thus allowing a cathartic effect. Second, social media can provide children with social support, which can act as a buffer against stressors. Technology, including Facebook postings and instant messaging, enables children to receive

(continued)

more, immediate, and diverse support from a wider range of people. Third, technology can allow children to find useful information that may help them to reduce their stress. Finally, technology may act as a distraction and a means of distancing children from the stressors, providing a respite from the stress and giving them the time and perspective to deal with the stress more effectively.

What Does This All Mean?

As I have often argued, technology is neither good nor bad, but, at the same time, it isn't neutral either. The impact that technology has on your children depends not on the technology itself, but rather on how you educate them about it and the experiences they have with it. It is your responsibility to become informed about the potential benefits and costs of this new digital age and then make deliberate decisions about the type and quantity of technology you expose your children to.

Source: Taylor, Jim, "The Bad, the Ugly, and the Good of Kids' Use of Social Media," *The Blog of Dr. Jim Taylor,* www.drjimtaylor.com, posted May 28, 2013. Copyright © Jim Taylor, Ph.D. Reprinted by permission of the author.

Check Your Comprehension of the Reading

Review your comprehension of the reading selection by answering the questions below. Use a separate sheet.

1. Can using social media be addictive? If so, how? Explain your answer.

2. How can using social media lead to depression?

3. How important is this topic for general readers? Might this information be more important to some readers than others? Which readers need the information in this article? Explain your answer.

4. What is one caution people should take with regard to their social media use? Explain your answer.

5. If you were advising parents about protecting their children from the negative effects of social media use, what advice would you give? Explain your answer.

3. Outline and Summarize the Reading

On a separate sheet, outline the reading's main ideas, and write a brief summary of the reading.

4. Prepare an Information Sheet for the Reading

Using your annotations and the outline and summary you prepared for step 3, create an information sheet for this article that includes the following headings: *Author, Title, Publication Information, How I Might Use This Source, Brief Outline, Brief Summary, Key Words,* and *Potential Quotes.* See "Step-by-Step Guidance for Integrated Reading and Writing Projects" for more help.

SOURCE 4 "Facebook's False Faces Undermine Its Credibility"

1. Preview the Reading and Think about the Topic

Jot down your notes for the Preview, Predict, Recall, and Ask strategies. For help with these strategies, see "Step-by-Step Guidance for Integrated Reading and Writing Projects."

2. Read and Annotate the Text

Read "About the Author." Then read and annotate the reading selection. You may need to read the selection more than once.

About the Author.   Somini Sengupta is a foreign correspondent for *The New York Times*. She is the author of numerous articles reflecting international issues in countries such as Liberia, Congo, Darfur, Iraq, and India. Her book, *The End of Karma: Hope and Fury among India's Young*, was on *The Economist's* Best Books of 2016 list. This article appeared in *The New York Times* on November 12, 2012.

Facebook's False Faces Undermine Its Credibility

By Somini Sengupta

YOUR ANNOTATIONS

The Facebook page for Gaston Memorial Hospital, in Gastonia, N.C., offers a chicken salad recipe to encourage healthy eating, tips on avoiding injuries at Zumba class, and pictures of staff members dressed up at Halloween. Typical stuff for a hospital in a small town. But in October, another Facebook page for the hospital popped up. This one posted denunciations of President Obama and what it derided as "Obamacare." It swiftly gathered hundreds of followers, and the anti-Obama screeds picked up "likes." Officials at the hospital, scrambling to get it taken down, turned to their real Facebook page for damage control. "We apologize for any confusion," they posted on Oct. 8, "and appreciate the support of our followers."

The fake page came down 11 days later, as mysteriously as it had come up. The hospital says it has no clue who was behind it.

Fakery is all over the Internet. Twitter, which allows pseudonyms, is rife with fake followers, and has been used to spread false rumors, as it was during Hurricane Sandy. False reviews are a constant problem on consumer Web sites.

Gaston Memorial's experience is an object lesson in the problem of fakery on Facebook. For the world's largest social network, it is an especially acute problem, because it calls into question its basic premise. Facebook has sought to distinguish itself as a place for real identity on the Web. As the company tells its users: "Facebook is a community where people use their real identities." It goes on to advise: "The name you use should be your real name as it would be listed on your credit card, student ID, etc."

Fraudulent "likes" damage the trust of advertisers, who want clicks from real people they can sell to and whom Facebook now relies on to make money.

(continued)

Fakery also can ruin the credibility of search results for the social search engine that Facebook says it is building.

Facebook says it has always taken the problem seriously and recently stepped up efforts to cull fakes from the site. "It's pretty much one of the top priorities for the company all the time," said Joe Sullivan, who is in charge of security at Facebook.

The fakery problem on Facebook comes in many shapes. False profiles are fairly easy to create; hundreds can pop up simultaneously, sometimes with the help of robots, and often they persuade real users into friending them in a bid to spread malware. Fake Facebook friends and likes are sold on the Web like trinkets at a bazaar, directed at those who want to enhance their image. Fake coupons for meals and gadgets can appear on Facebook newsfeeds, aimed at tricking the unwitting into revealing their personal information.

Somewhat more benignly, some college students use fake names in an effort to protect their Facebook content from the eyes of future employers.

Mr. Sullivan declined to say what portion of the company's now one billion plus users were fake. The company quantified the problem last June, in responding to an inquiry by the Securities and Exchange Commission. At that time, the company said that of its 855 million active users, 8.7 percent, or 83 million, were duplicates, false or "undesirable," for instance, because they spread spam.

Mr. Sullivan said that since August, the company had put in place a new automated system to purge fake "likes." The company said it has 150 to 300 staff members to weed out fraud.

Flags are raised if a user sends out hundreds of friend requests at a time, Mr. Sullivan explained, or likes hundreds of pages simultaneously, or most obvious of all, posts a link to a site that is known to contain a virus. Those suspected of being fakes are warned. Depending on what they do on the site, accounts can be suspended.

In October, Facebook announced new partnerships with antivirus companies. Facebook users can now download free or paid antivirus coverage to guard against malware. "It's something we have been pretty effective at all along," Mr. Sullivan said.

Facebook's new aggressiveness toward fake "likes" became noticeable in September, when brand pages started seeing their fan numbers dip noticeably. An average brand page, Facebook said at the time, would lose less than 1 percent of its fans.

But the thriving market for fakery makes it hard to keep up with the problem. Gaston Memorial, for instance, first detected a fake page in its name in August; three days later, it vanished. The fake page popped up again on Oct. 4, and this time filled up quickly with the loud denunciations of the Obama administration. Dallas P. Wilborn, the hospital's public relations manager, said her office tried to leave a voice-mail message for Facebook but was disconnected; an e-mail response from the social network ruled that the fake page did not violate its terms of service. The hospital submitted more evidence, saying that the impostor was using its company logo.

Eleven days later, the hospital said, Facebook found in its favor. But by then, the local newspaper, *The Gaston Gazette*, had written about the matter, and the

(continued)

fake page had disappeared. Facebook declined to comment on the incident, and pointed only to its general Statement of Rights and Responsibilities.

The election season seems to have increased the fakery.

In Washington State, two groups fighting over a gay marriage referendum locked horns over "likes" on Facebook. A group supportive of gay marriage pointed to the Facebook page of its rival, Preserve Marriage Washington, which collected thousands of "likes" in a few short spurts. During those peaks, the pro-gay marriage group said, the preponderance of the "likes" came from far-flung cities like Bangkok and Vilnius, Lithuania, whose residents would seem to have little reason to care about a state referendum in Washington. The "likes" then fell as suddenly as they had risen.

The accusations were leveled on the Web site of the gay marriage support group, Washington United for Marriage. Preserve Marriage Washington in turn denied them on its Facebook page. Facebook declined to comment on the contretemps.

The research firm Gartner estimates that while less than 4 percent of all social media interactions are false today, that figure could rise to over 10 percent by 2014.

Fake users and their fake posts will have to be culled aggressively if Facebook wants to expand its search function, said Shuman Ghosemajumder, a former Google engineer whose start-up, Shape Security, focuses on automated fakery on the Internet. If you are searching for a laptop computer, for instance, Facebook has to ensure that you can trust the search results that come up. "If the whole idea behind social search is to look behind what different Facebook users are doing, then you have to make sure you don't have fake accounts to influence that," he said.

The ubiquity of Facebook, some users say, compels them to be a little bit fake. Colleen Callahan, who is 25, is among them. She was a senior in college when she started getting slightly nervous about the pictures that a prospective employer might find on Facebook. Like the pages of most of her college friends, she said, hers had a preponderance of party pictures.

"It would be O.K. if people saw it, but I didn't want people to interpret it differently," she said. So Ms. Callahan tweaked her profile. She became Colleen Skisalot. ("I am a big skier," she explained.)

The name stuck. She still hasn't changed it, though she is no longer afraid of what prospective employers might think. She has a job—with an advertising agency in Boston, some of whose clients, it turns out, advertise on Facebook.

Check Your Comprehension of the Reading

Review your comprehension of the reading selection by answering the questions below. Use a separate sheet.

1. How did *Facebook* respond the second time the hospital's Facebook page was hacked?

2. What reasons does the writer provide to support the idea that *Facebook* needs to confront the problem of fake accounts? Explain your answer.

3. How important is this topic for general readers? Might this information be more important to some readers than others? Which readers need the information in this article? Explain your answer.

4. What is the purpose of this article? To inform? To analyze? To evaluate? To persuade?

5. How might fraudulent pages on *Facebook* be responsible for serious social problems? Explain your answer.

3. Outline and Summarize the Reading

On a separate sheet, outline the reading's main ideas, and write a brief summary of the reading.

4. Prepare an Information Sheet for the Reading

Using your annotations and the outline and summary you prepared for step 3, create an information sheet for this article that includes the following headings: *Author, Title, Publication Information, How I Might Use This Source, Brief Outline, Brief Summary, Key Words,* and *Potential Quotes.* See "Step-by-Step Guidance for Integrated Reading and Writing Projects" for more help.

Developing Your Essay

Follow these steps to plan, draft, revise, and edit your **essay.**

1. Synthesize Your Sources

Review your annotations of the four readings, and fill in the following issues chart. See Alex's example "Step-by-Step Guidance for Integrated Reading and Writing Projects" if you need to review how to create and use an issues chart.

ISSUES CHART				
Issues	Source 1	Source 2	Source 3	Source 4
	"Driven to Distrac-tion" by Larry Rosen	"A Harsh Truth about Fake News: Some People Are Super Gullible" by Callum Borchers	"The Bad, the Ugly, and the Good of Kids' Use of Social Media" by Jim Taylor	"Facebook's False Faces Undermine Its Credibility" by Somini Sengupta

2. Prewrite to Develop Your Ideas

Complete the following steps to develop your ideas.

Review the Assignment. Review your annotations on the project assignment. Compose a question for every statement that provides a specific requirement. List your questions here. Use a separate sheet if necessary.

My questions:

1. _____

2. _____

3. _____

4. _____

5. _____

Select a Topic. Look over your questions. Select a topic that interests you and write it here.

My essay topic: _____

Use a Prewriting Method to Generate Ideas. On a separate sheet, use these prewriting strategies—listing, clustering, asking 5 W's + 1 H questions, free-writing, freetalking, or discussion—to generate ideas.

3. Construct a Thesis Statement

For this assignment, your purpose is to inform. Make sure your thesis statement does not signal a persuasive essay—that is, make sure it does not express your opinion or propose a course of action. If it does, reword the statement so that it is appropriate for an informative essay. Examine the following examples for guidance.

Persuasively focused thesis statement: Parents should not allow their children to use the Internet unsupervised because of the many dangers to which children are exposed.

Informative thesis statement: Children's unsupervised use of the Internet can be dangerous in a variety of ways.

Review your prewriting notes and compose a thesis statement for your essay. Write your thesis statement here.

My thesis statement:

_____

_____

_____

4. Develop Support for Your Thesis Statement

Review your prewriting notes, and choose your major supporting points. List at least three major supporting points here. Add lines if you will use more than three major supporting points.

My major supporting points:

Point 1 _____

Point 2 _____

Point 3 _____

Think about Text Patterns You Can Use.   Determine which patterns you will use in your essay. You may use more than one pattern. Determine which patterns (narration, definition, illustration, classification, comparison-contrast, cause and effect, process analysis) you will use in your essay. You may use more than one pattern. On a separate sheet, create a chart with the headings *Text Pattern* and *How I Could Use the Pattern*. Fill in the chart with ideas about how each pattern might help you to create supporting details. See "Step-by-Step Guidance for Integrated Reading and Writing Projects" for an example chart..

5. Create an Outline to Organize Your Essay

Determine the order in which you will present your ideas—order of importance, chronological or sequential order, or spatial order. Then, on a separate sheet, create an enhanced outline for your essay. Your outline should follow the format shown in "Step-by-Step Guidance for Integrated Reading and Writing Projects." It should include your topic, your thesis statement, and major supporting points and supporting details for your introduction, body, and conclusion paragraphs.

6. Add Source Materials to Your Outline

Return to your outline, and write down where you will insert source materials. Include citation information for each source.

7. Write a Complete Draft of Your Essay

Follow these steps to write a complete draft of your essay.

Keep an Audience in Mind.   Reread your outline and answer this question:

> *Have I included all the important information that my readers will want to know about my topic?*

Yes or no? _____

If your answer is no, on a separate sheet, write down additional questions that your reader will want answered. Do additional prewriting to develop answers for those questions, and insert your new information into your outline.

Write an Introduction Paragraph.   On a separate sheet or in your computer file, write your introduction paragraph. Select a method of introduction, and include your thesis statement in your introduction paragraph.

Write Body Paragraphs According to Your Outline.   On a separate sheet or in your computer file, write your body paragraphs.

End with an Effective Conclusion.   On a separate sheet or in your computer file, write your conclusion paragraph. Use a method of concluding that brings closure to your essay.

Create a Title.   Think of an effective title and add it to your essay. A title can ask a question, present your main idea, or simply present the topic. Write your title here.

My title: _____

8. Integrate Ideas and Quotes from Sources Correctly

Check that you have used sources correctly. Look for comma splices, run-on sentences, and quotations that lack an introduction. Use attributive tags to help readers see where ideas come from. Make any changes necessary.

Finishing Your Assignment

Use the remaining steps to finish your integrated reading and writing assignment.

1. Check That You Have Met Assignment Requirements

Reread your annotated assignment and create a self-assessment list. See Alex's example in "Step-by-Step Guidance for Integrated Reading and Writing Projects" if you would like to see an example of how to do this.

An Informative Reading and Writing Assignment

The primary purpose of informative writing is to provide readers with information in a clear and organized way. Your assignment is to find an aspect of social media about which readers need more information and to write an informative essay on that aspect.

You will select a social media concern you wish to communicate to readers. Keep in mind that the purpose of your essay is to present information, not to persuade readers about a particular point of view. You will not be writing your own argument about why we should take privacy more seriously, for example. Rather, your essay will simply present the major points readers should consider about the social media issue you select. Your essay will provide the information readers need to know about an issue and, if applicable, what some writers have suggested be done about it.

Finally, your essay should be written in standard English, be free from grammatical, spelling, and formatting errors, and conform to MLA or APA style.

Answer each question that you wrote about your assignment and then answer the following:

Have I met my assignment requirements?

Yes or no? _____

If your answer is no, make the necessary corrections to your draft.

2. Revise for Organization and Unity

As you read your draft, answer these questions: (1) Do my major supporting points support my thesis statement? (2) Are my ideas organized in a logical and convincing way? (3) Have I used transitions to show relationships between ideas? (4) Does my writing have a successful introduction and conclusion? See "Checklist: Revising for Unity" in "Step-by-Step Guidance for Integrated Reading and Writing Projects" for more help.

If you answer no to any questions, make the necessary revisions to your draft.

3. Revise for Development

As you read your draft, answer these questions: (1) Have I answered my reader's potential questions? (2) Have I provided enough support (definitions, examples, comparisons, causes, effects, and so on) for the main idea? (3) Are there places where I could add more support? (4) Do I make unjustified assumptions about what the reader knows? See "Checklist: Revising for Development" in "Step-by-Step Guidance for Integrated Reading and Writing Projects" for more help.

If you answer no to any questions, make the necessary revisions to your draft.

4. Revise for Clarity

As you read your draft, answer these questions: (1) Does the sentence communicate the idea effectively? (2) Is the tone appropriate? (3) Would I normally use the particular words I'm using to communicate this idea? (4) If I were explaining the idea to a friend, how would I say it? See "Checklist: Revising for Clarity" in "Step-by-Step Guidance for Integrated Reading and Writing Projects" for more help.

5. Create a Works Cited or References List

Create a works cited or references list, and answer this question:

Is my documentation list correctly formatted?

Yes or no? _____

If you are unsure or you answer no, ask your instructor or tutor for help.

6. Check for Plagiarism

Double-check your essay and answer this question:

Is the source for every summary, quotation, and paraphrase correctly identified in my essay?

Yes or no? _____

Correct any errors and omissions.

7. Edit Your Essay Using SMART TRACS

Use the "SMART TRACS" guidelines—**S**pelling, **M**echanics, **A**ccurate punctuation, **R**epeated or missing words, **T**erminal punctuation, **T**ense and other verb issues, **R**eference of pronouns, **A**postrophe use, **C**onfusing words, **S**ources—to edit your essay. See "Step-by-Step Guidance for Integrated Reading and Writing Projects" for more help.

Correct any errors. List the types of errors that appear more than once in your essay.

Types of errors:

_____

_____

Make a point of learning how to correct these recurring errors.

Incorporate all of the changes you have made and write a final draft of your essay. Answer the following question:

Does this essay present my best work?

Yes or no? _____

If you answered no, do not stop working on your essay. Go back and work on it until you have created an essay you are proud of.

8. Put Your Essay in the Proper Format

Review your essay to make sure the following elements are correctly formatted: heading, header (and page numbers), spacing, margins, title, font type and size, quotations, and works cited or references list. Answer the following question:

Is my essay correctly formatted?

Yes or no? _____

If you answered no, make any needed corrections.

Turn In Your Completed Assignment

Congratulations! You have completed your integrated reading and writing assignment. Follow your instructor's guidelines for submitting your finished essay.

Project 3: Completing an Argument Project
The Impact of Walmart

An argument essay presents a *claim*—a person's opinion on a topic—along with reasons and evidence to support the claim. Because argument essays are generally complex, readers need strong critical reading skills to analyze them. Similarly, writers need strong critical thinking skills to write an argument that is sound, that resonates with readers, and that presents the very best support available for a claim. In this chapter, you will use your critical reading and writing skills to analyze sources and to create your own argument essay.

If you are not familiar with the controversies surrounding Walmart, you may be surprised to learn that many people debate whether Walmart, a huge retailer with stores all over the world, has been good for society. Some people believe the retailer's enormous power has hurt jobs for workers in the United States, that it treats employees unfairly, and that Walmart's business practices are unethical. Other writers, however, point out that Walmart is a perfect example of a successful business. They acknowledge that some of Walmart's business strategies may seem harsh but say that the company has managed to sell products for prices that would not otherwise be available to consumers.

The readings in this project present several viewpoints on Walmart. As you read these selections, you will be prompted to think critically about the content with an eye toward understanding the concerns raised in each one. You will also be asked to create reading notes that will eventually help you write your own argument essay. The sources you read will stimulate your thinking about the issues, and they will provide you with key words and potential quotations to help you enter into the dialogue about Walmart. After you finish the four readings, you will be prompted to think about the concepts that unify them. Finally, you will use your knowledge, notes, and creative ideas to write your own argument essay.

©tupungato/123RF RF

Walmart, the world's largest retailer, employs 1.5 million people in the U.S. and 2.3 internationally.

Getting Started

Follow these steps to get started on your reading and writing assignment.

1. Analyze Your Assignment

Read and annotate your assignment.

An Argument Essay Assignment	YOUR ANNOTATIONS
The readings in this project present a variety of debated issues involving Walmart. Select one of these issues, and write an essay in which you argue your viewpoint. You will need to clearly define the issue, explain both sides of the issue, write a claim stating your opinion, and write supporting paragraphs in which you provide sound evidence to back up your claim. Use information from the sources in this chapter as one way to support your claim. Finally, your essay should be written in standard English, be free from grammatical, spelling, and formatting errors, and conform to MLA or APA style.	

2. Identify Your Purpose

Recognize why you are reading the project texts. Write your purpose here.

Purpose: _____

Working with Readings

Use the steps that follow to read the source carefully and critically.

SOURCE 1 "WATCHING WAL-MART"

1. Preview the Reading and Think about the Topic

Preview the reading by looking over it and noticing the title, bold-faced words, repeated words, and headings. After you have previewed the reading, jot down your notes for the Preview, Predict, Recall, and Ask strategies. For help with these strategies, see "Step-by-Step Guidance for Integrated Reading and Writing Projects."

2. Read and Annotate the Text

Read "About the Author." Then read and annotate the reading selection. You may need to read the selection more than once.

About the Author.   Liza Featherstone, a college professor and journalist, is the author of *Selling Women Short: The Landmark Battle for Workers' Rights at Wal-Mart*, published in 2004. She frequently writes about labor and student activism. "Watching Wal-Mart" was published in the *Columbia Journalism Review* (vol. 44, no. 5, Jan./Feb. 2006, pp. 58–62).

Watching Wal-Mart

By Liza Featherstone

Until a couple years ago, press coverage of Wal-Mart—the nation's largest private employer, and its most powerful retailer—was fawning and sycophantic, and largely limited to the financial pages. Often, the company was presented as an icon of business success: HOW WAL-MART KEEPS GETTING IT RIGHT was a typical headline. All that has changed. Thousands of lawsuits against the company allege serious workers' rights violations, ranging from child labor to sex discrimination. Labor unions, church leaders, economists, state governments, and many other players have been raising questions about Wal-Mart's low wages and light benefits: Are they a helpful efficiency passed on to the consumer; inhumane and exploitive to the worker; burdensome to the taxpayer, who must foot the bill when the company's workers need supplemental Food Stamps and Medicaid? Now, the press is far more vigilant in covering the retailer's flaws and its economic impact.

Stories potentially embarrassing to Wal-Mart appear just about every day. . . .

In November 2004, PBS's *Frontline* aired "Is Wal-Mart Good for America?" Hedrick Smith's substantive exploration of the real-world implications of the company's "Everyday Low Prices" shows that Wal-Mart puts intense pressure on suppliers to lower labor costs, forcing many manufacturers to move production offshore. We meet a worker who used to make television sets in a plant in Ohio, which was forced overseas when Wal-Mart demanded cheaper TVs. The man is not sure where he'll find work or what will become of future generations in his small town. Without the plant, jobs are scarce, except, as Smith poignantly points out, at the local Wal-Mart, where wages and benefits aren't even half as good.

CNBC's *The Age of Wal-Mart*, which aired the same month and won a Peabody Award, was narrated by the reporter David Faber, whose ironically affable manner will be familiar to any regular viewer of the financial cable news channel. Faber presents the company in a more favorable light, yet his report is hardly a puff piece. He gives a sense of the breathtaking logistics and technology behind Wal-Mart's success: the distribution centers the size of twenty-four football fields, and the detailed data the company collects on what products are selling, where, and why.

Wal-Mart's computer geeks even track the weather. Learning, for instance, that people buy more strawberry Pop Tarts during a hurricane, the folks at Arkansas headquarters, seeing a hurricane predicted in Florida, could place a massive order for that coveted comfort food. Yet Faber doesn't shy away from the company's dark side, highlighting its many lawsuits, as well as the arrogant and fraudulent tactics Wal-Mart has used in political battles with community activists. He makes decent use of his access to the company's CEO, Lee Scott,

(continued)

asking some tough questions. Noting the company's less-than-generous employee health-care plans, Faber asks Scott, "Would Sam be proud?" ("Sam" is Sam Walton, the company's legendary founder.) Faber also challenges Scott's assertion that he's unconcerned about the company's bad press, noting Wal-Mart's numerous ads asserting its praiseworthy corporate citizenship. At points during the interview Scott becomes testy; it's clear that he expected kid-glove treatment from the business network, and was disappointed. . . .

The public debate surrounding Wal-Mart's business practices is now even fiercer. Two major national organizations, Wal-Mart Watch and Wake Up Wal-Mart, both attempting to press the company toward greater social responsibility, have been successful in influencing media coverage. It is fitting, then, that [recently], two more documentaries, far more polemical in tone, emerged to sharpen the debate over Wal-Mart.

Robert Greenwald's *Wal-Mart: The High Cost of Low Price*, strenuously argues that Wal-Mart's low-cost model is bad for America. In contrast to the PBS and CNBC documentaries, Greenwald interviews only people whose lives are directly affected by Wal-Mart's practices: former employees, small-business people, community opponents, former managers. This strategy has some limitations, yet it is also the source of the film's power.

Greenwald opens with a story about a small family-owned store in Middlefield, Ohio, H&H Hardware, which closed when Wal-Mart began breaking ground for a supercenter. The local real estate market anticipated that downtown businesses would suffer, so the value of the land plummeted, and the family was unable to refinance its commercial mortgage. Wal-Mart—along with conservative commentators sympathetic to the company—has relentlessly attacked this part of the film, correctly pointing out that the store closed three months before the Middlefield Wal-Mart opened, and that a new hardware store has reopened in the same spot and is thriving. The film doesn't actually say that the store folded because of direct competition with Wal-Mart. It's clear, however, that H&H is a flawed example, and that's unfortunate, because no one—not even Wal-Mart—disputes Greenwald's larger point that when Wal-Mart comes to town, small businesses are often forced to close their doors. Kenneth Stone, an Iowa State University economist, has extensively documented this phenomenon. Yet the segment also suffers from a lack of attention to this broader picture; Greenwald doesn't ask why we should care about small businesses being crushed by Wal-Mart. Of course it's disappointing for the entrepreneurs and their families, but does it affect life in the region in any significant way? We know, for example, that when small businesses suffer, the local newspaper is often hurt as well, for the steep loss in advertising dollars is far from offset by Wal-Mart, which does little print promotion. What do small businesses offer a community that big businesses can't, and vice versa? Greenwald doesn't say, and here exclusive reliance on personal stories seems to hinder an exploration of important issues.

At other points, however, Greenwald's focus on individuals works magnificently. Interviews with former and current employees—who describe sex discrimination and many other abuses—are powerful. The former managers in the film are riveting; some describe practices they were pressured into (including falsifying time cards to cheat employees of overtime pay), of which they are

(continued)

now deeply ashamed. The film's biggest surprise—especially in contrast to Smith's *Frontline* documentary, in which the Chinese exist only as a backdrop, an anonymous force stealing American jobs—is Greenwald's intimate, humanizing segment on a young couple who work in a factory in China making products for Wal-Mart, under harsh conditions. In an eloquent misconception—illustrating the vast distance between producers and consumers—a Chinese worker imagines that Wal-Mart shoppers in the United States must be very rich.

Ron Galloway's *Why Wal-Mart Works (And Why That Drives Some People Crazy)* is by far the most amateurish of these efforts, as well as the most ideologically extreme. It is hard to believe that anyone who was not being paid by Wal-Mart would make this lengthy infomercial, but Galloway has repeatedly said that he took no money from the company. In this film, analysis of Wal-Mart—and of the hostility to the company—is delivered only by conservative free-market zealots. The only Wal-Mart critics in the film are inarticulate young people who don't have much knowledge of the company's practices. Some are stereotypical hippies who wouldn't think highly of any large business. Elsewhere, Galloway's film verges on dishonesty, as when he dismisses talk of Wal-Mart's plan to cut down on "unhealthy" employees, suggesting that it's unfounded gossip, when in fact the proposal to save on health-care costs by "dissuad[ing] unhealthy people from coming to work at Wal-Mart" was earnestly discussed in an internal company memo.

The two workers Galloway chooses to profile—a ninety-year-old retired nurse and a former drug addict—are remarkably unrepresentative of the nation's working population. The retiree came to work at Wal-Mart because she still had plenty of energy and needed something to do—not because she needed money or health benefits. The recovered drug addict, who had no work history when Wal-Mart hired her, is tearfully grateful to the company for giving her a chance. Galloway's choice to emphasize their experiences over any others unintentionally raises a question: Shouldn't we be worried when the nation's largest private employer provides jobs that work well only for people with few needs and low expectations?

All these documentaries add to the debate, but reporting on the company can go further. Clearly, Wal-Mart is not merely a source of problems—it is a symptom of broader problems. In Greenwald's documentary—and to a more subtle extent, *Frontline*'s—Wal-Mart is a threat to everything rightfully and authentically American. For Ron Galloway, it represents what's greatest about America. Neither is quite true: Wal-Mart has emerged from the contradictions and paradoxes of American culture. We have created Wal-Mart, rather than the other way around. David Faber is right when he declares, at the end of *The Age of Wal-Mart*: "Wal-Mart is a near-perfect example of capitalism, which itself can bring both good and bad." This seems more promising as a point of departure than a conclusion; perhaps we will begin to see more coverage of the company as a window on the intensely marketized nature of contemporary life in the United States, rather than as an isolated example of corporate evil-doing.

Check Your Comprehension of the Reading

Review your comprehension of the reading selection by answering the questions below. Use a separate sheet if necessary.

1. Featherstone discusses four documentary films. List each film, and then write a sentence explaining the film's attitude toward Walmart.

2. Choose two potential topics—issues—that you found in this article that interest you. Turn each issue into a question. For example, suppose you are interested in writing about hiring discrimination against unhealthy people. Your topic question might look like this: "Do Walmart's hiring practices discriminate against people with health problems?" For each potential topic, list any additional information you would need if you were to write about the topic.

3. What do you believe Featherstone means when she writes, "We have created Wal-Mart, rather than the other way around"? Explain in a paragraph.

4. Reflect on the criticism of Walmart you read about in this article. Before reading this, were you familiar with this issue? What do you think about Walmart after having read this article? Do you believe you have enough information at this point to make a decision on whether Walmart is an ethical company?

5. Documentaries often focus on the negative or problematic parts of an issue. What are some of the reasons people might defend Walmart, its practices, and its success? Explain your answer.

3. Outline and Summarize the Reading

On a separate sheet, outline the reading's main ideas, and write a brief summary of the reading.

4. Prepare an Information Sheet for the Reading

Using your annotations and the outline and summary you created in step 3, create an information sheet for this article that includes the following headings: *Author, Title, Publication Information, How I Might Use This Source, Brief Outline, Brief Summary, Key Words,* and *Potential Quotes.* See "Step-by-Step Guidance for Integrated Reading and Writing Projects" for more help.

SOURCE 2 "DISCUSSION CASE: WAL-MART"

1. Preview the Reading and Think about the Topic

Preview the reading by looking over it and noticing the title, bold-faced words, repeated words, and headings. After you have previewed the reading, jot down your notes for the Preview, Predict, Recall, and Ask strategies. For help with these strategies, see "Step-by-Step Guidance for Integrated Reading and Writing Projects."

2. Read and Annotate the Text

Read "About the Author." Then read and annotate the reading selection. You may need to read the selection more than once.

About the Author.   Joseph DesJardins serves as the Vice Provost of College of St. Benedict and St. John's University in Minnesota, where he is also a philosophy professor. He has written a variety of books in the fields of ethics, environmental ethics and policy, and business ethics. He received his PhD from the University of Notre Dame. "Discussion Case: Wal-Mart" appears in *An Introduction to Business Ethics*, 5th edition (McGraw-Hill, 2014, pp. 49–52).

Discussion Case: Wal-Mart

By Joseph DesJardins

YOUR ANNOTATIONS

On April 21, 2012, *The New York Times* reported that a six-year internal investigation by Wal-Mart had uncovered evidence of widespread bribery and corruption within their Mexican operations. The investigation discovered that Wal-Mart employees had paid more than $24 million in bribes to promote the expansion of its business in Mexico. Furthermore, the *Times* reported that Wal-Mart executives in Mexico were not only aware of the bribes, but also had intentionally hidden them from the Wal-Mart corporate office in the United States.

More damaging than even the reports of bribery in Mexico, *The New York Times* report also alleged that when the internal investigation was shared with corporate headquarters, Wal-Mart executives terminated the investigation. The *Times* also reported that only upon learning of the newspaper's own investigation and plans to write a story did Wal-Mart executives notify legal authorities. As a result, the U.S. Justice Department began an investigation of possible violations of the U.S. Corrupt Foreign Practices Act in 2011.

Few corporations generate as much controversy and have as many vocal critics and defenders as Wal-Mart. Few corporations would generate as much debate as Wal-Mart on the question of corporate social responsibility. Part of this no doubt is due to its sheer size and influence. Wal-Mart is the world's largest retail business; it claims to have over 200 million customer visits per week at more than 8,100 retail stores in fifteen countries. Its total sales for fiscal year 2011 were $418 billion. Worldwide, Wal-Mart employs more than 2.1 million people. It is the largest private employer in both the United States and Mexico, and the single largest employer in twenty-five U.S. states.

In many ways, Wal-Mart is a socially responsible corporation, describing itself as a business that "was built upon a foundation of honesty, respect, fairness and integrity." What is described as the "Wal-Mart culture" is based on three "basic beliefs," attributed to founder Sam Walton: respect for individuals, service to customers, and striving for excellence. Defenders point out that Wal-Mart is regularly recognized as among the "most admired" companies in the *Fortune* magazine annual survey.

By all accounts Wal-Mart is among the most financially successful companies in the world. Defenders would point out that this economic success is itself

(continued)

evidence of how well Wal-Mart is fulfilling its social responsibility. Wal-Mart has created immense value for shareholders, consumers, suppliers, and employees. Stockholders, both individual and institutional investors, have received significant financial benefits from Wal-Mart. Consumers also receive financial benefits in the form of low prices, employees benefit from having jobs, many businesses benefit from supplying Wal-Mart with goods and services, and communities benefit from tax-paying corporate citizens.

Beyond these economic benefits, Wal-Mart regularly contributes to community and social causes. The Wal-Mart Foundation, a philanthropic arm of Wal-Mart, is the largest corporate cash contributor in the United States. For fiscal year 2009, Wal-Mart donated more than $378 million in cash and in-kind gifts to charitable organizations. It contributed more than $45 million to charities outside the United States, and its instore contribution programs added another $100 million to local charities. Wal-Mart has focused its charitable giving in areas such as disaster relief, food and hunger programs, and education.

More recently, Wal-Mart has begun an initiative to promote sustainability both in its own operations and in the products it sells. In 2005, Wal-Mart announced major sustainability goals for its own operations, including becoming more energy efficient, reducing its carbon footprint, reducing wastes and packaging, and finding more sustainable sources for its products.

Despite these positive aspects, not everyone agrees that Wal-Mart lives up to high ethical standards. The allegations of widespread bribery in Mexico are only the most recent charges that have been raised against Wal-Mart's ethical standards. In contrast to *Fortune* magazine's claim, critics portray Wal-Mart as among the least admired corporations in the world. Ethical criticisms have been raised against Wal-Mart on behalf of every major constituency—customers, employees, suppliers, competitors, and communities—with whom Wal-Mart interacts.

For example, some critics charge that Wal-Mart's low-priced goods, and even their placement within stores, are a ploy to entice customers to purchase more and higher-priced goods. Such critics would charge Wal-Mart with deceptive and manipulative pricing and marketing.

But perhaps the greatest ethical criticisms of Wal-Mart have involved its treatment of workers. Wal-Mart is well-known for its aggressive practices aimed at controlling labor costs. Wal-Mart argues that this is part of their strategy to offer the lowest possible prices to consumers. By controlling labor costs through wages, minimum work hours, high productivity, and keeping unions away, Wal-Mart is able to offer consumers the lowest everyday prices. One of the most infamous cases of employee treatment involved health care benefits.

In October 2005, *The New York Times* published a story detailing a Wal-Mart internal memo that outlined various proposals for reducing health care costs paid for Wal-Mart employees. The memo recommended two major areas for action: increasing reliance on part-time workers who do not qualify for health care benefits and seeking ways to encourage healthier and discourage unhealthy job applicants and employees. The memo also acknowledged long-standing criticisms of Wal-Mart's treatment of its employees and offered

(continued)

suggestions for a public relations strategy that would deflect criticism of these proposed changes.

The memo was written by Susan Chambers, Wal-Mart's executive vice president for employee benefits, and pointed out that Wal-Mart employees "are getting sicker than the national population, particularly in obesity-related diseases," including diabetes and coronary artery disease. In one passage, Chambers recommended that Wal-Mart would arrange for "all jobs to include some physical activity (e.g., all cashiers do some cart-gathering)" as a means to deter unhealthy employees and job applicants. "It will be far easier to attract and retain a healthier work force than it will be to change behavior in an existing one," the memo said. "These moves would also dissuade unhealthy people from coming to work at Wal-Mart."

Recognizing that young workers are paid less and require fewer health benefits than older workers and are equally productive, the memo recommended strategies, including reducing 401(k) retirement contributions and offering education benefits for attracting younger employees and discouraging older employees. The memo stated "the cost of an associate with seven years of tenure is almost 55 percent more than the cost of an associate with one year of tenure, yet there is no difference in his or her productivity. Moreover, because we pay an associate more in salary and benefits as his or her tenure increases, we are pricing that associate out of the labor market, increasing the likelihood that he or she will stay with Wal-Mart."

The memo pointed out that 46 percent of the children of Wal-Mart's 1.33 million U.S. employees were uninsured or on Medicaid. "Wal-Mart's critics can easily exploit some aspects of our benefits offering to make their case; in other words, our critics are correct in some of their observations. Specifically, our coverage is expensive for low-income families, and Wal-Mart has a significant percentage of associates and their children on public assistance."

Wal-Mart has also been criticized for paying its workers poverty-level wages. The average annual salary for a Wal-Mart sales associate in 2001 was $13,861, and the average hourly wage was $8.23. For the same year, the U.S. federal poverty level for a family of three was $14,630. Wal-Mart offers health care benefits to full-time workers but, relative to other employers, Wal-Mart employees pay a disproportionately high percentage of the costs. According to critics, these low wages and benefits result in many Wal-Mart employees qualifying for government assistance programs such as food stamps and health care, effectively creating a government subsidy for Wal-Mart's low wages.

Wal-Mart has also been sued by employees in nine U.S. states for illegally requiring employees to work overtime without pay and to work off-the-clock. The U.S. National Labor Relations Board filed suit against Wal-Mart stores in Pennsylvania and Texas charging illegal anti-union activities. Maine's Department of Labor fined Wal-Mart for violating child labor laws. Wal-Mart has also been sued in Missouri, California, Arkansas, and Arizona for violating the Americans with Disabilities Act.

Wal-Mart employs more women than any other private employer in the United States. Women comprise over 70% of Wal-Mart's sales associates, but

(continued)

men hold 90% of the store manager positions. Less than one-third of all managerial positions are held by women, significantly lower than the 56% among Wal-Mart's competitors Target and K-Mart. Only one of the top twenty positions at Wal-Mart is held by a woman. In June 2004, a federal judge in California ruled that a class-action lawsuit could proceed on behalf of all female employees of Wal-Mart, noting that "plaintiffs present largely uncontested descriptive statistics which show that women working at Wal-Mart stores are paid less than men in every region, that pay disparities exist in most job categories, that the salary gap widens over time, that women take longer to enter management positions, and that the higher one looks in the organization the lower the percentage of women."

U.S. federal agents raided sixty Wal-Mart stores in twenty states in October 2003. The raids resulted in arrests of over 250 illegal aliens who were working as janitors at Wal-Mart stores. All of the workers were employed by third-party sub-contractors that Wal-Mart had hired for overnight janitorial services. A lawsuit was filed on behalf of several of these workers claiming that Wal-Mart knowingly employed illegal workers as part of a scheme to pay below minimum wages, deny overtime pay, and otherwise exploit their illegal status.

Many local communities also criticize Wal-Mart as a major factor in the demise of small towns and local businesses. Small retail businesses find it difficult to compete with Wal-Mart's pricing and marketing strategies, and local communities suffer when Wal-Mart builds giant stores in suburban and rural locations. This not only encourages sprawl and places additional burdens on roads and transportation, it can undermine the local tax base. Further, the loss of local business has a trickle-down effect when local suppliers, and professionals such as accountants, lawyers, and banks, suffer the loss of local business to Wal-Mart's national and international suppliers. The problem is compounded when Wal-Mart receives tax subsidies and tax breaks offered by local governments hoping to attract a Wal-Mart store.

Wal-Mart's aggressive strategy to lower costs also is criticized for the harms it can cause suppliers both nationally and internationally. Wal-Mart has been known to force suppliers to bid against each other in a type of "reverse auction" in which suppliers compete to see who can offer their products at the lowest costs. Because Wal-Mart controls such a large market segment, many suppliers cannot survive if Wal-Mart declines to carry their product. This practice has caused some suppliers to go out of business and has most others finding ways to send production offshore. One result is that Wal-Mart, which promoted a "Buy American" marketing campaign in the 1980s, is responsible for the loss of uncounted American jobs as American businesses have been forced to outsource their production as the only means available to meet Wal-Mart's price targets. Finally, the labor practices of Wal-Mart suppliers in China, Central America, and Saipan have all been accused of sweatshop conditions in factories manufacturing clothing produced for Wal-Mart.

Source: DesJardins, Joseph, *An Introduction to Business Ethics*, 5th ed. 49–52. Copyright © 2014 by McGraw-Hill Education. Used with permission of McGraw-Hill Education.

Check Your Comprehension of the Reading

1. Why do critics believe Walmart is an unethical company? List at least three reasons.

2. The article points out some of the positive aspects of Walmart. List at least three.

3. Why might this article be important to understand? Explain your answer.

4. What experiences have you had with Walmart stores? Do you think Walmart's existence in your town or a town nearby is a good thing or not? Explain your answer.

5. Explain one way that Walmart is discriminatory, according to the article.

3. Outline and Summarize the Reading

On a separate sheet, outline the reading's main ideas, and write a brief summary of the reading.

4. Prepare an Information Sheet for the Reading

Using your annotations and the outline and summary you created in step 3, create an information sheet for this article that includes the following headings: *Author, Title, Publication Information, How I Might Use This Source, Brief Outline, Brief Summary, Key Words,* and *Potential Quotes.* See "Step-by-Step Guidance for Integrated Reading and Writing Projects" for more help.

SOURCE 3 "WALMART CUT MY HOURS. I PROTESTED. THEY FIRED ME."

1. Preview the Reading and Think about the Topic

This selection is the first of two first-person accounts of what it is like to work at Walmart.

After previewing the selection, jot down your notes for the Preview, Predict, Recall, and Ask strategies. For help with these strategies, see "Step-by-Step Guidance for Integrated Reading and Writing Projects."

2. Read and Annotate the Text

Read "About the Author." Then read and annotate the reading selection. You may need to read the selection more than once.

About the Author. Josh Harkinson, a staff writer at the *Houston Press* for three years, currently covers tech, labor, drug policy, and the environment for *Mother Jones* magazine and is a contributing writer for *The Atlantic*. The following article was published in *Mother Jones* on February 4, 2015.

Walmart Cut My Hours. I Protested. They Fired Me.

By Kiana Howard, as told to Josh Harkinson

Today, the union-backed Our Walmart campaign will hold demonstrations across the country calling on Walmart managers to reverse disciplinary actions against 35 workers in nine states who participated in Black Friday protests against the retailer. Our Walmart will also add claims of illegal retaliation against the workers to an existing case filed with the National Labor Relations Board in October. One of the workers being added to the case is 26-year-old Kiana Howard of Sacramento, California. This is her story, edited for length and clarity, as told to Mother Jones:

. . . I started working at the local Walmart. I love working around people and having conversations while ringing them up. You could be having a bad day and one customer in line says a joke and changes your whole day. My coworkers there were like family. We took care of each other because we were all going through the same situation. The managers, on the other hand, they don't give a damn about us. I started off at $8.40 an hour. Then California raised the minimum wage, and I got my yearly raise, which put me up to $9.80. But the most hours I could get in any week after picking up extra days and taking extra shifts was 36. After paying rent and utilities, I was barely scraping by. I was on welfare, getting $300. When they cut that off, I really started struggling. And then they cut my food stamps down by more than half, to $136, so I started having to spend money on food. I went to food banks to make sure I fed my seven-year-old son.

I live an hour away. I don't have a car. I have to catch the bus and the light rail every day. My schedule was all over the place. Some days I would have to be at work at 5:30 in the morning, and then some days I would work from 8 p.m. to midnight. I was tired all the time. It was just madness. Especially because there's no buses that run after 10 p.m.

Sometimes coworkers would give me rides home, but sometimes they would be like, "Oh, I can't go that way, I don't have the gas." And I didn't have gas money for them. Other times I would get on Facebook and ask people to give me rides.

Or there was this dating website called Tagged. I would write on my status: "Could anybody give me a ride home? Stranded at work." And then people would message me. "Well, what time are you off?"

Some of the guys were people that I knew. Other guys I didn't know. A lot of times I was scared but I had pepper spray and I was ready for whatever. I just had to make sure I got home. I was not spending the night at Walmart.

At the time, I was trying to get promoted to customer service. The manager kept telling me she was going to pick me, but then she takes somebody who has been at Walmart for a month and puts her there instead because she hadn't missed any days. But she doesn't have a child like I do. I missed three days

(continued)

because my son was sick, and I was late three days. They hold that against us for a whole year, and I feel like that's just too long.

I actually started applying at different jobs. I applied at Burlington Coat Factory, Macy's, Sears. But I just wasn't getting calls back from those people. I just kind of gave up and kept working at Walmart.

Around August of last year, I'd had enough and put in an availability change with my supervisor. I told them I could only work between 5:30 a.m. and 8:00 p.m. That way I could get home to my son. People who had worked there for years told me, "Oh, they are going to cut your hours back for a while, and then you will get them back again." But they cut my hours back—to just 23 a week—and they kept them cut back. It went on for a good month or two. That's one reason I decided to join Our Walmart.

I feel like we were overworked and underpaid. When my customer service manager, who is in Our Walmart, told me we are going to be fighting for $15 and full time, I just felt like it needed to be done. A lot of associates were like, well, isn't that too much for Walmart? I'm like, "No, dude! This is the richest family in America! What do you mean that's too much? Really?" Walmart, I call it the devil's palace. That's how I feel.

On Black Friday we went on strike. The organizers picked us up in a white van and drove us to a picket at the Rancho Cordova store. It was me and a couple of other Our Walmart people. They had balloons; they tied them on our wrists. They had posters. And we stood out there for a minute, we talked, and we had people get on the mic and speak. We had a DJ out there. It was like a little party. I did an interview on the news.

Then we started marching. They had me and my son in the front. We were chanting and singing and people were jumping and dancing. Then the police came. The people that got arrested, they were sitting down in the street. Santa Claus got arrested as well. They didn't put handcuffs on Santa Claus, though. We took lots of pictures. It was good. I felt great. Everybody was like, "I saw you on the news!"

They retaliated on January 13, which was the day I got fired. I had a four-hour shift. Thirty minutes before I was about to get off, they pulled me off the register and brought me in the office. It was like, "You went on strike for Black Friday . . ." I wasn't listening because I was upset. She said it counted as my fourth unexcused absence and that rolls over into me being terminated. I signed my papers and I gave her my badge and my vest and I left.

Since then, it has been hard. Our Walmart is going to help out with the retaliation fund, but that only lasts six months. With my last check I was able to pay my rent, but I can't do laundry, I can't pay any bills. I ran out of food and I had to go to the food bank once again. I feel like I'm going into a depression. I just try to keep myself humble, because my son needs me. I can't show him that I'm going through a lot right now.

Some employees don't want to join Our Walmart because they don't want to be in a predicament like I am. But I know they believe we're fighting for a good cause. I'm just trying to stay prayed up and hope for the best.

Check Your Comprehension of the Reading

Review your comprehension of the reading selection by answering the questions below. Use a separate sheet if necessary.

1.   Why did Howard's supervisor cut her hours to 23?

2.   What are Howard's reasons for believing her pay should be raised?

3.   How important is this topic for general readers? Might this information be more important to some readers than others? Which readers need the information in this article? Explain your answer.

4.   What is the purpose of this article? To inform? To analyze? To evaluate? To persuade?

5.   Write a few sentences in which you reflect on Howard's situation. What is your response to her article?

3. Outline and Summarize the Reading

On a separate sheet, outline the reading's main ideas, and write a brief summary of the reading.

4. Prepare an Information Sheet for the Reading

Using your annotations and the outline and summary you prepared for step 3, create an information sheet for this article that includes the following headings: *Author, Title, Publication Information, How I Might Use This Source, Brief Outline, Brief Summary, Key Words,* and *Potential Quotes.* See "Step-by-Step Guidance for Integrated Reading and Writing Projects" for more help.

SOURCE 4 "I WORKED AT WAL-MART FOR TWO YEARS AND I ACTUALLY REALLY LIKED IT"

1. Preview the Reading and Think about the Topic

The next reading selection is the second of two first-person accounts of what it is like to work at Walmart. After you have previewed the reading, jot down your notes for the Preview, Predict, Recall, and Ask strategies. For help with these strategies, see "Step-by-Step Guidance for Integrated Reading and Writing Projects."

2. Read and Annotate the Text

Read "About the Author." Then read and annotate the reading selection. You may need to read the selection more than once.

About the Author.   Travis Okulski is the Site Director of RoadandTrack.com. He worked for Walmart during his years in college. The following article was published by *BusinessInsider.com* on April 23, 2012.

I Worked at Wal-Mart for Two Years and I Actually Really Liked It

By Travis Okulski

I'm a former Wal-Mart associate.

Not only did I work there once, but I liked the job so much that I actually returned for three more tours of duty during college.

About six months before I started, a Wal-Mart opened near my hometown to fanfare from a number of residents and scorn from a majority of local businesses.

When my summer job ended, I decided to apply to Wal-Mart. The first thing you notice is the application: it's time consuming and actually difficult.

I sat at a kiosk in the store for about an hour filling out a questionnaire which mainly was intended to see how I would react in certain situations that employees would face, such as confrontations with coworkers and observing theft.

Soon after, I got a call back for an interview, which was also surprisingly grueling. I passed and was soon onboard as an associate in the automotive department, starting around $9 per hour. But before I hit the sales floor, I spent the majority of my first few days in the training room on computer terminals, learning proper store practices. They are actually useful, and if you pay attention, you learn a great deal about being on the floor.

Furthermore, you are encouraged by management to go back to the training room at any time during your employment to use the computers and learn more. Time on the computers does not count as break time, and associates are paid while using the training systems.

At Wal-Mart, you are assigned a department to work in, but that is not the only place you will be working. As you learn in training, there is a heavy emphasis on the customer. If someone is within 10 feet, you are supposed to greet the person and ask if you can help. If the customer is looking for something, you are then to take him or her to the item, not just vaguely point.

Wal-Mart taught me exactly how to deal with customers, and in my personal life I have people who could be considered difficult to handle.

Days at Wal-Mart are long. A full-time shift is nine hours. You get two fifteen-minute breaks and a one-hour lunch when you must clock out. The break room was always lively, clean, and stocked with good reading material. During my tenure, overtime was almost nonexistent. You were to work during your shift and to make sure you punched out on time. The company wanted to pay you but didn't want to pay for more than you were scheduled. It made sense.

The good thing was that weekend shifts went by quickly since so many people were in the store. A Tuesday afternoon during June felt like it lasted for years.

Wal-Mart works to make each associate feel like an owner. Each is given a scanning gun that could check stock levels. If something is out, the average employee on the floor orders goods to be in the department. This really encourages associates to know what sells in their departments since it's up to them to make sure the hottest sellers are in stock.

The company also wanted us to know what was going on from a broader perspective. Every evening I would go to a meeting with the store manager, who would tell us the stock price, how much we had sold that day, and whether there were other duties before we left for the night.

(continued)

The best thing that I learned at Wal-Mart was that hard work was recognized and rewarded. I worked hard and came back during a break from college to be promoted to work in the photo lab (more responsibility, higher rate of pay). I also saw many full-time employees that I worked with move up to become department managers, assistant store managers, and even move on to the corporate office.

However, I also saw the opposite end of the spectrum. Some fellow associates seemed content to do the bare minimum and didn't go anywhere in the company because of it. In fact, they are still at the same level.

In my opinion, these are also the employees that you hear speaking negatively of Wal-Mart's employment practices. They want something for nothing from the company and they aren't getting it.

Over all, I spent about two years at Wal-Mart. It was a great experience that I wouldn't trade for anything.

Source: Okulski, Travis, "I Worked At Walmart For Two Years And I Actually Really Liked It" *Business Insider*, April 23, 2012. Copyrighted 2012. Business Insider, Inc. 129228. 1017PF Used with permission.

Check Your Comprehension of the Reading

Review your comprehension of the reading selection by answering the questions below. Use a separate sheet if necessary.

1. Why does Okulski value his time working at Walmart? Explain your answer.

2. What is one factor that might have made Okulski's experience at Walmart different from Howard's? Explain your answer.

3. How important is this topic for general readers? Might this information be more important to some readers than others? Which readers need the information in this article? Explain your answer.

4. Okulski believes that the employees who complain about Walmart probably "want something for nothing from the company and they aren't getting it." Do you agree with Okulski?

5. While Okulski and Howard have differing points of view, they probably do share some similar values. Based on their articles, what values might they hold in common?

3. Outline and Summarize the Reading

On a separate sheet, outline the reading's main idea, and write a brief summary of the reading.

4. Prepare an Information Sheet for the Reading

Using your annotations and the outline and summary you prepared for step 3, create an information sheet for the article that includes the following headings: *Author, Title, Publication Information, How I Might Use This Source, Brief Outline, Brief Summary, Key Words,* and *Potential Quotes.* See "Step-by-Step Guidance for Integrated Reading and Writing Projects" for more help.

SOURCE 5 "WAL-MART IS GOOD FOR THE ECONOMY"

1. Preview the Reading and Think about the Topic

After you have previewed the reading, jot down your notes for the Preview, Predict, Recall, and Ask strategies. For help with these strategies, see "Step-by-Step Guidance for Integrated Reading and Writing Projects."

2. Read and Annotate the Text

Read "About the Author." Then read and annotate the reading selection. You may need to read the selection more than once.

About the Author.   John Semmens is a research fellow at the Independent Institute. He writes political satire from a libertarian-conservative perspective and contributes columns to *The Arizona Conservative*. He is a contributing author to *Street Smart: Competition, Entrepreneurship, and the Future of Roads,* edited by Gabriel Roth. "Wal-Mart Is Good for the Economy" was published on October 1, 2015, in *The Freeman* (vol. 55, no. 8, pp. 8–10).

Wal-Mart Is Good for the Economy

By John Semmens

YOUR ANNOTATIONS

To some, Wal-Mart is a "corporate criminal." Loni Hancock, a California legislator, asserts that Wal-Mart's fortune "has been built on human misery." A variety of critics have accused the company of engaging in questionable and exploitive practices on its way to becoming the largest business in the world. (Its $250 billion in annual sales means that Wal-Mart has more revenues than legendary giants like Exxon, General Motors, and IBM.)

To get this big, Wal-Mart allegedly exploits its own employees by paying "poverty wages" and forcing them to work unpaid overtime. It also allegedly "squeezes" vendors, forcing them to lay off American workers and ship their jobs to foreign "sweatshops." On top of this supposed economic rapacity is the charge that Wal-Mart disregards the concerns of small communities. While such charges fuel the passions of competitors who are losing customers to Wal-Mart, unions that have been unsuccessful in organizing the company's employees, and ideologues who despise the free market, they are without merit.

The nature of competition is to produce winners and losers. Those who lose can be expected to bemoan their fate. The remedy is to improve one's own competitive offering. The strategy and tactics of the leading competitor can be observed, analyzed, and, if warranted, imitated. Countermeasures can be devised. Since competition in the free market is continuous, today's losers can be tomorrow's winners. Instead of fomenting political opposition to Wal-Mart, its rivals should be improving their own game.

Unions in America have been granted ample privileges in their quest to enlist members. Under regulations established by the National Labor Relations Board, they can convert businesses to "union shops." A union shop means the union

(continued)

speaks and bargains on behalf of all workers—even those who don't belong. Non-members may even be compelled to pay fees to the union for unwanted bargaining "services." The rules governing elections to determine whether a union will be instituted are slanted in favor of the union's case. If Wal-Mart employees decline to form unions they are certainly within their rights to do so.

Ideologues who rant against Wal-Mart do not understand economics. In a market economy, success goes to those businesses that best and most efficiently serve consumer needs. Businesses must induce customers to hand over money in exchange for the merchandise. Customers are completely free to ignore the offerings of any business. Every business, Wal-Mart included, must win its customers' patronage anew each day.

We all know that consumers like bargains. Getting something for less money is considered savvy shopping. Wal-Mart has opted to ensure that its prices are as low as can be. This focus has enabled the company to promise "always low prices, always."

Low prices benefit both the consumers and the overall economy, besides being a winning strategy for Wal-Mart. Every dollar a consumer saves on a purchase enables him or her to buy other items. More of consumers' needs and wants can be fulfilled when prices are lower than when prices are higher. Because a consumer's dollars go further at lower prices, more merchandise can be manufactured and sold. All the businesses making and selling these other products and services are helped.

The sheer size of Wal-Mart attests to the success of its strategy and the benefits to the economy. Growing into the largest business on the planet indicates that it is accurately interpreting consumer needs and efficiently serving them. This is exactly what we want businesses to do. This is what the free market encourages them to do. It is estimated that Wal-Mart's impact on prices accounted for 12 percent of the economy's productivity gains in the 1990s. This also helped reduce the effect of the Federal Reserve's inflation of the money supply.

But what about the methods Wal-Mart uses to achieve its goal of low prices? What about its exploitation of labor? The free market requires that transactions be carried out voluntarily between the parties. No one is forced to work for Wal-Mart. The wages it pays must be adequate to secure the services of its employees. Would Wal-Mart's employees like to be paid more? Sure, everyone wants higher pay. If its employees could get higher pay elsewhere, Wal-Mart would lose its best workers to the businesses paying those higher wages.

The same goes for the alleged uncompensated overtime. Wal-Mart can't force its employees to work overtime without compensation. Employees are not chained to their stations. They are free to leave and take other jobs if the pay or working conditions at Wal-Mart are less than satisfactory.

Neither can Wal-Mart "squeeze" vendors, compelling them to accept deals that they would prefer to refuse. Of course, sellers would like to get as high a price for their wares as they can. Likewise, buyers would like to get as low a price as they can. Both have to settle on a price that is mutually agreeable. Wal-Mart has a reputation for keeping its word and paying promptly. This enables its suppliers to plan their production and provides a reliable cash flow to help fund operations.

(continued)

If some of Wal-Mart's suppliers choose to manufacture their products overseas, that is because doing so lowers their costs. Sure, the costs may be lower because the wages demanded by foreign workers in places like Bangladesh are low and the workplaces may be "sweatshops" compared to conditions in U.S. factories. But this is hardly the cruel exploitation that Wal-Mart's critics describe. The relevant comparison is not to the working conditions Americans have become accustomed to after two centuries of industrial progress and wealth beyond the wildest dreams of inhabitants of the less-developed countries. The relevant comparison is to the alternatives available in these less-developed economies.

Companies that employ people in factories in less developed economies must offer a compensation package sufficient to lure them from alternative occupations. So as bad as these "sweatshop" wages and working conditions may appear to Americans who have a fabulous array of lucrative employment opportunities, they are obviously superior to the alternatives that inhabitants of less-developed economies are offered. If the "sweatshop" jobs weren't superior, people wouldn't take them.

The claim that Wal-Mart "disregards the concerns of small communities" is also contradicted by the evidence. If Wal-Mart's stores were not in tune with the concerns of shoppers in small communities, the stores wouldn't make a profit and would eventually shut down. If Wal-Mart's stores were not in tune with the concerns of job seekers in those communities, the stores wouldn't be able to staff their operations. The concerns that Wal-Mart rightly disregards are those of local businesses that would prefer not to have to deal with new competition. The absence of rigorous competition leads to high prices in many small communities. While this may be good for the profit margins of established businesses, it is not necessarily a condition to be preferred over the benefits for the majority of the inhabitants of the community that result from robust competition.

Wal-Mart runs the largest corporate cash-giving foundation in America. In 2004 Wal-Mart donated over $170 million. More than 90 percent of these donations went to charities in the communities served by Wal-Mart stores.

From an economic perspective, when all the claims are dispassionately evaluated it looks like Wal-Mart promotes prosperity. The company is helping consumers get more for their money. It is providing jobs for willing employees. It is stimulating its suppliers to achieve greater economies in manufacturing. It is encouraging trade with less-developed economies, helping the inhabitants of Third World nations to improve their standards of living. Far from "disregarding the concerns of small communities," Wal-Mart offers an appealing place to shop and work.

Wal-Mart is doing all these good things and making a profit of around $9 billion a year. This is a profit margin of less than 4 percent. That's mighty efficient. To call Wal-Mart a "corporate criminal" is slander. Wal-Mart is a model of how successful capitalism is supposed to work. It is a company that should be emulated, not reviled.

Source: Semmens, John, "Wal-Mart Is Good for the Economy," *The Freeman*, vol. 55, no. 8, October 1, 2005. 8. © 2005 Foundation for Economic Education. Reprinted by permission of Foundation for Economic Education (FEE).

Check Your Comprehension of the Reading

Review your comprehension of the reading selection by answering the questions below. Use a separate sheet if necessary.

1. What is the main idea of Semmens's article? State it in your own words.

2. What does Semmens' mean by a "free market economy?" Explain your answer.

3. How important is this topic for general readers? Might this information be more important to some readers than others? Which readers need the information in this article? Explain your answer.

4. What is one criticism someone may make in response to Semmens's article?

5. What is Semmens's view of competition, since competition creates winners and losers?

3. Outline and Summarize the Reading

On a separate sheet, outline the reading's main ideas, and write a brief summary of the reading.

4. Prepare an Information Sheet for the Reading

Using your annotations and the outline and summary you prepared for step 3, create an information sheet for this article that includes the following headings: *Author, Title, Publication Information, How I Might Use This Source, Brief Outline, Brief Summary, Key Words,* and *Potential Quotes.* See "Step-by-Step Guidance for Integrated Reading and Writing Projects" for more help.

Developing Your Essay

Follow these steps to plan, draft, revise, and edit your **essay**.

1. Synthesize Your Sources

Review your annotations of the four readings, and fill in the following issues chart, using a separate sheet if necessary. See Alex's work in "Step-by-Step Guidance for Integrated Reading and Writing Projects" if you need to review how to create and use an issues chart.

PROJECT 3 ISSUES CHART					
Issue	Source 1	Source 2	Source 3	Source 4	Source 5
	"Watching Wal-Mart" by Liza Featherstone	"Discussion Case: Wal-Mart" by Joseph DesJardins	"Walmart Cut My Hours. I Protested. They Fired Me" by Josh Harkinson	"I Worked at Wal-Mart for Two Years and I Actually Really Liked It" by Travis Okulski	"Wal-Mart Is Good for the Economy" by John Semmens

2. Prewrite to Develop Your Ideas

Complete the following steps to develop your ideas.

Review the Assignment.   Review your annotations on the project assignment. Compose a question for every statement that provides a specific requirement. List your questions here. Use a separate sheet if necessary.

Questions:

1. _____

2. _____

3. _____

4. _____

5. _____

Select a Topic.   Look over your questions. Select a topic that interests you and write it here.

Essay topic: _____

Use a Prewriting Method to Generate Ideas.   On a separate sheet, use one of these prewriting strategies—listing, clustering, asking 5 W's + 1 H questions, freewriting, freetalking, or discussion—to generate ideas.

3. Construct a Thesis Statement

In this assignment, your purpose is to write a persuasive essay. A persuasively focused thesis statement will offer a *claim*, a sentence with which people may agree or disagree. Make sure your thesis statement is arguable. Notice how the first statement presents an arguable claim, while the second statement provides only information.

Persuasively focused thesis statement: We should lower the drinking age to eighteen and teach teenagers to drink responsibly.

Readers may agree or disagree with this idea.

Informative thesis statement: In many European countries, it is legal for teenagers to drink alcohol.

This statement simply expresses a fact. It is not an arguable statement.

Review your prewriting notes and compose a thesis statement for your essay. Write your thesis statement here.

Thesis statement: _____

4. Develop Support for Your Thesis Statement

Review your prewriting notes, and choose your major supporting points. List at least major three supporting points here. Add lines if you will use more than three major supporting points.

Supporting points:

Point 1 _____

Point 2 _____

Point 3 _____

Think about Text Patterns You Can Use.   Determine which patterns you will use in your essay. You may use more than one pattern. Determine which patterns (narration, definition, illustration, classification, comparison-contrast, cause and effect, process analysis) you will use in your essay. You may use more than one pattern. On a separate sheet, create a chart with the headings *Text Pattern* and *How I Could Use the Pattern*. Fill in the chart with ideas about how each pattern might help you to create supporting details. See "Step-by-Step Guidance for Integrated Reading and Writing Projects" for an example chart.

5. Create an Outline to Organize Your Essay

Determine the order in which you will present your ideas—order of importance, chronological or sequential order, or spatial order. Then, on a separate sheet, create an enhanced outline for your essay. Your outline should follow the format shown in "Step-by-Step Guidance for Integrated Reading and Writing Projects." It should include your topic, your thesis statement, and major supporting points and supporting details for your introduction, body, and conclusion paragraphs.

6. Add Source Materials to Your Outline

Return to your outline, and write down where you will insert source materials. Include citation information for each source.

7. Write a Complete Draft of Your Essay

Follow these steps to write a complete draft of your essay.

Keep an Audience in Mind.   Reread your outline and answer this question:

> *Have I included all the important information that my readers will want to know about my topic?*

Yes or no? _____

If your answer is no, on a separate sheet, write down additional questions that your reader will want answered. Do additional prewriting to develop answers for those questions, and insert your new information into your outline.

Write an Introduction Paragraph.   On a separate sheet or in your computer file, write your introduction paragraph. Select a method of introduction, and include your thesis statement in your introduction paragraph.

Write Body Paragraphs According to Your Outline.   On a separate sheet or in your computer file, write your body paragraphs.

End with an Effective Conclusion.   On a separate sheet or in your computer file, write your conclusion paragraph. Use a method of concluding that brings closure to your essay.

Create a Title.   Think of an effective title and add it to your essay. A title can ask a question, present your main idea, or simply present the topic. Write your title here.

Title: _____

7. Integrate Ideas and Quotes from Sources Correctly

Check that you have used sources correctly. Look for comma splices, run-on sentences, and quotations that lack an introduction. Use attributive tags to help readers see where ideas come from. Make any changes necessary.

Finishing Your Assignment

Use the remaining steps to finish your integrated reading and writing assignment.

1. Check That You Have Met Assignment Requirements

Reread your annotated assignment and create a self-assessment list. See Alex's example in "Step-by-Step Guidance for Integrated Reading and Writing Projects" if you need a refresher on how to do this.

An Argument Essay Assignment	SELF-ASSESSMENT LIST
The readings in this project present a variety of debated issues involving Walmart. Select one of these issues, and write an essay in which you argue your viewpoint.	

An Argument Essay Assignment

SELF-ASSESSMENT LIST

The readings in this project present a variety of debated issues involving Walmart. Select one of these issues, and write an essay in which you argue your viewpoint.

You will need to clearly define the issue, explain both sides of the issue, write a claim stating your opinion, and write supporting paragraphs in which you provide sound evidence to back up your claim. Use information from the sources in this chapter as one way to support your claim.

Finally, your essay should be written in standard English, be free from grammatical, spelling, and formatting errors, and conform to MLA or APA style.

Answer each question that you wrote about your assignment and then answer the following:

Have I met my assignment requirements?

Yes or no? _____

If your answer is no, make the necessary corrections to your draft.

2. Revise for Organization and Unity

As you read your draft, answer these questions: (1) Do my major supporting points support my thesis statement? (2) Are my ideas organized in a logical and convincing way? (3) Have I used transitions to show relationships between ideas? (4) Does my writing have a successful introduction and conclusion? See "Checklist: Revising for Unity" in "Step-by-Step Guidance for Integrated Reading and Writing Projects" for more help.

If you answer no to any questions, make the necessary revisions to your draft.

3. Revise for Development

As you read your draft, answer these questions: (1) Have I answered my reader's potential questions? (2) Have I provided enough support (definitions, examples, comparisons, causes, effects, and so on) for the main idea? (3) Are there places where I could add more support? (4) Do I make unjustified assumptions about what the reader knows? See "Checklist: Revising for Development" in "Step-by-Step Guidance for Integrated Reading and Writing Projects" for more help.

If you answer no to any questions, make the necessary revisions to your draft.

4. Revise for Clarity

As you read your draft, answer these questions: (1) Does the sentence communicate the idea effectively? (2) Is the tone appropriate? (3) Would I normally use the particular words I'm using to communicate this idea? (4) If I were explaining the idea to a friend, how would I say it? See "Checklist: Revising for Clarity" in "Step-by-Step Guidance for Integrated Reading and Writing Projects" for more help.

5. Create a Works Cited or References List

Create a works cited or references list, and answer this question:

Is my documentation list correctly formatted?

Yes or no? _____

If you are unsure or you answer no, ask your instructor or tutor for help.

6. Check for Plagiarism

Double-check your essay and answer this question:

Is the source for every summary, quotation, and paraphrase correctly identified in my essay?

Yes or no? _____

Correct any errors and omissions.

7. Edit Your Essay Using SMART TRACS

Use the "SMART TRACS" guidelines—**S**pelling, **M**echanics, **A**ccurate punctuation, **R**epeated or missing words, **T**erminal punctuation, **T**ense and verb issues, **R**eference of pronouns, **A**postrophe use, **C**onfusing words, **S**ources—to edit your essay. See "Step-by-Step Guidance for Integrated Reading and Writing Projects" for more help.

Correct any errors. List the types of errors that appear more than once in your essay.

Types of errors:

_____

_____

Make a point of learning how to correct these recurring errors.
Incorporate all of the changes you have made and write a final draft of your essay.

Answer the following question:

Does this essay present my best work?

Yes or no? _____

If you answered no, do not stop working on your essay. Go back and work on it until you have created an essay you are proud of.

8. Put Your Essay in the Proper Format

Review your essay to make sure the following elements are correctly formatted: heading, header (and page numbers), spacing, margins, title, font type and size, quotations, and works cited or references list. Answer the following question:

Is my essay correctly formatted?

Yes or no? _____

If you answered no, make any needed corrections.

Turn In Your Completed Assignment

Congratulations! You have completed your integrated reading and writing assignment. Follow your instructor's guidelines for submitting your finished essay.

Additional Skills

Chapter 12
Using Sources

AVAILABLE ONLY IN

Strategies for Reading
and Writing Exams

©Phanuwat Nandee/123RF RF

Using Sources

©senkaya/123RF RF

Professionals know that for the best outcome, they must use good sources and position their materials with care, whether they are building a house, catering a party, or writing an essay.

Many—if not most—of the writing assignments you will do in college and at work will include the use of source materials. What should be the connection between a source's ideas and your own ideas? When should you refer to sources in your writing? How do you use sources without plagiarizing? How do you integrate quotes and source references smoothly? These are a few of the questions we will consider in this chapter to help you use sources accurately, ethically, and effectively.

Chapter Objectives

After completing this chapter, students will be able to do the following:

- Prepare to use source materials.

- Work with readings for a source-based essay.

- Develop a source-based essay.

- Create in-text references in MLA and APA styles.

- Format an MLA paper and prepare a works cited list.

- Format an APA paper and prepare a references list.

- Check an essay for plagiarism.

Getting Started: Preparing to Use Source Materials

The best way to start any reading and writing task is to analyze and annotate the assignment itself. In the simple example that follows, the student's annotations point out the specific parts of the assignment that will help him determine exactly what to focus on when reading the sources.

English 0301 Reading and Writing Project

Most cities have recycling programs of some sort. In the essays that follow, you will learn about the cities with the best recycling programs in the United States. As you read about these cities, determine the factors that help them rank high in their recycling initiatives. Once you have determined these factors, think about the recycling program in your own city. How does it compare with the programs in the cities you have read about? Write an essay in which you use the factors you have identified to compare your city's recycling program to those you have read about. Evaluate how good a job your city is doing with its recycling program, and provide your evaluation in your essay. Your essay should have two parts: an analysis of your city's recycling program based on the factors you have read about, and an evaluation of the quality of your city's recycling program.

Read sources.

Determine factors used to judge recycling programs.

Compare my city's recycling program with the programs of cities in the articles.

Write an essay and use the factors for the comparison.

Evaluate my city's program.

Include an analysis and an evaluation.

By annotating the assignment, the student has identified the tasks he must focus on when he reads the source material. He is clear about his purpose: to figure out what makes the recycling programs of particular cities good. He must also figure out the factors that are used to judge the recycling programs (such as percentage of waste recycled, public awareness and participation, and so on). With these things in mind, the student can read in a more focused way.

Working with Readings

When you are ready to start reading the sources, use a previewing process to guide your work. Start by considering who wrote the source, for whom it was written, and when and where it was published. After previewing, read and annotate the sources. Next, create an outline, a summary, and an information sheet for each source. As you work with sources, keep in mind the information that follows.

Examining Authors for Bias and Credibility

One way to assess the credibility of a source is to evaluate the author: her position, her reputation, and the subjects she often writes about. A quick Internet search may help you obtain this information. Knowing the writer's background will help you understand her authority on the subject—as well as her biases. For example, if a writer has a reputation as an advocate of prison reform, you can expect her article to reflect that point of view. If she teaches criminology at a university or is a prison warden, her position lends credibility to her writing. Researching the writer's background will enable you to refer to her credentials later when you draft your essay. Doing so will tell your readers that the source you are using is credible.

Reputable Web sites go to some trouble to be transparent about who runs them and who writes for them. If you cannot find information about the source of the information on a Web site, be wary about using it for research. If you learn only that an article on a site is authored by Millard Wentworth, for example, you have not really learned anything (unless the name Millard Wentworth is meaningful to you!). If author biographies are provided, you have a bit more information and can rank the site a bit higher in terms of credibility. To determine more about a site's author or sponsoring organization, conduct a search using *Google* or another search engine.

Examining Audience

Examining the potential audience for a source will add to your understanding. Consider an article about diabetes that appears in a journal for doctors. The writer has made certain assumptions about the medical knowledge of the audience. When you read the article, you may need to consult dictionaries or other sources to understand it. An article that appears on the Web site of People for the Ethical Treatment of Animals (PETA) will be written for an audience that, for the most part, shares PETA's views. Knowing the beliefs of the audience will help you more accurately understand the writer's point.

Examining Date and Historical Context

Another aspect of the source to consider is when it was published. If the source is not current, consider its historical context. Suppose you are reading an article about the oil industry, and you notice that it was written in 1976. If you know that the United States experienced an energy crisis in the mid-1970s, you will better understand the issues discussed in the article. If you notice that an article about hurricane preparedness was written in 2006, you will have more insight into the article by realizing that Hurricane Katrina—one of the most deadly hurricanes to hit the United States—occurred in 2005. In general, unless a source is important or ground-breaking in its field (for example, a work on psychology by Sigmund Freud), use sources written within the last five years.

Examining the Source for Bias and Credibility

A source is *biased* if it advocates or promotes a particular view on an issue. For example, suppose you want to determine whether high-fructose corn syrup is good for you. If you look at the Web site of a company that produces high-fructose corn syrup, you would expect to find information that is biased in favor of the product and the many ways it improves foods and beverages. Likewise, it is unlikely that you would find arguments against the product. Therefore, you would be unwise to base your determination solely on the evidence of that biased Web site.

At times, reading biased sources might suit your writing task. For instance, in a persuasive essay, you might want to present the viewpoint of the corn syrup company as well as the viewpoint of those opposed to the wide use of corn syrup as a sweetener (a viewpoint that will also be biased). Comparing these two biased sources may be helpful in such a paper. Often, however, writers are best served by looking for sources that are neutral and do not have an interest in promoting a particular point of view.

Examining the Source for Bias.   Sources may come from general magazines, scholarly journals, Web sites, and a variety of other publications. Knowing a source's origin will help you predict potential biases. Some journals and magazines directly reveal their biases. For example, just the name of *The American Conservative* gives you a clue about the magazine's political orientation. If you go to the magazine's Web site, you will find a definitive statement of the magazine's biases. The magazine says, "To solve the country's seemingly intractable—and, in the long-term, lethal—strategic, economic, and socio-cultural problems requires a rediscovery of traditional conservatism. That's the mission of *The American Conservative*." Similarly, if you do an Internet search on book publishers, you also may be able to detect biases. Ignatius Press, for example, describes itself as the "primary publisher in U.S. of Pope Benedict XVI's books." We can expect books from Ignatius Press to have a Roman Catholic bias.

Determining the bias of Web sites can be a bit trickier. One way to do so is to examine its **domain name**—the last part of its Web address. Common domain names are *.com, .gov, .edu,* and *.org*. If a Web site address ends in *.com*, it is a commercial Web site, and you should suspect it will contain biases in favor of the product or service it is selling. Web sites whose domain is *.org* (meaning that it represents an organization) may be less biased, but *.org* sites often promote ideas. For example, PETA has this on its home page (www.peta.org): "Animals are *not* ours to eat, wear, experiment on, use for entertainment, or abuse in any other way." The bias of PETA's organizational Web site is clearly stated. Note that having a bias does not mean a source is disreputable; it simply tells you the source is not neutral.

Web sites sponsored by federal, state, and local governments have the domain *.gov*. Much of the information on government Web sites—in particular, statistical information—is simply factual. However, the Web site of a particular agency or department (for example, the US Environmental Protection Agency) may advocate for activities such as conservation and more regulation, which other organizations (for example, energy companies) do not favor. Additionally, individual senators and congressional representatives have Web sites that end in *.gov*. These sites will be biased because they will present the senator's or representative's point of view.

Web sites that end in *.edu* are educational—that is, associated with colleges, universities, and other recognized educational institutions. While these sites may be less biased than *.com* sites, it is important to remember that professors and even students often have personal Web sites sponsored by their institution. Those personal Web sites often present points of view about issues. Thus, these sites will also present bias.

In the end, you—as a consumer of information—must always be the one to make a careful choice about the bias of a particular Web site or source. Bias is not necessarily a bad thing, but as a researcher, you must know whether your sources are biased or take a neutral point of view.

Examining the Source for Credibility.

One way to determine the **credibility** of a source—its trustworthiness—is by examining its origin. For example, we expect articles in *The New York Times* to be written ethically and credibly. Similarly, we expect articles that appear in **peer-reviewed** journals (journals that have a stringent process for selecting what they publish) to be credible. On the other end of the credibility spectrum are tabloids that present celebrity gossip and news items that are often unverifiable—ranging from accounts of alien landings to reports of six-headed babies. You can often do an Internet search of a source's name to learn more about its reputation and credibility.

To assess a source that comes from a Web site, you must assess the Web site itself. Study the Web site that follows and the clues that are pointed out as you review the following factors. First, a professional Web site will be well edited and will not contain errors in spelling or grammar. Ideally, it should not carry advertising. There is one exception to this rule. Newspapers have historically depended on advertisements as one source of funding. The presence of advertisements in newspapers is not an indication of bias. Some credible Web sites do allow advertising, but unless you are looking

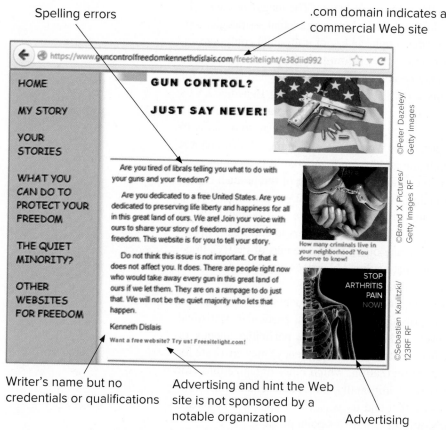

Spelling errors

.com domain indicates a commercial Web site

Writer's name but no credentials or qualifications

Advertising and hint the Web site is not sponsored by a notable organization

Advertising

A Web site that is biased and is *not* credible.

at reputable newspapers online, look for sites that do not permit advertising. Advertising is a sign that the owner of the Web site wants to make money by luring people to the site; thus, the owner may decide to post the content that draws in the most people, which may not necessarily be the most authoritative content on a subject. Additionally, a credible Web site will offer support for the information it posts. For example, some Web sites provide bibliographies to show the sources the authors consulted, a practice that allows readers to evaluate the credibility of the information.

Clearly, the Web site shown on the previous page is biased, but its bias is not the problem. The real question is whether we should regard its writer, Kenneth Dislais, as a credible or qualified source for information about gun control. He offers no biographical information about himself; in fact, we have no information about the sponsors of the Web site either. The only information we have is that it was created by means of a free Web site generator. Why should we believe that Kenneth Dislais knows *anything* about the issue of gun control? We do know one thing: he did not use a spell-checker to proofread his Web site! Further, the site includes advertisements that are not related to the content. In summary, when you encounter sites like this one, question the value of the information. Can you verify that it is anything other than a mouthpiece for one unknown individual? If not, the site lacks credibility and is a poor source.

Now, take a look at another Web site for an organization that opposes gun control, shown at the top of the next page. Notice that this site, sponsored by Citizens for Responsible Gun Ownership, is biased but credible.

The Web site goes to some trouble to let viewers know who sponsors it, where the organization is located (its physical address), and the group's philosophy and

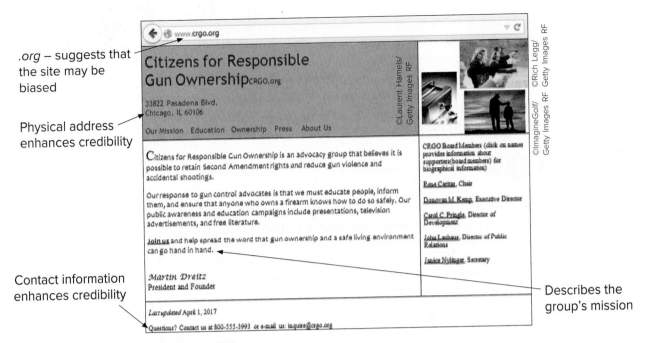

.org – suggests that the site may be biased

Physical address enhances credibility

Contact information enhances credibility

Describes the group's mission

A Web site that is biased but is also credible.

mission. Also, the clear identification of the site's founder and president and easy availability of information about its supporters (board members) lend it credibility. Moreover, the site provides ways for the sponsoring organization to be contacted, which suggests that the group is well-established. While we know that the site will be biased because it exists to promote the rights of gun owners, we can have some confidence that it may ultimately prove to have trustworthy information.

Finally, let's examine a Web site that is both credible and unbiased regarding the issue of gun ownership. Notice the characteristics of this objectively oriented site, Yes-or-No.org.

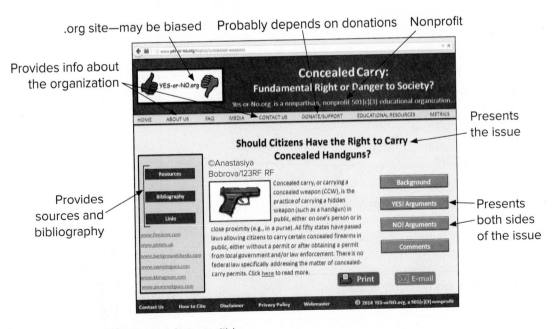

.org site—may be biased

Probably depends on donations

Nonprofit

Provides info about the organization

Provides sources and bibliography

Presents the issue

Presents both sides of the issue

A Web site that is *not* biased and is credible.

Yes-or-No.org provides numerous clues that it is credible and seeks to be objective. Its name suggests that we will learn about both sides of issues. The site confirms this idea by providing a neutral introduction to the issue of carrying concealed guns and then offering both sides of the argument. Also, the Web site enhances its credibility by giving resources and bibliographies. We can see that Yes-or-No.org is a nonprofit educational organization that depends on donations and is not funded by people on a particular side of an issue. These facts help establish the site as both credible and objective.

PRACTICE 1

Examining Sources

Bibliographic information is given below for one text source and two Web site. All of these sources concern the effects of aspartame, the artificial sweetener used in many products, including NutraSweet. Using this information and an Internet search engine to look up information about the publication and the writers, answer the questions that follow each source.

1. Author: Joe Graedon and Teresa Graedon

    Title: "How Safe Is Aspartame?"

    Source: www.tuscaloosanews.com/news/20060112/peoples-pharmacy-how-safe-is-aspartame

    Date: 12 Jan. 2006

    a. How credible are these writers?

    _____

    _____

    b. Does anything about the publication (*TuscaloosaNews.com*) suggest bias?

    _____

    _____

2. Author: John Briffa

    Title: "Aspartame and Its Effects on Health: Independently Funded Studies Have Found Potential for Adverse Effects"

    Journal: *BMJ* (*British Medical Journal*), vol. 330, no. 7486, pp. 309–10

    Publisher: BMJ Publishing Group

    Date: February 2005

    a. How credible is this writer?

    _____

    b. Does anything about the publication (*British Medical Journal*) suggest bias?

    _____

    _____

    c. For what audience was this probably written?

    _____

(continued)

3. http://www.aspartame.org

    a. How credible is this Web site?

    _____

    b. Does anything about this Web site suggest bias?

    _____

    _____

    c. What did you learn about the authors of this Web site?

    _____

Reading and Annotating Sources

The best way to work with sources is to print them out and have a pen, pencil, and highlighter ready. Read the source, using a pencil to annotate the ideas that seem to be important. It is difficult to recognize the most important ideas in a text the first time you read it, so using a pencil will enable you to go back and make changes.

Read the source a second time, this time using your pen and highlighter to annotate the text. Mark the major supporting points, the thesis statement, nuggets of information you find interesting or useful, potential quotes, and any passages about which you have questions. Write questions and comments in the margin. If you are reading more than one source, annotate any connections you notice between the sources.

If, after you have read the source several times, you are confused or unsure about its meaning, read it again. There is nothing wrong with reading a source several times; in fact, doing so is quite common and always useful. Another idea to help with your comprehension is to write down the topic on a piece of paper. Next, write down the main point the writer is making about the topic. Put this information into a sentence. What you have written _should_ be the writer's thesis statement. Work with your course instructor or a lab instructor if you need additional help comprehending a text.

As you search for potential quotes, think about the assignment. If you keep in mind the kind of paper you will be writing, you are more likely to select appropriate quotes. You cannot be totally certain about which parts of your sources you will actually use in your paper until you create an outline and work on a draft. To select quotes you think you may use, look over your annotations. You should have noted the main idea, major supporting points, and particularly interesting minor supporting details. These are potentially useful passages to use as quotations. It is vitally important to copy these passages _word-for-word_. A quote must include the exact words you find in the original source.

Outlining, Summarizing, and Preparing Information Sheets for Sources

Once you have read and understood a source, prepare a brief outline and a brief summary. Create an _information sheet_ that includes the outline and summary and enough information to render the source useful as a reference as you write your essay. At the top, write all the bibliographic information you have (author, title, publication, date of publication, city of publication, publisher or sponsoring organization, and pages or URL if you are using a Web source) and comment on any points of interest to you. For example, you could note an essay idea that the source suggests to you. Here's a sample format for an information sheet.

Model for an Information Sheet

Author

Title

Publication Information

How I Might Use This Source

Brief Outline

Thesis statement:
Major supporting point 1:
Major supporting point 2:
Major supporting point 3:

Brief Summary

Issues

Key Words

Potential Quotes

When you have created an information sheet for each source, you are ready to start the next phase of the integrated reading and writing process: developing your essay.

PRACTICE 2

Selecting Information to Use from Sources

What follows is one of the articles referred to in Practice 1.

- Read and annotate the article.

- On a separate sheet, prepare a simple information sheet. Include bibliographic information, a simple outline, a brief summary, and three quotes.

How Safe Is Aspartame?

By Joe Graedon and Teresa Graedon

People love to hate artificial sweeteners. Starting with saccharin in the late 1950s, some have enthusiastically embraced the idea of sweets without calories. Others have warned that saccharin, cyclamate and aspartame are too dangerous for human consumption.

The debate is often intensely emotional. Cyclamate was removed from the market in 1969 when animal studies showed an excess of tumors in rats exposed to the sweetener. This remained controversial for the next 20 years, but the Food and Drug Administration did not reverse itself.

The FDA proposed pulling saccharin off the market in the mid-1970s, also on the suspicion that it might cause cancer. The agency let those plans drop due to public outcry and congressional outrage.

The most popular noncaloric sweetener for the past few decades has been aspartame. This artificial sweetener was introduced with great fanfare in 1981 as one of the safest alternatives to sugar ever created. The FDA announced when

YOUR ANNOTATIONS

saccharin: an artificial sweetener commonly sold in pink packets under brand is Sweet'N Low.

cyclamate: an artificial sweetener approved for use in many countries but banned in the United States.

aspartame: an artificial sweetener most often sold in blue packages and initially marketed as NutraSweet. Its health effects are widely debated.

(continued)

it approved aspartame, "Few compounds have withstood such detailed testing and repeated, close scrutiny, and the process through which aspartame has gone should provide the public with additional confidence of its safety."

That's their story, and they're sticking to it. Through the years, though, frightening tales of aspartame toxicity have circulated on the Internet.

One reader wrote: "I know from firsthand experience that there are very serious problems with aspartame. In 1996 I was diagnosed with epilepsy. At that time I was trying to lose weight and eating a lot of products with aspartame.

"I became suspicious and stopped eating aspartame-laced products. Even though my neurologist was skeptical, I was able to discontinue my seizure medicine and have not had further seizures."

Others have blamed aspartame for a wide variety of health problems including headaches, dizziness, confusion, memory loss, depression, blindness, ADD, ALS, lupus and multiple sclerosis.

With dozens of symptoms attributed to aspartame, it is easy to discount the diatribes. We were skeptical about the more exaggerated claims, especially regarding links to cancer.

Recent research by a European foundation has forced us to look at aspartame in a new light, however. A study published online in the journal *Environmental Health Perspectives* (Nov. 17, 2005) involved 1,800 rats and six dosage levels of aspartame in their chow.

The rats in this study were not sacrificed but lived out their natural lives and were examined upon death. The authors report an excess of leukemias, lymphomas and malignant tumors among rats fed aspartame at several dosage levels.

Critics charge that the researchers did not follow standard protocols for this type of study. The investigators respond that "the findings speak for themselves."

Developing Your Source-Based Essay

Once you have read, annotated, analyzed, and prepared information sheets for all your sources, you are ready to start thinking about your own essay. It is wise to go back to the assignment and reread it before going on. You should look frequently at the assignment during the reading and writing process to stay on track. After you have reviewed the assignment, follow these steps to start developing your essay.

Synthesizing Sources

Begin by creating an *issues chart* to categorize your sources according to focus or point of view. For example, assume you are reading about the changing definition of the family in the United States. Some of your sources discuss types of families (such as single-parent families and multigenerational families). Others discuss why our definitions of the family are changing. You could categorize your sources into "types" and "explanations."

Or imagine you are reading about a controversial topic, such as the effects of violent video games. Some sources claim that such games enhance problem-solving skills and hand-eye coordination. Others claim that these games have little to no effect on participants. Still others claim that there is a direct relationship between playing violent video games and being violent in real life. You might put these sources into the groups "pro," "con," and "neutral/other." Once you have a clear picture of the points of view of your sources, you can choose the best categories. If you categorize your sources, you will more easily be able to locate the source you need to support a particular point while writing.

Another way to synthesize your sources is to create a table that is designed specifically for your assignment. For instance, if you were working on the recycling assignment, you would need to know details about the various recycling programs from each city. You would also need to know which factors the writers analyzed to judge the effectiveness of the programs. Thus, you could make a table like the one that follows to synthesize your information.

ISSUES CHART			
Issues	Source 1	Source 2	Source 3
	Mattaville, Washington	Westerson, Florida	Rio Terra, California
Percentage of community that participates in recycling program	81	88	84
Percentage of trash recycled	78	82	82
Recycling of glass?	Yes	No	Yes
Recycling of paper and plastic?	Yes	Yes	Yes
Recycling of furniture?	Yes	No	No
Recycling of wood?	Yes	Yes	Yes

This kind of table will help you see how each recycling program compares to the others, and it will help you determine the criteria (in the left column) you can use in your analysis of your own city's recycling program. Of course, the content of the chart you create will depend on the content of the sources you are analyzing.

Prewriting to Develop Your Ideas

As you read your sources, make notes, and synthesize the source material, you will start to have an idea of what you want to communicate in your thesis statement. Use a prewriting method to generate ideas about the topic. One way to start is to prewrite about each of the elements you need to include in your paper. For example, in the assignment we analyzed earlier, these are the required elements:

- Factors used to judge recycling programs
- Comparison of my city's recycling program with the programs of cities in the articles
- Analysis of my city's program using factors for comparison
- Evaluation of my city's program

Use prewriting to generate ideas for each of the elements that will be in your essay.

Constructing a Thesis Statement and Support

Once you believe you understand the issues well enough to know what point you would like to make, construct a thesis statement. Make sure your thesis statement is grammatically correct and that it communicates the main message you want to express in your paper.

After writing a thesis statement, you will choose your major supporting points. Let's take the example of Krystal, a student who is writing an essay about the dangers of concussions from playing football. She has read a number of sources on the topic, and her prewriting has led her to compose this thesis statement.

Thesis statement: The effects of concussions sustained while playing football are so serious that players should demand changes or refuse to play the game.

On the basis of her reading and thesis statement, Krystal lists the information she needs to support her position. What will her readers need to know? As she determines her readers' needs, she jots them down in the left column. Then she writes a complete sentence for each need in the right column, making sure the sentence supports her thesis statement.

Readers will need me to . . .	Major supporting points
Explain the effects of concussions	Scientists have learned that concussions have serious long-term effects on the brain. [List effects.]
Suggest changes that can decrease these negative effects	Players and those who care about them should demand changes. • The first thing that can be done is to reduce the number of concussions by changing some of the rules in football. • A second solution is to require the use of a new type of helmet. • Third, football coaches, trainers, physicians, players, and the families of players must be trained to identify concussions and consult the appropriate health-care professionals so that concussions are treated correctly.
Convince players to refuse to play unless such changes are made	Players must educate themselves about the realities and then stand up for themselves—if necessary, by refusing to play—for the sake of their long-term health and for those who care about them.

Notice how the major supporting points in the second column are directly related to both the thesis statement and to the readers' needs.

Creating an Outline

Krystal is now ready to create an outline. An outline does not have to be formal to be effective, but it does need to be written with care. The thesis statement and the major supporting points must be included in the form of well-written, complete sentences. Ideally, Krystal should be able to simply copy those sentences from her outline and put them directly into her paper.

As Krystal creates her outline, she determines how many body paragraphs she will need for each major supporting point. Some major supporting points can be expressed in a single paragraph, but others may need more than one body paragraph. Krystal's outline, which follows, demonstrates this idea.

Outline for a Source-Based Essay

Topic: Concussions in football

Thesis statement: The effects of concussions sustained while playing football are so serious that players should demand changes or refuse to play the game.

Introduction

Paragraph 1: Explain why so many people are talking about this issue these days. Start with the story of Dave Duerson. End with thesis statement.

Body

Paragraph 2 (major supporting point 1—effects): Scientists have learned that concussions have serious long-term effects on the brain.

Paragraph 3 (major supporting point 2—changes): Players and those who care about them should demand changes. The first thing that can be done is to reduce the number of concussions by changing some of the rules in football.

Paragraph 4 (major supporting point 3—changes): A second solution is to require the use of a new type of helmet.

Paragraph 5 (major supporting point 4—changes): Third, football coaches, trainers, physicians, players, and the families of players must be trained to identify concussions and consult the appropriate health-care professionals so that concussions are treated correctly.

Paragraph 6 (major supporting point 5—refuse to play): Players must educate themselves about the realities and then stand up for themselves—if necessary, by refusing to play—for the sake of their long-term health and for those who care about them.

Conclusion

Paragraph 7: Explain how this issue affects not only NFL players but also kids across the country. Urge a solution.

Adding Source Material and Details to Your Outline

Now that she has an outline, Krystal can start adding minor supporting details, including source materials. She has to consider carefully when and where to use quotes from her sources. She will not want to overuse her research by including too many quotes or by merely summarizing a variety of sources. The result would be a paper that jumps from quote to quote or from summary to summary without tying the information together in a way that represents her perspective and insights. Professors want to see *your* writing. So remember that quotes are best used sparingly and only when they truly support the point you are making.

Remember that when you use specific ideas from *any* source, even if you put them into your own words, you *must* give credit to the author of those ideas. Many students wonder whether they need to cite sources for well-known ideas, or **common**

knowledge. Krystal may write, for instance, that football is a dangerous sport. Because many others have said the same, this is common knowledge; so she does not have to cite other people who have made this general statement. In contrast, a statistic on the number of head injuries in football *would* need to come from a cited source because a statistic is not common knowledge. In her paper, Krystal will include specific information about the effects of concussions and solutions to the concussion problem that she learned about from her sources, and she will cite these sources when she uses them.

As Krystal considers how best to support her thesis statement, she selects several sources that will be advantageous and adds them to her outline. She uses the last name of the writer to refer to the source materials she will incorporate in her essay.

Essay Outline Annotated to Include Sources

Topic: Concussions in football

Thesis statement: The effects of concussions sustained while playing football are so serious that players should demand changes or refuse to play the game.

Introduction

Paragraph 1: Explain why so many people are talking about this issue these days. Start with the story of Dave Duerson. End with thesis statement. *Use Jackson source for Duerson's story.*

Body

Paragraph 2 (major supporting point 1—effects): Scientists have learned that concussions have serious long-term effects on the brain. *Use Monroe source and CDC source for quotes and statistics.*

Paragraph 3 (major supporting point 2—changes): Players and those who care about them should demand changes. The first thing that can be done is to reduce the number of concussions by changing some of the rules in football. *Use Davidson source to explain possible rule changes.*

Paragraph 4 (major supporting point 3—changes): A second solution is to require the use of a new type of helmet. *Use Jackson source and Monroe source for new helmet innovation information.*

Paragraph 5 (major supporting point 4—changes): Third, football coaches, trainers, physicians, players, and the families of players must be trained to identify concussions and consult the appropriate healthcare professionals so that concussions are treated correctly. *Use quotes from CDC source.*

Paragraph 6 (major supporting point 5—refuse to play): Players must educate themselves about the realities and then stand up for themselves—if necessary, by refusing to play—for the sake of their long-term health and for those who care about them. *Use the story of the Melville City League as an example—Monroe source.*

Conclusion

Paragraph 7: Explain how this issue affects not only NFL players but also youth football players across the country. Urge that a solution be found.

PRACTICE 3

Choosing Source Materials

Mark is a student writing an essay about artificial sweeteners. He plans to use the article you read in Practice 2, "How Safe Is Aspartame" by Joe and Teresa Graedon, as a source.

Read Mark's outline, below, and then reread "How Safe Is Aspartame?" Select two passages (these may be brief passages, such as one or two sentences) that support a section of Mark's outline. Choose passages that provide helpful information and would make good quotes for the essay. Underline each passage you would quote, and note where you would put each one in the outline.

Mark's Outline

Introduction

Thesis statement: The FDA should ban all artificial sweeteners since research has shown that no artificial sweetener is absolutely safe.

Body

Major supporting point 1: One of the earliest artificial sweeteners, cyclamate, was appropriately banned by the FDA, in spite of consumer pressures to make the sweetener legal.

Major supporting point 2: Saccharin, another artificial sweetener, is still legal, but it should be banned.

Major supporting point 3: Another artificial sweetener, aspartame, may be the most dangerous one yet, but it is not banned by the FDA.

Major supporting point 4: Finally, one of the newest artificial sweeteners, sucralose, is not safe for human consumption, yet it remains legal for use.

Conclusion

Writing a Complete Draft of Your Essay

Once you have an outline ready, you can use it to compose a first draft. Keep in mind that an outline is a plan, and as such it is changeable. If you write a body paragraph and find that you have not planned for enough support, change your outline by adding more examples or perhaps an anecdote or a comparison.

Use a recursive process when you draft. To *recur* means "to happen again." Recursive drafting means that you go back and reread what you have written, make changes, and resume drafting. After completing each paragraph, read your essay from the beginning. You will find areas that need more development, are unclear, and so on. Make changes as you draft.

Integrating Ideas and Quotes from Sources Correctly

As you draft your paper, integrate source material carefully. The key to using quotes effectively is knowing *when* to use them and *how* to integrate them. During the process of reading source materials, you annotated your sources and identified significant passages.

You also wrote down possible quotations on your information sheets. Keep in mind that because you wrote your notes before you knew exactly what you would be saying in your paper, the quotes you chose may not be the best ones to support your points. Be willing to go back to the source to choose the most appropriate quotes for your purpose.

A **quotation** consists of the exact words of a source. Even if the writer of the source made a grammatical error, you must reproduce the source exactly, errors included. You must acknowledge the source in the body of the text as well as in a list of references or works cited, which you will learn about later in this chapter.

Determining When to Use Quotations

Using quotations carefully can help you write an impressive, well-researched paper. However, if you use quotes like seasoning salt—sprinkling them here and there at random—you will have a paper that makes little sense. Use quotations only in the following situations.

- **You need to support your point of view with authoritative information.** The most common reason for using a quote is to back up your own ideas by citing professionals or experts who agree with you.

  Example: Some serious psychological disorders show up during the early adult years. Ian Christopher, director of the Psychiatry Department at Hudson University Hospital, points out that "schizophrenia, generalized anxiety disorders, and bipolar disorder commonly manifest in early adulthood."

- **You wish to provide complex or technical explanations.** Sometimes only experts can explain complex phenomena. Carefully select quotes when an expert can offer a better explanation than you can.

  Example: According to the Center for Genetic Origination, mutation consists of "the moment when a nucleotide sequence of the genome of an organism or related being undergoes change."

- **Using your own wording of a concept or idea would not be as effective as quoting the source's wording.** When you find a source that words an idea perfectly, it is fine to quote that source as long as you give credit.

  Example: George Orwell writes, "Doublethink means the power of holding two contradictory beliefs in one's mind simultaneously, and accepting both of them."

- **The source has used a particularly important phrase, and you do not want to change the wording of that phrase.** In the following example, the last name of the source's writer is provided in parentheses.

  Example: The detective refers to himself as "the lone ranger of the casino industry" (Cavanaugh).

Let's consider Krystal's project and her decision to quote from experts. Krystal is arguing that football players must demand changes to the game because the effects of concussions are so serious. Since she is not a doctor or a medical researcher, she needs support from experts to prove that concussions are truly as bad as she says. She has chosen a source from the Centers for Disease Control and Prevention, a credible authority on medical topics, but now she must choose quotes she could use in her paper. The source, "The Lystedt Law: A Concussion Survivor's Journey," was published in *Guide to Writing about Traumatic Brain Injury in News and Social Media* (2015, p. 7). Here is the source, with annotations by Krystal that show her reasoning process.

The Lystedt Law: A Concussion Survivor's Journey

By the Centers for Disease Control and Prevention

> There is no one tougher than my son. Sometimes players and parents wrongly believe that it shows strength and courage to play injured. Battling pain is glamorized. Zack couldn't swallow or hold his head up. Strength is seeing Zack stand up out of his wheel-chair and learning to talk again.
>
> —Victor Lystedt, Zack's Dad

Although most people with a concussion have a good recovery, for some the effects of this injury can last weeks, months, or longer. Concussions, a type of traumatic brain injury, are all serious. That is why the choices we make immediately following a concussion can decide life or death or whether an injured athlete will have a good recovery and return to play. The state of Washington stepped in to help make this choice more clear for coaches, parents, and athletes. In May 2009, the state of Washington passed a new bill called the Lystedt Law, which protects young athletes from the life-threatening or potentially lifelong consequences that can be caused by returning to the game too soon. The law is named after Zackery Lystedt, a young athlete who, in 2006, was permanently disabled after prematurely returning to a game after sustaining a concussion. It requires any youth showing signs of concussion to be examined and cleared by a licensed health care provider before returning to play.

Zack Lystedt's story, which led to what is sometimes referred to as the "shake-it-off" law, emphasizes why "shaking-it-off" puts players at risk for serious injury. Zack was a gifted athlete who played both offense and defense on his junior high school football team. He was injured at age 13 when his head struck the ground after tackling an opponent. A video of the game shows Zack lying on the ground with his hands clutching both sides of his helmet. The official called a time out, and Zack was sidelined for just three plays before half-time. His father recounts the moments following the injury, "Zack was not knocked out, but he did grab his head and rocked back-and-forth in pain." Despite the blow, Zack shook-it-off and, by the start of the third quarter, was back in the game. "He always wanted to be part of the play," his father recalls.

After a hard-played second half, Zack collapsed on the field and was airlifted to Harborview Medical Center where he underwent emergency life-saving surgery to remove the left and right side of his skull to relieve the pressure from his injured and swelling brain. He experienced numerous strokes and spent 7 days on a ventilator and 3 months in a

The use of 'life or death' shows how serious concussions can be.

Also a good phrase to use to point out seriousness Zack was 'permanently disabled.'

So 'shaking-it-off' can result in death – might be a good quote/idea to use.

I could summarize Zack's story

(continued)

coma before he awoke to his parents and a new reality. Prematurely returning to the game had resulted in the battle for Zack's young life that included 4 weeks in a nursing home, 2 months in a children's hospital for rehabilitation, 9 months before speaking his first word, 13 months before moving a leg or an arm, and 20 months on a feeding tube. It would be nearly 3 years before Zack would stand, with assistance, on his own two feet, and Washington would pass the Lystedt Law to help protect other young athletes in their state.

Shows how serious Zack's injury was.

Zack's recovery has been long and difficult by many accounts. He has again proven himself a fierce competitor. CDC, the Brain Injury Association of Washington, and the Seattle Seahawks launched Washington Heads Up: Concussion in Sports, a campaign to highlight the effects of concussion and the importance of being evaluated by a medical professional to prevent serious brain injury.

Protect your young athlete. Learn about the symptoms of a concussion and why the brain needs time to heal before your child returns to play at https://www.cdc.gov/headsup/index.html.

After thinking carefully, Krystal decides to use this quote to point out the seriousness of concussions: "[T]he choices we make immediately following a concussion can decide life or death or whether an injured athlete will have a good recovery and return to play."

Effective writers are selective about using quotations. The following guidelines will help you make decisions about when and what to quote.

- **Do not use a quote just to use a quote.** Always have a good reason for quoting a source.

- **Avoid using quotes too often.** If you pepper your essay with too many quotes, your voice will be lost, and you will not communicate your message effectively.

- **Use a lengthy quote only when you have a very good reason to do so.** Quotations—especially those that are more than two or three sentences long—take up a lot of space. You may be tempted to fill your paper with long quotations (and thus more easily reach a required word count), but do not yield to this temptation.

- **Avoid starting a paragraph with a quote.** Take ownership of the paragraphs in your paper by starting them with your own words. Use quotes very selectively to supplement your voice and your ideas; *your* voice should be the dominant voice heard in an essay.

- **Avoid using dialogue-style quotations.** Instead of repeating the dialogue as you might in a story, use a single quotation or your own words, as in the following example.

| **Dialogue:** | Colleen said, "You're always making irresponsible choices." "Maybe you're right," I replied. |
| **Better:** | Colleen told me I am always making irresponsible choices. Maybe she was right. |

PRACTICE (4)

Determining When to Use Quotations

The following paragraphs are from a student's essay about the positive effects of learning to play an instrument. Rihanna has used research to support her ideas. Each direct quote is shown in bold and numbered. Read through these paragraphs, and determine when her use of research is appropriate and when it is not appropriate. Use the guidelines in this chapter to help you decide.

Rihanna's Paragraphs

[1]**"Learning piano taught me persistence," claims Benjamin Briggs.** Briggs is a classical pianist living in Chicago. Many musicians who have achieved an impressive level of mastery find that their practicing habits have influenced their ability to persist in other tasks. Some musicians become adept at other skills, such as cooking, painting, or writing poetry. For Briggs, the persistence skills he gained as a musician have affected other parts of his life:

> [2]**I have used the same persistence techniques in other areas of my life. When I began running, I didn't even think about giving up after that first, awful day of heavy breathing and sweating. I simply got up the next morning and did the same thing: ran three miles that nearly killed me. I think my persistence at piano kind of taught me not to give up in anything. I am always surprised when my children give up so easily after a failed attempt at something. I remember my first time working through a Rachmaninoff piece. It was futile, I thought. But some months later, I was playing the piece decently, and by the end of a few more months, I got it.**

Not all musicians begin their musical careers enjoying practice time. Jan-Lin Chu has also benefited from the persistence required to master her instrument, the cello, but she did not always enjoy the process. Chu says that her hours of practice each day at first made her feel trapped, but she had little control over her time: her mother strictly required three hours of practice daily (Chu 15). [3]**Chu eventually became "a happy little prisoner," as she says in her journal, when she made peace with her practice responsibilities and grew to even enjoy the time (15).** She credits her persistence in practicing cello with her recent mastery of Spanish, a language she had hoped to learn for a long time. [4]**Learning Spanish, says Chu, "is much like learning pieces for cello. It requires persistence, daily work, patience, and practice" (17).**

Assess Rihanna's use of quotes. Which quotes should she leave in? Which should she take out? Explain your answers.

1. Quote 1: _____

_____

2. Quote 2: _____

_____

3. Quote 3: _____

_____

4. Quote 4: _____

_____

Determining How to Use Quotations

As you might have gathered by now, good writing requires authors to integrate quotes smoothly. You can quote in two ways. The first is to use the actual words from a source. The second is to put the source's ideas into your own words.

Whether you use a **direct quotation** (the exact words from a source enclosed in quotation marks) or an **indirect quotation** (the ideas of a source put into your own words), you must follow these guidelines.

Represent the Source Fairly.   When you quote, you are providing readers with another person's ideas, and you must do so accurately. Be thoroughly familiar with the entire source—the main idea, major supporting points, minor supporting details, examples, and so on—so that you do not misrepresent the writer's ideas.

Present the Source Accurately.   When you use the ideas of a source in a direct quote, you must restate the words *exactly as they appear* in the original source. Check and double-check to make sure your transcription is accurate.

Even if the author has made a spelling or grammatical error in the words you are quoting, you must include it in your quote. You can indicate that the error was in the original source by using the Latin adverb *sic,* which means "that's how it was written."

Example: Trenton Wiley writes that coaches still "fail to take concushins [sic] seriously enough."

Use Attributive Tags.   An **attributive tag** gives credit to the author of the quote you are using in your essay. These tags can be used to introduce a quote, to interrupt a quote, or at the end of a quote. In addition to giving credit to the author, attributive tags can provide information about the source or about the author's credibility or viewpoint, as the examples in the table show.

ATTRIBUTIVE TAGS FOR QUOTATIONS		
Location of attributive tag	**Example**	**Explanation**
Before the quote: *According to*	According to Shannon Kelly-Prince, a neurologist at Taugt-Creighton Hospital, "It is always a good idea to have a health professional evaluate a child who has had a concussion."	The attributive tag goes before the name, and the name is followed by a comma. The writer's degree (MD) or job title and position or affiliation are also included to lend credibility to the doctor's words. Since the quote is a complete sentence, the first word is capitalized. The period at the end of the sentence goes inside the quotation marks.
Before the quote: *As . . . writes,* *As . . . says,* *As . . . notes,* *As . . . claims,* *As . . . states,* *As . . . remarks,* *As . . . shows,* *As . . . contends,*	As the neurologist Shannon Kelly-Prince writes in Acute Care Journal, "We know from the CDC that traumatic brain injury is the leading cause of injury-related death in the U.S."	This attributive tag emphasizes where the doctor's writing was published.

(continued)

ATTRIBUTIVE TAGS FOR QUOTATIONS *(continued)*		
Location of attributive tag	**Example**	**Explanation**
After the quote: —*claims* . . . —*according to* . . . —*as* . . . *writes*	"If parents and coaches were more educated about post-concussion symptoms and care, fewer young people would die from sports-related traumatic brain injuries," <u>claims the neurologist Shannon Kelly-Prince.</u>	The sentence begins with the quote. At the end of the quote, a comma and then quotation marks are used. These are followed by the attributive tag (*claims*) and the writer's credentials. Notice that the attributive tag is followed with a comment about the doctor's viewpoint, which further helps the reader understand the doctor's position.

Use Indirect Quotes Correctly.   When you want to briefly summarize a source or refer to an idea from a source, you can create an indirect quote by using your own words. When you put ideas in your own words, you do not use quotation marks. However, you still have to give credit to the source. One way to create an indirect quote is to use attributive tags.

> **Example:** According to Samara Johnston, those who voyaged to the Americas had to learn methods for dealing with illness and death.

Another way is to state the idea and follow it with a reference in parentheses.

> **Example:** Those who voyaged to the Americas had to learn methods for dealing with illness and death (Johnston).

Note that the period goes *after* the parenthetical reference. Later in the chapter, you will find an explanation of when and how to use parenthetical references in your writing.

Avoid Run-on Sentences and Sentence Fragments When Using Quotes.   You know that run-on sentences and sentence fragments are all errors. But did you know that if you use quotes incorrectly, you can create these kinds of errors?

For example, this quote is a complete sentence: "If parents and coaches were more educated about post-concussion symptoms and care, fewer young people would die from sports-related traumatic brain injuries." If you joined this quotation to another complete sentence without appropriate punctuation, you would create a type of run-on sentence known as a *comma splice*. To avoid run-ons and sentence fragments when using quotes, follow these guidelines.

- **When the quote is a complete sentence, do not add it to another complete sentence. Use correct punctuation to separate the two complete sentences.**

> **Incorrect, with comma splice:** Shannon Kelly-Prince, a neurologist, would like to see increased education for coaches and <u>parents,</u> "If parents and coaches were more educated about post-concussion symptoms and care, fewer young people would die from sports-related traumatic brain injuries."

(continued)

Corrected by creating two complete sentences: Shannon Kelly-Prince, a neurologist, would like to see increased education for coaches and <u>parents. According</u> to Kelly-Prince, "If parents and coaches were more educated about post-concussion symptoms and care, fewer young people would die from sports-related traumatic brain injuries."

Note: When you quote complete sentences, capitalize the first word of the quoted sentence.

■ **When a quote is *not* a complete sentence, it cannot stand on its own, even with an attributive tag. Add your own words to the fragment to make it into a complete sentence. Clearly identify the source's words by using quotation marks around the quote.**

Incorrect, with fragment: The neurologist Shannon Kelly-Prince cites evidence of serious damage from concussions. <u>"Significant changes in brain structure."</u>

Corrected by adding words to make a complete sentence: The neurologist Shannon Kelly-Prince cites evidence of serious damage from concussions. In post-mortem analysis, <u>"significant changes in brain structure"</u> have been observed.

Note: Do not capitalize fragments that you quote.

■ **You can interrupt a quote with an attributive tag, but you cannot put a complete sentence on one side of the attributive tag and a complete sentence on the other side.**

Incorrect, with a comma splice: "The idea that athletes should just 'shake-it-off' after a concussion is dangerous," according to the neurologist Shannon Kelly-Prince, "'<u>Shaking</u>-it-off' and returning to the game can be deadly."

Corrected by inserting attributive tags: "The idea that athletes should just 'shake-it-off' after a concussion is dangerous," according to the neurologist Shannon Kelly-Prince. "'<u>Shaking</u>-it-off' and returning to the game can be deadly."

Apply Correct Punctuation Rules for Quotations.   Most of the time, punctuation goes inside the quotation marks.

Example: A more effective form of punishment, writes Dr. Brennan, "is intentional exclusion."

If a question mark is part of the quotation, put it inside the quotation marks.

Example: She asked, "Why should we bother to learn this?"

When you have a quote within a quote, use single quotation marks for the internal quote, and double quotation marks for the outer one.

Example: According to Marilyn Jackson, "County officials called the new ordinance 'a necessary evil' at the meeting."

Learn to Use Ellipses. An ellipsis is a mark made up of three spaced dots (. . .) that indicates the omission of words from quoted material. Study the list that follows to see how to use ellipses correctly. If you have additional questions about the use of ellipses, refer to a style manual such as the *MLA Handbook* or the *Publication Manual of the American Psychological Association*.

- **Original source:** On the voyage to the Americas, illness was a common cause of death.

  Material to omit from the middle of the sentence: On the voyage ~~to the Americas,~~ illness was a common cause of death.

  Use an ellipsis to show omission: "On the voyage . . . illness was a common cause of death."

- **Original source:** With little to no medicine available, not much could be done for those who became ill.

  Material to omit from the end of the sentence: With little to no medicine available, not much could be done ~~for those who became ill.~~

  Use an ellipsis to show omission: "With little to no medicine available, not much could be done. . . ."

Note: The ellipsis follows the period at the end of the sentence.

- **Original source:** On the voyage to the Americas, illness was a common cause of death. With little to no medicine available, not much could be done for those who became ill. Consequently, mariners had to solve the problem of disposing of the dead.

  Entire sentence to be omitted: On the voyage to the Americas, illness was a common cause of death. ~~With little to no medicine available, not much could be done for those who became ill.~~ Consequently, mariners had to solve the problem of disposing of the dead.

  Use an ellipsis to show omission: "On the voyage to the Americas, illness was a common cause of death. . . . Consequently, mariners had to solve the problem of disposing of the dead."

Give Credit to the Source to Avoid Plagiarism. As you learned earlier, *plagiarism* is using someone else's words or ideas without giving that source proper credit. To avoid plagiarism, you must make sure every source you use in your essay is credited both in the text itself and in a list of sources at the end of the essay. Neglecting to properly credit sources is plagiarism, even if you do not intend to plagiarize.

Just as with quotations, every time you use a writer's idea—even when you put it into your own words—you must give the writer credit by using an attributive tag or by putting the writer's name in parentheses after the idea.

Example: Christa Brennan writes that children who have to earn video gaming privileges are better equipped for hard work later in life.

Example: Children who have to earn video gaming privileges are better equipped for hard work later in life (Brennan).

If you continue to use information from the same source, make sure that you consistently give credit to the source. Do not move between your own ideas and the source's ideas without making it clear where the source's ideas start and end. Here is an example. Notice how the underlined phrases clarify the sources for readers.

Unclear	Clear
Christa Brennan writes that children who have to earn video gaming privileges are better equipped for hard work later in life. Children who earn those privileges begin to associate leisure time with work. By making this connection, children come to expect that they will have to earn certain recreational privileges. As a result, these children have a less difficult time accepting the hard work that is required in college and in the workplace. Parents should consider having children earn privileges such as video gaming by completing some kind of work or chore.	Christa Brennan writes that children who have to earn video gaming privileges are better equipped for hard work later in life. According to Brennan, children who earn those privileges begin to associate leisure time with work. By making this connection, children come to expect that they will have to earn certain recreational privileges; as a result, these children have a less difficult time accepting the hard work that is required in college and in the workplace (Brennan). Clearly, parents should consider having children earn privileges such as video gaming by completing some kind of work or chore.

PRACTICE 5

Constructing Accurate and Effective Quotations

Krystal is using material from a Centers for Disease Control and Prevention (CDC) pamphlet entitled *Get a Heads Up on Concussion in Sports Policies* in her writing. An excerpt ("State Laws") from this source document is given below, and Krystal's draft follows it.

In her draft, Krystal inserted the information from the source but did not use attribute tags or quotation marks where they were necessary. On a separate sheet, rewrite Krystal's paragraph. Add attributive tags and quotation marks to indicate the information that came from the CDC.

State Laws

Beginning in 2009, the state of Washington passed the first concussion in sports law, called the Zackery Lystedt Law. One month later, Max's Law passed in Oregon. In total, between 2009 and 2012, 43 states, and the District of Columbia, passed laws on concussion in sports for youth and/or high school athletes, often called Return to Play Laws. So far in 2013, four additional states have also passed Return to Play Laws. Some organizations, such as the National Conference of State Legislatures, have created online maps to track and update concussion in sports laws by state.

Most Concussion in Sports Laws Include Three Action Steps:

1. **Educate Coaches, Parents, and Athletes:** Inform and educate coaches, athletes, and their parents and guardians about concussion through training and/or a concussion information sheet.

(continued)

2. **Remove Athlete from Play:** An athlete who is believed to have a concussion is to be removed from play right away.

3. **Obtain Permission to Return to Play:** An athlete can only return to play or practice after at least 24 hours and with permission from a health care professional.

These action steps are based on recommendations presented in the International Concussion Consensus Statement. First created in 2002 and most recently updated in 2008, the Consensus Statement was developed by experts in the field and includes the latest science available on concussion in sports.

Krystal's Draft Paragraph

As school districts become more aware of the seriousness of concussions, they are taking steps to make sure student athletes, their parents, and coaches know what to do if a concussion occurs. Sometimes there are clear laws about the protocol that should be followed in the case of a concussion. For example, the state of Washington passed the first concussion in sports law, called the Zackery Lystedt Law. In Oregon, a law known as Max's Law addresses concussions, and many other states have passed similar laws. States that do not have specific laws can rely on ideas in the International Concussion Consensus Statement. First created in 2002 and most recently updated in 2008, the Consensus Statement was developed by experts in the field and includes the latest science available on concussion in sports.

Creating In-Text References in MLA and APA Styles

Giving proper credit for sources involves (1) creating in-text references at the places in your essay where you use sources and (2) supplying complete information about each source in a list at the end of the essay. Both the Modern Language Association (MLA) and the American Psychological Association (APA) have published guidebooks with instructions on how to properly credit sources—the *MLA Handbook,* 8th Edition and the *Publication Manual of the American Psychological Association,* respectively. Your instructor will very likely have you use one of these style guides. Following are basic guidelines for creating in-text references.

Using MLA Style for In-Text References

Parenthetical documentation is the term given to the MLA's method for giving in-text credit to sources. The parenthetical reference (information in parentheses) gives the reader enough information to locate full bibliographic information for the source in the list of works cited at the end of the essay.

Let's say that one of your sources is an article by Jeanette LeFarve titled "Understanding Anorexia." Because you found this article in a magazine in the library (not in a computer database), you can see the article's original page numbers. You wish to quote this passage from page 15 of the article: "Anorexia is actually a mental disorder that manifests in physical symptoms." To use this quote, you would find an attributive tag that fits into your sentence. The first time you use a source, you should give the writer's first and last name in the attribution. If you use the source again, you can use only the last name, since readers have already been introduced to the source. Here is an example.

MLA Style for an In-Text Reference (When Author's Name Is in the Sentence)

> According to Jeanette LeFarve, "Anorexia is actually a mental disorder that manifests in physical symptoms" (15).

Notice that the end quotation marks appear *before* the parenthetical reference and that the period follows the parenthetical reference. Notice also that LeFarve's name does not appear in the parentheses because it is used in the attributive tag. Thus, readers will understand that the quote comes from LeFarve and that it appears on page 15 in the source. If readers want to find the original source, they can look at the list of works cited at the end of your essay, find Jeanette LeFarve's name, and use the bibliographic information to look up the article.

If you refer to LeFarve's article without using her name in an attributive tag, you will need to put her last name in the parenthetical reference. Here is an example.

MLA Style for an In-Text Reference (When Author's Name Is Not in the Sentence)

> "Anorexia is actually a mental disorder that manifests in physical symptoms" (LeFarve 15).

Notice that the parenthetical reference follows the end quotation mark and is followed by a period. Notice also that there is no comma between the writer's name and the page number.

Sources obtained from a Web site or from an online database often do not include the original page numbers, so when using those sources, you will not be able to include page numbers in your in-text reference. Do not use the page numbers from a printout of an article from the Web; they are not the original page numbers. If you use a source that does not have page numbers, you can either include just the writer's last name in a parenthetical reference or simply use an attributive tag to credit the writer. When readers do not see a page number, they will know that the source you used did not contain page numbers, as in the following examples.

MLA Style for an In-Text Reference to a Source without Page Numbers

One scientist claims that anorexia can be cured by behavioral therapy (Mallin).

or

Mallin claims that anorexia can be cured by behavioral therapy.

Remember that you should not use quotation marks when you are putting an idea into your own words. Notice that at the end of the first example, the period follows the parenthetical reference.

If you use an article that has no author listed, use the full title of the work, if brief, in quotation marks, in place of the author's name. If the title is long, use the first few significant title words. For example, for a quote on page 25 of an anonymous article entitled "Fighting Anorexia," you would refer to the source as in the following example.

MLA Style for an In-Text Reference to a Source with No Author

"The clinics that specialize in anorexia often treat the disorder with a variety of treatment modalities" ("Fighting Anorexia" 25).

Finally, you will sometimes want to use a source that is quoted by another source. For instance, imagine that in Mallin's article about anorexia, she quotes this statistic from a treatment center: "approximately 1% of female teenagers have anorexia." If you would like to use this quote in your paper, you may do so, but you will need to add *qtd. in* (for "quoted in") to your parenthetical reference, as shown in the following example.

MLA Style for an In-Text Reference to a Source Quoted in Another Source

Few people realize that "approximately 1% of female teenagers have anorexia" (qtd. in Mallin).

In the list of works cited, you will include an entry for Mallin's article. Readers can then locate Mallin's article if they wish to find information about the original source.

For more information on MLA style for in-text references, consult the latest edition of the *MLA Handbook*.

Using APA Style for In-Text References

When you cite sources in APA style, two pieces of information are essential: the last name of the author and the date of the source. As with MLA style, you use parentheses to show where quotes and ideas came from.

When you use a writer's idea and include the writer's name in the sentence, put the date of the source in parentheses; in another set of parentheses, include the page number where the information was found, as in the following example.

APA Style for an In-Text Reference (When Author's Name Is in the Sentence)

According to Heinmann (2004), the prevalence of anorexia nervosa among girls in grades 7 and 8 rose by 5% from 1998 to 2002 (p. 21).

Because the author of this essay is using her own words rather than quoting from Heinmann directly, she does not use quotation marks. The date of Heinmann's article (in this case, a year) follows his name in parentheses. The end of the sentence contains a parenthetical reference with the page number. Note that in APA style, you use the abbreviation *p.* for "page" (or *pp.* for "pages") and then insert the number. The sentence period follows.

If you do not mention the name of the writer in your text, include the writer's last name in the parenthetical reference with the date and the page number, as in the following example.

APA Style for an In-Text Reference (When Author's Name Is Not in the Sentence)

> The prevalence of anorexia nervosa among girls in grades 7 and 8 rose by 5% from 1998 to 2002 (Heinmann, 2004, p. 21).

Notice that the writer's name is followed by a comma, the date of publication, another comma, and the page number.

If no author is indicated in the source, cite the first significant word or words of the title instead, as shown below.

APA Style for an In-Text Reference to a Source with No Author

> Several girls reported feeling uneasy with their bodies ("Why Girls," 2006, pp. 31–32).

Notice that the abbreviated title is in quotation marks to indicate that the source is an article (or other short work) with no author indicated. The comma goes inside the end quotation mark, and the date and the page numbers follow.

Page numbers should be included only when you have the original page numbers from the source. If you are looking at a book, you can see the original page numbers. If you are looking at a journal article online, you will probably not see page numbers, so you cannot use them in your parenthetical references. For more information on APA style for in-text references, consult the latest edition of the *Publication Manual of the American Psychological Association.*

The differences between the MLA and APA citation systems may seem minor—whether you need a comma, whether you use *p.* before the page number, and so on. However, using these systems properly shows your instructor that you take your research seriously and that you are good at following instructions.

Setting Off a Long Quotation

Both MLA and APA give guidelines for setting off long quotations so that they stand out in the text of an essay.

In MLA style, set off a quotation of more than four lines by indenting it a half inch from the left margin (the same indentation required by a new paragraph). Do not use quotation marks and do not indent the first line of the long quote. Follow the quote with a period and then the parenthetical reference, as in the following example.

MLA Style for a Long Quotation

> Educational researchers are calling for innovative ways to deal with misbehaving children in public schools:
>
>> There are alternatives to meting out punishment that treats our school children like criminals. Instead of sending students to the principal's office or worse—calling police into classrooms to deal with disorderly conduct—schools can

equip their teachers with tools proven to create safe, supportive learning environments and defuse disruption. The very things that mitigate student stress and bad behavior make a school what it's supposed to be: a healthy and productive place to learn. (Cantor 341)

In APA style, set off a quotation of forty words or more by indenting it a half inch from the left margin (the same indentation required by a new paragraph). Omit the quotation marks, and after the period at the end of the quoted passage, insert a parenthetical reference that includes the writer's last name, the date, and any page numbers.

APA Style for a Long Quotation

Educational researchers are calling for innovative ways to deal with misbehaving children in public schools:

> There are alternatives to meting out punishment that treats our school children like criminals. Instead of sending students to the principal's office or worse—calling police into classrooms to deal with disorderly conduct—schools can equip their teachers with tools proven to create safe, supportive learning environments and defuse disruption. The very things that mitigate student stress and bad behavior make a school what it's supposed to be: a healthy and productive place to learn. (Cantor, 2013, p. 341)

MLA Style: Formatting a Paper and Preparing a Works Cited List

For a source-based paper in an English class, most instructors require the use of MLA style. The following section covers a few of the basic MLA style requirements. For complete information about how to use MLA style, see the latest edition of the *MLA Handbook*. Your library or writing center is likely to have a copy.

Formatting a Paper in MLA Style

Most instructors who require MLA style can immediately tell whether a paper adheres to the MLA guidelines just by glancing at it. MLA style requires the following formatting elements:

- One-inch margins on all sides
- A header in the top margin area that includes the student's last name and the page number (with no *p.* abbreviation)
- On the first page of the paper, an additional header includes the student's full name, instructor's name, course information, and date
- The date in this format: 12 February 2012
- A centered title—regular text font, not bold or underlined
- Double-spacing throughout, with no additional space between the heading, title, or body of the paper
- Left-justified text, with no end-of-line hyphenation
- Half-inch indentions to begin new paragraphs

If you are unfamiliar with word processing and think you may have trouble formatting your paper, ask for assistance from someone in your library or writing center. A staff member there should be able to help you learn how to format your paper using word-processing software. See also the student paper later in this chapter for an example of MLA formatting.

The second and following pages of a source-based essay in MLA format must also conform to MLA requirements. These pages should (a) have the same header as the first page (your last name and page number), (b) have the same one-inch margins on all sides, and (c) be double-spaced. Only the first page of an essay should have the heading and title.

In general, do not use folders, plastic binders, or any sort of cover for source-based essays. A source-based essay should not have a title page unless your instructor directs you otherwise. Use black ink and a simple 12-point font such as Times New Roman. If your instructor has not given you specific directions regarding how to bind your paper, use a staple or a paper clip. And always keep a copy of your paper.

Creating Entries for an MLA Works Cited List

For each source you refer to in your essay, full bibliographic data must appear in a works cited list. Only sources you used within your paper for ideas or quotes should be included. If you read a source but did not refer to it in your paper, do not add it to your works cited list.

The sources on your works cited list are called *entries*. If you have referred to five sources in your paper, you will have five entries on your works cited list. Each type of source has its own format. The following sections present a few of the most common formats for entries. If you use other types of sources than those listed here, consult the latest edition of the *MLA Handbook* for guidance.

An Article in a Scholarly Journal

Last name, first name. "Title of article." *Title of publication*, vol. and volume number, no. and issue number, month or season (if available) and year of publication, p. or pp. and page numbers (for print articles).

Martin, Louise. "The Nature of Anorexia." *Journal of Disease Therapies*, vol. 255, no. 3, 2005, pp. 13–21.

Note: The specific punctuation *counts*! Do not forget the period after the writer's name, after the article's title, and at the very end of the entry. Also, notice where the commas appear in the example above. In addition, pay attention to which words are capitalized. In MLA style, the first and last words of titles are capitalized, as are all principal words. If you accessed the journal article in a database, then see "A Periodical in an Online Database" later in this chapter. If you accessed an online-only journal, then see "A Work Found Only on the Web" later in this chapter.

An Article in a Newspaper

Last name, first name. "Title of article." *Name of newspaper* [city], day month year of publication, p. or pp. and page numbers (for print articles).

Hernandez, Simon. "What You Need to Know about Your Teenage Daughter." *Daily News* [Marysville], 13 June 2007, pp. D1+.

Note: If the newspaper title includes the city's name (for instance, the *Chicago Tribune*) or it is a national newspaper, then there is no need to supply the city in the works cited entry. Also, if a newspaper article extends beyond one page, use a plus sign (+) to indicate this fact. If you accessed the article on the Web, then include the publication date provided online and use a URL in place of page numbers, like this:

Ellin, Abby. "In Fighting Anorexia, Recovery Is Elusive." *The New York Times,* 25 Apr. 2011, nyti.ms/1ONQc4y.

An Article in a Magazine

Last name, first name. "Title of article." *Name of magazine,* month (abbreviated) and year of publication, p. or pp. and page numbers (for print articles).

Washington, Misa. "Not Eating?" *Good Housekeeping,* Dec. 2007, pp. 35–37.

Note: When listing a month as part of the publication date for a source, abbreviate all months except for May, June, and July. A magazine differs from a journal in that magazines usually publish less scholarly items.

A Book

Last name, first name. *Title of book.* Name of publisher, year.

Durmond, William. *Clinical Studies of Anorexia.* Tranham Press, 2006.

Note that if the publisher's name includes the words *University Press*, then abbreviate those words as *UP* (with no period).

If there are two authors, list the first author's name in reverse order (last name first), and then give the second author's name in regular order (first name first), as shown below:

Durmond, William, and Martina McDaniel. *Clinical Studies of Anorexia.* Tranham Press, 2006.

A Work in an Anthology

Last name, first name. "Title of the specific work." *Title of the anthology,* edited by and editor's name, name of publisher, year of publication, p. or pp. and page numbers of the specific work.

Capps, Li. "Brooklyn's Story." *Stories of Girls in Crisis,* edited by Ann-Marie Tillich, Chicago Media Publishers, 2000, pp. 90–95.

Note: An anthology is a collection of writings.

An Article in a Reference Book

"Title of article." *Title of reference work,* number or type of edition (if available), name of publisher, year of publication.

"Anorexia Nervosa." *Taber's Cyclopedic Medical Dictionary,* 22nd ed., F. A. Davis, 2013.

Note: If a reference book has entries or articles organized alphabetically, then you do not need to include a page number in your citation.

A Work Found Only on the Web

Information from Web sites can be difficult to document, especially if the item is not from an online newspaper, journal, or database. For these other kinds of items, provide as much of the following information as you can:

1. Name of the author or editor of the work
2. Title of the work (if the work's title is the same as the title of the Web page, skip this step)
3. If the work is a Web page, title of the Web page (italicized)
4. Version or edition used (if you can find this information)
5. Publisher or sponsor of the site; if the publisher or sponsor is the same name as the title of the Web site (as in the example below), then skip this element
6. Date of publication or date the Web page was last updated (day, month, and year); if unavailable, then you can add the date you retrieved the work at the end of the entry, like this: Accessed 1 May 2016.
7. A URL; do not include *http://* and *https://* when you list the URL into your works cited entry

Here is an example of an article from the Cleveland Clinic's Web site:

> "Anorexia Nervosa." *Cleveland Clinic,* 29 Mar. 2012, my.clevelandclinic.org
> /services/neurological_institute/center-for-behavioral-health/disease-conditions
> /hic-anorexia-nervosa.

A Periodical in an Online Database

Use the same format you would use for an article obtained in print, except conclude the entry with the following information:

1. Title of the database (italicized)
2. A URL or a DOI for the article. A DOI (digital object identifier) is an alphanumeric code assigned by some publishers to online scholarly texts. If your source has a DOI, then use that in your entry instead of a URL.

Here is a source you saw previously (for an article in a newspaper). It has been converted to the format used for an online database, *General OneFile*:

> Ellin, Abby. "In Fighting Anorexia, Recovery Is Elusive." *The New York Times,*
> 26 Apr. 2011, p. D5. *General OneFile,* go.galegroup.com/ps/i.do?id=GALE
> %7CA254713336&v=2.1&u=nysl_me_wls&it=r&p=GPS&sw=w&asid=
> 9305cab421f0450c61419847a4863acf.

A Sample Paper in MLA Style

What follows is a source-based essay that uses MLA style written by a student, Meg Almond. You can use this model to format your own papers in MLA style. Note that your works cited list should start on a new page and should be the last item in your paper. It should include the same header as the rest of the paper (your last name and the page number). The list should be double-spaced and alphabetized. The first line of each entry should start at the left margin, and subsequent lines in the entry should be indented one-half inch.

Model Student Paper: "Causes of Anorexia Nervosa" by Meg Almond

Almond 1

Meg Almond

Dr. Hoeffner

English 0301

26 May 2017

Causes of Anorexia Nervosa

In a land with an overabundance of food, some people starve themselves to death. These people are victims of anorexia nervosa, defined by the Mayo Clinic as "an eating disorder that causes people to obsess about their weight and the food they eat." Anorexia, as it is often called, is usually seen as a mental disorder that affects the body. People who have it tend to "equate thinness with self-worth" (Mayo Clinic). While the Mayo Clinic's description is correct, it is not complete. The causes of anorexia are more complex than most people realize.

To begin, some researchers think there might be a medical basis for anorexia. Swedish researchers have learned some interesting things from studying people with anorexia. According to Thea Jourdan of the *Daily Mail,* a London newspaper, "The Swedish research showed that sufferers of anorexia and bulimia have unusually high levels of certain antibodies in their blood. These antibodies are produced by their own immune system in response to infections." Jourdan goes on to explain that the antibodies have an effect on brain chemicals, and a by-product is that one's appetite is affected. Jourdan points out that it may be wise to reclassify anorexia "as an auto-immune disease (a bit like rheumatoid arthritis)." If anorexia is found to be caused by a virus or if it is classified as an autoimmune response, the treatment of sufferers would change dramatically.

Another possible cause for anorexia is genetics. A National Institutes of Health study called the Genetics of Anorexia Nervosa is designed to research the role genetics plays in anorexia

---

Double-spacing throughout; 1-inch margins; 1/2-inch paragraph indent

Title centered

Introduction

Quotation as part of a sentence

Parenthetical reference to a Web source without page numbers

Thesis statement

Transition ("To begin") to major supporting point 1

Attributive tag giving author and source

Quotation as evidence

Major supporting point 2

Almond 2

("Researcher"). The genetic theory is that certain people have a set of genes that work together to create a genetic tendency toward anorexia. These genes are often found in more than one person in a family, according to the genetic theory ("Researcher"). Craig Johnson directs the eating disorders unit at Laureate Psychiatric Hospital in Tulsa, Oklahoma. He claims that "if a person has a family member who has had anorexia nervosa, she or he is 12 times more at risk of developing the illness." In his words, "Genetics loads the gun. Environment pulls the trigger" (qtd. in "Researcher").

Understanding that researchers are not sure about the causes of anorexia is very important. When a person develops anorexia, she is often blamed for the disease. She is told "Just eat!" as if she had complete control over her destiny. Since people think anorexia is a disease that is only in the mind, they think anorexia sufferers must *want* to be sick, or they must want to be thin.

Reba Loftin, a friend from high school, has suffered from anorexia for three years and is desperate to get better. She has been in and out of treatment for the disorder. "It's frustrating when people say things like 'She just wants attention.' They really don't know what it's like. I mean, if I eat two or three french fries, I feel guilty all day" (Loftin). At 5 feet 4 inches and 101 pounds, Reba is very thin, but she cannot look at herself without feeling disgusted. "I know it's not rational, but I can't control my feelings" (Loftin). People like Reba do not want attention. They simply cannot control the irrational thoughts that flood their minds.

Many disorders and conditions are caused by brain chemistry problems. People who are depressed take medicines to help the brain work right, and people who have other disorders such as autism or ADHD also have medicines to help change their brain chemicals. Maybe someday researchers will discover a medicine that will help change the brain chemicals responsible for anorexia. If

— Parenthetical reference to a source listed by title (no author name)

— Quote integrated into a sentence with *that*

— Major supporting point 3

— Personal example as evidence

Conclusion

Almond 3

people learn that the causes of anorexia are more complex than they realized, those who suffer from the condition, as well as their families, will have an easier time fighting it. As Robert Finn says, "Rethinking the purely psychoanalytic model has a number of implications. For one thing, parents can quit blaming themselves, family dysfunction, or careless comments for causing their children's anorexia." Research and science may someday give us the answer, but until we have it, blame is not the solution.

Ending with a quote and a speculation

Works cited list starting on a new page; title centered

Almond 4

Works Cited

Entries alphabetical and flush left, with subsequent lines indented 1/2 inch

Finn, Robert. "Fallacies about Anorexia Undermine Treatment." *Clinical Psychiatry News,* vol. 33, no. 8, Aug. 2005, doi:10.1016/ S0270-6644(05)70609-3.

Article in a journal, found online

Jourdan, Thea. "Anorexia Is a Real Disease." *Daily Mail,* 27 Sept. 2005, www.dailymail.co.uk/health/article-363643/Anorexia-em-real -em-disease.html.

Article in a newspaper, found online

Loftin, Reba. Personal interview. 3 Mar. 2017.

Personal interview

Mayo Clinic. "Anorexia Nervosa: Overview." *Patient Care and Health Information,* 5 Jan. 2012, www.mayoclinic.org /diseases-conditions/anorexia/home/ovc-20179508.

Organization as author

"Researcher Says Anorexia May Be Genetic." *AP Online,* 21 Feb. 2007. *HighBeam Research,* www.highbeam.com/doc/1Y1-103448899.html.

Listed by title (no author)

APA Style: Formatting a Paper and Preparing a References List

Professors of sociology, psychology, and other social science disciplines often prefer APA style to MLA style. As you saw earlier for in-text citations, the two styles are similar, but there are a few differences. We will look at the basic principles of APA style here. For a more comprehensive explanation, consult the latest edition of the *Publication Manual of the American Psychological Association.*

Formatting a Paper in APA Style

In APA style, source-based essays must conform to the following formatting guidelines:

- The paper starts with a separate title page that includes a running head, the page number, the complete title of the work, the writer's name, and the writer's affiliation (such as a university or a company), if any. See the sample paper later in this chapter for an example.
- A running head (the title in shortened form) appears at the top left of each page. On the first (title) page, the words *Running Head* and a colon precede the title. Subsequent pages have just the shortened title.
- A page number appears in the upper right corner on all pages, including the title page.
- An abstract appears on the second page. An abstract is a 150- to 250-word summary of your paper. It is often easiest to write this brief summary after you are finished writing the paper. Type "Abstract" on the top line of page 2. On the next line, without indenting, start writing the abstract.
- The body of the paper begins on the third page. It starts with the title centered on the top line of the page, followed by a double space.
- The paper must be double-spaced.
- All margins are one inch.
- Paragraphs are indented a half inch (except for the abstract, which is not indented).

Do not use folders, plastic binders, or any sort of cover for your source-based essay. Use a simple 12-point font such as Times New Roman, and print in black ink. If your instructor has not given you specific directions regarding how to bind your paper, use a staple or a paper clip. Remember always to keep a copy of your essay. See the sample APA paper later in this chapter for an example of APA formatting.

Creating Entries for an APA References List

A paper in APA style ends with a list of references, which are the sources you have used in the paper. A reader should be able to flip to the references page of your essay and easily find information for every source mentioned in your paper. The list of references should be organized alphabetically by author or, if the work has no author, by the first significant word of the title. If you used several works by the same author, they should be listed in chronological order of publication date.

The sources you include on your reference page must be formatted correctly. A few of the APA guidelines differ in significant ways from the MLA guidelines. In particular, in APA, the author's last name is spelled out, but initials are used for the first and middle names. Additionally, APA capitalization guidelines differ from those for MLA. For titles of journals, magazines, and newspapers in a references list, capitalize the main words, as usual. But for article and book titles, capitalize only the first word and any proper nouns. The titles of articles are not italicized and are not put in quotation marks, but the titles of books, journals, magazines, and newspapers are italicized.

The information below provides only a few of the many types of source formats specified by the APA. For complete information, consult the latest edition of the *Publication Manual of the American Psychological Association.*

An Article in a Scholarly Journal

Last name, initial. (Date of publication). Title. *Periodical title, volume*(issue), page numbers.

Martin, L. (2005). The nature of anorexia. *Journal of Disease Therapies, 255*(3), 13–21.

As in MLA style, the details *matter*! Use periods and commas correctly. Notice the rules regarding spacing—for example, there's no space between the volume and issue numbers. Also notice what is and is not italicized here and in the following examples.

An Article in a Newspaper

Last name, initial. (Date). Title of article. *Name of newspaper,* page numbers.

Hernandez, S. (2007, June 13). What you need to know about your teenage daughter. *New York Times,* pp. B11–12.

An Article in a Magazine

Last name, initial. (Date). Title of article. *Name of magazine,* page numbers.

Krantz, M. (2007, December). New solutions for daycare. *Good Housekeeping,* 35–37.

A Book by a Single Author

Last name, initial. (Date). *Title of book.* City of publication, state abbreviation: name of publisher.

Durmond, W. (2006). *Clinical studies of anorexia.* New York, NY: Tranham.

A Book with More Than One Author

List each additional author (up to seven total); use an ampersand (&) before the last author.

Williams, W., O'Connell, T., & Rouch, M. (2006). *Environmental factors in eating disorders.* Chicago, IL: United Medical Publishers.

A Work in an Anthology

Last name of article author, initial. (Date). Title of work. "In" editor of the anthology (Ed.), *title of the anthology* (page numbers). City of publication, state abbreviation: publisher.

Kennedy, D. (2002). Sustaining thought in brain injury patients. In J. T. Crasch (Ed.), *The brain and regenerative transformation* (pp. 332–335). Washington, DC: Collman Brothers.

A Work Found Only on the Web

APA requires an entry to include retrieval information—either a Web page or, preferably, a DOI designation. A **DOI (digital object identifier)** is an alphanumeric code that identifies a specific online reference. Most articles in databases are assigned a DOI. If you can find the DOI of a source, follow the instructions here for referencing that source.

An Online Article with DOI

> Author's last name, initial. (Date of publication). Title of article. *Title of periodical, volume*(issue), page numbers. doi: unique identifier

> Martin, J. (2003). Toward a theory of consciousness. *Journal of Neuroscience, 112,* 313–321. doi: 10.1033/0005-022X.30.8.750

An Online Article without DOI

If an article retrieved from an online source does not have a DOI, use the URL for the site from which you retrieved the item:

> Braggar, B. (1997). A view from the top. *Journal of Progress, 31,* 244–247. Retrieved from http://jopd/archives/ava

Research from a Web Site

Start with the name of the Web site and the date the Web site was last updated—if available (and if not, use *n.d.*). Then give the name of the document and the URL, as in the following example.

> Brady Center to Prevent Gun Violence. (2008, November 30). *Brady background checks: Fifteen years of saving lives* [Report]. Retrieved from http://www.bradycampaign.org/sites/default/files/brady-law-15years.pdf

A Sample Paper in APA Style

The references page should include a running head and page number, and the title *References* should be centered at the top. Each of the entries should be double-spaced and formatted with hanging indentation, as seen in this sample paper in APA style.

Title Page

Running Head: CAUSES OF ANOREXIA NERVOSA   1

Causes of Anorexia Nervosa

Megan Almond

Marshall Community College North

Title, writer's name, and institution centered top to bottom and left to right

Paper

1-inch margins all around; double-spacing throughout

Running head and page number
Title centered

Causes of Anorexia Nervosa

In a land with an overabundance of food, some people starve themselves to death. These people are victims of anorexia nervosa, defined by the Mayo Clinic (2012, para. 1) as "an eating disorder that causes people to obsess about their weight and the food they eat." Anorexia, as it is often called, is usually seen as a mental disorder that affects the body. People who have it tend to "equate thinness with self-worth" (Mayo Clinic, 2012, para. 4). While the Mayo Clinic's description is correct, it is not complete. The causes of anorexia are more complex than most people realize.

Paragraph number in a parenthetical reference for a source without page numbers

Source, date, and paragraph number in a parenthetical reference after integrated quote

To begin, some researchers think there might be a medical basis for anorexia. Swedish researchers have learned some interesting things from studying people with anorexia. According to Thea Jourdan (2005) of the *Daily Mail,* a London newspaper, "The Swedish research showed that sufferers of anorexia and bulimia have unusually high levels of certain antibodies in their blood. These antibodies are produced by their own immune system in response to infections" (para. 6). Jourdan goes on to explain that the antibodies have an effect on brain chemicals, and a by-product is that one's appetite is affected (para. 7). Jourdan points out that it may be wise to reclassify anorexia "as an auto-immune disease (a bit like rheumatoid arthritis)" (para. 7). If anorexia is found to be caused by a virus or if it is classified as an autoimmune response, the treatment of sufferers would change dramatically.

Date of publication after attributive tag

Another possible cause for anorexia is genetics. A National Institutes of Health study called the Genetics of Anorexia Nervosa is designed to research the role genetics plays in anorexia ("Researcher," 2003, para. 2). The genetic theory is that certain people have a set of

Parenthetical reference for a source listed by title

CAUSES OF ANOREXIA NERVOSA   3

genes that work together to create a genetic tendency toward

anorexia. These genes are often found in more than one person in a

family, according to the genetic theory ("Researcher," 2003, para. 4).

Craig Johnson directs the eating disorders unit at Laureate Psychiatric

Hospital in Tulsa, Oklahoma. He claims that "if a person has a family

member who has had anorexia nervosa, she or he is 12 times more at

risk of developing the illness." In his words, "Genetics loads the gun.

Environment pulls the trigger" (as cited in "Researcher," 2003, para. 4).

Understanding that researchers are not sure about the causes of

anorexia is very important. When a person develops anorexia, she is often

blamed for the disease. She is told "Just eat!" as if she had complete control

over her destiny. Since people think anorexia is a disease that is only in the

mind, they think anorexia sufferers must *want* to be sick, or they must want

to be thin.

Reba Loftin, a friend from high school, has suffered from anorexia

for three years and is desperate to get better. She has been in and out

of treatment for the disorder. "It's frustrating when people say things

like 'She just wants attention.' They really don't know what it's like. I

mean, if I eat two or three french fries, I feel guilty all day" (personal

interview, March 3, 2017). At 5 feet 4 inches and 101 pounds, Reba is

very thin, but she cannot look at herself without feeling disgusted. "I

know it's not rational, but I can't control my feelings" (personal

interview, March 3, 2017). People like Reba do not want attention. They

simply cannot control the irrational thoughts that flood their minds.

Many disorders and conditions are caused by brain chemistry

problems. People who are depressed take medicines to help the brain

work right, and people who have other disorders such as autism or

ADHD also have medicines to help change their brain chemicals. Maybe

someday researchers will discover a medicine that will help change the

Parenthetical reference for a personal communication (APA does not require an entry in the references list)

CAUSES OF ANOREXIA NERVOSA   4

brain chemicals responsible for anorexia. If people learn that the causes of anorexia are more complex than they realized, those who suffer from the condition, as well as their families, will have an easier time fighting it. As Robert Finn (2005) says, "Rethinking the purely psychoanalytic model has a number of implications. For one thing, parents can quit blaming themselves, family dysfunction, or careless comments for causing their children's anorexia" (para. 16). Research and science may someday give us the answer, but until we have it, blame is not the solution.

CAUSES OF ANOREXIA NERVOSA   5

References

Finn, R. (2005). Fallacies about anorexia undermine treatment. *Clinical Psychiatry News, 33*(8), 50. doi: 10.1016/S0270-6644(05)70609-3

Jourdan, T. (2005, September 27). Anorexia is a real disease. *Daily Mail.* Retrieved from http://www.dailymail.co.uk/health /article-363643/Anorexia-em-real-em-disease.html

Loftin, R. (2017, March 3). Personal interview.

Mayo Clinic. (2012, January 5).: Anorexia nervosa: Overview. *Patient Care and Health Information.* Retrieved from http://www .mayoclinic.org/diseases-conditions/anorexia/home/ ovc-20179508

Researcher says anorexia may be genetic. (2007, February 21). *AP Online.* Retrieved from https://www.highbeam.com/doc /1Y1-103448899.html

References list starting on a new page; title centered

First line of entry at left margin with subsequent lines indented 1/2 inch

Scholarly article with a DOI

Newspaper article from a Web site

Entry for a personal interview, if required by instructor

Organization as author

Article listed by title (no author given)

Checking Your Essay for Plagiarism

Plagiarism—using another person's words or ideas without giving proper credit—is a serious offense in academic writing. It can lead to a failing grade and even to dismissal from college. Certainly, submitting a paper you have not written and claiming it as your own work is plagiarism—and professors can recognize such intentional plagiarism right away. But plagiarism can also be unintentional; it can result from paying insufficient attention to how you credit your sources. To make sure you have properly credited your sources, use the following checklist.

Checklist for Documentation

1. Reread your entire paper. Underline each section where you used an idea or a quote from a source. Now, for each of these underlined sections, answer the following questions:
   - Have you provided the necessary attribution so that it is clear to readers where the quotation or idea came from?
   - Have you provided a parenthetical reference for the source that will enable readers to find the corresponding entry in your works cited or references list?
2. Compare the amount of source information to the amount of your own writing. What is the ratio? Aim to have no more than 30 percent of your paper come from source information.
3. Make a list of the sources you used in your paper. Is there an entry with complete information for each source on the works cited or references list?
4. Proofread each works cited or references entry. Do the entries conform to the appropriate style—MLA or APA?

Remember that if you have trouble understanding either MLA or APA style, you can seek assistance from tutors, learning center instructors, librarians, your instructor, and online resources.

Text Credits

Page 462: Graedon, Joe and Teresa, "How Safe Is Aspertame?" *The People's Pharmacy®*, January 9, 2006. © 2006 The Peoples Pharmacy—Distributed by King Features Syndicate, Inc.; Page 469: Source: Orwell, George, *1984*. London: Harvill Secker, 1949; Page 470: "The Lystedt Law: A Concussion Survivor's Journey," *Guide to Writing about Traumatic Brain Injury in News and Social Media*, National Center for Injury Prevention and Control, Centers for Disease Control and Prevention, 2015. 7; Page 477: *Get a Heads Up on Concussion in Sports Policies*, National Center for Injury Prevention and Control, Centers for Disease Control and Prevention, 3–4; Page 481: Source: Cantor, Pamela, "Police and Punishment: Strategic Alternatives for Schools," *District Administration*, August 2013. http://www.districtadministration.com.

Well-Crafted Sentences

©Dimitri Otis/Getty Images RF

Sentence Combining: Phrases and Clauses

©BananaStock/Jupiterimages RF

Combining sentences adds interest and variety to writing, just as combining different elements adds interest and variety to a visual display.

Unit Objectives

After completing this unit, students will be able to do the following:

- Combine sentences using prepositional phrases (and punctuate correctly).

- Combine sentences using verbal phrases (and punctuate correctly).

- Combine sentences using coordinating conjunctions (and punctuate correctly).

- Combine sentences using dependent words (and punctuate correctly).

- Combine sentences using conjunctive adverbs (and punctuate correctly).

Have you ever been amazed at how eloquently some people write? Some people put together sentences in such a way that their writing is a rhythmic, flowing cascade of thoughts. These people have a wealth of tools at their fingertips when they write, and many of these tools include strategies for combining sentences. Combining sentences not only adds variety and clarity to writing but also helps guide the reader in following the writer's course of ideas.

Look at the following paragraph, which does not make use of any sentence-combining strategies.

Paragraph A: Our planet is composed of four different layers. These layers have varying physical and chemical properties. The outer layer is called the *crust*. It averages about fifty miles in thickness. It consists of about a dozen large, irregularly shaped sections. These sections are called tectonic plates. The plates slide over one another. They slide under one another. They slide past one another. These sliding events take place on top of a second layer of the Earth called the *mantle*.

The sentences in the paragraph above are complete sentences, and they express the writer's thoughts adequately. But they are boring! Notice how similar they are in length. Combining some of the sentences results in a much more eloquent (and more pleasing to read) version.

Paragraph B: Our planet is composed of four different layers that have varying physical and chemical properties. The outer layer, which is called the *crust*, averages about fifty miles in thickness, and it consists of about a dozen large, irregularly shaped sections. These sections, referred to as *tectonic plates*, slide over, under, and past one another on top of a second layer, known as the *mantle*, that lies beneath the crust.

Can you tell the difference between the two paragraphs? To write the second paragraph, the writer did three things.

- Combined short, choppy sentences into longer ones. Paragraph A has ten sentences; paragraph B has three.
- Changed wording so that fewer sentences start with *it* or *they* (words the author repeated too frequently).
- Created sentences of varying lengths. The first sentence in paragraph B is considerably shorter than the two that follow it.

These changes made the paragraph *much* easier to read and greatly improved the writing style.

The explanations and exercises in this unit present sentence-combining strategies that will help you learn new ways to create sentences. The goal of this section of the text is to give you additional tools to use as a writer. If you like a particular sentence-combining strategy, annotate it or put a sticky note on the page. Intentionally use the strategy in your next writing assignment. Experiment with these strategies. The more adept you become at combining sentences, the more impressive, eloquent, and effective your writing will become.

Combining Phrases to Create New Sentences

Phrases are sets of words that function as a group but do not include both a subject and a verb. Because phrases lack either a subject or a verb or both, they cannot stand alone as complete sentences. Two important types of phrases are prepositional phrases and verbal phrases.

Combining Sentences Using Prepositional Phrases

Prepositions are words that connect a noun or a pronoun to other elements in a sentence. A preposition is always a part of a *prepositional phrase*. In the following example, the prepositional phrase is underlined, and the preposition is in bold print.

> **In** the textbook, a chart illustrates important terminology.

Prepositional phrases are useful because they enable writers to communicate more information in a sentence than would be possible otherwise. For example, consider the information presented by the following sentences:

- Many monarch butterflies spend each winter in the same particular location.
- They winter in Mexico.

- They live <u>in huge colonies</u>.
- They stay all winter <u>in trees</u>.
- These trees are located <u>in the mountains</u>.
- The mountains are <u>in southern Mexico</u>.

These sentences convey a great deal of information, but reading them is cumbersome. These choppy little sentences require the reader to start and stop repeatedly. What if all of these ideas could be combined into one single, smooth sentence? By taking the prepositional phrases (underlined) out of the short sentences and joining them together, the writer can produce a longer, smoother sentence that conveys the same ideas:

> Monarch butterflies spend each winter <u>in huge colonies</u> <u>in trees</u> <u>in the mountains</u> <u>of southern Mexico</u>.

By combining prepositional phrases, we can create a much more compact, interesting sentence.

Common Prepositions. The chart below lists the most common prepositions. Notice that some prepositions are single words, and some are made up of two words.

COMMON SINGLE-WORD PREPOSITIONS					
about	as	by	in	on	to
after	at	during	into	out	under
against	before	for	like	over	with
around	between	from	of	through	without

COMMON DOUBLE-WORD PREPOSITIONS			
according to	close to	inside of	out from
ahead of	due to	instead of	out of
aside from	except for	near to	outside of
because of	far from	next to	regardless of

A prepositional phrase contains *at least* a preposition and its **object,** which is a noun or pronoun. In the example that follows, you will see four prepositional phrases. The prepositions are in bold print, and the objects are underlined and identified.

> **Examples: at** the <u>dance</u>, **over** the <u>moon</u>, **with** <u>Timothy,</u> **because of** the <u>storm</u>
>   object   object   object   object

Prepositional phrases function like adjectives and adverbs. They typically answer questions such as these: *What kind? Which one? When? Where? How?* Using prepositional phrases effectively makes writing more descriptive, precise, and interesting.

EXAMPLES OF PREPOSITIONAL PHRASES			
Sentence without prepositional phrase	A reader's question	Answer	Expanded sentence using prepositional phrase
My favorite reading materials are books.	What kind of books?	books about science	My favorite reading materials are books <u>about science.</u>
The truck is for sale.	Which truck?	the truck by the fence	The truck <u>by the fence</u> is for sale.
The shopping rush will end.	When?	after the holiday season	The shopping rush will end <u>after the holiday season.</u>
They need to show up on time.	Where?	at the worksite	They need to show up on time <u>at the worksite.</u>
She paid for the calculator.	How?	with cash	She paid for the calculator <u>with cash.</u>

How to Use Prepositional Phrases.   First, use prepositional phrases to add interesting and pertinent details to your writing. Read the following paragraph, which has two prepositional phrases (underlined). Can you think of details a reader might want to know that would make the passage more interesting and informative?

> **Paragraph A:** We have all seen litter accumulate. It ends up <u>as marine debris</u> and is deposited ashore. Indeed, take a walk <u>along any beach</u> and you are likely to encounter ocean garbage.

Perhaps a reader would want to know exactly *where* litter accumulates and exactly *how* it gets deposited on the shore. We can add such details in individual sentences, as in paragraph B. Notice that these added sentences have prepositional phrases (underlined).

> **Paragraph B:** We have all seen litter accumulate. It accumulates <u>in cities</u>. It accumulates <u>along roadways</u>. Much of it collects together. It collects <u>in storm drains</u>. It collects <u>in canals</u>. It flows <u>through streams</u>. It flows <u>through rivers</u>. It flows <u>into our oceans</u>. It is driven <u>by currents</u>—sometimes thousands <u>of miles from its origin</u>. It ends up <u>as marine debris</u> and is deposited ashore. It is driven <u>by wind and tide</u>. Indeed, take a walk <u>along any beach</u> <u>in the world</u> and you are likely to encounter ocean garbage.

The additional sentences give much more information. However, because all the new sentences are short and constructed in the same way, the writing is choppy and repetitive. Glance back at all of the uses of *it*. The writer can use sentence-combining strategies to write less repetitive, choppy sentences. Notice how in paragraph C, the writer combines prepositional phrases to create an effective and detailed passage.

> **Paragraph C:** We've all seen litter accumulate <u>in cities</u> and <u>along roadways</u>. Much of it collects <u>in storm drains and canals</u> and eventually flows <u>through streams and rivers</u> and <u>into our oceans</u>. Driven <u>by currents</u>—sometimes thousands <u>of miles from its origin</u>—some marine debris is deposited ashore <u>by wind and tide</u>. Indeed, take a walk <u>along any beach</u> <u>in the world</u> and you are likely to encounter ocean garbage.

The power of prepositional phrases lies in their ability to add meaningful descriptive information to passages.

TIP

Prepositional Phrases

Generally speaking, a prepositional phrase that begins a sentence should be followed by a comma, especially if the phrase contains three or more words.

Examples: <u>Before the flood</u>, our house was in beautiful condition.

<u>Around the first of each year</u>, tax preparers become busy.

Note that commas are *not* used when prepositional phrases appear in the body of sentences, even if one prepositional phrase follows another one.

Examples: The hands <u>on the clock</u> <u>on the wall</u> seemed to move incredibly slowly.

Monarch butterflies winter <u>in huge colonies</u> <u>in trees</u> <u>in the mountains</u> <u>of southern Mexico</u>.

PRACTICE (1)

Adding and Combining Prepositional Phrases

A. Add prepositional phrases to the simple sentences that follow. Add at least three prepositional phrases to each sentence. Underline each prepositional phrase.

Example: The chapter was short.

The chapter <u>about podiatry</u> <u>in my medical textbook</u> <u>from 1972</u> was short.

1. Students eat.

    _____

2. The class will travel.

    _____

3. Moving was difficult.

    _____

4. Diana passed.

    _____

5. Women can vote.

    _____

B. Combine each group of sentences below into one sentence using prepositional phrases. Be sure to follow the punctuation guidelines. Underline each prepositional phrase.

Example:

*   She found her wallet.
*   It was in her jacket.
*   Her jacket was on the washing machine.

    She found her wallet <u>in her jacket</u> <u>on the washing machine</u>.

(continued)

1. Some people enjoy hunting for coins.

   They do their searching on weekends and holidays.

   Hunting for coins is a hobby for these folks.

   _____

   _____

2. Caches of coins are sometimes buried in open fields or forests.

   Usually, coins buried in such locations are hidden near landmarks.

   Landmarks are features like tall trees or boulders.

   _____

   _____

3. Coins are sometimes hidden underground but merely stashed unburied.

   Treasure hunters have found hoards of coins in caves.

   A deserted mine could be the location of a treasure trove.

   Old, abandoned cellars have been known to be the spot where hidden coin stashes were located.

   _____

   _____

4. Coin hoards have been found in old, unused sheds and barns.

   Ghost towns are filled with buildings that would make good hiding places for a trove of coins.

   Any structure can be a location for a hidden coin cache.

   _____

   _____

5. Even a house can potentially be a hiding place for hidden treasure.

   Within a house, coins can be hidden in the walls.

   They can be hidden under floorboards or in an attic.

   Attics are full of nooks and crannies.

   _____

   _____

6. Metal detectors can facilitate locating hidden coins.

   Treasure seekers use metal detectors in searching the ground in fields and forests.

   Metal detectors are used when treasure hunters explore underground sites.

   They are useful even within structures for scanning inside walls, floors, and attics.

   _____

   _____

Combining Sentences Using Verbal Phrases

A **verbal** is a verb form that functions in a sentence as a noun, an adjective, or an adverb. In a sense, a verbal is both a verb and some other part of speech. It may have its own modifiers and objects, and the verbal plus the words that accompany it together form a **verbal phrase.** Three types of verbal phrases occur in English:

- *to + verb* phrases
- *-ing* phrases
- *-ed/-en* phrases

Verbal phrases provide you with a tool for creating sentence variety, one of the characteristics of good writing. Learning to use verbal phrases will expand your sentence-writing ability. In addition, verbal phrases help you accomplish other writing goals.

***to + verb* Phrases.**   Form a *to + verb* (also known as an **infinitive**) by putting the word *to* in front of a verb stem.

> to + write = to write
> to + sleep = to sleep
> to + speak up = to speak up

A *to + verb* phrase is composed of the *to + verb* and any accompanying words. In the following examples, the verbal is in bold print and the *to + verb* phrase is underlined.

> **To acquire** the entire collection is a worthy goal.
>
> He is the man **to call** about a job.

***-ing* Phrases.**   To form an *-ing* verbal, add *-ing* to the end of the verb. Sometimes the final *-e* of a verb must be deleted (see the verb *leave* below) or the final letter of a verb must be doubled (see *plan* below) before the *-ing* is added.

> find + ing = finding
> leave − e + ing = leaving
> plan + n + ing = planning

An *-ing* verbal phrase consists of the verbal together with its accompanying words. In these examples, the *-ing* verbal is in bold print and the verbal phrase is underlined.

> **Finding** the lost keys made her day.
>
> **Planning** efficiently, Luis was able to complete his work on time.
>
> The hardest part of college for some teenage students is **leaving** home.
>
> The **winding** path disappeared into the woods.

***-ed/-en* Phrases.**   An *-ed/-en* phrase consists of the *-ed/-en* form of a verb and the words that accompany it. (The *-ed* or *-en* form, sometimes called the **past participle,** appears in verbs such as *has written* and *will have talked.* Occasionally, the form is irregular; for example, *buy* becomes *bought* in *has bought* and *do* becomes *done* in *have done.*) In these examples, the verbal is in bold print and the verbal phrase is underlined.

The young widow, **supported** lovingly by her family, worked through her grief.

A drain **clogged** with hair is one of a plumber's most common problems to solve.

Done with the assignment, the children were free to play outside.

She could work any sudoku puzzle **given** enough time.

How to Use Verbal Phrases.   Verbals of all three types can be used for a variety of purposes. The following explanations and exercises show the process of identifying when to create verbal phrases to accomplish particular purposes.

Using Verbal Phrases to Add Information.   Verbal phrases can perform some of the same functions as prepositional phrases. The questions *what kind, which one,* and *how* are often addressed using *-ing* and *-ed* verbals. For example, Consider this sentence:

Chenille Café is an unusual restaurant.

It's a complete sentence; nothing is wrong with it. However, you may wish to say more about how the restaurant is unusual. You could add these sentences to do so.

- The restaurant offers specialty desserts.
- It has French toast cheesecake.
- It offers banana meringue cookies.
- It sells caramel pie.

Now the reader has more information, but the string of short sentences makes for choppy writing. Using a verbal, you can write one sentence combining all these ideas. Note how the underlined verbal phrase below incorporates the ideas into the sentence.

Offering specialty desserts such as French toast cheesecake, banana meringue cookies, and caramel pie, the Chenille Café is an unusual restaurant.

The following chart shows ways in which verbal phrases can answer questions.

Sentence without verbal phrase	A reader's question	Answer	Expanded sentence using verbal phrase
My favorite reading materials are books.	What kind of books?	books by athletes	My favorite reading materials are books **written** by athletes.
		books about investigations	My favorite reading materials are books **involving** investigations.
The truck is for sale.	Which truck?	the truck on the lot	The truck **sitting** on the lot is for sale.
		the truck our family once owned	The truck once **owned** by our family is for sale.
She paid for the calculator.	How?	with a credit card	She paid for the calculator **using** a credit card.

PRACTICE 2

Using Verbal Phrases to Add Information

Combine each group of sentences below by creating a verbal phrase that answers *what kind, which one,* or *how.* An example has been provided.

Example:

- Margie was touched by the generosity of her coworkers.
- She could not speak without crying.

Margie, touched by the generosity of her coworkers, could not speak without crying.

1. Children of undocumented immigrants live in the United States.

    They need the chance for a college education.

    _____

    _____

2. The children of undocumented immigrants are affected by their parents' legal status.

    The children often believe they cannot be admitted to a college in the United States.

    _____

    _____

3. Undocumented students are not legally prohibited from enrolling in college.

    No such federal law exists.

    _____

    _____

4. Colleges write their own policies about the admission of undocumented students.

    These policies vary from college to college.

    _____

    _____

5. Many undocumented students hope to obtain a college education in the United States.

    Opportunities exist for them to do so.

    _____

    _____

Using Verbal Phrases to Express Purpose.   Verbal phrases allow you to explain a reason concisely. Consider these sentences:

- Building a new house takes time.
- It also requires a lot of planning.

- It is often more expensive than buying an existing house.
- It is wasteful.
- Buy an existing home rather than build a new one!

These sentences convey the writer's reasoning, but they take a lot of space, repeat words, and offer no sentence variety. A more effective alternative is to combine the sentences using verbal phrases (underlined below, with verbals in bold).

To save time and money and **to reduce** planning and waste, potential homeowners should buy an existing home rather than build a new one.

Notice that *to* + *verb* phrases are often used to express purpose or, as shown in the following chart, to answer the question *why*.

Sentence without verbal phrase	A reader's question	Answer	Expanded sentence using verbal phrase
The deer scrambled up the embankment.	Why?	because of the rising floodwaters	The deer scrambled up the embankment **to escape** the rising floodwaters.
Lori locked the door.	Why?	for some peace and quiet	Lori locked the door **to get** some peace and quiet.
We went to the market.	Why?	We needed some fresh vegetables.	We went to the market **to buy** some fresh vegetables.

PRACTICE 3

Using *to* + *verb* Verbal Phrases to Express Purpose

Combine each group of sentences below by creating a *to* + *verb* phrase to answer the question *why*. An example has been provided.

Example:

- Searle-Gorley Industries will produce a new kind of radar.
- They will use space-related technology as the basis for this production.

To produce a new kind of radar, Searle-Gorley Industries will use space-related technology.

1. The Supplemental Nutrition Assistance Program (SNAP) was created by the federal government.

   It reduces hunger in America.

   _____

   _____

2. SNAP provides food resources for struggling Americans.

   It helps them while they are between jobs or unemployed.

   _____

   _____

(continued)

3. SNAP needs continued government funding.

    Approximately fifteen million children live in food-insecure households.

    _____

    _____

4. The program expands and contracts.

    It responds to the ebb and flow of the economy.

    _____

    _____

5. SNAP assists the food banks that so many people depend on.

    More people can be helped that way.

    _____

    _____

Using Verbal Phrases to Name Activities.   Verbals can act as nouns to name activities or actions: *singing, hoping, lifting, thinking.* The verbals most commonly used as nouns are *-ing* and *to + verb* verbals. Notice how the *-ing* verbal (in bold print) acts as a noun in the following example.

> **Plowing** is a basic task of most farmers.

Because *plowing* is a verbal and not an ordinary noun, an object (such as *field*) and other words can be included as a part of a verbal phrase, as in the sentence below.

> **Plowing** a field on a hot summer day is an unpleasant task at best.
>   object

The following shows that *to + verb* verbal phrases can also function as nouns.

> **To plow** a field on a hot summer day is an unpleasant task at best.
>   object

Verbals that function as nouns often answer the question *what.*

> *What* is the greatest human endeavor?
>
> **To pursue** wisdom is the greatest human endeavor.
>
> The writer could just as well use an *-ing* verbal:
>
> **Pursuing** wisdom is the greatest human endeavor.

PRACTICE (**4**)

Using Verbal Phrases to Name Activities

Combine each group of sentences below by creating a verbal phrase that names an activity. Use either *-ing* or *to + verb* verbal phrases.

Example:

- People who counsel others must be sensitive.
- People who counsel others must have good listening skills.

To counsel others, a person must be sensitive and have good listening skills.

1. Veterans return from military service.

   They look for jobs.

   However, they find that landing a job is difficult.

   _____

   _____

2. In the civilian world, a veteran may not qualify for the same type of job she held in the military.

   That is the case when the veteran lacks the civilian certifications or licenses needed for employment in a given field.

   _____

   _____

3. Veterans often must repeat education or training.

   Doing so provides them with the "piece of paper" needed for employment.

   _____

   _____

4. We should find a method for officially certifying veterans' skills in the civilian setting.

   We should make veterans' transition to civilian life as smooth as possible.

   _____

   _____

5. We should show our appreciation to veterans for their service.

   One way to show our appreciation is to facilitate their re-entry into the workforce.

   _____

   _____

Using Verbal Phrases to Replace Unclear Pronouns.   Sometimes writers use words such as *it, that, this, these,* and *those* without making clear what these words refer to. Consider this example:

> The students planned to survey the freshman class. However, it would take time.

Readers are left confused. What would take time—the planning, the survey, or both? Replacing *it* with a verbal phrase (underlined) can eliminate this confusion. Note the differences in meaning in the following sentences.

> The students planned to survey the freshman class. However, **planning** the survey would take time.
>
> The students planned to survey the freshman class. However, **conducting** the survey would take time.
>
> The students planned to survey the freshman class. However, **planning** and **conducting** the survey would take time.

In all these sentences, the verbal phrase acts as a noun, replacing the pronoun *it* as the subject of the sentence.

Even when pronoun reference is not a problem, using verbal phrases to replace pronouns can make for clearer and more precise writing—a goal of every good writer. Look at the following example:

> Mika hopes to make it through the shift without incident. **That** is her only goal.

What is Mika's only goal? *To make it through the shift without incident.* The following sentence replaces the vague pronoun *that* with a verbal phrase.

> **To make** it through the shift without incident is Mika's only goal.

Combining the two sentences in this manner both clarifies and condenses.

PRACTICE (5)

Using Verbal Phrases to Clarify Pronoun Reference

Combine each group of sentences below. Use verbal phrases to replace the unclear pronouns. An example has been provided.

Example:

- Mark would rather read than mow the lawn.
- He sometimes neglects it for a long time.

Mark would rather read than mow, so he sometimes neglects mowing the lawn for a long time.

(continued)

1. Many students put off selecting a major and starting a degree program.

    They say it is too stressful.

    _____

    _____

2   After a year or two of dabbling in different courses, students may feel comfortable about selecting a major.

    They are more confident about it.

    _____

    _____

3. Of course, many students later change their majors.

    They should not feel bad about this.

    _____

    _____

4. College is a good time to consider career options.

    It will affect a person's future happiness.

    _____

    _____

5. Fortunately, career exploration workshops can help in the process.

    Attending them can help students make better decisions.

    _____

    _____

Using Verbal Phrases to Create Variety in Sentence Structure.   Using verbal phrases enables you to vary the structures of sentences but keep their meanings. We have seen how verbal phrases can introduce variety into a series of short, simple sentences. In addition, verbal phrases can introduce variety into any paragraph dominated by one type of sentence structure. Consider these sentences:

Jill, who had to be taken to the hospital against her wishes, was upset.

Her car, which had been totaled in the wreck, had to be towed away.

The emergency room doctor, who reassured Jill's family, quickly explained that Jill would be fine.

Jill's father, who sat in the waiting room, chattered incessantly.

Jill's mother, who was satisfied with the care her daughter was receiving, read the newspaper.

Notice that every sentence has the same basic structure. The group of sentences makes for tedious reading. Using some verbal phrases makes the passage easier to read and more interesting. The verbal phrases are underlined in the following examples.

Jill, who had to be taken to the hospital against her wishes, was upset.

Her car, **totaled** in the wreck, had to be towed away.

To reassure Jill's family, the emergency room doctor quickly explained that Jill would be fine.

Jill's father sat in the waiting room, **chatting** incessantly.

Satisfied with the care her daughter was receiving, Jill's mother read the newspaper.

PRACTICE 6

Using Verbal Phrases to Create Variety in Sentence Structure

Combine the sentences in each sentence group below using a verbal phrase to replace all or part of one of the sentences, as the example illustrates.

Example:

- ECON 101 was the course about which I knew the least.
- ECON 101 was required for graduation.

ECON 101, required for graduation, was the course about which I knew the least.

1. A ceremonial blessing of the fleet, which is given by a local Catholic priest, is a custom in Biloxi, Mississippi.

   It marks the beginning of shrimp fishing season.

   _____

   _____

2. The Blessing of the Fleet is a tradition that has its origins in Europe.

   Its purpose was to transmit God's grace for a safe and bountiful fishing season.

   _____

   _____

3. Fishermen travel long distances to reach Biloxi.

   They want to participate in the blessing.

   _____

   _____

4. A procession that passes by the anchored "Blessing Boat" begins.

   More than thirty shrimp boats are in the procession.

   _____

   _____

5. The priest, who stands on the "Blessing Boat," sprinkles holy water.

   He sprinkles it on each of the passing shrimp boats.

   _____

   _____

TIP

Misplaced Modifiers

A modifying phrase should be located as close as possible to the word it describes. Descriptive phrases that are not properly positioned are called *misplaced modifiers* and can create confusion for the reader. This issue is of special concern with regard to verbal phrase modifiers. In the following examples, the verbal phrases are underlined and the words that the phrases modify are in bold print.

Correct:	<u>Driving home</u>, **Jim** saw the old tree swing.
Misplaced modifier:	**Jim** saw the old tree swing <u>driving home.</u> (The swing was not driving home.)
Correct:	<u>Coming down the stairs for dinner</u>, **Rita** smelled the oysters.
Misplaced modifier:	**Rita** smelled the oysters <u>coming down the stairs for dinner.</u> (The oysters were not coming down the stairs.)

Similarly, if the modified word is missing from the sentence, the result, called a *dangling modifier*, can create confusion and even misreading.

Dangling modifier:	<u>Walking down the street</u>, a car hit a bicyclist. (Neither the car *nor* the bicyclist was walking down the street. The phrase "walking down the street" refers to no word at all in the sentence.)
Correct:	<u>Walking down the street</u>, **they** saw a car hit a bicyclist.

Combining Clauses to Create New Sentences

A **clause** is group of words containing a subject and a verb. Here are some examples:

- the engineer is drawing a blueprint
- that the intersection is busy
- when a coyote howled at the moon

Some clauses are also sentences. A **sentence** has at least one clause, starts with a capital letter, has end punctuation, and can stand alone as a complete thought.

> **Sentence with one clause:** The engineer is drawing a blueprint.
> capital letter   end punctuation

A sentence can have more than one clause. In the following example, the two clauses (underlined) are joined by a connecting word (*so*).

> **Sentence with two clauses:** The intersection is busy, **so** traffic is moving slowly.
> clause   connecting word   clause

Imagine an entire paragraph made up of single-clause sentences. What would the effect be? Read paragraph A, which is made up of single-clause sentences.

Paragraph A: Registered nurses spend much of the day walking and standing. They also bend and stretch quite a bit. They must often lift and move patients. They are vulnerable to back injuries. Registered nurses work closely with people. The people may have infectious diseases. Nurses often come in contact with hazardous drugs. They often come into contact with other dangerous substances. Registered nurses must follow strict, standardized guidelines.

Now read paragraph B, in which some single-clause sentences have been joined together. The connecting words are underlined.

Paragraph B: Registered nurses spend much of the day walking and standing, and they also bend and stretch quite a bit. They must often lift and move patients, so they are vulnerable to back injuries. Registered nurses work closely with people who may have infectious diseases. Because they often come in contact with hazardous drugs and other dangerous substances, registered nurses must follow strict, standardized guidelines.

The variety in sentence length and type make paragraph B more interesting to read. Also, the ways in which the sentences are connected give the reader more information. In paragraph A, the cause and effect relationships are only implied. The causes are listed separately and are not tied to their effects, as they are in paragraph B. In the revised paragraph, the second sentence uses *so* and the fourth sentence uses *because*. These words clarify the cause and effect relationships.

Paragraph A:

- Registered nurses spend much of the day walking and standing.
- They also bend and stretch quite a bit.
- They must often lift and move patients.

  In this paragraph, the causes are listed separately and not tied to the effect.

- They are vulnerable to back injuries.

  Effect

Paragraph B:

- Registered nurses spend much of the day walking and standing, and they also bend and stretch quite a bit.
- They must often lift and move patients, so they are vulnerable to back injuries.

  The combined sentences do a better job at helping readers notice the causes and effect.

Additionally, combining the following two sentences with the word *who* emphasizes the fact that nurses work with certain types of people.

Paragraph A:

- Registered nurses work closely with people.
- The people may have infectious diseases.

  Presenting these ideas separately makes the second sentence seem unimportant.

Paragraph B:

- Registered nurses work closely with people who may have infectious diseases.

  Combining the sentences shows readers why the information is important: nurses work with such people.

By carefully selecting clauses to connect, writers can produce texts that are clearer and that convey meaning more effectively.

Combining Sentences Using Coordinating Conjunctions

One way to join two or more clauses to create a sentence is by using a **coordinating conjunction (CC).** You may already be familiar with the seven coordinating conjunctions, often referred by the acronym FANBOYS: *for, and, nor, but, or, yet, so.*

Think of these seven coordinating conjunctions as sentence connectors. In the same way that physical tools such as hammers and crowbars have specific purposes, coordinating conjunctions do also. For example, *but* is used to join two clauses to show that the clauses (underlined below) mean opposite things, as this example shows:

Some Americans believe extreme measures should be taken for airport security, **but** others believe the measures violate their privacy rights.

The first clause (*Some Americans . . . security*) expresses agreement with the use of extreme measures. The second clause (*others believe . . . rights*) expresses disagreement with extreme measures. Using *but* enables the writer to alert readers to the contrasting information in the two clauses.

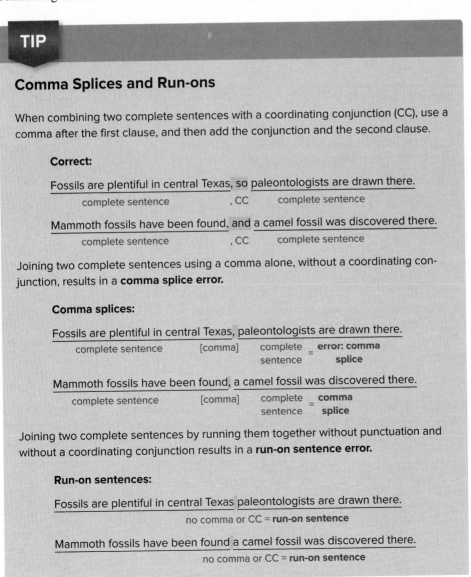

TIP

Comma Splices and Run-ons

When combining two complete sentences with a coordinating conjunction (CC), use a comma after the first clause, and then add the conjunction and the second clause.

Correct:

Fossils are plentiful in central Texas, so paleontologists are drawn there.
complete sentence   , CC   complete sentence

Mammoth fossils have been found, and a camel fossil was discovered there.
complete sentence   , CC   complete sentence

Joining two complete sentences using a comma alone, without a coordinating conjunction, results in a **comma splice error.**

Comma splices:

Fossils are plentiful in central Texas, paleontologists are drawn there.
complete sentence   [comma]   complete _ **error: comma**
                                        sentence   **splice**

Mammoth fossils have been found, a camel fossil was discovered there.
complete sentence   [comma]   complete _ **comma**
                                        sentence   **splice**

Joining two complete sentences by running them together without punctuation and without a coordinating conjunction results in a **run-on sentence error.**

Run-on sentences:

Fossils are plentiful in central Texas paleontologists are drawn there.
no comma or CC = **run-on sentence**

Mammoth fossils have been found a camel fossil was discovered there.
no comma or CC = **run-on sentence**

What follows are explanations of when to use coordinating conjunctions and guidelines for using them, followed by practice opportunities.

Using *for*

When to Use *for*:   When you want to provide an explanation.

Why to Use *for*:   To make clear which sentence is being explained.

> **Example:** Solar technology works well in Arizona, <u>for</u> Arizona has very few cloudy days.

For tells the reader *why* solar technology works well in Arizona. If the sentences are separated, readers might see them as two unrelated facts:

- Solar technology works well in Arizona.
- Arizona has very few cloudy days.

When the sentences are combined using *for,* readers can see that the second clause is an explanation of the first.

How to Use *for*:   Find sentences that are related because one sentence explains the other. Use *for* to join the sentences.

PRACTICE ⑦

Using *for* to Join Sentences

Read each pair of sentences. Does one sentence answer the question *why* about the other sentence? If so, use *for* to write a single sentence that combines the two sentences. If not, explain why combining the sentences would not be appropriate.

1. One hazard of a volcano is a lahar. A lahar is a mixture of volcanic ash, rock, debris, and water.

   _____

   _____

2. A lahar can be incredibly destructive to people who live nearby. It occurs quickly and can travel down the slopes of a volcano.

   _____

   _____

3. Lahars are generated when a high volume of hot or cold water mixes with ash and rock and starts downslope. When most people think of volcanoes, they envision a mountain with a lahar.

   _____

   _____

(continued)

4.   Rainfall or melting snow can be hazardous during a volcanic eruption. The combination of water and the eruption produces a lahar.

_____

_____

5.   When moving, a lahar looks like a mass of wet concrete. As a lahar rushes down the sides of a volcano, the speed at which it moves as well as the amount of water and rock debris it carries constantly change.

_____

_____

6.   The beginning surge of water and rock debris is forceful. It often erodes rocks and vegetation from the side of a volcano and along any river valley it enters.

_____

_____

7.   If a lahar enters a river, the hazards will increase. The eroding rock debris and additional water can cause the lahar to grow to more than ten times its initial size.

_____

_____

8.   As a lahar moves farther away from a volcano, it will eventually begin to lose its heavy load of sediment. It will also decrease in size.

_____

_____

Using *and*

When to Use *and*:   When you want to add information or to join two sentences that are related in meaning.

Why to Use *and*:   To put together clauses that contain related information.

> **Example:** Geothermal heat is a major source of energy in Iceland, <u>and</u> it is used there both to produce direct heat for homes and businesses and to generate electricity.

And allows us to combine two related facts: that geothermal heat is a major source of energy in Iceland and that it is used there both to produce direct heat for homes and businesses and to generate electricity.

Writing often requires us to provide related pieces of information. Technically, we could write complete sentences for each separate piece of information, but doing so would result in very choppy writing, such as this:

Choppy writing: Wind technology works well in western Texas. It has been used there extensively since 1975. In certain parts of western Texas, wind turbines are visible as far as the eye can see.

Combining information that is related in meaning reduces choppiness and shows that the elements joined together are related. We can revise the previous sentences as follows. (Notice that the last sentence was *not* added to the combined sentence because it is not closely enough related in meaning to the previous sentences.)

Wind technology works well in western Texas, <u>and</u> it has been used there extensively since 1975. In certain parts of western Texas, wind turbines are visible as far as the eye can see.

How to Use *and*:   Find sentences that each provide related pieces of information about the same subject. Use *and* to combine them.

PRACTICE (8)

Using *and* to Join Sentences

Read each pair of sentences. Does one sentence provide additional related information about the other sentence? If so, use *and* (preceded by a comma) to create a single sentence that combines the two sentences. If not, explain why combining the sentences would not be appropriate.

1. Africanized honeybees get part of their genetic code from European honeybees. They get another part from African honeybees.

    _____

    _____

2. Many questions about Africanized bees remain a mystery. Researchers have learned about some of the traits of Africanized bees.

    _____

    _____

3. Beekeepers are especially concerned about the traits of Africanized bees. Managing the bees in a hive is important in promoting their production of honey.

    _____

    _____

4. Beekeepers want to know whether Africanized bees produce as much honey as European bees. They want to know whether Africanized bees require more care than European bees.

    _____

    _____

(continued)

5. Africanized bees have a combination of African and European traits. It appears that African traits are showing themselves to be the dominant ones.

_____

_____

6. Both types of bees share some characteristics. Six biological and behavioral factors set Africanized bees apart from European bees.

_____

_____

7. One of these factors is especially significant. European queen honeybees mate disproportionately with African drones.

_____

_____

8. Thus, more of the genes in the colony are from African honeybees. The genetic makeup of the entire bee population is slowly affected.

_____

_____

Using _nor_

When to Use _nor:_ When you want to connect negative statements in a series, or, in conjunction with _neither,_ when you want to connect two equally negative possibilities.

Why to Use _nor:_ To avoid stringing together clause after clause of similar—but negative—statements _and_ to show that two or more alternatives are equally negative.

> **Example:** The bureaucrat was not very kind, <u>nor</u> was he particularly helpful.

1. Use _nor_ to link two negative statements. _Nor_ functions like _and_ except that the two statements being joined are both negative. In the example above, we have two negative statements:

   - The bureaucrat was not very kind.
   - The bureaucrat was not particularly helpful.

   These statements are similar because they both point out things the bureaucrat was _not._ Thus, we can use _nor_ to link them.

2. Use _nor_ together with _neither,_ as in the following example.

> **Example:** The committee members will <u>neither</u> phone Mark, <u>nor</u> will they interview him.

The *neither/nor* combination negates two different options. In the case of the example, the options are phoning and interviewing. By joining these ideas together in one sentence, the writer emphasizes that each option is equally rejected.

How to Use *nor*: Find two negative statements in a series. Use *nor* to join the clauses. Also, find two options that are equally negative; use *neither/nor* to join them.

PRACTICE 9

Using *nor* to Join Sentences

Read each pair of sentences. Are they both negative statements? If so, use *nor* or *neither/nor* to write a single sentence combining the two. If not, explain why combining the sentences would not be appropriate.

1. In democratic societies like the United States, the voting process is protected by federal laws. The Federal Bureau of Investigation (FBI) is responsible for analyzing all cases of suspected election crimes.

    _____

    _____

2. The FBI does not investigate all potential election crime cases. They investigate only cases involving potential violations of federal law.

    _____

    _____

3. For example, an individual may not give more than $4,600 to a federal candidate. Committees and groups may not exceed the limits set by law when making donations to federal candidates.

    _____

    _____

4. A donor may not ask a friend to give money to a federal candidate and then reimburse the friend. To do so is a federal election crime.

    _____

    _____

5. A voter may not intentionally give false information when registering to vote. A voter may not cast more than one ballot in a federal election.

    _____

    _____

6. When civil rights are alleged to have been violated in an election, the incidents are investigated by the FBI. For example, a scheme designed to keep minorities from voting would be under FBI jurisdiction.

    _____

    _____

(continued)

7. While many federal election offenses exist, some common actions are not against the law. For instance, giving voters a ride to the polls is not illegal. Encouraging friends, neighbors, and acquaintances to cast a ballot is not against the law.

_____

_____

8. Offering stamps to voters does not violate any law. Giving voters time off from work is not illegal.

_____

_____

Using *but*

When to Use *but*: When you want to show a difference in two ideas; when you want to indicate a change of direction.

Why to Use *but*: To help readers understand that one sentence is different (and perhaps opposite) in meaning from another sentence.

> **Example:** Senators and representatives love the idea of a law to make college education free, <u>but</u> they will not vote for one.

But indicates a complete change in direction in this sentence. Readers see *but* and are notified that the meaning of the sentence is about to change direction. In the example, *but* functions to join two contradictory statements:

- Senators and representatives love the idea of a law to make college education free.
- They will not vote for a law to make college education free.

When *but* is used, readers can see that it is possible for two contradictory conditions to exist. Also, *but* leads readers to the more important point. The clause that follows *but* reflects the actual case, the truth of the matter.

How to Use *but*: Find two sentences that are related to each other because the idea in one *opposes* the idea in the other. Use *but* to show this opposition.

PRACTICE 10

Using *but* to Join Sentences

Read each pair of sentences. Are the ideas in these sentences related but opposed to each other? If so, use *but* to write a single sentence that combines the two sentences. If not, explain why combining the sentences would not be appropriate.

1. Most people in the United States live in cities. They depend on the agricultural production of the countryside.

_____

_____

(continued)

2. Fifty percent of the United States, 907 million acres, is cropland, pastureland, or rangeland. This land is owned and managed by farmers and ranchers and their families.

_____

_____

3. This 50 percent of the United States is owned and managed by less than 2 percent of US citizens. We rely on them to produce the food on which the American consumer depends.

_____

_____

4. Most of the time, our agricultural systems work. Shortages do sometimes occur.

_____

_____

5. California, for example, provides a steady supply of strawberries to the United States and beyond. Diseases such as Fusarium wilt threaten the strawberry supply.

_____

_____

6. When diseases affect large areas of cropland, supplies become limited and prices go up. Chemists and biologists work diligently to determine the causes of crop diseases.

_____

_____

7. In general, crops are planted in areas where the climate is favorable to growth. In recent years, extreme weather changes have threatened crops and made shortages inevitable.

_____

_____

8. Many people around the world depend on the United States to meet their food demands. Farmers, ranchers, and food scientists are determined not to let these people down.

_____

_____

Using *or*

When to Use *or*:   When you want to offer clear alternatives.

Why to Use *or*:   To indicate to readers two or more options from which to choose.

> **Example:** Geology students must participate in a field trip, <u>or</u> they must create a project.

Or reveals options to the reader. In the example, the use of *or* makes it clear that two alternatives are available: a field trip or a project.

The term *or* is very specific in its meaning. Read the sentence about a menu item below carefully, noticing what *or* tells you about the entrée:

> The grilled salmon can be served on a bed of rice pilaf, <u>or</u> it can be served atop grilled asparagus.

The use of *or* means diners will have to choose between rice pilaf and grilled asparagus.

Sometimes the combination *either/or* is used to present the alternatives in a sentence:

> <u>Either</u> the law should be repealed, <u>or</u> it should be changed.

Either/or puts a stronger emphasis on the fact that only two choices exist.

How to Use *or* and *either/or*:   Find two sentences that give alternatives for the same related content. Use *or* to connect them, or use *either/or* to connect them.

PRACTICE (11)

Using *or* or *either/or* to Join Sentences

Read each pair of sentences. Are these sentences related, and do they also provide different alternatives? If so, use *or* or *either/or* to write a single sentence that combines the two sentences. If not, explain why combining the sentences would not be appropriate.

1. One reason Congress created the Affordable Care Act was to make sure anyone who wants health care can get it. The Affordable Care Act improves existing insurance in a variety of ways.

   _____

   _____

   _____

2. In the past, consumers could get affordable insurance if their employers offered it. If they did not have employer-sponsored insurance, they would have to purchase insurance on the open market if they were to be insured.

   _____

   _____

   _____

(continued)

3. Under the Affordable Care Act, workers can continue to participate in their employer's plans. Alternatively, virtually all consumers can purchase affordable insurance plans on the open market.

_____

_____

_____

4. Before the Affordable Care Act became law, insurance companies could use consumers' premiums for administrative costs. They could use consumers' premiums to provide health-care services.

_____

_____

_____

5. Now, insurance companies must use consumers' premiums exclusively to provide health-care services. They will be out of compliance with the new law if they do not.

_____

_____

_____

6. Preventive care is now covered at no cost to the consumer. In the past, consumers had to pay for portions of preventive care.

_____

_____

_____

7. The new plan allows consumers to choose their own doctors. Those who want a doctor to be assigned can request one.

_____

_____

_____

8. Many old plans prohibited people from using emergency services out of their area health-care networks. Now, health-care plans cover the use of emergency services outside of network areas.

_____

_____

_____

Using *yet*

When to Use *yet*: When you want to strongly emphasize a contrast between two ideas.

Why to Use *yet*:   To focus readers' attention on the contrast itself rather than the ideas being contrasted.

> **Example:** Jared is a pilot, <u>yet</u> he is afraid of heights.

Yet emphasizes the irony of the contrast in this example. *Irony* means the use of words that mean the opposite of what a reader would ordinarily expect, typically for humorous or emphatic effect. Compare the sentence above with the sentences that follow:

- Jared is a pilot.
- He is afraid of heights.

While these two sentences communicate the same ideas as the single sentence that uses *yet*, the ideas do not seem as connected as they do when they are joined in a single sentence using the conjunction *yet*. Additionally, readers cannot see the intentional irony as easily when the construction used involves two sentences rather than one.

We could use *but* instead of *yet*. If we used *but*, the sentence would not emphasize the irony of the situation as clearly as if we used *yet:*

> Jared is a pilot, <u>but</u> he is afraid of heights.

Using *but* makes the sentence sound much more ordinary than using *yet*.

How to Use *yet*:   When you can join two sentences with *but*, try using *yet*. Be aware that *yet* provides a special emphasis on how the sentences offer contrasting information. Save the use of *yet* for when you want to draw attention to that contrast.

PRACTICE (12)

Using *yet* to Join Sentences

Read each pair of sentences. Does one sentence contrast with the other, and does the contrast emphasize irony? If so, use *yet* to write a single sentence that combines the two sentences. If not, explain why combining the sentences would not be appropriate.

1. Hackers are computer experts who are able to penetrate secure computer systems to get access to data. Some people who hack into computers use the information they find for illegal activities.

    _____

    _____

2. Most Americans know that hackers pose real threats to online activities. People continue to use the Internet for very important financial transactions.

    _____

    _____

(continued)

3. Ironically, private companies and government institutions have spent billions of dollars trying to outsmart the hackers. The hackers continue to break into even the most secure systems.

_____

_____

4. Some people classify hackers into two groups, crackers and hackers. Crackers are the bad guys, the ones who hack for personal gain, and hackers are those who hack for fun or to show where weaknesses in "the system" can be found.

_____

_____

5. Hackers may think they do no harm. Their activities can result in serious damage.

_____

6. Suppose, for example, that a hacker is able to break into a particular bank's computer system. If word gets out that the bank's system is vulnerable, crackers may begin to hack into it immediately.

_____

_____

7. Hackers acknowledge this possibility. They typically say that the good they do by alerting companies to their security vulnerabilities outweighs any possible negative consequences.

_____

_____

8. Perhaps the best thing a hacker can do is to take a job with a company that needs rigorous computer security. Such a position would be the perfect opportunity for an expert hacker.

_____

_____

Using so

When to Use so: When you want to show a cause and effect relationship.

Why to Use so: To join two clauses that are directly related by cause and effect.

> **Example:** The cost of living increased this year, <u>so</u> employees are asking for a 2 percent raise.

_So_ brings together a cause (the increase in the cost of living) and an effect (employees' request for a raise). Joining together the two clauses with _so_ makes it clear that the first clause is a reason for the second.

Sometimes it is difficult to see the cause and effect relationship between sentences without joining the ones that are related, as this example shows.

- The new manufacturing facility was completed.
- The company held a grand opening ceremony.
- Factory workers marched in protest.

Was the grand opening related to the completion of the new facility? We cannot be sure. Did the workers protest the completion of the facility or the ceremony or something else? We have no way of knowing. When some of the sentences are linked together, we can more clearly see the cause and effect relationships.

- The new manufacturing facility was completed, <u>so</u> the company held a grand opening ceremony.
- Factory workers marched to protest the lavishness of the ceremony.

How to Use so: Find sentences in which one sentence expresses a cause and the other sentence expresses its effect. Use *so* to combine them.

PRACTICE 13

Using *so* to Join Sentences

Read each pair of sentences. Does one sentence express a cause and the other sentence express its effect? If so, use *so* to write a single sentence that combines the two sentences. If not, explain why combining the sentences would not be appropriate.

1. Child labor has been tolerated in every country on earth. It still exists in many countries.

   _____

   _____

2. The United States has strict labor laws protecting children. All children have the opportunity to go to school.

   _____

   _____

3. Companies cannot hire children to do work that is harmful to a child's health and well-being. Teenagers younger than eighteen cannot be employed as coal miners, for example.

   _____

   _____

4. In general, teens must be sixteen or older to engage in most nonfarm work. Minors aged fourteen and fifteen may work outside of school hours in certain occupations under certain conditions.

   _____

   _____

(continued)

5. Minors of any age may be employed in certain jobs. They may deliver newspapers; perform in radio, television, film, or theatrical productions; or work in nonhazardous, nonfarm businesses solely owned by their parents.

_____

_____

6. The laws that govern agricultural work differ from those that cover nonfarm work. Teens who work on farms may have different rights than those who work in nonfarm jobs.

_____

_____

7. The federal government allows children over the age of fourteen to work on farms after school hours. Each state has particular laws governing farm work.

_____

_____

8. Child labor laws protect children and teenagers. Teens who want to work can do so without exploitation.

_____

_____

Now that you have used each coordinating conjunction individually, complete the next exercise by joining clauses using a variety of coordinating conjunctions.

PRACTICE 14

Using Coordinating Conjunctions to Combine Sentences

Some of the following groups of sentences can be combined using a conjunction from the FANBOYS list (*for, and, nor, but, or, yet, so*). Combine the sentences you believe should be joined. Keep in mind the reasons for joining sentences: to show how one sentence relates to another sentence; to avoid lists of short, choppy sentences; and to emphasize some ideas over others. Not all sentences need to be combined. For each set of sentences you join, be prepared to explain why you chose to join them. Be sure to combine at least five sets of sentences, but join more if you believe doing so would be effective.

1. Like cigarette smoking, hookah smoking uses tobacco to deliver the addictive drug nicotine.

Although not all scientists agree, hookah smoking may be as toxic as cigarette smoking.

_____

_____

_____

(continued)

2. Some hookah smokers believe that this practice is less harmful than smoking cigarettes.

    Hookah smoking actually carries many of the same health risks.

    _____

    _____

    _____

3. Smoking cigarettes is not a healthy practice.

    Hookah smoking is not beneficial to health.

    _____

    _____

    _____

4. Hookahs are water pipes that are used to smoke specially processed tobacco that is typically flavored.

    Hookahs are also referred to by a number of different names, including narghile, argileh, shisha, hubble-bubble, and goza.

    _____

    _____

    _____

5. Hookah smoking is frequently practiced in groups.

    It can properly be referred to as a social activity.

    _____

    _____

    _____

6. Health organizations are beginning to pay more attention to the health effects of hookah use.

    Hookah use has been on the rise around the world in recent years.

    _____

    _____

    _____

7. A Monitoring the Future survey found that in 2011, 18.5 percent of twelfth-grade students in the United States had used hookahs in the past year.

    An even higher percentage of university students—from 22 to 40 percent—have used hookahs in the past year.

    _____

    _____

    _____

(continued)

8. Hookah smoking has been associated with lung cancer, respiratory illness, low birth weight, and periodontal disease.

   It exposes the smoker to more smoke over a longer period of time as compared to typical cigarette usage.

   _____

   _____

   _____

9. Young people often believe hookah smoking is a healthy choice.

   Cigarette smoking may actually be *less* harmful.

   _____

   _____

   _____

10. An average cigarette lasts 20 puffs.

    A typical one-hour hookah-smoking session involves 200 puffs.

    _____

    _____

11. We need to increase public education about the dangers of hookah smoking.

    Another generation may suffer the same fate as did their cigarette-smoking parents and grandparents.

    _____

    _____

    _____

12. Do not use hookahs yourself.

    Spread the word to others about the dangers of hookah use.

    _____

    _____

    _____

Combining Sentences Using Dependent Words

The use of coordinating conjunctions (FANBOYS) is not the only way to join sentences. Another method is to use **dependent words**. Remember that a clause is a group of words containing a subject and a verb. A clause that can stand alone as a complete thought is sometimes called an **independent clause**. When an independent clause begins with a capital letter and has end punctuation, it is a sentence.

Independent clause: Accounting majors must take several math classes.

If we add a dependent word, such as *although*, the clause can no longer stand alone.

Dependent clause: <u>although</u> accounting majors must take several math classes
                        dependent word

When we add a dependent word, the clause—now a **dependent clause**—can no longer stand alone because it is now an *incomplete* thought. After reading a dependent clause, we wonder about the writer's point; we need more information.

Writers can use dependent clauses effectively by combining them with independent clauses. In the following example, the dependent clause is underlined and the dependent word is in bold print.

Although <u>accounting majors must take several math classes,</u> they do not need many English classes.

Dependent words have a variety of functions, as the following chart shows. (Be aware that many of these words can also function as prepositions or as other parts of speech.)

FUNCTIONS OF DEPENDENT WORDS					
To reveal causes and effects	**To show comparisons**	**To show contrasts**	**To show possibilities**	**To provide time information**	**To modify a noun or act as a noun**
because	as	although	if	after	that
for	in the same way	even though	in case	as	what
in order to	just as	in spite of	in the event	as long as	whatever
since	like	the fact	once	as soon as	which
so that	that	regardless of	unless	before	whichever
		the fact that	until	now that	who
		that	whether (or not)	once	whoever
		though		since	whom
		whereas		until	whomever
				when	whose
				whenever	
				while	

Using Dependent Words to Show How Ideas Are Related.   As the chart demonstrates, dependent words can help readers more accurately decipher the relationships between the ideas in sentences. Consider these sentences:

- Art history is interesting to Shawna.
- She enjoyed taking the art history class.

If we want to show that Shawna's interest in art history was the cause of her enjoyment in the class, we can use the dependent word *because* to combine the sentences. The word *because* signals readers to look for a cause and effect relationship.

> **Because** art history is interesting to Shawna, she enjoyed taking the art history class.
>   dependent clause (cause)   independent clause (effect)

Notice that the dependent clause (*because art history is interesting to Shawna*) provides the *cause,* and the independent clause (*she enjoyed taking the art history class*) provides the *effect:* the fact that art history is interesting to Shawna *caused* her to enjoy the art history class.

You can use dependent words to combine sentences to show different relationships. In these examples, the dependent clauses are underlined and the dependent words are in bold print.

- **To show cause and effect**

> Candidates rarely spend campaign time at schools **since** minors cannot vote.
>   effect   cause

- **To show comparison**

> **Just as** college is expensive, life without a college degree is also expensive.
>   situation A   (compared to)   situation B

- **To show contrast**

> We prepared for war **although** Congress had not authorized military engagement.
>   situation A   (contrasted with)   situation B

- **To show possibility**

> A student cannot graduate **unless** he or she passes an English course.
>   possibility   (related to)   condition

- **To show time**

> **When** they are young, children are often afraid of monsters.
>   time information   (related to)   situation or action

- **To modify a noun or act as a noun**

> The final exam, **which** was given yesterday, covered the semester's work.
>   modifies *exam*
> **Whoever** leaves the room last should turn out the light.
>   acts as a noun

> ### TIP
>
> ## Nonessential and Essential Modifier Clauses and Phrases
>
> A dependent clause that modifies a noun can be either essential or nonessential. Use commas around nonessential clauses only.
>
> **Nonessential modifier clauses:** A nonessential clause adds interesting, but not necessary, information about the noun it modifies and should be set off with commas. Clauses beginning with *which* are always nonessential. In the following example, the nonessential dependent clause (underlined) modifies the word *form*. Notice the commas around the clause.
>
> > The personnel form, which is required for all applicants, can be completed online.
>
> **Essential modifier clauses:** A clause is essential when it identifies the noun it modifies. If the meaning of the sentence would not be clear without the modifying clause, then the clause is essential and should *not* be set off with commas. Modifier clauses beginning with *that* are always essential. In the following example, the essential dependent clause (underlined) modifies the word *class*.
>
> > The English class **that** is required for graduation is offered only in the spring.
>
> **Essential and nonessential phrases:** Like clauses, phrases can also be essential and nonessential. In the following example, the underlined phrase is not set off by commas.
>
> > **Example:** The compass **displayed** in the glass case is the oldest one.
>
> If a customer asks, "Which compass is the oldest?" the phrase *displayed in the glass case* tells the customer which compass is being discussed. Therefore the phrase is essential to the meaning of the sentence and is not set off by commas. Consider, however, the following sentence.
>
> > **Example:** The compass, **battered** by years of use at sea, guided us home.
>
> In describing the compass as *battered by years of use at sea,* the writer is not identifying this particular compass as compared with some other compasses. Rather the writer is just providing extra information. Notice the commas around the verbal phrase. If a phrase merely provides additional information, then it is nonessential and should be set off by commas.
>
> When a proper noun is used, any phrase that describes the person or thing cannot be *identifying* because its identity has already been provided by its name. So, phrases modifying proper nouns are always nonessential and are thus set off by commas.
>
> > **Examples:** Abraham Lincoln, **born in** Kentucky and **raised** in Indiana, is claimed by both states as a "native son."
> >
> > Lincoln, **hoping** to avert war, modified the content of his first inaugural address.

Using Dependent Words to Emphasize Ideas.
Besides showing relationships, dependent words are used to emphasize the relative importance of one idea as compared to another. The separate clauses that follow do not give readers any clues about whether one idea is more important than the other.

- Sue had never missed a day of training.
- She could not finish the marathon.

Notice how the meaning of the sentences changes when we use the dependent word *although* to join the clauses.

Although Sue had never missed a day of training, she could not finish the marathon.

dependent clause = less important   independent clause = more important

The most important point in the sentence is that Sue could not finish the marathon.

We can change the emphasis of the sentence and suggest a different meaning by making the second clause dependent.

Although she could not finish the marathon, Sue had never missed a day of training.

dependent clause = less important   independent clause = more important

Now, the emphasis is on the fact that Sue had never missed a day of training. The point we might infer is that Sue is to be commended for her faithfulness to her training schedule.

TIP

Fragments

A dependent clause that stands alone is a sentence fragment. A dependent clause must be combined with an independent clause.

> **Fragment: After** I began to use a graphing calculator.
> dependent clause

When you make one clause dependent, joint it to an independent clause.

> **Correct: After** I began to use a graphing calculator, I scored higher on math tests.
> dependent clause   independent clause

In general, if the *dependent* clause comes first, put a comma after it.

> **Correct: After** I began to use a graphing calculator, I scored higher on math tests.
> dependent clause   comma   independent clause

If the *independent* clause comes first, a comma is not necessary and usually should not be used.

> **Correct:** I scored higher on math tests **after** I began to use a graphing calculator.
> independent clause   (no comma)   dependent clause

When to Use Dependent Words to Combine Sentences.   Making clauses dependent is a way for you, as a writer, to help your writing more clearly convey your thoughts. Use dependent word clause constructions in these cases:

- When showing the relationship between clauses will help readers better understand your ideas
- When two sentences are related and you wish to emphasize the importance of one over the other

PRACTICE (15)

Using Dependent Words to Reveal Relationships

For each group of independent clauses, follow these steps to practice using dependent words to combine sentences.

A. Read each group of sentences.

B. Determine whether the sentences in a group share one of these relationships:

Cause and effect	Contrast	Time
Comparison	Conditionality	Noun or Noun Modifier

C. If the clauses do share a relationship, choose a dependent word that expresses that relationship. Refer to the Functions of Dependent Words chart for a list of dependent words.

D. Check the punctuation rules, and make sure your combined sentences follow them.

1. People today from all walks of life have tattoos.

    The general public might believe that tattoos are completely safe.

    Relationship: _____

    Combined sentence: _____

    _____

    _____

    _____

2. Tattoo artists are, generally speaking, conscientious about their work.

    They take measures to make sure their practice is safe and hygienic.

    Relationship: _____

    Combined sentence: _____

    _____

    _____

    _____

3. Tattooists try to maintain a sanitized work environment.

    Not all risks can be eliminated.

    Relationship: _____

    Combined sentence: _____

    _____

    _____

    _____

(continued)

4. One microbe has been found in hospitals and has caused infections in patients after minor surgeries.

   The microbe is named nontuberculous mycobacteria (NTM).

   Relationship: _____

   Combined sentence: _____

   _____

   _____

   _____

5. NTM has been found in hospitals.

   NTM has been found in certain tattoo inks.

   Relationship: _____

   Combined sentence: _____

   _____

   _____

   _____

6. Some of these contaminated inks caused serious infections in tattoo recipients in at least four states in late 2011 and early 2012.

   The FDA is reaching out to tattoo artists, ink and pigment manufacturers, and public health officials to warn them of the potential for infection.

   Relationship: _____

   Combined sentence: _____

   _____

   _____

   _____

7. Getting the word out to tattooists is particularly critical.

   They are on the front lines.

   Relationship: _____

   Combined sentence: _____

   _____

   _____

   _____

8. A tattoo artist may diligently follow hygienic practices.

   The tattooist may not be aware that an ink itself is contaminated.

   Relationship: _____

   Combined sentence: _____

   _____

   _____

   _____

(continued)

9. Tattoo artists can minimize the risk of infection.

They can use inks that have been processed to ensure they are free from disease-causing bacteria.

Relationship: _____

Combined sentence: _____

_____

_____

_____

10. Awareness of the problem involving tattoo inks becomes widespread among tattoo parlor operators.

The problem of infection related to tattoos will be greatly reduced.

Relationship: _____

Combined sentence: _____

_____

_____

_____

Now that you have practiced using dependent words to show relationships between sentences, try your hand at using dependent words for emphasis.

PRACTICE 16

Using Dependent Words to Emphasize the Importance of Ideas

Below are eight groups of sentences. Add dependent words to combine the sentences in each group if you believe emphasizing one of the clauses over the other is important. Here are the specific steps to follow:

A. Read each group of sentences.
B. Determine which sentence you would like to make the most important in the group, and circle it.
C. Select an appropriate dependent word, and use it to combine the two sentences.
D. Check the punctuation rules, and make sure your combined sentences follow them.

1. European immigrants colonized North America. The forests were thick, game was abundant, the water teemed with life, and the air was pure and clean.

_____

_____

(continued)

2. The settlers had a pioneering spirit. The natural bounty of the land was what really invited them to push westward in the early eighteenth century.

_____

_____

3. They explored and built cities in the Southwest. They built cities in the Ohio Valley and Great Lakes regions.

_____

_____

4. Railroads were built to create easy passage across the country. Cities in the West and Midwest grew.

_____

_____

5. Forests were logged, and plains and prairies were devoted to grain production and livestock. The environment began to suffer.

_____

_____

6. Freshwater resources were threatened. Large sewer systems were needed for the collection of wastewater.

_____

_____

7. More and more coal was being burned. City skies were darkening.

_____

_____

8. People began to realize that the environment is fragile. It became less acceptable to continue to abuse the environment.

_____

_____

Combining Sentences Using Conjunctive Adverbs

Conjunctive adverbs (CA) are another type of sentence connector. Conjunctive adverbs are words such as *consequently, however,* and *finally.* In the examples that follow, the words in bold print are conjunctive adverbs. Notice the punctuation that sets off the conjunctive adverbs.

Separate clauses:

Robotics is a rapidly developing field. Job opportunities are increasing.

Combined using a conjunctive adverb:

Robotics is a rapidly developing field; **consequently,** job opportunities are increasing.
   clause   CA   clause

Separate clauses:

The flu vaccine is effective. Not everyone chooses to receive it.

Combined using a conjunctive adverb:

The flu vaccine is effective; **however,** not everyone chooses to receive it.
   clause   CA   clause

The chart below lists the most common conjunctive adverbs for each of six different functions.

FUNCTIONS OF CONJUNCTIVE ADVERBS					
Addition	**Alternative**	**Cause and Effect**	**Conditionality**	**Contrast**	**Time**
additionally	alternatively	consequently	otherwise	conversely	afterward
also	instead	hence		however	finally
besides	otherwise	therefore		nevertheless	meanwhile
equally		thus		nonetheless	previously
furthermore				rather	subsequently
moreover					
similarly					

Like coordinating conjunctions and dependent words, conjunctive adverbs help you show the relationship between two clauses. They are also effective methods of combining short, choppy sentences so that a text flows more smoothly.

However, conjunctive adverbs often have one attribute that other methods of combining clauses do not have: they elevate the diction of a sentence. **Diction** refers to the level of formality a writer establishes through word choice. In the example that follows, notice how the diction is affected by the use of a conjunctive adverb (in bold print):

Slang: Some people don't recycle 'cause it's a pain in the neck.

Casual diction: Some people think recycling is too difficult, so they don't do it.

Formal diction: Some people perceive recycling as a burden; **consequently,** these people do not participate in recycling.

The use of the conjunctive adverb *consequently* helps raise the diction level of the sentence.

Conjunctive adverbs are used more frequently in texts written on a formal level, such as scholarly articles, research papers, and legal and medical documents. Academic writing is formal writing, so using conjunctive adverbs is a perfectly acceptable—and often desirable—strategy to use in writing for college courses.

TIP

Conjunctive Adverbs

When you use a conjunctive adverb to connect two clauses, you must also use a semicolon before the adverb and a comma after it.

Correct:

Green tea is full of antioxidants**; thus,** many people drink it for their health.
　　independent clause;　　　　CA,　　　　　independent clause

White tea also has health benefits**; however,** it is not used as commonly as green tea.
　　independent clause;　　　　　CA,　　　　　independent clause

Commas alone may not be used with a conjunctive adverb to join two clauses. If a writer uses commas alone, the result is a comma splice.

Comma splice:

Green tea is full of antioxidants**, thus,** many people drink it for their health.
　　independent clause;　　　　CA,　　　　　independent clause

A conjunctive adverb cannot join two sentences without any surrounding punctuation or with just a comma. The result is a run-on sentence.

Run-on error:

Green tea is full of antioxidants **thus** many people drink it for their health.
　　　　　　　　(missing punctuation)

Green tea is full of antioxidants **thus,** many people drink it for their health.
　　　　　　　　(insufficient punctuation)

Using conjunctive adverbs correctly:

1. Make sure you are joining two independent clauses (complete sentences).

    Children need protection. Parents must provide it.
    　independent clause　　　　independent clause

2. Select a conjunctive adverb appropriate for the meaning of the sentences.

    Children need protection. **therefore** Parents must provide it.

3. Insert the correct punctuation marks around the conjunctive adverb, and use appropriate capitalization.

    Children need protection.**; therefore ,** p~~P~~arents must provide it.

    Children need protection; therefore, parents must provide it.

When to Use Conjunctive Adverbs to Combine Sentences.

As you know, combining sentences can help writers avoid using the same single-clause sentences over and over. Using conjunctive adverbs to combine sentences, when appropriate, contributes to sentence variety and more eloquent writing. When you see that you have written many simple sentences, consider using conjunctive adverbs to combine some of them.

In addition to providing sentence variety, conjunctive adverbs help you more clearly communicate meanings. A simple example is using a conjunctive adverb to help readers understand time relationships. Read the sentences that follow:

- Matthew was in an auto accident.
- Matthew was seen drinking beer.

The sentences may result in confusion about time order. Was Matthew drinking when he was in the auto accident? Was Matthew drinking before or after the auto accident? Using a conjunctive adverb can clarify the confusion:

> Matthew was in an auto accident; **afterward**, he was seen drinking beer.
>
> Matthew was in an auto accident; **previously**, he was seen drinking beer.

The use of either *afterward* or *previously* clears up the confusion about when Matthew had the accident in relation to when he was seen drinking.

As you practice using conjunctive adverbs, find sentences that could be confusing to readers. Determine whether a conjunctive adverb might help clarify the meaning of the sentences or even make the relationships between sentences clearer. Practice using conjunctive adverbs to link clauses together when appropriate.

Using Conjunctive Adverbs to Show How Ideas Are Related. As the Functions of Conjunctive Adverbs chart demonstrates, each conjunctive adverb indicates a particular relationship. The sentences that follow provide an example for each of the types of relationships conjunctive adverbs can demonstrate.

- **To add information**

> Videos can help explain concepts; **additionally,** online sites can be effective tools.
> statement A — added to — statement B

- **To reveal alternatives**

> Students can study in the library; **alternatively,** they can study at home.
> option A — compared with — option B

- **To indicate cause and effect**

> The sun emits radiation; **thus,** using sunblock provides important protection.
> cause — effect

- **To indicate conditionality**

> Children must be taught manners; **otherwise,** they will behave like animals.
> condition — related to — result

- **To show contrast**

> The flu shot is supposed to be effective; **however,** its effectiveness is never universal.
> idea A — contrasted to — idea B

- **To indicate a time relationship**

> The jurors filed out of the courtroom; **meanwhile,** the defendant sat anxiously.
> time information showing simultaneous events

PRACTICE (17)

Using Conjunctive Adverbs

Read each of the following groups of sentences. Use conjunctive adverbs to join the sentences when doing so will clarify meanings, show relationships, or eliminate choppiness. Using the Functions of Conjunctive Adverbs chart, select the appropriate conjunctive adverb for each group. Remember to use correct punctuation for each sentence you compose.

1. Millions of Americans are looking for jobs online.

   The Internet has become fertile ground for phony business opportunity schemes.

   _____

   _____

2. These schemes sound like excellent opportunities.

   The company names sound legitimate.

   _____

   _____

3. The wages promised by some of the employers are too good to be true.

   Desperate job seekers hold out hope that the jobs are real.

   _____

   _____

4. Unfortunately, most of these jobs are not good opportunities at all.

   They are actually schemes to swindle, not help, job applicants.

   _____

   _____

5. Often, to apply, one must provide a great deal of personal information.

   Applicants routinely give out their driver's license number or social security number.

   _____

   _____

6. People who are "hired" by these companies receive a paycheck from a company outside the United States.

   The explanation is that the employer does not have any banking set up in the United States.

   _____

   _____

(continued)

7. The check is for much more than the employee is owed for salary.

    The employee is told to deposit the check and wire the overpayment back to the employer's bank.

    _____

    _____

8. The employee does as instructed.

    The employer's check is found to be fraudulent, and the swindled "employee" loses his or her money.

    _____

    _____

COMBINED PRACTICE 1

Use coordinating conjunctions, dependent words, and conjunctive adverbs to combine the sentences in at least ten of the following groups. Be prepared to explain why you decided to combine the sentences and why you chose the method and the particular combining word that you used.

1. Cybersecurity, phishing, worms, Trojan horses, hackers, and viruses seem to be in the news every day.

    Are these threats really serious?

    _____

    _____

2. Internet experts say that these threats are serious.

    You should take steps to protect yourself from being a victim of online privacy theft.

    _____

    _____

3. The first step in protecting yourself is to recognize the risks.

    Become familiar with some of the terminology associated with cybersecurity.

    _____

    _____

4. Hackers are everywhere.

    The goal of most of them is to exploit weaknesses in software and computer systems for their own gain.

    _____

    _____

(continued)

5. Their intentions are sometimes benign and motivated mostly by curiosity.

    Their actions are typically in violation of the intended use of the systems that they are exploiting.

    _____

    _____

6. Their meddling often creates problems for users.

    These problems can include the downloading of malicious code such as viruses, worms, and Trojan horses.

    _____

    _____

7. Some people use the terms *viruses, worms,* and *Trojan horses* interchangeably.

    Each has unique characteristics.

    _____

    _____

8. A virus is a type of malicious code.

    A virus requires the user to actually do something before it infects a computer.

    _____

    _____

9. One action that could activate a virus is opening an e-mail attachment.

    Going to a particular Web page is another action that could trigger the downloading of a virus.

    _____

    _____

10. A worm is similar to a virus and is considered a subclass of a virus.

    Unlike a virus, worms have the capability to spread without any human action.

    _____

    _____

11. The victim computer becomes infected.

    The worm will attempt to locate and infect other computers.

    _____

    _____

(continued)

12. Worms can spread through your entire computer and others' computers.

Viruses cannot spread from one computer to another.

_____

_____

13. A Trojan horse program is software that appears to be legitimate and useful.

It will actually do damage once installed or run on a computer.

_____

_____

14. Users on the receiving end of a Trojan horse are frequently tricked into opening the program.

They believe that they are receiving files from a legitimate source.

_____

_____

15. For example, a program may claim to be speeding up your computer.

It may actually be sending your confidential information to a data thief.

_____

_____

16. Spyware is sneaky software.

It piggybacks on downloadable software like screen savers, games, and music files.

_____

_____

17. Spyware sends information about what you are doing on the Internet to a third party.

The third party can then target you with pop-up ads and other pesky intrusions.

_____

_____

18. Browsers enable you to block pop-up ads.

You can also install anti-spyware programs to stop other threats to your privacy.

_____

_____

(continued)

19. Viruses, worms, and Trojan horses are collectively referred to as malware.

The word *malware* is derived from a combination of *malicious* and *software.*

_____

_____

20. Having antivirus and spyware-removal software on your computer is a good start to protecting yourself.

A practical step is to stay away from questionable sites.

_____

_____

COMBINED PRACTICE (2)

What follows is the first draft of an essay. It contains very choppy sentences, many repeated words, and very few sentence connectors. Improve the draft by doing the following:

- Use coordinating conjunctions, dependent words, and conjunctive adverbs to combine some of the sentences in the essay.
- Make additional wording changes to clarify ideas.
- Make additional wording changes to avoid repetition.
- Rearrange ideas, if necessary.
- Make any other changes that will produce more eloquent writing.

Be sure to make at least six combined sentences. Write the finished draft on a separate sheet of paper.

True College Prerequisites

College students know what prerequisites are. They are courses. Students must take prerequisite courses before certain other courses. For example, English Composition I is a prerequisite. It must be taken before English Composition II. Other types of prerequisites exist as well. These other types of prerequisites are abilities that students should have developed even before starting college. They include a strong work ethic. The ability to be goal-oriented is a prerequisite. The ability to be organized is a prerequisite.

Not all college students are used to studying. Some high schools are not academically demanding. Others are. Some students enter college with a strong work ethic. Other students do not. *Work ethic* refers to a student's willingness to work hard. Passing college classes requires a work ethic. The work ethic should be strong. For example, learning a foreign language requires daily work. Some students have never studied on an everyday basis. This requirement will be a change for those students. The same requirement is true of other courses. Math requires daily study. Some fast-paced courses require daily study. Students will need a strong work ethic. It will be required of them each week. It may be required each day.

(continued)

Another prerequisite for college is to be goal-oriented. Students who are goal-oriented are good at setting goals. They set goals that are attainable. They create strategies to reach their goals. They troubleshoot their strategies to make sure their plans are working. For instance, goal-oriented students often plan out their semester class schedule far in advance of the registration period. They like to see what is coming. They like to plan for the future. Keeping the future in mind helps them be more motivated with the daily difficulties of college.

The ability to be organized is a prerequisite that can really be helpful in college. Organization alone can help students pass classes. Not being organized can cause students to miss due dates. It can cause students to misplace important papers. It can cause students to fail to set aside enough time for studying. Not being an organized thinker can also cause problems. Some students cannot organize their notes. They cannot organize the information presented in class. They cannot organize the information they read. Being able to organize course materials is important. It helps students manage the materials. It helps students condense the materials. It makes the materials easier to think about. It makes the materials easier to memorize.

Yes, some skills are prerequisites for college success. Students need these skills to succeed. Starting college with a strong work ethic is indispensable. Staying goal-oriented is vitally important. Being able to organize one's life is essential. Being able to organize one's course materials is crucial. These prerequisite skills are vital. They may make the difference between success and failure.

Spelling and Word Choice

"The travelers were ready for the desert/dessert." Choosing the right word can make a difference in how well you communicate your ideas.

Unit Objectives

After completing this unit, students will be able to do the following:

- Use four strategies for improving spelling.

- Apply four basic spelling rules.

- Use homophones and commonly confused words correctly.

- Avoid using clichés and slang in professional and academic writing.

Easy access to software and smartphone apps that check spelling as we write has made spelling a much less crucial skill than it once was. Even so, spelling remains significant. Indeed, the fact that technological tools have made correct spelling more commonplace makes it all the more important that writers get it right! Today's readers simply expect correct spelling.

In this unit we emphasize the aspects of spelling that computers cannot fix for us. First, we consider some broad strategies for improving spelling and look at a few spelling rules. Then, we present some specific words that are frequently confused. The unit concludes with a discussion of the use of clichés and slang.

Using Spelling Strategies

Here are four useful strategies for improving your spelling.

- **Read.** Reading has a huge impact on spelling. If you see a word over and over, your mind grips that visual representation of the word.
- **Use a spell-checker.** Most word-processing software includes a spell-checker.
- **Use a dictionary.** No longer do you need to lug around a twenty-pound dictionary. Free, excellent, and easy-to-use dictionaries are available online and as mobile apps. Three good online dictionaries are *Merriam-Webster, Oxford Dictionaries,* and the *American Heritage Dictionary.*
- **Make a list of words you often misspell.** You will be surprised how quickly you will remember the spelling of a word once you make a point of learning it.

Applying Spelling Rules

The spelling of a great many words follows specific rules. These four basic spelling rules will help you improve your spelling.

The Order of *i* and *e*

You probably remember the little rhyme about spelling words that contain *-ie* or *-ei:*

> Write *i* before *e,*
>
> Except after *c,*
>
> Or when it sounds like an *a,*
>
> As in *neighbor* and *weigh.*

Examples: *i* **before e:** relief, believe, niece, chief

except after c: receive, ceiling, conceit, deceit

when it sounds like an *a*: vein, sleigh, weigh, neigh

Several exceptions to the rule do exist. The list below contains virtually all of the exceptions that you are likely to use in your writing.

ancient	counterfeit	foreign	leisure	society
atheism	deficient	forfeit	neither	sovereign
caffeine	efficient	glacier	protein	sufficient
codeine	either	height	science	weird
conscience	feisty	heist	seize	

Final -e and Suffixes

Drop the final *-e* before a suffix that begins with a vowel, but retain the final *-e* before a suffix that begins with a consonant.

Examples: arrive + ing = arriving   brave + ly = bravely

guide + ance = guidance   achieve + ment = achievement

date + ing = dating   like + ness = likeness

Final -y and Suffixes

In general, change a final *-y* preceded by a consonant to *-i* before a suffix.

Examples: rely + -ance = reliance   study + -ed = studied

supply + -er = supplier   carry + -es = carries

beauty + -ful = beautiful   ugly + -est = ugliest

Exception: If the suffix begins with *-i*, then the final *-y* is retained:

rally + -ing = rallying   deny + -ing = denying

If the word ends in a -y that is preceded by a vowel, then add the suffix without making any change to the root word.

Examples: annoy + -ance = annoyance	destroy + -ed = destroyed
betray + -er = betrayer	monkey + -s = monkeys
joy + -ful = joyful	delay + -ing = delaying

Final Consonant and Suffixes

When adding a suffix that begins with a vowel, double a final single consonant if both of these criteria are met:

- A single vowel precedes the consonant.
- The word has only one syllable, or the last syllable is accented.

Examples in which both criteria are met:

grab + -ing = grabbing   submit + -ed = submitted   refer + -al = referral

Examples in which both criteria are *not* met:

pool + -ed = pooled (The final consonant is preceded by more than one vowel.)

mourn + -ful = mournful (The final consonant is preceded by another consonant.)

benefit + -ed = benefited (The last syllable is not accented.)

Mastering Common Usage Errors

Sometimes writing mistakes occur because a writer confuses one word for another; these kinds of missteps are called *usage errors*. Some spelling errors are usage errors; in other words, knowing which word is the proper one to use can often enable you to avoid a spelling mistake.

Homophones

Frequently, the kind of confusion involved is a function of two words that sound the same (or almost the same) but are spelled differently (and are two entirely different words). Each of the words in such a pair is called a **homophone.** (We will include in this category "near homophones"—words that are not properly pronounced in an identical manner but are close enough to create usage problems.) Spell-checkers will, at best, detect only a few homophone errors. That is why learning common homophones is crucial.

accept/except

accept = (verb) to receive; to take in

except = (preposition) other than

Examples: I *accept* your apology.

I will buy everything on this table *except* the vase.

QUICK CHECK   **Fill in the blanks with the correct words.**

_____ criticism! Doing so, while difficult, can pay huge dividends. If your boss tells you that everything in your performance is great _____ your punctuality, take that as encouragement to be on time rather than as condemnation of the job you are doing.

---

advice/advise

advice = (noun) a recommendation as a guide to action; words of counsel

advise = (verb) to give advice; to counsel; to offer a suggestion

Examples: I strongly recommend that you take his *advice.*

The attorney will *advise* you regarding this matter.

QUICK CHECK   **Fill in the blanks with the correct words.**

How would you _____ me to proceed? What is your _____? No matter what your instructions are, I will follow your _____.

---

affect/effect

affect = (verb) to influence or change

effect = (noun) result

Examples: The dark weather *affects* my moods.

Sunshine has a positive *effect* on me.

QUICK CHECK   **Fill in the blanks with the correct words.**

The sun can _____ different people in different ways. One _____ that the sun has on some people is to contribute to their being in a good mood. Another _____ it can have is to cause sunburn.

allot/a lot

allot = (verb) to provide

a lot = (noun) a group of items; many

Note: *Alot* is an incorrect spelling of *a lot* and is not a word.

> **Examples:** The professor will *allot* the students one hour for the exam.
>
> *A lot* of items are in the lost and found bin.

QUICK CHECK   Fill in the blanks with the correct words.

The judge will ___ each person six jars. The contest requires that we fill those jars with as many pennies as we can. Without question, each of the jars will hold ___ of pennies!

all ready/already

all ready = (adverbial phrase) entirely prepared; set to proceed

already = (adverb) has occurred previously

> **Examples:** The kids were *all ready* for the trip. (Better: All of the kids were *ready* for the trip.)
>
> I have *already* read this book.

QUICK CHECK   Fill in the blanks with the correct word.

We have _____ learned this material.

bare/bear

bare = (verb) to reveal

   (adjective) to be in a revealed state

bear = (verb) to support or carry (both literally and figuratively)

   (noun) a very large mammal with stocky legs, a long snout, and shaggy fur

> **Examples:** My *bare* arms were cold in the auditorium.
>
> The old *bear* is literally starving; I cannot *bear* to see it suffer so.

QUICK CHECK   Fill in the blanks with the correct words.

The refrigerator is ___, but the pantry shelves are so loaded with dry goods that I'm not sure that they can ___ the weight. However, I simply cannot ___ going to the grocery store during the weekend, so we will just need to make do with canned food for now.

brake/break

brake = (noun) the part of a vehicle that causes slowing and stopping

(verb) to slow or stop something, such as a vehicle

break = (noun) a recess period; a fracture (as in a bone)

(verb) to split into pieces; to interrupt; to take a recess

> **Examples:** The *brakes* in his jalopy were dangerously worn.
>
> When approaching a stop sign, you should *brake* smoothly.
>
> We should probably take a fifteen-minute *break*.
>
> The kids will *break* the glass figurines if they play with them.

QUICK CHECK   Fill in the blanks with the correct words.

I was afraid that my car would ____ down. I took it to the shop to have the ____ checked. They said it would be an hour before anyone could look at the car because all of the mechanics were on ____ . The shop boss said that before they do any work, they will drive the car and ____ hard to test the system.

breath/breathe

breath = (noun) a single inhalation and exhalation of air

breathe = (verb) to inhale and exhale air

> **Examples:** She took a *breath* of air.
>
> She needs to *breathe* the fresh air.

QUICK CHECK   Fill in the blanks with the correct words.

The bus was so hot that it was hard to _____. I felt as though I could not take even a single ____.

cite/sight/site

cite = (verb) to make reference to; to create a *citation*

sight = (noun) the faculty of vision; something seen

(verb) to see something; to adjust the aiming apparatus (as of a gun)

site = (noun) a location; a piece of land

Examples: You should always *cite* the sources used in an academic paper; in addition, you need to use the proper form for all of your *citations*.

The Christmas tree with all of its ornaments and lights was quite a *sight*.

The home is located at a very convenient *site*—near a bank, a pharmacy, and a grocery store. (The house is in a convenient *situation*.)

QUICK CHECK   **Fill in the blanks with the correct words.**

The ___ where the mammoths were found is a riverbed. It was quite a ____ to see so many people working to uncover the fossilized bones. The articles that the paleontologists write about the work being done there will no doubt frequently be ____ (past tense) in scholarly journals in the future.

---

clothes/cloths

clothes = (plural noun) attire, apparel, garments

cloths = (noun, plural of *cloth*) pieces of fabric, such as those used for cleaning

Examples: Back-to-school time means that we get to shop for *clothes*!

Cloths work far better than paper towels for some tasks.

QUICK CHECK   **Fill in the blanks with the correct words.**

When I am ready to clean the house, I put on some old _____, find some ____ to dust with, get out the vacuum cleaner, and line up all of my cleaning products on the table.

---

coarse/course

coarse = (adjective) rough; vulgar; unsophisticated (as in *coarse* humor)

course = (noun) route; sequence; an academic class
(verb) to run through (as in blood coursing through a person's veins)

Examples: The *coarse* sandpaper was perfect for the job.

Which *course* of action should we take?

I am taking a *course* at the local community college.

The river *courses* through the lush valley.

QUICK CHECK   Fill in the blanks with the correct words.

In one of my nursing _____, I learned something that pertained to my own health! I will need a _____ of antibiotics to get rid of a persistent rash. The rash dries out my skin and makes it feel _____.

complement/compliment

complement = (noun) something that completes or makes perfect

   (verb) to provide an addition that fits well or is appropriate

compliment = (noun) an expression of approval, esteem, or acknowledgment

   (verb) to offer praise, admiration, or respect

Examples: Some people think milk is a perfect *complement* to cookies in the same way that ice cream exquisitely *complements* apple pie.

I never expected to receive a *compliment* from my boss, so I was shocked when she said to me in front of the entire work group, "I'd really like to *compliment* you on your performance this quarter."

QUICK CHECK   Fill in the blanks with the correct words.

I couldn't wait to _____ the host on the reception, which was such a nice _____ to the lecture. I was delighted to receive several _____ for the dip and crackers I brought to the reception. Raspberry preserves are a wonderful _____ to cream cheese in a dip.

conscience/conscious

conscience = (noun) a person's intuitive sense of right and wrong

conscious = (adjective) awake; intentional

Examples: My *conscience* tells me that I really should donate blood.

The hockey player was *conscious* after his fall.

I made a *conscious* decision to give more to charity this year.

QUICK CHECK   Fill in the blanks with the correct words.

The defendant was _____ of the crowd of angry people behind him. Even so, his _____ did not prompt him to confess.

decent/descent/dissent

decent = (adjective) proper; appropriate; satisfactory

descent = (noun) downward movement; downward slope

dissent = (verb) to disagree; to differ in opinion

(noun) the expression of an opposing view

Examples: The dress code required everyone to wear *decent* clothing.

The airplane began its *descent* into Chicago.

The senator expressed her *dissent* regarding the proposed bill.

QUICK CHECK **Fill in the blanks with the correct words.**

The used book of mythology that I bought recently is in _____ condition. It includes my favorite myth—the story of Hercules's _____ into the underworld. Although almost all of the reviews were glowing, I did read a couple that expressed _____ as to its being a great collection of stories.

desert/dessert

desert = (noun) a dry, arid area, typically with a very warm climate

dessert = (noun) a sweet treat, usually the last course in a meal

Examples: Many types of cactus thrive in the *desert*.

I'd like strawberry cheesecake for *dessert*.

QUICK CHECK **Fill in the blanks with the correct words.**

A restaurant in the _____ would probably earn more revenue from selling cold drinks than from serving coffee and _____.

fair/fare

fair = (adjective) impartial or just; not cloudy (with reference to weather)

(noun) an exhibition or exposition, such as a county *fair*

fare = (noun) a fee

(verb) to experience good or bad fortune or treatment

Examples: Professor Hendricks is tough but *fair*.

The children want to go to the state *fair* because they love the rides.

I have money enough for train *fare*, but I don't have enough for an airline ticket.

Amy did not win a medal, but she did not *fare* too badly at the tournament.

> **QUICK CHECK**   **Fill in the blanks with the correct words.**
>
> Having the __ occur right after school starts in the fall is not __! School kids want to be able to attend. Moreover, for the city to raise the standard bus __ during this time of the year is also not __.

farther/further

farther = (adjective, adverb) to a greater length or distance (literally)

further = (adjective, adverb) to a greater degree (figuratively)

> **Examples:** The soldier said, "We marched *farther* today than you told us we would."
>
> The sergeant replied, "If you complain *further,* I'll make you do it again!"

> **QUICK CHECK**   **Fill in the blanks with the correct words.**
>
> I had to drive _____ to get to the college library than to the public library. However, going to the library on campus will enable me to go much _____ with my research than I could have gone at the public library.

forth/fourth

forth = (adverb) onward; forward

fourth = (adjective) something that is number four in a series

> **Examples:** She stretched *forth* her hands as she offered a blessing on the couple's marriage.
>
> The sprinter did not receive a medal because he finished *fourth.*

> **QUICK CHECK**   **Fill in the blanks with the correct words.**
>
> Although this campaign would represent their _____ attempt, the emperor exhorted his army: "Go ___ and conquer the enemy!"

hear/here

hear = (verb) to perceive sound

here = (adverb) in or at this place

> **Examples:** Her ability to *hear* was compromised by ear infections.
>
> We will have the trial *here* in our city.

> **QUICK CHECK** | Fill in the blanks with the correct words.
>
> The rafting guide said, "Look, someone drowns ___ every summer. So, it's vitally important that you let me know if you can't ___ the instructions I'm giving."

hole/whole

hole = (noun) gap; opening

whole = (adjective) entire; complete

Examples: Some people like to wear jeans with *holes* in them.

We have to read the *whole* book for this class.

> **QUICK CHECK** | Fill in the blanks with the correct words.
>
> The ___ house needed repair. The walls needed painting. The plumbing leaked. The roof even had a huge ___ in it.

its/it's

its = (adjective) possessive form of *it*

it's = (contraction) *it is*

Examples: The tree dropped *its* (possessive) leaves in a matter of a few days.

The grass is suffering from the drought; *it's* (*it is*) turning brown.

> **QUICK CHECK** | Fill in the blanks with the correct words.
>
> The house for sale looked promising, but ___ roof was in bad shape. I thought, "I don't know if ___ the house for us."

lead/led

The usage of these words is especially complicated, so we will lay out the variations in a chart.

Word	Part of Speech	Rhymes with	Definition
lead	verb, present tense	bead, deed, feed	to guide, especially by going in advance
lead	noun	head, dead, red	a type of metal; a pencil's marking substance
led	verb, past tense	head, dead, red	past tense of the verb *lead*

> **Examples:** You can *lead* a horse to water.
>
> The pencil required for standardized tests is one with a No. 2 *lead*.
>
> They *led* the donkeys to the feed trough.

> **QUICK CHECK**   **Fill in the blanks with the correct words.**
>
> The art teacher said, "Watch as I ___ you through this exercise. Sketch lightly so you don't break your pencil's ___. After I have ___ you through it once, you will be able to do it on your own."

loose/lose

loose = (adjective) not tight

lose = (verb) to not retain; to fail to win

> **Examples:** The *loose* shoestring caused Andrea to trip.
>
> We did *lose* the game, but we enjoyed ourselves anyway.

> **QUICK CHECK**   **Fill in the blanks with the correct words.**
>
> Some school districts are making rules prohibiting the wearing of clothing that is too ___. Students who violate these rules will ___ privileges.

passed/past

passed = (verb, past tense) proceeded; happened; exceeded

past = (adjective) a time ago
     (noun) a time before the present

> **Examples:** The runner who leads the marathon *passed* the halfway point minutes ago.
>
> The old man told delightful stories from his colorful *past*.

> **QUICK CHECK**   **Fill in the blanks with the correct words.**
>
> Once the deadline had ___, it was too late to apply for the grant. I'd like to put that lost opportunity out of mind and leave it entirely in the ___.

peace/piece

peace = (noun) tranquility; a sense of calm

piece = (noun) a part of something

Examples: Spreading *peace* throughout the world is a noble goal.

A *piece* of the jigsaw puzzle was missing.

QUICK CHECK   **Fill in the blanks with the correct words.**

Those kids made so much noise that no one had any _____ all night. I'd sure like to give them a _____ of my mind!

plain/plane

plain = (adjective) simple; unadorned

(noun) a vast area of mostly level land

plane = (noun) a flat surface; an airplane; a woodworking tool

(verb) to smooth or shape a wood surface by using a *plane*

Examples: While *plain,* Shaker furniture is nonetheless beautiful.

The open *plain* before us stretched as far as the eye could see.

In geometry, circles, squares, and triangles are figures that exist in a *plane.*

A carpenter can *plane* the uneven edge of a door.

QUICK CHECK   **Fill in the blanks with the correct words.**

From up in the _____ I could see the _____ below us. The landscape was _____ yet beautiful. The countryside was so flat that I was reminded of a _____ in my geometry textbook.

principal/principle

principal = (adjective) first; most important; highest in rank or degree

(noun) leader of an elementary or secondary school; headmaster

principle = (noun) a law, rule, truth, or guideline

Examples: The *principal* reason I stayed home was my broken leg.

Ms. Williams is the new *principal* of the high school.

There are five *principles* of good citizenship.

Spelling and Word Choice   **561**

> ### QUICK CHECK   Fill in the blanks with the correct words.
>
> This morning, the high school _____ discussed the _____ of civility, which she said should govern the way students treat one another.

quiet/quit/quite

quiet = (adjective) noiseless

quit = (verb) to stop

quite = (adverb) completely; wholly

> **Examples:** A *quiet* evening was just what I needed after my stressful day.
>
> I plan to *quit* eating sweets after New Year's Day.
>
> The dinner was *quite* wonderful.

> ### QUICK CHECK   Fill in the blanks with the correct words.
>
> The woman is ____ a conversationalist. She wouldn't ___ talking long enough for anyone else to say anything. The rest of us were ____ all night while we just listened to her.

right/rite/write

right = (adjective) correct; opposite of *left*

　　(noun) a just claim (as in civil rights or human rights)

rite = (noun) a ritual

write = (verb) to put words and ideas into a visual form

> **Examples:** Maria wants to do the *right* thing about her mistakes.
>
> One *rite* our culture observes is the celebration of birthdays.
>
> Anyone can learn to *write* with practice and diligence.

> ### QUICK CHECK   Fill in the blanks with the correct words.
>
> The ___ of fasting is part of many religions. Some believers like to ____ poetry to express their experience and understanding of God. Each person chooses a way to honor God that he or she believes is ___.

sale/sell

sale = (noun) an event where items are offered for purchase

sell = (verb) to offer for purchase

Examples: The electronics store is having a huge *sale*.

Rachel is going to *sell* her condo.

QUICK CHECK Fill in the blanks with the correct words.

I need to post a sign that says, "Tomatoes for ___." We have so many tomatoes this summer that if we don't ___ some soon, I'm afraid that they will rot.

---

set/sit

set = (verb) to place something down; to fix or arrange something

sit = (verb) to rest the body on the buttocks

Examples: The grandfather *set* the groceries on the counter.

The children will *sit* together at a separate table at the party.

QUICK CHECK Fill in the blanks with the correct words.

We will ___ the food on the counter and put all of the drinks in the refrigerator. After we eat, we can all ___ around and talk.

---

tail/tale/tell

tail = (noun) the often elongated appendage attached to the rear portion of an animal's body; something that resembles an animal's tail

(verb) to follow for surveillance purposes

tale = (noun) a story or fable (typically, a fictional story)

tell = (verb) to make known by speech or writing; to express (as a story, a lie, and so on)

Examples: Unfortunately, the car ran over our dog's *tail*.

FBI agents have been known to *tail* suspects for months.

Before beginning the fairy *tale,* the teacher will *tell* students about its historical background.

QUICK CHECK Fill in the blanks with the correct words.

I want to ___ you one of Aesop's fables. It's the ___ about the fox that lost its ___ in a trap.

their/there/they're

their = (adjectival pronoun) possessive form of *they*

there = (adverb) in or at that place (as opposed to *here*)

they're = (contraction) *they are*

Examples: *Their* insurance policy covered the cost of the wrecked car.

She drove the car *there* and then walked back here.

The children are hoping that *they're* (*they are*) going to the zoo today.

QUICK CHECK **Fill in the blanks with the correct words.**

My parents are visiting Colorado this month. They drove in ___ motor home, and they are planning to stay ___ for several weeks. However, _____ definitely planning on leaving before the snow starts to fall.

threw/through

threw = (verb) past tense of *throw*

through = (preposition) in one side and out the other side of something

Examples: The pitcher *threw* the ball over 100 miles per hour.

We took the subway *through* the tunnel under the San Francisco Bay.

QUICK CHECK **Fill in the blanks with the correct words.**

_____ his mask, the umpire clearly saw that the pitcher ____ the ball with the intention of hitting the batter.

to/too/two

to = (preposition) indicates movement toward something

too = (adverb) also; in addition to

two = (noun, adjective) the number 2

Examples: I decided to go *to* the mall.

Maria wanted to go *too,* so she rode with me.

Two eagles circled overhead.

QUICK CHECK **Fill in the blanks with the correct words.**

The man was ___ tired to continue hiking. He walked over __ a tree, where he slumped down, took out all the food he had left—just ___ cupcakes— and slowly ate them.

want/won't

want = (verb) to desire

won't = (contraction) *will not*

> **Examples:** We all *want* to see the film.
>
> We *won't* (*will not*) pay $20 per movie ticket.

QUICK CHECK   **Fill in the blanks with the correct words.**

I know you don't ____ to wait for the supervisor, but if you ____ to take your luggage with you, you must wait. We ____ allow your luggage on the plane otherwise.

---

wares/wear/where

wares = (plural noun) things that are being sold by someone

wear = (verb) to use a particular garment as clothing

where = (adverb) at; in what location (*Where* can also be used as an interrogative, a word used to ask a question, in the same manner as *who, what,* and *why.*)

> **Examples:** The peddler showed his *wares* to the crowd.
>
> She will *wear* that coat until the sleeves fall off!
>
> The restaurant *where* the crime occurred is close to our neighborhood.
>
> *Where* can we find another coat like it?

QUICK CHECK   **Fill in the blanks with the correct words.**

"____ can I find something special to ____ to the party?" I wondered. At that moment, an advertisement popped up on my computer screen. "Take a look at our ____!" the retailer's ad said just as I was struggling with the question as to ____ I could find a unique dress for the reception. It seems that everyone ____ the same traditional designs.

---

weak/week

weak = (adjective) not strong

week = (noun) a period of seven days

> **Examples:** He felt *weak* after skipping both breakfast and lunch.
>
> Next *week* is going to be a very busy time at work.

> **QUICK CHECK**   Fill in the blanks with the correct words.
>
> She felt _____ after having been sick in bed for a full _____ .

weather/whether

weather = (noun) the condition of the atmosphere during some period of time

(verb) to endure (as in *to weather a storm*)

whether = (conjunction) function word that introduces two alternatives

> **Examples:** The bad *weather* meant we had to delay the shopping trip.
>
> I didn't know *whether* (or not) you wanted cream in your coffee.

> **QUICK CHECK**   Fill in the blanks with the correct words.
>
> It doesn't matter _____ the _____ is nice. The postal service always
> delivers the mail.

we're/were

we're = (contraction) *we are*

were = (verb) a past tense form of the verb *to be*

> **Examples:** I hope *we're* (*we are*) going to get coffee after the play.
>
> The children *were* glad to go outside to play.

> **QUICK CHECK**   Fill in the blanks with the correct words.
>
> _____ going to the movies. We had planned to go yesterday, but we _____
> held up by the traffic.

who's/whose

who's = (contraction) *who is*

whose = (adjective) indicates possession (*Whose* can also be used as an interrogative, a word used to ask a question, in the same manner as *who, what,* and *why.*)

> **Examples:** I live near Mr. Carter, *who's* (*who is*) my dad's best friend.
>
> The donor, *whose* name will not be announced, deserves credit nonetheless.
>
> *Whose* scarf was left in the break room?

QUICK CHECK | Fill in the blanks with the correct words.

She is the woman _____ husband won the raffle. She's the same woman _____ going to be in charge of the fund-raiser.

---

your/you're

your = (adjective) indicates possession

you're = (contraction) *you are*

> **Examples:** I'd like to borrow *your* car.
>
> If *you're* going to sleep over, we will need to locate a cot.

QUICK CHECK | Fill in the blanks with the correct words.

I'm sorry that _____ not feeling well. Would you like me to pick ____ children up from school?

Other Commonly Confused Words

Sometimes as writers we face word choice challenges that are not related to the matter of homophones. We will address several cases in this section.

among/between

among = (preposition) points generally to a group of three or more

between = (preposition) relates one thing to one or more others

> **Examples:** The workers began to talk *among* themselves.
>
> *Between* you and me, I think Macy is the best candidate.
>
> Let's keep this secret just *between* the three of us for now.

QUICK CHECK | Fill in the blanks with the correct words.

The class members discussed the ideas _____ themselves. Meanwhile, Gabriella and I devised a plan _____ the two of us.

---

amount/number

amount = (noun) the quantity of something that *cannot* be counted

number = (noun) the quantity of something that *can* be counted

Examples: We received a large *amount* of rain over the weekend.

A large *number* of suggestions were submitted to the management staff.

QUICK CHECK   **Fill in the blanks with the correct words.**

We saw a great _____ of floats in the parade. The _____ of beer that people drank that day was astounding.

---

believe/feel

believe = (verb) to be convinced by logic or reason

feel = (verb) to experience an emotion; to touch

Examples: I *believe* that the defendant is guilty.

I *feel* sad for the victim's family.

QUICK CHECK   **Fill in the blanks with the correct words.**

My view of the accident causes me to _____ that the driver of the green car was at fault. I ___ a great deal of concern for all those who were injured.

---

can/may

can = (verb) to be able to doing something

may = (verb) to be permitted to do something

Examples: Coach, you know that I *can* run the entire distance without hurting myself, so *may* I please enter the marathon?

QUICK CHECK   **Fill in the blanks with the correct words.**

___ I swim in your pool? I ___ swim like a fish. I ___ dive well, too!

---

casual/causal

casual = (adjective) informal

causal = (adjective) responsible for causing

Examples: *Casual* dress will be appropriate for the meeting.

A *causal* factor in the fire was the use of a space heater.

QUICK CHECK | **Fill in the blanks with the correct words.**

Her attitude toward the interview was far too ____. In fact, her attitude was a ____ element in the company's decision to decline to offer her the job.

---

fewer/less

fewer = (adjective) not so many; smaller in number

less = (adjective) not so much; smaller in amount

> **Examples:** *Fewer* shoppers made major purchases this season than last season.
>
> The tank actually has *less* gasoline in it than the gauge indicates.

QUICK CHECK | **Fill in the blanks with the correct words.**

If we can make the vaccine readily available, the result will be ___ disease, ____ deaths, and consequently a much happier society.

---

lay/lie

Determining how to use these words is particularly complicated, so we will lay out the variations in a chart.

Word	Part of Speech	Definition	Past Tense
lay	verb	to set something down	laid
lie	verb	to recline	lay

> **Examples:** I *lay* the logs on the back porch every autumn.
>
> I *laid* the logs on the back porch last year but not this year. (past tense of *lay*)
>
> The cat *lies* on the rug every afternoon.
>
> The cat *lay* on the rug for an hour, but then it got up. (past tense of *lie*)

QUICK CHECK | **Fill in the blanks with the correct words.**

I need you to __ down in your bed and rest. Children who are ill must __ aside other activities until they are healthy. I know that yesterday you __ down most of the day, and I know that you ___ aside all of the things you wanted to do, but you still must __ in bed and rest today.

Avoiding Clichés and Slang

Most of us use clichés and slang in everyday speech. Thus, it is easy for these expressions to slide into our writing. Avoiding clichés and slang in your writing will make your writing more professional and will keep it in line with the standards of academic writing.

Clichés

A **cliché** is a phrase or sentence that is commonly used and often overused. For example, "better safe than sorry" is a common cliché, as is "peace of mind." There is nothing wrong with using clichés in casual conversation; we all do it. The primary complaint against clichés is that using them does not require us to think critically about language choices. Sometimes we reach for a cliché simply because it is handy, not because it fits our purpose better than other phrases. Thus, the writer who depends on clichés may be seen as lazy and considered less creative than the writer who does not.

Even worse than using a cliché is *misusing* a cliché. Here are just a few examples of how clichés are misused—and consequently do not make sense!

Standard Cliché	Confused Form of Cliché
It's not rocket science. (It's not brain surgery.)	It's not rocket surgery.
tough row to hoe	a tough road to hoe
dog-eat-dog world	doggy-dog world

You can avoid making mistakes with clichés simply by avoiding their use. Instead of using a cliché, create your own unique phrase. A common type of cliché is a simile—a comparison using *as* or *like*. By creating your own original expressions, you will avoid making embarrassing mistakes by misusing clichés, but just as importantly, you will be able to convey your thoughts more creatively and precisely.

Cliché (in Standard Form)	New Formation of the Cliché
as dry as a bone	as dry as a rock in the desert
as happy as a clam	as happy as a mouse in a grain silo
like a fish out of water	like a cat at the Westminster Dog Show

When you use a cliché, your readers will understand the meaning of the phrase, but you will have missed an opportunity to write in a fresh, original way. A much better option is create a new phrase.

Slang

Humans are very imaginative when it comes to language. Every culture and each new generation finds a way to bend linguistic rules a bit, and what results from that bending is *slang*. Slang is simply language used in a nonstandard way. For example, *croak* is a standard word when it refers to the sound a frog makes; however, when it is used as a synonym for *die,* the word is slang. (Example: "The old buzzard finally croaked.") Other slang words have no standard meaning; they are directly created as slang words. The word *scuzzy* is an example; its only use is as a slang word meaning "dirty" or "shabby in condition or character." (Example: "If you don't shave and do something with your hair, you'll just look scuzzy.")

Linguists, people who study language, will be quick to tell you that there is nothing wrong with slang. Most English professors agree. Slang wording becomes a problem when people use it in the wrong places. Most employers, for example, expect their employees to avoid slang in written communication and, in some work settings, in spoken communication also. Additionally, academic writing should never contain slang, and e-mails and other correspondence between students and instructors should be slang-free. In general, anytime you wish to establish a tone of seriousness, avoid slang.

So, what fits into that category we call *slang*? In "What Is Slang?" Robert Beard, a linguist, calls slang

> a code in which one vaguely related or unrelated word or phrase is substituted for a more common one. The words that are replaced in slang are the most common ones: good (*cherry, boss, phat, da bomb*), bad (*icky, yucky, jankety*), crazy (*nuts, bananas, crackers, bonkers*), smart (*brainy, savvy, sharp*), fast (*scream, tear out, fly, like greased lightning*), slow (*dragging, poky, crawling, creeping*).

One point Beard makes about slang is that it functions as a code: it separates the in-crowd from the outsiders. Because slang is a cultural code, its most appropriate use is within a particular cultural context. If you are hanging out with friends, using slang is probably not only common but actually expected.

If you are unsure whether a term is considered slang, look it up in a dictionary. Almost every dictionary will identify slang words in some fashion.

Text Credits

Punctuation and Mechanics

Punctuation marks are like road signs. They prepare people for what is ahead and point them in the right direction.

After completing this unit, students will be able to do the following:

- Use end punctuation correctly.
- Use commas correctly.
- Use apostrophes, colons, and semicolons correctly.
- Use hyphens, parentheses, dashes, quotation marks, and ellipses correctly.

Punctuation is a tool that helps writers communicate their thoughts. End punctuation signals the end of a complete thought and comes at the end of a complete sentence. Commas group sets of words together so readers can grasp the meaning of a sentence as well as the importance of certain elements in the sentence. In this unit, we will discuss the various types of punctuation available to writers, when to use each type, and how to use each type correctly.

Using End Punctuation Correctly

A sentence is a complete thought. End punctuation shows readers where one thought ends and where the next thought begins. Sentences can end in periods, question marks, or exclamation marks.

Type	Explanation	Examples
Period	A declarative (ordinary) sentence ends with a period.	*The sky is deep blue.* *She cooks lunch daily.*
Question mark	A question is a sentence that asks something and ends with a question mark.	*How are you?* *What time is it?*
Exclamation mark	A sentence that emphasizes a point or strongly expresses an emotion ends with an exclamation mark. An interjection or command also ends with an exclamation mark.	*My way is right!* *I am so happy!* *Wow! That's cool.* *Clean your room!*

Particular situations pose special problems for each of the three types of end punctuation, as the chart below illustrates.

Type	Trouble Spots	Examples
Period	Two complete thoughts that are combined without proper punctuation between them are called *run-on sentences*. This form is grammatically incorrect.	*The workers are <u>drained they</u> have labored all night.* (Period needed between *drained* and *they*.)
Question mark	Sentences in which the subject is wondering or asking about something should not end with a question mark. A question mark is only used when a question is being asked directly.	*I wonder if it will rain today.* *Ty asked whether the mail had come.* (No question mark needed.)
Exclamation mark	A sentence that is merely *reporting* strong emotion does not need an exclamation mark.	*Mira was excited about the news. Indeed, she was ecstatic.* (No exclamation mark needed.)

PRACTICE 1

Using End Punctuation Correctly

Read the paragraph below, adding the appropriate end punctuation to each sentence. (Capital letters indicate where new sentences begin.)

Close the door How many times do I have to tell you that Whether it's cold or hot outside doesn't matter You need to close the door regardless Have you ever looked at our utility bills Do you realize how much of our income goes to pay for heating and cooling Think If you would just think before you act, things would be so much better around here

Using Commas Correctly

Commas are primarily used to separate or to join elements within a sentence.

Commas after Introductory Elements

A comma should follow several types of words, phrases, and clauses that are used to begin a sentence.

Use	Examples
After a prepositional phrase of three or more words	After the Saint Patrick's Day parade (,) we had lunch at a pub. On my birthday (,) my mom always bakes a special cake.
After an introductory verbal phrase	Talking rapidly (,) the agent described every detail about the house. Tired to the bone (,) the rangers collapsed in the cabin.
After some single words to clarify meaning or insert a useful pause	Yes (,) I did think her apology was sincere. However (,) I have enjoyed staying at this hotel.
After a dependent clause that begins a sentence	Although my family was out of town (,) I still enjoyed the holidays. Until he left (,) no one realized how much of a pest he had been.

Note that when a dependent clause is placed at the *end* of a sentence, no comma is needed.

Examples: I still enjoyed the holidays <u>although my family was out of town.</u>
No one realized how much of a pest he had been <u>until he left.</u>

PRACTICE 2

Adding Commas after Introductory Elements

Read the paragraph below and consider the introductory elements in each sentence. If commas are needed, add them. Circle each comma you add.

By 4:00 p.m. the town was deserted. Across from Seawall Boulevard businesses had boarded up their windows and doors. Although the storm was not supposed to make landfall until the next day   most people were not waiting around. However   a few people intentionally remained on the island. Seeking one last bit of adventure before heading for the mainland   the surfers stayed to ride the waves a last time. Scared though they were   their excitement trumped their common sense.

Commas with Conjunctions

If two sentences are joined together with a FANBOYS conjunction (*for, and, nor, but, or, yet, so*), a comma is needed before the conjunction.

Conjunction	Examples
for	The parrot chattered constantly (,) for it hoped that a cracker would be presented.
and	The two boxers shook hands (,) and then they returned to their corners.
nor	The windows were not locked (,) nor were the curtains drawn shut.
but	Mr. Li wants to go the beach (,) but Ms. Li prefers taking a trip to the mountains.
or	He must do the assignment (,) or he will surely suffer the consequences.
yet	The heat was intense (,) yet the firefighters continued to battle the fire all night.
so	Tissa completed her homework (,) so she decided she could take time for some fun.

PRACTICE (3)

Using Commas and Conjunctions to Join Sentences

Guided by the examples in the chart above, write two sentences using each conjunction—*for, and, nor, but, or, yet, so*. Add commas appropriately. Use a separate sheet for your sentences.

Commas in a Series

Use commas to separate elements in a series.

Type of Series	Examples
adjectives	The cake is moist⚪ sweet⚪ and delicious.
nouns	The Broncos⚪ the Panthers⚪ the Redskins⚪ and the Cowboys are the best teams in the league.
verbs	The mayor ran for reelection⚪ won the race⚪ and continued his political career.

Note that omitting the comma before the word *and* or *or* in a series is grammatically acceptable in journalism and other types of writing. However, because leaving out the comma can sometimes cause confusion, many writers include it. In academic writing, a comma is always used before *and* or *or*.

Commas between Dual Adjectives

Sometimes a noun is preceded by two adjectives that modify the noun separately. A comma between such dual adjectives is required.

Examples: The grand⚪ glorious staircase makes the home seem regal.

Sweet⚪ sticky cakes were served with the tea.

She freely offered advice to the sincere⚪ curious girl.

PRACTICE (4)

Using Commas in a Series and between Dual Adjectives

Read the paragraph that follows, and add commas where necessary. Circle each comma you add.

I needed to take three science courses in college, so I chose to take anatomy physiology and microbiology. The intriguing stimulating courses provided me with information I use to this day. I learned about the bones in the human body the major body systems and the principal types of diseases. My interesting witty professor for all three courses was a retired cardiologist. He had years of surgical experience from which to draw wonderful stories, so he made the classes very entertaining. His classes convinced me that I would love to become a certified nursing assistant a licensed vocational nurse or a registered nurse, and so I am very glad that I took those courses.

Other Uses of Commas

Some commas are required simply as technical punctuation details based on rules developed by printers, who desired consistency in producing published works.

Function	Examples
To separate elements in addresses	811 Martin Drive(,) Richmond(,) VA
To separate the day of the month from the year and the year from whatever follows (when needed)	Wynn was born on May 16(,) 1887(,) and he died on May 17(,) 1989. The battle on March 3(,) 1777(,) was especially brutal.
To separate the day of the week from the month	I arrived on Tuesday(,) April 18.
To set off dialogue	Jayne said(,) "I wish I knew how to ice skate." "I took a year of lessons and then dropped out(,)" Ashley replied.
To introduce a quotation from a written source	In the words of Enrique Marquez(,) "An epidemic is a disease gone rogue."
To separate a person's name from a title that follows it	Soo Kim(,) mayor of Yuma(,) is the host for the week. Carrie Garza(,) MD(,) was the speaker at the conference.

Several situations involving comma usage require special attention, as the chart below illustrates.

Typical Usage	Trouble Spot
To separate the day of the month from the year **Example:** Wynn was born on May 15, 1887.	Do *not* use a comma to separate the month from the year. **Example:** He died in May 1989.
To set off dialogue **Example:** Jayne said, "I wish I knew how to skate!"	Do *not* use a comma when dialogue is described but not quoted directly. **Example:** Jayne said that she wished she knew how to skate. (Note the use of the word *that* and the absence of quotation marks.)
To introduce a quote from a written source **Example:** The CDC report stated, "No significant outbreak of the virus has occurred."	Do *not* use a comma when the word *that* is used to transition into a quotation. **Example:** The CDC report stated that no significant outbreak of the virus had occurred. (Note the use of the word *that* and the absence of quotation marks.)

PRACTICE ⑤

Using Commas Correctly

Read the paragraphs below, and add commas where necessary. Circle each comma you add.

Selena walked hurriedly into the classroom. She quickly took the nearest seat quietly unzipped her backpack and noiselessly removed her textbook. Opening her book she sighed anxiously. The test would be extremely difficult and she knew that she had not studied enough. Throughout the entire semester Biology 101 had been a tough course for her. Her professor Sue McGee MD was a retired surgeon and she was very demanding. Professor McGee had told the class that the exam would be challenging and Selena knew that she meant it.

Selena glanced backward and saw classmates studiously reading their notes. Her heart slowly sank as she realized that she had put herself into a very difficult situation. Nevertheless she summoned her inner strength closed her eyes and said to herself "Sellie you can do this. You know you can."

Using Apostrophes, Colons, and Semicolons Correctly

Apostrophes, colons, and semicolons play important roles in sentences.

Apostrophes

Apostrophes are used for two principal reasons: to create contractions and to show possession by a noun.

Apostrophe Use in Contractions.   A **contraction** is a word formed by the merging of two other words. When the words are merged, one or more letters are dropped. An apostrophe's role is to stand in the spot that the dropped letters have vacated. The key to forming contractions correctly is to use the apostrophe in *the very place* that the omitted letters once stood. Generally speaking, contractions should be used sparingly in academic or formal writing.

Original Words	Letters Omitted	Contraction
do + not	*o* (in *not*)	don't
should + have	*ha*	should've
he + will	*wi*	he'll

Apostrophe Use to Show Possession.   For a singular noun, simply add -*'s* to the noun in order to show possession. Names are treated in the same manner as other nouns.

Singular Noun	Possessive
the coach	the coach's cap
a truck	a truck's tires
a New York Yankee	a New York Yankee's hits
the scientist	the scientist's graph
a city	a city's schools

For a plural noun, follow these rules to show possession:

1. If the plural noun ends in -*s,* add only an apostrophe.
2. If the plural noun does not end in -*s,* add -*'s.*

Plural Noun	Possessive
coaches	coaches' caps
scientists	scientists' graphs
New York Yankees	New York Yankees' infield
children (no -*s*)	children's toys
women (no -*s*)	women's vote

PRACTICE (6)

Using Apostrophes Correctly

Read the paragraphs below, and add apostrophes where necessary. Circle each apostrophe you add.

Men s involvement in the construction industry is long established. However, women s participation is on the rise, so much so that some people have replaced the word *tradesmen* with *tradesworkers* because they don t want to suggest a gender bias.

Various members of the workforce are involved in the construction of a house. They specialize in various areas, and workers tools vary from trade to trade.

Concrete finishers principal role in building a house is pouring a foundation. Driveways and sidewalks are also the fruit of their labor. A concrete finisher has a tool called a "screed"; he ll use that to level and smooth poured concrete.

Carpenters tasks primarily involve the "framing" of a house. Carpenters build the wooden structures that support the house s walls, ceilings, and roof. Hammers, saws, and measuring tapes are probably the most important tools for carpenters.

Masons lay brick and do other kinds of stonework. Masons use mortar as a type of adhesive between the bricks. A mason s number one tool is a trowel.

Wiring houses is electricians assignment. An electrician relies on a special kind of pliers that can be used to cut, strip, and crimp wire; she ll never go to a job site without this special tool.

The responsibility of carpet layers is evident in the name of their trade. Carpet layers use a special tool called a "knee kicker" to stretch carpet for wall-to-wall installation.

A plumber s job in a house s construction is to install the pipes that carry water and the fixtures that provide outlets for water. Plumbers carry with them a set of tools that includes a propane torch, a hacksaw, and various wrenches.

Colons and Semicolons

Colons and semicolons help writers create interesting and varied sentences.

Colons.   A colon's function is to introduce an explanation, a list, or a long quotation.

Function of Colon	Examples
To introduce explanations	I decided to stay home for one good reason ⊙ the roads were frozen and the bridges icy. The result of the survey was clear ⊙ students want more parking.
To introduce lists	Campers will need the following ⊙ a flashlight, a backpack, and a knife. The car certainly had problems ⊙ bent frame, bad brakes, and bald tires.
To introduce long quotes	Mark Twain had this to say about books ⊙ "In a good bookroom you feel in some mysterious way that you are absorbing the wisdom contained in all the books through your skin without even opening them."

Semicolons.   A semicolon is used to connect two complete sentences. Its function is similar to that of a FANBOYS conjunction (*for, and, nor, but, or, yet, so*): it joins two complete thoughts that are equally weighted in the mind of the writer. The two most common situations in which semicolons are properly used are described below.

Function of Semicolon	Examples
To connect clauses that are clearly related in meaning or content	The plane was delayed ⊙ the airport was packed. The judge looked at the defendant ⊙ the defendant looked at his attorney.
To connect clauses using a conjunctive adverb	I took a wrong turn ⊙ consequently, I arrived at the party late. We slowly learned the truth ⊙ thus, we began to take action.

Note that each clause connected with a semicolon must be an *independent clause*—a complete thought capable of standing alone as a sentence. A comma used in place of a semicolon results in a *comma splice error*.

PRACTICE 7

Using Commas, Colons, and Semicolons Correctly

Insert the appropriate punctuation—comma, semicolon, or colon—in the sentences below. If no punctuation is needed, write *NP* in the blank.

1. We went to eat after the play___ we went home after we ate.
2. The instructions indicated ___ that each piece needed to be thoroughly cleaned before assembly.
3. Even though the theater company's interpretation of *Hamlet* was highly unusual___ I found the performance to be superb.
4. The types of art that could be submitted in the contest were strictly limited___ oil paintings, watercolors, pastels, or charcoal sketches.
5. We sailed for a day on rough seas ___ because a storm had just passed through our sea route.
6. The restaurant specializes in ham and beans___ buttermilk pie___ and grits casserole.
7. The play lasted for two hours___ consequently, we didn't get home until late.
8. The surgeons continued the operation ___ even though the outlook for the patient seemed grim.
9. This is one of my favorite lines from Jack Kerouac's *On the Road*___ "Why think about that when all the golden lands ahead of you and all kinds of unforeseen events wait lurking to surprise you and make you glad you're alive to see?"
10. The surface of the road ahead is smooth enough___ however, the curves and the ice and the wind will make it treacherous indeed.

Using Hyphens, Dashes, Parentheses, Quotation Marks, and Ellipses Correctly

Hyphens, dashes, parentheses, quotation marks, and ellipses are used less frequently than the punctuation marks covered above.

Hyphens

The hyphen, which is a small horizontal mark, has three main uses, as shown in the following table.

Use	Examples	Tip
In some compound nouns	mother-in-law six-pack	The rules about when to use hyphens with compounds are inconsistent, so check a dictionary if in doubt.
In fractions and numbers that consist of two words	two-thirds twenty-seven	Numbers higher than one hundred are usually written with numerals: 101, 237, and so on.
In ranges of numbers or years	pp. 25-32 1920-2011	Do not use a hyphen to replace *to* in a construction with *from:* "The civil unrest took place *from* 2010 *to* 2014."

Dashes and Parentheses

A dash is a horizontal mark that is longer than a hyphen. Both dashes and parentheses set off material that interrupts a sentence but adds to its meaning. The principal difference between dashes and parentheses is how they focus the reader's attention. Dashes highlight an interruption; parentheses deemphasize it.

Punctuation Type	Function	Examples
Dash	To set off emphasized information	The tiger — furious and roaring — leaped toward the tourists. The song — wistful and tender — touched his soul.
Parentheses	To set off understated information	The bus (which had seen better days) rolled along. Sammy (who had never liked school) joined the army.

Note that with word-processing software, you create a dash by typing two hyphens (--) without any spaces between them or on either side of them. Some word-processing software will automatically change the two hyphens into a dash (—). Both styles (two hyphens and a long dash) are acceptable, so there is no need to worry about this detail.

Quotation Marks

Double and single quotation marks serve different purposes.

Type	Function	Examples
Double quotes	To indicate a word-for-word quotation	According to Confucius, "Everything has beauty, but not everyone sees it."
Double quotes	To indicate dialogue in a narrative	They asked, "So what are you?" The Buddha simply replied, "I am awake."
Double quotes	To set off special terms	The term "scientific method" refers to a specific procedure used for investigation in the natural sciences.
Single quotes	To indicate a quote *within* a quote	The patient complained, "I told the doctor I was ill, but he muttered, 'It's probably all in your head.' Then he just walked away."

When you write, place periods and commas *inside* quotation marks, even inside single quotes.

Ellipses

In formal and scholarly writing, an ellipsis consists of three spaced periods that indicate the omission of words from quoted material. As a student writing academic papers, you may want to shorten a long quotation by using ellipses to show where you have omitted words. When the omission is at the end of a quoted sentence, the ellipsis is preceded by a period.

In informal writing and in some forms of literature, an ellipsis indicates a pause. Although you may never use an ellipsis for that purpose as a writer, you should be aware of this use as a reader. Why does the author want the reader to pause at the designated place? How does the pause affect the meaning being conveyed?

The chart below provides examples of different uses of ellipses.

Function	Examples
To show that words have been omitted from quoted material	"On the voyage (. . .) illness was a common cause of death." "With little to no medicine available, not much could be done. (. . .) The captain decided to head for port."
To show a pause in thinking or to show hesitation or uncertainty	I was wondering if maybe you'd be willing to loan me ten bucks (. . .) I was dreaming of a time long ago (. . .)

PRACTICE 8

Using Hyphens, Dashes, Parentheses, Quotation Marks, and Ellipses Correctly

In the sentences below, insert the appropriate punctuation.

1. Millions of Americans who are living with chronic pain rely on opioids available only by prescription   to improve their lives.

2. Recently, though, the Food and Drug Administration has noticed increased abuse and misuse of opioids that is, hydrocodone combination drugs, such as Vicodin .

3. Many drug dependent people are now obtaining opioids illegally.

4. The FDA announced, Due to the unique history of this issue and the tremendous amount of public interest, we are announcing the agency's intent to recommend to HHS that hydrocodone combination products should be reclassified to a different and more restrictive schedule.

5. The agency consulted a wide range of interested parties   health-care providers, patients, experts, and other agencies   before making the recommendation.

6. Changing the classification of opioids from Schedule III to Schedule II would, according to the announcement, increase the controls on these products.

7. I hope this doesn't make it harder for me to get my prescription, said one patient. She added, her voice trailing off, To deal with the pain

Thematic Anthology of Readings

PART 5

©Don White/Superstock

Theme
Triumphing over Adversity

Theme
Self-Segregation

Theme
Food for Thought

Theme
Planning for the Future

AVAILABLE ONLY IN **create**

Theme
Television and Stereotypes

Theme
The Rules of Attraction

Triumphing over Adversity | THEME

What qualities lead to resilience and perseverance? Can those qualities be cultivated? If so, how?

We all face times of adversity, moments when obstacles of different kinds threaten to ruin our happiness or keep us from realizing our dreams. For some people, adversity is a stepping-stone to success. Why are some people successful at overcoming hard times while other people are crushed by them?

The four readings that follow present ideas about the difficulties we might encounter in life and how we might handle them. As you read, think about your own experiences with adversity. Are there lessons in these readings that can help you overcome your own difficulties?

Author and Context. Melissa Balmain is a journalist whose writing has appeared in a variety of publications, including *The New Yorker, The New York Times,* and *McSweeney's.* "Bouncing Back" appeared in *Success* magazine in 2012.

Previewing. Have pen and paper (or a computer) on hand as you read. Think about the title, and then study the author's biography and the contextual information about the reading. Next, preview the selection. From the information you have gathered, determine the topic. What predictions can you make about the reading's content? Jot down your answers.

Reading Critically and Annotating.   As you read, annotate the main idea, the major supporting points, key words, and a few passages that would make good quotations. Either write in your book or make annotations on sticky notes.

As you find key ideas, annotate them. Do Balmain's suggestions sound reasonable? Does Balmain support her suggestions with information that convinces you to try them? While you read and question content, also notice Balmain's writing choices. How does she organize her essay? What role do illustrations play in her essay? What is effective about her writing? Use annotations to record your observations and questions.

After reading and annotating, create an information sheet on which you record and organize your annotations as well as your thoughts about the content of the reading.

Bouncing Back

By Melissa Balmain

No matter what troubles you face, at work or at home, it's worth asking yourself one question: What would Howie Truong do?   1

In 1977, as Truong fled postwar Vietnam with his wife, baby son and several other people, their motorboat was captured by pirates. The pirates forced everyone aboard their own boat; although brusque toward the adults, they doted on the baby and tried to buy him. After a few days, they shoved Truong into the sea. He nearly drowned before he was rescued by fishermen. Weeks later, in Thailand, he learned that his wife's body had washed ashore; he would spend 34 years wondering what had happened to his son.   2

How in the world did Truong survive the grief that followed his ordeal? How did he move to America, become an expert metalworker, remarry, raise four more children, and eventually find his firstborn? Truong, handsome and dark-haired at 54, smiles in his living room in West Henrietta, N.Y. "I told myself, 'Get going,'" he replies emphatically. "'Life has to go on.'"   3

If you think Truong's story has little to do with your own, think again. Resilience like his can be learned, experts say. And it can help you through just about any setback—a blow to your business or health, for instance; a death, a divorce, a disaster.   4

"Resilience is very important in today's uncertain world," says Harvard psychologist Robert Brooks, Ph.D., author of *The Power of Resilience: Achieving Balance, Confidence, and Personal Strength in Your Life*. It's a trait worth nurturing even when all is well, he believes, so you'll be better prepared for a crisis. But if hard times have already knocked you down, it's not too late to bounce back. "There are certain outlooks and skills we can develop," Brooks says, "so that regardless of what the adversity or challenge may be, we are able to deal with it."   5

And who better to coach us than Truong and others who have endured life at its worst?   6

Pulling Yourself Forward

Getting flattened by adversity is, of course, as common as adversity itself. Inertia, self-pity, junk-food binges: All are par for the course, experts say, and nothing to beat yourself up about. "I think of grief as ebbing and flowing rather than as a distinct phase that ends," says Karen Reivich, Ph.D., co-director of the Penn Resiliency Project at the University of Pennsylvania, which trains soldiers and others to manage stress. The more time passes after a major loss—of a job, a loved one, or home—the more you'll feel able to get up and at 'em, Reivich says. "The good periods get longer and the others, shorter." The trick is to take advantage of those good periods. "If there's   7 that voice inside you that says, 'I don't want to get out of bed, but I probably could,' listen to that voice," Reivich says. "Sometimes you may need to give yourself a little pep talk—'I know I don't feel like getting up, but if I get going it's going to feel better than if I don't get going.'"

Listening to those who love you is important, too: the buddy who says, "Grab your coat—we're taking you out." The brother who insists you start writing a new résumé. "Rely on people that you trust, who know you and know your style, to help pull you forward a bit," Reivich says.

8

Another powerful pulling force: obligation. For many who find themselves unemployed or bereaved, a desire to "be strong" for children or a spouse can help. For Truong, what yanked him free of despair—and of drinking himself to sleep—was remembering his role in his family. "In my country, the big brother is the main guy to take care of sisters and brothers," he says. After his nightmare at sea, he went to a Thai refugee camp. Then an uncle sponsored him to come to Louisiana. Within seven months of losing his wife and son, Truong was studying welding in upstate New York (home of his in-laws), determined to earn money, and bring his parents and seven siblings from Vietnam to live with him. "Sometimes I would buy beer, try to forget the past, but then that wasn't good," he says. "I said to myself, 'Go out, learn something. Keep busy.'" Burying himself in his studies—and, later, his career—distracted him from his woes for long stretches and filled him with hope.

9

Taking Control

Any positive step you take after a major loss, in fact, can curb anxiety and keep you moving forward. "One basic finding in resilience research is that resilient people will focus on what they have control over," Brooks says.

10

Something as simple as cooking a good meal can make you feel less helpless. So can taking a brisk walk, playing a musical instrument or writing a step-by-step plan for getting what you want. "When people feel overwhelmed, being able to break up a task in shorter- or longer-term goals is very important," says Brooks, who has known plenty of overwhelming times himself. "I've always liked to put a couple of easy things at the top of my to-do lists, so I could check them off quickly. I know it's only a mind game, but seeing a few things checked off, I could say, 'OK! At least I got this out of the way.'" Making backup plans and lists is important as well, to buoy your spirits if Plan A doesn't pan out.

11

Even at the most basic level, seizing control may help. Three years ago, financial planner Carl Richards found himself—ironically—in financial hot water after the stock market crashed and the housing bubble popped. He and his family wound up losing their $575,000 house in Las Vegas. Richards' main way of handling the stress was to ride his mountain bike—and focus on his breathing. "It was kind of empowering to realize everything else may be out of control, but I can control my breath," says Richards, who has since written *The Behavior Gap: Simple Ways to Stop Doing Dumb Things with Money,* and moved with his family to a rented home in Park City, Utah. "It gave me a sense of stability and 'I can do this the next minute and the next, and doors will keep opening for me.' It gave me the ability to say, 'I can make the tough decisions. I can face this other stuff.'"

12

Finding a Team

When dealing with your own problems, resist the urge to isolate yourself. Join a support group. Keep up your social life. Don't be shy about asking a neighbor to watch your kids while you go to an interview. "The myth of resilience is you go it alone," Reivich

13

says. "But resilience is really a team sport rather than an individual sport. Those people who have a board of advisers, a close-knit group—those people do better."

No one knows this more than Jennifer Loredo, a master sergeant in the Army. In 2010, while she and her husband, Edwardo, were serving in Afghanistan, a roadside bomb left her a single mother of two. Back in the United States, Loredo began seeking other widows to talk with; some were part of a military support group, some not. "It just felt really like a relief almost, like I'm not alone in this—other people are going through it and they're OK," says Loredo, who lives in Fayetteville, N.C. "It kind of confirmed that my kids and I were going to come out OK."

Counting Your Blessings

Odd as it may sound, something else that has helped Loredo—and countless others in desperate straits—is gratitude. Each night before bed, Loredo takes a few minutes to recall three pleasant moments of her day. She often jots notes on how they made her feel, what made them happen and how she might make such things happen again. One recent note was about learning that her 14-year-old daughter had aced an English test, another about hearing her 4-year-old son say, "Mommy, you're beautiful." Research suggests that this habit of reflection, taught to her by Reivich (from the Penn Resiliency Project), reduces symptoms of depression. "In the beginning it's kind of hard to come up with three good things that happened every day," Loredo says. "But after you do it for a while, you find yourself realizing there is a lot of good in your life and it definitely outweighs the bad." Partly as a result, she now tries harder to let family and friends know she treasures them: "It could be something as little as telling my mom that I love her and I appreciate the time we spent together the last time I was home."

All of which fits a common and welcome pattern known as "post-traumatic growth." "We're all familiar with post-traumatic stress," Reivich says. "But in post-traumatic growth, when people emerge on the other side of something horrible, they know what their passions are. They have a new commitment to life and a greater sense of spirituality and faith. It doesn't take away the suffering they feel, but some people experience this renewed sense of going after what matters in life. Research would support that that's a critical part of healing and resilience."

Lending a Hand

For Celeste Peterson, what matters in life is what mattered to her daughter. Erin Peterson was among 32 students and faculty shot to death in 2007 by a deranged student at Virginia Tech. More than anything, Erin—who died at 18—had wanted to work for a nonprofit that improves people's lives. So now that's what Peterson does. With donations that poured in after Erin's death, she co-runs a program for at-risk boys who attend Erin's high school in Fairfax County, Va. She takes the boys on outings, brings in speakers to inspire them, and gives them scholarships for books if they're accepted to college. "It keeps my mind going," she says. "I don't just sit there and act pitiful. I don't have the time to just feel sorry for myself."

Helping others is a great way to boost your resilience, studies show. Like religion and spirituality, it can give you a sense of community. Like paid work, it can bolster your belief that you have a positive effect on the world. "This belief reinforces a sense of purpose to one's existence," Brooks has written, "thereby impacting positively on emotional and physical health."

Peterson says amen to that: "Working with the boys does give me a sense of purpose. It's like I can hear Erin in my head, saying, 'Come on, Mom, we've got a job to do.'"

14

15

16 **post-traumatic stress disorder (PTSD):** a type of anxiety disorder that results from exposure to serious trauma, such as sexual assault, serious injury, the witnessing of traumatic events, or the threat of death. The disorder is characterized by severe anxiety symptoms, including panic attacks, inability to tolerate stressful situations, and suicidality.

17

18

19

Accepting and Adapting

Another key to climbing beyond self-pity, experts say, is a willingness to reinvent 20
yourself. Anna Hovind of Atlanta learned the truth of this six years ago, after losing
her longtime position as a newsroom manager at CNN. Although her layoff came soon
after her 25-year marriage dissolved, she found the divorce from her job even harder.
And it wasn't just because she missed the office camaraderie and excellent health benefits. "Before I got downsized, all I had to do was say, 'I work at CNN,' and people
were like, 'Wow'—and all of a sudden I didn't have that," she says. "I was just like an
ordinary Joe on the street and that was a little bit of a challenge." After she found a
new job in broadcast public relations, she continued struggling with her relative obscurity. But as she mastered the duties of an unfamiliar field, Hovind found a fresh identity to take pride in: that of the plucky middle-aged professional who could compete
with people in their 20s. "I kind of shook the dust of CNN off my sandals," she says.
"I said, 'I'm done grieving for what I lost, and this is my new reality.'"

Tricia Downing can relate. In 2000, she was a cyclist who rode in races through- 21
out the country. Then a bike accident left her paralyzed from the chest down. Downing
threw herself into rehab and—on top of learning how to care for herself—mastered the
challenge of using a handcycle and a racing chair. As a para-athlete, she finished 68
marathons and triathalons and many other races between 2001 and 2011. Now she's
training to make the U.S. Paralympic rowing team. "If I had thought, 'Gosh, I can
never come back from this injury,' I probably wouldn't have," says Downing, who lives
in Denver and has become a motivational speaker. "In the beginning I did have those
thoughts, but I let them dissipate. I realized, 'I can't do things the same way I used to
do them—I just have to find different ways.' Telling yourself, 'I can do this' is really
important to being resilient." Another mantra that keeps her going on the racecourse
and off: "Ride your own race." Instead of comparing herself to others, Downing takes
pride in beating personal records. "What it comes down to is focusing on what you do
have and not what you don't have," she says. And by her own estimation, she has a lot:
A nice house. Lucrative work. A loving husband she met seven years ago. And, of
course, the biceps of an Amazon. "I feel accomplished," Downing says. "I feel like I
stared down a demon and I won."

Forgiving, but Not Necessarily Forgetting

It's easy after a major setback to be angry—at the spouse who dumped you, the driver 22
who hit you, the boss who derailed your career. Yet one of the most important parts of
resilience, experts say, is deciding to forgive. This shouldn't be confused with forget-
ting, minimizing or denying hurtful actions, Brooks says. "Rather," he explains, "forgiveness ensures that our lives are not dominated by intense anger and thoughts of
revenge that lessen our own happiness."

And here, again, we look to Howie Truong. 23

As the decades passed, he couldn't shake the feeling that his stolen child, Khai, 24
was still alive. The pirates had been too fond of the boy to have killed him, he believed.
Last summer, after years of fruitless attempts to find him long-distance, Truong got his
family's blessing to take an extended trip to Thailand. Incredibly, thanks in large part
to his dogged questioning of strangers and to help from Thai officials and media, he
found Khai in a month. He turned out to be a father of two known as Samart Khumkhaw, who worked on a rubber plantation near the home of the couple who—
apparently ignorant of his kidnapping—had adopted him when he was a baby.

Now Khumkhaw, on his first visit to the United States, sits with Truong in his living 25
room. Father and son have matching eyes, matching mustaches, and, above all, matching
infectious grins. Truong, the only one adept at English, does most of the talking.

One thing he realized during his trip to Thailand, he says, is he could easily track down the pirates and press charges against them. But he won't. "I figure if I forgive them now," he says, "later somebody will forgive me for something." He glances at his recovered son, eyes widening as if he still can't believe he is right beside him. "He was lost for 34 years. It's time for me to make up for that."   26

Five More Secrets of Resilient People

1. Keep a journal and read through it now and then. You'll spot trends you may want   27
   to address ("I'm always sad around 6 p.m."), and feel proud when you read of obstacles you've since overcome.
2. Think about what your greatest strengths of character are—from kindness to persistence to a knack for humor. Then brainstorm approaches to your problems that revolve around those strengths.
3. Don't shield your partner or spouse from hard decisions you face. If you make them together, it will be easier for you both to live with the consequences.
4. As much as possible, even when times are hard, lift your spirits by keeping up with favorite hobbies or pastimes.
5. Stop asking, "Why me?" and start asking, "Why not me? How am I going to handle this? How do I help other people handle it?"

Using Your Annotations.   Use your annotations and key words to write a one-page summary of the reading. In your summary, identify the writer's thesis statement, the major supporting points, the support for the major supporting points, and any other information needed to complete the summary.

Thinking about the Text

1. What is Balmain's purpose for this article?
2. For what audience is this piece composed?
3. What does the writer mean by "pulling yourself forward"?
4. The writer shares the stories of several people who have overcome adversity. What character traits or behaviors do these people have in common?
5. Why do you think Howie Truong decided to forgive the pirates who killed his wife and stole his child?

The Writer's Techniques

1. Look at your annotations. Which of the following types of supporting details does Balmain use—comparison and contrast, cause and effect, definition, process analysis, classification, or illustration?
2. What method does Balmain use to introduce and conclude her essay? How might you use Balmain's introduction and conclusion methods in your own writing?
3. Identify at least two examples. What effect does the use of examples have on you as a reader? What do you think the essay would be like without the examples? Explain.

Brief-Response Assignments

1. Write a paragraph defining *resiliency* in your own words. To support your definition, describe the characteristics of resilient people.
2. What role does forgiveness have in resiliency? Explain your answer, and provide an example.

3. Write a paragraph in which you explain this assertion: *Overcoming adversity requires intentional actions and intentional thoughts.*

4. What is the role of work in overcoming adversity? In other words, how does working or staying busy contribute to overcoming adversity?

Essay Assignments

1. Imagine you are writing an essay to be published in *Success,* the magazine that published Balmain's essay. Write a detailed account of someone who has overcome adversity. The person can be a family member, a friend, or a public figure from the past or present. What situation did the person face? What approach helped the person successfully overcome the situation's challenges? Why do you think this approach was successful? Your essay should present the person, the problem, the person's method for handling the problem, and the outcome.

2. Write an essay in which you classify responses to a particular adverse situation, such as losing a loved one or being in a car accident. First, discuss the event. Next, discuss the types of reactions people have to the event. Finally, explain the consequences of each type of reaction. For example, consider the ways people react to failing a class. Some students overcome the situation and emerge stronger and more determined to pass classes in the future; other students give up and drop out or get angry and blame others for their failure.

3. When we face adversity, our lives feel out of control. Adversity reminds us that we truly cannot control everything that happens to us or to those we love. Dealing with adversity requires us to confront this lack of control. One way to be successful is to control that which we can control. Using the ideas in this article and other ideas you develop through prewriting, write an essay about how people triumph over adversity by taking steps to regain control of their lives. Explain the methods they use to regain such control. Explain how these steps are effective at helping people overcome their difficulties. You might find it helpful to use process analysis as a text pattern for this assignment. ↻

Author and Context.   Carlos C. Huerta is a major and a chaplain (rabbi) in the US Army 1st Battalion, 320th Field Artillery, 101st Airborne Division (Screaming Eagles). "Leaving the Battlefield" appeared as a news article on the US Army's Web page in April 2012.

Previewing.   Have pen and paper (or a computer) on hand as you read. Think about the title, and then study the author's biography and the contextual information about the reading. Next, preview the selection. From the information you have gathered, determine the topic. What predictions can you make about the reading's content? Jot down your answers.

Reading Critically and Annotating.   As you read, annotate the main idea, the major supporting points, key words, and a few passages that would make good quotations. Either write in your book or make annotations on sticky notes.

As you find key ideas, annotate them. When you read the essay, note the writer's occupation and think about how it may have affected him. Note any questions that come to mind.

After reading and annotating, create an information sheet on which you record and organize your annotations as well as your thoughts about the content of the reading.

Leaving the Battlefield: Soldier Shares Story of PTSD

By Chaplain (Maj.) Carlos C. Huerta

My name is Huerta. I am an American Soldier and I have PTSD [post-traumatic stress disorder]. I refused to admit it to myself even when the Army doctors told me I had it in 2004. I refused to talk to anyone about it even when Army health professionals told me I needed to in 2005. I was afraid how Army leadership would react if I had that on my record. I was a Soldier, I was tough, I just needed to rub the patch and drive on.

And drive on I did until one day in September 2010, five years after I last left the battlefield. I don't know what the trigger was. Maybe it was the young Soldier, a mother of two who was just redeployed, who I watched cut down after she hanged herself weeks after returning from battle earlier. Maybe it was the faces of the children I saw behind all the doors I knocked on to tell them their father or mother was not coming home. Maybe it was because it was the same time of year when my uniform was covered with the blood and brains of a 6-year-old Iraqi child who was caught in an IED during Ramadan.

I don't know what the trigger was, but it hit me hard. I went home one evening and all of a sudden, I felt a tightness in my chest, it was hard to breathe, and I felt closed in and panicky. I bolted out of bed thinking I was dying. I paced the room in the dark for hours before I exhausted myself. I almost went to the ER that night, but the Soldier in me said to stick it out.

The morning came and it hit again, a panic, a fear of being closed off, claustrophobia, and pains in the chest. I thought maybe I was having a heart attack and, if I was, I needed to see a doctor.

A heart attack was honorable, [but] PTSD was not. I went to sick call and they ordered a battery of tests to exclude any heart condition. When my heart was cleared, the doctors recommended I see someone in CMHS [Community Mental Health Services]. I thought to myself, "I wasn't crazy, why do I need to see them? If I see them, I know the 'big' Army will find out and tag me as 'broken.'"

I went home that night and the same thing happened. I knew I could not live like this so I talked, off the record, to someone in mental health. They looked at my records and after talking with me, said I had PTSD. They said there was probably some trigger that set it off. I did not want to believe it, but I knew that I needed something or I would face the same thing again that evening. I then "officially" saw them and was prescribed some psychotropic medication to help with the anxiety in order to help me function.

I thought when I got off the battlefield that I could heal and place the war behind me. As a chaplain, I soon realized that I could not. Within weeks of getting back in 2004, I was knocking on doors telling families a husband, wife, a father or mother, a daughter or son was not coming home. In 2008, I knocked on a door to tell a family that their husband, a father of three, was lost to them. To this day I can close my eyes and see the face of a teenage daughter who looked at me with hatred. She looked deep into my soul and said that she would never forget what I did to her and her family that day and turned away, too destroyed to even cry.

Even though I was home, I never left the battlefield. I brought the war home and it took a toll on me, my family, wife and children. I got to be good friends with Jim and Jack. You may know them as Mr. Beam and Mr. Daniels.

I did not want to get close to my new babies for fear I may get deployed again. A big piece of me wanted to go back to battle because the battlefield made sense; coming home to emails, memorandums and unit "politics" did not. I also knew that if I went back, a bigger piece of me would not want to come back home again.

The home I came back to was not the one I left. My family was not the same, I was 10
not the same. I felt that something important was stolen from me and there was nobody
I could talk to about it, nobody except the guys I was over there with. I would look for
combat patches, look for buddies to talk to, look for the Soldiers who went through
what I went through and felt the same way I did. There were many of us. Our experiences were very different but we had one thing in common. We felt different, but we
were not crazy and we did not have some defective genetic failing.

It just was hard for us to come to terms with all the death, destruction and pain we 11
had participated in and witnessed. We were all reluctant about "officially" talking to
someone. Even if we needed help, we would not go to it as we thought leadership
would use that against us for assignments and promotions.

We felt we were alone. We were trapped in our own memories, sometimes trying 12
to ignore them and often not being able to. We watched as our suicide numbers went
up and are still going up.

The Army leadership has tried and is trying to change this trend and is having 13
some success. I cannot say that a piece of me at one time did not wonder if the world,
my family, would have been better off without me.

For Soldiers with PTSD, we often felt the very act of seeking help from a mental 14
health professional could be information that could be used against us, to target us, and
make us feel we were burdens to the system. I felt that way and was afraid to get the
help I needed. I now fear that the problem may be made worse with the so-called discovery of a PTSD gene. If this data is used wrong or misinterpreted, those of us with
PTSD now could be considered genetically dysfunctional.

Instead of being a burden to the Army, I ended up being a burden to the most 15
important people in my life, my wife and children. Fearing being minimized as a
Soldier, I, like so many others, went underground. It seemed the very thing that
leadership was using to try to help me actually worked against me.

When I close my eyes at night, sometimes I still see myself picking up the body 16
parts of my Soldiers. I still see myself holding my Soldiers as they die in my arms on
the battlefield. I still see the blood of Iraqi children spattered all over my uniform as
they take their last breaths due to no fault of their own. In the quiet moments of the
day, when I am with my family, I see the faces of all the wives, children, husbands,
mothers and fathers whose lives I destroyed with the notifications I made.

My mind tells me that I did not cause their pain and grief, but my heart tells me 17
otherwise. I know I can't change their pain, but I can change mine and the pain I
inflicted on my family due to war. Only a Soldier understands that physically being
home doesn't mean coming home.

Coming home from battle seemed to be one of the easiest things to do. It seemed that 18
you just get on a plane. After spending hours, weeks and months getting help and talking
to someone about my wounds, I am only beginning to understand how to come home.

I am, in our Army culture, what some would identify as a broken or deadwood Sol- 19
dier. I have no bullet holes to show my wounds. I will not get any medal that will recognize them. If I did, I would be afraid and ashamed to wear it in our present culture. As
with so many of us, my wounds are the invisible kind, the type we bear in our souls. I am
not ashamed of them. For me and others like me, they are just as real as one that bleeds.

I am getting help because I'm tired of not being home. I am tired of being on the 20
battlefield I brought back with me. It is time for me to come home. It is time for all of
us to come home. My name is Huerta and I am a wounded American Soldier, and I am
not ashamed of my wounds and I have no genetic failing. I am proud of my service and
I am going home. Let's go home together.

Using Your Annotations.   Use your annotations and key words to write a one-page summary of the reading. In your summary, identify the writer's thesis statement, the major supporting points, the support for the major supporting points, and any other information needed to complete the summary.

Thinking about the Text

1. What obstacles is Huerta facing as he seeks to recover from PTSD?
2. How did the writer's particular job in the army contribute to his stress?
3. What message does he hope to send to other veterans and soldiers?
4. Based on Huerta's article, what are some of the steps one should take to overcome PTSD?
5. What is the writer's main idea? What major details does he use to support his main idea?

The Writer's Techniques

1. Where does Huerta use transitions in his essay to move from one point to the next? What effect do these transitions have on your experience or understanding as a reader? Explain your answer.
2. Which supporting details most effectively help you understand the pain Huerta is facing?
3. Reread the conclusion of Huerta's essay. Is the positive tone convincing? Explain your answer.

Brief-Response Assignments

1. What is PTSD? What situations other than combat might cause PTSD? Explain.
2. Explain this statement: *Because he was a soldier, Huerta had a more difficult time dealing with PTSD than he would have had dealing with a physical injury.*
3. What role does shame play in Huerta's struggle to overcome his wartime experiences? Explain in a paragraph.

Essay Assignments

1. Thousands of soldiers have returned from the wars in Afghanistan and Iraq with PTSD as well as other injuries, both physical and mental. Based on Huerta's essay, what are some solutions that can help soldiers adjust when they come home? How can civilians help make the transition easier for these soldiers? Write an essay in which you explain the methods soldiers can use as well as the ways civilians can help.
2. Because soldiers are trained to be tough, they sometimes use ineffective coping mechanisms to deal with adversity. How does a soldier's training actually become a barrier to dealing with PTSD or other physical or mental problems? Write an essay in which you explain how the qualities of a strong warrior might lead soldiers to select ineffective coping mechanisms to deal with stress.
3. Interview a person who has successfully coped with a major change, such as coming back from war, surviving a life-threatening situation, or learning to live with the loss of a loved one or with a significant disability. What coping mechanisms helped the person adjust? What lessons can be learned from this person's story? Write an essay in which you present the person's story and the lessons or insights the story provides. ↺

Author and Context. Benjamin B. Lahey is the Irving B. Harris Professor of Epidemiology, Psychiatry, and Behavioral Neuroscience at the University of Chicago. He is interested in the genetics, measurement, taxonomy, and behavioral neuroscience of child and adolescent psychopathology. The selection "Coping with Stress" is from Lahey's textbook *Psychology: An Introduction.*

Previewing. Have pen and paper (or a computer) on hand as you read. Think about the title, and then study the author's biography and the contextual information about the reading. Next, preview the selection. From the information you have gathered, determine the topic. What predictions can you make about the reading's content? Jot down your answers.

Reading Critically and Annotating. As you read, annotate the main idea, the major supporting points, key words, and a few passages that would make good quotations. Either write in your book or make annotations on sticky notes.

As you find key ideas, annotate them. Which methods have you used to cope with stress? Which methods are new to you? What kinds of events produce stress? Note any insights or questions you have as you read.

After reading and annotating, create an information sheet on which you record and organize your annotations as well as your thoughts about the content of the reading.

Coping with Stress

By Benjamin B. Lahey

We cannot always avoid stress in our lives. What are the best ways of coping with stress when we experience it?

1

Effective Coping

Effective methods of coping either remove the source of stress or control our reactions to it:

2

1. Removing or reducing stress. One effective way of dealing with stress is to remove or to reduce the source of stress from our lives. If an employee holds a job that is stressful, discussions could be held with the employer that might lead to a reduction in the pressures of the job, or the employee could resign. If the stress stems from an unhappy marriage, either marriage counseling could be sought or the marriage could be ended. In a variety of ways, effective coping with stress can take the form of reducing it. For example, Taylor and her colleagues randomly assigned college students to two groups at the beginning of the term. One group was asked to imagine themselves beaming with success when they received high marks in the class. The second group was asked to think of practical steps they could take to avoid failure and get a good grade (getting the book, reading assignments, studying in advance, and so on). They actually studied more and received higher grades, and as a result of reducing the stressful threat of failure, felt less anxious.

3

2. Cognitive coping. Our cognitions are intimately linked to our reactions to stressful events and a number of effective methods of coping involve cognitive strategies. Three effective cognitive coping strategies involve changing how we think about the stressful event, focusing attention away from stressful events that cannot be changed, and religious coping:

4

■ Reappraisal can be an effective method of coping. This refers to changing how we think about—or interpret—the stressful events that push and shove our lives. For example, I know a musician who had a successful first record, but his second

5

album was a flop—the critics panned it and the public didn't buy it. At first, he saw this as a sign that the first record was a fluke and that he had no real talent. As a result, the failure of the second album was a huge stress. However, a veteran musician convinced him that having an unsuccessful second album is a common "sophomore slump" among musicians who go on to be very successful. This conversation changed his interpretation of his unsuccessful album and allowed him to view it as a challenge to do better next time. Finding an interpretation that is realistic and constructive minimizes the stressfulness of negative events.

- In some cases, stressful events cannot be changed and reappraising their meaning is of limited help. For example, losing a spouse to death must be coped with in some other way. Focusing attention away from the death and moving on with life is associated with less depression and better physical health.

- Many individuals cope effectively by interpreting events in terms of their religious beliefs. For example, a study of Latinos with arthritis found that individuals who viewed their painful condition as being *en las manos de Dios* (in God's hands) experienced greater psychological well-being than did individuals who engaged in less religious coping.

3. Managing stress reactions. When the source of stress cannot realistically be   6
removed or changed, another effective option is to manage our psychological and physiological reactions to the stress. For example, an individual may decide to start a new business, knowing full well that the first year or two will be hectic. She would be unwilling, then, to remove the source of the stress (the new business) but could learn to control her reactions to the stress. One strategy might be to schedule as much time as possible for relaxing activities, such as aerobic exercise, hobbies, or time with friends. Another would be to seek special training from a psychologist in controlling the body reactions to stress by learning to deeply relax the large body muscles. Happily, psychological counseling that encourages all three methods of effective coping has even been successful in changing the Type A behavior pattern. Indeed, treated patients showed a 50% reduction in heart attacks and deaths compared with Type A individuals who did not receive treatment.

Ineffective Coping

Unfortunately, many of our efforts to cope with stress are ineffective. They may   7
provide temporary relief from the discomfort produced by stress but do little to provide a long-term solution and may even make matters worse. Three common, but ineffective, coping strategies are as follows:

1. Withdrawal. Sometimes we deal with stress by withdrawing from it. Many   8
students encounter courses in college that are far more difficult than anything they had experienced in high school. Attempting to study difficult material can be highly stressful, and that stress can lead to a withdrawal from studying—by playing electronic games, talking on the telephone, partying, and the like. Similarly, a husband may ineffectively cope with the stress of an unhappy marriage by withdrawing to the refuge of a bar every day after work.

Note that it is not what you do, but how and why you do it, that makes a coping   9
strategy effective or ineffective. Spending your time playing electronic video games actually may be an effective coping strategy if you only do it for reasonable periods of time to relax. It becomes withdrawal if you use it excessively as a way to avoid the necessity for more effective coping (studying).

In this context, it is also important to recognize that there is a big difference   10
between actually removing a source of stress and withdrawing from it. If you find that you have signed up for an extremely difficult course for which you are not prepared,

dropping that class until you are ready to take it would be an effective way to remove the stress. However, simply not studying for the tests in that course because you have withdrawn to the refuge of long philosophical discussions with friends would obviously be an ineffective solution.

2. Aggression. A common reaction to frustration and other stressful situations is aggression. The woman who has tried unsuccessfully to create romantic interest in a man may suddenly become hostile toward him. The man who cannot get a screw to fit into a curtain rod may throw a temper tantrum and hurl the rod to the floor in disgust.   11

3. Self-medication. It appears that many individuals cope ineffectively with stress by using tobacco, alcohol, and other drugs to soothe their emotional reactions to stress. For example, a study in which participants' emotions were measured daily showed that higher levels of anxiety during the day increased the likelihood of drinking alcohol later that day. Although alcohol temporarily reduces anxiety for some people, it does nothing to remove the source of stress and often creates additional problems in relationships, studying, job performance, and health that make things worse in the long run. Self-medication with alcohol or street drugs is a very poor method of coping indeed. It does seem clear, however, that some individuals benefit from professionally prescribed medications that reduce anxiety and depression far more effectively and safely than from alcohol and street drugs. Perhaps because of the stigma associated with mental health "problems," far too many people self-medicate instead of seeking medication from a competent physician in conjunction with assistance from a psychologist in developing effective coping strategies.   12

Defense Mechanisms

According to Freud, one of the key functions of the ego is to "defend" the person from a buildup of uncomfortable tension. Freud believed that the ego possesses a small arsenal of defense mechanisms that are unconsciously used to cope with tension. There is evidence that we use cognitive coping strategies that are very similar to the defense mechanisms described by Freud over 100 years ago. When they are not overused, such defense mechanisms can effectively reduce stress, but they create problems when they are overused. The major defense mechanisms identified by Freud: 13

Displacement: When it's unsafe or inappropriate to express aggressive or sexual feelings toward the person who is creating stress (such as a boss who pressures you), that feeling can be directed toward someone safe (such as yelling at your friend when you are really angry with your boss).   14

Sublimation: Stressful conflicts over dangerous feelings or motives are reduced by converting the impulses into socially approved activities, such as schoolwork, literature, and sports.

Projection: One's own dangerous or unacceptable desires or emotions are seen not as one's own but as the desires or feelings of others. A person who has stressful conflicts about sex might perceive himself as having little sexual desire but might view other people as being "obsessed" with sex.

Reaction formation: Conflicts over dangerous motives or feelings are avoided by unconsciously transforming them into the opposite desire. A married man with strong desires for extramarital sex might start a campaign to rid his city of massage parlors and prostitutes. A woman who wishes her hateful mother would die might devote herself to finding ways to protect her mother's health.

Regression: Stress may be reduced by returning to an earlier pattern of behavior, such as a business executive who has a stomping, screaming temper tantrum when her company suffers a major setback.

Rationalization: Stress is reduced by "explaining away" the source of stress in ways that sound logical. A man who is rejected by his lover may decide that he is glad because she had so many faults or because he really did not want to give up the single life.

Repression: Potentially stressful, unacceptable desires are kept out of consciousness without the person being consciously aware that the repression is occurring.

Denial: The conscious denial of upsetting feelings and ideas. For example, in an argument, an obviously angry person may shout: "I am not angry at you!" Similarly, a cigar smoker who was shown widely endorsed research on the dangers of all forms of tobacco use would be using denial if he or she flatly rejected the validity of the evidence.

Intellectualization: The emotional nature of stressful events is lessened at times by reducing it to cold, intellectual logic. For example, the person who learns that he has lost a large sum of money in an overly risky investment may think about it in a detached way as a temporary debit in a successful lifelong program of investment, rather than as a painful financial mistake that should be avoided in the future through more careful planning.

When overdone, defense mechanisms can inhibit long-term solutions to stress if 15 they distort reality. For example, suppose that a student copes reasonably well with the stress of failing a course in college by deciding that her instructor graded her test papers unfairly because she asks too many questions in class. If her instructor is actually fair and competent, she would be distorting reality by using the defense mechanism of rationalization. A simple change in study habits or test-taking strategies might make a big difference in her grades, but she will never see the need for change if she distorts reality through rationalization. The other defense mechanisms can be harmful in similar, reality-distorting ways.

———————————————————————————●

Using Your Annotations.   Use your annotations and key words to write a one-page summary of the reading. In your summary, identify the writer's thesis statement, the major supporting points, the support for the major supporting points, and any other information needed to complete the summary.

Thinking about the Text

1. What is Lahey's main idea? What major supporting points does the writer use to support his main idea?
2. Why is withdrawal an ineffective way of dealing with stress? Explain.
3. Choose three of the defense mechanisms the writer discusses. Provide an example of times when you used each one.
4. Lahey says, "Note that it is not what you do, but how and why you do it, that makes a coping strategy effective or ineffective." What does he mean by this? Make up an example to add to your explanation, and explain your example.
5. What is self-medication? What does the writer say about this method of reducing stress?

The Writer's Techniques

1. In what ways does Lahey use examples? Cite some of the examples he uses.
2. How does the writer organize his essay? What method does he use to present the content early in the essay, and how does he organize the remaining information?
3. Does this reading fit a specific text pattern, such as cause and effect, classification, or process analysis? Explain your answer.

Brief-Response Assignments

1. Imagine that a student fails an exam. Discuss an ineffective coping mechanism the student might use to deal with the stress of failure. What might be the negative results of using this coping mechanism?
2. Give an example of how displacement is used to deal with stress. What other methods of coping might be more beneficial when dealing with stressful situations?
3. Discuss a time in your life when you used an unhealthy method for dealing with stress. What method would have been a better choice?

Essay Assignments

1. Imagine that a tornado destroys a person's home, leaving him with only a box of personal belongings. Everything else is gone. Write an essay in which you present three or more effective coping mechanisms this person could use to deal with the stress of his situation.
2. Write a self-analysis. What is the greatest source of stress in your life right now? Explain. Now, imagine that you can see yourself from a friend's perspective. What methods would she say you have used to deal with your stress? Would she think your methods have been effective? Why or why not? Based on your analysis, what new methods should you use to handle the particular stress you are dealing with? Why might these new methods be more effective?
3. In stressful situations, we tend to think about our own pain and suffering. However, those around us often suffer also. How are people affected by the stress of a close friend or family member? What are some methods for reducing the effects of your stress on others? What advice would you offer to a person who lives with someone who is constantly stressed out? ↻

Author and Context.   Andria Ramon is a professor of political science at McLennan Community College, where she has also served as a sponsor of the Hispanic Student Association. She is the recipient of an Excellence Award from the National Institute for Staff and Organizational Development (NISOD).

Previewing.   Have pen and paper (or a computer) on hand as you read. Think about the title, and then study the author's biography and the contextual information about the reading. Next, preview the selection. From the information you have gathered, determine the topic. What predictions can you make about the reading's content? Jot down your answers.

Reading Critically and Annotating.   As you read, annotate the main idea, the major supporting points, key words, and a few passages that would make good quotations. Either write in your book or make annotations on sticky notes.

As you find key ideas, annotate them. Why do some people find Justice Sotomayor remarkable? In what way is Sotomayor like many other Americans? Note any insights or questions that come to mind as you read.

After reading and annotating, create an information sheet on which you record and organize your annotations as well as your thoughts about the content of the reading.

"To Do for Others": The Dream of Justice Sonia Sotomayor

By Andria Ramon

"After completing this exhaustive process, I have decided to nominate an inspiring woman who I believe will make a great justice: Judge Sonia Sotomayor of the great state of New York" (White House, 2009). With these words, President Barack Obama, himself a trailblazer, nominated the first Hispanic, and only the third woman, to the U.S. Supreme Court. President Obama called Sotomayor an example of the American dream who had "sterling credentials." Justice Sotomayor's compelling background, sheer dedication, resolute commitment to the law, and selfless love led to her position on one of the greatest judicial bodies in the world.   1

Sonia Maria Sotomayor was born in 1954 in New York City. Her Puerto Rican father, Juan Sotomayor, was a factory worker whose work ethic and love for his children—in spite of his alcoholism—influenced Sonia throughout her life. Sonia's mother, Celina Sotomayor, also born in Puerto Rico, was orphaned at the age of 9. She had come to New York through the U.S. military's Women's Army Corps at age 17. When Sonia was a child, Celina was a somewhat distant mother, no doubt in part because of her own difficult background. Celina had grown up in dire poverty and had not experienced the benefits of a warm and supportive family.   2

Juan and Celina married and struggled through poverty, Juan's alcoholism, and the demands of a large extended family. These situations created the self-sufficient person that Sonia became. As a young child, she acquired the nickname Aji, or "hot pepper" in English, for her curious and boisterous behavior. Aji was never shy and had an adventurous personality. Sometimes that led to mischief, as when she put a bucket on her head to listen to her voice, and her head got stuck (Sotomayor, 2013, p. 5).   3

A dramatic display of self-sufficiency came at a young age, when Sonia was diagnosed with type 1 diabetes. Daily insulin shots are required for type 1 diabetics. Although by this point Sonia's mother was working as a nurse in a local hospital, Celina could not bear giving her daughter the insulin shots she needed to stay alive. She simply could not endure hurting her daughter in that way. So, at the age of 6, little Aji began giving herself her own insulin shots.   4

Sotomayor later admitted that the primary reason for her perseverance was actually fear. She feared that she would not be able to sleep over at her grandmother's house unless she learned to administer her own insulin injections. Coping with diabetes helped her develop the discipline and self-awareness that she later credited in part with enabling her to achieve her life goals.   5

Juan Sotomayor eventually succumbed to his alcoholism; he died when Sonia was only 9 years old. His death strained the family but strengthened the relationship between Sonia and her grandmother, her *abuelita* (literally, "little grandmother," a term of endearment). Sonia's grandmother had always provided a safe haven from   6 the frequent arguments at her parents' house. Even when Sonia left her Bronx neighborhood to attend Princeton University, her grandmother sent her one dollar every week until the day she died (Sotomayor, 2013, p. 137). The relationship between the two of them had a profound effect on Justice Sotomayor. The nurture she received from her grandmother provided the sense of protection Sonia needed to defend herself against the cruelty of her neighborhood and the dysfunction of her family.

Sonia spoke primarily Spanish at home, loved the traditions of her Puerto Rican heritage, and visited Puerto Rico when her family could afford to make the trip. However, she experienced prejudice at the hands of those who did not understand her culture or who felt threatened by the advancements of Hispanic women. Her mother's answer to these difficulties and the impoverished world in which they lived was education. Sonia had what, as far as she knew, was the only set of encyclopedias in her neighborhood. Her mother purchased books with every little bit of extra money they acquired. Sonia read them insatiably, as well as any other books she could obtain. Reading transformed her world from the Bronx projects into a fantasy land created by words. Unfortunately, Sotomayor's poor neighborhood did not afford her the opportunity to read many classical works, nor did the poor private Catholic school that she attended. Only while attending Princeton did she realize that her exposure to the great literary works was deficient. In keeping with her self-reliant character, Justice Sotomayor found the time despite her academic requirements to read the classics while in college. She also challenged herself to learn and use ten new vocabulary words every day during summer vacations (Sotomayor, 2013, p. 135).

After graduating first in her eighth-grade class, Sonia attended Cardinal Spellman High School in the northeast Bronx. There, she enjoyed participating on the debate team and found that doing so helped her develop the skills necessary for structuring a good argument. Her teachers became her mentors and advisers. They pushed her to think critically and persuaded her to go to college. She graduated first in her high school class in 1972. A close friend suggested that she apply to the Ivy League school that he attended, and with the encouragement of her family, she did and was accepted into Princeton.

At Princeton, Sotomayor was one of the few minority students, as well as one of the few women, on the campus. (Princeton had only just become coeducational in the fall of 1969.) As the valedictorian of her high school class, she was a qualified applicant. However, she has made no secret of her belief that affirmative action played a role in her Princeton admittance. "It was a door opener that changed the course of my life" ("Sotomayor on Role," 2013). She wrote in her memoir that affirmative action students were routinely criticized for taking the place of a "deserving student":

> [T]here were vultures circling, ready to dive when we stumbled. The pressure to succeed was relentless, even if self-imposed out of fear and insecurity. For we all felt that if we did fail, we would be proving the critics right, and the doors that had opened just a crack to let us in would be slammed shut again. (Sotomayor, 2013, p. 145)

Sotomayor's initial semesters at Princeton revealed to her that, compared with her classmates' educations, her own suffered from several gaps. Her limited English, lack of writing skills, and dearth of exposure to critical thinking, together with the amount and level of academic work required, posed a major challenge for her. Her Princeton mentor, Peter Winn, recalled, "She was not the best student I taught in my seven years at Princeton—though she certainly was high on the list—but she was the one who took greatest advantage of the opportunities there and emerged most transformed by her experience" (Winn, 2009). Sotomayor's determination was the key to her success. Winn writes, "By graduation, Sonia could compete with anyone and succeed anywhere—including on the Supreme Court" (Winn, 2009). Sotomayor graduated from Princeton *summa cum laude* (with highest honor) in 1976.

Notwithstanding her impoverished upbringing and limited exposure to advanced academic experiences, her time at Princeton and her internal drive provided her with a strong sense of belonging at Yale Law School. She married her high school sweetheart and surrounded herself with a dynamic, diverse group of fellow-student friends, which contributed to her integration into the Yale environment.

12

Graduating from Yale Law School (in 1979) and passing the bar exam enabled Sotomayor to reach a lifelong dream. Since her childhood days watching *Perry Mason* (a dramatized courtroom television series broadcast in the 1950s and 1960s), Soto-mayor had dreamed of being a lawyer. In 1979, the district attorney in Manhattan offered her a job prosecuting criminals, many of whom were not unlike people she had known in her Bronx neighborhood. Her experiences in the Bronx enabled her to recognize the decency of many of these defendants, and this realization motivated her to protect her clients from overly aggressive prosecution (Stolberg, 2009). She received praise and at times criticism for her stalwart efforts to follow the rule of law and not be "pushed around" by judges or others (Stolberg, 2009).

13

For Justice Sotomayor, the "idea of heroism in action was a lawyer, the judge being a kind of superlawyer" (Sotomayor, 2013, p. 255). Her captivation with the concept of justice had grown during her adolescent years as she watched the nightly news depictions of courageous Southern judges defying mobs to improve civil rights. Her fighting spirit, her mother's humanity as a nurse, her grandmother's nurture, and her community and educational mentors' support combined to produce her desire to become a judge. Her goal was attained when she was nominated to the federal bench by President George H.W. Bush in 1991. Her judicial nomination received unanimous consent from the U.S. Senate, and Judge Sotomayor became the first Hispanic federal judge in the state of New York (Collins, 2010). After years of sterling performance in that role, Sotomayor was nominated by President Bill Clinton to the U.S. Court of Appeals for the Second Circuit, where she served from 1998 to 2009. President Obama nominated Sotomayor to serve on the U.S. Supreme Court in May 2009. Sotomayor's nomination was approved by the Senate on August 6, 2009, by a 68–31 vote, and thus she became the first Hispanic to serve on the Supreme Court ("Sonia Sotomayor," n.d.).

14

What insights can be gained from Justice Sotomayor's ascension to the Supreme Court? Of course, there are the usual lessons that one should have high aspirations and big dreams. Having those dreams—even though the odds are that they are unlikely ever to come true—is an essential ingredient for accomplishing remarkable feats. But as Sotomayor herself says, her success was more than just the result of having a dream. Was it her will, determination, and dedication to succeed that propelled her to accomplish her goal? Certainly, these attitudes were necessary. But Justice Sotomayor explains that something deeper than all those factors motivated her. She had "the desire to do for others." She saw this selfless love demonstrated by her *abuelita*, her mother, her helpful doctors, and her friends. This "synergy of love and gratitude, protection and purpose" planted and cultivated in her the desire to serve (Sotomayor, 2013, p. 255). That synergy eventually led her to assume one of the most prestigious and important positions in the world: associate justice of the Supreme Court of the United States.

15

References

Collins, L. (2010, January 11). Sonia Sotomayor's high-profile debut. *The New Yorker*. Retrieved from http://www.newyorker.com/reporting/2010/01/11/100111fa_fact_collins?currentPage=all

Sonia Sotomayor. (n.d.). The Oyez Project at IIT Chicago-Kent College of Law. Retrieved from http://www.oyez.org/justices/sonia_sotomayor

Sotomayor, S. (2013). *My Beloved World*. New York, NY: Knopf.

Sotomayor on role affirmative action played in her life. (2013, January 11). Retrieved from http://www.cbsnews.com/news/sotomayor-on-role-affirmative-action-played-in-her-life

Stolberg, S. G. (2009, May 26). Sotomayor, a trailblazer and a dreamer. *The New York Times*. Retrieved from http://www.nytimes.com/2009/05/27/us/politics/27websotomayor.html?pagewanted=all

The White House, Office of the Press Secretary. (2009, March 26). Remarks by the president in nominating Judge Sonia Sotomayor to the United States Supreme Court (Press Release). Retrieved from http://www.whitehouse.gov/the_press_office/Remarks-by-the-President-in-Nominating-Judge-Sonia-Sotomayor-to-the-United-States-Supreme-Court

Winn, P. (2009, July 12). Mentor at Princeton recalls Sotomayor's evolution. *The Washington Post*. Retrieved from http://www.washingtonpost.com/wp-dyn/content/article/2009/07/09 /AR2009070902391.html?sid=ST2009071302618

Using Your Annotations.   Use your annotations and key words to write a one-page summary of the reading. In your summary, identify the writer's thesis statement, the major supporting points, the support for the major supporting points, and any other information needed to complete the summary.

Thinking about the Text

1. What does Ramon hope to accomplish by writing this article?
2. What does she mean when she writes that "the primary reason for [Sotomayor's] perseverance was actually fear"?
3. Why was Sotomayor's diabetes diagnosis a turning point for her in her childhood?
4. What are some of the adversities Sotomayor had to overcome in her life?
5. Based on the text, how do you think a friend might describe Justice Sotomayor?

The Writer's Techniques

1. Why do you think the author uses quotes throughout her essay? What do these quotes add to readers' understanding of Justice Sotomayor?
2. What method of ordering information did the writer use to present Sotomayor's story?
3. Which parts of the reading did you find the most interesting? Why? What can you learn—as a writer—from analyzing the parts of the reading that you found interesting? Explain.

Brief-Response Assignments

1. The reading makes connections between events in Sotomayor's life and the effects of those events. Select one event in her life and discuss its effects, according to the reading.

2. How did the support that Sotomayor received from her grandmother translate into feelings of security and strength?

3. Write a paragraph in which you discuss what it means to persist even when facing adversity. Use an example from the reading to explore this subject.

Essay Assignments

1. Write an essay in which you identify three or four of the character traits that made Sotomayor successful in life. Why were these traits important? Provide examples from the reading to explain.

2. Sotomayor had a dream and worked hard to achieve it. Most children start life with dreams, but many of them eventually give up on their dreams and accept a life different from what they had planned. What enables some people to achieve their dreams while others never do? Write an essay in which you explore this topic.

3. Sotomayor believes affirmative action is a helpful policy. What is affirmative action? Why was it implemented? What is the controversy about affirmative action? Finally, how does Sotomayor defend affirmative action? Write an essay in which you answer these questions. If you use sources for ideas or quotes, be sure to give credit to the sources. ↺

Thematic Assignment

Use the readings in this thematic unit to write an essay that answers one of the following questions.

a. Read the following explanation of *resilience* from the American Psychological Association's Practice Central Web site:

> Resilience is the process of adapting well in the face of adversity, trauma, tragedy, threats or significant sources of stress—such as family and relationship problems, serious health problems, or workplace and financial stressors. Resilience is not a trait that people either have or do not have. It involves behaviors, thoughts and actions that anyone can learn and develop.

Resilience is not something people are born with; it is something that they can develop. Write an essay in which you explain how to develop resilience. Use the sources in this thematic unit for information. Provide concrete examples, and consider using hypothetical examples if you do not have real-life examples that fit your purpose.

b. Thousands of soldiers have returned from the wars in Afghanistan and Iraq with PTSD as well as other injuries, both physical and mental. Read the article entitled "Bouncing Back" in this section. Which of the suggestions Balmain presents might be helpful for soldiers who return with PTSD? Write an essay in which you present methods soldiers might use to overcome the stress that accompanies them as they return from war. Be sure to give credit to Balmain for each of the ideas you use from her essay.

c. Write an essay in which you present the best ideas you encountered in the readings about dealing with adversity. Select three to four ideas, and argue why they would be effective in dealing with adversity.

d. Write an argument essay on when *accepting* is the best way to deal with adversity and when *fighting back* is the best way. Which kinds of situations should be accepted, and which kinds of adversity are best met with resistance? Alternatively, when might a response include both acceptance and resistance? Write an essay in which you discuss hypothetical situations that fit into each of these three categories.

Be sure to cite any sources from which you obtain ideas or quotes. Include a works cited or references page with your essay. For additional information on source-based writing, follow the steps in the Quick Start Guide to Integrated Reading and Writing Assignments.

Text Credits

More than sixty years after the landmark US Supreme Court decision in *Brown v. Board of Education*, which made segregation in public schools illegal, the issue of segregation is still being debated. One question under debate is whether self-segregation in education and elsewhere holds advantages for minority groups in particular and society in general.

Self-segregation by race or ethnic group shows up in lunchrooms across America; it is seen in churches, prisons, college classrooms, and almost anywhere groups of people congregate. Is this common and sometimes unconscious separation good for minority groups in particular and society as a whole? Is it simply a natural impulse to segregate, and if so, are there any reasons for resisting this impulse?

These are the questions explored in the four readings that follow. As you read, think about your own experiences and the self-segregation you have participated in or observed.

Author and Context.   Debra Humphreys received her BA from Williams College and her PhD in English from Rutgers University. Dr. Humphreys is currently the vice president for policy and public engagement at the Association of American Colleges and Universities. "Campus Diversity and Student Self-Segregation: Separating Myths from Facts" appeared on the Diversity Web in December 2008.

Previewing.   Have pen and paper (or a computer) on hand as you read. Think about the title, and then study the author's biography and the contextual information about the reading. Next, preview the selection. From the information you have gathered, determine the topic. What predictions can you make about the reading's content? Jot down your answers.

Reading Critically and Annotating.   As you read, annotate the main idea, the major supporting points, key words, and a few passages that would make good quotations. Either write in your book or make annotations on sticky notes.

As you find key ideas, annotate them. In the article that follows, Debra Humphreys weighs in on the issue of segregation on college campuses. Determine Humphreys's viewpoint as you read.

After reading and annotating, create an information sheet on which you record and organize your annotations as well as your thoughts about the content of the reading.

Campus Diversity and Student Self-Segregation: Separating Myths from Facts

By Debra Humphreys

When students went off to college this Fall, they entered more diverse campuses than ever before. For many students, in fact, their college community is the most diverse they have ever encountered. Most students entering college today come from high schools that are predominantly or exclusively one racial or ethnic group. Given this reality, how are students interacting with one another educationally and socially in college? How socially segregated are college campuses? Is campus diversity leading to educational benefits for today's college students or are students too separated into enclaves on campus to benefit from campus diversity?   **1**

> **enclave:** a small, distinct area or group enclosed or isolated within a larger group.

A survey of the most recent research suggests that, indeed, campus diversity is leading to significant educational and social benefits for all college students. It also suggests that, contrary to popular reports, student self-segregation is not, in fact, a dominant feature of campus life today. This paper summarizes new research on campus diversity and on the actual extent of student self-segregation and interaction across racial/ethnic lines on college campuses today.   **2**

This new research is little known outside of the academic community and critics have ignored it as they describe campus life today to reflect their own political agendas. Critics of both affirmative action and campus diversity programs are skeptical about the educational benefits of campus diversity; they allege that racial and ethnic self-segregation among students is widespread and that it undermines the educational promise of a genuinely multicultural college community. In addition, some critics suggest that campus diversity programs themselves, including African American and Ethnic Studies programs, racial/ethnic student groups, theme houses and dorms, encourage separation rather than community and undermine intergroup contact and the learning that can result from it.   **3**

The latest educational research suggests a very different picture of campus life.   **4**

While the phenomenon does not appear to be widespread, given the degree of continuing segregation in America's schools and communities, it isn't surprising that college students today do sometimes choose to live, socialize, or study together with other students from similar backgrounds. Contrary to many commentators' claims, however, research suggests that this clustering isn't widespread; it doesn't prevent students from interacting across racial/ethnic lines; and it may be an essential ingredient in many students' persistence and success in college.   **5**

Is student self-segregation prevalent on today's diverse college campuses?

While there are situations in which college students may cluster in racial/ethnic groups, research suggests that there is a high degree of intergroup contact on college campuses and that self-segregation by race/ethnicity is not a dominant feature on diverse college campuses today.

6

In a recent study, Anthony Lising Antonio, assistant professor of education at Stanford University, examined the extent to which students perceive racial balkanization at the University of California, Los Angeles (UCLA) and whether their perceptions reflect the reality of actual close friendship patterns.

7   **balkanization:** the process of breaking into small groups.

Compared to many American colleges and universities, UCLA is a very diverse campus. When this study was conducted (between 1994 and 1997), the undergraduate student body was approximately 40% white, 35% Asian American, 16% Latino, 6% African American, and just over 1% Native American.

8

Antonio found that students at UCLA do, indeed, view their campus as racially balkanized.

9

More than 90% of students in his surveys agreed that students predominantly cluster by race and ethnicity on campus. A small majority (52%) said that students rarely socialize across racial lines.

10

Antonio, however, didn't stop at just measuring perceptions. He also calculated the actual racial/ethnic diversity or homogeneity of close friendship groups on campus. Antonio categorized the racial diversity of each student's friendship groups as one of the following: 1) Homogenous—the largest racial/ethnic group makes up 100% of the friendship group; 2) Predominantly one race/ethnicity—the largest racial/ethnic group makes up 75–99% of the friendship group; 3) Majority one race/ethnicity—the largest racial/ethnic group makes up 51–74% of the friendship group; and 4) No majority— the largest racial/ethnic group makes up 50% or less of the friendship group.

11   **homogeneity:** composition from like parts, elements, or characteristics; opposite of *diversity*.

Just 17% of UCLA students, or about one in six, reported having friendship groups that were racially and ethnically homogenous.

12

Homogenous groups and those groups with predominantly one race/ethnicity together account for about one-quarter of the sample.

13

The most common friendship group on campus (46%), however, was racially and ethnically mixed with no racial or ethnic group constituting a majority.

14

At the level of student friendship groups, then, racial and ethnic balkanization is not a dominant, overall campus characteristic at UCLA. Several other earlier studies also suggest a high degree of student interaction across racial and ethnic lines at campuses across the country, especially among students of color.

15

A 1991 study that examined patterns of intergroup contact at 390 institutions across the country confirmed that self-segregation is not a general pattern among students of color. The authors of this study examined the frequency with which students dined, roomed, socialized, or dated someone from a racial/ethnic group different from their own.

16

Chicano, Asian American, and African American students reported widespread and frequent interaction across race/ethnicity in these informal situations. White students were least likely to report engaging in any of these activities across race/ethnicity.

17

Sixty-nine percent of Asian Americans and 78% of Mexican American students frequently dined with someone of a different ethnic or racial background compared with 55% of African American students and 21% of white students.

18

Nearly 42% of Asian American students reported interracial or interethnic dating compared with 24% of Mexican Americans, 13% of African Americans, and 4% of white students.

19

What characterizes student interactions within and across racial/ethnic lines on campus? Why do some students cluster by race/ethnicity on college campuses?

Understanding student interactions across racial/ethnic lines requires an appreciation of the influence of the widespread residential segregation that characterizes American society. It also requires an appreciation of how white American higher education still is, despite its increasing diversity. Most students of color who do not attend historically black colleges or universities attend overwhelmingly white institutions.

20

A 1991 study of student life at [the University of California at] Berkeley, an unusually diverse college campus, describes the experience of campus life as a complex phenomenon that encompasses both some student-initiated racial/ethnic clustering and substantial amounts of interracial interactions.

21

This study also found, however, that 70% of all undergraduates agreed with the statement, *I'd like to meet more students from ethnic and cultural backgrounds that are different from my own.*

22

A forthcoming book by Richard Light of Harvard University also suggests that students from a wide array of racial/ethnic groups desire intergroup contact and see the educational and social benefits of such interactions.

23

The widespread segregation by race that still characterizes much of the rest of American life is, however, having an impact on how students interact with one another on college campuses.

24

A 1997 study at the University of Michigan found that students' friendship patterns closely reflected the make-ups of their high schools and home neighborhoods. This study confirmed that a majority of all students, but a very high percentage of white students, came from highly segregated high schools and neighborhoods.

25

The Michigan study also found that white students had the most segregated friendship patterns on campus of all ethnic groups.

26

The reality is that students of color have much more intergroup contact than do white students, but their patterns of interaction need to be understood in light of their psychological development. Research by psychologist Beverly Daniel Tatum, Dean of the College at Mt. Holyoke College, suggests that there are complex psychological reasons why college students may choose to cluster in racial/ethnic groups. She argues that racial grouping is a developmental process in response to an environmental stressor, racism. Joining with one's peers for support in the face of stress is a positive coping strategy. There is a developmental need on the part of many college students to explore the meaning of one's identity with others who are engaged in a similar process.

27

What difference does racial/ethnic clustering make when it does occur?

Recent research, including Tatum's and that of others, suggests that racial/ethnic clustering can be an important component contributing to the psychological health and educational success of many students. Research also suggests that this clustering need

28

not prevent students from achieving the educational benefits of intergroup contact within college classrooms and on college campuses.

The 1991 study of 390 institutions cited above found that ethnic-specific activities were not impeding intergroup contact for the students who participated in them. Programs like racial/ethnic theme houses and study groups seem to help students of color persist and succeed in college and seem to increase their involvement overall with other areas of college life in which they interact frequently across racial/ethnic lines.

29   **Impede:** to obstruct, hinder, or hamper.

Other studies confirm these findings:

30

A 1994 study of Latino students suggests that students belonging to Latino organizations increased their adjustment and attachment to their colleges and universities.

31

Two other studies, one in 1994 and another in 1996, also found positive benefits of participation in racial and ethnic groups and that these groups also fostered rather than impeded intergroup contact.

32

Another 1989 study found that a targeted student support program was positively related to African American students' persistence in college and their degree status.

33

Given the relatively high level of intergroup contact and the existence of some racial/ethnic clustering, what is the impact of campus diversity on today's college students?

Research suggests a variety of positive educational outcomes that result from being educated in a diverse environment. It also suggests a positive impact for those students with high degrees of intergroup contact.

34

Patricia Gurin, professor of psychology at the University of Michigan, recently compiled a report summarizing three parallel empirical analyses of university students. Her report suggests that,

35

> A racially and ethnically diverse university student body has far-ranging and significant benefits for all students, non-minorities and minorities alike. Students learn better in such an environment and are better prepared to become active participants in our pluralistic, democratic society once they leave school. In fact, patterns of racial segregation and separation historically rooted in our national life can be broken by diversity experiences in higher education.

36   **pluralistic:** having multiple aspects or parts. In this context, the term is a synonym for diverse.

Gurin's research demonstrates that the diverse environment provided by many colleges today contributes to students' intellectual and social development. She suggests that racial diversity in a college or university student body provides the very features that research has determined are central to producing the conscious mode of thought educators demand from their students.

37

Gurin also found that these positive effects of campus diversity extend beyond graduation.

38

> Diversity experiences during college had impressive effects on the extent to which graduates in the national study were living racially and ethnically integrated lives in the post-college world. Students with the most diversity experiences during college had the most cross-racial interactions five years after leaving college.

39

The study by Antonio mentioned above also confirms that campus diversity is having a positive impact on today's college students.

40

Antonio examined the impact of the diverse friendship groups he found to be com-   41
mon at UCLA. Controlling for important background information such as gender,
socio-economic status, and the racial diversity of pre-college friendship groups, Antonio found that friendship group diversity contributed to greater interracial interaction
outside the friendship group and stronger commitments to racial understanding.

Another important arena of college life, of course, is the classroom. On diverse   42
campuses, many students are now being educated in highly diverse classrooms in
which they are studying a much wider array of subjects that include content about
previously neglected groups. These classes are also having a significant positive educational impact on both majority and minority students as well.

Conclusions: Is there cause for alarm, hope, or celebration?

There is little cause for alarm, some cause for celebration and much hope for what lies   43
ahead. The reality is that while there is still a long way to go before American higher education will truly reflect the full diversity of American society, college campuses are
becoming much more diverse and their diverse campus environments are having a significant positive effect on this generation of students.

College campuses are not dominated by widespread racial/ethnic segregation and   44
the racial/ethnic clustering that does occur isn't impeding intergroup contact. In fact,
the existence of racial/ethnic groups and activities, along with other comprehensive
campus diversity initiatives, is contributing to the success of today's college students
and preparing them to help build a healthier multicultural America for the future.

Using Your Annotations.   Use your annotations and key words to write a one-
page summary of the reading. In your summary, identify the writer's thesis statement,
the major supporting points, the support for the major supporting points, and any other
information needed to complete the summary.

Thinking about the Text

1. What is Humphreys's position on self-segregation?
2. What educational or social benefits might college students gain by self-
   segregating into ethnic groups?
3. What does the writer say about the differences between self-segregation in high
   schools and self-segregation on college campuses?
4. What would the writer like to see campuses do about self-segregation?
5. How common is racial self-segregation, according to Humphreys?

The Writer's Techniques

1. Humphreys cites a variety of sources to provide proof for her claims. What kind
   of information does she quote from these sources? What function does she hope
   each type of information will serve?
2. Look at your annotations. Which of the following types of supporting details
   does the writer use—comparison and contrast, cause and effect, definition,
   process analysis, classification, illustration, or narrative?
3. What ordering strategy does the writer use to present her information?

Brief-Response Assignments

1. Write a paragraph discussing how college students might consciously try to be
   more inclusive of others outside their own racial group.

2. What can colleges do to encourage more intergroup interaction? Explain.
3. Have you ever observed or participated in self-segregation? If so, reflect on your observation or experience. If you are writing about your observations, why do you think some people choose to self-segregate? If you are writing about your experience, why did you choose to self-segregate? Explain.

Essay Assignments

1. Write an essay in which you discuss the self-segregation you have observed on your college campus or elsewhere. Discuss the potentially positive and potentially negative effects of the self-segregation you have observed.
2. People who are critical of self-segregation claim that it limits a person's full development. What, exactly, is their argument? What are the problems of self-segregation? Write an essay in which you explain the problems fully.
3. Write an essay giving ways to add diversity to the college experience. What can students do to experience more than their own culture? ↻

Author and Context.   As a contributing writer for *USA Today* and *The Huffington Post*, Ernest Owens writes on a range of social issues, including race relations, social media and policy, and entertainment. His work has also appeared on the *Good Men Project, Al Jazeera English, The Root,* and the Oprah Winfrey Network. "Equal When Separate" appeared in *The Daily Pennsylvanian* on September 13, 2012.

Previewing.   Have pen and paper (or a computer) on hand as you read. Think about the title, and then study the author's biography and the contextual information about the reading. Next, preview the selection. From the information you have gathered, determine the topic. What predictions can you make about the reading's content? Jot down your answers.

Reading Critically and Annotating.   As you read, annotate the main idea, the major supporting points, key words, and a few passages that would make good quotations. Either write in your book or make annotations on sticky notes.

As you find key ideas, annotate them. What is Owens's opinion on the topic of self-segregation? What are his reasons for his opinion? Note any questions that come to mind as you read.

After reading and annotating, create an information sheet on which you record and organize your annotations as well as your thoughts about the content of the reading.

Equal When Separate

By Ernest Owens

Some of my favorite moments at Penn have happened at 1920 Commons—most of them on a Saturday morning over brunch with friends.

We usually laugh loudly and take comical jabs at one another—each more intense than the last. But then comes a moment when our antics dim and someone in the group points out the fact that we're the only black students in the room and shouldn't be so loud about it.

Someone usually says, "I wonder what they think about us being so loud and black over here . . . we are being so self-segregating."

1   **Penn:** University of Pennsylvania.

2

3

For a long time, I felt the same way. Was I being culturally limiting by eating brunch every weekend with my black peers? Was this self-segregation?   4

Then I looked around the other tables at Commons and saw separate groups of white students and Asian students congregated over waffles and bacon. That made me wonder: do they ever have the same discussion that I just had with my friends?   5

I bet they don't. Otherwise, we would all mingle over pancakes every weekend like they do at the United Nations cafeteria. Fantasy aside, minorities on campus shouldn't feel a sense of guilt when they choose to hang out with friends from a similar background.   6

It didn't take a UMOJA, Makuu or Black Student League event for me to get together with my friends. We just found each other as a group of black students looking to kick start the weekend together.   7

UMOJA, Makuu, Black Student League: names of African-American student organizations.

Debates about self-segregation are nothing new. W.E.B. Du Bois, Penn's honorary emeritus professor of sociology and Africana studies, was a strong proponent of developing economic enterprises exclusive to blacks.   8

Coretta Scott King, however, spoke out vocally against the practice when she said that segregation "is still wrong when it is requested by black people."   9

This idea is also explored at length in one of my favorite novels, *Invisible Man* by Ralph Ellison, published in 1952.   10

While the media and politicians attempt to convince us that we live in a post-racial society, the truth is, self-segregation persists and is a natural instinct.   11

Not everyone is going to get along all the time. It is normal for people to gravitate toward those who are similar. It is necessary for each of us to find a "safe space" where we feel accepted and immune from misunderstandings.   12

Most Quakers devote a substantial amount of their time and energy to others. We're always working on group projects with people we'd rather never see again. Or we're involved in six different student groups where we have to interact with students from all walks of life.   13

Quakers: the name that the athletic teams of the University of Pennsylvania use. So the word is used to refer to Penn students in general.

While there is a lot to be learned from interacting with diverse people, the question arises: when can we take a step back from the face we strive so hard to display and be ourselves?   14

The fabric of Penn life is woven by strings of separate communities. While we work together to produce equality, especially in an academic setting, each community is distinct. Most of our successes have come from different groups that worked hard to achieve a goal.   15

There is something aesthetically and socially pleasing about seeing the internal workings of these individual groups. When I go to Hillel for lunch, it always amazes me to see a close-knit circle of Jewish students. I also appreciate the ability to see groups of exchange students from Germany, Israel and China occupy the floors of Du Bois College House every semester.   16

In essence, we should stop attempting to sacrifice our identities and embrace self-segregation.   17

By virtue of being members of the Penn community, we have already made strides to produce a more equal society. But in the words of Malcolm X, "We cannot think of uniting with others until after we have first united among ourselves."   18

Using Your Annotations.   Use your annotations and key words to write a one-page summary of the reading. In your summary, identify the writer's thesis statement, the major supporting points, the support for the major supporting points, and any other information needed to complete your summary.

Thinking about the Text

1. What does Owens say about self-segregation on college campuses?
2. Explain what the writer means by "culturally limiting."
3. For what purpose did Owens write this article? Explain your answer.
4. For whom did he write the article? Explain your answer.
5. The writer contends that self-segregation is a natural instinct. What reasons does he give for this belief?

The Writer's Techniques

1. How does Owens use quotations in his essay? What purposes do the quotations in his essay serve?
2. The writer uses first and third person in this essay. What is the effect of using first person where the writer does? What would be the effect of using only third person? Is the writer's choice to use first person in some places a good choice?
3. The writer uses an extended anecdote in his introduction. How does this anecdote set the tone for the rest of the essay?

Brief-Response Assignments

1. Based on this essay, define *self-segregation.*
2. The author presents one side of the self-segregation argument. Write a paragraph presenting the other side.
3. Write a paragraph in which you agree or disagree with this statement: *Minorities on campus shouldn't feel a sense of guilt when they choose to hang out with friends from a similar background.*

Essay Assignments

1. The writer quotes Malcolm X as saying, "We cannot think of uniting with others until after we have first united among ourselves." What do you think would be the long-term impact of following this rationale? Would it result in a greater sense of cooperation with others or a deeper entrenchment in our own social groups? Why? Write an essay explaining the potential effects of Malcolm X's idea.
2. Some people are hesitant to move out of their self-segregated groups, not because they have prejudices against others but because moving out of one's group means moving out of one's comfort zone. Why is such hesitancy common? What particular barriers must individuals address if they want to move out of their self-segregated circles? Write an essay explaining your answers.
3. What is the difference between self-segregation and the kind of racial segregation that used to be legal in the United States? Write an essay in which you contrast these two types of segregation. ↻

Author and Context.   The Australian journalist Michael Gawenda served as editor of *The Age* from 1997 to 2004. He was named the first director of the Centre for Advanced Journalism at the University of Melbourne in 2009. "What Happened to the Dream?" appeared in *The Age* in October 2005.

Previewing.   Have pen and paper (or a computer) on hand as you read. Think about the title, and then study the author's biography and the contextual information about the reading. Next, preview the selection. From the information you have gathered, determine the topic. What predictions can you make about the reading's content? Jot down your answers.

Reading Critically and Annotating.   As you read, annotate the main idea, the major supporting points, key words, and a few passages that would make good quotations. Either write in your book or make annotations on sticky notes.

As you find key ideas, annotate them. As an Australian, Gawenda can look at the United States from a unique perspective. How does his vantage point affect his ability to assess race relations in the United States? What insights does he have to offer? Make a note of these insights as you read.

After reading and annotating, create an information sheet on which you record and organize your annotations as well as your thoughts about the content of the reading.

What Happened to the Dream?

By Michael Gawenda

In Anacostia, on the street corners, outside the storefronts, along the littered pavements and in front of the rundown row houses, the young men of Washington's underclass spend their days. They do business, they huddle in groups. They look to outsiders dangerous and menacing; this is a place where whites are unwelcome. Here, in Washington's south-east, away from the grandeur of Capitol Hill or the simple, soaring optimism of the Washington Memorial, is one metaphor for race relations in America. 1

Travel a few kilometers north, through neighborhoods once like Anacostia but now gentrified, overwhelmingly white, inner-city suburbs, and you get to the Gold Coast, with its tree-lined streets and substantial houses and pretty gardens. This wealthy black neighborhood of Washington is another metaphor for America's race relations. 2

> **gentrification:** the process in which people buy inner-city properties and transform them into high-income residences or businesses.

Washington and its surrounding suburbs in the adjacent states of Virginia and Maryland is, in some ways, a microcosm of race relations in America. In this imperial capital of the world's greatest power, more than 50 years after the US Supreme Court ended school segregation—ruling that the concept of "separate but equal" when it came to education was unconstitutional—the city's public schools have virtually no white children. 3

It is a segregated city, with perhaps Silver Spring, one small neighborhood near the Maryland-DC border approaching something like an integrated community. 4

This segregation is not a matter of class; Washington's growing black middle-class lives in either the Gold Coast area of DC or, if they have children and want a suburban life, in Montgomery County where they send their children to predominantly black schools. They are a world away from the schools where the black and mostly poor children of DC go. 5

Across America, somewhere between 5 and 10 percent of American families live in integrated communities, and across America, the public school system is almost totally segregated. What does this mean and what does it say about race relations in America? More than 300 years after the first African slaves were brought here, black and white Americans, in the main, exist in parallel universes, separated by culture, language and history. 6

Like everything in this country where dreams and ideals bump up against harsh reality yet remain as potent as ever, where neighborhood still means something, where guns are invested with almost spiritual meaning, and where America as the promised 7 land remains the country's great unifying myth, no single metaphor can encompass relations between blacks and whites. When New Orleans was drowned by Hurricane Katrina a month ago, the most shocking and shaming images for Americans were of black poverty, helplessness and abandonment.

The New Orleans police chief and the city's mayor appeared on *The Oprah Winfrey Show* and told of murders, rapes and bodies stored in the basement of the Superdome while no one came to rescue the people inside. Mayor Ray Nagin told tales of armed gangs roaming the streets, looting and shooting anyone, including police, who stood in their way. Where, he cried, was the national guard? Where was the army, the marines?

Police Chief Eddie Compass, who has since resigned, Nagin and, of course, Winfrey are black, though her audience is predominantly white. Not once did she ask Compass or Nagin whether they had credible eyewitness testimony to all this horror. Like a game of broken telephone, the stories became increasingly lurid—and were mostly untrue.

There were no murders and no rapes in the Superdome. There were no bodies stacked in the basement. There were no armed gangs shooting at police and members of the Army Corps of Engineers. These were fantasies retold, without much checking, by hundreds of reporters in the chaos of Katrina's aftermath, in the rush to be first with the story and, crucially, because these fantasies played into half-conscious but widely held racial and class stereotypes.

Indeed the Katrina disaster offers a neat but ultimately simplistic and distorted encapsulation of black-white relations in America: poor and powerless African-Americans are left to suffer and die, preyed on by their own violent and lawless underclass, while their white compatriots look the other way.

In the days and weeks after Katrina, on cable television talk shows, on newspaper op-ed pages, even in Congress, race and poverty, for the first time in years, was a major issue.

When he gave his televised address to the nation from New Orleans, George Bush, for the first time in his presidency, said poverty and race were connected. Americans had seen that there was a "deep, persistent poverty and that poverty has roots in a history of racial discrimination which cuts off generations from the opportunity of America."

Both *Newsweek* and *Time,* for the first time since the O. J. Simpson trial, carried cover stories on race and poverty in America; all the major TV networks had current affairs specials on the subject; in Congress, politicians from both parties expressed dismay over what Katrina had revealed about the lives of the poor. But there is a weariness about all this talk, a lack of confidence that the intractable problems that Katrina revealed have solutions or even that there can be agreement across the great conservative-liberal divide on just what those problems might be.

Ten years ago this month, Louis Farrakhan, the Nation of Islam leader, led his Million Man March to Washington, and 10 years ago this month, in Los Angeles, O. J. Simpson was acquitted of the murder of his white wife Nicole and her friend Ronald Goldman.

The Simpson trial divided Americans along racial lines; 83 percent of blacks agreed with the verdict compared with 37 percent of whites. Farrakhan's march attracted hundreds of thousands of black men to Washington, despite the fact that he was seen as an extremist, a sexist and some argue, an anti-Semite. It was a powerful statement by black men that they wanted to take responsibility for their lives and the lives of their children.

Ten years on, the Simpson anniversary has passed without much notice; the trial and verdict, which many thought would have a profound effect on race relations, has

8

9

10

11

12

13

14

15

16

17

broken telephone: a game in which one person whispers a message to another person, who then whispers it to another, and so on. At the end of the game, the message is announced, and usually the message is different from the one that the first person whispered. The point of the game is to show how inaccuracies occur in the communication process.

intractable: impossible to solve; incurable.

been virtually forgotten and Simpson, living in obscurity in Florida, is the occasional butt of jokes by black stand-up comedians.

And 10 years on, Farrakhan's Millions More protest, . . . to mark the anniversary of the Million Man March, attracted just 20,000 people, in the main to protest the Bush Administration's response to Hurricane Katrina.   18

Polls show that support for Bush is down about the 2 percent mark among African-Americans, compared with the 11.9 percent of the black vote he received at November's presidential election, a 3 percent increase compared with 2000, mostly because of conservative African-Americans who shared his views on gay marriage and "culture of life" issues. Now, black leaders from Jesse Jackson to Al Sharpton to Farrakhan argue that in New Orleans, the world saw that if you're poor and black in the US, you end up invisible and abandoned.   19

But the black and poor of New Orleans were invisible not just to America's white middle-class and the conservative and liberal elites, but to the essentially black leadership of the city and to the growing black middle-class in the country, which now represents almost 40 percent of America's 39 million African-Americans.   20

The life journey of Reverend Charles White, the regional head of the National Association for the Advancement of Colored People, based in Atlanta, Georgia, and covering most of the Deep South encapsulates the success and the failure of 40 years of civil rights activism, of landmark civil rights legislation and of government programs that were meant to bridge the racial and economic divide between black and white America.   21

White is in his early 40s, passionate and outgoing, and articulate in the way people of great conviction often are, and he is both angry and optimistic about the future. The child of farm laborers in the rural hinterland of Charleston, South Carolina, White calls himself a poster child for what can be achieved through government programs and by building on the legacy of the great civil rights leaders of the '60s.   22

hinterland: a remote or outlying area.

"We are the first generation of African-Americans afforded opportunities and access to institutions that were closed to African-Americans just a generation ago," he says. "We have made giant strides. Look at me. Were it not for the civil rights movement and the federal government programs that followed the big civil rights changes, I would never have had the chance to go to college.   23

"Those programs gave me simple things like milk and cheese, took me out of my poor segregated high school on weekends to Charleston College, where a whole new world opened up for me and where I was shown that I could be more than a farm laborer like generations of farm laborers in my family.   24

"Those programs have been cut during the Bush presidency. There are a thousand young men like me wandering around in Charleston County and tens of thousands across the South who would give anything to have the opportunities I had who simply won't be afforded them."   25

Atlanta was the birthplace of Martin Luther King, Jr., the city where the first sit-ins by blacks at all-white lunch counters were held in the early '60s, and where King preached his message of non-violent protest at the Ebenezer Baptist Church. It was in Atlanta where he was arrested for the first time and jailed for breaking the city's rigidly enforced color bar.   26

This is no longer the Atlanta where King's great crusade for black civil rights began. It is a big, sprawling, growing city, the headquarters for a number of multinational corporations, including Coca-Cola, a magnet for mostly small-town white southern middle-class go-getters, young northerners and increasingly, Latinos attracted by job opportunities, low state taxes and relatively cheap housing.   27

Some time in the next few years, Atlanta will cease to be a majority black city, and when that happens, the political dynamics will change and a predominantly black city government, which has ruled Atlanta for decades, will be replaced by a white mayor and a majority white city council.

28

All over the south, this growing urbanization is changing the demographics and the economy of what has been America's poorest region and where black Americans, for more than a hundred years after the civil war freed them from slavery, lived like serfs, without rights, without economic opportunities, abused and discriminated against, at best patronized and treated like children and at worst, lynched and humiliated by an overwhelming racist white population.

29

serf: a slave who was attached to the lord's land and transferred with it from one owner to another.

On the streets surrounding the Martin Luther King Centre, just beyond the Martin Luther King museum and gift shop, past the Martin Luther King Memorial Pool in the center of which is King's white marble tomb and just beyond the renovated Ebenezer Baptist Church, there is black despair.

30

Panhandlers, unemployed young black men, young black women with ancient faces, battered apartment blocks, menace and hopelessness—indeed this could be Anacostia in Washington or the battered heart of Detroit or perhaps the 9th district of New Orleans before the great flood. For all the changes in Atlanta, the violent crime rate remains the highest in the country, just ahead of Detroit, and Atlanta has the third highest murder rate behind the black-majority cities of Baltimore and New Orleans.

31

Things change and things stay the same. Or get worse. More than 37 million Americans live below the official poverty line, set at $19,500 for a family of four and just under $9000 for people living alone; during every year of the Bush Administration, on average an extra 1 million people joined the ranks of the poor.

32

While the poverty rate for white Americans is about 8 percent, for African-Americans it is close to 25 percent. Most of that poverty is concentrated in the inner-city neighborhoods of America's cities from which the whites fled to the suburbs after the black riots of the '60s and which newly middle-class blacks abandoned as soon as they had the means to do so.

33

Professor Michael Giles is a political scientist at Emory University in Atlanta, who has worked on inner-city renewal programs and who is pessimistic about the prospect of solving the multitude of problems that afflict the mostly black inner-city communities that, in many ways, are the casualties of globalization and the decline of unskilled manufacturing jobs.

34

"There has been a huge growth in the black middle class, basically because of the good economic times in the '90s, but at the same time, all the government programs, all the development of so-called enterprise zones in our inner-city areas, all the work on addressing generational poverty and family dysfunction in these communities has been only marginally successful," he says.

35

"You know, there's been lots of talk after New Orleans about how the Federal Government was slow to respond because most of the victims in that city of Hurricane Katrina were poor and black. We were shocked by what we saw. We had developed amnesia about poverty in our country.

36

"But a lot of black middle-class people had amnesia as well. The leadership of New Orleans was black and they had amnesia. We have had black leadership in Atlanta for a long time but they have not significantly improved the lives of poor black people here."

37

Giles considers himself to be a liberal. The department of political science at Emory has several black professors. Giles tells of how delighted he is that some of his regular tennis partners are black—engineers, academics, businessmen.

38

Asked whether beyond playing tennis together, he meets his tennis partners   39
socially, Giles pauses and then says, no, he does not.

"Middle-class blacks mix with middle-class whites in the workplace but there's   40
still a comfort-level issue, a fear of being slighted, of racial put-downs that means
middle-class blacks prefer to live and even worship among their own.

"We have wonderful African-American middle-class communities here, with   41
great amenities, great homes, great schools. Yes, more than four decades after
desegregation, self-segregation rules so that our schools and our churches and our
neighborhoods remain as segregated as they ever were."

Eleanor Holmes Norton was a civil rights leader in the '60s and now represents   42
Washington DC in Congress. She worries that in the poorer black areas of Washington,
and in similar areas across America, a sea-change is taking place, a change that if it
continues, will mean "we will have whole non-viable communities."

"It is impossible to overestimate what has happened to our community in only a   43
couple of generations and what might happen to the next generation if it continues at
this pace," she says.

What she means is that there has been a fundamental breakdown of family life in   44
these communities—about 70 percent of babies are born outside marriage, to young
single mothers, many of them teenagers who are invariably abandoned by the fathers
of their children.

"Disintegration of the family is the greatest problem facing the African-American   45
community," she says. "And there are no simple, easy answers to this. Government has
a role, but you have to be careful. How do you get into someone's family and try and
save it, convince young men that they have responsibilities, young men who often feel
they have no future and no hope?"

Farrakhan's Million Man March was meant to inspire young black men to take   46
responsibility for their children, their families and perhaps it worked for some. What
cannot be denied is that more than a century-and-a-half after the end of slavery, more
than 50 years after the end of legal segregation, more than 40 years after landmark
civil rights legislation ended legal discrimination, black and white Americans live in
separate worlds, informed by their different histories and life experience, their different takes on what it means to be American.

For all the high-profile blacks in American life, the athletes, the black success   47
stories in politics such as Condoleezza Rice and Colin Powell, the genius of black
music and the success of black writers such as Alice Walker and Toni Morrison and a
host of others, blacks and whites in America do not, it seems, really want to share their
lives with each other.

In Atlanta, walking through the exhibits at the Martin Luther King Center that   48
mark the often bloody and yet inspiring history of the civil rights movement, listening
to King's mesmerizing speeches, his dream of an America where skin color no longer
mattered and where all Americans shared common dreams and aspirations, it was
impossible not to wonder what he would have thought of all this.

Chances are he would have been gratified and disappointed. Chances are that he   49
would have thought that America had not yet become the promised land.

Using Your Annotations.   Use your annotations and key words to write a one-
page summary of the reading. In your summary, identify the writer's thesis statement,
the major supporting points, the support for the major supporting points, and any other
information needed to complete the summary.

Thinking about the Text

1. According to Gawenda, what role does self-segregation play in the cycle of poverty?
2. Why does the writer believe race and poverty became newsworthy after Hurricane Katrina?
3. What does Gawenda believe about race relations in the United States? Express his beliefs in a paragraph.
4. In what ways was Charles White's upbringing different than that of young African Americans today, according to Gawenda?
5. The writer mentions globalization. What is globalization? Explain in a paragraph.

The Writer's Techniques

1. Why does Gawenda use a question for his title? What possible functions might such a title have?
2. How does the writer sequence his essay? Is it organized by time, by importance, or by some other method? Explain and cite examples of his ordering strategy.
3. The writer uses several quotes. Select one of these quotes, and write a paragraph about the person being quoted. What is the person's reputation, expertise, and status? You may need to do an Internet search to learn about the person.

Brief-Response Assignments

1. What is Gawenda's point about the aftermath of Hurricane Katrina? Explain.
2. How does Gawenda answer the question he poses in the title of this essay? Explain in a paragraph.
3. Gawenda points out a number of problems but does not discuss many solutions. What is one solution the writer might offer for a problem he discusses?

Essay Assignments

1. The writer states, "Blacks and whites in America do not, it seems, really want to share their lives with each other." Is this true? Write an essay in which you support, qualify, or refute Gawenda's statement based on the evidence you have seen in your community. Do not write a first-person essay explaining your own point of view. Rather, use observations of race relations to support your point.
2. Write an essay in which you explain this quote from the reading: "America as the promised land remains the country's great unifying myth." In what ways is the idea of America as a promised land a myth? Is it a myth for all people or for only some people? For whom is it a myth? Explain.
3. Gawenda's essay presents his point of view on the status of segregation in the United States, but he is not from the United States; he is an Australian journalist, viewing the situation as an outsider. Does his position as an outsider help him form a more accurate view of the American situation, or does it limit his knowledge of what life here is really like? Write an essay in which you answer this question. Defend your answer by analyzing Gawenda's observations. ↻

Author and Context.   Brett Buckner is an award-winning freelance writer in Alabama. Previously, Buckner, a graduate of Troy University, was a features writer (with a focus on religion) for *The Anniston Star* in Anniston, Alabama. "Color

Blind: Is Sunday Morning Still the Most Segregated Hour in America?" first appeared in *The Anniston Star* in May 2011. A slightly shortened version appears here.

Previewing. Have pen and paper (or a computer) on hand as you read. Think about the title, and then study the author's biography and the contextual information about the reading. Next, preview the selection. From the information you have gathered, determine the topic. What predictions can you make about the reading's content? Jot down your answers.

Reading Critically and Annotating. As you read, annotate the main idea, the major supporting points, key words, and a few passages that would make good quotations. Either write in your book or make annotations on sticky notes.

The essay contains five sections. Write a sentence that expresses the main idea of each one.

After reading and annotating, create an information sheet on which you record and organize your annotations as well as your thoughts about the content of the reading.

Color Blind: Is Sunday Morning Still the Most Segregated Hour in America?

By Brett Buckner

As a black woman in Anniston during the 1960s—a time of racism, segregation and bus burnings—Jean Martin knew what it was like to live in fear because of the color of her skin. "She saw and survived a lot of awful stuff," said her son, Marcus Dunn. "But she never put that poison in me to hate people just because they were different from me." 1

In 1962, when her son was 2 years old, Martin left Anniston "for a better life" in Oakland, Calif. She taught her son a simple rule: "Every white person isn't bad. Every black person isn't good. Good people come in all colors." 2

When Dunn returned to Anniston in 1989, her words still resonated. 3

Twelve years later, when he founded Kingdom Place Ministries, one of his main aspirations was to build a diverse congregation where people worshipped colorblind. 4

"We have an ingrained fear," Dunn said. "We fear loving one another outside of race, outside of culture, outside of tradition. We go to church where we're comfortable. That's not good enough. Too many of us have been raised in the church, when what we need is to be born into the kingdom of God. In the kingdom of God, we should only see God's people." 5

With a congregation that runs 80 percent black, 20 percent white, Dunn is working to achieve what he believes is the biblical mandate of "Love thy neighbor as thyself"— that the only way to truly worship God is to learn from all people of faith, no matter their race, culture, tradition, social or financial background. 6

"Since this ministry began, God has wanted us to be diversified . . . it's the only way to learn from one another," Dunn said. "We've done that by displaying love to one another or whoever comes through that door. If we show love in the church, we can't help but come together as men and women of God." 7

True diversity in Christian pews is a dream still under construction. The largest obstacles are differing opinions on music and style of worship, especially in the South, where the ghosts of racism and segregation linger just below the surface. 8

In order to exorcise those demons of the past, pastors must aggressively pursue 9
diversity, rather than praying it will resolve itself, said Carlton Weathers, pastor of
Grace Fellowship in Anniston, which in addition to a dozen or so black members also
numbers Hispanic, Indian and Japanese among its nearly 200 members.

"Racism is a sin," Weathers said. "To me, diversity is a gospel issue rather than a 10
social issue. Christians must be on the forefront of integration by attempting to bring
racial harmony to the community, but too often the church has been on the wrong side
of the issue. Sure, we've come a long way, but there's still a long way to go."

"The Most Segregated Hour"

It's been 53 years since Martin Luther King Jr. wrote in *Stride Toward Freedom: The* 11
Montgomery Story "that the most segregated hour in Christian America is 11 o'clock
on Sunday morning, the same hour when so many are standing to sing, 'In Christ there
is no East nor West.' Equally appalling is the fact that the most segregated school of
the week is Sunday school. How often the church has had a high blood count of creeds
and anemia of deeds."

King's indictment still rings true. According to a recent study conducted at Baylor 12
University, nine out of 10 congregations have a single racial group that accounts for
more than 80 percent of their membership.

"Socially, we've become much more integrated in schools, the military and busi- 13
nesses," said Kevin Dougherty, assistant professor of sociology at Baylor University,
who co-authored the study. "But in the places where we worship, segregation still seems
to be the norm. And it's not just an issue of attraction, of getting them into the door, but
of retention. Can we keep them? Our research indicates that we've not been able to."

It is a challenge that all mainstream Christian denominations must acknowledge, 14
said Will Willimon, bishop for the North Alabama Conference of the United Methodist Church.

"Look at the numbers and what Martin Luther King said still rings true," he said. 15
"Attending church tends to be one of the most culturally specific things we do. In most
of our churches where there is tension, it's usually over style of worship and music,
things that are as much generational as racial."

One big difference in worship styles is the length of the service. At black churches, 16
music, prayer, the reading of Scripture and other activities can run upwards of an hour
before the preacher starts preaching.

Some 20 years ago, Willimon served as a guest pastor at a historically black 17
church in South Carolina where the service lasted more than two hours. Afterwards,
Willimon asked the pastor why worship at black churches lasts so long. The answer
was, simply put, some black people have more to deal with come Sunday mornings.

"Male unemployment is running about 30 percent in this neighborhood. Young 18
male unemployment is running about 50 percent. That means when my people are
outside the church, every signal they receive from the culture is saying, 'You're nothing. You're nobody.' Then I get them into church and tell them, 'Jesus died for you.
You're God's people.' It takes about two hours for them to get their heads on straight."

Seeking Something Different

Tyler McDaniel's parents never sat in a pew beside a white person. 19

Having been raised in Oxford [Mississippi] at a time when it was dangerous to be 20
black, they attended a tiny C.M.E. [Christian Methodist Episcopal] church less than a
mile from their home. Every Sunday for as long as he could remember, McDaniel went
to that church, surrounded by friends and relatives. But when his parents died,
McDaniel, then 27, did something they never would have considered.

"I went to a white church . . . several, in fact," he said. "It was a different genera- 21
tion. I had white friends and co-workers, went to a racially mixed school at JSU [Jack-
sonville State University]. I even dated a white girl, so going to church with white
people wasn't that big a deal."

At first, he felt a bit out of place, McDaniel admitted. Not because anyone in the 22
pews treated him differently, but because he was in such a "total minority practically
everywhere I went." There were other black members at Word Alive, the church he
most frequently attended—"quite a few," in fact. But then he started talking to friends
who still attended predominately black churches.

"It was about going where they were raised," he said. "It wasn't just that I was in 23
the minority in terms of where I went to church, I was also in the minority as someone
who wasn't afraid to seek out something different. And I think that's the problem for
both blacks and whites. True diversity on Sunday mornings will forever be a problem
because we never stop to consider that where we are might not be where we belong.

"Faith is supposed to challenge us. We'll never really learn anything if we're 24
always surrounded by people who think and act just like we do . . . it's a dead end."

Church Leaders Encourage Diversity

Willimon and other United Methodist Church leaders have encouraged diversity by 25
making cross-racial appointments—placing a black minister in charge of a predominately white congregation, or vice versa. They have met with only limited success.

"Unfortunately, we can't point to a case where it dramatically energized or grew a 26
congregation, at least not repeatedly," Willimon said. "That's terribly disappointing."

Genia Garrett was one of those cross-racial appointments. Today, Garrett, who is 27
black, is the minister at the predominantly black Glen Addie Community Church—which
also has eight white members. For the previous three years, however, she was minister at
four churches in Iowa where she was the only black person in the congregation.

"I think sometimes we get too hung up on tradition, on what we think is right or 28
'normal,' and that means being surrounded by people who look and act like us,"
Garrett said. "In doing that, we can block out the power of what God is trying to do.
You can't keep God in a box. When it comes to worship, when it comes to getting
closer to God, we've all got to think outside the box we were raised in."

Born in Birmingham and raised in the Baptist church, Garrett felt called to preach 29
from a young age, but because she was Baptist her options were limited. Now, as a
Methodist, she has come to understand and respect various forms of worship, from the
conservative traditionalism common to white congregations to the enthusiastic worship of black churches.

At Glen Addie Community Church, the most important thing is the music, Garrett 30
said. "We have different members of various denominations—Holiness, Baptist,
Pentecostal—but they all want vibrant praise, especially in the music. They expect the
songs to take them off to heaven and just be off the chain, and they expect the preacher
to bring the word—dynamic with fire and brimstone," she said.

"I think blacks have been given the gift of freedom of worship, the power and the 31
gift of feeling the music and using that in their worship to God," Garrett said. "And
while that might look more dynamic, it's just different—not necessarily better."

"They Were Just Like Me"

Nita Jones considers herself to be quiet and reserved most of the time, but that 32
all changes when she steps into Kingdom Place Ministries, where she is one of a
handful of white members. Raised Methodist, Jones attended mostly nondenomina-
tional churches before being invited by a friend to visit Kingdom Place five years

ago. She never went anywhere else. During services, she claps, raises her hands to the heavens and praises the Lord "loudly."

It was the first time she'd ever been in the minority during worship services—but she didn't really notice. "It didn't really register," she said with a laugh. "I know it sounds strange, but color didn't exist for me. Everybody was kind and I felt right at home. The way I saw it, they were just like me. Inside, Christians are all the same . . . at least they should be." . . .

33

Using Your Annotations.   Use your annotations and key words to write a one-page summary of the reading. In your summary, identify the writer's thesis statement, the major supporting points, the support for the major supporting points, and any other information needed to complete the summary.

Thinking about the Text

1. What is the main idea of this article?
2. Buckner suggests that one difference between white and black churches is the typical length of worship services. He says that Will Willimon asked the pastor of a black church why worship there lasts so long. What answer did the pastor offer?
3. The writer quotes Tyler McDaniel as saying that his experience regarding race and church has been very different than that of his parents. What reason does McDaniel give for his being so much more comfortable in attending a predominantly white church than his parents would have been?
4. The author says that Willimon and other United Methodist Church leaders have encouraged diversity by making "cross-racial appointments." What does the expression "cross-racial appointments" mean?
5. According to Willimon, how successful have "cross-racial appointments" been in promoting racial diversity?

The Writer's Techniques

1. Which text pattern best fits this article? Explain.
2. What is the purpose of this article—to inform, analyze, evaluate, or persuade? Explain your answer.
3. Analyze the article's conclusion, paying particular attention to the quotes in the last paragraph. Why do you think Buckner ends with these quotes? Explain.

Brief-Response Assignments

1. In the body of the essay, Buckner provides the context for the title of the essay. What was the source? Why is it important to note the source?
2. Included in the quotation from Martin Luther King, Jr., at the beginning of the essay is this expression: "How often the church has had a high blood count of creeds and anemia of deeds." The word *anemia* is used in this context to mean the opposite of *high blood count*. What does King mean? Use a dictionary to look up *creed* and *anemia* and any other unfamiliar words in that sentence.
3. Several churches are mentioned in the article: Kingdom Place Ministries, Word Alive International Outreach, Grace Fellowship, and Glen Addie Community Church. Do an Internet search for each church, and determine where it is located. (For best results, enclose the church's name in quotation marks, and include the pastor's name, if provided.) Identify the location by city and state. Then, answer this question: Why are their locations relevant to this particular article?

Essay Assignments

1. Most of the voices heard in this essay suggest that racially integrated worship is a very desirable goal. However, some arguments for blacks worshipping with blacks and whites worshipping with whites are implied, if not explicitly stated. Using these implicit perspectives, argue that the self-segregation of worshippers not only is understandable but also can be a positive practice.

2. The writer includes stories of white people attending black churches and vice versa. Locate one of each story type, and compare and contrast the descriptions of the experiences each person had.

3. Select another religious tradition, such as Islam, Buddhism, or Orthodox Judaism. Is segregation a problem for the religious tradition you have selected? Write an informative essay explaining how integration issues exist or have been resolved in the religious tradition in question. ↺

Thematic Assignment

Use the readings in this thematic unit to write an essay on one of the following topics:

a. Write an essay discussing the advancements that have been made regarding race relations in the United States. Also discuss ways in which progress has been slow in coming.

b. Is self-segregation something we should eliminate? Should self-segregation be discouraged in some places and encouraged or seen as okay in others? Defend your answer.

c. Describe various steps mentioned in the readings in this thematic unit that might be taken to actively encourage desegregation.

d. Analyze the self-segregation practices at your college or university by observing and making notes about classroom and lunchroom behaviors. Write an essay about your observations, and evaluate your college. Is self-segregation prevalent on your campus? If it is, why? What are the effects of such segregation? What insights can you draw from your observations? Present them in your essay.

Be sure to cite any sources from which you obtain ideas or quotes. Include a works cited or references page with your essay. For additional information on source-based writing, follow the steps in the Quick Start Guide to Integrated Reading and Writing Assignments.

Text Credits

Food for Thought | THEME

Eating at fast food restaurants is a cultural pastime. But how does it affect our health? Are fast foods responsible for making us obese? If so, what can—and should—we do about that?

What's for dinner? For many Americans, the answer is some kind of fast food. But what, exactly, does that food do to us? To answer that question, the filmmaker Morgan Spurlock created a documentary that chronicled his experience eating only at McDonald's for a month. Since Spurlock's documentary, many people have discussed the effects of fast food, especially obesity. Some people have even proposed that we tax junk food so that obesity rates might decrease. Others question whether such a tax would be effective.

In the four selections that follow, you will read about Spurlock's experiment and about the issue of taxing junk food. As you read, identify the key questions that we—as a nation—need to ask about the food we eat and the policies that regulate it.

Author and Context.   Ty Burr writes for *Boston Globe* as a film critic, where he has been on staff since 2002. He studied film at Dartmouth College and New York University. Burr's review of the movie *Super Size Me* appeared in *The Boston Globe* on May 7, 2004.

Previewing.   Have pen and paper (or a computer) on hand as you read. Think about the title, and then study the author's biography and the contextual information about the reading. Next, preview the selection. From the information you have gathered, determine the topic. What predictions can you make about the reading's content? Jot down your answers.

Reading Critically and Annotating. As you read, annotate the main idea, the major supporting points, key words, and a few passages that would make good quotations. Either write in your book or make annotations on sticky notes. As you find key ideas, annotate them. What were the details of Spurlock's experiment? What criticism did Spurlock receive? What lessons can be learned from Spurlock's experiment? As you read, work on identifying the issues Spurlock's film confronts.

After reading and annotating, create an information sheet on which you record and organize your annotations as well as your thoughts about the content of the reading.

Super Size Me Makes for Meaty Viewing

By Ty Burr

Morgan Spurlock's outrageously amusing *Super Size Me* is the redheaded stepchild of Michael Moore and *Jackass*, a low-budget nonfiction stunt with a sharp point of view, a sheaf of alarming statistics, and the willingness to entertain us until we cry uncle. Like *Bowling for Columbine*, it's less a documentary than a provocumentary, and, like Moore, Spurlock is a born showman. It's one thing to rail against Fast Food America and the burgeoning obesity epidemic. It's another to eat nothing but Mickey D's for a solid month and record what happens. 1

Spurlock got the notion a few years back while watching news stories about two women who sued McDonald's over their weight gain, and lost. The company's defense was that its food is perfectly healthy, so the filmmaker, 33, put the matter to a test: three square meals of McDonald's food a day, and he *had* to accept a super-size portion if offered. 2

In the full spirit of deadpan mockery, Spurlock first gives himself a weigh-in: a cardiologist, nutritionist, and general physician look him over and pronounce him to be a fit, 185-pound ex-smoking New Yorker. Then it's off to the Golden Arches, to the horror of his vegan chef girlfriend and his own stomach lining: The *Super Size Me* crew captures Spurlock's first burger and fries coming back up in all their Technicolor splendor, a scene that should endear the movie to the teenagers who need to see it most. 3

As the 30-day diet wends onward and the director balloons into a dazed McNugget junkie, the film throws out dozens of greasy factoids: The number of people McDonald's feeds daily is greater than the population of Spain; 60 percent of Americans are overweight; 40 percent eat out each day; the average American child recognizes Ronald McDonald more easily than George Washington or Jesus; a 7-11 Double Gulp has 48 teaspoons of sugar in its half-gallon of soda. My favorite: French fries are this country's most consumed vegetable. 4

It's not all genial agitprop. Spurlock interviews Don Gorske, a Wisconsin McDonald's fanatic and Guinness record holder who claims to have eaten two Big Macs a day for 30 years; he's as skinny as a post, so there. The director also speaks to nutritionists and other specialists, discusses the compromised state of food in America's public schools, and muses on the perils of being a snack food executive: Baskin-Robbins heir John Robbins (author of *Diet for a New America*) talks about his ice-cream-related health problems and we hear about Ben's (of Ben & Jerry's) quintuple bypass. Spurlock also spends a lot of time trying to get McDonald's Jim Cantalupo on the phone; he never did and never will, since the CEO died of a heart attack on April 19 at 60. 5

agitprop: political propaganda.

Throughout, *Super Size Me* keeps returning in increasingly woozy circles to that diet, and the end results are enough to put you off the trough for good. Spurlock gains 6

25 pounds and suffers chest pains, depression, and "McStomach-aches." His cholesterol tests and other blood work set off air-raid klaxons, and one of his doctors proclaims the filmmaker's liver "obscene." Let's not talk about what it does to his libido.

klaxons: loud horns.

The company has an easy defense: No one's supposed to eat *only* at McDonald's. Except that many customers come close—the marketing department calls them "heavy users" and would dearly love to increase their numbers. Besides, if many Americans aren't eating at McDonald's, they're at Burger King or Taco Bell or KFC or any of the other lard barns across the country.   7

With *Super Size Me*, Spurlock gleefully martyrs his body to our sense of outrage. McDonald's announced . . . that it plans to phase out super-size portions . . . and has also launched a line of "Go Active! Adult Happy Meals" that includes salad, water, a pedometer, and a leaflet promoting the benefits of walking. In a remarkable coincidence, the new Happy Meals went on sale . . . a day before *Super Size Me* opened nationally.   8

Nice stab at corporate responsibility, but you may find more nutrition in the food for thought Spurlock offers; at the very least, there are more laughs. I don't usually make recommendations of this kind, but if you or your kids have gone to a burger joint in the last few weeks, you really do need to see this movie.   9

And maybe go easy on the Goobers while you're there.   10

Source: Burr, Ty, "*Super Size Me* Makes for Meaty Viewing," *Boston Globe*, May 7, 2004. Copyright © 2004 Boston Globe Media Partners. All rights reserved. Used by permission and protected by the Copyright Laws of the United States. The printing, copying, redistribution, or transmission of this Content without express written permission is prohibited.

Using Your Annotations.   Use your annotations and key words to write a one-page summary of the reading. In your summary, identify the writer's thesis statement, the major supporting points, the support for the major supporting points, and any other information needed to complete the summary.

Thinking about the Text

1. What does the writer mean by "provocumentary"?
2. What happened to Spurlock when he ate only foods from McDonald's?
3. How does the writer help the reader see why the topic of fast-food-related obesity is relevant?
4. What is one criticism of Spurlock's experiment?
5. What is the writer's opinion of the movie *Super Size Me*?

The Writer's Techniques

1. Look at your annotations. Which of the following types of supporting details does Burr mainly use—comparison and contrast, cause and effect, definition, process analysis, classification, or illustration?
2. What type of order (spatial, chronological, order of importance) does Burr use?
3. Most of the article is a summary of the movie. What other elements are in the article?

Brief-Response Assignments

1. Write a paragraph in which you discuss your attitude about fast food. How often do you eat it? What are your feelings about eating fast food?
2. Do you think Spurlock's experiment was helpful, or was it too extreme (eating fast food every day for a month) to be instructive? Explain your answer.

3. There is an epidemic of obesity in the United States. In your opinion, what role has fast food played in this epidemic? Explain your answer.
4. The author provides some suggestions for eating fast food more responsibly. What additional suggestions can you think of? Create at least three.

Essay Assignments

1. College cafeterias are increasingly becoming hubs for fast food outlets. Taco Bell, Chick-fil-A, McDonald's, and other restaurants are often part of the college cafeteria offerings. Should colleges continue to allow fast food to dominate their food services? Would it be a better idea to offer only cafeteria-style food on college campuses? Write an essay presenting and defending your point of view.
2. Some people believe that instead of focusing on fast food as a problem, we should figure out why so many Americans eat fast food. Is it because they have few other choices? Is it because people lack cooking skills or easy access to well-stocked grocery stores? Is it because we are addicted to the flavor of fast food? Write an essay in which you discuss the reasons why so many people eat fast food.
3. Watch Spurlock's documentary *Super Size Me*. Write an essay in which you summarize the movie and present criticisms of it. ↺

Authors and Context. The following article appears in the textbook *M: Advertising*, by William F. Arens, David H. Schaefer, and Michael F. Weigold. Arens has worked in the field of advertising for over 35 years. He is a graduate of Whittier College. Weigold is Associate Dean for Undergraduate Affairs and Enrollment Management at the University of Florida. Schaefer is Professor Emeritus of Business and Marketing at Sacramento City College, where he taught courses in business, marketing, advertising, customer service, and personal finance.

Previewing. Have pen and paper (or a computer) on hand as you read. Think about the title, and then study the authors' biographies and the contextual information about the reading. Next, preview the selection. From the information you have gathered, determine the topic. What predictions can you make about the reading's content? Jot down your answers.

Reading Critically and Annotating. As you read, annotate the main idea, the major supporting points, key words, and a few passages that would make good quotations. Either write in your book or make annotations on sticky notes. As you find key ideas, annotate them. Should fast food companies direct their advertising to children? Is it right to do so? Is advertising the problem, is the problem parental control, or are other problems associated with the obesity epidemic?

After reading and annotating, create an information sheet on which you record and organize your annotations as well as your thoughts about the content of the reading.

Is Ronald McDonald Bad for Kids? Are Parents?

By William F. Arens, David H. Schaefer, and Michael F. Weigold

Deborah Lapidus has found the "person" responsible for the childhood obesity epidemic that is sweeping the United States. While the culprit can often be found   1 visiting children's hospitals and performing at other charity events, Lapidus is unmoved. She wants him gone for good, or, in her words, "retired." Anyone interested in joining Ms. Lapidus's quest should be on the lookout for an easily recognized, flamboyantly dressed individual with flaming red hair and a bright round nose. Because Deborah Lapidus wants to retire Ronald McDonald.

To make her point, in 2010 she traveled all the way to Oak Brook, Illinois, the location of McDonald's annual meeting, to protest Ronald's prominence in the company's advertising. Her trip was funded by her 30,000-member advocacy group, named "Corporate Accountability."

Does McDonald's market to children? The evidence is pretty compelling. Like any smart family-oriented eatery, McDonald's knows that kids exercise enormous influence in family dining decisions. In response, it has created Happy Meals and playgrounds that make its restaurants fun places for kids to eat and play (and for mom and dad to relax). And, of course, kids love Ronald, one of the world's most recognized brand symbols.

And it is undeniable that America has a health problem, and food is a big part of it. [President Barack Obama's] Secretary of Health and Human Services Kathleen Sebelius suggests that one in three kids in the United States is overweight, a number that has grown 400 percent in just 20 years. Sebelius . . . urged the U.S. Conference of Mayors to join a program initiated by First Lady Michelle Obama called "Let's Move," aimed at encouraging healthier lifestyles among children.

So the problem that Lapidus is calling attention to is real. What is in question is her proposed solution. Will retiring Ronald make America's children skinnier?

Interestingly, McDonald's may be way ahead of Lapidus. The company has developed a broader line of healthy menus for its Happy Meals, ones that include fresh fruits and veggies. Playgrounds are slowly being phased out at McDonald's in favor of coffee bars. Ads that feature Ronald are difficult to find anymore, part of a recent trend toward reducing McDonald's ads that target children. In fact, while the company's overall ad spending in the first quarter of 2010 was up 30 percent from 2009, ads directed at kids were down 23 percent.

So McDonald's seems to be doing its part. Lapidus should be thrilled.

But one commentator, *Courier-News* writer Julia Doyle, thinks Lapidus has missed the real source of childhood obesity: moms and dads. Doyle writes,

> If our kids are fat, it automatically has to be because there's a goofy, smiley-faced clown telling them to eat cheeseburgers and French fries, right? It can't possibly have anything to do with Mom or Dad stopping for fried chicken, tacos or burgers every night rather than cooking a healthy dinner when they get home. And if our kids are fat, it has everything to do with the pizza, chicken fingers and hot dogs served in their school cafeterias and nothing to do with the fact that their parents can't be bothered to pack them a healthy lunch to take to school each day. I think it's high time these so-called watchdog groups get off their high horses and stop blaming corporate America for everything they think is wrong with us.

The ethical issues here are complex. Is it right for McDonald's, or any company, to advertise to children? Is it morally acceptable for a fast-food chain to feature playgrounds and brand symbols that kids find appealing? Would these activities be more ethically permissible if the company exclusively sold healthy food? Can the obesity problem affecting American children (and adults) be blamed on a single company? McDonald's has been using Ronald in its ads since the 1960s, a time when children were generally fitter and slimmer than they are today. So how can he be the root cause, or even a significant factor, of the problem? What about Doyle's points regarding the role of parents, both as role models for good eating and as gatekeepers for the types of foods their children eat? Does she have a fair point or not? America's children have a health problem. How significant is advertising as a cause?

Using Your Annotations.   Use your annotations and key words to write a one-page summary of the reading. In your summary, identify the writer's thesis statement, the major supporting points, the support for the major supporting points, and any other information needed to complete the summary.

Thinking about the Text

1.   This article presents several issues. What is the main topic?
2.   What does Deborah Lapidus believe about advertising fast food to children?
3.   What evidence in the article suggests that Ronald McDonald might not be to blame for obesity?
4.   Why does Julia Doyle object to Lapidus's mission?
5.   The article suggests that McDonald's might be making changes in its advertising to children. What specific details in the article provide this suggestion?

The Writer's Techniques

1.   Do the writers present their own points of view on the topics they discuss, or do the points of view belong to the people the writers discuss?
2.   In one of the paragraphs, the writers begin with the question "Does McDonald's market to children?" Why do you think they used a question to start this paragraph? Do they answer the question?
3.   The final paragraph contains several questions but few answers. What is the effect of offering so many questions? Why do you think the authors end their article this way?

Brief-Response Assignments

1.   Think about your experience as a child. Did advertising affect your desires? Explain in a paragraph and offer examples.
2.   How might fast food advertisements affect parental authority? Write a paragraph in which you explain.
3.   Write a paragraph in which you respond to this passage from the text: "McDonald's has been using Ronald in its ads since the 1960s, a time when children were generally fitter and slimmer than they are today. So how can he be the root cause, or even a significant factor, of the problem?"
4.   What could McDonald's do to market its products in an ethical way?

Essay Assignments

1.   The chief executive officer of McDonald's has asked you to create an advertising campaign. Specifically, she wants you to create ads that attract children to eat at McDonald's but to choose fresh fruit and vegetable sides. Discuss advertising techniques that might work for this purpose. Write an essay in which you explain in detail each advertising technique you create.
2.   Two points of view are offered in the article. First, Lapidus blames McDonald's for advertising to children by making Ronald McDonald a kid-friendly figure. Next, Doyle blames parents for not exercising authority over their children and

for not making sure their children eat healthfully. Who is to blame when children eat poorly? Write an essay in which you argue your point.

3. Analyze a current McDonald's advertisement, either one on television or one in print. In your essay, present the details of the advertisement. Discuss the intended audience of the advertisement. Talk about how you think McDonald's hopes the advertisement will work. What products are featured in the ad, if any? Does the ad promote healthy or responsible eating? For whom might the ad be effective? For whom might the ad be ineffective? ↻

Author and Context.   The following article, written by Jacob Goldin, appears on the Web site of the Tax Policy Institute, part of the Urban Institute and Brookings Institution. Goldin, Assistant Professor of Law at Stanford Law School, specializes in tax policy and how taxes affect people's economic behavior. On its Web site, the Urban Institute explains its mission: "We believe in the power of evidence to improve lives and strengthen communities. . . . We conduct sophisticated research to understand and solve real-world challenges in a rapidly urbanizing environment." The Brookings Institution's mission is similar. Its Web site describes the Institution as a "nonprofit public policy organization based in Washington, DC": "Our mission is to conduct in-depth research that leads to new ideas for solving problems facing society at the local, national and global level." The Tax Policy Institute is a joint venture between the Urban Institute and the Brookings Institution.

Previewing.   Have pen and paper (or a computer) on hand as you read. Think about the title, and then study the author's biography and the contextual information about the reading. Next, preview the selection. From the information you have gathered, determine the topic. What predictions can you make about the reading's content? Jot down your answers.

Reading Critically and Annotating.   As you read, annotate the main idea, the major supporting points, key words, and a few passages that would make good quotations. Either write in your book or make annotations on sticky notes. As you find key ideas, annotate them. What does the Tax Policy Institute say about taxing junk food? Will such taxes be effective? Why or why not?

After reading and annotating, create an information sheet on which you record and organize your annotations as well as your thoughts about the content of the reading.

Taxing Junk Food

By Jacob Goldin

One proposal to help finance health reform would tax fast food, salty snacks, and/or sugary drinks like soda. While critics see government meddling in citizens' private lives, supporters of a "junk food" tax say such a levy could help finance expanded insurance coverage as well as lower health care costs by inducing people to switch to healthier diets. Taxpayers pay much of the expense of obesity-related disease through Medicare and Medicaid. 1

Would a junk food tax really reduce obesity? Economic theory says that by raising the relative price of unhealthy foods that contribute to obesity, the tax would motivate people to spend more of their income on foods that are healthy. As consumers abandon 2 costlier junk foods, obesity rates would fall, and so would health-care costs. At least that's the theory.

In practice, a lot would depend on how the tax is designed. For example, a tax on chips could result in people choosing to buy more cookies for their afternoon snack. Similarly, a tax on soda might lead people to drink more beer. For a tax to be effective at reducing obesity, consumers must not respond by switching to other unhealthy foods not covered by the tax.

3

Lisa M. Powell and Frank J. Chaloupka recently combed the literature to find out what we know about how junk food taxes affect obesity. Their answer: not much. Most studies have concluded that changes in the price of unhealthy foods have relatively small effects on obesity rates, although one found that residents of states that repealed junk food taxes were more likely to experience subsequent obesity gains. Powell and Chaloupka concluded that it would probably require a "nontrivial" change in prices to significantly affect obesity rates. In other words, it would take a heavy tax to keep the weight off.

4

Like other sin taxes, a tax on junk foods would be regressive. That is, it would disproportionately affect low-income families who consume a greater share of those goods. However, this story may not be so clear-cut. Several studies have found that low-income households are especially sensitive to changes in the price of unhealthy foods, suggesting they will avoid much of the tax (and the financial hit) by reducing junk food purchases.

5

sin tax: a tax applied to items that are thought of as harmful, such as alcohol and tobacco.

Moreover, low-income communities are among the most affected by obesity-related diseases such as Type II diabetes and heart disease. If a junk food tax helped change that pattern while also providing revenue to improve access to health insurance, its net effect could be extremely progressive. . . .

6

regressive tax: a tax that is usually applied the same way to all situations. For example, a wealthy person and a low-income person would pay the same amount of tax on a bag of chips. However, the tax would claim a greater share of the low-income person's resources. Thus, a regressive tax hurts low-income people more than it hurts wealthy people.

A final stumbling block lies in defining junk food. Are high-calorie sports drinks junk foods or useful exercise aids? What makes a sugary drink healthy enough to avoid the tax? Do O.J. and apple juice make the cut? The United Kingdom has spent years trying to define a potato chip (the issue is still not fully resolved). Wherever policy-makers draw the line, food manufacturers will try to make their product appear to be on the right side of it. Thus a junk food tax might precipitate more changes to how foods are packaged and sold than to what people actually eat.

7

Using Your Annotations. Use your annotations and key words to write a one-page summary of the reading. In your summary, identify the writer's thesis statement, the major supporting points, the support for the major supporting points, and any other information needed to complete the summary.

Thinking about the Text

1. What answer does the article provide to this question: "Will a junk food tax work to lower obesity rates?"
2. Using the answer you wrote for the first question, explain what support the author provides.
3. What does the writer mean by a "regressive" tax?
4. Why might a tax on junk food affect low-income people more than higher-income people?
5. How might food manufacturers try to get around a junk food tax?

The Writer's Techniques

1. Look at your annotations. Which of the following types of supporting details does the author use—comparison and contrast, cause and effect, definition, process analysis, classification, or illustration?

2. The writer ends the second paragraph with this sentence: "At least that's the theory." What effect do you think this sentence might have on readers?

3. Why does the author bring up the topic of Medicare and Medicaid in the first paragraph? What are Medicare and Medicaid?

Brief-Response Assignments

1. Think about your favorite junk food item and what it costs. How much would the item have to cost before you would buy it less frequently? Write a paragraph and explain your answer.

2. The author mentioned several ways that people might get around a junk food tax and continue to buy unhealthy foods. Think of another way people might get around the tax and write a paragraph explaining your answer.

3. Are there ways other than taxing junk food that the government could reduce the consumption of such foods? Explain one way.

4. How important is junk food in your life or in the lives of people you know? Explain your answer and provide examples.

Essay Assignments

1. Reread this section of the article:

> While critics see government meddling in citizens' private lives, supporters of a "junk food" tax say such a levy could help finance expanded insurance coverage as well as lower health-care costs by inducing people to switch to healthier diets. Taxpayers pay much of the expense of obesity-related disease through Medicare and Medicaid.

   When should the government make new laws that affect our personal freedom, such as the freedom to buy junk food? Tobacco products are routinely taxed at higher rates because their health effects put a burden on US health-care costs. Provide examples of when it is okay (and good) for the government to make laws that affect our personal freedom, and present examples to show where the government should not interfere. You may use hypothetical examples.

2. Write an essay in which you define "junk food." In the final paragraph of the article you just read, the authors discuss how difficult it can be to define junk food. What criteria would you use to characterize a food as "junk food"? For example, is yogurt with added sugar "junk food"? Is a junior hamburger "junk food"? Provide examples as you create and explain your definition.

3. Write an essay in which you answer this question: Should public schools stop serving junk food such as pizza, burgers, ice cream, soda, and fried foods? Why or why not? Defend your answer by providing at least three reasons. For each reason, use supporting details that provide examples and explanations. ↺

Author and Context.   Michael Blanding is a Boston-based freelance writer and investigative journalist whose work has appeared in *WIRED, Slate, The Nation, Consumers Digest, The Boston Globe Magazine*, and *Boston Magazine*. He is the author of *The Coke Machine: The Dirty Truth behind the World's Favorite Soft Drink*. This article first appeared in the Winter 2015 issue of *Tufts Nutrition* magazine.

Previewing.   Have pen and paper (or a computer) on hand as you read. Think about the title, and then study the author's biography and the contextual information about the reading. Next, preview the selection. From the information you have gathered, determine the topic. What predictions can you make about the reading's content? Jot down your answers.

Reading Critically and Annotating. As you read, annotate the main idea, the major supporting points, key words, and a few passages that would make good quotations. Either write in your book or make annotations on sticky notes. As you find key ideas, annotate them.

After reading and annotating, create an information sheet on which you record and organize your annotations as well as your thoughts about the content of the reading.

●───────────────────────────────

Should We Tax Unhealthy Food?

By Michael Blanding

What does a 20-ounce bottle of soda cost? If you said 99 cents, you are only partly right. While that may be the price on the sticker at the store, it doesn't take into account the cost to public health. One study, for example, found for every extra can of soda a person drinks per day, he or she is 30 percent more likely to become obese—increasing the risk of heart disease, diabetes, and other diseases.

1

"Diet is now the leading cause of poor health in the country," says Dariush Mozaffarian, dean of the Friedman School, who notes health-care costs account for nearly one out of every five dollars in our national economy.

2

Friedman School: refers to the Gerald J. and Dorothy R. Friedman School of Nutrition Science and Policy at Tufts University.

Yet when cities and states have tried to enact so-called snack taxes on soda, candy, and other junk food, they've met resistance. Conservatives greet such attempts as evidence of the "nanny state" limiting personal choice, while hunger groups view the taxes as discriminatory against the poor, who consume more high-calorie foods.

3

That doesn't mean the policy of taxing foods should be abandoned, says Mozaffarian. In fact, as he argued in an editorial in the *Journal of the American Medical Association* . . ., it doesn't go far enough. Along with Boston Children's Hospital obesity researcher David Ludwig and Harvard economist Kenneth Rogoff, Mozaffarian expanded on the snack tax by proposing across-the-board food taxes combined with key food subsidies.

4

"We propose taxing pretty much everything with a food label or sold in chain restaurants," explains Mozaffarian, recommending a flat tax of anywhere between 10 and 30 percent. At the same time, he and his co-authors propose dramatically lowering the prices on unimpeachably healthy foods. "The modest tax would be used to subsidize minimally processed, mostly whole foods that the scientific evidence demonstrates are clearly healthy, such as fruits, vegetables, nuts, fish, vegetable oils and yogurt." The taxes would also support school lunch programs.

5

The radical step comes out of research Mozaffarian did on different strategies for improving diet, published by the American Heart Association. . . . "It showed us that education and knowledge alone have a pretty minimal effect," he says. On the other hand, "there is strong evidence that taxes reduce consumption, while subsidies increase consumption."

6

It's Public Safety

He compares changing food choices to efforts to reduce fatalities from car accidents over recent decades. "Did we simply say, 'Car accidents happen; let's just educate people about the risks'? No. We instituted driver's licensing, car crash standards,

7

antilock brakes, airbags, guard rails, speed limits and rumble strips, as well as seat belt, child seat, and motorcycle helmet laws," he says. "The food system is just as complex—we need to use all the tools at our disposal to address the consumer, industry, food environment, and food culture to be successful."

By providing subsidies for healthy foods, the proposal would avoid challenges that food taxes are punitive or regressive. "The subsidy in the beginning would be very large," he says. "Imagine an apple might cost 5 cents, a filet of salmon 25 cents. It would radically alter incentives for producers, retailers, restaurants, and the public." While those bargains would be offset by modestly higher prices on processed foods, Mozaffarian believes that with healthier choices, the average grocery bill for families could stay the same or even decrease—while at the same time reducing family medical costs.

8

Originally, Mozaffarian and Ludwig considered taxing foods at different amounts depending on their healthfulness. However, economist Rogoff counseled that such a scheme would be too open to lobbying by food companies for exemptions, undermining the system. Instead, the idea is to start with a simple flat tax, and later introduce scaled taxes to further increase incentives for food companies and restaurants to create healthier offerings.

9

"If Pepsi can sell an apple with 'Pepsi' on it and make the same amount of money as soda, they would be delighted to do that," says Mozaffarian. "I believe that over five to 10 years, it would transform the food system."

10

> **regressive tax:** a tax that is usually applied the same way to all situations. For example, a wealthy person and a low-income person would pay the same amount of tax on a bag of chips. However, the tax would claim a greater share of the low-income person's resources. Thus, a regressive tax hurts low-income people more than it hurts wealthy people.

Using Your Annotations.
Use your annotations and key words to write a one-page summary of the reading. In your summary, identify the writer's thesis statement, the major supporting points, the support for the major supporting points, and any other information needed to complete the summary.

Thinking about the Text

1. According to Mozaffarian, how effective are education and knowledge at reducing consumption of junk food?
2. What are "unimpeachably healthy foods"? Explain why some foods are in this category.
3. Mozaffarian would like to see a junk food tax that would go along with another new policy. What is the other new policy he would like to see?
4. What are two reasons why Mozaffarian thinks we should tax junk food?
5. What is a food "subsidy"?

The Writer's Techniques

1. What analogy does Mozaffarian use to support the idea that we should tax junk food? How does the analogy work? (Explain the comparison he makes.)
2. What method does the writer use to introduce the topic? Explain.
3. Sometimes the writer refers to the words (quotes) or ideas of other people. How can you tell when the writer is referring to other people's ideas?

Brief-Response Assignments

1. Reread this sentence from the first paragraph: "While that may be the price on the sticker at the store, it doesn't take into account the cost to public health." Write a paragraph in which you explain what the writer means by this statement.
2. One of the ideas this article implies is that people care about costs when they select snack items. Is this true in your opinion? Cite examples to prove your point.

3. Mozaffarian asks readers to imagine paying 5 cents for an apple or 25 cents for a filet of salmon. If healthy foods were significantly reduced from their current prices, do you think more people would consume them? Would you? Write a paragraph explaining your answer.

4. There are probably some people who would not purchase healthy foods even if snacks were expensive and healthy foods were affordable. Why might some people be resistant to eating healthy foods? Write a paragraph to respond.

Essay Assignments

1. Write an essay in which you respond to the ideas in this article. In particular, the writer believes that by making unhealthy food more expensive and healthy food less expensive, Americans will change their purchasing and eating habits. Do you agree? Why or why not? Write an essay in which you present reasons for your opinion.

2. When talking about subsidies for healthy foods, Mozaffarian says, "there is strong evidence that taxes reduce consumption, while subsidies increase consumption." Imagine that Congress passed a new law that would create food subsidies for ten healthy foods. Which foods would you argue need to be subsidized? For instance, you might argue that salmon should be subsidized because it is healthy and expensive. Explain your reasoning in your essay.

3. Some food companies work diligently to make sure their products are healthy. Other companies work to make their high-sugar and high-fat snacks almost addictive by using food science. Should companies be able to produce unhealthy junk food that clearly has a negative effect on health? If so, should they have to label such foods? Write an essay in which you present your point of view and discuss how snack food companies should behave. ↻

Thematic Assignment

Use the readings in this thematic unit to write an essay that answers one of the following questions.

a. Do fast food companies have a corporate responsibility to control the healthfulness of their products? Some people think that fast food restaurants should not have to worry about the calories, fat, or sugar content of their foods. These people believe that consumers must be responsible for making the right choices about what to eat. Other people believe that fast food companies need to be good corporate citizens by watching out for the health of those they serve. These people believe that it is reasonable for fast food companies to prepare and serve tasty food that is healthy. Write an essay in which you present your opinion on this topic and the reasons for your opinion.

b. When you compare the arguments in favor of a junk food tax to the arguments against such a tax, which arguments are the most convincing? Why? Write an essay in which you compare and contrast both sides of the argument and defend your point of view.

c. Is fast food really more affordable, more convenient, and more flavorful than healthy or home-prepared meals? Write an essay in which you present your point of view and the reasons for it.

d. In a perfect world, parents would make sure their children consumed only the best, healthiest foods. But we do not live in a perfect world, and parents often give in to their children's demands for junk food. If you were advising a parent on rules to set up to make sure children eat healthfully, what rules would you advise? Write an essay in which you present at least three rules that can help parents make sure their children eat more healthfully.

Be sure to cite any sources from which you obtain ideas or quotes. Include a works cited or references page with your essay. For additional information on source-based writing, follow the steps in the Quick Start Guide to Integrated Reading and Writing Assignments.

Text Credits

Planning for the Future | THEME

The American inventor and engineer Charles Franklin Kettering said, "We should all be concerned about the future because we will have to spend the rest of our lives there." What responsibilities do we have, to ourselves and to the rest of the world, to take care of the future?

Mass exterminations, super volcanoes, nuclear holocaust! Is it time to settle down in our bomb shelters, or are we making mountains out of nanobot hills?

In the following selections, you will read about what some people believe the future holds and how we should plan for it. Some of the writers bemoan the advent of technology and fear what future generations of supercomputers may mean for the human race. Other writers are optimistic about our ability to prepare for and handle the challenges of the future. As you read these selections, keep an open mind so you can look at the future in a new way.

nanobot: an incredibly tiny, self-propelled machine. The word is a blend of *nano-* (tiny, literally one-billionth) and *robot.*

Author and Context. Cahal Milmo, chief reporter of *The Independent,* has been with the London newspaper since 2000. He was born in London and previously worked at the Press Association news agency. "*Google* Search and Destroy" was published in *The Independent* on December 16, 2013.

Previewing. Have pen and paper (or a computer) on hand as you read. Think about the title, and then study the author's biography and the contextual information about the reading. Next, preview the selection. From the information you have gathered, determine the topic. What predictions can you make about the reading's content? Jot down your answers.

Reading Critically and Annotating. As you read, annotate the main idea, the major supporting points, key words, and a few passages that would make good quotations. Either write in your book or make annotations on sticky notes.

As you find key ideas, annotate them. If you think of robots as toys, you will be surprised to learn about how far robotics technology has advanced. As you read, think about what you know about robotics. How does the information in the reading differ from your assumptions or knowledge?

After reading and annotating, create an information sheet on which you record and organize your annotations as well as your thoughts about the content of the reading.

Google Search and Destroy: Rise of the Machines

By Cahal Milmo

1   Big Dog is capable of many things of interest to its new owners at *Google*. What remains to be seen is whether the quadruped robot's ability to pick up a breeze block and hurl it across a warehouse with impressive dexterity and speed is among them.

> 1 **breeze block:** British term for *cinder block*.

2   The computer search giant has completed the purchase of Boston Dynamics, the maker of a cutting-edge menagerie of walking and crawling robots including Big Dog, which counts America's Department of Defense (DoD) among its major sources of income.

3   The robotics firm is the eighth company in the same field to be snapped up by *Google* in the past six months under a project headed by Andy Rubin, the executive responsible for turning Android into the world's most widely used smartphone software and whose first love is robots. Mr. Rubin, an engineer by training, last week used Twitter to declare that "the future is looking awesome!"

4   But what is as yet unclear is just to what use *Google*, whose motto is famously "Don't be evil," plans to put its new stable of walking, sprinting and rock-throwing machines.

5   Boston Dynamics has won contracts worth $140m (£86m) since 2000 from the DoD and its agencies. The company boasts that it advises and assists the "US Army, Navy and Marine Corps" on developing "the most advanced robots on earth." By comparison, *Google's* income from defense work over the same period was $300,000.

6   Experts and campaigners yesterday voiced concern that despite *Google's* insistence that it does not intend to become a defense contractor, the acquisition of a company with established links to the military might make such work hard to resist in the future.

7   With inventions such as Big Dog, which is primarily designed to carry loads over rough terrain and has the uncanny ability to recover from a human kick, Boston Dynamics could move into the sphere of transporting weaponry rather than producing it. Professor Noel Sharkey, the leading artificial intelligence and robotics expert, based at the University of Sheffield, told *The Independent:* "I would like to think that *Google* will actually use the advanced technology to build an astonishing civil robot—maybe one that can deliver parcels or help in the home. But the multi-million dollar lure of military contracts may push them into the dark side. Let us hope not."

The Boston Dynamics deal, for an undisclosed sum, brought inevitable—if overblown—comparisons between *Google* and Skynet, the rogue computer system which manages to wipe out much of humanity in the *Terminator* film series. The robotics company has blazed a trail in producing some extraordinary machines capable of operating in harsh environments, including the Cheetah, which can run at 29 mph—faster than Usain Bolt—and Atlas, a humanoid robot built under a $10.8m deal with the Pentagon's Defense Advanced Research Projects Agency.   8

But rather than hunting down hapless *Homo sapiens* for some sort of robotic genocide, the maker of Atlas and its stablemates insists they are designed to help humanity out of self-inflicted disasters such as the Fukushima nuclear meltdown by working in environments where people would perish.   9

Dr. Marc Raibert, a former professor at the Massachusetts Institute of Technology who became fascinated with re-creating animal biology in mechanical form and founded Boston Dynamics, has insisted his company does not exist to be a military contractor and is motivated by advancing robotics. For his part, Mr. Rubin has described his project as a "moonshot"—the term *Google* applies to its slightly more outlandish schemes, such as self-driving cars and using a network of blimps to bounce Internet signals to remote regions. But while a world of autonomous cars remains some way off, it is likely *Google* is expecting a quicker return on its robotic investments. Amazon has already spent nearly £500m [$852m] on automating its warehouses and announced earlier this month—amid a lot of skepticism about the feasibility of such a scheme—that it is developing delivery drones designed to drop a package on doorsteps for use within the next five years.   10

Amid such accelerating interest in the potential of what Mr. Rubin has described as computers that are "starting to sprout legs," it is likely that *Google* will focus its attentions on manufacturing and logistics, with its first products ready within several years. While it is unclear whether the *Google* robotics venture will sail forth under the name of the mother ship or be hived off as a separate subsidiary, the pattern of spotting an everyday need—such as Internet search—and expanding dynamically to fulfill it may sound familiar.   11

Mr. Rubin told *The New York Times:* "I feel with robotics it's a green field. We're building hardware, we're building software. We're building systems, so one team will be able to understand the whole stack."   12

The question is whether the company avowed to "make money by doing good things" can finesse Big Dog and its brethren sufficiently to assist an old person out shopping or run to a stricken hiker's aid, rather than launching bits of masonry like a siege engine.   13   **siege engine:** an ancient machine, such as a catapult, used to sling stones and other projectiles over fortified walls.

Boston Dynamics: The Brains behind the Beasts

They sound like characters from a sci-fi series: SandFlea can leap 30 ft into the air; Big Dog can lug a 340 lb load up steep slopes and muddy trails, moving mammal-like on its four legs; LS3 can do even better, with the strength to shoulder 400 lb cargos; and the tiny claws in RiSE's feet allow it to crawl up walls, trees and fences.   14

But they are, in fact, the eerily agile robotic creations of Boston Dynamics, the Massachusetts-based company that's been snapped up by *Google*. Its roots lie at MIT, where founder Marc Raibert first worked on machines that could mimic the movement of animals. Spun off from the university in 1992, the business has since produced a line-up of robots that can leap and bound with astonishing nimbleness.   15   **MIT:** Massachusetts Institute of Technology, a highly respected research university.

Though the company doesn't sell its creations to the public, it does upload videos of its robotic army on *YouTube*. One, showing the four-legged Cheetah, a machine that Boston Dynamics says can run faster than Usain Bolt, has been viewed over seven million times. Another, demonstrating the agility of WildCat, a bulkier quadruped that   16 is shown darting around what appears to be a car park, has received close to 15.8 million hits. Among the company's collaborators is the Defense Advanced Research Projects Agency, or DARPA, which was involved in the creation of the Internet.

car park: British term for *parking lot.*

Earlier this year, Boston Dynamics unveiled Atlas, an advanced humanoid robot created for a DARPA-run competition that is meant to spur the development of robots that can help in responding to natural disasters.

17

Mr. Raibert was quizzed about the company's association with the military in 2010, when *The Engineer* magazine asked him if he had any concerns over how his creations might be deployed in the future. "I'm an engineer who builds robots; I don't know why people would be interested in my views on the ethical question," he replied.

18

"The big thing is that some people think the designer should be responsible for all possible uses of the system, and others think that the designer is just building a platform and someone else is responsible for the ethics of how it's used. I look at our systems and I say they're vehicles. You could put sacks of rice on them. You could put bullets on them. Their use is to go to places on Earth where you can't put vehicles now—and there are a lot of uses that can be put to."

19

Using Your Annotations.   Use your annotations and key words to write a one-page summary of the reading. In your summary, identify the writer's thesis statement, the major supporting points, the support for the major supporting points, and any other information needed to complete the summary.

Thinking about the Text

1. What are Milmo's main idea and major supporting points?
2. Why are some people concerned with the potential uses of robotics?
3. How might robots help humankind, according to this article?
4. What is the relationship between the military and Boston Dynamics?
5. Based on the information in this essay, explain why a company like *Google* might be interested in robotics.

The Writer's Techniques

1. Is the subject presented in a biased way, or does Milmo attempt to present the information objectively? Explain your answer, using examples from the text as support.
2. How does the essay's title help readers anticipate the content?
3. What is the primary type of support the writer uses in this article? Which text pattern or patterns does the writer use?

Brief-Response Assignments

1. Reread the section called "Boston Dynamics: The Brains behind the Beasts." Write a paragraph to explain how robots could be used for malevolent or criminal purposes.
2. In one or two paragraphs, explain some of the potentially positive uses of robots. Use the article for ideas, and come up with some ideas of your own.
3. When asked about his personal responsibility to create technologies that do no harm, Raibert said he is merely an engineer who builds robots; how people use them is not his concern. Does the person who builds a potentially harmful machine have any responsibility if someone uses that machine for criminal purposes? Write two or three paragraphs defending your point of view.

Essay Assignments

1. If you have never seen one of the robots referred to in this article, go to *YouTube* and do a search for the "Cheetah robot" or the "Big Dog robot." From what you see in the videos and what you have read in this article, do you think there should be rules that govern the things people can program robots to do? Defend your position.

2. How would the use of robots in warfare transform the rules of war? Explain some of the new issues that would arise from using robots, including advantages, disadvantages, and ethical issues.

3. Make a list of the potential evil that robots could do. Make another list of ways robots could help the human race. Compare and contrast your lists and decide whether developing robots is a good idea. Write a paper arguing your position. ↺

Author and Context. As a Los Angeles–based journalist and writer, Andrew Gumbel has been a longtime foreign correspondent for British newspapers. After covering the collapse of communism in eastern Europe, the wars in Yugoslavia, and the rise of Silvio Berlusconi in Italy—mostly for *The Independent* of London—he came to the United States in 1998 and has written extensively about politics, the criminal justice system, and pop culture. The following article appeared in *The Independent* in March 2000.

Previewing. Have pen and paper (or a computer) on hand as you read. Think about the title, and then study the author's biography and the contextual information about the reading. Next, preview the selection. From the information you have gathered, determine the topic. What predictions can you make about the reading's content? Jot down your answers.

Reading Critically and Annotating. As you read, annotate the main idea, the major supporting points, key words, and a few passages that would make good quotations. Either write in your book or make annotations on sticky notes.

As you find key ideas, annotate them. Which of the issues are you most interested in? Which ones do you think are important enough to prepare for? Make a note of any questions or insights that come to mind as you read.

After reading and annotating, create an information sheet on which you record and organize your annotations as well as your thoughts about the content of the reading.

Homo sapiens RIP (or Why One of the Leading Gurus of the Technological Age Believes That the Future Doesn't Need Us)

By Andrew Gumbel

Bill Joy is not a Luddite. He is not afraid of new technology. On the contrary, as chief scientist at Sun Microsystems, the Silicon Valley company that devised JavaScript and countless other Internet-era computer innovations, he has been in the vanguard of the high-tech revolution for more than 20 years: a geek's geek if ever there was one. But recently Joy took a glimpse into the future and it scared him to death.

1   **Luddite:** a person who is opposed to technological changes.

What he saw was a world in which humans have been effectively supplanted by machines; a world in which super-powerful computers with at least some attributes of human intelligence manage to replicate themselves and develop their own autonomy; a world in which people become superfluous and risk becoming extinct.

What he saw, in short, was something resembling the nightmare universe of the *Terminator* movies. Previously, Joy had dismissed such scenarios as sci-fi fantasy, but then he listened to his friends who were experts in robotics and realized that this brave new world is much closer than any of us might imagine—as close as 30 years away. What spooked him most was this passage, quoted in a book called *The Age of Spiritual Machines* by the computing innovator Ray Kurzweil: "As society and the problems that face it become more and more complex and machines become more and more intelligent, people will let machines make more of their decisions for them, simply because machine-made decisions will bring better results than man-made ones. Eventually a stage may be reached at which the decisions necessary to keep the system running will be so complex that human beings will be incapable of making them intelligently. At that stage the machines will be in effective control. People won't be able to just turn the machines off, because they will be so dependent on them that turning them off would amount to suicide."

The way Kurzweil's book was laid out, Joy did not know who had written this passage until he had read most of it and found himself nodding in agreement. As he turned the page, however, he realized with a start that the author was Theodore Kaczynski, the notorious Unabomber who so hated technology that he sent mail-bombs to leading scientists to try to deter them from furthering their research. Joy had spent most of his professional career bitterly opposed to everything the Unabomber stood for.

"Kaczynski's actions were murderous and, in my view, criminally insane," Joy writes in a remarkable explanation of his misgivings in this April's *Wired* magazine. "He is clearly a Luddite, but simply saying this does not dismiss his argument; as difficult as it is for me to acknowledge, I saw some merit in the reasoning in this single passage. I felt compelled to confront it."

And confront it he did. The further Joy dug into the cutting edge of research in the new technologies—robotics, genetic engineering and nanotechnology—the more horrified he became. He began thinking about what would happen to the mass of humanity if labor became obsolete (the scenarios he read about ranged from mass extermination, Nazi style, to a world in which most human beings would be reduced to the level of domestic animals). In a book by Hans Moravec, a leading researcher in robotics at Carnegie Mellon University, he read how "in a completely free marketplace . . . robotic industries would compete vigorously among themselves for matter, energy and space, incidentally driving their price beyond human reach. Unable to afford the necessities of life, biological humans would be squeezed out of existence."

Not only did he see scenarios in which robots would take on a life of their own and exterminate the human race, but he began to perceive ways in which other staples of sci-fi horror might come to pass: the ability to download consciousness into a computer and so effectively merge human beings and machines into a new organism; the proliferation of so-called White Plagues, in which malevolent scientists or governments could unleash diseases that would strike widely but selectively; genetically engineered bacteria or plants that could dominate and wipe out existing species.

In fact, Joy argues, the technological age could usher in the same terror of human self-destruction as the nuclear age did 55 years ago, with one crucial difference. While the 20th-century weapons of mass destruction required the sponsorship of governments and highly skilled scientists to become a reality, the nightmares of the 21st century will be accessible to anyone with the educational skills to know how to manipulate them. Joy describes this as the potential for "knowledge-enabled mass destruction."

"We have yet to come to terms with the fact that the most compelling 21st-century   9
technologies . . . pose a different threat than the technologies that have come before," Joy writes. "Specifically, robots, engineered organisms, and nanobots share a dangerous amplifying factor: they can self-replicate. A bomb is blown up only once—but one bot can become many, and quickly get out of control. . . .

"I think it is no exaggeration to say we are on the cusp of the further perfection of   10
extreme evil, an evil whose possibility spreads well beyond that which weapons of mass destruction bequeathed to the nation-states, on to a surprising and terrible empowerment of extreme individuals."

Using Your Annotations.   Use your annotations and key words to write a one-page summary of the reading. In your summary, identify the writer's thesis statement, the major supporting points, the support for the major supporting points, and any other information needed to complete the summary.

Thinking about the Text

1. According to this article, what is Bill Joy afraid of?
2. How does Gumbel feel about artificial intelligence? Use portions of the article to identify his fears.
3. Why did Gumbel write this article? For whom did he write it? Explain your answer.
4. Explain what *artificial intelligence* is, based on this article.

The Writer's Techniques

1. What is Gumbel's purpose in writing this article—to inform, analyze, evaluate, or persuade? Explain your answer.
2. How does the writer present Bill Joy as a credible source? What information does he include that demonstrates Joy's credibility?
3. Would the article have been as effective if Gumbel had given the information without presenting Bill Joy's ideas? Explain.

Brief-Response Assignments

1. Why was Bill Joy reluctant to recognize the insights of Theodore Kaczynski?
2. What does it mean to be a Luddite? Does our culture revere or revile Luddites (or neither)? Explain in a paragraph.
3. Write a paragraph in which you discuss how the world would be different today without the proliferation of machine intelligence.
4. What do you think Joy means when he says, "We are on the cusp of the further perfection of extreme evil"?

Essay Assignments

1. Write an essay discussing the development of artificial intelligence. Discuss three areas in which artificial intelligence has replaced human intelligence.
2. Bill Joy believes that teaching computers to "think" may be opening up a world that could destroy us. Should we be performing research regarding self-replication and nanotechnology? Why or why not?

3. The writer quotes Ray Kurzweil as saying, "Machine-made decisions will bring better results than man-made ones." Write an essay comparing and contrasting decisions that are better made by machines and those in which a human's experience is beneficial. ↻

Authors and Context.   Volpe, The National Transportation Systems Center, is a federal agency that works under the US Department of Transportation. The center partners with public and private organizations to assess transportation needs, evaluate research, and implement state-of-the-art transportation technologies. On September 29, 2016, the Volpe Center held a panel discussion as part of its series "The Future of Transportation: Safety, Opportunity, and Innovation." Panel participants were Robin Chase, co-founder of the car-sharing company Zipcar, as well as other car-sharing companies worldwide, and Dr. Anthony Townsend, a senior research scientist at New York University's Rudin Center for Transportation Policy and Management. The panel was moderated by Austin L. Brown of the White House Office of Science and Technology Policy. This article appeared on the Volpe Center Web site on October 18, 2016.

Previewing.   Have pen and paper (or a computer) on hand as you read. Think about the title, and then study the speakers' biographies and the contextual information about the reading. Next, preview the selection. From the information you have gathered, determine the topic. What predictions can you make about the reading's content? Jot down your answers.

Reading Critically and Annotating.   As you read, annotate the main idea, the major supporting points, key words, and a few passages that would make good quotations. Either write in your book or make annotations on sticky notes.

As you find key ideas, form questions about them. What does the article say about how transportation will change in the near future? What changes might happen in your lifetime? Find and underline key passages that help you understand the reading, and use annotations to record your observations and questions.

After reading and annotating, create an information sheet on which you record and organize your annotations as well as your thoughts about the content of the reading.

Automated Vehicles and Urban Mobility

By the Volpe Center

Automated vehicles are coming sooner than you might think, according to two leading thinkers in transportation who spoke recently at Volpe.   1

Robin Chase: Automated Vehicles Are Here

No longer the stuff of science fiction, cars and trucks that drive themselves are nearly a reality.   2

"Someone said to me, 'So [are automated vehicles] five years away? Everything is five years away,'" said Robin Chase, co-founder and former CEO of ZipCar and co-founder of Veniam. "I said, 'Not only is it not five years away; it's three-and-half years away—three years away.'"   3

Two Autonomous Futures: Heaven or Hell

There are two available futures for tomorrow's automated vehicle revolution, Chase said. One future is what she calls "hell," where automated vehicles are a nearly one-to-one replacement for current personal vehicles. The other future is "heaven," where shared vehicles are the norm.   4

"We have autonomous vehicles that we are going to swap out for our internal combustion engines," Chase said. "They may be electric; it's not guaranteed. Or they can be something I'm calling FAVES: Fleets of Autonomous Vehicles that are Electric and Shared. This is really a huge choice."   5

In the "hell" scenario, automated vehicle owners go to work or to the store, and their vehicles drive around until needed or they drive home. Businesses, too, may replace traditional storefronts with automated vehicles that go where customers are. Taxi drivers and truckers may lose their jobs, and more vehicles on the road rather than in parking spaces means more wear and tear on roads and bridges.   6

The "heaven" scenario takes a proactive approach, Chase said. The FAVES concept combines car sharing and ride hailing using mobile devices or computers, with these net benefits: 7

- Car sharing eliminates the need for parking.   8
- Ride sharing reduces congestion.   9
- Individuals save thousands of dollars per year by not owning a personal vehicle.   10
- Only 10 percent of cars currently in cities would be needed.   11

Despite these potential benefits, there would still be major challenges related to loss of employment in industries that depend on cars with human drivers, Chase said.   12

"No matter what people say, economics leads them," Chase said. "If they can get someplace for cheaper and the quality is still there, they will go for the cheaper path."   13

A Blueprint for Getting to FAVES

The five-years-or-less path to autonomous vehicles could look something like this, according to Chase: A pilot project with a 100-vehicle fleet of FAVES begins in a major city. It's mostly used by students, tourists, and people who work nights.   14

Between years two and five, the pilot expands to 1,000 vehicles. More people have a reason to try it out—maybe their second car breaks down, for example. They'll find the shared autonomous vehicle system works, and works well. The next time they have to make a major financial decision, such as buying a new car, they may opt instead to rely solely on cheaper, reliable FAVES, Chase said.   15

"That's why I think it will be a very fast transition," Chase said. "Within five years, people will be able to reflect, 'What the heck? Why am I owning a second car? And why am I owning a first car?'"   16

Anthony Townsend: The Emerging Policy Landscape for Autonomous Vehicles and Cities

Cities and automation go hand-in-hand, according to Anthony Townsend, senior research scientist at New York University's Rudin Center for Transportation Policy and Management. With vehicle automation, cities are safer, more efficient, and more connected. But automated vehicle technology has caught many cities by surprise, and their policies have not kept up, Townsend said.   17

"What we're confronting ahead is this 20-year period of automation," Townsend said. "It's primarily about reinventing the automobile. It's involving a massive amount of private investment and I don't think we really have an urban lens yet."   18

Urban Policy Implications of Autonomous Vehicles

Townsend proposed a policy framework that promotes accessibility and allows cities to confront challenges related to automated vehicles. An ideal policy framework for cities preparing to manage an influx of automated vehicles would address safety, economics, and land use, Townsend said.

19

Safety is the top governmental and industry priority, Townsend explained. If the technology is not safe, the conversation around automated vehicle policy can't happen. Loss of ridership and revenue for transit agencies, and a decrease in employment for workers in vehicle-related industries, could happen concurrently, Townsend said.

20

Leaders in cities will also need to rethink how they repurpose land currently used for vehicle infrastructure. How cities use their physical space is among the most important open questions related to vehicle automation, and will take the most time to develop, Townsend said.

21

"It's useful to think from the point of view of the user," he said. "This [change] is about providing accessibility and getting people where they need to go. It's not about transportation."

22

A Discussion on Urban Mobility: Streetscape Visions and Access to Opportunity

Following their introductory remarks, Chase and Townsend sat down with the White House's Austin Brown for a wide-ranging dialogue on how automated vehicles are poised to fundamentally change the look and feel of cities.

23

"One of the visions for what the vehicle might look like is the mobile living room, and it could be compatible with the FAVES concept, but the very nature of that vehicle is isolating from the streetscape," Brown said. "That kind of worries me. Is that something that should worry me?"

24

Automated vehicles should not replace all modes [of transportation],", Chase said. Pedestrians and bicyclists spur retail shopping, and an active public environment where people are not in vehicles is needed to maintain healthy urban economies.

25

"[Retail is] one of the lobbies we need to get back into this discussion," Chase said. "We can re-partition the streets [so that] not everybody . . . is in their enclosed AV looking at their laptop. We want people out."

26

Positive outcomes from discussions among city leaders and citizens on what urban streets will look like will rely on a city having the authority to act on its designs for public space, Townsend said. "There has to be some vision to allow city authorities to say, 'Repair shops? Totally consistent with our vision of public space. Amazon picking up your shoes to take them to a warehouse in New Jersey to get fixed there and then dropped back off? Not consistent with our use of public space,'" Townsend said.

27

An undercurrent of the discussion was that transportation provides access. Things traditionally associated with transportation, like mobility and movement, are simply means to provide access. Chase explains: "There was a Harvard longitudinal study and another study that said the single largest barrier to escaping poverty was access to quality transportation." Chase continues: "And I think [FAVES] are completely game-changing on that. I see these vehicles going everywhere and being the price of a subway ticket."

28

Using Your Annotations.   Use your annotations and key words to write a one-page summary of the reading. In your summary, identify the writer's thesis statement, the major supporting points, the support for the major supporting points, and any other information needed to complete the summary.

Thinking about the Text

1. What are FAVES?
2. What do you think is meant by "a city's infrastructure"?
3. What are the differences between the "heaven" and "hell" scenarios described in the article?
4. How might retail shopping be affected by transportation changes?
5. Based on the article, what does "automation" mean?

The Writers' Techniques

1. Examine the use of quotation marks in the statement that follows. Why does the writer use single quotation marks *and* double quotation marks?

   "There has to be some vision to allow city authorities to say, 'Repair shops? Totally consistent with our vision of public space. Amazon picking up your shoes to take them to a warehouse in New Jersey to get fixed there and then dropped back off? Not consistent with our use of public space,'" Townsend said.

2. Why do you think the article uses so many quotations?
3. Some of the concepts in this reading such as *infrastructure, automation,* and *streetscape visions* can be difficult to understand. How does the article help readers understand difficult concepts? Provide one example.

Brief-Response Assignments

1. Write a descriptive paragraph in which you imagine what transportation in a major city might be like twenty years from now. Use the ideas in the article, but also use your imagination.
2. What jobs might be threatened by the changes that are taking place in transportation? Explain your answer in a paragraph.
3. Explain this idea: "There was a Harvard longitudinal study and another study that said the single largest barrier to escaping poverty was access to quality transportation." What is the connection between transportation and poverty? Explain in a paragraph.

Essay Assignments

1. The Volpe Center tries to find solutions for transportation problems and issues. Think of a transportation problem that needs to be solved in your city or community. Write an essay in which you present a method for solving this problem. You may discuss how the futuristic ideas in the article could solve the problem you present.
2. What would be the advantages of having cars that are intelligent enough to drive themselves? Write an essay in which you explain at least three advantages of self-driving cars.
3. According to the article, using FAVES would have advantages and disadvantages. Write an essay in which you imagine a city that primarily uses FAVES for transportation. What would be the advantages of living in that city? What would be the disadvantages? Explain your thoughts in an essay. ↻

Author and Context. The American Preppers Network (APN) is a nonprofit corporation and part of a growing international movement of people who call themselves preppers. The social network is organized by state and regional blogs and forums.

The members are volunteer contributors who are dedicated to providing free information on survival, preparedness, self-sufficiency, and sustainability. "The Five Principles of Preparedness," inspired by a talk by James E. Faust, appears on the APN Web site (americanpreppersnetwork.com). It was written by Phil Burns, a co-owner of the APN.

Previewing.   Have pen and paper (or a computer) on hand as you read. Think about the title, and then study the author's biography and the contextual information about the reading. Next, preview the selection. From the information you have gathered, determine the topic. What predictions can you make about the reading's content? Jot down your answers.

Reading Critically and Annotating.   As you read, annotate the main idea, the major supporting points, key words, and a few passages that would make good quotations. Either write in your book or make annotations on sticky notes.

As you find key ideas, annotate them. What is "prepping"? Why do people participate in it? Is prepping something that everyone should do? Think about these questions as you read and annotate the selection.

After reading and annotating, create an information sheet on which you record and organize your annotations as well as your thoughts about the content of the reading.

The Five Principles of Preparedness

By Phil Burns, the American Preppers Network

There are basic principles that keep us and our families grounded that are key to   1
our happiness as a family unit while we walk the path of the prepper. By getting started in prepping, or continuing in prepping as the case may be, and following these five principles of preparedness we can provide our families with the assurance that we will be able to maintain a certain standard of living. This standard of living is dictated by the level of preparedness we are able to achieve and maintain.

Principle One: Practice Thrift and Frugality

The depression era saying of "Use it up, wear it out, make it do, or do without" sums up   2
the practice of thrift. Living thriftily is not a popular concept in our "staying up with the Joneses" mentality, but the folly of that mentality is that if one thing goes wrong and your family slips into crisis, you will have to learn all about "staying above water." Living thriftily is a very simple, effective and immediate method to increase your spending power. Imagine being, instead of a consumer, a creator, a repairer, or simply abstaining. Thrift is a practice of not wasting anything including time and money.

Why do Americans work themselves so hard and as soon as the paycheck comes   3
in, throw it to the wind as quickly as they can—leaving themselves with no reserves, no safety and no peace? It is because we have come to accept abundance as our standard. We foolishly assure ourselves that there will be a check next pay period—and there normally is—until there is not. It is the high possibility that at some point something critical will happen in our lives that brings us to the conclusion that it is very likely that at some point, that check will not be there.

One massive waste that Americans have become very comfortable with is living   4
on credit. We have become extremely complacent with our finances in this regard. Instead of doing without for a short time while we save, we finance everything and as a consequence, pay financing fees and interest that we somehow justify as necessary.

It is not necessary that we ever pay financing fees or interest for anything, even a house, if we are willing to be prudent.

Preppers who successfully follow this principle for a few years will find themselves in a position where they are able to spend time not working without affecting their families in an adverse manner. 5

Principle Two: Seek to Be Independent

Debt can be crippling and crushing to a family, making them unable to move forward due to the demands of making payments on things they potentially don't even own anymore. Seek to become independent from debt. Learn to abhor the idea of being forced to labor and earn money that is not yours as a consequence of choosing to "live a little better" by going into debt. Living independently means being free to choose what is pertinent for you and your family to do with your money. Establish savings that will grow and serve you as you become the master of your money. Learn to budget and responsibly manage your money as it is a very powerful tool to either enslave or empower you. 6

Independence doesn't just mean money though. Seek to be independent of the influences of the world such as caffeine, alcohol, drugs, tobacco, unhealthy yet addictive food, medications (where possible) and so on. All of these things not only make you a personal slave to addictions, but indenture your wallet and cause you to spend wasteful amounts of money to satiate your personal weaknesses. Strive to become independent of all these things and you will not only be healthier, but you will also increase your income as you free a daily outgo to servicing your demons. 7

Live independent of the entrapping influences of society as much as possible. Free your mind of thinking you need a better looking car, a prettier house or better clothes. Do what works for *you*, not what you think others will think highly of. Live independently of the fear of judgment of others and become secure in your own person. Prepper families who learn to live independently will find themselves prospering greatly—in ways that may not be apparent to the enslaved masses of society. 8

Principle Three: Become Industrious

Learn, explore, do. When opportunity presents itself, work hard at redefining and reshaping yourself, your position and your knowledge to be worthy of the success that opportunity can provide. Be resourceful, always looking for a new way to create what you need in order to succeed. 9

Common ways to be industrious include furthering your education and constantly working to develop new skills. By exploring opportunities, we are able to assess their potential, weigh risks and make decisions as to whether our conclusions merit committing to an opportunity or walking away from it. By improving ourselves constantly, we open up even more opportunity; and opportunities can potentially bring success. 10

Idly standing by and waiting for success to land in your lap is a poor strategy. Being industrious means getting up and attempting something, even if it has the potential to fail. The farmer who fails to put in a crop because he doesn't think there was enough snowfall during the winter loses out when spring rains finally bring plenty of water. When you commit to something, work hard at it; throw in everything you've got. Getting up and going is truly the only way to end up somewhere else. 11

Preppers who industriously seek out opportunity will soon find the one that will create a change in the direction their lives have been heading. 12

Principle Four: Strive towards Self-Reliance

The principle of self-reliance is predicated by and builds upon the first three principles. Self-reliance is, in its simplest form, being able to create or provide all needed things 13 as the result of labor using a developed skill or talent and being able to provide resources as a result of a judicious practice of storing needful things. Therefore, becoming self-reliant is the actual process of developing skills and talents while putting away resources.

When combined with thrift and frugality, self-reliance helps you to obtain what you need without having to pay exorbitant amounts of money for those things such as growing a garden, sewing or repairing clothes, building furniture, building a home, fixing your vehicle and so on. It is being willing to enjoy the fruits of your labor versus the blandness of buying something commercially produced. It is accepting things for their functionality, not for the logo that was stamped on them in a plant somewhere. It is being willing to use something that may be less than perfect in its manufacture but is functional.   14

Self-reliance, when combined with independence, drives us to be truly reliant on ourselves in all areas. Self-reliance can involve learning how to make soap, grow your own food, provide your own energy, defend yourself, and create the things you need and so on. It requires research, learning, experimenting, failing, experimenting more and finally succeeding. By being self-reliant, you succeed in gaining a new skill, accomplishing something new or developing a new vocation. An industrious and self-reliant person is truly a creator and experiences the joy of creation on a daily basis.   15

Principle Five: Aspire to Have a Year's Supply of Every Needful Thing

The natural outgrowth of becoming truly self-reliant is to feel compelled to store things up that are essential for our family's ensured safety, comfort and existence. The "every needful thing" concept teaches us to consider the possibility of storing up a supply of every item that we purchase which we truly need. What is a need? Simply put, it is something that it would be difficult to not have or to live without. This includes food, clothing, water, heat, power, home medical supplies, fire starters, and so on.   16

It is obviously not prudent to simply purchase a year's supply of every needful thing. For example, it is quite inexpensive and easy to acquire a year's supply of ketchup; at most a family will use two bottles a month. Therefore, purchasing 24 bottles would give you a year's supply. However, a year's supply of something like water, which is consumed every day, requires a very different approach. It is not feasible to store a year's supply of water unless you have your own water tower. There are other options available, though, which include such things as drilling a well, installing a rain catchment system, or being situated near a body of water.   17

Preppers who are striving to build a year's supply of every needful thing will experience a dramatic reduction in stress and an increase in peace as they begin meeting goals on the path to achieving this principle.   18

The Impact of Living the Principles of Preparedness

When teaching these principles, the question is inevitably asked: "What if nothing ever happens that I need my supplies for?" To which I respond, "That would be wonderful!"   19

As you live by these principles, you will experience breaking free of the slavery of debt, a "career," of "keeping up with the Joneses" and most importantly, the stress of trying to live month to month. What you will find instead is that you are able to fully experience life and truly enjoy the blessings of your family, all the while knowing that the secret to a happy life is wrapped up in a little concept called being a "prepper"!   20

Using Your Annotations.   Use your annotations and key words to write a one-page summary of the reading. In your summary, identify the writer's thesis statement, the major supporting points, the support for the major supporting points, and any other information needed to complete the summary.

Thinking about the Text

1. What is the main idea of this essay?
2. What does the writer mean in stating that "we have come to accept abundance as our standard"?
3. Why does the writer believe the elimination of debt is so important?
4. What is self-reliance, according to the essay?
5. What does the writer say are the benefits of becoming industrious?

The Writer's Techniques

1. Preppers are sometimes thought of as radical people who have outlandish ideas. How does this article help to change that stereotype?
2. Think of some examples the writer could use to enhance the article. Where would examples make the writer's ideas clearer?
3. How does the writer conclude the essay? What is the conclusion trying to convey?

Brief-Response Assignments

1. Of the five principles mentioned in the essay, which one would be the most difficult for most people to accomplish? Why?
2. Reflect on what the average American might need for a year's worth of supplies. What would be the most important supplies to have on hand to be self-reliant?
3. In what ways would a prepper's lifestyle be different from the lifestyle of most Americans today?

Essay Assignments

1. The writer suggests that a key to living a happy life is being a prepper. Write an essay discussing how being a prepper could make one's life either happier or more miserable.
2. This writer, as well as other famous writers in history, discusses the importance of self-reliance. What is self-reliance, and how can the average American become more self-reliant?
3. Select one of the principles offered in this essay that would improve the lives of Americans if followed. Write an essay defending your advocacy of this principle. Provide reasons for your belief, and include examples. You may use hypothetical examples. ↻

Thematic Assignment

Use the readings in this thematic unit to write an essay that answers one of the following questions.

a. To what extent should all Americans become "preppers"? What prepping behaviors are reasonable? Write an essay in which you answer these questions. Provide proof for your point of view, and provide examples of the kinds of prepping you believe people should undertake, based on your understanding of the articles in this theme. Use two or more of the readings as support for your point of view.

b. We have limited time, limited resources, and limited energy to solve the problems of the future. Thus, we have to prioritize the projects that need our attention. Many of the articles in this section emphasize problems: transportation needs of growing cities, a divided government, global warming, consumer debt, the potential dangers of computer technology, and more. Select the three most important issues we should tackle. Use the readings in this unit to support your assertion that these are the three most important issues.

c. The essays in this unit present at least two responses to the future: one is to withdraw to an extent and become a prepper, and the other is to collaborate with others to try to solve the problems that face us. Compare and contrast these two responses. In what ways are they similar? In what ways are they different? Write an essay presenting your comparison.

d. The articles in this thematic unit present both problems and prospects for the future. How can some of the ideas presented here—such as robots and prepping—solve some of the problems we are facing? For example, can robots solve any climate change problems? Select a problem presented in this unit that may be solved by one of the prospects presented here. Explain how the prospect may affect the problem.

Be sure to cite any sources from which you obtain ideas or quotes. Include a works cited or references page with your essay. For additional information on source-based writing, follow the steps in the Quick Start Guide to Integrated Reading and Writing Assignments.

Text Credits

Page 637: Milmo, Cahal, "Google Search and Destroy: Rise of the Machines," *The Independent*, December 16, 2013. Copyright © 2013 Independent Print Ltd. Reprinted with permission. http://www.independent.co.uk; Page 640: Gumbel, Andrew, "Homo Sapiens RIP (or Why One of the Leading Gurus of the Technological Age Believes That the Future Doesn't Need Us)," *The Independent*, March 15, 2000. Copyright © 2000 Independent Print Ltd. Reprinted with permission. http://www.independent.co.uk; Page 643: Source: "Robin Chase and Anthony Townsend on Automated Vehicles and Urban Mobility," October 18, 2016. Volpe: The National Transportation Systems Center, U.S. Department of Transportation; Page 647: Abridged from Phil Burns, "The Five Principles of Preparedness," American Preppers Network, http://americanpreppersnetwork.com. © American Preppers Network. Reprinted with permission.

Index